Anonymous

The King and the Kingdom

A study of the four Gospels. Vol. 3

Anonymous

The King and the Kingdom
A study of the four Gospels. Vol. 3

ISBN/EAN: 9783337183585

Printed in Europe, USA, Canada, Australia, Japan

Cover: Foto ©Lupo / pixelio.de

More available books at **www.hansebooks.com**

THE KING

AND

THE KINGDOM:

A STUDY OF THE FOUR GOSPELS.

'To the present age is ascribed productiveness and changeableness of opinions, and at the same time indifference to opinions. But that cannot arise from this: no man in all corrupted Europe can be indifferent to truth as such, for it, in the last resort, decides upon his life; but every one is at last become cold and shy towards the erring teachers and preachers of truth. Take the hardest heart and brain which withers away in any capital city, and only give him the certainty that the spirit which approaches him brings down from eternity the key which opens and shuts the so weighty gates of his life-prison, of death, and of heaven,—and the dried-up worldly man, so long as he has a care or a wish, must seek for a truth which can reveal to him that spirit.'—RICHTER's *Levana*.

'Hasten the time when, unfettered by sectarian intolerance, and unawed by the authority of men, the Bible shall make its rightful impression upon all; the simple and obedient readers thereof calling no man Master, but Christ only.'—Dr. CHALMERS.

'I speak as to wise men; judge ye what I say.'—1 Cor. x. 15.

THIRD SERIES.

NEW YORK: G. P. PUTNAM'S SONS.
LONDON: WILLIAMS AND NORGATE.
1893.

PREFACE.

Many thoughtful and honest minds cannot but feel that under the pressure of a systematised theology the gospel of Christ has lost much of its freshness and power. The very reverence paid outwardly to Scripture has tended towards this result. By every generation, throughout eighteen centuries, the divine Truth has been expounded, weighed, measured, attacked, defended. This ceaseless handling could scarcely fail to soil and dim its native brightness. The atmosphere of Christian thought, necessary and life-giving though it be, is always more or less weighted with foreign particles, emanations of the human mind, which have settled into a thick film of dogmatic teaching, blurring in no small degree the truth which lies beneath. There is surely no irreverence in the touch which would brush away these accretions of centuries.

Probably they whose profession it is to preach the gospel are of all men least likely, in the ordinary course of theological study, to accept it in its simplicity. This involves no disparagement of their learning or sincerity. It arises from the fact that they are bound down to creeds and articles of religion, and that their minds have been nourished and developed by the ideas of spiritual fathers and doctors of the Church. So it comes to pass that their interpretations of Scripture are tinged unconsciously with traditional beliefs. Their expositions of the New Testament have a definiteness which did not exist in the teaching of Jesus, and almost every parable he spoke has had impressed upon it some settled, orthodox meaning.

There is indeed much in the present aspect of Christianity to occasion sorrow and perplexity. On the one side are clashing creeds and sects, seeming but to rend and disfigure the

Truth at which they clutch; on the other side is a band of honest, fearless sceptics, acute in the exercise of criticism, and so self-confident that they scruple not to adopt unhesitatingly the conclusions of their own minds, to the utter rejection of whatever appears miraculous in the gospel narratives. Yet surely the compilers, who wrote in apostolic times, were not destitute of common sense and powers of judgment, and they must have had infinitely better means of arriving at the facts than can be claimed by any investigator after the lapse of eighteen centuries.

Disregarding alike dogmatic interpretations and hostile criticisms, it is no small comfort to turn to the narratives themselves, seeking with patient study their true import. Independent and unprejudiced enquiry is the best preservative against the two extremes of believing too easily or doubting too much. To do full justice to the authors of the Gospels we must take their work as it were fresh from their own hands. If the gospel histories are worth anything, they will be self-luminous, and by their own light alone should they be interpreted. If in the main points and circumstances they are held to be not reliable, they can scarcely be deemed worthy of serious study.

In this spirit the following investigation has been conducted. Everything is sought to be taken as it stands, without abatement and without addition, the simple object being to arrive at the facts intended to be conveyed by the evangelists, and to grasp the truths and doctrines taught by Jesus.

Not scholarship, as may easily be seen, but only earnestness of thought and sincerity of purpose, can be urged in favour of this work. It is the outcome of many years of painstaking, loving labour, the foundation having previously been laid by a similar methodical and careful review of each of the four gospels separately. Not until that apprenticeship to the subject was ended, did the author venture to undertake the more important task of combining the four narratives, pondering them as before verse by verse, phrase by phrase, and when necessary word by word. No preconceived ideas, his own or of others, were voluntarily allowed to influence the investigation; no theories or doctrines had to be upheld, no reasonable conclusions needed to be shrunk from or evaded, no fear of adverse judgment or criticism, no dread of blame, no hope of praise or profit have been at work to interfere with the expression of free and honest thought. That fact may serve, it is hoped, to extenuate any apparently undue boldness of utterance: if the writer seems, as may often be the case, to undervalue the opinions of other men, it is not out of disrespect, but simply because truth is to be prized above everything; whenever the conclusions arrived at are strongly stated, it is because they have been as strongly felt. A careful reader will note the gradual growth of opinion from first to last. The true nature of Christ's gospel, of the kingdom of heaven, and of real discipleship to Jesus, must needs dawn more and more, here a little and there a little, on the mind which sets itself to the study of his divine teaching.

All Scriptural quotations are from the Revised Version, unless otherwise stated.

Frequent references will be found to the following works:

THE HOLY BIBLE. Literally and idiomatically translated out of the original languages. By Robert Young, D.D. A. Fullarton & Co., Edinburgh, Dublin and London.

THE NEW TESTAMENT. With various readings from the most celebrated manuscripts of the original Greek Text. By Constantine Tischendorf. Tauchnitz Edition. Volume 1000. Sampson Low, Son & Marston, London.

THE NEW TESTAMENT. Translated from the critical text of Von Tischendorf. By Samuel Davidson, D.D. Henry King & Son, London. (*All readings and renderings mentioned as being those of Von Tischendorf are from this work, the renderings, of course, being by Dr. Davidson.*)

THE NEW TESTAMENT FOR ENGLISH READERS. By Henry Alford, D.D. Rivingtons, London.

THE HOLY BIBLE. Translated by Samuel Sharpe. Williams & Norgate, London.

THE ENGLISHMAN'S GREEK NEW TESTAMENT, together with an interlinear Translation. S. Bagster & Sons, Limited, London.

THE ENGLISHMAN'S CONCORDANCE OF THE GREEK NEW TESTAMENT. S. Bagster & Sons, Limited, London.

THE
KING AND THE KINGDOM:
A STUDY OF THE FOUR GOSPELS.
PART III.

In the Authorised Version the 24th chapter of Matthew begins with the words, 'And Jesus went out, and departed from the temple.' In the two oldest MSS. the order is reversed: 'went out from the temple and departed.' The Revised Version stands: 'And Jesus 24 Mat. 1 went out from the temple, and was going on his way.' But some of his disciples were anxious that he should take the opportunity of inspecting the building, and offered their services as guides. 'And ,, 1 his disciples came to him to shew him the buildings of the temple.' Jesus appears never to have resided in Jerusalem. He went there only occasionally, and while there was fully occupied with his work, and spent the nights in Bethany. Mark describes one of the disciples as calling his attention to the magnificent material and style of the buildings. 'And as he went forth out of the temple, 13 Mark 1, 2 one of his disciples saith unto him, Master (or, Teacher), behold, what manner of stones and what manner of buildings!' In the Authorised Version the words 'are here' are added, in italics. They were superfluous, and the Revisers have omitted them; the literal rendering is: 'what stones and what buildings!' Luke represents several persons as expressing their admiration at the sight. 'And as 21 Luke 5 some spake of the temple, how it was adorned with goodly stones and offerings . . .' Jesus, who had been moved to enthusiasm by the poor widow's gift of two mites, manifested something like apathy with respect to these 'goodly stones and offerings.' To his foreseeing eye, this massiveness was deceptive: it promised a permanence which would not be realised. No gradual process of decay would come over the building: it would be destroyed by violence, ruthlessly and utterly. 'And Jesus said unto him, Seest thou these great buildings? there 13 Mark 2 shall not be left here one stone upon another, which shall not be thrown down.' The word 'answering,' after 'Jesus,' has been omitted by the Revisers, not being in the two oldest MSS. They have inserted after 'left' the word 'here,' following a reading adopted by Lachmann and Tregelles. They have done the same in Luke, on the authority of the two oldest MSS. According to Matthew, the remark of Jesus was addressed, not to one person only, 'Seest thou?' but to the disciples generally: 'But he answered and said unto them, See 24 Mat. 2

B

ye not all these things? verily I say unto you, There shall not be left here one stone upon another, that shall not be thrown down.' Tischendorf modifies the phraseology by using 'will' instead of 'shall.' The latter word might be mistaken by some, as indicating a purpose in the mind of Jesus, especially as some Commentators have not scrupled to assert that the Roman soldiers were fulfilling his will in the destruction of Jerusalem. Luke also gives the words as spoken to all, not to one individual : 'He said, As for these things which ye behold, the days will come, in which there shall not be left here one stone upon another, that shall not be thrown down.' That two evangelists should record an observation as made to several persons, and that another evangelist should state it to have been addressed to one person, in reply to an enquiry put by him, is rather evidence of truthfulness than of inaccuracy. Conversation in the presence of many listeners naturally tends to become general : one begins it, is answered, and gradually all are, or appear to be, addressed by the principal speaker. Mark seized the point at which the talk commenced, 'as he went forth out of the temple,' rendered by Young, 'as he was going out of the temple;' Luke refers to a subsequent moment, when all present were observing, and many talking, 'and as some spake of the temple;' Young renders : 'and certain saying about the temple, that with goodly stones and offerings it hath been adorned.' When one of them uttered a remark to that effect to Jesus, and he replied thereto, all who listened are properly described as collectively addressed by Jesus. As to the fulfilment of his prediction, Alford quotes the following from Josephus : 'Cæsar gave orders to pull down the whole city and the temple . . . and all the area of the city was so levelled by the workmen, that a traveller would never believe that it had been inhabited.'

The disciples were naturally anxious to learn more from Jesus as to the evils he foresaw and foretold, and they took the opportunity, when he was elsewhere, of obtaining further information in private. 'And as he sat on the Mount of Olives, the disciples came unto him privately, saying . . .' Mark tells us that the time chosen was when Jesus was seated in view of the temple, and the names of the disciples are recorded. 'And as he sat on the mount of Olives over against the temple, Peter and James and John and Andrew asked him privately . . .' Luke says nothing of time, place or persons, but simply, 'And they asked him, saying . . .' In Matthew the question is thus recorded : 'Tell us, when shall these things be? and what *shall be* the sign of thy coming (Gr. presence), and of the end of the world (or, the consummation of the age)?' Knowing the sense in which the expression 'the end of the world' is generally taken, we may be grateful to the Revisers for giving the alternative rendering. Young and Sharpe render it, 'the end of the age,' and the 'Englishman's Greek New Testament,' 'the completion of the age.' Alford and Tischendorf retain, 'the end of the world,' and Luther adopted the same form, 'der Welt Ende.' The erroneous rendering is much to be regretted. In the Authorised Version five Greek words are translated by the word 'world.' The word here is *aiōn*; elsewhere it is *kosmos*; but it is obvious that even where the latter is used, it is not to be understood of the material world, as it is apt to be by many. 'If ye were of the world (*kosmos*), the world [15 John ⁊] (*kosmos*) would love its own: but because ye are not of the world (*kosmos*), but I chose you out of the world (*kosmos*), therefore the world (*kosmos*) hateth you.' 'We know that we are of God, and [5 I. John 1⁊] the whole world (*kosmos*) lieth in the evil one.' In these and many such passages it is impossible to understand the physical world. *Kosmos* is thus defined: ' order, good order, a set form of order: *of states* government: the mode or fashion of a thing; II. an ornament, an honour;' and lastly: 'the world or universe,' with the explanation: '*from its perfect* arrangement.' The end or ends of the ages would seem to have been a recognised form of expression, for Paul used it: 'They are written for our admonition, upon whom the [10 I. Cor. 11 (A. V.)] ends of the world (*aiōn*) are come,' rendered by Young, 'to whom the ends of the ages came,' and by the Revisers, 'upon whom the ends of the ages are come.' The first coming of Jesus is said to have been ' in the end of the world,' in a passage in which both words occur. It stands in the Authorised Version as follows: ' For [9 Heb. 26] then must he often have suffered since the foundation of the world (*kosmos*); but now once in the end of the world (*aiōn*) hath he appeared to put away sin by the sacrifice of himself;' Young renders: 'Since it would have behoved him many times to suffer from the foundation of the world, but now once, at the end of the ages, for the putting away of sin through his sacrifice, he hath been manifested;' the Revisers render: ' Else must he often have suffered since the foundation of the world: but now once at the end (or, consummation) of the ages hath he been manifested to put away sin by the sacrifice of himself (or, by his sacrifice).' It is clear, therefore, that the question of the disciples, as recorded in Matthew, had no reference to the destruction of the physical universe. Mark states it as follows: ' Tell us, when shall these things be ? and what *shall* [13 Mark 4] *be* the sign when these things are all about to be accomplished ?' The Revisers have replaced 'fulfilled' by 'accomplished,' the consummation or final accomplishment of things being intended, not the fulfilment of a prophecy. Luke is to the same effect: ' Master (or, [21 Luke 7] Teacher), when therefore shall these things be ? and what *shall be* the sign when these things are about to come to pass ?' The Revisers, agreeing with Young, Tischendorf and Alford, have altered ' shall come to pass ' to ' are about to come to pass,' and a similar rectification of the Authorised Version has been made in Mark, ' about to be ' instead of ' shall be.' We must observe that 'the sign' of the approaching consummation was enquired about, and that Matthew connects it also with the 'coming' or 'presence' of Jesus, implying that his 'coming' could not be anticipated until the 'end of the age.'

Jesus began his reply by warning them against deception. Matthew: ' And Jesus answered and said unto them, Take heed that [21 Mat. 4, 5] no man lead you astray.' Mark: ' And Jesus began to say unto [13 Mark 5] them, Take heed that no man lead you astray.' Luke: ' And he [21 Luke 8] said, Take heed that ye be not led astray.' In Mark, the Revisers, following the two oldest MSS., have omitted ' answering ' before ' began.' Many persons would lay claim to the authority and work of Jesus, holding themselves out as Messiahs. ' For many shall come [21 Mat. 5] in my name, saying, I am the Christ; and shall lead many astray.'

Mark: 'Many shall come in my name, saying, I am *he*, and shall lead many astray.' The word 'for' before 'many' has been omitted by the Revisers, on the authority of the two oldest MSS. Luke: 'For many shall come in my name, saying, I am *he*; and, The time is at hand; go ye not after them.' We have not, nor do we need, any historical corroboration with respect to this prediction. Alford says: 'Of such persons, before the destruction of Jerusalem, we have no distinct record; doubtless there were such: but I believe the prophecy and warning to have a further reference to the latter times, in which its complete fulfilment must be looked for. The persons usually cited as fulfilling this (Theudas, Simon Magus, Barchochab, &c.) are all too early or too late, and not correspondent to the condition, *in my name*, with my name as the ground of their pretences.' The expression 'in my name' occurs in several other passages. 'Whoso shall receive one such little child in my name receiveth me.' 'Where two or three are gathered together in my name, there am I in the midst of them.' 'There is no man which shall do a mighty work in my name, and be able quickly to speak evil of me.' 'Whatsoever ye shall ask in my name, that will I do.' In every instance the words 'in my name' denote a recognition of Jesus and an action having reference to him. The deceivers of whom Jesus spoke would so acknowledge him and profess their adherence to him. 'Many shall come in my name:' this must be taken as explaining and modifying the following words, 'saying, I am the Christ.' As representatives of Jesus they would claim his Christhood or anointing, holding themselves out as dispensers of his salvation. Only Matthew introduces the words, 'the Christ.' In Mark and Luke the translators have supplied the word 'he.' Omitting it, 'Many shall come in my name, saying I am,' is clear enough from its very vagueness: 'I am'—whatever one coming in Christ's name can claim to be, clothed with his authority, ministering his gifts, in a sense, myself 'the Christ,' at least to this extent, that without me you cannot have him. Jesus foretold not a few, but 'many' such; and we must needs believe that self-deception on their part is antecedent to their leading 'many astray.' Every perversion of the true gospel of Christ is pointed at in this prophecy, and every unwarranted assumption of priestly and sacramental power. 'Take heed that no man lead you astray:' that counsel is even more needful for us than for the apostles. Misconceptions abound, and we can only be delivered from them by reverting to the pure and simple gospel of Jesus: that, apart from all that men have added to it and taken from it, should be all our salvation and all our desire. For eighteen centuries the 'gospel' has been proclaimed, with such a multitude of accretions and disfigurements, and with such an absence of the essential and primary requirements imposed by Jesus on his 'disciples,' that it is no wonder honest preachers have to wring their hands over the result, with the heartrending admission: 'We have not wrought any deliverance in the earth; neither have the inhabitants of the world fallen (or, been born).' The cry of our spiritual guides has ever been, 'the time is at hand:' but what, or what manner of time, the Spirit of Christ signifies, mankind has still to learn: assuredly it has not yet dawned upon the nations. They stand always armed to the teeth and ready for war, every people in Europe oppressed by the weight of military service, or by the taxation necessary to maintain a standing army. It is impossible to admit that the gospel of Christ has free course, runs and is glorified, while such a condition of society continues. Jesus alluded to it as the foremost indication of the world's hostility to his kingdom of righteousness, peace and joy, and as a phenomenon which must needs exercise the minds of his disciples. 'And ye shall hear of wars and rumours of wars: see that ye be not troubled.' Mark: 'And when ye shall hear of wars and rumours of wars, be not troubled.' Luke: 'And when ye shall hear of wars and tumults, be not terrified.' It might well seem to them, as it should to us, that the cause of their Master must either be lost or indefinitely postponed, so long as men fight like beasts, biting, devouring, destroying each other, and actually glorying in war and carnage. That could not be helped: society could not be transformed in a day, and time was required for the triumph of the gospel. 'For *these things* must needs come to pass: but the end is not yet.' The Revisers have omitted 'all' before the italicised words 'these things.' The two oldest MSS. have, 'for it must come to pass.' Tischendorf renders: 'For they must come to pass.' The 'end' (*telos*) is obviously 'the end (*suntelia*) of the age' previously mentioned (verse 4), the two words having the same sense. Mark: '*These things* must needs come to pass first; but the end is not immediately.' The last word stands in the Authorised Version as 'yet.' Viewing the then existing state of the world, Jesus did not anticipate, under the most favourable circumstances, the speedy prevalence of his doctrine. But did he anticipate that throughout and at the end of eighteen centuries, the world would be what it has been and now is? Are we to assume that he calmly acquiesces in that state of things which we contemplate with an indifference bordering on complacency? Let us not mistake his words, as though they imported the gradual unfolding of a scheme of providential government, the times and seasons of which are beyond human control. The world is what we make it, and the things of the world must remain unchanged until we change them. The universe, physical and moral, was in a state of convulsion, and the disciples of Jesus, few and weak, however ardent and hopeful, could no more expect to control potentates and armies than the forces of nature. 'For nation shall rise against nation, and kingdom against kingdom: and there shall be famines and earthquakes in divers places.' Mark: 'For nation shall rise against nation, and kingdom against kingdom: there shall be earthquakes in divers places; there shall be famines.' The Revisers, following the two oldest MSS., have here omitted twice the conjunction 'and.' Luke: 'Then said he unto them, Nation shall rise against nation, and kingdom against kingdom: and there shall be great earthquakes, and in divers places famines and pestilences; and there shall be terrors and great signs from heaven.' In the Authorised Version 'fearful sights' stands in place of 'terrors.' Young renders it 'fearful things.' In proportion to men's ignorance of science and want of faith, is their terror at anything irregular and abnormal. Blazing comets, and falling stars, and meteoric stones, are in that respect to be classed with earthquakes, famines and pestilences. Jesus taught his disciples to take a calm and rational view of all such things, regarding them as means to an end, indications and premonitions of the changes incident to the constitution and evolution of the world. 'But all these things are the beginning of travail.' The last word is 'sorrows' in the Authorised Version. Alford explains that the literal meaning is 'birth-pangs.' Mark: 'These things are the beginning of travail.' Luke omits the saying. The word 'all' in Matthew makes it include national and dynastic troubles, the rising of nation against nation and kingdom against kingdom. These are the natural, inevitable outcome of man's earthly history, crises indicative of change and inseparable from progress, birth-pangs of humanity, when the old order gives place to the new, and fresh ideas and forms of government are born into the world. This social childbirth has its curse of suffering, and only the plan of salvation devised by Jesus can regenerate society apart from it. His kingdom rests not upon physical force, but on its opposite, gentleness, love, long-suffering. The course of action he laid down was to 'disciple all the nations' (that is Dr. Young's literal rendering) so that through his disciples, men living by his precepts—not to resist evil, not to lay up treasure upon earth—his light might permeate the world's darkness, his spirit of love and self-sacrifice abolish strife, and leaven earth with heaven's own peace and righteousness. Thus to redeem mankind from inherent evil, was no light task, and would involve to these apostles and ministers of Jesus persecution, suffering and death. 'Then shall they deliver you up unto tribulation, and shall kill you : and ye shall be hated of all the nations for my name's sake.' Young renders, 'because of my name;' the 'Englishman's Greek New Testament,' 'on account of my name.' Strange, that the harmless Jesus, and those who devoted themselves to the proclamation of his beneficent purposes, should thus draw down upon themselves the universal hatred of Gentiles as well as Jews. The world was averse to any attempt at change, even in this heavenward direction. The secret springs, the motive power of social influence, were then, as ever since, in the hands of a privileged class, and the hold which these men had gained over the world's affairs they would suffer no man to loosen. Reform was abhorrent to them, especially when it threatened to interfere with their self-will and self-interest. It suited some to play upon the prejudices and passions of the multitude, as when 'the Jews, being moved with jealousy, took unto them certain vile fellows of the rabble, and gathering a crowd, set the city in an uproar ; and assaulting the house of Jason, they sought to bring them forth to the people. And when they found them not, they dragged Jason and certain brethren before the rulers of the city, crying, These that have turned the world upside down are come hither also ; whom Jason hath received : and these all act contrary to the decrees of Cæsar, saying that there is another king, *one* Jesus.' A similar instance happened at Ephesus. 'For a certain man named Demetrius, a silversmith, which made silver shrines of Diana, brought no little business unto the craftsmen ; whom he gathered together, with the workmen of like occupation, and said, Sirs, ye know that by this business we have our wealth. And ye see and hear, that not alone at Ephesus, but almost throughout all Asia, this Paul hath persuaded and turned away much people, saying that they be no gods which are made with hands : and not only is there danger that this our trade come into disrepute; but also that the temple of the great goddess Diana be made of no account, and that she should even be deposed from her magnificence, whom all Asia and the world worshippeth. And when they heard this, they were filled with wrath, and cried out, saying, Great is Diana of the Ephesians.' Whenever a Reformer's hand touches and shakes an error of creed or an abuse of power, the instinct of self-defence and self-preservation rises up in opposition, for those who not only acquiesce in an evil but profit by it, are not likely to forego without a struggle their own advantage. Something more than a mere sentiment of reverence for their deities must have been at work in the bitter persecutions of Christians under the Roman emperors. Were Christ's doctrine of non-resistance to evil now to be adopted by any considerable number of believers, there would be reason to anticipate a somewhat similar outburst of persecution. For such persons would refuse to serve in the army, and would feel bound to declare that under no compulsion would they shed the blood of a fellow-creature. We can imagine what that would lead to in countries where the law of conscription is still in force, as in France, Germany and Russia. The fact that Count Leon Tolstoi's religious works are prohibited in Russia, is significant enough. If any large body of Christians adopted the non-militant doctrine broached in the Sermon on the Mount, not only would autocrats and statesmen seek out and persecute them, but the clergy would be compelled either to side with the ruling powers or to confess that their own teachings in that matter had been erroneous and anti-christian. Such a crisis is as possible now as it was in the days when Jesus foresaw it, and warned his disciples to be prepared for it: 'But take ye heed to yourselves: for they shall deliver you up to councils; and in synagogues shall ye be beaten; and before governors and kings shall ye stand for my sake, for a testimony unto them.' Young readers 'councils,' literally, by 'sanhedrims;' spiritual and secular rulers would combine to accuse and condemn the followers of Jesus. The Authorised Version has, 'for a testimony against them,' now rendered, 'for a testimony unto them:' the disciples would thus bear witness 'unto' the truth of Jesus, not 'against' their persecutors. Luke stands as follows: 'But before all these things, they shall lay their hands on you, and shall persecute you, delivering you up to the synagogues and prisons, bringing you (Gr. *you being brought*) before kings and governors for my name's sake. It shall turn unto you for a testimony.' The notoriety of the accusation and defence would further the cause of the gospel. But not all who professed the faith would stand firm therein. There would be a grave defection among believers generally, traitors in their own ranks, and hatred in the church. 'And then shall many stumble, and shall deliver up one another, and shall hate one another.' The Revisers have altered 'be offended' to 'stumble,' and 'betray' to 'deliver up.' The Sinaitic MS. adds, after 'another,' 'to tribulation,' and omits 'and shall hate one another.' A system of erroneous teaching also would prevail, and many would thereby be turned away from the truth as it is in Jesus. 'And many false prophets shall arise, and shall lead many astray.' 'Prophets' is equivalent to 'teachers,' and 'prophecy' to 'teaching,' the foretelling of future events being altogether subordinate. In

'Helps to the study of the Bible' it is stated: *prophetic* means *instructive*, as well as *predictive*, Acts xiii. 1, 1 Cor. xiii. 2, 8.' By using the word 'many' Jesus let it be understood that the false teaching of Christianity would be widespread; how long it might continue would necessarily depend upon the characters of unborn generations, and the consequent developments of human history. What eighteen centuries of 'teaching' have made of Christianity, doctrinally and practically, is now before our eyes. It behoves us to judge it by its fruits, to investigate it dispassionately, and to compare it carefully with the recorded teaching of Jesus himself. He foresaw that corruptions would creep into the church, and that the prevalence of iniquity therein would undermine its professed love and devotion. 'And because iniquity shall be multiplied, the love of the many shall wax cold.' The Revisers have replaced 'abound' by the stronger expression 'be multiplied:' evil has a power of generation: the longer it exists the more difficult becomes the task of extirpation. Mark and Luke do not allude to the false teaching, but enlarge upon the hatred and persecution. 'And brother shall deliver up brother to death, and the father his child; and children shall rise up against parents, and cause them to be put to death (or, put them to death). And ye shall be hated of all men for my name's sake.' The Revisers have altered 'son' to 'child,' which agrees with Young. Luke: 'But ye shall be delivered up even by parents, and kinsfolk, and friends; and *some* of you shall they cause to be put to death (or, shall they put to death). And ye shall be hated of all men for my name's sake.' Jesus knew well that his new doctrine would be so hateful to mankind generally that the promulgators of it would be held in universal detestation. Whatever came upon them they must bear patiently, with quiet confidence that all would be well with them at the last. 'But he that endureth to the end, the same shall be saved.' Instead of 'endureth' the Authorised Version has 'shall endure;' Young renders: 'But he who hath endured to the end—he shall be saved;' Tischendorf: 'But he that endured unto the end, the same will be saved.' Often the end would be death, but death to them would be safety and life, for nothing about them was perishable. Luke records an additional saying to that effect: 'And not a hair of your head shall perish. In your patience ye shall win your souls (or, lives).' The Authorised Version has, 'In your patience possess ye your souls.' Tischendorf renders: 'And there will not an hair of your heads perish. By your patience acquire your lives.' The hope of a resurrection to life, here and elsewhere held forth by Jesus, differs from the view commonly entertained. He does not distinguish between 'soul' and 'body,' as we are taught to do, for the words 'soul' and 'life' are interchangeable. He does not say, the body will perish, but the soul will live: on the contrary, he declares that not a hair of the head will perish, the body in its entirety will be preserved. Nor does he adjourn that bodily resurrection to a remote future, as some suppose. The only state of existence we know or can really conceive of, is in connection with a bodily organisation. The separate existence of the departed in a disembodied state is never even hinted at by Jesus. 'That the dead are raised' was his doctrine. His picture of Dives and Lazarus represents them with all their corporeal attributes. At his last meal

he assured his disciples : 'I will not drink henceforth of this fruit of 26 Mat. 29
the vine, until the day when I drink it new with you in my Father's
kingdom.' After death he himself was revealed in a bodily form, and
the apostle John wrote : 'We know that, if he shall be manifested, 3 i. John 2
we shall be like him : for we shall see him, even as he is.' With his
hands outstretched in blessing, his resurrection body was uplifted
from the earth and carried off in a cloud ; and while the disciples
'were looking stedfastly into heaven, as he went, behold, two men 1 Acts 10, 11
stood by them in white apparel ; which also said, Ye men of Galilee,
why stand ye looking up into heaven? this Jesus, which was received
up from you into heaven, shall so come in like manner as ye beheld
him going into heaven.' Whenever angelic beings have visited
mankind, it has been in bodily form, and the fashion and lustre of
their clothing have been described. The apostle Paul emphatically
rejected the idea of disembodiment in the future state of existence,
saying : 'For we know that if the earthly house of our tabernacle 5 ii. Cor. 1-3
(or, bodily frame) be dissolved, we have a building from God, a house
not made with hands, eternal, in the heavens. For verily in this we
groan, longing to be clothed upon with our habitation which is from
heaven : if so be that being clothed we shall not be found naked.'
In another passage he represents a doubter of the resurrection he
preached asking, not how a departed soul can exist without a body,
but 'How are the dead raised ? and with what manner of body do 15 i. Cor. 35
they come ?' and he declares : 'If there is a natural body, there is   ,,   44
also a spiritual *body*.' The idea of a separate existence of soul apart
from body is not derived from Scripture, but appears to have been
grafted on to the Christian hope of a resurrection from the teaching
of heathen philosophy. It is found in Plato's 'Phædo,' where
Socrates asks Simmias : 'Do we think that death is anything ?
Certainly, replied Simmias. Is it anything else than the separation
of the soul from the body ? and is not this to die, for the body to be
apart by itself separated from the soul, and for the soul to subsist
apart by itself separated from the body ? Is death anything else
than this ? No, but this, he replied.' That stands in direct opposition to the teaching of Paul. It was but a guess of Socrates, the
best he could make, and ably reasoned out ; but Jesus spoke of the
resurrection as one who knew, and his doctrine does not harmonise
with such conceptions. That is not the only point in which Jesus
differed from Socrates, and wherein Christians have followed the
latter rather than the former. In the same discourse Socrates
observed : 'As long as we are encumbered with the body, and our
soul is contaminated with such an evil, we can never fully attain to
what we desire ; and this, we say, is truth. For the body subjects us
to innumerable hindrances on account of its necessary support, and
moreover if any diseases befal us, they impede us in our search after
that which is ; and it fills us with longings, desires, fears, all kinds
of fancies, and a multitude of absurdities, so that, as it is said in real
truth, by reason of the body it is never possible to make any advances
in wisdom . . . And while we live, we shall thus, as it seems,
approach nearest to knowledge, if we hold no intercourse or communion at all with the body, except what absolute necessity requires,
nor suffer ourselves to be polluted by its nature, but purify ourselves
from it, until God himself shall release us.' There we have the

foundation on which the practice of asceticism rests, a practice altogether out of harmony with the example and teaching of Jesus and his apostles. Our Lord declared, not the body but the heart, to be the seat and source of all wrong-doing : ' For out of the heart come forth evil thoughts, murders, adulteries, fornications, thefts, false witness, railings ; these are the things which defile the man.' What the skin is to the nerves and flesh, the body is to heart and mind. The source of evil and of good lies deeper than the bodily organs through which the will of the spirit within is worked out and manifested. The apostle Paul expressed the opinion : ' Every sin that a man doeth is without the body,' and went on to instance a sin which men commit against their own bodies. The source of corruption lies within, working outwards. Jesus put the figurative case of an eye or a hand becoming so diseased through sin as to call for amputation : why ? in order to save the other eye or the other hand : but if both were naturally evil, of what avail to extirpate the one ? Sin is the disease of the body : if the whole cannot be delivered, save at least as much of it as possible : ' It is profitable for thee that one of thy members should perish, and not that thy whole body go into Gehenna.' No, argued Socrates : the body is an unmitigated evil ; the mind would be good, without it ; the less we care for it now, and the sooner we are separated from it, the better. We must answer, in the words of Jesus, ' What God hath joined together, let not man put asunder.'

When Jesus first told his disciples, ' Then shall they deliver you up into tribulation, and shall kill you,' and afterwards assured them, ' Not a hair of your head shall perish,' he promised them, in fact, that resurrection-body to which Paul looked forward as 'our habitation which is from heaven.' It by no means follows that we are to restrict that promise to those disciples, or to those who afterwards should believe in Jesus. He once said to his disciples, ' Shall he not much more clothe you, O ye of little faith ? ' not at all implying thereby that God would not clothe and feed others, for he maketh his sun to rise on the evil and the good, and sendeth rain on the just and on the unjust, and clothes the flowers of the field. Freedom from anxiety, a sure hope for this life and the next, distinguish Christians from those who lack their faith and quiet confidence : but all men share the same physical and mental destiny here and hereafter, modified only by their particular character and actions, alike in this world and the next. Lazarus and Dives both entered into the same condition of existence after death, and if—as we doubt not—that parable of things in the heavens is true to nature as all those were which related to earthly things, of both men it can be said that not a hair of the head had perished. The dread of death, simply as death, had no place in the mind of Jesus, and he could only feel wonder and pity for those who entertained it. When the disciples in the storm cried out hysterically, ' Save, Lord ; we perish,' he expostulated against their unreasoning terror : ' And he said unto them, Why are ye fearful, O ye of little faith ? ' Death should be no more the bugbear of our existence than sleep is : the one is as natural, as necessary, as inevitable as the other. Jesus sought to raise the minds of his disciples above the dread of death, his only care being that it should not be prematurely brought about through sin, but that his followers should have life 'age-during.' All who will may take hold of the hope he has set before them; only, life in the world to come is of neither more nor less importance than life in this world: neither of them can be worth much to us apart from the guiding spirit of Jesus. That is why only those devoted to him and anxious to be led by him, can contemplate the future without dismay, and with tranquil, hopeful eyes.

Jesus had far-reaching plans for the welfare of mankind. Amidst all the strife, confusion, devastation prevailing in the world, and as the only effectual antidote of its sad condition, it was essential that the gospel should be universally proclaimed. 'And the gospel must first be preached unto all the nations.' Matthew is fuller: 'And this gospel (or, these good tidings) of the kingdom shall be preached in the whole world (Gr. inhabited earth) for a testimony unto all the nations; and then shall the end come.' The gospel must be received and preached under its social aspects, as 'the gospel of the kingdom.' That—its true nature—has been too much lost sight of. It is regarded rather as a panacea for individual sins and woes, than as a scheme and system of communistic life on earth. The 'kingdom' must needs have a visible, tangible existence, with Jesus as its ruler and his laws for its government. The ecclesiastical polity which calls itself 'the Church,' with its spiritual hierarchy, does not satisfy the requirements of humanity, or answer to the idea of a heavenly kingdom established in the earth. Ministers of religion deem it their chief business to labour for the salvation of men's 'souls' in the next world. There is the only 'kingdom of heaven' they contemplate or aim at; there, not here, the wrongs, evils, inequalities of life, are to be rectified. Meantime, mankind are to be 'saved' through faith, baptism, holy communion, prayers, praises, Bible reading and teaching; society generally, it is admitted, is in a most unsatisfactory and terrible condition, but in spite of that, to every individual member thereof the offer of 'salvation' is made, and it is his own fault if he does not accept it, so as to escape damnation hereafter, whatever his earthly lot may be. While such conceptions prevail of 'the gospel of the kingdom,' and the means at present adopted for its development are deemed sufficient, there is small hope, or rather none at all, of its establishment. We have only, and can have only, the form of Christianity without the power thereof. Civilisation makes headway; education does its work towards elevating the masses; republicanism and democracy mitigate to some extent that habit of war and conquest which is the ingrained inheritance of dynastic and autocratic rulership: and at every step of progress, there is a clapping of hands among religionists, and a shout sent forth by them, See what 'the gospel' has done and is doing! Yes: they will have it, that all our hospitals and modes of caring for the poor—workhouses perhaps excepted—are to be attributed to Christianity: where the Bible is not, or where a false religion —non-protestant—is, there, they say, darkness covers the earth and gross darkness the people. The day for such a style of argument is past. Let us look with honest eyes upon the world and its history. If the evil does not preponderate over the good, it is not because of our profession of Christianity. Look round upon the armaments and hosts of fighting men in Europe; think of the low, degraded, unhappy condition of huge masses of our population: what influence has been produced upon the lust of War or upon the greed of Commerce, by the propagation of what is called 'the gospel?' Absolutely none. Peace, goodwill and equity are the fundamentals of human brotherhood: in the 'inhabited earth' of our day, these virtues are conspicuous by their absence. What may be the triumphs of Christianity in heaven, we know not: but it is time for us to face, and utter, the solemn, startling truth, that the influence of Jesus Christ in the nations of the world is small indeed. His spirit is not in them: the gospel preached is not his gospel, not the 'gospel of the kingdom.' When that has been made 'a testimony unto all the nations,' his promise will come to pass: 'then shall the end come': 'the end of the age,'—of 'wars and rumours of wars,' of sin, and wrong, and misery.

That the preaching of the gospel by the apostles would draw down upon them the hostility of the world, was a foregone conclusion, and Jesus counselled them as to the manner in which he would have them meet the charges brought against them. He bade them dismiss all anxiety on that score, not troubling themselves even to frame their defence beforehand, but to trust, as we should express it, to the inspiration of the moment. 'And when they lead you *to judgement*, and deliver you up, be not anxious beforehand what ye shall speak: but whatsoever shall be given you in that hour, that speak ye: for it is not ye that speak, but the Holy Ghost.' In the Authorised Version the word 'you' after 'lead' is italicised, but the Revisers instead have introduced in italics 'to judgement'; and they have replaced 'take no thought' by 'be not anxious.' They have also omitted, 'neither do ye premeditate,' on the authority of the two oldest MSS. Luke records the same counsel and promise, but in words entirely different: 'Settle it therefore in your hearts, not to meditate beforehand how to answer: for I will give you a mouth and wisdom, which all your adversaries shall not be able to withstand or gainsay.' The Authorised Version has, 'gainsay nor resist:' in the two oldest MSS. the order of those words is reversed, as in the Revised Version. Young renders, literally, 'how to answer,' by 'to make a defence.' The marked difference between Luke and Mark in this particular passage, and its omission by Matthew, lead to the conclusion that more than one original record of the discourse existed from the first. The four disciples to whom it was delivered may each have given his own version of it; or one of them may have supplemented the account prepared by another of them. The words introduced by Luke at this point do not appear to represent the saying of Jesus as given by Matthew, but constitute an additional saying, the latter immediately following upon and strengthening the former.

How are we to understand the words, 'whatsoever shall be given you in that hour, that speak ye: for it is not ye that speak, but the Holy Ghost'? We are not to suppose that a miracle was to be worked at such times: in every emergency of life, when the heart is touched and the mind is full, a power of utterance is given to us, which rises to the level of the occasion. That power may, and often does, fail us, owing to our miserable self-consciousness, making us morbidly sensitive about how we shall look in the eyes of others, or to a want of self-reliance, arising out of our inexperience: for although speech is as intuitive as walking, they are both matters of habit and

13 Mark 11

21 Luke 14, 15

practice. The advice of Jesus was sound and wise. If his disciples were to hold their ground, they must have courage, moral and mental as well as physical. To rehearse their defence beforehand would be the surest way of weakening it : the charges against them might not, probably would not, be formulated till the moment of trial, and a prepared speech might prove wholly inapplicable when the crisis came. It was enough for them to have a clear conscience, a definite aim, an honest purpose : they must learn to front their foes with unembarrassed heart and mind, assured that the tongue would not fail of its office, inasmuch as 'out of the abundance of the heart the month speaketh.' The expression, 'it is not ye that speak, but the Holy Ghost,' is not to be interpreted according to the views of orthodox Trinitarians, for at the time when Jesus first uttered it, those to whom it was addressed could not possibly have understood it in that sense, if even they came to do so after, which must not by any means be taken for granted. Translators, by capitalising Holy and Ghost, have introduced the conception of divine personality : the import does not necessarily seem quite the same when the words are printed, as in Samuel Sharpe's version, 'holy spirit,' without capitals. Instead of adopting current views as a matter of course, let us make a careful study of the scriptural usage and meaning of both words. It has already appeared, from the examination of a multitude of passages, that the term 'holy' denotes anything specially and entirely devoted to the service of God. Let us hold fast to that fact. Jesus was regarded by the company of his disciples as ' thy holy Servant Jesus, whom thou didst anoint :' the word 'holy' there obviously does not refer, as some assume, to moral purity, but to the devotion of Jesus to God's will and purposes. The same significance attaches to the word in the passage, ' ye holy apostles and prophets,' rendered by the Revisers according to the Sinaitic and Vatican MSS., 'ye saints, and ye apostles, and ye prophets.' Zacharias alluded to God's ' holy prophets which have been since the world began.' ' Holy ' is equivalent to ' separate,' ' apart,' and is so applied to God himself : ' Holy, holy, holy *is* the Lord God, the Almighty.' It is not going too far to say, and an examination of the word and its cognates in the many hundreds of passages in which it occurs will justify the assertion, that such is its fixed and invariable meaning. Whenever men, women, angels, apostles, prophets, brethren, are spoken of as ' holy,' it is with reference to their dedication to God and aloofness from the world. In conjunction with the word 'spirit,' whether capitalised or uncapitalised, 'holy' must be admitted to bear the same sense. The 'holy spirit' is for 'holy' people. The apostle John contrasts the spirit of God and the spirit of antichrist, the spirit of truth and the spirit of error. The word 'spirit' is often thus applied in Scripture according to modern usage : as we speak of the 'spirit of patriotism,' the 'spirit of friendship,' the 'theological spirit,' the 'scholastic spirit,' the 'spirit of brotherhood,' and so on, so we read of the 'spirit of adoption,' the 'spirit of bondage,' the ' spirit of fearfulness,' the 'spirit of power and love and discipline,' the 'spirit of counsel,' the 'spirit of glory and of God,' the 'spirit of grace,' the 'spirit of meekness,' the 'spirit of promise,' the 'spirit of prophecy,' the 'spirit of slumber,' the 'spirit of wisdom and revelation.' The apostle Paul asserted : ' In one spirit we were all baptized into one body, whether Jews or Greeks, whether bond or free: and were all made to drink of one spirit:' the meaning of that passage is clear, especially when the capitals introduced by translators are disregarded. To reject and curse Jesus, proves us to be without God's spirit; to acknowledge him as Lord over us, demonstrates that we have 'the holy spirit.' 'No man speaking by the spirit of God calleth Jesus accursed; and no man can say that Jesus is the Lord but by a holy spirit.' That is Sharpe's rendering. The apostle gave a careful explanation about 'spiritual things:' wisdom, knowledge, faith, gifts of healing, miracles, teaching, discernment, languages, were manifestations of the spirit; and he added: 'But all these worketh one and the same spirit, dividing to each man severally as it will.' That is Sharpe's rendering; in the Greek there is no pronoun, and 'he' or 'it' may be adopted, by preference the latter, for the apostle was describing the nature and working of the spiritual influence; he was not contending that the holy spirit which was in all of them was the third person of a divine Trinity. Such an assumption lies wholly outside of Paul's argument, and we must be careful not to introduce it, either into his words or into those of Jesus when he said: 'it is not ye that speak, but the holy spirit.' 'It is not ye that speak:' you have not to argue your own cause, to defend your own interests, to justify and uphold a personal policy and course of action; 'but the holy spirit'—of devotion and self-sacrifice, which will come to you through my teaching and example; the spirit within you being mine, your words also will be mine: 'for I will give you a mouth and wisdom, which all your adversaries shall not be able to withstand or gainsay:' the 'mouth and wisdom' given by Jesus to his disciples, would be the manifestation of his spirit; they being 'holy' to him, the 'holy spirit' would be revealed in their utterances. There is a mystery connected with the impartation and manifestations of that spirit, whether considered as a divine personality or as a supernatural energy or influence, which it is as yet beyond our power to fathom. The first step towards a clearer comprehension of the subject, must be to clear away the dogmatic teaching connected with that doctrine of the Trinity which was elaborated by theologians subsequently to the times of the apostles, and which has been for generations pressed upon the acceptance of the Church by means of a creed bristling with recondite logical arguments and damnatory clauses, one of them being, 'He therefore that will be saved: must thus think of the Trinity.' There can be no freedom of thought, no ripening of judgment, no advance towards perfect truth, for those who bow down their necks to such a yoke of theological assumption and censure.

Reverting to the question of the disciples as to the time of the overthrow of the temple, Jesus told them: 'But when ye see Jerusalem compassed with armies, then know that her desolation is at hand.' Alford renders, 'being compassed,' and observes that the expression 'graphically sets forth the scene now before them, as it should then appear.' Only Luke has recorded this sentence. Matthew is as follows: 'When therefore ye see the abomination of desolation, which was spoken of by (or, through) Daniel the prophet, standing in the (or, a) holy place (let him that readeth understand). .' Young renders 'when' as 'whenever.' Mark: 'But when ye see the abomination of desolation standing where he ought not (let him that readeth understand) .' In Mark the Revisers have omitted the words, 'spoken of by Daniel the prophet,' on the authority of the two oldest MSS. Alford has summarised the ideas of commentators and given his own, as to the meaning of 'the abomination of desolation:' Antiochus Epiphanes, the eagles of the Roman legions, some internal desecration of the temple by the Zealots. The expression occurs twice in Daniel: 'They shall profane the sanctuary, even the fortress, and shall take away the continual *burnt offering*, and they shall set up the abomination that maketh desolate.' Again: 'And from the time that the continual *burnt offering* shall be taken away, and the abomination that maketh desolate set up, there shall be a thousand two hundred and ninety days.' *Burnt offering* has been interpolated; Young inserts '*sacrifice*:' the Authorised Version has '*daily sacrifice*.' What was there, at the time when the sanctuary was profaned, answering to the description of 'the abomination that maketh desolate?' Alford states that Josephus referred the prophecy to *the desolation by the Romans*. We need scarcely seek for any other explanation: the military power was a desolating power, and we are sure that in the eyes of Jesus, who preached love, brotherhood and peace, there could not be a greater abomination. On the words '(let him that readeth understand)' Alford observes: 'This I believe to have been an ecclesiastical note, which, like the doxology in ch. vi. 13, has found its way into the text. If the two first Gospels were published before the destruction of Jerusalem, such an admonition would be very intelligible.' Understanding the allusion to be to the Roman armies, the words recorded by Luke, 'then know that her desolation is at hand,' correspond in sense with Matthew and Mark: the 'desolation' would be accomplished by that 'abomination of desolation.' When entrance had been gained to the city by the soldiery, instant escape must be the only thought. Until the gates were forced, there would have been no possibility of egress, and the favourable moment for departure would be before they were again closed, while the troops were busy wrecking the fortress and the temple. 'Then let them that are in Judæa flee unto the mountains; and let them that are in the midst of her depart out; and let not them that are in the country enter therein.' The Revisers have altered 'countries' to 'country.' Alford explains: '*the fields*, not *the countries*, or *the provinces*. It is in the original the same word as our Lord uses in John iv. 35, where he commands his disciples to lift up their eyes on the fields.' There would be no safety anywhere: home and property must be forsaken if bare life was to be preserved. In Matthew the words are even more urgent. 'Then let them that are in Judæa flee unto the mountains: let him that is on the housetop not go down to take out the things that are in his house: and let him that is in the field not return back to take his cloke.' The Revisers have replaced 'any thing' by 'the things,' and 'clothes' by 'cloke,' following the two oldest MSS. Mark: 'Then let them that are in Judæa flee unto the mountains: and let him that is on the housetop not go down, nor enter in, to take anything out of his house: and let him that is in the field not return back to take his cloke.' The flight must be rapid, for the pursuit would be hot, and the sword unsparing. 'But woe unto them that are with child and to them that give suck in those days.' Luke prefaces that with the words : 'For these are days of vengeance, that all things which are written may be fulfilled.' Whenever the word 'vengeance' occurs, we must eliminate from its sense all idea of hatred and vindictive retaliation : divine vengeance, unlike human vengeance, as the latter is generally understood, is simply divine justice working out a wise and necessary law of retribution. The doom was irrevocable, inevitable, the fulfilment of 'all things which are written.' Luke adds : 'for there shall be great distress upon the land (or, earth) and wrath upon this people.' If we understand this to refer to divine wrath, the same remark applies as to the word vengeance ; if to the wrath of the conquerors, the apostolic reflection applies : 'the wrath of man worketh not the righteousness of God :' it wrecked Jewish nationality, but it did nothing towards, but retarded for many centuries, the establishment of Messiah's kingdom. From that day to this, military prowess has been the strength and the curse of nations, even of those which have deemed themselves 'christianised.' Jesus foresaw no hope of the triumph of his cause among the Gentiles ; they would thus subjugate the Jews, and afterwards work out their own destinies, in their own way, which would not be his, nor would their times be his times. 'And they shall fall by the edge of the sword, and shall be led captive into all the nations : and Jerusalem shall be trodden down of the Gentiles until the times of the Gentiles shall be fulfilled.' Alford renders, 'shall remain trodden down,' and explains that 'the construction of the word in the original is unusual, and is made use of to signify a state of duration,—a condition which shall continue.' He adds : 'The *times of the Gentiles* are the *end of the Gentile dispensation*, just as the *time* of Jerusalem was the end, fulfilment, of the Jewish dispensation ; the great rejection of the Lord by the Gentile world, answering to its type, His rejection by the Jews, being finished, the *time* shall come, of which the destruction of Jerusalem was a type. *Times* has the same meaning as *time :* no essential difference is to be insisted on. It is plural, because the Gentiles (nations) are plural : each Gentile people having in turn its *time*.' Only Luke has recorded this forecast of Jesus. Matthew and Mark report the sorrowful words in which he dwelt on the miseries which would overtake the Jewish fugitives. 'And pray ye that your flight be not in the winter, neither on a sabbath : for then shall be great tribulation, such as hath not been from the beginning of the world until now, no, nor ever shall be.' In Mark the wording is somewhat different : 'And pray ye that it be not in the winter. For those days shall be tribulation, such as there hath not been the like from the beginning of the creation which God created until now, and never shall be.' Matthew says, 'from the beginning of the world ;' Mark : 'from the beginning of the creation which God created.' We can hardly suppose that Jesus used both expressions ; probably the one most out of the common was his ; the other evangelist caught the sense, although the exact words escaped his memory. Alford observes that the allusion to the sabbath referred 'to the positive impediments which might meet them on that day, the shutting of the gates of cities &c., and their own scruples about travelling further than the ordinary sabbath day's journey (about a mile English).'

How must we understand the words, 'Pray ye that your flight be not in the winter, neither on a sabbath'? Jesus spoke of the catastrophe as inevitable, but urged his disciples to pray that its attendant evils might to this extent be mitigated. Surely, unless he believed the prayer would be heard, he would not have counselled it; neither would he have done so, if that boon was sure to be vouchsafed without the asking. Neither was any assurance coupled with the counsel: the prayer might, or might not, be granted. Still it was a thing, if not the only thing, they would feel justified in praying for. And being forewarned to desire that much, and pray for that much only, their own efforts would be turned towards that object. In the midst of the siege, that would be their one clue as to the best policy; either to urge surrender before the winter set in, or the holding out until it had passed, and so to hasten or defer the last crisis as to avoid its occurrence on the eve of the sabbath. All to whom these words of Jesus came, would remember them at that fateful period, and exert their influence accordingly. What men pray for, they must needs strive for; and what faithful souls earnestly desire, and feel to be beyond the reach of their own powers, they must needs pray for. Uncertainty, difficulty, danger, helplessness: these are the incentives to prayer. We do not pray for power to use our limbs or minds, so long as we are conscious of possessing bodily and mental vigour; nor when accident or ill-health befalls us do we pray for recovery, until we have first availed ourselves of surgical or medical assistance. But when the lamp of life burns low, and human aid and skill have done their utmost, and the need of a higher power is felt, then, and not till then, do we feel justified in praying, either for relief, or deliverance, or whatever other issue God may please to vouchsafe. Weakness, faith, hope, submission: these are the elements of prayer. The prayer which is taught us, deals only with the things which it is certain God desires for men and is willing to bestow upon them. That is true of every petition in the Lord's prayer: it brings our mind into harmony with the divine will and purposes. 'All things whatsoever ye pray and ask for, believe that ye have received them, and ye shall have them.' Our only certainty in prayer is with respect to those things which we are assured God has already granted. That applies to 'common' prayer: 'whatsoever ye,' as a community, not as individuals, 'pray and ask for'; but that private and personal petitions, touching only our individual welfare, have no such assurance, is evident from two instances: Jesus in Gethsemane prayed with a reservation, 'that, if it were possible, the hour might pass away from him,' but his own will therein was not accomplished: Paul also 'besought the Lord thrice' that his 'thorn in the flesh' might depart from him, but in vain. The philosophy of prayer,—its basis, instinctiveness, reasonableness, efficacy and disappointments,— call for independent, honest, reverential investigation. The ideas current with respect to it are crude, unsettled, uncertain; some of us are apt, and most of us are urged, to resort to prayer in a spirit and fashion not wholly free from superstition and false assumptions: the bent knee, the cross made by the fingers, the repetition of the Church Service, the words learnt by rote and uttered in public or private, are regarded too much in the light of charms, acceptable to God and the saints, and of virtue to ward off evils and draw down divine blessings. In order to obtain the broadest and truest possible view

[11] Mark 24

[14] Mark 25

[12] ii. Cor. s

of this important subject, let us examine methodically the references to prayer in the New Testament. They may be classed under the following heads: 1. Prayers of Jesus. 2. Apostolic prayers. 3. Exhortations to prayer. 4. Answers to prayer. 5. Habit of prayer. 6. Forms of prayer. 7. Ostentation in prayer. 8. Imperfection in prayer. 9. Intercessory prayer.

^{3 Luke 21}
^{14 Mat. 23}
^{9 Luke 18}
^{11 Luke 1}
^{9 Luke 28}
^{26 Mat. 36,}
^{39, 43}
^{17 John}

(1). Jesus prayed at his baptism. After feeding the multitudes 'he went up into the mountain apart to pray.' He prayed alone and with his disciples: 'As he was praying alone, the disciples were with him.' Again: 'As he was praying in a certain place.' Again: 'He took with him Peter and John and James, and went up into the mountain to pray.' He prayed in Gethsemane for himself and for

^{1 Mark 35}

his disciples. Once, 'in the morning, a great while before day, he rose up and went out, and departed into a desert place, and there

^{5 Luke 16}
^{22 Luke 32}
^{,, 44}

prayed.' In the midst of his labours 'he withdrew himself into the deserts, and prayed.' He said to Simon, 'I made supplication for thee, that thy faith fail not.' In Gethsemane, 'being in an agony he prayed more earnestly.' The writer to the Hebrews alludes to his

^{5 Heb. 7}
^{14 John 16}

'having offered up prayers and supplications with strong crying and tears.' He promised his disciples: 'I will pray the Father, and he shall give you another Comforter.'

(2). *The instances of apostolic prayer are numerous.* They prayed

^{1 Acts 21}
^{6 Acts 4}
^{8 Acts 15}
^{9 Acts 40}
^{13 Acts 3}
^{9 Acts 11}
^{16 Acts 25}

before electing an apostle to take the place of Judas. They said, 'We will continue steadfastly in prayer, and in the ministry of the word.' When Peter and John visited the Samaritans, they 'prayed for them, that they might receive the Holy Ghost.' Peter prayed over the body of Tabitha. Certain prophets and teachers 'fasted and prayed and laid their hands on' Barnabas and Saul. Paul prayed at his conversion: 'Behold, he prayeth.' In prison, 'Paul and Silas were praying and singing hymns unto God.' Parting from the elders

^{20 Acts 20}

of the church of Ephesus, Paul 'kneeled down, and prayed with them all.' At Tyre the parting of the disciples is thus described:

^{21 Acts 5}
^{22 Acts 17}
^{28 Acts 8}
^{1 Rom. 9-11}

'and kneeling down on the beach, we prayed, and bade each other farewell.' Paul relates that in Jerusalem, 'while I prayed in the temple, I fell into a trance.' At Melita, Paul prayed over the father of Publius, and healed him. To the Romans Paul wrote: 'Unceasingly I make mention of you, always in my prayers making request, if by any means now at length I may be prospered by the will of God to come unto you. For I long to see you, that I may

^{13 ii. Cor. 7}
^{1 Phil. 4}

impart unto you some spiritual gift.' Again: 'Now we pray to God that ye do no evil.' To the Philippians he wrote: 'Always in every supplication of mine on behalf of you all making my supplication with joy, for your fellowship in furtherance of the gospel from the

^{,, 9}

first day until now. . . . And this I pray, that your love may abound yet more and more in knowledge and all discernment; so that ye may approve the things that are excellent; that ye may be sincere and void of offence unto the day of Christ, being filled with the fruits of righteousness, which are through Jesus Christ, unto the

^{Col. 9, 10}

glory and praise of God.' To the Colossians: 'We . . . do not cease to pray and make request for you, that ye may be filled with the knowledge of his will in all spiritual wisdom and understanding, to walk worthily of the Lord unto all pleasing, bearing fruit in every good work, and increasing in the knowledge of God.' To the Thessalonians: 'Night and day praying exceedingly that we may see your face, and may perfect that which is lacking in your faith.' Again: 'The God of peace himself sanctify you wholly; and may your spirit and soul and body be preserved entire, without blame at the coming of our Lord Jesus Christ.' Again: 'We pray always for you, that our God may count you worthy of your calling, and fulfil every desire of goodness and *every* work of faith, with power.' To Timothy: 'At my first defence no one took my part, but all forsook me: may it not be laid to their account.' For his unbelieving countrymen Paul prayed: 'My heart's desire and my supplication to God is for them, that they may be saved.'

(3). *Exhortations to prayer abound.* Jesus counselled his disciples: 'Pray for them that persecute you.' 'Pray ye therefore the Lord of the harvest, that he send forth labourers into his harvest.' 'Pray ye that your flight be not in the winter, neither on a sabbath.' 'Watch and pray that ye enter not into temptation.' 'And he spake a parable unto them to the end that they ought always to pray, and not to faint.' Peter bade Simon the sorcerer, 'Pray the Lord, if perhaps the thought of thy heart shall be forgiven thee.' Paul desired the Romans to be, 'patient in tribulation, continuing instant in prayer.' Again: 'Strive together with me in your prayers to God for me; that I may be delivered from them that are disobedient in Judæa, and that my ministration which *I have* for Jerusalem may be asceptable to the saints.' He wrote to the Corinthians: 'Let him that speaketh in a tongue pray that he may interpret.' Again: 'Ye also helping together on our behalf by your supplication.' Again: 'While they themselves also, with supplication on your behalf, long after you by reason of the exceeding grace of God in you.' To the Ephesians: 'With all prayer and supplication praying at all seasons in the spirit, and watching thereunto in all perseverance and supplication for all the saints, and on my behalf.' To the Philippians: 'Rejoice in the Lord alway: again I will say, Rejoice. Let your forbearance be known unto all men. The Lord is at hand. In nothing be anxious; but in everything by prayer and supplication with thanksgiving let your requests be made known unto God. And the peace of God, which passeth all understanding, shall guard your hearts and your thoughts in Christ Jesus.' To the Colossians: 'Continue steadfastly in prayer, watching therein with thanksgiving; withal praying for us also, that God may open unto us a door for the word, to speak the mystery of Christ.' To the Thessalonians: 'Rejoice alway; pray without ceasing; in everything give thanks; for this is the will of God in Christ Jesus to youward. . . . Brethren pray for us.' To Timothy: 'I exhort, therefore, first of all, that supplications, prayers, intercessions, thanksgivings, be made for all men; for kings and all that are in high place; that we may lead a tranquil and quiet life in all godliness and gravity. This is good and acceptable in the sight of God our Saviour; who willeth that all men should be saved, and come to the knowledge of the truth.' Again: 'I desire therefore that the men pray in every place, lifting up holy hands, without wrath and disputing.' James wrote: 'Is any among you suffering? let him pray. . . . Is any among you sick? let him call for the elders of the church; and let them pray over him, anointing him with oil in the name of the Lord. . . . Confess therefore believers, who were bidden to let their moderation or gentleness be conspicuous, and to take the consequences of renouncing self-defence or retaliation, knowing that the Lord was near them, and that such a course of conduct was matter for rejoicing instead of anxiety, and would fill their hearts and thoughts with the peace of Christ Jesus. In the same way, the exhortation 'that supplications, prayers, intercessions, thanksgivings be made for all men, for kings and all that are in high place,' had reference to the peace of the church, 'that we (believers) may lead a tranquil and quiet life in all godliness and gravity.' The apostle goes on to say that such a state of affairs would be acceptable to Jesus, as tending to promote his salvation and truth among mankind. (4) The recorded answers to prayer are connected with the spread of the gospel. When the element of personality comes in, it is either in connection with apostolic work, or at a crisis in individual experience: 'Through your prayers I shall be granted unto you.' 'The prayer of faith shall save him that is sick.' (5) Prayer, as a simple habit, was rather discouraged than encouraged by Jesus. With the Jews, as with ourselves, it was necessarily more or less a matter of custom and routine, as when 'Peter went up upon the housetop to pray, about the sixth hour,' and as Cornelius 'prayed to God alway.' Prayer cannot always be spontaneous, instinctive, born of an urgent sense of need, any more than letters to relatives and friends can always be prompted by outbursts of affection and regard: but the charm and virtue and value of prayer are gone, whenever it becomes merely perfunctory, just as intercourse with our fellows deteriorates when goodwill, courtesy, or vivacity are absent. Better say nothing, than not say it from the heart and with sincerity. Earnestness of spirit, as in the case of Epaphras, when engaged in the work of God in Christ, may naturally and constantly find vent in prayer. Paul asserted that our very food is 'sanctified through the word of God and prayer:' the 'word of God' apparently meaning the removal or absence of divine restrictions, such as had been imposed upon the Jews in regard to certain meats, and 'thanksgiving' and 'prayer' denoting rather the recipient's habitual frame of mind than any set form of words at meal time. The custom of saying grace may perhaps be based upon some idea originally arising out of this passage. That habit comes to us by inheritance, descending from father to son; it is so widely recognised, so simple, harmless, spontaneous, that none, or very few, would seek to discourage it, although to minds of deepest faith and reverence it may appear unimportant, not altogether free from superstition, often degenerating into a senseless, formal gabble. Those who insist upon it should give more care to its form and manner: the shorter it is, the better; a thanksgiving seems more appropriate than a prayer: 'For what we are about to receive may the Lord make us truly thankful,' is not praise, has no note of joy or thanksgiving, but of self-depreciation and lack of gratitude. Well suited to it are the folded hands and downcast eyes: but when Jesus gave thanks before the multitude, 'looking up to heaven, he blessed.' Why not choose some short outburst of melody, fit either to be sung or spoken: 'Thanks be to God.—Praise God for all.—Lift up your hearts.—For what we receive let us be thankful.' There is, however, a growing tendency towards the omission of grace: it is now generally restricted to the principal meal of the day; the custom of saying it after dinner as well as before, may next be dropped; and as we attain to wider views of God's providence, we shall ask ourselves, why thank him for food only, and at a set time only? Are we not equally indebted to him for raiment, for books, and everything that nourishes the intellect, for medicine, for sleep, for daylight and for darkness? Yet for none of these things do we think of saying grace. Why select one form only of his gifts, as calling for repeated devout acknowledgment? Not irreverence, but a deeper reverence, not ingratitude, but an ampler and more abiding sense of gratitude, must needs more and more tend to abolish the custom which has come to be described as 'asking a blessing' on our food.

An analogous custom, to which the same ideas apply, is that of bowing at the name of Jesus. The number of worshippers in church who neglect doing so is on the increase, although where the ritual is high the genuflexions are more frequent and punctilious than formerly. Anything between these two extremes is to be deprecated rather than encouraged. If obeisance is to be made at all, it should be as formal and reverential as possible. The careless, shame-faced, sudden nod at mention of the name, is no honour to Jesus, no credit to those who offer it. Better nothing, than only that. That is why some of us avoid it: we do not choose to be conspicuously formal, yet feel that nothing less than a profound and solemn inclination of the body can properly express the honour we owe to Jesus. Why should we be taught to bow at mention of the name of One who is invisible? Probably through some misapplication of Paul's magnificent words: 'Wherefore also God highly exalted him, and gave unto him the name which is above every name: that in the name of Jesus every knee should bow, of *things* in heaven, and *things* on earth, and *things* under the earth, and that every tongue should confess that Jesus Christ is Lord, to the glory of God the Father.' It were worse than pueri e to understand that as obliging us to curve the knee and lower the head whenever Jesus is spoken of. The one occasion on which that has been chiefly insisted upon and observed, namely in the saying of the Creed, is precisely the occasion on which it is logically wrong. For Jesus has laid down the rule: 'that all may honour the Son, even as they honour the Father,'—not 'above the Father,' which is certainly the case when we fail to bow at the words, 'I believe in God the Father Almighty,' and the next moment bow at the words, 'and in Jesus Christ his only Son our Lord.'

(6) With respect to forms of prayer, Jesus by precept and example insisted upon brevity, and there is no instance of prolonged formal prayer, or intimation of any benefit therefrom, to be found in the New Testament. (7) Any over-estimate of prayer is apt to lead to hypocrisy, some exhibiting their performances and others admiring them. (8) The things we most need are those we are unable to ask, and which the Spirit entreats on our behalf. (9) Intercession on behalf of others, as regards simply their individual welfare, finds small countenance in the New Testament. The apostle John restricts the efficacy of prayer by saying, 'If we ask ANYTHING ACCORDING TO HIS WILL, he heareth us: and IF WE KNOW that he heareth us whatsoever we ask, we know that we have the petitions which we

have asked of him.' Then he speaks of intercession for a brother's sin, but limits it to 'them that sin not unto death.' If the offence is one against which capital punishment has been decreed, he could not hold that any intercession should be made for it: 'There is a sin (or, sin) unto death: not concerning this do I say that he should make request.'

1. John 16

The ideas current and the advice given with respect to prayer, are often not in harmony with these Scriptural teachings and examples. From the opinions expressed about prayer: its absolute necessity, its acceptableness to God, its undoubted efficacy, the danger of neglecting it, the blessings it draws down, the evidence it affords of our spiritual condition, one would imagine it had been imposed upon us by divine command, and that our clerical teachers would be able to prove all the assertions they so positively make on the subject. That is far from being the case. Prayer is an instinct of humanity, and as long as man is man and human life is what it is, prayer for divine help and guidance will never cease. Prayer at its best is neither more nor less than the asking from God something we have not and earnestly desire. Let us have the same confidence in our heavenly Father as our own children have in us. The request to Jesus, 'Lord, teach us to pray, as John also taught his disciples,' is just as though a tutor should be asked by the family he taught, Sir, teach us what to ask our father for. What could he say except, in effect, Ask what you are sure he means to give you as being right and best for you? To prescribe a set form of prayer, is to meet a craving of human nature arising out of a sense of distance from God and a desire to call his attention to us, our wants and cravings. In proportion as we realise his presence and loving providence, prayer ceases and is replaced by praise, and that not necessarily formal and verbal, but the overflowing in mind and heart of a joyful confidence. Our children are not ever asking us to supply their wants, knowing well our daily, hourly care for them; but what we fail to give them, and they,—naturally or unwisely,—wish to have, that they will ask, and we shall grant or refuse according to our better judgment. Take that as an illustration of the whole theory and practice of prayer. It must needs spring out of human wants and wishes, and therefore does not rest upon any divine command. How much less can its presence or absence be regarded as an indication of either our love or disregard of God! The infant, nestling in its mother's bosom, prays not; children, having all that heart could wish, and knowing neither care nor grief, pray not, except so far as they are taught to bend the knees and repeat phrases they have learned by rote. Are they less dear on that account to the heavenly Father, than we are who lay before him the burden of our anxieties and sorrows, with our smitings on the breast and cries of 'God be merciful to me, a sinner?' In no wise, surely. Prayer, from first to last, in its inception and through all its phases, is purely and entirely human, and, like every other outcome of our nature, is liable to aberrations of judgment and morbid developments. . The Pharisees who plumed themselves on the perfection of their prayers, were enslaved by a system and mode of thought the very reverse of heavenly or divine. We have reason to guard against the same spirit of hypocrisy; for in the length of public prayer on sabbath-days, the members of the

Church of England have outstripped the intentions of their pious forefathers, by rolling two or three services into one morning service, in the course of which the Lord's prayer is repeated twice or thrice. The strain of such prolonged formalities would be more acutely realised than it is, were it not that to a greater or less degree inattention and mind-wandering have become habitual to most or all of us, and can neither be reproved nor detected. If our clergy would only think what a hotbed for the growth of hypocrisy these long services are, they would soon resolve on shortening them. But instead of that, these wearying exercises are regarded as normal modes of 'divine worship,' appointed 'means of grace,' the instinctive relaxation and revolt of our minds being by some denounced either as infirmities of the unregenerate nature or as temptations of the devil. Let us form and cherish healthier, wiser, broader views of prayer. What earthly father would think the better of a child who asked most, most often, and with most words? The very idea is an absurdity: yet we have admitted it into our conceptions of the relationship between God and man! God is to be worshipped, not with the mouth only, nor with the mind and mouth together only, but through all our faculties and actions, by a life spent in accordance with his laws and will. Is prayer a great matter in his sight? Surely not, unless when it is natural, spontaneous, unforced, unhypocritical. As we continue daily to bow our knees before him, let us aim at two things: sincerity and brevity, the latter being essential to the former. 'Be not rash with thy mouth, and let not thine heart be hasty to utter anything before God; for God is in heaven, and thou upon earth: therefore let thy words be few.' The Mosaic ritual was a divinely appointed mode of ceremonial worship: altars, sacrifices, censers, incense, sprinklings, washings, signs and symbols there were in abundance, but prayer was chiefly conspicuous by its absence. God did not enjoin it, and the first recorded words of Jesus with respect to it were words of warning: 'When ye pray, ye shall not be as the hypocrites.' Let us put a watch upon ourselves, lest prayer degenerate into a slovenly pretence, a mere perfunctory custom, a lowly posture without the sense of reverence, words without thoughts, expressions without desires. Right living is true praying, for it draws down the divine blessing. 'The eyes of the Lord are upon the righteous, and his ears unto their supplication.' 5 Eccl. 2 6 Mat. 5

Jesus intimated that even in the downfall of Jerusalem, the time of slaughter would be shortened for the elect's sake. 'And except those days had been shortened, no flesh would have been saved: but for the elect's sake those days shall be shortened.' The Authorised Version has 'should be shortened,' instead of 'had been shortened;' the original reading of the Sinaitic MS. was 'were shortened.' Mark is as follows: 'And except the Lord had shortened the days, no flesh would have been saved: but for the elect's sake, whom he chose, he shortened the days.' Young renders: 'And if the Lord shortened not the days, no flesh had been saved; but because of the chosen, whom He chose for Himself, He shortened the days.' The French and German versions indicate that the word 'elect' is plural: a divine interposition would be vouchsafed on behalf of the remnant of the people, out of regard for those who had devoted themselves to the will of God in Christ. Or perhaps the words have a wider 21 Mat. 22 13 Mark 20 application, meaning for the sake of the Jewish nation generally, the 'children of Jacob, his chosen ones.' But they must not expect any manifestation of the Christ in those days: 'Then if any man shall say unto you, Lo, here is the Christ, or, Here; believe *it* (or, him) not.' The Revised Version replaces 'there' by 'here,' before 'believe,' which agrees with Young's rendering, the original word (*hōde*) being the same in both places. Mark stands: 'And then if any man shall say unto you, Lo, here (*hōde*) is the Christ; or, Lo, there (*ekei*); believe *it* (or, him) not.' Alford observes that these words 'would tend to correct the idea of the Christians that the Lord's coming was to be simultaneous with the destruction of Jerusalem.' That seems to be quite irreconcilable with the opinion elsewhere expressed by Alford, to the effect that the destruction of Jerusalem was itself a coming of the Lord. There would rise up imitators of Jesus, deceptive teachers, able to give striking, startling evidences in their own favour, basing their claims on works or methods of deliverance so apparently convincing that even those who followed Jesus and were chosen by him would be in danger of being misled. 'For there shall arise false Christs, and false prophets, and shall shew great signs and wonders; so as to lead astray, if possible, even the elect.' Mark corresponds, except that the word 'great' is omitted, and instead of 'so as to' the words 'that they may,' stand before 'lead.' Obviously, the warning against 'false Christs' did not refer to any persons who would come under the assumed personality of Jesus himself. The word 'Christ' must be understood in the sense in which it was then generally used. The Samaritan woman said, 'I know that Messiah cometh (which is called Christ): when he is come, he will declare unto us all things.' Whoever hold themselves out as divinely anointed Teachers, or Saviours, or Messiahs, assume to themselves the office of the Christ. Jesus foretold that some would present themselves in that character, false Christs and false teachers. Such men would probably be self-deceived; nothing is said to the contrary: the huge mass of false doctrine throughout the world has been accumulated and is upheld by men working earnestly, and more or less honestly, on a wrong foundation of faith and practice. Jesus intimated some subtle danger which would need to be watched against. 'But take ye heed.' He foresaw that there would be an inevitable development of humanity in that direction: 'Behold, I have told you all things beforehand.' 'Behold, I have told you beforehand.' Any teaching contrary to the teaching of Jesus, which claims to be his, is a false teaching; any hope held out to mankind in his name, which is contrary to the hope of the gospel he proclaimed, is a false Christianity, and its expounders are to that extent 'false Christs.' The warning of Jesus is very solemn and emphatic: 'If therefore they shall say unto you, Behold, he is in the wilderness; go not forth: Behold, he is in the inner chambers; believe *it* (or, him) not.' Christendom is full of such cries: He is here, in these ordinances and modes of worship; he is here, in these creeds and dogmas; he is here, in the persons of his ministers and his chief representative the pope; he is there, 'in the wilderness' of retirement from the world; he is there 'in the inner chambers' of personal love and consecration; he is here, there, everywhere, anywhere, except in the place where he has told us the kingdom of God must be sought and only can be found,—'within you,' 'in the midst of you,' not as individuals, each intent on saving his own soul, but as a community swayed throughout by the laws of the heavenly kingdom. When Christ comes into the world, when his presence is among us, there will be no doubt or question about the fact, which will be seen and known of all men. 'For as the lightning cometh forth from the east, and is seen even unto the west; so shall be the coming (Gr. presence) of the Son of man.' The word 'also' after 'shall,' and the word 'for' at the beginning of the next verse, have been omitted by the Revisers on the authority of the two oldest MSS. Jesus added: 'Wheresoever the carcase is, there will the eagles (or, vultures) be gathered together.' He had previously used that metaphor, and in the same connection. Whenever and wherever the Son of man is revealed and present, there will be an utter annihilation of the corruptions that are in the world. So long as they continue—wars, crimes, oppressions, and the degradation of the masses—so long does Christ remain absent, in spite of all assurances that he is to be found outside the community, 'in the wilderness,' or within it secretly, 'in the inner chambers.'

The remaining portion of this discourse of Jesus presents unusual difficulty, and its interpretation involves more or less uncertainty. The language is highly figurative, and to disentangle the metaphors from the solemn realities connected with them, to say where symbolism ends and literalism begins, is a task hard if not impossible, with our present imperfect knowledge. Matthew begins as follows: 'But immediately, after the tribulation of those days, the sun shall be darkened, and the moon shall not give her light, and the stars shall fall from heaven, and the powers of the heavens shall be shaken.' The word 'immediately' must not be disregarded. The Revisers have prefaced it with 'but,' rendered 'and' by Young, Tischendorf and Sharpe. The 'and' or 'but' (Greek *de*) is a connecting link with what precedes. The Revisers have inserted a comma after the word 'immediately,' possibly with the object of giving that word the sense of 'suddenly,' but that has not been done by other translators. Alford observes: 'All the difficulty which this word (immediately) has been supposed to involve has arisen from confounding the *partial* fulfilment of the prophecy with its *ultimate* one. The important insertion in Luke (xxi. 23, 24) shows us that the *tribulation* includes *wrath upon this people*, which is yet being inflicted; and the treading down of Jerusalem by the Gentiles, still going on: and immediately after *that tribulation* which shall happen *when the cup of Gentile iniquity is full*, and *when the Gospel shall have been preached in all the world* for a witness, *and rejected by the Gentiles* (in Luke, *the times of the Gentiles be fulfilled*) shall the coming of the Lord Himself happen. . . . The expression in Mark is equally indicative of a considerable interval. *In those days, after that tribulation.*' Even supposing that to be a correct view, it scarcely touches upon the word 'immediately.' The tribulation which Alford *assumes* to happen when the times of the Gentiles shall be fulfilled, had not been mentioned by Jesus, and therefore his words, 'immediately after the tribulation of those days,' cannot apply to that period. But the expresion 'those days' had already been used: 'And except those days had been shortened, no flesh would have been saved:' therefore when, only seven verses lower down, we read: 'And immediately after the tribulation of those days,' it is most natural to refer 'those days' and 'the tribulation' to the time of the destruction of Jerusalem, which must have been the only idea then in the minds of the listeners. Simultaneously with that event, the sun would be darkened, the light of the moon fail, the stars fall, and the powers of heaven be shaken: all these similes of celestial influences denote the deprivation of heavenly light previously granted to the world. The Mosaic economy came then to a sudden end, the Jewish ritual ceased with the destruction of the temple and the dispersion of the people. This was both instantaneous and prolonged, the word 'immediately' in Matthew indicating the former, and Mark's record more clearly bringing out the latter: 'But in those days, after that tribulation, the sun shall be darkened, and the moon shall not give her light, and the stars shall be falling from heaven, and the powers that are in the heavens shall be shaken.' The Authorised Version has, 'the stars of heaven shall fall,' altered by the Revisers to 'the stars shall be falling from heaven,' on the authority of the three oldest MSS. Understanding these celestial prodigies to signify the overthrow of that system of divine worship and revelation which Jehovah had granted to the Israelites alone of all people on the earth, and the sealing up of vision and prophecy with regard to them,—a state of things which has continued from that day to this,—the interpretation of what follows becomes clear and accords therewith. Matthew's record continues: 'And then shall appear the sign of the Son of man in heaven:' sun, moon and stars being blotted out, 'the Son of man' would take their place 'in heaven.' They were set for 'lights in the firmament of the heaven,' and to 'be for signs,' but the only sign now needed in the heavens for the illumination and preservation of the world is Jesus, the foretold 'sun of righteousness' who should 'arise with healing in his wings.' Luke's record contains some additional touches denoting the confusion and terror incidental to the passing away of the old order of things and the introduction of the new. 'And there shall be signs in sun and moon and stars; and upon the earth distress of nations, in perplexity for the roaring of the sea and the billows; men fainting (or, expiring) for fear, and for expectation of the things which are coming on the world (Gr. the inhabited earth); for the powers of the heavens shall be shaken.' Matthew is brief in referring to the national distress: he reports simply the saying, 'and then shall all the tribes of the earth mourn.' The next sentence is given by all three evangelists. Matthew: 'And they shall see the Son of man coming on the clouds of heaven with power and great glory.' Mark: 'And then shall they see the Son of man coming in clouds with great power and glory.' Luke: 'And then shall they see the Son of man coming in a cloud with power and great glory.' Observe the difference between the evangelists: Matthew says 'in the clouds,' Mark, 'in clouds,' Luke, 'in a cloud.' The symbolism is still carried on; sun, moon and stars being obliterated, the Son of man will be seen instead, rising as the sun in a cloudy sky, with all the effulgence and glory of the early dawn. And the dawn is the prelude of the day: shining more and more, like the sun in its strength, the influence of the Son of man will extend throughout the universe: 'And then shall he send forth the angels, and shall gather together his elect from the four winds, from the uttermost part of the earth to the uttermost part of heaven.' The words 'and then,' repeated, may be taken to indicate the consecutiveness rather than the simultaneousness of the events foretold: each must come in due order, one leading the way to the other, a wide interval of time elapsing between the first appearance of 'the sign of the Son of man in heaven' and the final gathering of his elect. Matthew has recorded one more trope introduced by Jesus: 'And he shall send forth his angels with a great sound of a trumpet (or, a trumpet of great sound), and they shall gather together his elect from the four winds, from one end of heaven to the other.' Here again the evangelists differ in a form of expression, one reporting 'from one end of heaven to the other,' the other 'from the uttermost part of the earth to the uttermost part of heaven.' The sense may be the same, but we cannot suppose both phrases were uttered by Jesus: it is enough for us that the narrators are true to the spirit, in spite of such slight discrepancies as to the letter of the discourse. [24 Mat. 31]

From first to last the truths here disclosed are shrouded in figures of speech: the darkened sun and moon, the falling stars, the sign in heaven, the clouds, the trumpet of great sound, the four winds, the roaring sea and billows: there is no reason for taking any one of these in a literal sense. We must deal with prophecy as we find it; there is a system of recondite symbolism running throughout the scriptural revelations of futurity, and some clue is yet wanting to guide our minds to a right interpretation. In all cases we must be careful not to mistake the metaphors for the things they signify. Jesus had previously dealt with the subject of 'the consummation of the age' in the same figurative way: 'As therefore the tares are gathered up and burned with fire; so shall it be in the consummation of the age.' That parable touches on the gathering together of the wicked; this last discourse of Jesus on the gathering together of the elect. In both, the angels of the Son of man are represented as the agents of his purposes; over what period of time this their ministry may extend, we know not, nor in what manner and by what means their task may be executed. The allusion to 'the Son of man coming in clouds with great power and glory,' must not be pressed too literally, any more than the analogous passage, 'Then shall the righteous shine forth as the sun in the kingdom of their Father.' Here is Alford's interpretation of some of the figures of speech: 'The *Sun* of this world and the church is the Lord Jesus—the *Light*, is the knowledge of Him. The *moon*—human knowledge and science. . . . The *stars* (see Dan. viii. 10) are the leaders and teachers of the Church.' No definition is attempted of the *clouds* and the *trumpet*; indeed, Alford takes everything literally as well as figuratively. He says: 'The physical signs shall happen as accompaniments and intensifications of the awful state of things which the description typifies. . . . The knowledge of God shall be obscured—the Truth nigh put out— worldly wisdom darkened—the Church system demolished, and her teachers cast down. And all this in the midst of the fearful signs here recounted: not *setting aside*, but *accompanying*, their literal ulfilment.' This blending of the literal with the symbolical is very [13 Mat. 40] [13 Mat. 43] puzzling and unsatisfactory: we need better guidance than is to be found in the views of Alford.

Luke does not allude to the sending forth of the angels, but records instead the following words of Jesus. 'But when these things begin to come to pass, look up, and lift up your heads; because your redemption draweth nigh.' Amidst all the distress, perplexity and fears of the world, the disciples of Jesus would have reason to be hopeful and confident: his elect were not of the world, and being chosen out of the world would be redeemed from it and gathered together. Is not that process of selection ever going on, not visibly before the eyes of men, but invisibly in the world beyond the grave, even as Lazarus was carried by the angels into Abraham's bosom?

The counterpart of these things might be discerned in the ordinary operations of nature. Jesus said, 'Now from the fig tree learn her parable.' Mark records the same words; Luke is as follows: 'And he spake to them a parable: Behold the fig tree, and all the trees.' Matthew: 'When her branch is now become tender, and putteth forth its leaves, ye know that the summer is nigh.' Mark gives the same words. Luke: 'When they now shoot forth, ye see it and know of your own selves that the summer is now nigh.' One obvious change in the condition of things is the sure indication of others to follow. The budding branches and the foliage foretell the summer, with all that appertains to it,—its heat, brightness, shortened nights and lengthened days, the fruits in their season, and the time of harvest. The coming of the Son of man could be anticipated with equal certainty from the opening scenes of those events which Jesus had now foretold. 'Even so ye also, when ye see all these things, know ye that he (or, it) is nigh, *even* at the doors.' Mark agrees, simply adding after 'things' the words 'coming to pass.' Luke: 'Even so ye also, when ye see these things coming to pass, know ye that the kingdom of God is nigh.' The signs of Christ's coming, and the consummation of the age, would be within the experience of the generation then living: 'Verily I say unto you, This generation shall not pass away, till all these things be accomplished.' Mark records precisely the same words, and Luke simply omits 'these' before 'things.' Alford gives this explanation: 'As regards the parable,—there is a reference to the *withered fig-tree which the Lord cursed.*' The reference was in Alford's mind only, for there is nothing to indicate such a connection. He continues: 'And as that, in its judicial unfruitfulness emblematized the Jewish people,' (that is another unproved assumption), 'so here the putting forth of the fig-tree from its state of winter dryness, symbolizes the *future reviviscence* of that race which the Lord declares shall not pass away till all be fulfilled.' Alford omits to notice the words in Luke, 'and all the trees,' and also the fact that the withered fig tree was doomed never to revive: 'No man eat fruit from thee henceforward for ever.' Alford observes further: 'As this is one of the points on which the rationalizing lay most stress to show that the prophecy has *failed*, I have taken pains to shew, in my Gr. Test., that the word here rendered *generation*, has the meaning of *a race or family of people*. In all the places there cited, the word necessarily bears that signification: having it is true a more pregnant meaning, implying that the character of one generation *stamps itself upon the race*, as here in this verse also. The continued use of *pass away* should have saved the Commentators from the blunder of imagining that the then living generation was meant, seeing that the prophecy is by the next verse carried on to the end of all things: and that, as matter of fact, the Apostles and ancient Christians *did continue to expect the Lord's coming, after that generation had passed away.* The idea that the Jewish race only was alluded to, scarcely accords with the mention of 'the times of the Gentiles,' and the 'distress of nations.' If the word 'generation' is to be taken here as signifying 'a race or family of people,' it would seem rather to mean the human race or family. But unless we overstrain the similes and their application, the then existing generation beheld their verification in the downfall of Jerusalem and Judaism, the troublous times, and the glorious uprising of Christianity. The sending forth of the angels with a trumpet of great sound to gather the elect from the four winds, has never come within the sight and hearing of those dwelling upon earth, but may become visible and audible enough to each successive generation as it passes into the world to come where Jesus rules and reigns. His words, 'this generation shall not pass away, till all these things be accomplished,' compel us to take that view, unless we can adopt Dean Alford's, whose argument that in all the passages cited 'the word necessarily bears' the signification he would have us here attach to it is by itself a proof that the context must fix the sense. The fancy of Alford that the fig tree denotes the Jewish people is the basis of the argument; apart from that idea, the word 'generation' here carries the same meaning as in the passage, 'Whereunto shall I liken this generation?' which 11 Mat. 16 obviously signifies the generation then living. The emphatic declaration of Jesus, 'Verily I say unto you, this generation shall not pass pass away till all these things be accomplished,' should lead to the reinvestigation and modification of the prevalent doctrine concerning his coming to judge the world. He would have us 'from the fig tree learn her parable.' Do not 'the fig tree and all the trees,' season after season, repeat the process which Jesus bids us regard as the illustration of the nearness of his coming? The generations of mankind are renewed, the world's history repeats itself, the sign of the Son of man in heaven is ever visible, all that the apostolic generation saw was seen by our forefathers, and is now seen by us: to all alike the words apply, 'When ye see all these things, know ye that he is nigh, *even* at the doors.' Jesus had previously illustrated the same crisis under the figure of a 'harvest:' 'The harvest is the consumma- 13 Mat. 39 tion of the age, and the reapers are angels.' As long as the English Version stood simply, 'the harvest is the end of the world,' without the alternative reading introduced by the Revisers, it was not possible for most of us to conceive the idea of a reference to anything except the literal destruction either of the earth, or of the universe, or of all mankind simultaneously. As we know but one 'world,' its 'end' could come but once. The word 'age' is totally different in character: its 'end' or 'consummation' conveys simply the idea of the closing up of the past and the opening out of a new future. The simile of harvest-time is akin to that of the budding trees: both figures of speech denote consecutiveness, an endless series of repetitions in the course of nature. Such were the parables chosen by Jesus to symbolise his coming and his judgment of mankind. The Revisers have altered another passage. 'Upon whom the ends of the world are come,' now reads, 'Upon whom the ends of the ages are come,' rendered by Young, 'To whom the ends of the ages came,' and by Tischendorf, 'Unto whom the ends of the ages have reached.' The word 'age' is elastic: it may signify a longer or shorter period, or be pluralised, as here. Let us review some other passages by the light of our Lord's declaration that the first 'generation' of Christians would experience all he foretold in relation to his coming.

_{1 i. Cor. 11}

_{1 i. Cor. 7, 8} 'Waiting for the revelation (coming—A. V.) of our Lord Jesus Christ; who shall also confirm you unto the end, *that ye be* unreproveable in the day of our Lord Jesus Christ.' Why should we assume that these Corinthian converts were disappointed of their hope? that Jesus Christ has not been revealed to them, because not yet to the world? The apostles taught plainly that our experiences are not to be confined to this present life, which is but the border-

_{3 Col. 3, 4} land of futurity. 'Your life is hid with Christ in God. When Christ, our life, shall be manifested, then shall ye also be manifested with him in glory.' Is it to be supposed that there is no manifestation of Christ and his elect in glory, nor can be until at some yet more or less remote period in this world's history? The possible fulfilment of Christ's words in another world than this, has been well

_{5 ii. Pet. 4} nigh lost sight of, and gives rise to the unbelieving scoff. 'Where is the promise of his coming (Gr. presence)? for, from the day that the fathers fell asleep, all things continue as they were from the beginning of creation.' The apostle goes on to argue that the apparent stability of nature is no proof of its unalterableness, and he asserts that as the earth was once overwhelmed and destroyed by water, so it will here-

_{„ 10} after be by fire. He alludes to that catastrophe as ' the day of the the Lord,' but so far from identifying it with his promise, concerning

₉ which there is no slackness (rendered by Young, ' the Lord is not slow in regard to the promise '), the apostle refers that promise to

_{„ 13} another world and a better life : ' But, according to his promise, we look for new heavens and a new earth, wherein dwelleth righteousness.' Our comprehension and interpretation of such passages must necessarily depend on the ideas we bring to them; and the question which now arises in connection with them is, whether each successive generation of believers does not realise all that Jesus foretold and promised concerning his coming and the gathering together of his elect? whether the new heavens and new earth wherein dwelleth righteousness, are not now in actual existence, ruled by Jesus and peopled with his elect? That entirely accords with the words of the

_{1 i. Pet. 3, 4} same apostle : ' Blessed *be* the God and Father of our Lord Jesus Christ, who according to his great mercy begat us again unto a living hope by the resurrection of Jesus Christ from the dead, unto an inheritance incorruptible, and undefiled, and that fadeth not away, reserved in heaven for you, who by the power of God are guarded through faith unto a salvation ready to be revealed in the last time.' The heavenly inheritance exists, and the salvation, *ready to be revealed in the last time.*

In several passages the word 'coming' in the Authorised Version is 'presence' in Greek, and is so noted in the margin by the

Revisers: 'Christ the firstfruits; then they that are Christ's, at his coming (Gr. presence).' 'For what is our hope, or joy, or crown of glorying? Are not even ye, before our Lord Jesus Christ at his coming (Gr. presence)?' 'To the end he may stablish your hearts unblameable in holiness before our God and Father, at the coming (Gr. presence) of our Lord Jesus with all his saints.' 'Touching the coming (Gr. presence) of our Lord Jesus Christ, and our gathering together unto him.' 'Be patient, therefore, brethren, until the coming (Gr. presence) of the Lord.' 'Be ye also patient; stablish your hearts: for the coming (Gr. presence) of the Lord is at hand.' 'When we made known unto you the power and coming (Gr. presence) of our Lord Jesus Christ.' 'Where is the promise of his coming (Gr. presence)?' 'Looking for, and earnestly desiring (or, hastening) the coming (Gr. presence) of the day of God.' 'That, if he shall be manifested, we may have boldness, and not be ashamed before him at his coming (Gr. presence).' 'We that are alive, that are left unto the coming (Gr. presence) of the Lord, shall in no wise precede them that are fallen asleep.' This passage requires examination. The Authorised Version has 'we which are alive *and* remain,' instead of 'we that are alive, that are left;' but Young renders: 'we who are living—who remain over.' Luther agrees therewith: 'die wir leben und überbleiben,' 'we who live and remain over.' Those who 'remain over,' not having been brought through death 'to the presence of the Lord,' are alluded to: this surplus or remnant of Christ's flock 'shall in no wise precede (in no wise may anticipate —Englishman's Greek New Testament) them that are asleep. For the Lord himself shall descend from heaven, with a shout, with the voice of the archangel, and with the trump of God: and the dead in Christ shall rise first: then we that are alive, that are left (who are living, who remain over—Young), shall together with them be caught up in the clouds, to meet the Lord in the air.' This descent of the Lord from heaven and the gathering together to him both of dead and living, is not synonymous with his 'presence,' but appears to constitute that crisis in the history of the universe elsewhere described as the 'revelation' and 'the day' of the Lord. 'Waiting for the revelation of our Lord Jesus Christ; who shall also confirm you unto the end, *that ye be* unreproveable in the day of our Lord Jesus Christ.' The Authorised Version stands: 'waiting for the coming,' altered by the Revisers and Young to 'revelation:' the Greek word here is *apokalupsis*, and out of 18 passages in which it occurs this is the only one in which the Authorised Version renders it as *coming*. The Greek word in the previous passages is *parousia*, which in the following instance the Revisers have failed to render as 'presence:' 'Without blame at the coming (or, appearance) of our Lord Jesus Christ,' although the expression *en tēi parousiāi* would be literally rendered by *in the presence*, instead of *at the coming*. The scriptural doctrine of the 'coming' of the Lord cannot be rightly understood without taking into account these verbal distinctions. The whole subject needs to be reviewed carefully, impartially, from another standpoint than that taken by expounders who look no further than the Authorised Version, and are more intent on building up and clinging to their faith than on testing its foundations.

After saying, 'Verily I say unto you, This generation shall not pass

24 Mat. 35	away, till all these thing be accomplished,' Jesus added : ' Heaven
13 Mark 31	and earth shall pass away, but my words shall not pass away.' This
21 Luke 33	saying is recorded by the three evangelists.. Jesus had used the
5 Mat. 18	same expression in his sermon on the Mount : ' Till heaven and earth pass away, one jot or one tittle shall in no wise pass away from the law, till all things be accomplished.' In these passages there is a deeper meaning than the merely verbal preservation of the law and sayings of Jesus by means of written documents. 'My words' is
8 Mark 38	equivalent to ' my commands ' or ' my will.' ' Whosoever shall be ashamed of me and of my words . . . the Son of man also shall be
14 John 24	ashamed of him.' ' He that loveth me not keepeth not my words.'
15 John 7	' If ye abide in me, and my words abide in you, ask whatsoever ye will, and it shall be done unto you.'
24 Mat. 36	Jesus continued : ' But of that day and hour knoweth no one, not even the angels of heaven, neither the Son, but the Father only.' The words ' neither the Son ' are not in the Authorised Version ; but they are in the two oldest MSS. ; the Revisers note : ' Many authorities, some ancient, omit *neither the Son.*' In Mark the
13 Mark 32	passage stands : ' But of that day or that hour knoweth no one, not even the angels in heaven, neither the Son, but the Father.' Alford's note on Matthew is : ' *That* day, viz. of heaven and earth passing away ; or perhaps referring to verse 30. *Day and hour*—the exact time—as we say *the hour and minute.*' There is no reason for supposing the allusion to be to the coming of the Son of man in verse 30 : that is included in the words, ' all these things.' The passing away of heaven and earth is the consummation of another age, about ' the day and hour,' or ' the day or hour ' of which Jesus could only speak vaguely. He knew no more than the angels of heaven respecting it, and only the Father could forecast the event. This is a very plain declaration, and very puzzling to those who have formulated theories concerning the doctrine of the Trinity. Alford observes : ' This is one of those things which the Father hath *put in his own power,* Acts i. 7, and with which *the Son,* in his mediatorial office, is not acquainted. We must not deal unfaithfully with a plain and solemn assertion of our Lord by such evasions as " He does not know it so as to *reveal* it to us," or as Aug. " He did not so know it as then to indicate it to his disciples." Of such a sense there is not a hint in the context, nay, it is altogether alien from it. The account given by the orthodox Lutherans, as represented by Meyer, that our Lord knew this by *possession,* but not by *use,* is right enough, if at the same time it is carefully remembered, that it was this *possession* of which He emptied Himself when he became man for us, and which it belongs to the very essence of his mediatorial kingdom to hold in subjection to the Father.' Alford observes further : ' All attempts to soften or explain away this weighty truth must be resisted : it will not do to say with Commentators, " He knows it not *as regards us,*" which, however well meant, is a mere evasion : in the course of humiliation undertaken by the Son, in which He increased in wisdom (Luke ii. 52), learned obedience (Heb. v. 8), uttered desires in prayer (Luke vi. 12 &c.), *this matter was hidden from him ;* and as I have already remarked, this is carefully to be borne in mind, in explaining the prophecy before us.' It is, indeed, one of the evils and difficulties of the various accepted and

contradictory systems of dogmatic theology, that very often things have 'carefully to be borne in mind' with respect to them in interpreting the Scriptures, the result being that the true sense of a multitude of passages is either perverted, or ignored, or explained away, or lost in a cloud of haze and uncertainty. Dean Alford here protests against the attempts of other Commentators to reconcile this passage with their own preconceived opinions, but he does the same thing himself, and adopts Meyer's quibble, that 'our Lord knew this by *possession*, but not by *use*,' adding thereto the idea that 'it was this *possession* of which He emptied Himself when he became man for us.' In effect Alford says: Yes; Jesus did not know, but he must originally have known the day and hour of the passing away of heaven and earth. Why? On what ground is that assumption made? Giving full significance to the declaration, 'All things were made by (or, through) him, and without him was not anything made that hath been made,' it follows not that Jesus anticipated the period of their dissolution. The doctrine of divine omniscience is easily expressed in words, but it is really beyond the grasp of our intelligence, and the more enquiring and reverential our minds the less will be our presumption of certainty with respect thereto: for divine revelation and human history alike attest the influence of man's free-will, and we are assured that the divine plans have often been changed to correspond therewith. We are bound to give as much weight to the Scriptural passages which set limits to the power of Jehovah over the human will, and announce the modification or relinquishment of his plans for human benefit, as to those which assert his infinite knowledge and irresistible might. Our science of 'Divinity,' than which a term more arrogant and misleading does not exist in the language of mankind, is far from perfect, and needs to be purged from its misconceptions and brought into harmony with the realities of nature and the teachings of experience. Let us be content to accept in its simplicity, apart from theories and dogmas which have arisen since the words were first uttered, the assertion of Jesus: 'Of that day or that hour knoweth no one, not even the angels in heaven, neither the Son, but the Father.' 1 John 3

Without a break, Matthew's narrative continues: 'And as were the days of Noah, so shall be the coming (Gr. presence) of the Son of man.' That seems to relate to the previous topic; Jesus is now speaking, not 'of that day or that hour,' but of his own days, which on a former occasion also he had compared to the days of Noah: 'And as it came to pass in the days of Noah, even so shall it be also in the days of the Son of man.' In what respect does the comparison hold good? 'For as in those days which were before the flood they were eating and drinking, marrying and giving in marriage, until the day that Noah entered into the ark, and they knew not until the flood came, and took them all away; so shall be the coming (Gr. presence) of the Son of man.' The point here turns upon the words, 'and knew not until the flood came.' The revelation of the Son of man will be by a sudden break in the avocations and interests of the present life. It is not compared to the flood, as a catastrophe to be dreaded, but simply with respect to its instantaneousness and inevitableness. It will involve a process of selection and separation: of two persons, engaged in precisely the same employments, one will be 24 Mat. 37

17 Luke 26

24 Mat. 38,

^{24 Mat 40, 41} chosen and the other rejected. 'There shall two men be in the field: one is taken, and one is left: two women *shall be* grinding at the mill; one is taken, and one is left.' This appears to refer to the gathering together of the elect by the angels (verse 31). Where and when and how this event will happen, is hidden from us. We do not know, and it is rash to assume, that it will take place on this earth. Is there not a world beyond the grave? Is the power of Jesus over human destinies restricted to the present life? Has he no sphere of action in the world to come, and have we no interest in its concerns? It is too narrow an interpretation of all these repeated parables and exhortations of Jesus, to refer them to incidents and experiences which are merely mundane. That view of them takes away all personal interest in the matters urged so solemnly, not only from the present but from all preceding and subsequent generations of mankind, up to the last generation existing upon earth, to which alone the incidents of Christ's coming are generally assumed to appertain. Is there not some fundamental error in the common method of interpreting and applying these revelations of futurity? Is there now no 'coming' or 'presence' of Jesus to his elect anywhere in the universe? And shall we continue to assert, or tacitly assume, that there never will be until he revisits the earth on the eve of its destruction? Those who hold the notion of a purely spiritual existence after death, the unbodied soul living by itself for an indefinite stretch of time up to a moment of general resurrection, unless they take the words 'in the field' and 'grinding at the mill,' as hyperbolical, cannot possibly emancipate themselves from the idea that this prophecy of Jesus must be accomplished here on earth. But when our apprehension of the doctrine of the resurrection becomes modified to the extent of believing that our personality remains after death in human form and with all the attributes of humanity, a spiritual body taking the place of the earthly body, then all the promises and teachings of Jesus become as applicable to the next life as to this, and his 'coming' or 'presence' is a certainty in the experience of each individual, at whatever times and by whatever methods the elect are taken and gathered together and the rest of mankind passed over and left. Some kind of selection and separation is to be looked for at death, for Jesus represented Lazarus as carried by the angels into Abraham's bosom; but it must not therefore be imagined that the coming of Jesus is coincident with death, or can be in any way identified therewith. The coming of the Lord is at a time or times of his own appointment, but death may happen at any moment, and is brought about often by man's own folly or crime, being precipitated by intemperance, or suicide, or murder, or by the wholesale legalised butchery of war. On the other hand, however uncertain and remote the time of Christ's coming, our mode of life on earth is all-important with respect to it. A depraved mind and course of action here, must be carried with us hence, and ^{21 Luke 34, 35} must unfit us for the day of Christ. 'But take heed to yourselves, lest haply your hearts be overcharged with surfeiting, and drunkenness, and cares of this life, and that day come on you suddenly as a snare: for *so* shall it come upon all them that dwell on the face of all the earth.' The word 'this' before 'life' is not in the original, and does not appear in Young's version. The Authorised Version reads:

'that day come upon you unawares. For as a snare shall it come.' The Revisers, following the two oldest MSS., have attached 'a snare' to 'unawares,' now rendered 'suddenly,' but they have at the same time retained the former meaning by inserting the italicised word 'so' after 'for.' Tischendorf and Alford, on the contrary, render, 'and that day come upon you unawares as a snare: for it will come on all them that dwell on the face of all the earth': not upon all 'as a snare,' but 'suddenly as a snare.' Young's rendering of 'earth' by 'land,' whilst indicating the universality of the judgment, at the same time obviates the idea of a necessary allusion to this earth. Jesus continued: 'But watch ye at every season, making supplication, that ye may prevail to escape all these things that shall come to pass, and to stand before the Son of man.' Tischendorf renders: 'But be awake at all times, praying that ye may be able to escape.' There is no time for sinful, slothful slumber; there are outward dangers which can only be warded off by inward virtue, perils of various kinds which must be met with vigilance and prayer, not for deliverance from evil simply, but for that perfection of character and life which will enable us 'to stand before the Son of man,' that 'we may have boldness, and not be ashamed before him at his coming.' The words of this exhortation are peculiar to Luke. Each of the three evangelists here records different sayings, all impressing the necessity of watchfulness. Matthew: 'Watch therefore: for ye know not on what day your Lord cometh.' The Revisers have substituted 'day' for 'hour,' following the two oldest MSS. Mark: 'Take ye heed, watch and pray; for ye know not when the time is.' The Revisers note: 'Some ancient authorities omit *and pray*': the words are not in the Vatican MS. 21 Luke 36

24 John 28

24 Mat. 42

13 Mark 33

The Authorised Version continues: '*For the Son of man is*,' the six words being italicised. The Revisers have inserted only three words, altogether different: '*it is . . . when.*' Young renders literally, without any such needless addition: 'As a man who is gone abroad.' The Revised Version stands: '*It is as when* a man, sojourning in another country, having left his house, and given authority to his servants (Gr. bondservants), to each one his work, commanded also the porter to watch.' This parable represents in brief the position and duties of Christians in the absence of their Lord. He has gone abroad; his house is left in charge; his servants are commissioned to rule in his absence; each one has an appointed task to fulfil; and the gatekeeper especially is warned to be vigilant, lest strangers and robbers should enter in. This last-named office figured that of the apostles, and on it Jesus dwelt. There must be no slumbering on their part: in order that the household may rest securely, the watchmen must be awake from the first shades of evening till after daylight. There is no one to overlook him at his post, to say whether he really watches or whether he sleeps in the night. Let him remember that at any moment his lord may return, either at twilight, or midnight, or early dawn, or later when the sun is up. 'Watch, therefore; for ye know not when the lord of the house cometh, whether at even, or at midnight, or at cockcrowing, or in the morning; lest coming suddenly he find you sleeping.' ,, 34

13 Mark 35. 36

The words 'commanded also the porter to watch' seem to indicate a change of duty for the time being, the day porter being transformed into a night-watchman, unless we assume a combination of duties, the easy task of a doorkeeper admitting of sufficient repose being taken during the day. This last idea may, however, be dismissed as improbable, inasmuch as only one watchman is appointed in the household, and the recognised office of a watchman is to secure the safety of others when they are unable to protect themselves. For that purpose 'the watchman waketh,' and men are entitled to ask, 'Watchman, what of the night?' The parables which speak simply of watching must be distinguished from one in which the allusion is to a marriage feast: 'Let your loins be girded about, and your lamps burning; and ye yourselves like unto men looking for their lord, when he shall return from the marriage feast; that, when he cometh and knocketh, they may straightway open unto him. Blessed are those servants, whom the lord when he cometh shall find watching.' There is another kind of watching, having a different object: 'But know this, that if the master of the house had known in what hour the thief was coming, he would have watched, and not have left his house to be broken through.' Both parables illustrate the same truth: 'Be ye also ready; for in an hour that ye think not the Son of man cometh:' but the parable of the marriage feast refers only to that coming, and the other parables to the duty of watchfulness in general for the protection of the house. The words 'lest coming suddenly he find you sleeping,' indicate detection in the non-fulfilment of an appointed duty: the master had given 'to each one his work,' and 'commanded also the porter to watch,' and returning suddenly he finds the latter asleep, instead of guarding the household. The watching enjoined was more than a mere waiting and looking out for the master; it was an office of trust, the safety of the house and household being dependent on its due fulfilment. The same sense attaches to the added words: 'And what I say unto you I say unto all, Watch.' Jesus commands every member of his household to exercise vigilance for the common welfare, to guard against the approach of evil, and when necessary to raise the note of warning. The apostle Paul's exhortation is conceived in the same spirit: 'Not looking each of you to his own things, but each of you also to the things of others.' And again: 'Looking carefully lest *there be* any man that falleth short of the grace of God; lest any root of bitterness springing up trouble *you*, and thereby the many be defiled.' Not errors of doctrine, but moral evils, were in the writer's mind, for he went on to say, 'lest *there be* any fornicator, or profane person, as Esau, who for one mess of meat sold his own birthright,' as though immorality and gluttony were most to be dreaded. The warning of Jesus was to the same effect: 'But take heed to yourselves, lest haply your hearts be overcharged with surfeiting, and drunkenness, and cares of life, and that day come on you suddenly as a snare.' Those are the things which unfit men for the coming of the Lord; and they who themselves avoid them, and watch for their prevention in others, are doing their part to prepare for his appearing. An attitude of habitual watchfulness is our only safeguard. There can be no foreknowledge of an approaching crisis, no opportunity of remaining careless up to the moment of danger, and then on a sudden rising up to resist and overcome it. Matthew here records the parable which conveys that lesson. 'But know this (or, But this ye know), that if the master of the house had known in what watch the thief was coming, he would have watched, and would not have suffered his house to be broken through (Gr. digged through). Therefore be ye also ready: for in an hour that ye think not the Son of man cometh.' The idea of oversight for the general good and of responsibility towards others is continued by another parable. 'Who then is the faithful and wise servant (Gr. bondservant), whom his lord hath set over his household, to give them their food in due season? Blessed is that servant (Gr. bondservant), whom his lord when he cometh shall find so doing. Verily, I say unto you, that he will set him over all that he hath. But if that evil servant (Gr. bondservant) shall say in his heart, My lord tarrieth; and shall begin to beat his fellow-servants, and shall eat and drink with the drunken; the lord of that servant (Gr. bondservant) shall come in a day when he expecteth not, and in an hour when he knoweth not, and shall cut him asunder (or, severely scourge him), and appoint his portion with the hypocrites: there shall be the weeping and gnashing of teeth.' The right performance of our social duties, a conscientious care for the temporal welfare of those about us, will best prepare us for the coming of our Lord, and prove our fitness for enlarged responsibilities. Violence, oppression, excess in self-indulgence, will draw down upon us certain retribution when he comes. There is nothing in this teaching of Jesus to justify the widespread notion that his favour is to be secured and his coming prepared for by what are held to be acts of piety and devotion, such as frequent prayers, confession, churchgoing, communion, abstention from the ordinary business or enjoyments of life. On the contrary, he represents our proper sphere of activity as existing and consisting in our intercourse with others, and our concern in their interests. The doctrines of socialism, whatever be the errors attaching to them, and however much they may be derided, are in many points more consonant with the mind and will of Jesus, more impregnated with the true spirit of Christianity, than are the current systems of theological belief and the professions and practices incidental to Church-membership.

These parables of the watchful householder, the faithful and wise servant and the evil servant, have been considered previously. They occur in the 12th chapter of Luke, and form part of what the Reverend J. J. Halcombe * considers the 'displaced section.' If the arrangement of Luke's narrative is to be disturbed, their proper place would seem to be in conjunction with this 24th chapter of Matthew, the verbal agreement between the two being remarkably close. The same remark applies to other portions of the 'displaced section.' One fits into the sermon on the mount; another may be read in connection with the 23rd chapter of Matthew, and others in the same way seem to belong to different periods. Other portions stand alone, not being recorded by Matthew, Mark or John. All that Luke could do was to compile according to the best of his ability. He may have been in doubt as to the proper place for some of the

---

* "Gospel Difficulties."

material in his hands; this he would naturally group together, and other sayings of Jesus recorded without reference to time or place he might feel justified in inserting wherever their introduction seemed most appropriate. We find indications of this in the 'displaced section' and elsewhere.

Jesus illustrated by another parable his coming and its consequences, not to mankind generally, but to those within his kingdom.

25 Mat. 1 'Then shall the kingdom of heaven be likened unto ten virgins, which took their lamps (or, torches), and went forth to meet the bridegroom.' The scene was pictured from an ordinary wedding ceremony. Alford explains: 'In a passage from Rabbi Salamo, cited by Wetstein, he mentions ten lamps or torches as the usual number in marriage processions.' The ten maidens made every preparation for taking part in the festival, and they all looked forward to it with equal joy and confidence. But their dispositions

„ 2 were different: 'And five of them were foolish; and five were wise.' The Authorised Version stands: 'And five of them were wise, and five *were* foolish.' The Revisers have reversed the order on the authority of the two oldest MSS. Their respective folly and wisdom

„ 3, 4 were manifested in one particular. 'For the foolish, when they took their lamps (or, torches), took no oil with them: but the wise took oil in their vessels with their lamps (or, torches).' Alford notes: 'The object of the marriage procession was to fetch the bride to the bridegroom's house.' These maidens would therefore be waiting for his return from the wedding: the time could only be fixed approximately, and was liable to be delayed by a variety of circumstances. On this occasion the period of waiting was so prolonged that the whole party were overcome by drowsiness, and actually fell asleep.

„ 5 'Now while the bridegroom tarried, they all slumbered and slept.' Not till midnight did he come, and then, suddenly, warning of his approach was given, and the ten maidens were summoned to attend

„ 6 him. 'But at midnight there is a cry, Behold the bridegroom! Come ye forth to meet him.' The word 'cometh,' after 'bridegroom,' is omitted by the Revisers, on the authority of the two oldest MSS., wherein also the last word 'him' is omitted, although retained by the Revisers and Tischendorf. The virgins were to meet, not the bridegroom specially, but the bridal procession. The Revisers have altered 'Go ye out' to 'Come ye forth.' Tischendorf retains 'Go ye out,' and Young renders 'Go forth.' Roused by the cry, the ten

„ 7 maidens at once proceeded to trim their lamps. 'Then all those virgins arose, and trimmed their lamps (or, torches).' But five of them, finding their lights on the point of extinction, begged the

„ 8 others to supply them with oil from their vessels. 'And the foolish said unto the wise, Give us of your oil; for our lamps (or, torches) are going out.' The Authorised Version has 'gone out.' To divide the oil, would be to run the risk of utter failure for the whole company, the unexpected delay having already diminished the supply

„ 9 provided. 'But the wise answered, saying, Peradventure there will not be enough for us and you.' In the Authorised Version the words '*Not so*' are introduced in italics, followed by 'lest there be not enough.' Tischendorf renders: 'There might not be enough;' Young, literally, 'Lest there may not be sufficient.' The brightness of the bridal procession would suffer from the temporary absence of half the lamp bearers, but there might be yet time for them to repair the failure, and if not, it were better to make certain of the five lights than to endanger the continuance of the ten. 'Go ye rather to them that sell, and buy for yourselves.' The word 'but' before 'go' is omitted by the Revisers, on the authority of the two oldest MSS. That was the only sensible course: of two evils to choose the least, of two risks to avoid the greater. But the want of foresight proved irreparable to those who were guilty of it. They started off to purchase oil; the bridegroom came; the five lamp-bearing maidens joined the procession; his house was reached; those ready to enter were admitted to the feast; and then the door was closed. 'And while they went away to buy, the bridegroom came; and they that were ready went in with him to the marriage feast: and the door was shut.' When the other five arrived, they could only knock and beg for admission. 'Afterwards come also the other virgins, saying, Lord, Lord, open to us.' They besought in vain. He could not recognise them as members of the procession of which they had not formed a part. 'But he answered and said, Verily I say unto you, I know you not.' Jesus summed up the lesson and scope of the parable in a single sentence: 'Watch therefore, for ye know not the day nor the hour.' The words, 'wherein the Son of man cometh,' are omitted by the Revisers, on the authority of the three oldest MSS. The aim of the parable was to illustrate and impress that particular truth, and no other. We are not at liberty to press the parable beyond its natural incidents and limits. The result to the five foolish maidens was simply exclusion from the marriage feast: there is nothing to justify the inference that tremendous consequences are here prefigured, nothing less indeed than utter ruin of body and soul to all eternity. The thoughtless girls lost their opportunity, and by that sharp experience were left to learn wisdom for the future. If we venture at all outside the range of the parable, our steps must tend in that direction; but it is wiser to keep strictly to the application of it which was made by Jesus himself: 'Watch therefore, for ye know not the day nor the hour.' Expositors are in the habit of introducing their own preconceived opinions into their interpretations of the parables. Alford assumes that the period here referred to is 'the coming of the Lord to His personal reign—not his final coming to judgment;' and, as usual, he discerns a variety of parables within the parable: the bride, who is not mentioned, is the church: 'We may perhaps say that she is here, in the strict interpretation, the Jewish Church, and these ten virgins Gentile congregations accompanying her.' The lamps represent 'the inner spiritual life fed with the oil of God's Spirit.' On 'they all slumbered and slept' Alford observes: 'I believe no more is meant here than that all, being weak by nature, gave way to drowsiness ... Some understand this verse of sleep in death.' On, 'lest there be not enough' he refers to two passages: 'None *of them* can by any means redeem his brother,' and 'Each one of us shall give account of himself to God.' On 'them that sell,' he says: 'These are the ordinary dispensers of the means of grace—*ultimately* of course God Himself, who alone can give His Spirit ... Observe that those who sell are a *particular class* of persons—no mean argument for a *set and appointed ministry*; and

25 Mat. 9

„ 10

„ 11

„ 12

„ 13

49 Ps. 7

14 Rom. 12

moreover for a *paid* ministry.' This method of dealing with the parables may be expanded indefinitely. The resemblances between natural objects and spiritual ideas are infinite, may be turned and twisted in any desired direction, and may be adduced in support of whatever theories their authors wish to formulate. We can, if we choose, attribute symbolical meanings to the lamps, the vessels, the midnight, the feast, the door: because Alford passes them by, others need not: and if once these fanciful suggestions of theologians are worked into their system of doctrines, there is no end to the conclusions thence drawn and apparently justified. Let us be careful to distinguish between the parables of Jesus and those which commentators have invented out of them: the former come to us with his authority: the latter pass current with many, but are without his stamp, and need to be weighed, tested, often depreciated, and sometimes rejected as base and spurious. The safest plan is to repudiate them altogether, as human and unauthorised additions to the divine teaching of Jesus. His similes we are prepared to accept, in their simplicity, without abatement or addition, but not this later coinage which lacks his image and superscription.

The next parable begins in Young's literal translation with the words: 'For—as a man going abroad.' In the Authorised Version additional words are introduced: 'For *the kingdom of heaven is* as a man travelling into a far country.' The Revisers introduce three italicised words instead of five: 'For *it is* as *when* a man going into another country, called his own servants (Gr. bondservants), and delivered unto them his goods.' That is the aspect under which Jesus would have his disciples contemplate his absence and their responsibilities. Until his coming, whatever goes wrong in his business will be the result either of their neglect or of their errors in judgment and conduct. Not the outside world but the church, not mankind in general but disciples ('his own bondservants') are here alluded to. The expression 'delivered unto them his goods,' carries a very wide meaning: for it seems to include, if not all the master possessed, certainly all that he intended to be utilised in the business left in their charge. His property was portioned out among the servants with care and discretion. 'And unto one he gave five talents, to another two, to another one; to each according to his several ability.' The words of Paul may be taken as an apostolic comment and explanation: 'To each one is given the manifestation of the Spirit to profit withal.' Having made these arrangements the master departed: 'And he went on his journey.' The servant to whom most was entrusted lost no time in employing the money, and by judicious trading succeeded in doubling it. 'Straightway he that received the five talents went and traded with them, and made other five talents.' The holder of the two talents pursued a course of like activity, and he also doubled his trust. 'In like manner he also that *received* the two gained other two.' The word 'and' at the beginning of this verse, and the words 'he also'. before gained, are omitted by the Revisers on the authority of the two oldest MSS. The man of least ability, to whom least had been committed, pursued a different course. He did not trade, he did not stay in his former place, but departed elsewhere, and hid away the money. 'But he that received the one went away and digged in the earth, and hid his lord's money.' The Revisers have altered 'went' to 'went away:' the verb in the original is *aperchomai*, which is defined: 'to go away, depart from.' The two oldest MSS. have, instead of 'digged in the earth,' simply 'digged the earth,' and Tischendorf has adopted that rendering, which conveys a different idea. The verse contains three statements: (1) the man went away; (2) he digged the earth; (3) he hid the money. It is not to be assumed that the sole object of digging was to make a hole for burying the treasure: the omission of the word 'in' obviates that meaning. In order to bring out that sense Luther gave a free translation: 'und machte eine Grube in die Erde, und verbarg seines Herrn Geld—and made a hole in the earth, and hid his lord's money.' A similar addition to the literal text is made, mentally, by those who suppose it to mean what Luther did. The true sense seems to be, that the man threw up trading, for which purpose only the money had been placed in his hands, departed from his appointed sphere of duty, chose rather to labour elsewhere as a mere tiller of the ground, and therefore hid the money—actually buried it in the earth (verse 25)—having resolved not to be at the trouble of dealing with it. He is represented as shirking the responsibility thrown upon him, choosing a course for himself contrary to his master's will, and caring nothing about his master's plans and interests. He had no thought of stealing the money; he used none of it for himself; he kept it intact, but neglected the trust involved in its possession. In this and other parables the word 'servant' is literally 'bondman;' Samuel Sharpe always renders it 'slave,' a term which throws a somewhat different light upon the parable. The slaves were absolutely bound to their master; their service could not be terminated, nor could they have any personal interest apart from their lord; they themselves were his, all their time and skill at his command. When this slave 'went away,' it must have been to some other part of his lord's estate, for he was not a runaway; when he changed his occupation, and 'digged the earth,' he was still engaged in a lawful and useful labour, only it was not that which his master had seen fit to impose on him. The simile of 'bondmen' or 'slaves' was deliberately chosen by Jesus, and was not too strong a figure of speech to represent the obligations of his followers towards himself. He demanded, he will ever demand of them, entire, unquestioning obedience: 'Why call ye me, Lord, Lord, and do not the things which I say?' He would have them regard him in that character: 'Ye call me Master (or, Teacher), and, Lord: and ye say well; for so I am.' And again: 'One is your master, *even* the Christ.' So the apostle Paul spoke of him as 'Christ Jesus my Lord: for whom I suffered the loss of all things;' so he alluded to his Master's work as an imperative obligation: 'Necessity is laid upon me; for woe is unto me, if I preach not the gospel. For if I do this of mine own will, I have a reward: but if not of mine own will, I have a stewardship entrusted to me.'

The second scene of the parable opens with the return of the Master and his investigation of his servants' conduct. 'Now after a long time the lord of those servants (Gr. bondservants) cometh, and maketh a reckoning with them.' The first was able to produce a satisfactory account. 'And he that received the five talents came and brought other five talents, saying, Lord, thou deliveredst unto me five talents: lo, I have gained other five talents.' The Authorised Version adds the words 'beside them' after 'gained,' which are now omitted on the authority of the two oldest MSS. The Master's commendation was emphatic. 'His lord said unto him, Well done, good and faithful servant (Gr. bondservant).' His successful fidelity demonstrated his fitness for ampler trusts. 'Thou hast been faithful over a few things, I will set thee over many things.' His willing, active service proclaimed his entire sympathy with his master's aims and purposes, and the joy of successful effort would henceforth be shared by them in common: 'enter thou into the joy of thy lord.' As regarded the second slave, a similar enquiry led to the same result. 'And he also that *received* the two talents came and said, Lord, thou deliveredst unto me two talents: lo, I have gained other two talents. His lord said unto him, Well done, good and faithful servant (Gr. bondservant); thou hast been faithful over a few things, I will set thee over many things: enter thou into the joy of thy lord.' Again at the end of verse 22 the Revisers have omitted the words 'beside them' after 'talents,' on the authority of the two oldest MSS. The third servant came in a very different spirit. He had no gain to show, no account to make up. He had known from the first that everything he might gain would be for his master, who was accustomed to find his property increase by the labours of others; fearing therefore that the risk of loss by trading might be visited upon him, and that there could be no hope of personal profit, he had thrown up his office of trust, careful only to keep the money intact, and to return it whenever called upon. 'And he also that had received the one talent came and said, Lord, I knew thee that thou art a hard man, reaping where thou didst not sow, and gathering where thou didst not scatter: and I was afraid, and went away and hid thy talent in the earth: lo, thou hast thine own.' The excuse was lame, wrong, foolish: the character of the master could not justify the slave's neglect of duty; there had been deliberate and utter disregard of the owner's interests; 'thou hast thine own' was no true saying, for the money might have been invested with bankers, thereby avoiding any risk of trading and obtaining the customary interest. The presumptuous critic deserved severest criticism: his evil mind and slothful habits were the real cause of his inactivity, and his absurd attempt to accuse his lord and justify himself recoiled upon his own head. 'But his lord answered and said unto him, Thou wicked and slothful servant (Gr. bondservant), thou knewest that I reap where I sowed not, and gather where I did not scatter; thou oughtest therefore to have put my money to the bankers, and at my coming I should have received back mine own with interest.' Let the money be taken from him, and placed in worthier and more efficient hands. 'Take ye away therefore the talent from him, and give it unto him that hath the ten talents.' The improvement of the gift was the one thing aimed at, not its equal distribution. The capital would increase most rapidly in the hands of the first slave, and to him therefore this additional amount should be entrusted. Jesus made this the salient point of the parable by introducing a saying of his own which he had uttered to his disciples on previous occasions.

'For unto every one that hath shall be given, and he shall have abundance: but from him that hath not, even that which he hath shall be taken away.' There is no escape from that law. 'To each one is given the manifestation of the Spirit to profit withal.' At the coming of Jesus he will bestow his highest gifts and largest trusts on those who have shown the greatest faithfulness and ability in labouring for his cause. As for the slothful servant, he was excluded from that joy of his lord in which the others were invited to participate. 'And cast ye out the unprofitable servant (Gr. bondservant) into the outer darkness: there shall be the weeping and gnashing of teeth.' This form of expression Jesus himself had adopted, having used it on several occasions in connection with the kingdom of God and the separation which must take place between men at the last as the result of their respective characters and works. Within his kingdom will be light and joy; outside of it, darkness and misery.

    There is a resemblance between this parable and that in the 19th chapter of Luke which has been previously considered; but the differences between them are also very marked and significant. That in Matthew appears to have been spoken to the disciples on the mount of Olives; Luke states that the one recorded by him was spoken to the people on approaching Jerusalem. The points of difference are as follows. (1) In Luke ten bondservants are mentioned; in Matthew the bondservants generally, although in both three only are specially alluded to as examples of all. (2) In Luke each had an equal sum, one mina, altogether ten minæ; in Matthew different sums were given, to one five talents, to another two, to another one: 'to each according to his several ability.' (3) In Luke the value was very little, the mina being the $\frac{1}{60}$th of a talent, and equal to about £3 of our money; therefore in Matthew the servants received respectively 300 times, 120 times, and 60 times as much as those in Luke. Obviously the object in the one case was to depreciate, and in the other to augment, our conception of the relative importance of the trusts committed to the servants, especially as, in contrast to the trifling amount in Luke, Matthew represents the whole of the property to have been apportioned among the servants, the master having 'delivered unto them his goods.' The one master placed all his servants on the same low level, giving to each alike, and as little as possible: the other handed over to them all his estate, having careful regard to each man's capabilities. Luke's parable represents the incidents of earthly rulership; Matthew's represents the heavenly kingdom and the rule of Christ. (4) The servants were rewarded in different fashions. In Luke, ten minæ conferred absolute authority over ten cities, five minæ over five cities, the recompense having no connection with, and being out of all proportion to, the services rendered; in Matthew 'cities' are not mentioned, but 'things:' 'thou hast been faithful over a few things, I will set thee over many things:' the trust is extended, but its nature remains unaltered. (5) Luke represents the nobleman as hated by his citizens, and his departure to have been the signal of open rebellion, and the parable closes with the terrible tragedy of a wholesale destruction of the rebels; these episodes find no place in Matthew; doubtless the object of introducing them was to paint the irresponsible, high-handed, remorseless autocracy of the then existing system of this world's government, in its natural sombre, hideous, hateful colours. (6) Luke says nothing about the unfaithful servant going away and digging the earth; those points are brought out prominently in Matthew, and may be taken to typify a departure from the high ideal of professed discipleship, and the degradation involved in a subsequent return to merely secular hopes and aims. The incidental resemblances between the two parables must not be taken to indicate that they relate to the same subject. Faithful and unfaithful service must be judged by the same rules, whether it relates to earth or heaven, the world or Christ. For instance : 'To whom they commit much, of him will they ask the more:' that is equally true of temporal rulers, of Jesus, and of God the judge of all. Alford states: 'Many modern Commentators maintain that the two parables represent one and the same;' and he adds: 'If so, we must at once give up, not only the pretensions to *historical* accuracy on the part of our Gospels, but all idea that they furnish us with the words of our Lord anywhere: for *the whole structure and incidents of the two are essentially different.*'

_{12 Luke 48}

In the Authorised Version the next verse begins, 'When the Son of man.' The Revisers have placed the word 'But' before 'when,' therein agreeing with Alford, Tischendorf and Luther. Young has 'and' instead of 'but.' The word indicates a connection with what precedes: we have now the application of the parable to the coming and judgment of Jesus. 'But when the Son of man shall come in his glory, and all the angels with him, then shall he sit upon the throne of his glory.' Alford explains that the word 'when' is literally 'whenever,' 'setting forth the indefiniteness of the time.' He couples this with the word 'then,' as marking 'a precise time when all this shall take place—a day of judgment.' Alford seems to mean that there will only be one time or day of judgment, although that time is indefinite. That by no means follows from the wording of the passage, but rather the reverse: 'Whenever he shall come . . . then shall he sit on the throne,' is quite as applicable to repeated comings as to one coming. Take, as an analogous expression, this: 'When the judge comes, he will sit on the bench, and execute judgment.' It could not be thence inferred that the judge would never come again,—that he would hold but one sitting. Alter 'when' into 'whenever,' and the idea of repeated sittings becomes a matter of course. 'The Son of man' is here represented as a King and a Judge: surely not king and judge for one day, one occasion only. By introducing at the outset that conception, or misconception, of his words, we are likely to fall into a wrong system of interpretation altogether. But it may be argued that the New Testament contains many allusions to a particular time or 'day' of judgment, and to only one such period or event. True: here are some instances. 'But after thy hardness and impenitent heart treasurest up for thyself wrath in the day of wrath and revelation of the righteous judgment of God.' 'He which began a good work in you will perfect it until the day of Jesus Christ.' 'It shall be more tolerable for the land of Sodom and Gomorrah in the day of judgement, than for that city.' 'The Lord knoweth how to deliver the godly out of temptation, and to keep the unrighteous under punishment unto the day of judgement.' 'The day of the Lord so cometh as a thief in the night.' 'The day of the

25 Mat. 31

2 Rom. 5

1 Phil. 6
10 Mat. 15
2 ii. Pet. 9

5 i. Thes. 2
3 ii. Pet. 10

Lord will come as a thief, in the which the heavens shall pass away with a great noise, and the elements shall be dissolved with fervent heat, and the earth and the works that are therein shall be burned up.' It would be absurd, in these and similar passages, to restrict the word 'day,' to a space of twenty-four hours. It must be understood to denote the incoming of a new period and stretch of time. In that sense the apostle Paul used it. 'The night is far spent, and the day is at hand.' 'He again defineth a certain day, saying in David, after so long a time, To-day, as it hath been before said, 13 Rom. 12

4 Heb. 7

To-day if ye shall hear his voice,
Harden not your hearts.

For if Joshua had given them rest, he would not have spoken afterward of another day.' 'For he saith, At an acceptable time I hearkened unto thee, and in a day of salvation did I succour thee: behold, now is the acceptable time; behold, now is the day of salvation.' These last two passages are decisive as to the meaning of the term 'day.' *To-day* embraces a lengthened period; the 'day of salvation' extends through successive generations, each in turn passing into it, none—possibly—passing out of it until the 'day of judgment,' which also is to be understood of a continuous period: the apostle Peter represents the final day of judgment as including the destruction and passing away of the universe and the manifestation of 'new heavens and a new earth wherein dwelleth righteousness.' The word *day* itself is sufficiently expressive, not only of definite duration affording scope for varieties of action and experience, but also of changes and recurrence, dawn, noon, sunset, and then, after night, another day. The 'hour of death' which comes to every man, is not the same hour; the 'day of judgment' is not of necessity the same day. A reconsideration of the Scriptural passages relating to it, will tend to modify our inherited opinions on the subject. A more accurate translation enables us to understand the 'coming' of Jesus to be identical with his 'presence,' as in the passage of the Revised Version: 'The coming (Gr. presence) of the Lord is at hand.' The apostles were not mistaken, as seems to be generally assumed, when they declared themselves to be very near to the 'coming,' that is the 'presence' of Jesus. Successively and individually we pass through death, and 'must all be made manifest before the judgement-seat of Christ; that each one may receive the things *done* in the body, according to what he hath done, whether *it be* good or bad.' Now we can better comprehend the exhortation of the apostle John, to 'abide' in Jesus, in order that 'if (in the Authorised Version *when*) he shall be manifested, we may have boldness, and not be ashamed before (Gr. from) him at his coming (Gr. presence).' Were this world the only world, and this life the only life for mankind, we should be constrained to believe that the 'manifestation' 'coming' or 'presence,' and judgment of Jesus must take place on earth or not at all, and at one particular time or never. But that is not the case: Jesus 'is on the right hand of God, having gone into heaven, angels and authorities and powers being made subject unto him'; as we troop, through death, into that world of his, we must taste 'the powers of the age to come'; there we shall be under his jurisdiction; there, unquestionably, he already sits 'on the throne of his glory,' and we know not to what extent his judgment of mankind may be there, continuously, now and

6 ii. Cor. 2

3 ii. Pet. 13

5 James 5

5 ii. Cor. 10

2 i. John 28

3 i. Pet. 22

6 Heb. 5

always, in progress, or to what extent it may be postponed to a future day. Jesus having told us that the Father 'hath given all judgement unto the Son,' it ill becomes us to assert, except upon clearest evidence, that he will judge no man until some pre-appointed day when he will descend again to earth for the purpose. The declaration of Athanasius: 'From whence he shall come to judge the quick and the dead. At whose coming all men shall rise again with their bodies: and shall give account for their own works,' must be taken only for what it may be worth. It was the interpretation put upon the Scriptures by himself and others, and having been imposed as a creed upon the Church, it has been, generation after generation, adopted without question as a settled article of belief, not only requiring no investigation, but all free thought upon the subject being prohibited by the damnatory clause: 'This is the Catholick Faith: which except a man believe faithfully, he cannot be saved.' However learned, eloquent, and positive the originators of our theological doctrines may have been, they were far from infallible; and when their teaching comes to us in such 'persuasive words of wisdom,' it behoves us to remember the apostolic counsel that our 'faith should not stand in the wisdom of men, but in the power of God.'

Whenever Jesus, in his representative character of 'Son of man,' takes to himself that supreme and recognised exaltation expressed by the words 'then shall he sit on the throne or his glory,' he will act as the judge of mankind in general: 'and before him shall be gathered all the nations.' He will then discriminate between man and man with the same unerring ease and sagacity as the shepherd of a mixed flock of sheep and goats distinguishes the one from the other: 'and he shall separate them one from another, as the shepherd separateth the sheep from the goats (Gr. kids).' The illustration implies an obvious difference in the characteristics of the two classes, between whom thenceforth there must be no further intercourse. 'And he shall set the sheep on his right hand, but the goats (Gr. kids) on the left.' Then this king of men will own and take, as the subjects of his sway and the objects of his care, those whom he has thus selected and grouped together for the purpose. 'Then shall the King say unto them on his right hand, Come, ye blessed of my Father, inherit the kingdom prepared for you from the foundation of the world.' The phrase 'inherit the kingdom,' imports that they will thenceforth live under his sole government, forming a community regulated entirely by his will and laws, all opponents thereto being excluded, and only fit and loyal subjects admitted. National distinctions will then be abolished, 'all the nations' becoming merged into two nations only, one constituting Christ's flock, and the other rejected by him and excluded from his fold. The Christian society will be the realisation of the divine purpose, the state of existence natural and proper to mankind, designed by God himself 'from the foundation of the world.' Jesus lays down his own test of fitness for admission to that 'kingdom.' 'For I was an hungred, and ye gave me meat: I was thirsty, and ye gave me drink: I was a stranger, and ye took me in: naked, and ye clothed me: I was sick, and ye visited me: I was in prison, and ye came unto me.' On the words 'took me in,' Alford notes: 'the idea of the word is "numbered me among your own circle."' To have shown practical sympathy with the king to this extent, will ensure participation in his kingdom, which the apostle Peter also held out as the final hope and goal of redeemed humanity, in the exhortation: 'Wherefore, brethren, give the more diligence to make your calling and election sure: for thus shall be richly supplied unto you the entrance into the eternal kingdom of our Lord and Saviour Jesus Christ.' Jesus not only minimises the terms of admission, but rests them upon grounds so peculiar and slender, that he represents the elect as deprecating their applicability to themselves. They never saw him in any such depressed and necessitous condition, and therefore could not be conscious of any action on their part towards him deserving his eulogium. 'Then shall the righteous answer him, saying, Lord, when saw we thee an hungred, and fed thee? or athirst, and gave thee drink? And when saw we thee a stranger, and took thee in? or naked, and clothed thee? And when saw we thee sick, or in prison, and came unto thee?' Here the word 'thee' occurs eight times; the Authorised Version italicises the four which are not in the original, and Young omits them. The following verse requires careful consideration. 'And the king shall answer and say unto them, Verily I say unto you, Inasmuch as ye did it unto one of these my brethren, *even* these least, ye did it unto me.' In the Authorised Version the word 'it' is italicised in both places, not being in the original. Luther renders: 'Was ihr gethan habt einem unter diesen meinen geringsten Brüdern, das habt ihr mir gethan.' 'What ye have done to one among these my least (lowest, meanest, least important) brethren, that ye have done to me.' To whom does the word 'brethren' refer? To some who are represented as present—'these my brethren.' Yet not to those, or any of them, on the king's right hand, for it is they who ask the question, and the answer must not be taken in the sense, Inasmuch as ye have done it among yourselves. The 'brethren' of Jesus, styled and owned by him as such, are his disciples. Brotherhood, in his eyes, was synonymous with discipleship. On one occasion 'He stretched forth his hand towards his disciples, and said, Behold, my mother and my brethren! For whosoever shall do the will of my Father which is in heaven, he is my brother, and sister, and mother.' The expression 'do the will of my Father which is in heaven' denotes here much more than the living of an ordinary moral life; it signifies an entire dedication to the cause of Jesus and his Father in heaven: the words as well as the hand of Jesus pointed to his disciples. To the end of his career he spoke of them as 'brethren.' 'Go unto my brethren, and say to them, I ascend unto my Father and your Father, and my God and your God. Mary Magdalene cometh and telleth the disciples, I have seen the Lord; and *how that* he had said these things unto her.' Again: 'Go tell my brethren that they depart into Galilee, and there shall they see me. . . . But the eleven disciples went into Galilee, unto the mountain where Jesus had appointed them.' The term 'brethren' being thus applied, and thus restricted, to professed 'disciples,' we must be careful not to misunderstand and misapply the latter word. Disciples of Jesus were those who not only believed in him, but devoted themselves to his cause and accepted all his precepts as their rule of life, including his unworldly and to other men impossible doctrines of constant poverty and absolute non-

E

resistance, the forsaking of everything and the suffering of anything for his name's sake. By such men the gospel was first proclaimed, and by such men only can it be perpetuated, spread throughout the world, and accomplish the regeneration of mankind. The command, 'Go ye therefore, and make disciples of all the nations,' is rendered literally by Young, 'Having gone, then, disciple all the nations.' Luther renders: 'lehret alle Völker,' and Beza in the Latin version, 'docete omnes gentes,' simply 'teach all people.' The true sense lies between the two extremes of mere teaching on the one hand, and a proclamation of universal discipleship on the other; the former is insufficient, the latter is impossible. The scheme of Jesus for the evangelisation of the world was the sending forth of a band of disciples imbued with his doctrine, possessing his characteristics, illustrating the heavenly life as much by example as by precept; such a class would constitute his leaven in society, the salt of the earth, the light of the world, a city set on a hill which cannot be hid. That was not designed as a temporary expedient, suited to the apostolic age but not to later generations; for it must continue up to the time 'when the Son of man shall sit on the throne of his glory.' Is it not an obvious inference, that there can be no such manifestation of Jesus, in the absence of such a body of disciples? They must be in existence at the time of his appearing, seen and known of all men, the recognised representatives of Christ, 'partakers of Christ's sufferings—that at the revelation of his glory also' they 'may rejoice with exceeding joy.' In the first days of Christianity such sufferings for Christ's sake overflowed the church generally; but it must ever be on the heads of the leaders and teachers that the full force of the storm of persecution will burst. Jesus here represents them as exposed to hunger, thirst, homelessness, nakedness, sickness and imprisonment. How exactly did the experience of Paul and others agree with that description: 'Even unto this present hour we both hunger, and thirst, and are naked, and are buffeted, and have no certain dwellingplace.' And again he says: 'In prisons more abundantly, in stripes above measure, in deaths oft.' To such ministers and disciples of Jesus the expression 'these my brethren' referred. There is the king on his throne, the righteous are on his right hand, the others on his left, and the brethren of the king are spoken of as a class by themselves, present and separate. To understand this allusion to 'these my brethren,' we must bear in mind the opening words: 'But when the Son of man shall come in his glory, and all the angels with him.' Young here and elsewhere gives the literal sense of the Greek word *angelos*, rendering it 'messenger.' That alteration throws upon us the necessity of discriminating the import of the word in accordance with the context. Generally the sense may appear to be synonymous with our word 'angel,' as commonly understood; but there are passages to which evidently that will not apply. For instance: 'Was not also Rahab the harlot justified by works, in that she received the messengers (*angelous*) and sent them out another way?' The literal meaning, 'messenger,' is always applicable, as denoting one who is sent, which also is the equivalent of the word 'apostle.' In the passage: 'Our brethren, *they are* the messengers of the churches,' the Revisers have noted that the word 'messengers' is

in Greek 'apostles;' Young renders literally, 'apostles of assemblies.'
It is stated that Jesus 'steadfastly set his face to go to Jerusalem, and [Luke 52]
sent messengers (*angelous*) before his face:' of course angelic beings
are not referred to. Again: 'the messengers (*angeloi*) of the seven [Rev. 20]
assemblies,'—Young—may be taken to denote simply the apostles or
elders, although that idea is unfamiliar by reason of the translation,
'angels of the seven churches.' It is not supposable that John would
have been commissioned to write to angelic beings. We are justified
in assuming that the expression 'all the messengers with him,' is
properly, necessarily, to be understood as referring to the disciples of
Jesus, rather than to angelic beings. The word 'holy' before
'messengers' does not appear in the oldest MSS.; but its insertion
would make no difference, for it merely denotes special and entire
dedication to God, and the apostle Paul wrote to Timothy that God
'saved us, and called us with a holy calling.' The word 'messenger' [ii. Tim. 9]
or 'angel,' appertains to all who are emissaries of God, engaged in
working out his will.

'Bless the LORD, ye angels of his: 103 Ps. 20
    Ye mighty in strength, that fulfil his word,
    Hearkening unto the voice of his word.'
This is rendered by Young:
    'Bless the LORD, ye His messengers,
    Mighty in power—doing His word,
    Hearkening to the voice of His word.'

Do not the apostles and disciples of Jesus stand in that category?
'How shall they preach, except they be sent?' and will they be his [10 Rom. 15]
'messengers' on earth only, and not in heaven also? Ponder this
passage, in Young's literal rendering: 'I fell down to bow before the [22 Rev. 8]
feet of the messenger who is showing me these thing; and he saith
to me, See—not; for fellow-servant of thee am I, and of thy brethren
the prophets.' And this: 'The measure of a man, that is, of the [21 Rev. 17]
messenger.' Passages which seem at first sight to point the other
way may, when carefully considered, be found in harmony. 'For we [4 i. Cor. 9]
are made a spectacle to the world, and to angels (*angelois*), and to
men.' The Revisers give the alternative rendering, 'both to angels
and men:' the messengers' and 'men' are both 'in the world.' 'If [13 i. Cor. 1]
I speak with the tongues of men and of angels (*angelōn*):' that is,
with the eloquence of ordinary men and of prophets or disciples: we
cannot speak the language of angelic beings. 'He who was mani- [3 i. Tim. 16]
fested in the flesh, justified in the spirit, seen of angels (*angelois*),
preached among the nations.' The expression 'seen of messengers'
tallies with the apostle John's statement: '(And the Life was mani- [1 i. John 2, 3]
fested, and we have seen, and testify, and declare to you the Life
the age-during, which was with the Father, and was manifested to
us): that which we have seen and heard declare we to you.' (Young.)
A vision granted to angelic beings,—'seen of angels,'—would have
no connection with the preaching of Jesus among the nations.'
'Having become by so much better than the angels (*angelōn*), as he [1 Heb. 1]
hath inherited a more excellent name than they.' The context fixes
the meaning of the word 'angels' as 'messengers:' 'God having of [,, 1, 2]
old time spoken unto the fathers in the prophets by divers portions
and in divers manners, hath at the end of these days spoken unto us
in his (Gr. a) Son:' the 'messengers' are the prophets. Of the Son

it is said: 'God, thy God, hath anointed thee with the oil of gladness above thy fellows:' that is, thy fellow messengers. The essence of angelship or messengership is ministration to the service of mankind: 'Are they not all ministering spirits, sent forth to do service for the sake of them that shall inherit salvation?' In that work Jesus stands foremost, recognised as supreme over all others: 'And when he again bringeth the firstborn into the world, he saith, And let all the angels (*angeloi*) of God worship him.' Elsewhere also the apostle speaks of the Son as 'the firstborn among many brethren.' Take another passage. 'For verily he took not on *him the nature of* angels; but he took on *him* the seed of Abraham.' That is the Authorised Version, and it contains five inserted words, on which the sense is made to depend. Young renders: 'For verily of messengers (*angelōn*) it layeth not hold, but of the seed of Abraham it layeth hold;' which gives a very different meaning. The Revised Version is as follows: 'For verily not on angels doth he take hold, but he taketh hold of the seed of Abraham.' Tischendorf renders: 'For verily he helps not angels; but it is the seed of Abraham that he helps.' Sharpe: 'For verily it taketh not hold of angels, but taketh hold of the seed of Abraham.' The question is as to whether 'it' or 'he' is to be understood. If, however, we take the Revised Version, simply altering 'angels' to 'messengers,' the words 'take hold' are equivalent to 'help,' and the meaning given by Tischendorf comes out: 'Jesus helps not messengers, but Abraham's children.' Who are these messengers? They have been already alluded to in this chapter: 'The word spoken through messengers (*angelōn*) proved steadfast, and every transgression and disobedience received a just recompense of reward.' That is the Revised rendering, only altering 'angels' to 'messengers.' The word of God was not spoken to mankind by angelic beings, but by prophets and teachers, who are here called 'messengers.' Yet not to them was supremacy to be granted in the new organisation of society: 'For not unto messengers did he subject the world (Gr. the inhabited earth) to come, whereof we speak.' But a Son of man was foretold to whom all things would be subjected, and 'we behold him who hath been made a little lower than the' messengers (*angelous*). '*even* Jesus, because of the suffering of death crowned with glory and honour.' The wording of the Psalm from which the apostle quotes is peculiar:

'For thou hast made him but little lower than God (or, the angels, Heb. Elohim)
And crownest him with glory and honour.'

Young renders:

'And causest him to lack a little of Godhead,
And with honour and majesty compassest him.'

Sharpe renders: 'For thou hast made him a little lower than the gods.' Luther: 'Du wirst ihn lassen eine kleine Zeit von Gott verlassen sein.' 'Thou wilt leave him a little time of God to be forsaken.' But the writer to the Hebrews interprets the passage as referring to 'messengers.' In suffering and degradation Jesus was, for the moment, brought lower than any of God's messengers, but he is one with them: 'For both he that sanctifieth and they that are sanctified are all of one: for which cause he is not ashamed to call them brethren.' Here again we reach the truth that the messengers are the brethren of Jesus, and the brethren of Jesus his messengers. Not for them, as restricted to them, are his help and his salvation, but for a far larger number, for all 'the seed of Abraham,' who are 'as the stars of heaven in multitude, and as the sand, which is by the sea shore, innumerable.' The disciples, brethren, messengers of Jesus, are his coadjutors in the great work of taking hold on all mankind.

Some passages which seem clearly to refer to another race of beings bear a different meaning when the translation is revised. 'Man did eat angels' food:' that is the reading of the Prayer Book and Authorised Version. In modern editions of the latter issued with marginal notes the alternative rendering is given: 'Or, Every one did eat the bread of the mighty.' The text of the Revised Version is: 'Man (or, every one) did eat the bread of the mighty.' Young renders: 'Food of the mighty each hath eaten :
Venison he hath sent them to satiety.'
And Sharpe: 'Every man did eat the food of princes ;
He sent them flesh-meat to the full.'

The allusion is not to the manna, 'the corn of heaven,' mentioned in the previous verse 24, but to the 'flesh' and 'winged fowl' mentioned in the following verses 26 and 27. Again, in the same psalm the Authorised Version has: 'He cast upon them the fierceness of his anger, wrath, and indignation, and trouble, by sending evil angels *among them*.' The Revised Version alters the sense by personifying the evils as evil angels:

'He cast upon them the fierceness of his anger,
Wrath, and indignation, and trouble,
A band (Heb. a sending) of angels of evil.'

Young's rendering corresponds therewith :

'He sendeth on them the fury of His anger,
Wrath, and indignation, and distress—
A discharge of evil messengers.'

Sharpe, however, adopts the Authorised rendering: 'by sending evil angels;' the Prayer Book Version has: 'and sent evil angels among them.' Only a strictly literal and idiomatic version of the original, on the same lines as that of Dr. Robert Young, can deliver us from these idiosyncrasies of translators, which are really alterations or modifications of the text.

We can get a clue to the idea attached by the Jews to the word 'angel' or 'messenger,' by comparing other passages. They had a notion of 'spirits' or 'apparitions,' visible but intangible, just as we have of 'ghosts.' When the disciples saw Jesus 'walking on the sea, they were troubled, saying, It is an apparition (*phantasma*); and they cried out for fear.' Tischendorf, Young and Sharpe render the word 'apparition:' in the Authorised Version it is 'spirit.' When Jesus appeared to the disciples after his resurrection 'they were terrified and affrighted, and supposed that they beheld a spirit (*pneuma*).' To convince them to the contrary he said: 'See my hands and my feet, that it is I myself: handle me, and see; for a spirit hath not flesh and bones, as ye behold me having.' A distinction was drawn between an angel or messenger and a spirit. 'The Sadducees say that there is no resurrection, neither angel (*angelon*) nor spirit (*pneuma*): but the Pharisees confess both.' And that resurrection as an angel or messenger was understood to be in the visible, substantial form of humanity, appears from the following passage. Peter had been put in prison, delivered to 'four quaternions of soldiers to guard him.' When he knocked at the door of the house where many of the disciples were assembled, the damsel Rhoda 'ran in, and told that Peter stood before the gate. And they said unto her, Thou art mad. But she constantly affirmed that it was even so. And they said, It is his angel (*angelos*).' It may be inferred from this that the Jews supposed that angels were men who had been raised from the dead. The title angel or messenger appears to have a wide application, denoting any one sent by God, either in earth or from heaven; and so far from angels being of an entirely different race or order from mankind, supernatural manifestations of angels or messengers, however majestic in bearing and countenance, have been in human form; they have spoken as man to man, and sometimes their garb has been described. Here is an account given by Daniel: 'I lifted up mine eyes, and looked, and behold a man clothed in linen, whose loins were girded with pure gold of Uphaz: his body also was like the beryl, and his face as the appearance of lightning, and his eyes as lamps of fire, and his arms and feet like in colour to burnished brass, and the voice of his words like the voice of a multitude.' Again: 'And, behold, one like the similitude of the sons of men touched my lips.' Again: 'Behold, there stood other two, the one on the brink of the river on this side, and the other on the brink of the river on that side. And one said to the man clothed in linen, which was above the waters of the river, How long shall it be to the end of these wonders? And I heard the man clothed in linen, which was above the waters of the river, when he held up his right hand and his left hand unto heaven.' Ezekiel had a marvellous vision of the cherubim, and he described their wings, the form of a man's hand under their wings, their four whirling wheels, full of eyes round about, and the four faces of each—cherub, man, lion, eagle. 'Every one had four faces apiece, and every one four wings: and the likeness of the hands of a man under their wings.' All that is far removed from our human nature. But on the same occasion Ezekiel saw one in human form. 'And behold, the man clothed in linen, which had the inkhorn by his side, reported the matter, saying, I have done as thou hast commanded me.' At the ascension of Jesus we read: 'And while they were looking steadfastly into heaven as he went, behold, two men stood by them in white apparel.' It would be unjustifiable to assume that these supermundane beings were not revealed in their actual and natural forms. Two suppositions are reasonable: heaven may contain another human-like race, not descended from Adam: or the supernatural men occasionally revealed may have been of his posterity, who having passed through death, have been thus transformed and glorified. That was the case with Moses and Elijah on the mount of transfiguration, and the visions of Jesus granted to Saul near Damascus and to John in Patmos, point to that conclusion. The latter describes 'one like unto a son of man (or, the Son of man), clothed with a garment down to the foot, and girt about at the breasts with a golden girdle. And his head and his hair were white as white wool, *while* as snow; and his eyes were as a flame of fire; and his feet like unto burnished brass, as if it had been refined in a furnace; and his voice as the voice of many waters. And he had in his right hand seven stars: and out of his mouth proceeded a sharp two-edged sword: and his countenance was as the sun shineth in his strength.' The seven stars were explained to be mystical, representing 'the angels (*angeloi*) of the seven churches,' rendered by Young 'the messengers of the seven assemblies.' There is a hint also of the symbolism of the sword: 'I will make war against them with the sword of my mouth.' But the person, voice and dress of Jesus—we have no ground for imagining them to be a phantasmal and simply figurative representation. Doubtless he was manifested as he was. He had shone forth upon Saul as 'a light out of heaven,' and even on earth on one occasion 'his face did shine as the sun, and his garments became white as the light.' The apostle John made bold to say: 'It is not yet made manifest what we shall be. We know that, if he shall be manifested, we shall be like him; for we shall see him as he is.'

1 Rev. 3
2 Rev. 10
9 Acts 4
17 Mat. 2
3 i. John 2

This survey of the Scriptural revelations justifies the conclusion that the angels or messengers of the Lord Jesus are men—his disciples—whether tabernacling in Adam's earthly likeness or clothed upon with their house which is from heaven. We need have no hesitation in applying the passage, 'all the angels with him,' to the disciples of Jesus. Their earthly history, from the nature of their profession and calling, must ever be exposed to experiences of poverty, loneliness and persecution, beyond the common lot; and the reception of these messengers of Jesus will be a sufficient test of character. Those who have sympathised with them, supported them, comforted them, thereby prove their own fitness for participation in Messiah's kingdom. For it is that, and only that, of which Jesus here speaks: the blessedness of living under his personal rule and of membership in his society. When the Son of man comes with his messengers, it will be that they may assist in the inauguration and development of his kingdom. As explained in another parable, it will be to 'gather together out of his kingdom all things that cause stumbling, and them that do iniquity;' but the slightest disposition shown to help forward the cause of Christ, will be laid hold of as evidence of fellowship and a title to the privileges of citizenship. On the other hand, an utter absence of sympathy with the doctrine, plans and purposes of the Messiah, evidenced by neglect of and estrangement from his messengers, will be deemed sufficient reason for exclusion: for all must be loyal subjects in that kingdom, and there must be no longer a blending of the world's goats with the sheep of Jesus. 'Then shall he say also unto them on the left hand, Depart from me, ye cursed (or, Depart from me under a curse), into the eternal fire which is prepared for the devil and his angels (*angelois*): for I was an hungred, and ye gave me no meat: I was thirsty, and ye gave me no drink: I was a stranger, and ye took me not in; naked, and ye clothed me not; sick, and in prison, and ye visited me not.' Young renders: 'Go ye from me, the cursed, into the age-during fire, which hath been prepared for the Devil and his messengers.' The word 'cursed' stands in opposition to 'blessed' in verse 34. No idea of vindictiveness or revenge should be asso-

13 Mat. 41
25 Mat. 41-43

ciated with 'cursed:' it denotes the absence of that divine blessing and approval without which nothing can prosper and no true happiness be realised. 'Behold, I set before you this day a blessing and a curse: the blessing, if ye shall hearken unto the commandments of the LORD your God, which I command you this day: and the curse, if ye shall not hearken unto the commandments of the LORD your God, but turn aside out of the way which I command you this day, to go after other gods, which ye have not known.' The practical exemplification and teaching of the gospel of Jesus can only be manifested to the world by the lives of his disciples or 'messengers,' who must necessarily stand forth in opposition to the spirit and practice of the world, not in all things or in things indifferent, but with respect to those peculiar doctrines of non-resistance and voluntary poverty which are the distinctive features of Christian discipleship, the method designed by Jesus, the lever placed in the hands of his followers wherewith, in the power of his Spirit, they may hope to 'bring to nought the things that are.' The world has ever been a seething cauldron of crimes and sufferings, dominated by the military spirit, which relies on brute force and courage, and secures its triumphs by rapine and carnage. Such a remedy for the rectification of social wrongs is worse than the disease. The system of Jesus is entirely different: to plant in every nation disciples in his name, living exemplars of the heavenly virtues of harmlessness, long-sufferance, unselfishness, strong as iron to preach and practise righteousness, truth and peace, but in all else weak as water, in the judgment of the world, nerved for martyrdom but not for fighting, even in self-defence. By a few men of that stamp the gospel of Jesus was first preached and planted. Where are their successors? Before the Son of man can sit on the throne of his glory, they must be again among us, seen and known of all men: and our treatment of them, the warmth of our sympathy or the coldness of our neglect, will prove our fitness or unfitness for his presence and his kingdom. If we despise the blessing, we must remain under the curse: if we reject the messengers, we must depart from their Master: 'Go ye from me, the cursed, into the age-during fire, which hath been prepared for the Devil and his messengers.' The apostle John taught: 'To this end was the Son of God manifested, that he might destroy the works of the devil.' Jesus here speaks of the devil's 'messengers.' Who are they? 'He that doeth sin is of the devil, for the devil sinneth from the beginning.' And what is the most noteworthy characteristic of the devil? 'He was a murderer from the beginning, and stood not in the truth, because there is no truth in him. When he speaketh a lie, he speaketh of his own: for he is a liar, and the father thereof.' Murder and lying are pre-eminently the works of the devil. The wholesale slaughter of mankind by war is wholly contrary to the spirit of Jesus, 'for the Son of man is not come to destroy men's lives, but to save *them*.' 'Wars and rumours of wars must needs come to pass,' but the ending of such things is the hope and scope of the gospel, and the disciples of Jesus must not be of those 'that take the sword.' That is not generally admitted. It is argued that it is as natural for men as for animals to fight; which is, alas! only too true, and must continue true, until we rise to a higher level of Christian doctrine and practice. Nation has risen against nation and kingdom against kingdom, from the earliest times; neither is the fact to be overlooked that the Israelites also were a fighting people, that they engaged in battle under the leadership of Moses, Joshua, and David, that Jehovah himself not only justified but commanded war for the conquest of Canaan, and later sent Saul the anointed king of Israel 'on a journey, and said, Go and utterly destroy the sinners the Amalekites, and fight against them until they be consumed.' God allowed war, commanded war, promised and gave victory in battle, although the title 'God of battles' is not a Scriptural one, as might be supposed from the way in which it is sometimes used. We must not blink these facts. Yet it should be remembered that the nations overcome by the Israelites were evil ones: 'For every abomination to the LORD, which he hateth, have they done unto their gods; for even their sons and their daughters do they burn in the fire to their gods.' And the policy of the Israelites was not, except as regards those nations, an aggressive one, their object being to preserve their own land, and their utmost ambition, with that view, to extend their borders: 'For I will cast out nations before thee, and enlarge thy borders: neither shall any man desire thy land, when thou goest up to appear before the LORD thy God three times in the year.' The hope of victory by divine aid went no further: 'Be strong and of a good courage, be not afraid nor dismayed for the king of Assyria, nor for all the multitude that is with him: for there is greater with us than with him: with him is an arm of flesh; but with us is the Lord our God to help us, and to fight our battles.' But if God in his wisdom chose thus to interfere and overrule the destinies of mankind, raising up and preserving a peculiar people to himself in the only way by which, in the existing condition of the world, it could be done, that affords no justification for war in the abstract, nor for the waging of it permanently and universally. Because God once, under a certain condition of society some thousands of years ago, permitted and used war, are we to argue or assume that he designs its continuance throughout all time, at the will of the world's successive rulers, and that we are free to disregard his voice when he says through his Son to the raging nations, making 'wars to cease unto the end of the earth:'

'Be still, and know that I am God:
I will be exalted among the nations,
I will be exalted in the earth?'

God made known his abhorrence of bloodshed to David, who told Solomon his son: 'The word of the LORD came to me, saying, Thou hast shed blood abundantly, and hast made great wars: thou shalt not build an house unto my name, because thou hast shed much blood upon the earth in my sight.' The great Ruler of the universe works out, advances, modifies his plans, according to his wisdom and the progressive needs and possibilities of humanity. The views of the apostle Paul on this question were sound and wise. He tells how God 'made of one every nation of men for to dwell on all the face of the earth, having determined *their* appointed seasons, and the bounds of their habitation.' But mankind, being left to themselves, lapsed into idolatry. 'The times of ignorance therefore God overlooked; but now he commandeth men that they should all everywhere repent (reform—Young); inasmuch as he hath appointed a day, in the which he will judge the world (Gr. the inhabited earth) in righteousness by the (or, a) man whom he hath ordained.' This relates to national life, 'every nation of men,' national worship, which had degenerated into idolatry, national reformation, of 'all men everywhere,' national judgment, of 'the inhabited earth.' The gospel is a message of reform to the nations from God, 'who in the generations gone suffered all the nations to walk in their own ways.' The divine purposes of blessing to mankind have always been nationalistic, not individual. The promise to Abraham was: 'Thou shalt be the father of a multitude of nations.' When God threatened to cast off the rebellious Israelites, the same purpose was still kept in view: he said to Moses: 'I will smite them with the pestilence, and disinherit them, and will make of thee a nation greater and mightier than they.' At the intercession of Moses they were not disinherited, but their future national career was not according to the divine intention, so that they were repeatedly brought into subjection by other nations, the two remaining tribes out of the twelve were at the coming of Jesus under foreign rule in their own land, that remnant was scattered soon after, and from that day to this Israel as a nation has not existed: the divine plan was thwarted by human perversity. That truth should be laid to heart. Man's free will is not interfered with, but is a potent factor in the world's history. The experiment with the Israelites having failed, the method was changed. The idea of a heavenly kingdom upon earth was not to be relinquished. The Son of God was sent to found it. It was first offered to the Jews, and being by them rejected, was proclaimed among the Gentiles. 'It was necessary that the word of God should first be spoken to you. Seeing ye thrust it from you, and judge yourselves unworthy of eternal life, lo, we turn to the Gentiles.' That was the design of Jesus, who commissioned his apostles to 'disciple all the nations:' 'Go ye into all the world, and preach the gospel to the whole creation.' The world must be interspersed with disciples preaching the gospel of the kingdom, gathering assemblies of believers in it and in Jesus as its king, but not bringing about its establishment; for it is evident that until the king himself is present his kingdom in its completeness cannot be: the utmost to be done in his absence is to prepare the hearts and lives of men for his coming and his rule. The apostle Paul admitted the apparent inadequacy of the means to the end: 'It was God's good pleasure through the foolishness of the preaching (Gr. thing preached) to save them that believe ... But we preach Christ (or, a Messiah) crucified, unto Jews a stumblingblock, and unto Gentiles foolishness.' The true preaching of the gospel is even more by example than by precept. Before the eyes of the Galatians 'Jesus Christ was openly set forth crucified.' In what sense? By the example, in the person, of Paul his messenger: 'I have been crucified with Christ; and it is no longer I that live, but Christ liveth in me.' The preaching of Christ must be not so much verbal and doctrinal as actual and practical, by living demonstration of the spirit and power of the gospel: 'And my speech (or, word) and my preaching (Gr. thing preached) were not in persuasive words of wisdom, but in demonstration of the Spirit and of power.' The gospel is not Judaism, not the precepts of the Mosaic law or ritual; it was a novelty, equally startling both to Jews and Gentiles: 'Howbeit we speak wisdom among the perfect (or, full-grown); yet a wisdom not of this world (or, age), nor of the rulers of this world (or, age), which are coming to nought.' Jesus deliberately enlarged, repealed, reversed, such of the divinely-given Mosaic laws as he deemed necessary, saying with respect to murder, adultery, divorce, oaths, retaliation, estrangements: 'Ye have heard that it was said . . . but I say unto you.' This important fact has been, generation after generation, overlooked, or misunderstood, or forgotten, or explained away, hidden from men's eyes, absent from their thoughts, so that those new and few precepts of Christianity on which alone its power and influence are based, are precisely the maxims to which the whole policy and practice of society in 'Christian' nations stand opposed. The world's code of morals, laws, government, does not recognise the commands, prohibitions, counsels of Jesus, with respect to slaughter, oaths, retaliation: it is assumed that these things must always exist as part and parcel of national life. But what legislators cannot insist upon, or even attempt, was made incumbent upon all professed 'disciples,' 'brethren,' 'messengers' of Jesus: the name by which they are called matters not, but their calling lays upon them the obligation to take his precepts in their entirety, literally and truly, as their rule of conduct. The absence from the world of any such class of men is sufficient to account for the fact that Christ's special commands are deemed too high and exacting, visionary or figurative, magnificent considered simply as ethical doctrines of perfection, but impracticable generally, and beyond the range of our earthly surroundings. It is held that so far as we can see along the vista of futurity, there must ever be wars, and law suits, and oath taking, and national animosities, divorce also, we have lately been persuaded, and so on. Society indeed progresses, but at a rate monotonously slow, beating out its advances by centuries instead of years and days. There is no open demonstration of the spirit and power of Christ, no living exemplification of him in the persons of disciples adhering to *all* his commands. Had there been such a band of followers of Jesus, how much of blundering and bloodshed would the world have been spared! In Cromwell's time there was an earnest effort made to live and rule according to the revealed will of God. But the Puritans imbibed the spirit of the Old Testament, and disregarded that of the gospel, talked about 'smiting Amalek,' thought they were fighting the Lord's battles when they slaughtered, ravaged, burnt, after the old, old fashion. That could not have come to pass if there had existed in their midst a nucleus exhibiting the true doctrine and life of Christians, round which might have gathered all who were earnest seekers of salvation, and by means of which they might have learnt that 'the wrath of man worketh not the righteousness of God,' and have imbibed the spirit of the angelic carol, 'Glory to God in the highest, and on earth peace among men in whom he is well pleased.' Oliver's Ironsides might then have become Christian martyrs; they could never have developed into so-called 'Christian' soldiers. There had been a similar turning-point in history at the time of the crusades. Religious enthusiasm was kindled, and the spirit of devotion and self-sacrifice was all that could be desired: but the forces of Christendom were wrongly directed and applied; instead of helping forward the cause of our Redeemer upon earth, they resulted only in an enormous expenditure of blood and treasure in fighting over his sepulchre; these warriors thought they were doing God service, but in fact they were doing the Devil's work, who ' was a murderer from the beginning, and stood not in the truth.' These things could not have been, it the doctrine and aims of Jesus had been rightly apprehended, which must have been the case if his professed brethren and followers had formed a class apart from the world, not of monks and nuns and religionists anxious through prayers, praises, fastings, sacraments, to save their own souls and those of others *hereafter*, but of men living the apostolic life, holding fast to Christ's command, ' Resist not him that is evil: but whosoever smiteth thee on thy right cheek, turn to him the other also.' There would have been no preaching of the crusades if Christians had known what manner of spirit they are of. There has ever been an anti-christian spirit in the world. ' Every spirit which confesseth not Jesus is not of God:' the Revisers note that in place of ' confesseth not Jesus ' ' some ancient authorities read *annulleth Jesus*.' Have not some of the commands of Jesus to his disciples been practically annulled, and especially that of non-resistance to evil ? The rectification of evil by wholesale slaughter is not Christ's work, if it be not Devil's work : ' This is the *spirit* of the antichrist, whereof ye have heard that it cometh ; and now it is in the world already.' We must apply that dictum of the apostle John to whatever opposes or annuls the teaching of Jesus, and we still need to take to heart the warning, ' Beloved, believe not every spirit, but prove the spirits, whether they are of God : because many false prophets are gone out into the world.'

It is clear from the parable of the sheep and the goats that Jesus contemplated the existence among mankind, up to the time of his manifestation in glory, of a distinct class of ' brethren ' of himself, who would be exposed by their profession to poverty, rejection, and even imprisonment. They being his representatives, callousness to their wants and infirmities must be taken as evidence of indifference to Jesus. The world to the very last will be slow to discern that connection. The righteous, who have done such small services as they could to these preachers of righteousness, are represented as astounded at the value placed upon their sympathy, and those who have kept wholly aloof from Christ's ' brethren ' can scarcely be brought to admit that they are rightly excluded on that account from his kingdom. ' Then shall they also answer, saying, Lord, when saw we thee an hungred, or athirst, or a stranger, or naked, or sick, or in prison, and did not minister unto thee ? Then shall he answer them, Verily I say unto you, Inasmuch as ye did it not unto one of these least, ye did it not unto me.' In verse 44 the word ' him ' has been omitted after 'answer,' on the authority of the three oldest MSS. The Revisers in verses 40 and 45 have altered ' least of these ' to ' these least,' indicating not comparison between one and another of the brethren, ' one of the least of these,' but the small esteem in which all the brethren are held by the world,—' these least.' Potentates, statesmen, warriors, politicians, regard them not : ' Behold your calling, brethren, how that not many wise after the flesh, not many mighty, not many noble,' are engaged in the effort ' to bring to nought the things that are.'

In what sense are the words in verse 41 to be understood: 'Depart from me, ye cursed, into the eternal fire which is prepared for the devil and his angels'? Is the 'age-during fire' to be taken literally or figuratively? That Jesus should have introduced it as a figure of speech is perfectly natural, and consistent with his usual mode of teaching, which overflowed with metaphors. So much was this the case that the apostles themselves were sometimes in doubt whether he was speaking literally or figuratively, as when he said, 'I have meat to eat that ye know not. The disciples therefore said one to another, Hath any man brought him *aught* to eat? Jesus saith unto them, My meat is to do the will of him that sent me, and to accomplish his work.' Once he warned them: 'Take heed and beware of the leaven of the Pharisees and Sadducees'; at first they took his words literally, to his astonishment. 'How is it that ye do not perceive that I spake it not to you concerning bread? But beware of the leaven of the Pharisees and Sadducees.' Then understood they how that he bade them not beware of the leaven of bread, but of the teaching of the Pharisees and Sadducees.' It was no new thing for Jesus to speak of 'fire' figuratively. 'I came to cast fire upon the earth; and what will I, if it is already kindled?' The word had been used by prophets in the same way. 'Behold, all ye that kindle a fire, that gird yourselves about with firebrands: walk ye in the flame of your fire, and among the brands that ye have kindled.' Does not that carry precisely the same significance as, 'Go ye from me, the cursed, into the age-during fire, which hath been prepared for the Devil and his messengers'? Again: 'Behold, is it not of the LORD of hosts that the peoples labour for the fire, and the nations weary themselves for vanity?' Instead of 'for the fire,' the Authorised Version has 'in the very fire.' We must interpret the words of Jesus in this place in accordance with his accustomed style, with the context, and with the similitudes in the prophetic writings. The 'age-during fire' in verse 41 is opposed to 'the kingdom' in verse 34. Both have been 'prepared.' Those who oppose the kingdom of God are ever labouring in the very fire, and for the fire, together with the supreme opponent of God, the devil and his messengers. To the end of existence, and age after age, the weariness and vanity must needs continue. That must be the inevitable, ceaseless doom, the punishment, whenever the righteous are taken away and the wicked are left to themselves. 'And these shall go away into eternal punishment,' rendered by Young, 'And these shall go away to age-during punishment.' But to the righteous, thus gathered together and separated from others, there will be granted age-during life apart from punishment: 'but the righteous into life eternal,' rendered by Young, 'but the righteous to age-during life.' No need to promise anything more; for life under the rule of the glorified Son of man implies the utmost blessedness of which man's nature is capable. This parable coincides with that of the tares of the field: 'The good seed, these are the sons of the kingdom; and the tares are the sons of the evil *one;* and the enemy that sowed them is the devil; and the harvest is the consummation of the age; and the reapers are angels (messengers—Young). . . . The Son of man shall send forth his angels (messengers) and they shall gather out of his kingdom all things that cause stumbling, and them that do iniquity, and shall cast them into the furnace of fire: there shall be the weeping and gnashing of teeth. Then shall the righteous shine forth as the sun in the kingdom of their Father.' Life prolonged to its utmost bound under the rule and guardianship of Jesus, is the ultimatum of Christian hope and progress.

A very different construction is generally put upon the parable of the sheep and the goats. The true significance of the expression 'these my brethren' is lost sight of, and a sense altogether erroneous is adopted. It is assumed, as a matter of course, that 'these MY brethren' is synonymous with 'these YOUR brethren,' all mankind being deemed 'brethren' of the Christ by virtue of his participation in our human nature. This grave misapprehension is not much to be wondered at, for two reasons: (1) The true sense and application do not lie upon the surface, and all experience proves that when a wrong notion has once been started among theologians, it is apt to be laid hold of and spread abroad, with all the self-satisfied certainty of conviction, as an admitted and irrefragable conclusion. (2) There is no distinct class of persons before the eyes and in the minds of men, and has not been during many hundreds of years, answering to the description given of 'these my brethren' in this parable. In the days when the gospel was first preached, there existed no such difficulty of identification. Jesus could appeal to his first missionaries: 'When I sent you forth without purse, and wallet, and shoes, lacked ye anything?' And they said, Nothing.' The apostle Paul could say: 'In everything commending ourselves, as ministers of God, in much patience, in afflictions, in stripes, in imprisonments . . . as poor, yet making many rich.' That high ideal of a Christian ministry, that brotherhood to Jesus, has become lost to the church and the world. The fact is undeniable, be the causes what they may, by which it may be either justified or explained. Ministers of the gospel do not now attain to that level, or need not now descend to that depth of poverty and degradation: put it which way you will, so only the fact be admitted and realised. The preaching of the gospel now is committed to men who simply perform functions analogous to those rendered by priests, Levites, scribes, doctors of the law. Availing ourselves of their services, it becomes us not to criticise their office, or disparage their conscientious efforts and labours. Their position, their creed, their practice, come to them, as to all of us, by inheritance, subject to such modifications in doctrine and life as the light and leading of our own generation may supply. But whether we, as a professed Christian community, are living up to the doctrine of Christ, is another question, a very solemn one, applicable alike to the clergy and the laity. The promised salvation of Jesus seems to have been relegated, by common consent, to the next world: we appear to have lost all hope of it in this. The wrongs and evils, the sufferings and inequalities of society are regarded as stereotyped pages in human history. Teachers and preachers of what ought to be, we have in abundance; but exemplars of the heavenly life, the life of Jesus and his apostles,—where are they? The sheep we know, and the goats we know, or think we do, but the 'brethren' of Jesus we discern not, because they are not,—no recognised fraternity devoted to the cause of Christ in such a way that it may at all times be said by each of them to those who minister to their necessities : ' I was an hungred, and ye gave me meat : I was thirsty, and ye gave me drink : I was a stranger, and ye took me in ; naked, and ye clothed me : I was sick, and ye visited me : I was in prison, and ye came unto me.' Yet such wants and infirmities are part and parcel of the normal daily existence of multitudes about us, men, women, helpless children, together with not a few outcasts and criminals,—all of whom we are taught to class under the designation of Christ's poor, Christ's ' brethren ' ! If we accept that common application and interpretation of the parable, we must needs believe that the final salvation or condemnation of each one of us will depend upon the giving or witholding of our alms to the necessitous. That idea is of itself sufficient to throw Christian faith and practice into confusion. Indiscriminate almsgiving tends to perpetuate pauperism : yet if all the poor are Christ's brethren, dare we refuse them at any time the help and succour we are able to give ? Moralists and political economists, who have studied the subject, warn us that a constant stream of gratuitous benevolence is the surest way to bring about the degradation of the recipients : it robs them of energy, self-reliance, self-respect. Are these hard-thinking students of social problems wrong in their conclusions ? Or did Jesus blunder when he laid down the rule of giving and visiting as a sufficient test of fitness for admission to his kingdom ? Neither : the political economists on this point are right, and Jesus never made it incumbent upon all who have, to give to all who have not. To suppose he did, introduces another anomaly. Political economy is a hard and ' dismal ' science, because resting too entirely upon the basis of self-interest. Christianity introduced a higher principle of action, transforming every master into a bond-servant to Jesus, a ' faithful and wise steward whom his lord ' has ' set over his household, to give them their portion of food in due season.' That is the foremost responsibility of every Christian employer of labour. But in the race for wealth it has been sadly disregarded. Manufacturers, merchant-princes, have not scrupled to cut down wages to the lowest point, justifying themselves by the law of supply and demand, and disregarding the law of Christ, ' Masters, render unto your servants that which is just and equal.' The result of this selfish policy is seen in the permanently degraded condition of the toiling masses everywhere. And that very poverty which neglect of a primary obligation of Christian duty has imposed and perpetuated, is assumed to be the proper field of action for the benevolence of those to whom it is really owing ! Having made paupers, the help we dole out to them, however scanty, is imagined to be—and if the common view of this parable is correct, must be—our highest if not sole claim for admission into Christ's kingdom ! In face of such a *reductio ad absurdum*, is it not high time for all of us to review and revise our traditional systems of theology and Christianity, and set ourselves to the task of studying and comprehending the true doctrines of Jesus ? With respect to those of almsgiving and discipleship, fundamental errors exist which have made Christianity a puzzle even to its professors, several of its precepts standing apparently at variance with their deliberate practice, and being to men of independent thought, be they half-believers or disbelievers, sufficient to stamp the loftiest doctrines of Jesus as ideals impossible of attainment, a scheme of morality and action impracticable upon earth, 'a view of life . . . which if carried into effect by the whole world—a test which any doctrine professing to be at once true and universal ought to stand—would speedily bring the world to an end.'* A painstaking, unprejudiced investigation of the gospels and epistles, leads us to a point of view at which these anomalies, difficulties and uncertainties disappear. To see the gospel in its proper light, we must bear in mind the following truths to which we have attained. (1) Jesus did not invite all men to become his 'disciples,' but dissuaded some, and bade every man count the cost before he enrolled himself as a disciple. (2) Certain commands given to disciples were never intended for universal adoption. (3) Yet those commands, without exception, were intended to be put in practice by the professed disciples. (4) Such disciples are Christ's 'leaven' in the world; without them the world cannot be saved, converted, changed, Christianised, made Christlike: the term chosen is unimportant, if only we lay hold on the thing signified. (5) Such disciples, from the nature of their undertaking and the prescribed method of carrying it out, must face poverty, obloquy, ill-treatment; sacrificing their own prospects in this life, they must ever be more or less dependent on the good will and charity of those among whom they perform their ministry. (6) To sympathise with and assist such disciples is to help forward the cause of Christ; to hold aloof from them, indicates indifference to him and unfitness for his kingdom.

How can the gospel of Jesus be expected to triumph, when its primary requisite—a body of 'disciples' or 'brethren' pledged to an implicit obedience to *all* his commands—is wanting in the world? So long as his plan of evangelisation is not adhered to, but is actually overlooked and forgotten, his merciful designs for mankind must remain in abeyance. Let us not imagine that the advancement of the gospel is retarded by some mysterious divine purpose: the delay is not chargeable to God or to Jesus, but to ourselves. We seem to be repeating the history of the Israelites, of whom God could only say:

* Ps. 13 15

'Oh that my people would hearken unto me,
That Israel would walk in my ways!
I should soon subdue their enemies,
And turn my hand against their adversaries.
The haters of the LORD should submit themselves unto him;
But their time should endure for ever.'

There must be some failure of 'hearkening' to Jesus, some neglect of 'walking in his ways,' to account for the non-success of his gospel. Errors of heart and life there are, we admit; let us search out also and not be blind to errors of judgment and of system.

These startling discourses were delivered by Jesus in Jerusalem. They must have seemed all the more solemn to the twelve apostles when they remembered how near must now be the accomplishment

---

* "Civilization and Progress." By J. B. Crozier.

of his sad and mysterious prediction about himself : 'Behold, we go up to Jerusalem, and all the things that are written by the prophets shall be accomplished unto the Son of man. For he shall be delivered up unto the Gentiles, and shall be mocked, and shamefully entreated, and spit upon : and they shall scourge and kill him : and the third day he shall rise again.' But Jesus was still pursuing his work of teaching with the utmost calmness. The manner of his life at this period has been recorded. The day was spent in discoursing in the temple, and every night he left the city for his lodging in the mount of Olives. 'And every day he was teaching in the temple ; and every night he went out, and lodged in the mount that is called *the mount of Olives*.' His labours began with the early morn, large numbers of the people attending him betimes in the temple at Jerusalem. 'And all the people came early in the morning to him in the temple, to hear him.'

At the close of his teaching Jesus prepared the minds of his disciples for the approaching crisis of his fate, telling them plainly that he would be delivered up for crucifixion at the approaching festival. 'And it came to pass, when Jesus had finished all these words, he said unto his disciples, Ye know that after two days the passover cometh, and the Son of man is delivered up to be crucified.' The Revisers and Young have altered 'sayings' to 'words ;' 'betrayed' is now rendered 'delivered up,' agreeing with Young, Tischendorf and Alford. The word 'betray,' according to modern usage, characterises the heinousness of the deed ; the expression 'deliver up' simply describes the fact. Mark and Luke allude to the nearness of the passover, but have not recorded the prophecy of Jesus. 'Now after two days was *the feast of* the passover and the unleavened bread.' Young's rendering is equally clear without the italicised words : 'But the passover and the unleavened bread were after two days.' Luke : 'Now the feast of unleavened bread drew nigh, which is called the Passover.' The enemies of Jesus now finally resolved to make an end both of his teaching and of himself. A conclave of the chief priests and principal citizens was held in the high priest's palace, at which the question was debated how best to apprehend and kill him. 'Then were gathered together the chief priests, and the elders of the people, unto the court of the high priest, who was called Caiaphas ; and they took counsel together how they might take Jesus by subtilty, and kill him.' Young renders 'subtilty,' 'guile,' Tischendorf 'craft.' Rulers can easily persuade themselves that actions are justifiable, in carrying out their policy, which are deemed wrong, mean and despicable in private persons. It was decided that either the plot must be carried out before the passover, or adjourned till afterwards, so that there might be no risk of a tumult whilst the populace were free from their labours and increased in numbers. 'But they said, Not during the feast, lest a tumult arise among the people.' The Revisers have altered 'on the feast *day*' to 'during the feast,' which agrees with Young and Alford. Tischendorf renders 'at the feast.' As it lasted seven days, the introduction of the word 'day' was misleading. Only Matthew mentions the holding of the council. Mark describes in similar words their purpose and policy. 'And the chief priests and the scribes sought how they might take him with subtilty, and kill him ; for they said, Not during the feast, lest haply there shall be a tumult of the people.' 'But they said' is altered to 'for they said,' on the authority of the two oldest MSS. The word ' for' indicates the reason which impelled them to act secretly and treacherously. They could be as open and bold as they chose when all danger of uproar and rescue was over. Luke also attributes their timidity to the same cause. 'And the chief priests and the scribes sought how they might put him to death; for they feared the people.' At the critical moment, a tool rose up before them, fit for their purpose and fashioned for their hand. One of the twelve apostles turned traitor to his Master, went over to his enemies, and lent himself to their designs. 'Then one of the twelve, who was called Judas Iscariot, went unto the chief priests, and said, What are ye willing to give me, and I will deliver him unto you?' The Revisers and Young have improved the translation by rendering, 'What are ye willing to give' in place of 'What will ye give.' Mark is briefer. 'And Judas Iscariot, he that was one of the twelve (Gr. the one of the twelve), went away unto the chief priests, that he might deliver him unto them.' Luke attributes the conduct of Judas to Satanic agency. 'And Satan entered into Judas who was called Iscariot, being of the number of the twelve. And he went away, and communed with the chief priests and captains, how he might deliver him unto them.' Young renders 'Satan,' 'the Adversary,' and 'captains,' 'magistrates.' Matthew states that Judas bargained for money. Luke intimates that a pecuniary bond was drawn up between the parties. 'And they were glad, and covenanted to give him money.' Mark also refers, not to an actual payment but to a promise. 'And they, when they heard it, were glad, and promised to give him money.' Matthew, however, states, according to the Revised Version, not only that something was paid, but the exact sum. 'And they weighed unto him thirty pieces of silver.' The Authorised Version stands, ' And they covenanted with him for thirty pieces of silver.' Alford explains: 'The verb rendered *covenanted . . for*, may mean either *weighed out*, or *appointed*.' Tischendorf renders, 'And they weighed unto him thirty shekel-pieces.' Young: 'And they weighed out to him thirty silverlings.' The verbs used by the evangelists differ: Matthew *histēmi*; Mark: *epangellomai*; Luke: *suntithēmi*. Luther renders the words respectively by *bothen*, *verhiessen* and *gelobten*. Alford notes: 'Thirty shekels, the price of the life of a servant, Ex. xxi. 32. Between three and four pounds of our money.' The bargain having been struck, the traitorous Judas watched for an opportunity of effecting his purpose. 'And from that time he sought opportunity to deliver him *unto them*.' The Revisers have added the two last words, in italics, apparently because the word 'deliver,' which formerly stood 'betray,' is susceptible of the opposite meaning, 'save.' They have done the same in Mark, probably for the same reason. 'And he sought how he might conveniently deliver him *unto them*.' He fully agreed with the priests as to the importance of avoiding a crowd or commotion. 'And he consented, and sought opportunity to deliver him unto them in the absence of the multitude (or, without tumult).' Alford explains that the concluding words might bear either meaning. Tischendorf introduces 'a good' before 'opportunity.' Young renders, 'a favourable season.'

Among those who had journeyed to Jerusalem to worship at the passover were certain foreigners. 'Now there were certain Greeks [12 John 20] among those that went up to worship at the feast.' Alford explains: 'The *Greeks* were not *Grecian Jews*,—who would not have been so called: but *Gentiles*, "proselytes of the gate," who were in the habit of coming up to the feast.' These men being desirous of an interview with Jesus sought to obtain an introduction through one of his disciples. 'These therefore came to Philip, which was of Bethsaida [,, 21] of Galilee, and asked him, saying, Sir, we would see Jesus.' Tischendorf here renders 'Sir,' by 'Lord;' this is peculiar, and may serve to show that Young's habitual rendering of 'Sir,' even when the title was applied to Jesus, ought to be followed. Alford observes: 'What they here requested was evidently a private interview.' Remembering the words of Peter: 'Ye yourselves know that it is an [10 Acts 28] unlawful thing for a man that is a Jew to join himself or come unto one of another nation,' we can understand why the apostle Philip should hesitate about yielding to the request. Jesus already stood in great peril, and any intercourse between him and Gentiles would add one more to the 'unlawful' things charged against him. In doubt and anxiety, Philip consulted a fellow apostle. 'Philip cometh and [12 John 22] telleth Andrew.' Alford notes: 'Andrew was of the same city as Philip (ch. i. 45): and this reason of Philip conferring with him is perhaps implied in the words *which was from Bethsaida of Galilee*.' Together they went to Jesus, and informed him of the desire which these Greeks had expressed. 'Andrew cometh, and Philip, and they [,, 22] tell Jesus.' It is not stated or implied that the interview was granted. Alford says: 'Certainly *not*, if I understand His discourse rightly.' But, in reference to the application, Jesus made certain observations, which are here recorded by the apostle John, whose gospel is a collection of various discourses of Jesus preserved and handed down by this apostle only. 'And Jesus answereth them, say- [,, 23] ing, The hour is come, that the Son of man should be glorified.' The Revisers have altered 'answered' to 'answereth,' on the authority of the two oldest MSS. If the discourse was written down at the time of its delivery, this use of the present tense would be very natural. Young renders: 'The hour hath come, that the Son of Man may be glorified.' Hitherto the experience of Jesus had lain in the contrary direction. He had been treated with contumely: 'I honour my Father, [8 John 49, 50] and ye dishonour me. But I seek not mine own glory: there is one that seeketh and judgeth.' At an earlier period he had recognised the same fact: 'I receive not glory from men,' and had protested against [5 John 41] the prevalent folly of seeking the praise of men rather than the praise of God: 'How can ye believe, which receive glory one of another, [,, 44] and the glory that *cometh* from the only God ye seek not?' Only through dishonour could true honour be attained. On the eve of his betrayal and mocking and crucifixion, Jesus felt that his career of rejection and contempt would soon be closed, and 'the glory that *cometh* from the only God' be manifested in him. His death would ensure nobility to himself and vitality to the cause to which his life had been consecrated. 'Verily, verily, I say unto you, Except a grain [12 John 24] of wheat fall into the earth and die, it abideth by itself alone: but if it die, it beareth much fruit.' The Revisers, agreeing with Alford, have strengthened the rendering by adding 'by itself,' before 'alone.' Young renders: 'If the grain of wheat having fallen into the earth may not die, it remaineth itself alone; but if it may die, it beareth much fruit.' Jesus had come into the world to die for the world, just as the wheat is sown in order to decay, spring up and supply abundance of food for man. If the planted wheat die not in the soil, neither could it germinate anew: its true life would be lost to itself and the world. The simile contained a truth of general application. 'He that loveth his life (or, soul) loseth it, and he that hateth his life (or, soul) in this world shall keep it unto life eternal (age-during —Young).' The Revisers, following the two oldest MSS., have altered 'shall lose' to 'loseth.' A merely barren, personal existence, 'by itself alone,' is not the life which God designs and man needs. Keeping close to the parable, we must bear in mind that it applies to corn actually sown for the purpose of reproduction, not to that which is consumed for food. The former represents Jesus and his disciples, the latter may stand for mankind in general, to whom Jesus is not alluding. Both must perish, for the law of death is universal; but discipleship involves a design and results which are not aimed at and cannot be brought to pass otherwise. That this was in the mind of Jesus is evident from his next words: 'If any man serve me, let him follow me.' Young renders: 'If any one may minister to me, let him follow me;' Tischendorf: 'If any one minister to me, let him follow me.' The term 'serve' or 'minister' carries here the same sense as in the parable of the sheep and the goats, where the latter say: 'Lord, when saw we thee an hungred, or athirst, or a stranger, or naked, or sick, or in prison, and did not minister unto thee?' The verb is the same in both passages: *diakoneō*. Jesus here distinguishes between ministering to him and following him, and he counsels his apostles that whoever may perform the former office is also to be at liberty, if not exhorted, to assume the latter. That there is no imperative command intended, transforming of necessity the minister into the follower, seems obvious from what follows: 'And where I am, there shall also my servant be,' where Young and Tischendorf render 'servant' as 'minister.' The two classes must ever remain distinct, as followers or disciples and ministers or helpers. We have already learnt that the followers or 'brethren' of Jesus are his representatives among mankind, and that ministration to their necessities will be regarded as done to himself.

This discourse may be taken as referring and replying to the application of the Greeks. Their request for an interview was evidence of a desire to come into some closer connection than ordinary with Jesus. Whether they designed to express sympathy, offer help to him and his disciples, as others who had 'ministered unto him of their substance,' or hoped to join the ranks of his followers, we know not, and possibly the two apostles themselves were not told. But the rule now laid down by Jesus meets the case of all who seek to ally themselves with his cause. If any one helps his 'followers' he becomes thereby his 'minister;' and whoever so ministers is thereby fitted to become his 'follower.' If he chooses the higher grade he must be prepared for the sacrifices it entails: 'Whosoever he be of you that renounceth not all that he hath, he cannot be my disciple.' If he takes the lower ground of sympathy, his ministry, however slight, will be accepted and recompensed: 'For whosoever shall give you a cup of water to drink, because ye are Christ's, verily I say unto you, he shall in no wise lose his reward.' Jesus now puts this truth in another form. 'If any man serve me, him will the Father honour.' Young and Tischendorf render the word 'serve' as 'minister to.' Jesus had begun by saying, 'The hour is come that the Son of man should be glorified,' and immediately went on to speak of the necessity and advantage of death. His passage to glory lay through death and suffering. 'Now is my soul troubled.' Young renders literally : 'Now hath my soul been troubled,' as alluding rather to a troubled existence than to the present moment. Alford notes that the word 'soul' in this verse is the same as that rendered 'life' in verse 25, and although he there preferred to translate the word as 'soul' twice and as 'life' once, he added : 'Notice, that the *soul* involves the *life* in both cases, and must not be taken in the present acceptation of that term.' The life of Jesus had indeed been a troublous one, and the hour upon which he had now entered must constitute the crisis of his sufferings prior to his glorification. In what way did it behove him to meet it ? 'And what shall I say ? Father, save me from this hour.' The Revisers intimate that a note of interrogation may be added after 'hour.' Alford observes that the words, 'Father, save me from this hour,' 'must not be taken interrogatively, as if our Lord were doubting whether to say them or not : for thus the whole sense is destroyed, besides the sentiment being most unworthy of Him who uttered it. The prayer is a *veritable prayer.*' Young combines the two sentences : 'And what shall I say Father, save me from this hour ?' The same word *ti*, 'what,' is used with the same emphasis and object elsewhere : 'What shall we say ? Is God unrighteous who visiteth with wrath ?' In both passages the idea is started only with the view of its dismissal, as something which cannot be admitted or contemplated for an instant. The career of Jesus had been deliberately chosen, and its culmination in rejection and crucifixion foreseen. 'But for this cause came I unto this hour.' Young renders : 'But because of this I came to this hour.' Alford observes : 'The misunderstanding of these words has principally led to the erroneous punctuation just noticed. *For this cause* really means, *in order that I may be saved from this hour*: i.e. I came to this hour for this very purpose,—*that I might be safe from* this hour : i.e. the going into, and exhausting this hour, this cup, is the very appointed way of my glorification.' In seeking to obviate one error, Alford has apparently fallen into another. He takes the meaning to be 'safe,' instead of 'saved' or delivered from the hour. But it seems right to understand the expression in the sense of the subsequent prayer of Jesus, 'that, if it were possible, the hour might pass away from him.' Alford observes further : 'The other interpretation of the words *for this cause,* that of Meyer and others, is, *that Thy Name may be glorified.* But surely this is to do violence to the order of thought. This particular does not come on till the next clause, and cannot without an improbable transposition be drawn into this.' Let that be admitted : the question remains, whether the words *for this cause* refer, as Alford supposed, to safety *in* the hour, or to something else antecedent to the words. Must not the reference obviously be to that which was to happen at the hour ? And what was that ? 'The hour is come, that the Son of man should be glorified.' For that cause Jesus had come to that hour, and now 'we behold him . . .

because of the suffering of death crowned with glory and honour.' The glorification of Jesus was bound up with the glory of God. In his last prayer Jesus said, 'Father, the hour is come; glorify thy Son, that the Son may glorify thee.' So he says here: 'Father, glorify thy name.' That was the cry of submission, of self-dedication to the divine will, which had made 'the suffering of death' the medium and harbinger of glory. And the cry was answered instantly, miraculously. 'There came therefore a voice out of heaven, *saying*, I have both glorified it, and will glorify it again.' The Revisers and Young have altered the word 'then' of the Authorised Version to 'therefore.' Alford explains : ' This *voice* can no otherwise be understood, than as a plain articulate sound, miraculously spoken, heard by all, and variously interpreted. So all the ancients, and the best of the modern expositors.' A similar phenomenon is related at the baptism and the transfiguration of Jesus. To the latter, the apostle Peter, many years later, bore deliberate and solemn testimony, stating that they had been ' eye-witnesses of his majesty. For he received from God the Father honour and glory, when there came such a voice to him from the excellent glory, This is my beloved Son, in whom I am well pleased : and this voice we *ourselves* heard come out of heaven, when we were with him in the holy mount.' If all human testimony is not to be discredited, this evidence must be received ; and if the possibility of a divine revelation is admitted, or, at the least, held to be admissible, we must expect to find connected with it things outside the range of human experience. That such things lie ordinarily above and beyond us, is no more a reason for disbelief when they are vouched for by honest men, than the invisibility of stars is a proof of their absence, or the rarity of comets an argument for their non-existence. On the words, 'I have glorified it,' Alford notes: 'In the manifestation hitherto made of the Son of God, imperfect as it was ; in all Old Testament type and prophecy ; in Creation ; and indeed before the world was made.' Should we not rather understand the reference to be to the personal history of Jesus ? Upon that his prayer touched, and to that the answer must apply. He had told the Jews : 'The works that I do in my Father's name, these bear witness of me ;' and we read 'that the multitude wondered, when they saw the dumb speaking, the maimed whole, and the lame walking, and the blind seeing ; and they glorified the God of Israel.' That answers to the words, 'I have glorified it.' But these works were now to cease ; Jesus could no more go about doing good, but must face his baptism of suffering and death. To that the words may be applied, 'I will glorify it again.' The voice out of heaven was loud and sonorous, and to many of the crowd which stood about sounded like a thunderclap. Others of them detected articulate words, and as no human lips could have uttered them, the opinion was expressed that an angel had spoken to Jesus. 'The multitude therefore, that stood by, and heard it, said that it had thundered ; others said, An angel hath spoken to him.' Young's rendering is more graphic : 'The multitude therefore that were standing and hearing, were saying that there had been thunder ; others said, A messenger hath spoken to him.' Alford notes : 'Some *heard words*, but did not apprehend their meaning ; others *a sound* but no words.' If there were similar differences between those who were present at Paul's vision, that fact may account for the obvious discrepancy between two descriptions of it, one stating: 'The men that journeyed with him stood speechless, hearing the voice, but beholding no man;' the other: 'They that were with me beheld indeed the light, but they heard not the voice of him that spake to me.' 9 Acts 7

22 Acts 9

The Authorised Version continues: 'Jesus answered and said, This voice came not because of me, but for your sakes:' altered by the Revisers to: 'Jesus answered and said, This voice hath not come for my sake, but for your sakes.' Young renders: 'Not on my account hath this voice come, but on your account.' The truth thus revealed and attested was of interest to mankind at large: not the mere sound as of thunder in the ears of the multitude, but the import of the words to those who heard and understood. Twice before had a declaration concerning Jesus been vouchsafed from heaven: 'Lo, a voice out of the heavens, saying, This is my beloved Son, in whom I am well pleased.' Again on the mount: 'Behold, a voice out of the cloud, saying, This is my beloved Son, in whom I am well pleased; hear ye him.' The three audible, supernatural manifestations of the divine approval of Jesus were given that they might be recorded, and are recorded for our instruction. The voice having come for our sakes, we ought to understand the why and wherefore. It behoves us to ponder the import of the phenomenon. A similar revelation had been granted to the Israelites: 'Behold, the LORD (literally, Jehovah) our God hath shewed us his glory and his greatness, and we have heard his voice out of the midst of the fire: we have seen this day that God doth speak with man, and he liveth.' This unique experience was granted in connection with the giving of a law and the introduction of a system of a divine national government. That system was now relinquished by its Author, and another was to be set up in its place; the kingdom of Israel was to be replaced by the kingdom of heaven, the law of Moses by the law of Jesus. 'The law and the prophets *were* until John: from that time the gospel of the kingdom of God is preached.' Was it not necessary that the withdrawal of what had gone before should be notified, and the introduction of the new scheme for man's salvation attested, by the same divine voice speaking from heaven? Twelve Israelites were chosen to proclaim the Messiah and to inaugurate the conversion of the world. Any one of them might well have faltered, in spite of other signs and wonders, if this particular testimony had been wanting. They asserted the paramount authority of Jesus, who 'if he were on earth, he would not be a priest at all, seeing there are those who offer the gifts according to the law.' The high-priesthood of Jesus is heavenly, and involves an utter overthrow of the Mosaic ritual. These are bold words for the ambassadors of Christ to utter: 'For there is a disannulling of a foregoing commandment because of its weakness and unprofitableness (for the law made nothing perfect), and a bringing in thereupon of a better hope, through which we draw nigh unto God.' The divinely-appointed priesthood, which had endured and been venerated for ages, was set aside as a thing of the past, a better ministry organised, a new covenant established between God and his people. 'But now hath he obtained a ministry the more excellent, by how much also he is the mediator of a better covenant, 12 John 30

3 Mat. 17

17 Mat. 5

5 Deu. 24

16 Luke 16

8 Heb. 4

7 Heb. 18, 19

8 Heb. 6

which hath been enacted upon better promises.' There was no shrinking from the declaration that the first handiwork of God was defective : ' For if that first *covenant* had been faultless, then would no place have been found for a second. For finding fault with them, he saith '—Young renders : ' For finding fault, he saith to them ; ' Sharpe : ' For when finding fault it saith to them : ' and then follows this quotation from the 31st chapter of Jeremiah :

' Behold the days come saith the Lord,
 That I will make a new covenant with the house of Israel and
  with the house of Judah,
Not according to the covenant that I made with their fathers
 In the day that I took them by the hand to lead them forth out
  of the land of Egypt ;
For they continued not in my covenant,
And I regarded them not, saith the Lord.'

The old system had long shown signs of feebleness and decay : ' In that he saith, A new *covenant*, he hath made the first old. But that which is becoming old and waxeth aged is nigh unto vanishing away.' The argument and the forecast have been borne out by the facts. The Jews still exist, but they have simply synagogues without a temple, no priests, no sacrifices offered according to the law ; the covenant and the ritual have together become obsolete. Yet inasmuch as they had been ratified on mount Sinai by a voice speaking from heaven, could they, a Jew might ask, be repealed on any less authority ? That voice came, and Jesus exclaimed : ' This voice hath not come for my sake, but for your sakes.' In Peter's mind it ranked as the foremost evidence. He wrote : ' We did not follow cunningly devised fables, when we made known unto you the power and coming (Gr. presence) of our Lord Jesus Christ.' In proof thereof he referred first to the fact that ' there came such a voice to him from the excellent glory,' and secondly to ' the word of prophecy made more sure.' Only the most irrefragable evidence could have nerved the apostles to face obloquy and death for the purpose of enunciating the doctrine concerning Jesus, his kingdom and his priesthood.

The glorification of the Son of man and of the divine name was connected with the opening of a new chapter in human history. ' Now is the (or, a) judgement of this world : now shall the prince of this world be cast out.' Young renders ' prince ' by ' ruler.' The word ' now ' may be taken to mean both at this time and from this time ; it certainly cannot indicate an indefinite period in the distant future. The impression prevails that the judgment of the world, that is, of mankind, by Christ has not yet commenced. That is contrary to this declaration of Jesus. We talk of the coming of the Lord to judge the world, overlooking the fact that the word rendered ' coming ' is properly ' presence,' and taking the expression ' day of the Lord ' rather as a literal ' day,' not yet come, than in its scriptural sense of a continuous stretch of time. Our ideas on the subject are often as hazy and indefinite as they are hasty and positive. ' The judgment of the world ' must surely signify ' the judgment of mankind.' In this earth Jesus does not ' now ' exercise such judgment ; yet it is ' now ' exercised. Do we ask, Where ? In that world beyond the grave, whither he has gone and whither we all go at death.

There, not here, he judges 'now;' there his work on behalf of mankind is carried on and perfected, 'to the intent that now unto the principalities and the powers in the heavenly *places* might be known through the church (assembly—Young) the manifold wisdom of God.' His rule and judgment will hereafter be extended to this present world: that also is revealed: 'He hath appointed a day, in the which he will judge the world (Gr. the inhabited earth) in righteousness by the man whom he hath ordained.' But Jesus assures us that now, before that consummation, 'Now is the (or, a) judgement of this world: now shall the prince of this world be cast out.' He speaks as conversant with unseen spiritual realities. No earthly prince is alluded to, but the Being termed by Paul 'the god of this world (or, age),' 'the prince of the power of the air, of the spirit that now worketh in the sons of disobedience.' Here is a mystery beyond our power to fathom. As there is a holy Spirit of God, so there is an evil Spirit of the Devil, who is the adversary both of God and man. The expression 'cast out' denotes the deliverance of mankind from the devil's power, as in the passage, 'If Satan cast out Satan (If the Adversary casteth out the Adversary—Young) he is divided against himself; how then shall his kingdom stand? But if I by the Spirit of God cast out devils (Gr. demons), then is the kingdom of God come upon you.' It would not be within the bounds of common sense and truth to assert that any judgment and casting out such as Jesus speaks of, are now at work and prevalent on earth. Still we must not alter the present tense into the future: somewhere in the universe the judgment now is of this world, although not in this world, and has been since the glorification of Jesus, and following thereupon—'now'— the casting out of the ruler of this world. Jesus will assume that supremacy over mankind which the devil had usurped. The present tense is now dropped: 'And I, if I be lifted up from (or, out of) the earth, will draw all men unto myself.' In the Authorised Version the word 'men' is in italics; Tischendorf omits it. An explanation is here interpolated: 'But this he said, signifying by what manner of death he should die.' This is obviously an addition by the evangelist, and does not prove that Jesus himself attributed that recondite sense to his words. The uplifting of the body of Jesus on a cross can certainly be connected with them, and we know that he had foreseen and foretold his crucifixion. The expression 'lifted up' had been previously applied by Jesus to himself: 'As Moses lifted up the serpent in the wilderness, even so must the Son of man be lifted up.' There, 'lifted up' can scarcely be held to point to crucifixion, for the serpent was not crucified: the exaltation of Jesus permanently in the sight and for the salvation of men is the idea there conveyed. But here the words are taken as indicative of 'what manner of death he should die,' rendered by Young 'by what death he was about to die.' Alford observes: 'St. John does not say that this was *all* that the *lifting up* meant, but that it was the first and obvious reference.' By the light of a previous prophecy, or of the subsequent event, the words may be taken in that enigmatical way, but it must be the secondary, not the primary sense of them, and the multitude who heard them could not possibly attach to them that significance. They understood the expression 'lifted up from the earth' to mean exalted above, removed from, the world. 'The multitude therefore answered him. We have heard out of the law that Christ abideth for ever: and how sayest thou, The Son of man must be lifted up?' The word 'therefore' has been introduced by the Revisers, on the authority of the two oldest MSS. Young renders 'abideth for ever' as 'remaineth for the age.' Alford observes: 'The actual words, *the Son of man must be lifted up*, had not been on this occasion used by Jesus.' Inferentially they had: Jesus alluded to 'the Son of man' in the beginning of the discourse (verse 23), and it was obvious that the application was personal to himself. The form of the question also indicates that the terms 'the Son of man' and 'the Christ' were held to be synonymous. Alford observes: '*The law* must be taken in its wider sense, as including the whole of the Old Testament,' and he refers to the saying of Jesus: 'Is it not written in your law, I said, Ye are gods,' where the reference is to one of the Psalms of Asaph. The people may have had in mind such passages as the following:

'I will not lie unto David;
His seed shall endure for ever,
And his throne as the sun before me.'

Messiah's reign was to be perpetual. What kind of Son of man or Messiah was Jesus telling of? 'Who is this Son of man?' Young renders: 'Who is this—the Son of man?'

Apart from the idea of crucifixion, the expression 'lifted up from (or, out of) the earth,' may naturally be taken as applying either to the resurrection or ascension of Jesus, or to both. The result of his death and uprising will be to 'draw all' to himself. This certainly has not been realised on earth. Again we are compelled to turn our thoughts to those 'heavenly places' alluded to by the apostle. There is the scene of his career, the sphere of his activity, 'the heavenly Jerusalem' (that is, 'the habitation of peace'), 'the company of myriads of messengers . . . the assembly of the firstborn in heaven enrolled' (Young); there his work is going on and his attractive power is in fullest exercise. Paul, in the Epistle to the Hebrews, argues very forcibly that the high-priesthood of Jesus on behalf of mankind must be exercised by him in heaven: 'Now if he were on earth he would not be a priest at all.' His true and proper functions are not performed in this world. 'For Christ entered not into a holy place made with hands, like in pattern to the true, but into heaven itself, now to appear before the face of God for us.' Contemplating with boldness our own entrance into that 'holy place by the blood of Jesus, by the way which he dedicated for us,' the writer exhorts, 'let us draw near with a true heart in fulness of faith.' living and walking as Christian brothers, 'and so much the more, as ye see the day drawing nigh.' The progress of our earthly life is a drawing nigh, and the close of it our day of entrance into the holy place where Jesus manifests his priestly power and glory, and where his words must needs come true: 'I, if I be lifted up from the earth, will draw all men unto myself.'

In the Authorised Version the next verse begins, 'Then Jesus said unto them . . .' The Revisers have altered 'then' to 'therefore,' agreeing with Young, Tischendorf and Alford. The word 'therefore' indicates the connection with what precedes. 'Jesus therefore said unto them, Yet a little while is the light among (or, in) you.' The Authorised

Version has 'with you:' the reading of the two oldest MSS. is 'among you.' The light must alternate with darkness. Let them take the day and the night for a parable, and avail themselves of God's truth, as of his sunlight, while they had it. 'Walk while ye have the light, that darkness overtake you not.' The Authorised Version stands, 'lest darkness come upon you,' which might be taken to signify that the walking in light would prevent the coming on of darkness. Alford and Tischendorf agree with the Revisers in using the word 'overtake.' No advance can be made except by the use of existing opportunities. To-morrow, when it comes, may be as this day: but the night must intervene, and if the day be lost, the night cannot be utilised to repair that loss. 'And he that walketh in the darkness knoweth not whither he goeth.' When the light is with us, we should trust to its revelations, and direct ourselves accordingly. 'While ye have the light, believe in the light, that ye may become sons of light.' [12 John 35, 35, 36]

This was the last public discourse of Jesus, the close of his ministry. He left the multitude and returned no more. 'These things spake Jesus, and he departed and hid himself (or, was hidden) from them.' As long as he could hope to benefit them, his teaching had been continued; but it was worse than useless to persevere with it, for though it had been accompanied by many miracles, he gained no credence with them. 'But though he had done so many signs before them, yet they believed not on him;' they could not regard him as 'the Son of man,' the Messiah, a heaven-sent Teacher and Saviour. Therein they justified the accuracy of a prediction of Isaiah: 'That the word of Isaiah the prophet might be fulfilled, which he spake, [36, 37, 38]

Lord, who hath believed our report?
And to whom hath the arm of the LORD (literally, Jehovah) been revealed?'

In our version of Isaiah the word 'Lord' at the beginning does not appear. Alford notes: 'Beware of understanding the words to mean merely *so that the saying of Esaias was fulfilled*, which the original will not bear.' This remark is corroborated by what follows: 'For this cause they could not believe, for that Isaiah said again, [53 Isa. 1; 12 John 39]

He hath blinded their eyes, and he hardened their heart;
Lest they should see with their eyes, and perceive with their heart, And should turn,
And I should heal them.' [40]

The Revisers, as well as Alford and Tischendorf, have strengthened the assertion of the evangelist by rendering, instead of 'Therefore,' 'For this cause.' Young renders, 'On account of this.' This obviously refers to what precedes, namely the question, 'To whom hath the arm of Jehovah been revealed?' Failing to discern 'the arm,' or as we should say, 'the hand' or 'the finger' of Jehovah in the teaching and working of Jesus, it was impossible for the people to place their confidence in him as the promised Messiah. More than that: as Isaiah had further foretold, they were blind and obdurate, in no fit state of mind and heart for conversion and reformation. The Revisers and Sharpe have altered 'be converted' to 'should turn,' rendered by Young 'turn back.' Coupled with the word 'heal,' the expression evidently alludes to reformation of heart and life, which was the object Jesus ever aimed at. Alford observes : 'The prophecy is freely cited, after neither the Hebrew nor the LXX. What God *bids* the prophet *do*, is here described as *done*, and by Himself: which is obviously *implied* in the Hebrew text.' The passage in Isaiah stands: 'Make the heart of this people fat, and make their ears heavy, and shut their eyes,' which Young renders :

6 Isa. 10

> 'Declare fat the heart of this people,
> And its ears declare heavy ;
> And its eyes declare dazzled.'

Shrinking from the words, 'He hath blinded their eyes and he hardened their heart,' Samuel Sharpe replaces ' He ' by ' (This people),' in brackets. The retributive consequences of men's own conduct are as much from God as are their powers of thought and action. Our unused faculties grow 'fat :' whether we say God makes them so, or simply declares them so, matters little : the effect arises from the constitution of our nature as moulded by divine Providence ; the ears kept closed against unwelcome truths become hard of hearing, and eyes long shut against the light of heaven lose, if not their power, at least their accuracy of vision : ' for this cause they could not believe.'

12 John 41

The evangelist had no hesitation in applying these prophecies of Isaiah to the history of Jesus. 'These things said Isaiah, because he saw his glory ; and he spake of him.' The Authorised Version reads, 'when he saw his glory, and spake of him.' The Revisers, Tischendorf and Alford have altered 'when ' to ' because,' on the authority of the three oldest MSS. Alford explains : 'The last clause is independent of *because*, and contains another assertion—*and he spake concerning him*.' The Revisers have indicated this by the semi-colon and inserting the word ' he ' before ' spake.' We have no difficulty in accepting the opinion expressed by the evangelist: the 53rd chapter of Isaiah is unmistakably Messianic, from first to last, and indicates that the glory of the Messiah lay through suffering and death ; and the 6th chapter alludes to the rejection of a heaven-sent messenger, the obduracy of the nation, and the desolation of the land. The primary reference appears to be to Isaiah himself, but if so, the experiences of Jesus were identical and the national disaster was repeated. Yet although the people generally ignored the claims of Jesus, some believed on him, and many even of the ruling class.

,, 42

'Nevertheless even of the rulers, many believed on him.' The Authorised Version stands, 'among the chief rulers also,' but Alford's rendering agrees with that of the Revisers, and Young translates : ' Still, however, even out of the rulers . . .' But the fear of consequences withheld them from any open confession of faith, the penalty of excommunication having been threatened against all who espoused

,, 42

the cause of Jesus. ' But because of the Pharisees they did not confess it (or, him), lest they should be put out of the synagogue.' Young avoids the doubtful ' it ' or ' him ' by rendering, ' were not confessing.' Alford notes that the word is ' not expressed in the original.' The timorous and time-serving policy of those who shrank from any open admission of their convictions sprang from their preference of human applause to the divine approval: 'For they loved the glory of men more than the glory of God.' The Revisers have altered 'praise' to 'glory,' therein agreeing with Young, Tischendorf and Alford. Luther renders the word 'Ehre,' 'honour.' Jesus had previously detected and exposed that cause of some men's want of faith in him: 'How can ye believe, which receive glory one of another, and the glory that *cometh* from the only God ye seek not?' 12 John 43
5 John 44

The remaining seven verses of this chapter comprise various sayings of Jesus, which seem at first sight somewhat out of place after the statement of the evangelist: 'These things spake Jesus, and he departed and hid himself from them.' Alford observes: 'It was by the older Commentators generally thought, that these verses formed part of some other discourse delivered at this period. But this is improbable, from no occasion being specified,—from verse 36,—and from the form and contents of the passage, and its reference to the foregoing remarks of the Evangelist, I take it—with almost all modern Commentators—to be a *continuation of these remarks, substantiating them by the testimony of the Lord Himself*. The words are taken mostly, but not altogether, from discourses *already given* in this Gospel.' The explanation of this insertion and combination of previous declarations of Jesus becomes sufficiently apparent on a consideration of the context. The first quotation from Isaiah begins, 'Lord, who hath believed our report?' The evangelist proceeds to specify the nature of the report which Jesus had made, but which had not been believed: 'And Jesus cried and said . . .' The expression is peculiar, equivalent to that of the Baptist, 'I am the voice of one crying in the wilderness:' the reference in both cases is to a crying, a proclamation or 'report.' The Revisers have inserted 'and' before 'Jesus,' which agrees with Young. Tischendorf, Alford and Luther have 'but.' The word, omitted in the Authorised Version, is a connecting link between what precedes and follows. The 'report' of Jesus is summarised in two sentences: (1) 'He that believeth on me, believeth not on me, but on him that sent me.' (2) 'And he that beholdeth me, beholdeth him that sent me.' The precise words are not recorded elsewhere, but their spirit pervades the teaching of Jesus. 'That all may honour the Son, even as they honour the Father. He that honoureth not the Son honoureth not the Father which sent him. Verily, verily, I say unto you, He that heareth my word, and believeth him that sent me, hath eternal life.' 'Whosoever receiveth me, receiveth not me, but him that sent me.' 'He that hath seen me hath seen the Father.' The second quotation from Isaiah, beginning, 'He hath blinded their eyes, and he hardened their heart,' is illustrated by various statements made in effect by Jesus at different times: (1) 'I am come a light into the world, that whosoever believeth on me may not abide in the darkness.' That corresponds with the passage: 'I am the light of the world: he that followeth me shall not walk in the darkness, but shall have the light of life.' (2) 'And if any man hear my sayings, and keep them not, I judge him not: for I came not to judge the world, but to save the world.' The Revisers have altered 'words' to 'sayings,' agreeing with Young, and 'believe not' to 'keep them not,' on the authority of the three oldest MSS. The word 'them' should be italicised, not being in the original. These ideas are contained in the following passages. 'Think not that I will accuse you to the Father.' 'For God sent not the Son into the world to judge the world; but that the world should be saved through him.' (3) 'He that rejecteth me, and receiveth not my sayings, hath one that judgeth him: the word that I spake, the same shall judge him in the last day.' Analogous passages: 'He that rejecteth me rejecteth him that sent me.' 'I have many things to speak and to judge concerning you.' 'My teaching is not mine, but his that sent me.' 'If a man keep my word, he shall never see death.' (4) 'For I spake not from myself; but the Father which sent me, he hath given me a commandment what I should say, and what I should speak.' This corresponds with the following passages. 'Ye seek to kill me, because my word hath not free course in you. I speak the things which I have seen with *my* Father ... But now ye seek to kill me, a man that hath told you the truth, which I heard from God.' (5) 'And I know that his commandment is life eternal (age-during—Young): the things therefore which I speak, even as the Father hath said unto me, so I speak.' To that effect are the following sayings. 'This is the will of my Father, that every one that beholdeth the Son, and believeth on him, should have eternal life.' 'The words that I say unto you, I speak not from myself: but the Father abiding in me doeth his works.'

The last seven verses of this 12th chapter appear to be the evangelist's epitome of the doctrine of Jesus, based upon declarations uttered by him at various times. He presented himself as God's ambassador and representative to mankind, as a new light come into the world to lead believers on him out of the prevailing darkness; his sayings, words, commandment, doctrine—the terms appear to be synonymous—will be to every man the final and decisive test of character, will 'judge him in the last day:' his teaching is God's teaching, embodying the divine will and introducing 'life age-during.' Now, after the lapse of eighteen centuries, the question still applies:

'Lord, who hath believed our report?
And to whom hath the arm of the Lord been revealed?'

Has not the method of Jesus for the regeneration of society been partly perverted and partly lost sight of? The very idea of a perfect adherence by his disciples to all his precepts in their literal meaning, is dismissed by most of us as visionary and impracticable. Yet they all stand firm as his word or teaching, and only by the exhibition of those peculiar Christian virtues which all admire and praise but none profess to follow, can the world become leavened with the spirit of Jesus, and the kingdom of heaven be established upon earth. The living of the ideal life by the few is the appointed means of salvation to the many. A body of disciples will generate a community of believers; but a community of believers without disciples must degenerate from the high standard of the gospel, the profession thereof remaining, but its spirit and power becoming more and more lost. That the Lord's prayer should be taught to every child, repeated constantly and generally by all classes, as a matter of course, if not a Christian duty, is by itself an evidence that the true conception of discipleship has become obscured and wellnigh lost to the church and the world. The fact is overlooked that the prayer was taught to disciples. In Matthew's gospel it is found in the Sermon on the mount, which was spoken to disciples, [5 Mat. 1] and follows those precepts of non-resistance to evil, abstention from [6 Mat. 9] oath-taking and from law, which if not restricted to a distinct class of professed 'disciples must perforce fall into desuetude, as has actually come to pass, and upon the ears of the world as mere rhetorical flourishes, doctrines of perfection never designed by him who spoke them to be understood literally or obeyed implicitly. Luke records the giving of the prayer at a later period, in answer to the request of a disciple: 'Lord, teach us to pray, even as John [11 Luke 1] also taught his disciples.' The prayer was given to disciples, for disciples, as a badge of discipleship; and it contains a phrase which can only carry its natural and proper meaning when uttered by a disciple, that is, by one who has actually, practically, literally accepted and complied with Christ's own terms, 'Whosoever he be of [14 Luke 33] you that renounceth not all that he hath, he cannot be my disciple.' Here is the sentence in Matthew: 'Give us this day our daily bread [6 Mat. 11] (Gr. our bread for the coming day).' In Luke: 'Give us day by [11 Luke 3] day our daily bread (Gr. our bread for the coming day).' Young renders Matthew: 'Our appointed bread give us to-day,' and Luke: 'Our necessary bread be giving us daily.' 'Our bread the needed,' is the rendering of both passages in the 'Englishman's Greek New Testament.' That petition is appropriate to those who, like the apostles, 'suffered the loss of all things' for Christ's sake; its full, [3 Phil. 8] true, honest sense is lost when uttered by those who have never resolved and do not feel themselves bound to carry out Christ's precepts, 'Lay not up for yourselves treasures upon the earth,' and [6 Mat. 19] 'Sell that ye have, and give alms; make for yourselves purses which wax not old, a treasure in the heavens that faileth not, where no thief draweth near, neither moth destroyeth. For where your treasure is, there will your heart be also.' However strange it may seem to us, impecuniosity was made a badge of discipleship. Jesus must have had a deliberate and serious purpose when he sent forth first twelve preachers, commanding them 'Get you no gold, nor [10 Mat. 9] silver, nor brass in your purses,' and afterwards seventy others, charging them also, 'Carry no purse.' That petition in the Lord's [10 Luke 4] prayer, which we repeat so glibly, 'Give us this day our daily bread,' points in the same direction. There are multitudes, indeed, whose involuntary, constant and crying need gives literalism and pathos to the utterance; but this daily want of all things was regarded by Jesus as the normal condition of his followers or disciples, universally, without exception, and the form of prayer he bequeathed to them contains this evidence of his intention and their duty. All who are not professed disciples are free to labour for a competency, for advancement in the world, to nourish an honourable ambition for the best things of life, fair fame, an assured position, and so much of wealth as they can honestly earn, to be wisely used, and handed down for the benefit of those near and dear to them. Only let the fact be recognised, that they who seek such things do not stand upon the platform of discipleship, have not attained or sought to reach that high level of fellowship with Jesus, and cannot properly use, as applicable to their own case and expressive of their own necessities and entire helplessness and dependence, the disciples' entreaty, 'Give us this day our daily bread.' We take the words euphemistically, if not as figurative, yet with a stretch of the imagination, thinking, when we think at all about them, that God's providence provides sustenance for us all, and that it is well to recognise in this way the fact, realising and acknowledging our dependence upon the divine bounty. But that is not the spirit, the aim, the right motive of prayer. True prayer is based upon the sense of a want which is felt and pressing. Surely Jesus would not have us pray, never taught us to pray, for that which is already in our own hands and power. The whole structure of the Lord's prayer points to the conclusion that it was not designed for universal adoption. The first words, 'Our Father,' are decisive on that point, if we bear in mind the apostolic declaration: 'As many as received him, to them gave he the right to become children of God, even to them that believe on his name.' It is only faith in Jesus which justifies our calling upon God as Father : 'Because ye are sons, God sent forth the Spirit of his Son into our hearts, crying, Abba, Father.' Baptism without faith, which infant baptism must needs be, cannot confer this sonship, which Jesus makes contingent upon character : 'Love your enemies, and pray for them that persecute you ; that ye may be the sons of your Father which is in heaven.' The whole tone of the Lord's prayer is in unison with the high keynote struck by the opening words. Each succeeding petition indicates a heart and life devoted to the cause of God : the hallowing of his name, the doing of his will on earth after the heavenly fashion, the daily recurring impoverishment and need, the Christlike habit of forgiveness, the immanence of temptation to fall below a high standard, and the exposure to evil with only God for a deliverer : such utterances beseem disciples, but not mankind in general, and not all professing Christians, except in their loftiest mood of devotion and as a verbal recognition of the duties and desires of Christ's true followers. The endless, perfunctory, matter of course repetitions of the Lord's prayer, by persons of every class and age, can neither be acceptable to God nor salutary to mankind. The thoughtless and inconsiderate use of it, as though it were a charm possessing some intrinsic virtue recommending us to God and ensuring his favour and protection, cannot be too strongly deprecated. Rightly viewed and understood, it stands forth as an ideal rather than a common prayer, and whenever we repeat it the thought should be prominent in our minds, that it was framed for disciples, and is ours only so far as we have the spirit of discipleship, not ours at all in its full and literal import. The world waits, the church waits, Christ waits, the kingdom of heaven waits for a body of 'disciples,' in the true sense of the term, and for them, when they shall be manifested, for their daily use, not for ours meantime, the Lord's prayer must wait its perfect application. Until then, the prophet's cry remains without any adequate response :

'Lord, who hath believed our report ?
And to whom hath the arm of the Lord been revealed ?'

Jesus was now at Jerusalem with his disciples. It was the time of the passover, and as yet no preparations had been made by them with respect to it. They therefore enquired of Jesus where he proposed to keep the feast. 'Now on the first *day* of unleavened bread the disciples came to Jesus, saying, Where wilt thou that we make ready for thee to eat the passover?' The Revisers have omitted the words 'the *feast of*' before 'unleavened bread.' They have also omitted 'unto him' after 'saying,' on the authority of the two oldest MSS. Mark is to the same effect. 'And on the first day of unleavened bread, when they sacrificed the passover, his disciples say unto him, Where wilt thou that we go and make ready that thou mayest eat the passover?' The Revisers, Young and Tischendorf have rendered 'said' by 'say,' which is the literal translation. Luke: 'And the day of unleavened bread came, on which the passover must be sacrificed.' The word 'sacrificed' is adopted by the Revisers instead of 'killed.' Alford observes: 'By *came* we must of course understand that the day *was come*, not, as some would interpret it, *was at hand*.' Luke records the question: 'And they said unto him, Where wilt thou that we make ready?' but represents it to have been asked by the two disciples he mentions in the previous verse, whereas Matthew and Mark indicate that it was put by the disciples generally. Either Luke misplaced the question, or the accounts are to be reconciled by supposing it to have been put twice, which might naturally occur, first by the twelve, and again by the two who had been selected by Jesus to make the preparations. 'And he sendeth two of his disciples.' Luke mentions their names: 'And he sent Peter and John, saying, Go and make ready for us the passover, that we may eat.' His instructions were very definite and peculiar. 'And he said unto them, Behold, when ye are entered into the city, there shall meet you a man bearing a pitcher of water.' Mark: 'And saith unto them, Go into the city, and there shall meet you a man bearing a pitcher of water.' Alford observes: 'There can, I think, be no question that this direction was given in super-human foresight, just as that in ch. xix. 30: see also 1 Sam. x. 2-8, and Matt. xvii. 27.' These references are to the obtaining of the ass for the triumphal entry, the payment of the tribute by a coin found in the fish's mouth, and Samuel's prophetic instructions, which it will be interesting to transcribe. 'When thou art departed from me to-day, then thou shalt find two men by Rachel's sepulchre, in the border of Benjamin at Zelzah; and they will say unto thee, The asses which thou wentest to seek are found: and, lo, thy father hath left the care of the asses, and taketh thought for you, saying, What shall I do for my son? Then shalt thou go on forward from thence, and thou shalt come to the oak of Tabor, and there shall meet thee there three men going up to God to Beth-el, one carrying three kids, and another carrying three loaves of bread, and another carrying a bottle of wine: and they will salute thee, and give thee two loaves of bread; which thou shalt receive of their hand. After that thou shalt come to the hill of God, where is the garrison of the Philistines: and it shall come to pass, when thou art come thither to the city, that thou shalt meet a band of prophets coming down from the high place with a psaltery, and a timbrel, and a pipe, and a harp, before them; and they shall be prophesying: and the spirit of the LORD will come mightily upon thee, and thou shalt prophesy with them, and shalt be turned into another man.... And it was so, that when he had turned his back to go from Samuel, God gave him another heart: and all those signs came to pass that day.' The belief in such a power of second-sight dates back to very remote times, and is not confined to one nation. Admitting its existence, it involves another mystery, that is, the over-ruling of the human will by supernatural influence. We are as unable to disprove as we are to explain such possibilities: they lie outside the range of our faculties and knowledge, and to deride and dismiss them as superstitious and wholly incredible, is rather the presumption of ignorance than the dictum of science or philosophy. We are assured that Jesus foresaw and foretold the time and manner of his death, with some of its incidents. The evangelists did not, would not, dared not shrink from recording that and similarly attested facts, on the ground that they pass our comprehension; they relate with simple gravity what actually happened, and we have no choice between either rejecting the gospel in its entirety or accepting it in the form in which it was first handed down. Any attempt to exclude the miraculous, the unearthly, the supernatural, from these histories would dismember them, destroy their symmetry, and kill the life, the spirit, the essence of Christ's teaching. The disciples had so much confidence in Jesus, that they went unhesitatingly in search of the man bearing the pitcher of water, who should meet them when they entered Jerusalem. Jesus gave them precise instructions. 'Follow him; and wheresoever he shall enter in, say to the goodman of the house, The Master (or, Teacher) saith, Where is my guest-chamber, where I shall eat the passover with my disciples.' The word 'my' replaces 'the,' in the Revised Version, on the authority of the two oldest MSS. Luke evidently compiled from the same record. ' Follow him into the house whereinto he goeth. And ye shall say unto the goodman of the house, The Master (or, Teacher) saith unto thee, Where is the guest-chamber, where I shall eat the passover with my disciples?' Young renders 'goodman' by 'master;' Tischendorf by 'master of the house' (literally 'house-master') in Mark, and 'householder' (literally 'house-master of the house') in Luke. Alford explains: "The *goodman of the house* was a man of some wealth, and could not be *identical with* the water-carrier . . . It was the common practice during the feast for persons to receive strangers into their houses gratuitously, for the purpose of eating the Passover.' Matthew does not allude to the means adopted for bringing the disciples into communication with the householder, but states that they were sent 'to such a man,' as we might say 'to a certain person,' and the wording of the message seems to indicate some prior knowledge on his part of Jesus and of the catastrophe impending over his life. 'And he said, Go into the city to such a man, and say unto him, The Master (or, Teacher) saith, My time is at hand; I keep the passover at thy house with my disciples.' The Revisers have omitted the word 'will' before 'keep,' therein agreeing with Young and Tischendorf; the ' Englishman's Greek New Testament ' agrees with the Authorised Version. Alford observes: 'The Lord spoke not from any previous arrangement, as some have thought, but in virtue of his knowledge, and command of circumstances.' That is a matter of opinion, not of certainty. The expression, 'My time is at hand,' points to some previous discourse on that subject; 'I keep the passover at thy house with my disciples,' sounds like the acceptance of an invitation given beforehand and still remaining open, and this idea is corroborated by the question, 'Where is my guest-chamber, where I shall eat the passover with my disciples?' Nothing could more clearly indicate some prior acquaintance and friendly understanding between Jesus and his host. We need not add a miracle of supernatural compulsion even if we assume a miracle of supernatural foresight on the part of Jesus. The course adopted may have been absolutely necessary for the peace and safety of all concerned. Consider the circumstances of the time. Jesus was now hiding himself from the multitude, and Judas was watching to deliver him up to the chief priests and captains in the absence of the multitude. If the traitor knew in advance where his Master would be at a particular time, he might in the hours which intervened inform the enemies of Jesus where to effect his capture. The treachery of Judas was known to Jesus—foreknown by him—and the surest if not the only way of securing a quiet interval with his disciples before his sufferings, was to keep the betrayer in his sight and by his side. Their movements were therefore involved in uncertainty, and when the question was put, at the last moment, where they were to hold the passover, even the two disciples who were sent to prepare it were not told where the place was, but simply desired to follow a water-carrier. The work of preparation would occupy some hours, and when Peter and John returned, it would be merely to announce that all was in readiness and for the disciples, Judas among them, to accompany Jesus straight to the place. The chief priests were relying upon Judas to watch for and announce the desired opportunity, and so long as his purpose was baffled Jesus was safe from intrusion and arrest. But if, as seems probable, Jesus had a deliberate purpose in keeping secret their next meeting-place, everything relating to the carrying out of his plan may have been attributable to natural causes. The host had reserved the room for the purpose, seemingly in expectation of a message, and as he was prepared for the intimation 'My time is at hand,' he must have understood the danger hanging over the head of Jesus, who evidently relied upon his kindly offices. It is more reasonable to suppose that he was known to Jesus as a friend, than to assume that he was an utter stranger, impelled by some supernatural influence to lend his room on a sudden demand. And if there was any previous arrangement between Jesus and himself, it may have included the sending out the servant with a pitcher of water on a certain day and hour. The question of the disciples, 'Where wilt thou that we go and make ready that thou mayest eat the passover?' may be taken to imply that they knew he had determined on the place, and on sending them thither at the fitting moment. Jesus was waiting to give the intimation, and the host sent out his servant at the appointed time in order that, unconsciously to himself, he might guide the messengers of Jesus to the house. The necessity for such precautions may be inferred from the fact that it was dangerous for any one to harbour Jesus, or to refrain from informing the rulers of his whereabouts: 'Now the chief priests and the Pharisees had given commandment, 11 John 57 that, if any man knew where he was, he should shew it, that they might take him.' The evangelists relate what actually happened, without giving any clue to the interpretation of the narrative, and without adding one word indicative of supernatural prescience on the part of Jesus. Probably the apostles themselves never learnt anything on the subject beyond the facts handed down to us. The crisis was too solemn and the time with Jesus too short to admit of any questions to him on a point of such comparative indifference, and at a time when they were all beset by peril and sorrow. Matthew seems to have been of opinion that the sending of an ordinary message, 'Go into the city to such a man,' best describes the event: he omits all mention of that which might be taken to convey a different impression. The details supplied by Mark and Luke are quite consistent with the idea of a pre-arrangement between Jesus and the householder. 'And he himself will shew you a large upper room furnished and ready: and there make ready for us.' The Revisers have introduced the word 'himself' before 'he,' as though the importance of secrecy would be recognised by him and nothing relating to the expected guests entrusted to servants. The word 'and' before 'there' has been inserted on the authority of the two oldest MSS. The italicised *and* is omitted by Young and Tischendorf, not being in the original. Luke's wording varies little. 'And he will shew you a large upper room furnished: there make ready.' Tischendorf renders 'furnished' by 'spread.' Alford notes: 'i.e. spread for the feast.' Everything happened as Jesus had led them to expect. 'And they went, and found as he had said unto them: and they made ready the passover.' Mark: 'And the disciples went forth, and came into the city, and found as he had said unto them: and they made ready the passover.'

In the evening all the apostles went with Jesus to the place. 'And when it was evening he cometh with the twelve.' The thirteen sat down to the meal. 'Now when even was come, he was sitting at meat with the twelve disciples.' Young here and elsewhere renders, 'he was reclining (at meat.)' The Revisers have inserted the word 'disciples' on the authority of the two oldest MSS., and they note: 'Many authorities, some ancient, omit *disciples*.' Luke's account indicates that the meal commenced at the proper time, the hour appointed for eating the passover. 'And when the hour was come, he sat down, and the apostles with him.' Here the Revisers, Tischendorf and Alford, following the two oldest MSS., have omitted 'twelve' before 'apostles.' Luke informs us that Jesus told them how earnestly he had longed to partake with them of this last passover before his approaching death. 'And he said unto them, With desire I have desired to eat this passover with you before I suffer.' This is sufficient to explain the precautions taken to keep the place and the preparations secret from the eyes of the world. Although Jesus had delivered his last public discourse, he had yet much to say to his disciples privately, and some special reason for wishing to celebrate this feast in their company. He proceeded to explain that he would not again eat the paschal lamb until—but let us take his own words.

'For I say unto you, I will not eat it, until it be fulfilled in the kingdom of God.' The Authorised Version stands, 'I will not any more eat thereof,' altered by the Revisers to 'I will not eat it,' in accordance with the three oldest MSS., except that the Vatican has 'thereof' instead of 'it.' Tischendorf and Alford agree with the Revised reading. It is clear from the words, 'I have desired to eat this passover with you,' and from the narratives generally, that Jesus did actually eat it, and that the words 'I will not eat it,' referred only to the future. 'Until it be fulfilled in the kingdom of God' is rendered by Young, 'till the time that it may be fulfilled in the reign of God.' The passover itself was about to receive its fulfilment enlargement, full and complete significance under that new condition of human life and divine government described by the phrase 'the reign of God.' Having made that statement, Jesus received the cup, gave thanks, handed it to the disciples, bade them share it between them, and made with respect to it a similar remark. 'And he received a cup, and when he had given thanks, he said, Take this, and divide it among yourselves: for I say unto you, I will not drink from henceforth of the fruit of the vine, until the kingdom of God shall come.' The Authorised Version has 'took the cup,' rendered by the Revisers 'received a cup.' 'Gave thanks' is now rendered 'when he had given thanks.' Young renders: 'having taken a cup, having given thanks.' The Revisers and Tischendorf have added 'henceforth' after 'drink,' on the authority of the two oldest MSS. Young renders instead of 'fruit,' 'produce:' the 'fruit' of the vine is the grape itself, not the wine which is extracted from it. The following extract from a work on the manners and customs of the Jews, published by the Religious Tract Society, will enable us better to understand the narrative. 'Before they sit down they wash their hands very carefully. A blessing is then asked. The master, or chief person, takes a loaf, and breaking it, says, " Blessed art thou, O Lord, our God, the King of the world, who produced bread out of the earth." The guests answer him " Amen," and the bread is distributed to them. He then takes the vessel which holds the wine in his right hand, and says, " Blessed art thou, O Lord, our God, King of the world, who hast created the fruit of the vine.' The twenty-third Psalm is then repeated. When the meal is finished, the master takes a piece of bread which has been left for the purpose, and filling a glass or cup with wine, says, " Let us bless Him of whose benefits we have partaken." The company reply, " Blessed is He who has heaped His favours on us, and has now fed us on His goodness." The master then repeats a prayer, thanking God, entreating Him to restore the throne to David, to send Elias and the Messiah, and to deliver them from their low state. The guests all answer, " Amen," and repeat Psalm xxxiv. 9, 10. Then each guest drinks a little of the wine, and goes from the table.' Here is another account, extracted from a work by N. L. Herschel, a converted Jew, 'The master of the house sits down at the head of the table, the whole family being assembled round it. On the table are placed three plates: one contains three passover-cakes, another horse-radish and bitter herbs, and a third a bone of lamb, or small piece of roast meat, and a roast egg; the two last in commemoration of the paschal lamb and the offering that accompanied it. Besides these three plates there are two other dishes: one containing vinegar or salt water, the other a mixture of various ingredients worked up to the consistence of lime in remembrance of the time in which our fathers worked in Egypt. Each individual is provided with a glass or some cup for wine, which is filled four times in the course of the service. The service commences by a repetition of several blessings, and then they drink the first cup of wine. Then the master of the house dips some of the bitter herbs in the vinegar, and gives a small portion to each one. He then takes the middle cake, leaves one half in the dish, and hides the other until

22 Luke 17. 18

after supper. Then they lay hold of the dish containing the passover-cakes and bitter herbs, and say. Lo, this is the bread of the affliction which our ancestors ate in the land of Egypt! The unleavened bread is shown to all, and a portion of it is received and eaten by each. They again eat bitter herbs dipped in the mixture that represents lime. This concludes the first and the greater service. Supper is then put on the table, and is a meal of social rejoicing. The supper being ended, two large cups are filled with wine. One of these is taken by the master of the house, and a blessing is pronounced. After the blessing the head of the family gives the cup to all those sitting round. He then brings forth the hidden cake and distributes a piece to each. The second cup of wine is called Elijah's cup, and is then placed before him; the door is opened, and a solemn pause of expectation ensues. It is at this moment that the Jews expect the arrival of Elijah to announce the glad tidings that Messiah is at hand. The passover has been celebrated by the Jews, without intermission, since the Babylonish captivity; and as we are not a people given to adopt modern innovations, it is probable the mode has never been changed in any other way than by the addition or substitution of different prayers suited to the state of the dispersion. It is, therefore, most probable that our Lord and His disciples, in all the ceremonial part, commemorated it in the same manner as we do now.' The cup of which Luke has spoken, and of which Jesus said, 'Take this, and divide it among yourselves,' appears to have been 'the first cup of wine,' which was shared before the meal. The words, 'Take this, and divide it among yourselves,' must naturally, in the absence of anything to the contrary, signify that Jesus omitted to drink of it himself, and merely passed it on to them, desiring them to drink the whole of it. That intention is clear from his next words: 'For I say unto you, I will not drink from henceforth of the fruit of the vine.' If we had been told that Jesus partook of the cup, as he did of the meal, the words 'from henceforth' would import merely 'after this occasion.' As it is, there is no such reservation, and they are equivalent to, 'from this time,' or 'from this moment.' In that respect Jesus departed from the custom of the feast. Although acting as 'the master, or chief person,' he would not participate in the drinking of the wine. If the ordinary observances had been followed, there would have been no reason for giving any special instruction: 'Take this, and divide it among yourselves,' betokens an innovation, and called for the explanation that he had resolved to pass the cup untasted. His desire to eat that passover with them, and his resolution not to drink of the wine, although opposite actions, were conceived in the same spirit. The eating of the paschal lamb and of the unleavened bread was in obedience to the divine command, the spiritual significance—fulfilment—of which was on the point of manifestation. This last participation of Jesus was to be the bidding adieu to the old symbol and the introduction to the new reality. The feast in remembrance of deliverance from Egyptian bondage would thenceforth be transformed into a feast of remembrance of deliverance from the more enduring and degrading bondage of sin. The drinking of wine was the human addition to the prescribed ceremony, and that emblem and medium of rejoicing Jesus deliberately postponed for himself in testimony of his assurance, now expressed to the disciples, that when the purpose of his life and death had been accomplished, opportunities would exist for that high form of social rejoicing in the kingdom of God.

This last passover was full of anxiety and grief to those present. They knew the imminent danger in which Jesus stood, his enemies having plotted against his life, and he himself having foretold his sufferings and death. Now he tells them something which saddens them still more. 'And as they were eating, he said, Verily I say unto you, that one of you shall betray me.' The Revisers have altered 'did eat' to 'were eating': at some time during the progress of the meal. Mark adds a sentence which gives additional pathos. 'And as they sat (Gr. reclined) and were eating, Jesus said, Verily I say unto you, One of you shall betray me, *even* he that eateth with me.' In both Matthew and Mark, Young and Tischendorf render instead of 'betray me,' 'deliver me up.' The word 'betray' calls up the idea of the infamy of the action, as when a man is styled 'traitor,' whereas 'deliver up' describes the act itself. That one of themselves should be the means of handing him over to his enemies, was an announcement which filled them with dread and consternation. It was terrible to think of, and each, conscious of his innocence, begged Jesus to say if it were himself. 'And they were exceeding sorrowful, and began to say unto him every one, Is it I, Lord?' Young renders, 'Is it I, Sir?' Bent on ascertaining, they were not content to put the question simultaneously, but after an interval of sorrowful meditation and discussion asked it consecutively. 'They began to be sorrowful, and to say unto him one by one, Is it I?' The word 'and' is omitted by the Revisers before 'they,' and after 'I' the words 'and another *said, Is* it I?' on the authority of the two oldest MSS. Although Jesus disclosed the fact, he refrained from naming the person, replying simply that it was one of themselves then sharing in the meal. 'And he said unto them, *It is* one of the twelve, he that dippeth with me in the dish.' The words 'answered and' are omitted before 'said,' on the authority of the two oldest MSS. The italicised words 'it is' are omitted by Young; their insertion is needless, and mars the terseness and force of the saying, which sounds less like a reply than a sorrowful reflection on the blackness of such a deed committed by such a person at such a time. 'And he answered and said, He that dipped his hand with me in the dish, the same shall betray me.' Young renders: 'He who dipped with me the hand in the dish, he will deliver me up.' Here is the same tone of reproach and grief as in the words of David: 'Yea, mine own familiar friend, in whom I trusted, which did eat of my bread, hath lifted up his heel against me.' That such was the appointed destiny of the Messiah, was no justification for the treachery. 'For the Son of man goeth, even as it is written of him: but woe unto that man through whom the Son of man is betrayed; good were it for that man if he (Gr. for him, if that man) had not been born.' Matthew records precisely the same words, only omitting 'for' at the beginning. Young and Tischendorf adopt the Greek idiom as in the margin, and they render 'betrayed' as 'delivered up.' The Authorised Version indicates only one possible sense: the 'woe' to the traitor appears to be emphasised by the words, 'good were it for that man if he had not been born.' But the literal expression now given in the margin suggests a different sense. A reader of Young or Tischendorf would naturally understand the words as applying to Jesus: 'good were it for him' (the Son of man) 'if that man' (the betrayer) 'had not been born.' That is equally true of Luther's rendering of Matthew: 'Es wäre ihm besser, dass derselbige Mensch noch nie geboren wäre.' 'It were better for him that the same man had never yet been born.' But although the Greek is the same in both passages, he translates it differently in Mark: 'Es wäre demselben Menschen besser, dass er nie geboren wäre.' 'It were better for the same man, that he had never been born.' The rendering of this passage in two ways seems to indicate that either sense may be accepted; and that conveyed by the marginal reading seems the more natural. Let not Judas deceive himself by thinking that some overmastering fate impelled him to betray Jesus into the hands of his enemies. His devilish compact with the chief priests did but expedite the crisis, which must have been reached in any case. Jesus being bent on preaching, and the chief priests equally determined on silencing him, his death was only a question of time. The treachery of the disciple not only precipitated the catastrophe, but added greatly to the anguish of his Master, for whom it would indeed have been good if such a man had not been born. The form of expression is significant, seeming to point him out as a monster of iniquity, one in a million, whom failing, there would not have been found among his contemporaries another capable of so base an action. Even while that damnation was ringing in his ears, Judas with unabashed duplicity maintained an air of seeming innocence, and put to Jesus the same question as the rest of the company. 'And Judas, which betrayed* him, answered and said, Is it I, Rabbi?' Jesus answered him in the affirmative: 'He saith unto him, Thou hast said.' Only Matthew records the question and reply. The other evangelists do not represent Jesus to have responded to any one of the twelve questioners. 'He saith unto him,' imports that the words were uttered to Judas himself, and it by no means follows that they were intended to be heard by all. It is quite reasonable to assume that they may have been spoken in a low tone, and that only one of the disciples overheard them. If Jesus had not only denounced the traitor but also disclosed his name, the indignation of the eleven would doubtless have been manifested then and there, and the solemn quietude of this last meeting would have been interrupted by the ignominious expulsion—or worse—of Judas. If Jesus had not been predetermined to adopt a policy of long-suffering silence with respect to his betrayer, he would have identified him and have appealed to the loyalty of the eleven. He deliberately chose the opposite course, and all he said and did, or refrained from saying and doing, was in harmony with that intention.

Matthew and Mark state that the conversation about the betrayal took place during the meal, 'as they were eating,' 'as they sat and were eating.' Both evangelists use again the same expression with respect to another incident. Matthew: 'And as they were eating, Jesus took bread (or, a loaf), and blessed, and brake it; and he gave to the disciples, and said, Take, eat: this is my body.' The Revisers have omitted the italicised word 'it' after 'blessed' and after 'gave,'

---

* How much finer, 'who was betraying,' and more literal!—(Note by a friendly critic).

and have retained the 'it,' but without italics, after 'brake.' Alford explains that 'the definite article is before *bread* in the original,' adding, 'but no especial stress must be laid on it; it would be *the bread which lay before Him*.' Tischendorf, adopting another reading which omits 'the,' has 'a loaf.' Young renders literally: 'having taken the bread, and having blessed, brake, and was giving to the disciples.' Mark is as follows: 'And as they were eating, he took bread (or, a loaf), and when he had blessed, he brake it, and gave to them, and said, Take ye: this is my body.' After 'eating' the Revisers have replaced 'Jesus' by 'he,' on the authority of the Sinaitic and Vatican MSS., the former having been so altered by a later hand. Instead of 'and blessed, and brake *it*' the revised rendering is, 'and when he had blessed, he brake it.' Young renders: 'having taken bread, having blessed, brake.' The Revisers, Tischendorf and Alford have omitted the word 'eat' after 'take,' on the authority of the three oldest MSS. Luke, having first mentioned the handing of the wine cup to the disciples, records the giving of bread. 'And he took bread (or, a loaf), and when he had given thanks, he brake it, and gave to them, saying, This is my body which is given for you.' The Revisers note that 'Some ancient authorities omit *which is given for you*.' Luke adds the words: 'This do in remembrance of me.' There can be no doubt as to the fact that the bread or loaf which Jesus broke was the unleavened passover cake. That being so, the word 'this,' which is used by all three evangelists, is important. 'This,' the passover bread, 'is my body.' 'This do' refers to the breaking and eating of the passover bread. On the word 'is' in 'This is my body,' Alford has the following note: 'On this much-controverted word *itself* no stress is to be laid. In the original tongue in which probably our Lord spoke, *it would not be expressed*.' The broken passover cake was handed to the disciples as a symbol of the body of Jesus, and he desired that whenever that ceremony was repeated they should do it in remembrance of him. He selected the latter portion only of the passover rite, not the flesh of the lamb but the bread distributed at the close of the feast. As Jesus foresaw and foretold the destruction of Jerusalem and the dispersal of the Jews, he knew that the passover festival could not continue in its entirety subsequently even at Jerusalem; and elsewhere, in the time of Jesus, the paschal lamb could not be slain and eaten. Although the Jews still keep the passover, it is in a mutilated form, the 'bone of lamb, or a small piece of roast meat, and a roast egg,' being put on a plate as representing the absent sacrificial joint. The following account was given by a distinguished Jewish authority in answer to an enquiry on the subject: 'December 19th, 1876. The paschal lamb, which constituted the Pesach, or passover of Scripture, could only be offered in Jerusalem, and within the Temple. Out of the Holy City it could not be slain. The Rabbis strictly interdicted it. All Israelites, wherever they lived, kept, as they still do, the feast of unleavened bread, which was an expansion of the real Pesach or Pascha. The Jews always, on the evening of the passover, place a shankbone of a shoulder of lamb on the table, in commemoration of the paschal sacrifice. There are other ceremonies connected with the feast, but they are entirely of Rabbinical origin.' We see, therefore, that the passover cake could be broken anywhere and everywhere, and Jesus having bidden his apostles regard it thenceforth as significant of his body, he proceeded to make the remaining part of the ceremony also a memorial of himself, of his death and of its object. 'And he took a cup, and gave thanks, and gave to them, saying, Drink ye all of it: for this is my blood, of the covenant (or, testament), which is shed for many unto remission of sins.' The Revisers have altered 'the cup' to 'a cup,' noting that 'Some ancient authorities read *the cup.*' The word 'new,' before 'covenant,' is omitted on the authority of the two oldest MSS., the Revisers noting that 'Many ancient authorities insert *new*.' Tischendorf adopts both these alterations; Alford the latter only. 'For remission' is now rendered, 'unto remission.' Alford renders 'shed' as 'being shed.' Young's version stands: 'And having taken the cup, and given thanks, he gave to them, saying, Drink ye of it—all: for this is my blood—that of the new covenant—which is poured out for many—for remission of sins.' The expression 'poured out' points to the symbolical outpouring of the wine into the cup, which the the word 'shed' does not. The following apostolic statement may be safely taken as an explanation of these words of Jesus: 'But now once at the end of the ages hath he been manifested to put away sin by the sacrifice of himself.' Remission appears to be synonymous with forgiveness. Luther always so renders it—*Vergebung*. Young does so occasionally. Only our notion of the word 'forgiveness' needs to be rectified and expanded. It is not merely mental, verbal, forensic, an assumption of innocence where guilt exists, an imaginative, vicarious transference of sin to the sinless and of virtue to the wicked. It is actual and involves realities. Jesus came to 'put away sin,' with all that appertains to it. 'For by one offering he hath perfected for ever (to the end—Young) them that are sanctified.' Forgiveness comprehends a change of character conjointly with a change of destiny. A sin punished cannot be a sin forgiven, and a forgiven sin repeated calls for the infliction of a previously remitted punishment. The remission of sin cannot be apart from sanctification, that is, a submission to the divine will, and a constant progression towards perfection. Jesus made the outpoured wine an emblem of his blood shed as a covenant unto remission of sins. The nature and effect of that covenant are explained in the Epistle to the Hebrews by a quotation from the 31st chapter of Jeremiah:

'Behold, the days come, saith the Lord,
That I will make a new covenant with the house of Israel and with the house of Judah; . . .
For this is the covenant that I will make with the house of Israel After those days, saith the Lord;
I will put my laws into their mind,
And on their hearts also will I write them: . . .
For I will be merciful to their iniquities,
And their sins will I remember no more.'

The argument is closed with the words: 'Now where remission of these is, there is no more offering for sin.' The word 'Lord' in the Epistle to the Hebrews is 'Jehovah' in the prophecy, when rendered literally.* The writer to the Hebrews asserts and proves nothing less

---

* The word 'literally,' here and elsewhere, is not intended to endorse the opinion of the 'Jehovists,' who maintain that the vowel-points annexed to the word Jehovah, in Hebrew, express the true pronunciation.

than a change of procedure on the part of the God of Israel—Jehovah. The prophecy quoted is styled a 'finding fault' with the previous covenant and the gifts and promises attached thereto; and it is argued that the mention of a new covenant makes the first covenant an old one, leading to the conclusion: 'But that which is becoming old and waxeth aged is nigh unto vanishing away.' All that must have been in the mind of Jesus, of whom we are assured:

'When he cometh into the world, he saith,
  Sacrifice and offering thou wouldest not,
  But a body didst thou prepare for me;
  In whole burnt offerings and *sacrifices* for sin thou hadst no pleasure:
  Then said I, Lo, I am come
  (In the roll of the book it is written of me)
  To do thy will, O God.
Saying above, Sacrifices and offerings and whole burnt offerings and *sacrifices* for sin thou wouldest not, neither hadst pleasure therein (the which are offered according to the law), then hath he said, Lo, I am come to do thy will. He taketh away the first, that he may establish the second. By which will we have been sanctified through the offering of the body of Jesus Christ once for all.' The writer to the Hebrews laboured to prove, and demonstrated effectually, the fact that a change had been foretold in the divine plan with respect to the ritual which had been given through Moses to the Israelites, and that Jesus was sent and commissioned to bring about that revolution. 'Now hath he obtained a ministry the more excellent, by how much also he is the mediator of a better covenant, which hath been enacted upon better promises.' The handing of the wine to the disciples, and the words of Jesus accompanying the action, were a solemn intimation of this ministry of Jesus to mankind, and of the object contemplated in the offering up of his body and the shedding of his life-blood. In Mark's account the words closely correspond with those in Matthew. 'And he took a cup, and when he had given thanks, he gave to them: and they all drank of it. And he said unto them, This is my blood of the covenant (or, testament), which is shed for many.' Here also the word 'new' is omitted before 'covenant,' on the authority of the two oldest MSS. Young and Alford render 'shed' as 'being shed.' Luke is briefer: 'And the cup in like manner after supper, saying, This cup is the new covenant (or, testament) in my blood, *even* that which is poured out for you.' The Revisers have replaced 'likewise' by 'in like manner,' agreeing with Young; and 'is shed' by 'is poured out,' rendered by Young 'is being poured out.' The Revisers note that 'Some ancient authorities omit *which is poured out for you*.' Tischendorf retains those words, which are found in the three oldest MSS. In the Communion Service of the Church of England the quotation runs, 'which is shed for you and for many.' Luke says 'you,' and Matthew and Mark 'many.' It is not unreasonable to combine the words, as it must be assumed that Jesus used both. To Jewish ears the expression, 'this is my blood of the covenant,' conveyed a distinct reference to the Mosaic ritual, for, as stated in the Epistle to the Hebrews, Moses 'sprinkled both the book itself, and all the people, saying, This is the blood of the covenant which God commanded to

you-ward.' The words of Jesus were obviously full of deep and solemn significance. His hearers were familiar with the fact that 'almost all things are by the law purged with blood; and without shedding of blood is no remission.' The blood of Jesus was to be thenceforth all that the blood of slain offerings was in Jewish eyes and in the sight of Jehovah. That the apostle Peter then or later laid hold of that truth is evident from his words: 'In sanctification of the Spirit, unto obedience and sprinkling of the blood of Jesus Christ.' That the apostle John did, is clear from his saying: 'The blood of Jesus his Son cleanseth us from all sin.' That the writer to the Hebrews did, we have already seen. That epistle is attributed by some to the apostle Paul, and his doctrine is also elsewhere plainly declared, as in the passage: 'Through him to reconcile all things unto himself, having made peace through the blood of his cross.'

Matthew states that Jesus, in handing the cup to his disciples, said, 'Drink ye all of it,' and Mark observes, 'and they all drank of it.' Not a word is added to the effect that Jesus himself drank of the wine, but on the contrary Matthew records his words: 'But I say unto you, I will not drink henceforth of this fruit of the vine, until that day when I drink it new with you in my Father's kingdom.' Young renders: 'But I say to you, that I may not drink henceforth of this produce of the vine, till that day when I may drink it with you new in the reign of my Father.' Mark records the saying thus: 'Verily I say unto you, I will no more drink of the fruit of the vine, until that day when I drink it new in the kingdom of God.' This is rendered by Young: 'Verily I say to you, that no more may I drink of the produce of the vine till that day when I am drinking it new in the reign of God.' Luke's record of a similar saying appears not to be identical with the foregoing, but to have been uttered previously, on handing to the disciples the first wine cup before the meal, whereas that in Matthew and Mark was spoken in presenting to them the second wine cup after the meal. Alford annotates Matthew as follows: 'This declaration I believe to be distinct from that in Luke xxii. 18. That was spoken over the first cup—this over one of the following.' And again: 'Thus much seems clear,—that our Lord blessed and passed round *two cups*, one before, the other after the supper,—and that he distributed the unleavened cake during the meal.' The words spoken by Jesus lead to the inference that he partook neither of the bread nor of the wine. Alford observes that 'they seem to shew us that the Lord did *not himself partake of the bread or wine*. It is thought by some, however, that He *did*: e.g., Chrysostom, "He Himself drank His own blood." But the analogy of the whole, as well as the words *Take, eat,* and *Drink ye all of it,* lead us to a different conclusion.' But with respect to the first cup Alford expresses the opposite opinion. He says in a note on verse 17 in Luke: 'Some suppose that it is here implied that our Lord *did not drink of the cup Himself*. But surely this cannot be so. The two members of the speech are strictly parallel: and if He desired to *eat* the Passover with them, He would also *drink of the cup*, which formed a usual part of the ceremonial.' To this it must be replied that the expression 'eat the passover' referred only to the lamb and, at most, to the unleavened bread and bitter herbs taken with it: the eating of the bread by itself and the drinking of wine formed no part of the ceremonial as ordained by Moses. Alford however continues: 'This seems to me to be implied in *He* TOOK *the cup*, where the original has a different word from that used by all *afterwards*, when he did *not* partake of the bread and wine.' The Revisers have brought out the distinction alluded to by rendering in Luke 'received a cup,' and in Matthew and Mark 'took a cup.' But receiving is not synonymous with drinking, and the drift of the narrative leads to the conclusion that Jesus did not take up of his own accord the first cup, but that when it was placed, probably by some one present conversant with the ceremonial, in his hand, he 'received' it, but immediately handed it over to the disciples, saying, 'Take this, and divide it among yourselves.' Is not that by itself a plain intimation that they were to take the whole of it, excluding him? The reason is given in the following words, 'For I say unto you, I will not drink from henceforth of the fruit of the vine.' After the supper also, he desired that they should all drink of the second cup, and explained his own abstinence from it on the same grounds: 'Verily I say unto you, I will no more drink of the fruit of the vine.' On the idea that Jesus drank of the first cup but not of the second, Alford founds an argument as follows: 'This most important addition in our narrative, amounts, I believe, to a solemn declaration of the *fulfilment of the Passover rite*, in both its usual divisions,—the eating of the flesh of the lamb, and drinking the cup of thanksgiving. Henceforward, He who fulfilled the Law for man will no more eat and drink of it. I remark this, in order further to observe that *this division* of the cup is not only not *identical with*, but has *no reference to*, the subsequent one in ver. 20. That was the *institution of a new rite*; this the *abrogation of an old one*, now fulfilled, or about to be so, in the person of the true Lamb of God.' Alford distinguishes the first cup from the second, not simply as a question of historical accuracy in an account every point and detail of which is interesting, but to insist upon the inference that wine out of the first cup was drunk by Jesus in 'the abrogation of an old rite,' and that wine out of the second cup was not drunk by him in 'the institution of a new rite.' But it has been admitted by Alford himself that the cup after was as much a part of the passover ceremony as was the cup before the meal, and we have evidence of the fact, which he does not allude to, that the breaking and distributing of a passover cake was also a customary proceeding. Instead, therefore, of instituting a new rite, Jesus merely gave a new significance to the old one. The cup spoken of as 'this cup,' was the passover cup, the broken loaf of which he said, 'this is my body,' was the passover loaf. When he added, 'this do in remembrance of me,' the twelve disciples could not possibly have imagined that he referred to any other ceremony or period than the annually recurring feast of the passover. If the Lord's supper had been adopted as a yearly festival, it might naturally and properly be considered as replacing the Jewish passover, and to that extent as answering to the design of Jesus when he said, 'this do in remembrance of me.' But its constant celebration, the elaborate ceremonials and startling dogmas which have become connected with it, the assumed right of the priesthood only to administer it, the theological quarrels, anathemas and bloody persecutions by which it has been surrounded and upheld, any one of these things,—and how much more all of them together!—is sufficient proof that our doctrine and practice of 'Holy Communion' are of human invention, a departure from the simple command of Jesus, altogether different from that household rite of the passover on which it was based, and in which 'the master of the house sits down at the head of the table, the whole family being assembled round it.' No evidence exists in the New Testament indicating a regular, daily or weekly celebration of the death of our Lord. A notion prevails that the expression 'breaking of bread' is an allusion to some such ceremony. Alford observes: 'It was a round cake of unleavened bread, which the Lord broke and divided . . . Hence the act of communion was known by the name *the breaking of bread*, Acts ii. 42. See 1 Cor. x. 16, also Isa. lviii. 7; Lam. iv. 4.' That last quotation indicates plainly that the breaking of bread was a recognised form of speech: 'The young children ask bread, and no man breaketh it unto them.' The following passage has been by some considered to refer to the Eucharist: 'And they continued steadfastly in the apostles' teaching and fellowship, in the breaking of bread and the prayers.' Alford's comment is as follows: 'This has been very variously explained. Chrysostom, " In mentioning *bread* here he seems to me to signify fasting, and *ascetic life*: for they partook not of luxuries, but simply of subsistence." And similarly Bengel: "The breaking of bread, that is, a frugal diet, common among them all." But on verse 46 he recognizes a covert allusion to the Eucharist.' That verse stands in the Revised Version as follows: 'And day by day, continuing steadfastly with one accord in the temple, and breaking bread at home, they did take their food with gladness and singleness of heart, praising God, and having favour with all the people.' The expression 'from house to house' is now rendered 'at home,' agreeing with Alford and Tischendorf. Young renders 'at every house.' Alford notes: 'Privately, as contrasted with their public frequenting of the temple: not *from house to house*, as A. V.: the words *may* bear that meaning, but we have no trace of such a practice, of holding the *agapæ*, or love-feasts, successively at different houses. The *breaking of bread* took place at their *house of meeting*, wherever that was. *Did eat their meat*, i.e. they *partook of food*: viz. in these *agapæ*, or breakings of bread.' If not a contradiction, this must at least be taken as a modification of Alford's previous assertion: 'the act of communion was known by the name of *the breaking of bread*.' The *agapæ* and the Eucharist are not identical. On verse 42 Alford continues: 'The interpretation of the *breaking of bread* here as *the celebration of the Lord's supper* has been, both in ancient and modern times, the prevalent one. Chrysostom himself, in another place, interprets it, or at all events the whole phrase, of the Holy Communion. And the Romanist interpreters have gone so far as to ground an argument on the passage for the administration *in one kind only*. But barely to render (*the*) *breaking of* (*the*) *bread* to mean the breaking of bread in the Eucharist, *as now understood*, would be to violate historical truth. The Holy Communion was at first, and for some time, till abuses put an end to the practice, *inseparably connected with the* agapæ, or *love-feasts*, of the Christians, and *unknown as a separate ordinance*. To these *agapæ*, accompanied as they were at the time by the celebration of the Lord's supper, the

2 Acts 42

„ 46

breaking of (the) bread refers,—from the custom of the master of the feast breaking bread in asking a blessing: see ch. xxvii. 35, where the Eucharist is out of the question.' But the act of breaking bread is not necessarily connected, as Alford seems to assume, with the *agape*, or with any special feast or meeting. Take the passage to which he last refers: 'And when he had said this, and had taken bread, he gave thanks to God in the presence of all: and he brake it, and began to eat.' No special significance can be attached to the words 'he brake it,' which simply introduce 'and began to eat,' those present following his example: 'themselves also took food.' Bishop Pearce wrote: 'In the Jewish way of speaking, *to break bread* is the same as *to make a meal*.' One more passage remains to be considered. 'And upon the first day of the week, when we were gathered together to break bread ... And when he was gone up, and had broken the bread, and eaten.' Alford notes as follows: 'The breaking of bread in the Holy Communion was at this time inseparable from the *agape* or *love-feasts*. It took place apparently in the evening (after the day's work was ended), and at the end of the assembly, after the preaching of the word (verse 11).' Alford's tacit assumption that the Lord's Supper was celebrated on this occasion, though no wine is mentioned, is probably correct, for the following reasons. (1) The purpose of the disciples is specially mentioned: 'we were gathered together to break bread.' (2) It is explained in the previous verses that certain persons had left Paul and his companions, and 'had gone before and were waiting for us at Troas.' Then it is said: 'And we sailed away from Philippi after the days of unleavened bread, and came unto them to Troas in five days.' It was therefore about passover time. Instead of 'and upon the first day of the week,' Young begins verse 7, 'and on the first of the sabbaths.' The same form of expression occurs six times in the Gospels, always in connection with passover time. It was on that 'first of the sabbaths' that Jesus rose from the dead. That day was chosen for the gathering together of the disciples and breaking of the bread, Paul's departure being postponed till the morrow. He did not sail with the others 'from Philippi after the days of unleavened bread,'—'intending himself to go on foot,' so that his departure would necessarily precede theirs, the intention being 'to take in Paul' at Assos. It was, therefore, what we call Easter day, when this breaking of bread was appointed. The fact points to a yearly, instead of a more frequent celebration of the Lord's supper in apostolic times. (3) The expression, 'when he was gone up, and had broken the bread, and eaten,' denotes a meal in an upper room and the breaking of the passover cake. Tischendorf renders: 'And when he went up, and broke the bread and tasted.' Alford allows the word 'tasted,' but says that 'usage decides for the other meaning—*eaten*.'

Although this is the only occasion mentioned in the New Testament on which it can be inferred that the Lord's supper was celebrated, it is evident from the following passage that the rite was practised and well known. 'The cup of blessing which we bless, is it not a communion of (or, participation in) the blood of Christ? The bread (or, loaf) which we break, is it not a communion of (or, participation in) the body of Christ?' Young and Tischendorf render 'communion' as 'fellowship.' That seems best to agree with what follows: 'Seeing that we, who are many, are one bread, one body: for we all partake of the one bread (or, loaf).' Tischendorf renders: 'Because we the many are one bread, one body: for we all partake of the one bread.' Young: 'for one bread, one body, are we the many—for we all of the one bread do partake.' The apostle evidently uses the words 'bread' and 'body' in a figurative sense: 'one bread, one body, are we the many'; that is the truth to be laid hold of, and which is symbolised by all eating one bread (or, loaf), which is emblematic of Christ's body. The nature and extent of our participation in or communion with Christ's body is thus illustrated: 'Behold Israel after the flesh: have not they which eat the sacrifice, communion with the altar?' Tischendorf renders: 'See Israel after the flesh: are not they who eat the sacrifices fellow-partakers of the altar?' Young: 'See Israel according to the flesh! are not those eating the sacrifices in the fellowship of the altar?' The eating of the sacrifice which had been offered on the altar denoted a fellowship with the altar. That applies to the eating by the household of the paschal lamb which had been sacrificed: the fellowship of the participants thereof with the altar was ideal, not material and actual. The participation of believers in the body of Christ is of the same character, nothing more, nothing less. The apostle puts the eating of the bread representing Christ's body on the same level as the eating of the paschal lamb, and the participation in Christ's body on the same level as the participation in the altar on which the lamb was offered. Much more than that has been made, and is still made, of the Holy Communion. Alford reprobates, with all Protestants, 'the caricature of this real union with Christ, which is found in the gross materialism of transubstantiation.' But the question still is, What is 'this real union'? The doctrine of the 'real presence' of Christ in the Lord's supper was first lowered from Transubstantiation, believed in as an actual although invisible and imperceptible transformation of the bread and wine into the actual body and blood of Jesus,—whether in whole or in part, with or without bones, nerves and other bodily adjuncts, alive and breathing, or dead and breathless, none could presume to say, and few cared to pause and think,—to the lower platform of Consubstantiation, understood as opposed to any material transmutation of the substance of the bread and wine, yet at the same time by their medium and effect imparting to faithful recipients veritably and literally, not merely ideally and figuratively, an actual incorporation with themselves of the flesh and blood of Jesus. The Church of England goes one step lower than that. The 28th Article says: 'Transubstantiation (or the change of the substance of Bread and Wine) in the Supper of the Lord, cannot be proved by holy Writ: but it is repugnant to the plain words of Scripture, overthroweth the nature of a Sacrament, and hath given occasion to many superstitions. The Body of Christ is given, taken, and eaten, in the Supper, only after an heavenly and spiritual manner. And the mean whereby the Body of Christ is received and eaten in the Supper is Faith.' The words were carefully chosen: it is not said, 'only after a figurative and symbolical manner,' but 'only after an heavenly and spiritual manner.' Who is to define what is meant by 'heavenly and spiritual'? It is asserted that 'the Body of Christ is given, taken, and eaten,' subject to the two qualifications,—the eating is 'heavenly and spiritual' and must be through 'Faith.' Who can say what meaning is here to be attached to 'Faith'? The word may be defined in a variety of ways, to suit the theological ideas of those who use it. The 29th Article seems to make the reception of Christ's body in the Supper dependent both on faith and character: 'The Wicked, and such as be void of a lively faith, although they do carnally and visibly press with their teeth (as Saint *Augustine* saith) the Sacrament of the Body and Blood of Christ, yet in nowise are they partakers of Christ.' There is a vagueness in these statements sufficient to allow of an indefinite latitude in their interpretation. The Catechism was conceived in the same spirit, and a similar haze of uncertainty and mystery hangs about its phraseology. The sacrament is defined as 'an outward and visible sign of an inward and spiritual grace given unto us, ordained by Christ himself, as a means whereby we receive the same.' That can only mean that some spiritual gift is imparted through the eating and drinking of the bread and wine. In reply to the question, 'What is the inward part, or thing signified? the child is taught to answer: 'The Body and Blood of Christ.' If the reply had stopped there, the mind could fix on the word 'signified,' and regard the bread and wine as simply representative or significant; but that is impossible, for it is added : 'which are verily and indeed taken and received by the faithful in the Lord's Supper.' Not 'figuratively and spiritually,' but 'verily and indeed.' The next question and answer seem to tone down somewhat that high doctrine. 'What are the benefits whereof we are partakers thereby? The strengthening and refreshing of our souls by the Body and Blood of Christ, as our Bodies are by the Bread and Wine.' That may indicate that the body and blood of Christ, 'verily and indeed taken,' are received by the soul only, not by the body, which is nourished by the bread and wine only. But what is 'the soul'? How is it to be distinguished from 'the life'? This style of teaching is all verbiage and mysticism, an attempt to define the indefinable, a feeble imitation, a travesty rather, a degradation and materialisation of that sublime figurative language used by Jesus when he said, 'I am the bread of life . . . I am the living bread which came down from heaven . . . The bread which I will give is my flesh, for the life of the world . . . Except ye eat the flesh of the Son of man and drink his blood, ye have not life in yourselves. . . . For my flesh is true meat, and my blood is true drink.' All these deep symbolical sayings have been rashly connected with and appropriated to the Lord's supper, regardless of the fact that the evangelist in whose gospel they are recorded made no allusion to that rite, and that the three evangelists who relate its institution did not record these sayings. The arbitrary and unwise assumption, that the 6th chapter of John's gospel is to be taken as explanatory of the Holy Communion, and that the significance and benefits of that ceremony are to be taken as defined in that chapter, has led us into this maze of confusion and uncertainty. The framers of the Church of England Services had no deliberate intention of using language of doubtful or double meaning ; but the task of connecting together certain metaphors uttered by Jesus with a ceremony having no relation to them, and at the same time of broaching and attempting to explain inexplicable mysteries,—this was altogether beyond the power of human wisdom, and led naturally and inevitably to that positive dogmatic teaching on the matter with which the minds of our forefathers were saturated through many generations. There are only two views of this sacrament which can be clearly conceived and expressed: the words, 'This is my body, This is my blood,' must be taken either literally, or figuratively. The Romanists assert the former to be the case, and do not shrink from the startling and miraculous conclusions that opinion involves. If the Church of England had been content to attach a simply figurative meaning to the words uttered by Jesus at the table, as well as to those recorded in the 6th chapter of John's gospel, no difficulty or uncertainty would have been found in the wording of the Articles or Catechism. This one question and answer in the latter would have sufficed: 'Why was the sacrament of the Lord's supper ordained? For the continual remembrance of the sacrifice of the death of Christ, and of the benefits which we receive thereby.' That places the rite on precisely the same level as that of the Passover, and if nothing more had been attempted, it would not have been necessary to add the footnote at the end of the Communion Service about kneeling: 'Lest the same kneeling should by any persons, either out of ignorance and infirmity, or out of malice and obstinacy, be misconstrued and depraved: It is hereby declared, That thereby no adoration is intended, or ought to be done, either unto the Sacramental Bread or Wine there bodily received, or unto any Corporal Presence of Christ's natural Flesh and Blood. For the Sacramental Bread and Wine remain still in their very natural substances, and therefore may not be adored; (for that were Idolatry, to be abhorred of all faithful Christians;) and the natural Body and Blood of our Saviour Christ are in heaven, and not here; it being against the truth of Christ's natural body to be at one time in more places than one.' How is that statement to be reconciled with the assertion that 'the Body and Blood of Christ are verily and indeed taken and received by the faithful in the Lord's Supper?' What an intellectual puzzle is here set before us! Christ's natural Body and Blood cannot be present or received, yet the Body and Blood of Christ are verily and indeed taken and received! Not figuratively; mark that: for it is said that the result of participation is 'the strengthening and refreshing of our souls *by* the Body and Blood of Christ.' These word-quibblings and contradictions in terms proceed from the determination to attach a certain virtue, power, influence, or benefit either to the consecrated bread and wine, or to the act of participation. And inasmuch as that belief is entertained, and these efforts have been made to give expression to it, in all sincerity and good conscience, and from no unworthy motives, the subject demands the fullest and most careful consideration. We must turn therefore to the Apostle Paul's teaching with respect to the Lord's supper. He had been expressing his satisfaction with the Corinthians for their adherence to what he had delivered to them. 'Now I praise you that ye remember me in all things, and hold fast the traditions, even as I delivered them to you.' But with respect to one observance laid upon them, he could not praise them. 'But in giving you this [1 i. Cor. 17] charge, I praise you not.' Young renders: 'But this declaring, I give no praise.' Tischendorf: 'Now while enjoining this I praise you not.' Alford: 'Now this precept I give unto you not praising you.' The matter had reference to some church-assembly of Christians, and the occasion had not been conducive to improvement, but the reverse: 'that ye come together not for the better but for the worse.' In the [,, 17] first place, their meeting had promoted not union but disunion. 'For [,, 18] first of all, when ye come together in the church (or, in congregation), I hear that divisions (Gr. schisms) exist among you; and I partly believe it.' 'Come together in the church (or, in congregation),' is rendered by Young, 'ye, coming together in the assembly:' by Alford: 'when ye come together in assembly:' by Tischendorf: 'when ye come together in a church-assembly.' The expression seems to denote some special occasion, not any regular weekly or other gathering together of detached portions of believers in synagogues or elsewhere for worship or preaching, but the meeting of the whole body of Christians at a set time and place, 'a church-assembly,' a congregational union. The tendency at such times to divisions or schisms must needs assume some practical shape, and result in the formation of sects under various chosen leaders. 'For there must be also [,, 19] heresies (or, factions) among you, that they which are approved may be made manifest among you.' Young and Tischendorf render 'heresies' as 'sects.' The spirit of disunion and segregation evinced on such occasions, made any observance of the Lord's supper impossible. 'When therefore ye assemble yourselves together, it is not [,, 20] possible to eat the Lord's supper.' It is evident that this special 'church-assembly' was the recognised opportunity for keeping that rite. The fact must not be overlooked that a large proportion of the Corinthian believers were Jews, who had always been accustomed to celebrate the passover annually, and who would naturally and necessarily associate the Lord's supper with the sharing of the passover cake and 'the cup of blessing' at the close of that ceremony. Jesus certainly gave no instructions for commemorating his death at any other time. It is not to be assumed that any of the apostles, or any believing Jew, could have conceived it possible or desirable to obey Christ's behest, 'Take ye, this is my body.—Drink ye all of it; for this is my blood,' except by eating the paschal bread and drinking the paschal cup. The Lord's supper was bound up with that institution, and the idea of celebrating it otherwise than annually and at passover time, would not find favour, even if it occurred at all to a Jewish mind. That Jews abounded at Corinth appears from the following passages. 'And after these things he departed from Athens, [18 Acts] and came to Corinth. And he found a certain Jew named Aquila, a man of Pontus by race, lately come from Italy, with his wife Priscilla, because Claudius had commanded all the Jews to depart from Rome: and he came unto them; and because he was of the same trade, he abode with them, and they wrought; for by their trade they were tentmakers. And he reasoned in the synagogue every sabbath, and persuaded Jews and Greeks. But when Silas and Timothy came down from Macedonia, Paul was constrained by the word, testifying to the Jews that Jesus was the Christ. And when they opposed themselves and blasphemed, he shook out his raiment, and said unto them,

Your blood *be* on your own heads: I am clean: from henceforth I will go unto the Gentiles. And he departed thence, and went into the house of a certain man named Titus Justus, one that worshipped God, whose house joined hard to the synagogue. And Crispus the ruler of the synagogue believed in the Lord with all his house; and many of the Corinthians hearing believed, and were baptized.' Although the Church at Corinth included 'many of the Corinthians,' Jews preponderated therein. Paul, writing to the Corinthians, said: 'For I would not, brethren, have you ignorant how that our fathers were all under the cloud, and all passed through the sea.' It is not credible, scarcely conceivable, that such a community, having learnt how and when the Lord's supper was first instituted, should have disregarded its connection with the paschal bread and 'cup of blessing,' and have celebrated it except through their medium. An annual observance was all that Jews could have deemed necessary or proper. Alford says: '*The cup of blessing which we bless* is the Christian form of the Jewish cup in the Passover, over which thanks were offered after the feast;' and he boldly adds: 'Observe, the first person plural is the *same throughout*: the blessing of the cup, and the breaking of the bread, the acts of consecration, were *not the acts of the minister, as by any authority peculiar to himself, but only as the representative* of the whole Christian congregation. The figment of the sacerdotal consecration of the elements by transmitted power, is as alien from the apostolic writings as it is from the spirit of the Gospel.' The Revisers have altered the wording of '*this* is not to eat the Lord's supper,' to 'it is not possible to eat the Lord's supper.' Young renders: 'it is not to eat the Lord's supper;' Tischendorf: 'there is no eating of the Lord's supper;' Alford the same, with Young's rendering in the margin. Why there could not be any eating of the Lord's supper, the apostle proceeds to explain. 'For in your eating each one taketh before *other* his own supper; and one is hungry, and another is drunken.' Why the italicised word *other* should be introduced does not appear. Young, Tischendorf and Luther omit it. Tischendorf renders: 'For in eating each takes his own supper beforehand; and one is hungry and another is drunken.' Young renders 'filled' instead of 'drunken.' Alford observes: 'There is no need to soften the meaning of this latter word.' The word 'before' or 'beforehand' apparently means, before the distribution of the one passover cake and the sharing of the cup of blessing among all present. There was no table common to all, no social meal, which was the very essence of the passover feast, but each individual 'took first his own supper,' some being too poor to satisfy their natural appetite, and others indulging to repletion. That was but a mockery of Christian fellowship. 'The cup of blessing which we bless, is it not a fellowship of the blood of Christ? The bread which we break, is it not a fellowship of the body of Christ?' But what kind of fellowship was that, in which only the last loaf and the last cup were shared in common, one participant being actually hungry, and another having passed the bounds of moderation? If only an ordinary meal was desired, instead of a feast of brotherhood, it should be eaten at home. 'What? have ye not houses to eat and to drink in?' But for all to meet, and eat, in one place, yet in such a selfish and uncommunicative way, was to cast contempt upon their act of assembling, and to put to the blush those who could provide themselves with but a scanty meal, or none at all. 'Or despise ye the church (or, congregation) of God, and put them to shame that have not (or, have nothing)?' What must be thought and said of those who could look with equanimity on such a practice? 'What shall I say to you? shall I praise you in this? I praise you not.' It must be excepted from the praise he had accorded for their observance in general of what he had delivered to them. That was a very solemn and touching ceremony. 'For I received of the Lord that which also I delivered unto you.' On the words 'I received,' Alford observes : 'By special revelation (see Gal. i. 12).' Not necessarily, for Paul alludes to this as one of the 'traditions' delivered by him to the Corinthians, and which he praises them for holding fast. The Authorised Version has 'ordinances.' Young renders : 'According as I delivered to you, the deliverances ye do keep.' Luke's gospel alludes to narratives relating to certain matters 'even as they delivered them unto us, which from the beginning were eyewitnesses and ministers of the word.' Therefore the term 'delivered' seems to relate to and denote the 'traditions' which were 'received of the Lord' through the eleven apostles, and which Paul, having so received them in common with others, also 'delivered' to the Corinthians. The account he gives coincides so nearly with that of Luke that it may be well to place them side by side.

22 Luke.	11. i. Cor.
19. 'And he took bread, (or, a loaf), and when he had given thanks, he brake it, and gave to them, saying, This is my body which is given for you : this do in remembrance of me.	23. 'How that the Lord Jesus in the night in which he was betrayed took bread ; 24. and when he had given thanks, he brake it, and said, This is my body which is for you : this do in remembrance of me.
20. And the cup in like manner after supper, saying, This cup is the new covenant (or, testament) in my blood, *even* that which is poured out for you.'	25. In like manner also the cup after supper, saying, This cup is the new covenant (or, testament) in my blood : this do, as oft as ye drink *it*, in remembrance of me.'

Such was the tradition delivered by Paul, from which it is evident that each occasion of eating the paschal loaf and drinking the paschal cup was a remembrance and representation of the death of Jesus : 'For as often as ye eat this bread, and drink the cup, ye proclaim the Lord's death till he come.' The apostle's words, 'in the night in which he was betrayed,' and the allusion to 'this bread' and 'the cup,' certainly point to an annual repetition of the ceremony, to which the words 'as often' must be restricted. Alford observes : 'Not a *general* rule, for all common meals of Christians ; but a precept that as often as *that cup* is drunk, it should be in *remembrance of him*.' That overlooks entirely the paschal ceremony, to which alone 'this bread' and 'the cup' refer. The word 'shew' in the Authorised Version is rendered by the Revisers 'proclaim,' by Young 'shew forth,' by Tischendorf and Alford 'declare,' by Luther 'verkundigen' to announce or proclaim. The service was thenceforth to be an annual commemoration, a memorial banquet of the death of Jesus.

The question occurs: How did it come to pass that the Corinthians came 'together in congregation' for the observance of the Lord's supper? The Jewish passover was kept at home, by the members of each separate family, or in hired furnished apartments, the guests sharing the meal and afterwards the loaf and cup. That would have been the natural, proper manner for all Jews, and would have corresponded to the ceremony observed by Jesus and his disciples. But as individuals, not families, became converts to Christianity, there could be no possibility of remembering the death of Jesus in that way: it must have been absolutely necessary for converted Jews to assemble by themselves, away from their own homes; if the meal itself was taken there, either they must have retired before the closing portion of the ceremony, or having joined in it must have repeated it elsewhere, with its new significance, among fellow believers. As regards Gentiles, they could not introduce the passover feast into their own homes, nor celebrate there the Lord's supper, the very central idea of which was the fellowship of all present with their common Lord and Saviour. We should expect, therefore, to find the custom springing up of which this chapter gives evidence. The Jews would bring their own provisions to the appointed place of meeting, leaving the Gentiles to do the same. If all had arrived, begun, and ended at the same time, it would have been feasible to break and distribute one loaf and pass round one cup, as we now sometimes share the 'loving-cup' at the end of a banquet. But no arrangement was made for a simultaneous eating; on the contrary, the apostle complained, 'in your eating each one taketh before his own supper.' The want of unanimity and fellowship in the meal, brought out strong contrasts. Those Jews who were well off provided for themselves abundantly; the poorer Jews, shut out from their family feast, brought what they could; the Gentiles naturally followed the example thus set them, probably forming a group by themselves, for to this day the Jews at passover time avoid food which is not properly prepared. The inevitable result was as stated by the apostle: 'one is hungry, and another is filled.' Dr. Macknight justified that rendering, saying: 'As the word sometimes signifies only to drink so freely as to cheer the spirits, and is rendered "well drunk," John ii. 10, and is used by the LXX. much in the same sense, Gen. xliii. 34, and Cant. v. 1, there is no necessity of thinking that any of the Corinthians used to make themselves drunk at the Lord's supper. "Filled" or "plentifully fed," opposed to one who is hungry.' * The milder translation appears most suitable: if drunkenness had been the meaning of the apostle, he would surely not have alluded to the vice in that incidental, easy, matter of fact way, seeing how he was in the habit of lashing and condemning it, having written in this very epistle: 'Now I write unto you not to keep company, if any man that is named a brother be . . . a drunkard . . ; with such a one no, not to eat;' and again in this epistle he had classed drunkards among vilest criminals, asserting that none such 'shall inherit the kingdom of God.' Elsewhere he says: 'They that be drunken are drunken in the night.' If Paul had become aware of drunkenness practised openly by believers in their most solemn

5 i. Cor. 11

6 i. Cor. 10
5 i. Thes. 7

---

* Dr. Macknight on the Epistles.

assembly, is it conceivable that he would have alluded to the scandal with such equanimity? No: we must needs adopt Dr. Young's rendering, however much it may interfere with the views generally entertained in connection with this passage. The eating and the meeting together brought into offensive prominence the inequalities existing among the professed Christian brotherhood, put them to shame that had nothing, and became to the others so little more than an ordinary meal that the apostle sharply enquired of them, 'Have ye not houses to eat and to drink in?' He had in the previous chapter insisted on the fact that the communion of Christ's body meant a common participation in one loaf, as significant of the truth that all were one in Christ. As to what should be eaten and drunk before, he gave no directions; but all must partake of the one loaf and drink of the one cup. That was no small thing to insist upon in a mixed congregation. The orthodox Jew might ask how he could join with Gentiles in the passover feast? The Gentile might ask why he should keep a feast at passover time? The expression 'do this in remembrance of me' is equivalent to 'keep this in remembrance of me.' The Greek verb *poieō*, here rendered 'do,' is often translated 'keep' in the New Testament in connection with a feast. 'Witness Matt. xxvi. 18, where our Lord is represented as saying, *I will* keep *the* passover. It is used by Paul in Acts xviii. 21, where he says, *I must* keep *the feast*, and where he says in Heb. xi. 28, *He* kept *the passover*. In conformity therefore with this rendering of the word in the authorised version we may translate 1 Cor. xi. 24, *Keep ye this*, or in reversing the terms in the passages referred to, and translating them in conformity with the authorised translation of *do* in 1 Cor. xi. 24, 25, the words in Matt. xxvi. 18 might be rendered, *I will* do the passover; those of Paul in Acts xviii. 21, might be rendered, *I must* do *the feast*; and those in Heb. xi. 28, *He did the passover*. This would sound, perhaps, oddly, but still it would be in conformity with the authorised translation of the word in 1 Cor. xi. 24, 25. We might, therefore, render in 1 Cor. xi. 24 (the direction given *during* the supper) *Keep ye this in remembrance of me*; that is, *Keep ye this* (the passover) *in remembrance of me*; and in 1 Cor. xi. 25 (the direction given *after* the supper) *Keep ye this* (the passover) *in remembrance of me, as often as ye may drink of this cup*, that is, the passover cup. The use of the demonstrative pronoun, this, seems significant in the case. Christ did not simply say, *Eat bread in remembrance of me—drink wine in remembrance of me.* No. What he referred to as being ate, as stated by St. Paul, in 1 Cor xi. 26, was *this bread* (that is, *this passover bread*); and what he referred to as being drunk of, as stated by St. Paul in 1 Cor. xi. 26, was *this cup* (that is, *this passover cup*), which represented the new covenant in His blood, adding, *as often as ye may drink of it* (that is, *as often as ye may drink of the passover-cup*).'* The connection of the Lord's supper with the passover is evident and insuperable. Christian Jews would never dream, at first, of separating the two, and the celebration could only take place annually. As they dropped,

---

* "The Two Sacraments, so called, no Institutions of Christ."
By W. Blackley, M.A.

by degrees, the Mosaic ordinances, changes with respect to the time and method of keeping the Lord's supper might be introduced. Gentiles must have begun the observance by adopting at least some portion of the paschal ceremony at passover time: from Paul's account it is evident that they assembled to eat and drink in one place. But from the first there were difficulties and conscientious scruples in Jewish minds about eating with Gentiles. The apostle Peter tried to please both parties, and the apostle Paul condemned his indecision and lack of a settled principle of action. 'But when Cephas came to Antioch, I resisted him to the face, because he stood condemned. For before that certain came from James, he did eat with the Gentiles: but when they came, he drew back and separated himself, fearing them that were of the circumcision.' That the question was not an easy one to decide, and was beset with doubts and conflicting arguments, appears from the fact that Peter's hesitating and evasive policy was adopted by others also. 'And the rest of the Jews dissembled likewise with him; insomuch that even Barnabas was carried away with their dissimulation.' The eating and drinking together of Jews and Gentiles was a standing difficulty, and it must necessarily have arisen in connection with the Lord's supper. Peter, although quite willing to put aside Jewish prejudices, thought it better to obviate contention and respect the scruples to which others clung, by arranging at Antioch for Jews and Gentiles to eat apart. That may have been the case in Corinth. The expression 'come together in congregation' applies equally, whether the meeting was in two or more places or in one only. That might be a question of convenience, as to whether a building sufficiently large was available, or a matter of feeling, as to whether the two nationalities were accustomed to meet at the same time and for the same object, but apart. The latter would be as natural then as it is now for Romanists and Protestants, Ritualists, Low Churchmen and Dissenters to worship separately. The Jews had their synagogues, the Gentiles their temples, but in neither of them could any act of professedly Christian worship be performed. Converted Jews still attended their synagogues; there was no reason why they should not. Whether converted Gentiles continued to attend their temples, although with changed heart, hope and object, we know not: probably they did, for all that the apostle warned them against, as a thing which might happen without any intention of wrong doing, was the partaking of food therein. 'But take heed lest by any means this liberty of yours become a stumblingblock to the weak. For if a man see thee which hast knowledge sitting at meat in an idol's temple, will not his conscience, if he is weak, be emboldened to eat things sacrificed to idols?' The Jews did not eat in their synagogues, neither might the Gentile Christians eat in their temples: special arrangements therefore had to be made about the Lord's supper. The plan adopted had not worked well. The meal was taken by each individually, and served chiefly to bring into prominence the inequalities of condition which existed among the participants. In face of that, the apostle recalled the solemn circumstances under which the rite was first ordained, the sacred symbolism attaching to the bread and wine, and the fact that the ceremony was nothing less than a representation, a display, a showing forth, a proclamation of the Lord's death. To do that in an unworthy manner, to make it a feast of self-indulgence to some, and suffer it to be the mere pretext of a feast to others, was to desecrate the occasion, to dishonour the broken bread and outpoured wine, and thereby the body and blood they were designed to typify. 'Wherefore whosoever shall eat the bread or drink the cup of the Lord unworthily, shall be guilty of the body and the blood of the Lord.' The word 'or' now replaces the word 'and' before 'drink,' on the authority of the two oldest MSS. The death of Christ was not to be memorialised lightly, but with searchings of heart, and in a spirit suited to the nature and design of his self-sacrifice. 'But let a man prove himself, and so let him eat of the bread, and drink of the cup.' The word 'prove' instead of 'examine' is adopted by the Revisers and Tischendorf. To obey the command of Jesus, 'This do in remembrance of me,' was equivalent to the taking of an oath of fealty to his name and cause: it was no common repast, and veiled under the figures of bread and wine there must be a discernment of *the body*, 'For he that eateth and drinketh, eateth and drinketh judgement unto himself, if he discern (Gr. discriminate) not the body.' The Revisers have omitted the word 'unworthily,' and also before 'body' the words 'the Lord's,' on the authority of the three oldest MSS.; and they have altered 'damnation' to 'judgement.' Alford notes: 'The word *unworthily* is spurious, not occurring in our most ancient MSS., and having found its way into the text by repetition from ver. 27. . . . The *judgment* meant, as is evident by vv. 30—32, is not *damnation*, as rendered in our A.V., a mis-translation which has done infinite mischief.' What did the apostle mean by 'the body?' He had already explained that, telling them that the wine and the bread were 'a communion of (or, participation in) the body of Christ, seeing that we, who are many, are one bread (or, loaf): for we all partake of (Gr. from) the one bread (or, loaf).' Later on, also, he says: Now ye are the body of Christ, and severally members thereof.' To the Ephesians also he wrote: 'The Gentiles are fellow-heirs, and fellow-members of the body.' This significance of the term was ever in the apostle's mind, and must not be excluded from his allusion here to 'the body.' The body which they failed to discriminate was not the material earthly or resurrection heavenly body of Jesus, which was not present, nor only its emblematical representation in the bread and wine, beyond which no further identification or discrimination of it was possible, but the body of Christ in the sense of one union and fellowship among themselves. Some of them were living in self-indulgent abundance, and others in poverty, hungring for a meal; and so little was this regarded that even in the congregation of believers for the purpose of remembering their Lord's death, the scandal existed as a matter of course, uncared for and unreproved, 'one is hungry, and another is filled.' Repletion, if not excess, in some, and dire poverty and want in others, were working, as they ever must, physical deterioration, ill-health, premature death. 'For this cause many among you are weak and sickly, and not a few sleep.' Tischendorf renders: 'and a considerable number fall asleep.' Alford understands the allusion to be to 'the present sicknesses and frequent deaths amongst the Corinthian believers.' He adds: 'We may distinguish *weaklings*, persons whose powers have failed spontaneously, from *invalids*, persons whose powers are enfeebled by sickness. Both words refer to *physical*, not *moral* weaknesses.' That the words, 'for this cause,' rendered literally by Young, 'because of this,' refer to the failure to 'discriminate' the general body of believers, their needs and claims as Christian brethren, appears from the words which immediately

^{11 i. Cor. 31} follow : ' But if we discerned (Gr. discriminated) ourselves, we should not be judged.'* Alford explains : ' This *discerned* is the same word in the original as that rendered *discern* in ver. 29, and should be carefully kept the same in the translation, the idea being the same.' It was not possible to get at the sense from the Authorised Version, which has 'judged' in place of 'discerned' or 'discriminated.' Young renders literally : ' For if ourselves we were discerning, we would not be being judged :' there was an habitual failure to recognise the fact and duties of Christian fellowship, and a consequent prevalence in their community of the evils naturally resulting from such neglect. That was a providential judgment, constantly at work in the world, and which Christians should be far from bringing on themselves. On the contrary, they should be careful to submit themselves only to the Lord's judgment, to that chastening which he laid upon them as the result of their separation from the world, and which would be an evidence of their freedom from condemnation with the world. ' But when we are judged, we are chastened of the Lord (or, when we are judged of the Lord, we are chastened) that we may not be condemned with the world.' Young's literal rendering brings out the sense more clearly. ' For if ourselves we were discerning, we would not be being judged, but being judged, by the Lord we are chastened, that with the world we may not be condemned.' The contrast is drawn between the judgment thus naturally brought upon them by their conformity to the world's standard, with its saddening extremes of poverty and wealth, low living and high living, one hungry and another filled, and that judgment of Jesus which fell upon those who rose with him above the world's level, suffered like him in the world, and so escaped condemnation with the world. The chastening of the Lord which was in the apostle's mind was that which results from the strife

^{12 Heb. 4} with sin, as explained in the Epistle to the Hebrews : ' Ye
" 5 have not yet resisted unto blood, striving against sin : and ye have forgotten the exhortation, which reasoneth with you as with sons,

> My son, regard not lightly the chastening of the Lord,
> Nor faint when thou art reproved of him ;

" 6 For whom the Lord loveth he chasteneth,
And scourgeth every son whom he receiveth.

" 7 It is for chastening that ye endure.'

The apostle Peter expressed a similar view of the Lord's 'judge-
^{4 i. Pet. 17} ment' of his people. ' For the time *is come* for judgement to begin at the house of God : and if *it begin* first at us, what *shall be* the end of them that obey not the gospel of God ?' The judgment he meant

---

* An able critic of the author's MS. suggests the following note. "If, however, we had been setting ourselves apart, we had not, in that case, been coming under judgment."—N. T. Critically Emphasised (Bagster).

was not that arising from wrong doing, from any conformity to the customs and crying evils of the world, but the reverse; for he had just said: 'For let none of you suffer as a murderer, or a thief, or an evil-doer, or as a meddler in other men's matters: but if *a man suffer* as a Christian, let him not be ashamed; but let him glorify God in this name.' If only these Corinthians had discerned themselves in the light of that their high calling of God in Christ Jesus, then, however severe the Lord's judgment and chastening, none would have originated out of their own misconduct and lack of Christian fellowship, and the apostle would not have had reason to utter the reproachful words, 'For this cause many are weak and sickly among you, and many fall asleep.' The highest, if not the first duty of the Christian brotherhood is to change and elevate the tone and condition of social life, not less in its physical than in its moral aspects. 'Who then is the faithful and wise bondservant, whom his lord hath set over his household, to give them their food in due season?' Wherever and whenever that primary obligation is overlooked and overridden, be it in Corinth or in England, in Asia or in Europe, in the first or the nineteenth century, there and then Christianity has deteriorated from its proper standard, has imbibed the spirit, the maxims, the policy of the world, and the professed church of Christ must fall a prey to the evils, with their judgments— or consequences—which are rampant in the world. That generation of believers had inherited, as our own has, the social—or rather unsocial—curse of abject poverty and destitution, with their concomitant evils, existing among degraded masses of the community. That state of society is contrary to the spirit of Jesus, and only by the presence and power of his spirit in the dealings of man with man, can the real origin of the social disease be recognised and a true and effectual remedy be applied. Alford states that the Lord's supper 'was an inseparable adjunct, in the apostolic times, to their agapæ or feasts of love. Chrysostom and Tertullian give an ample description of these feasts, which were of the nature of mutual contributions, where each who was able brought his own portion, and the rich additional portions for the poor. *During* and *after* this feast, as shewn by the institution, by the custom at the passover, by the context here, and by the remnants of the ancient custom and its abuse until forbidden by the council of Carthage, the ancient Christians partook of the Supper of the Lord. It was necessary for the celebration of the Lord's supper, that all should eat of the same bread and drink of the same cup; and in all probability, that a prayer should be offered, and words of consecration said by the appointed ministers. Hence cessation of the feast itself, and solemn order and silence, would be necessitated even by the outward requirements of the ordinance.' No custom of that kind existed at Corinth: there was no preliminary feast of love, there were no mutual contributions; the rich brought no additional portions for the poor. These arrangements were wanting there, and arose out of those necessities which the Corinthians overlooked. The following explanation is given by Parkhurst: 'Such of the heathens as were converts to Christianity were obliged to abstain from *meats offered to idols*, and these were the main support of the poor in the heathen cities: *the poor are supported by the sacrifices* says the old scholiast on Aristophanes, Plut., ver. 594. The Christians, therefore, who were rich, seem very early to have begun the custom of these *love feasts*, which they made on every first day of the week, chiefly for the benefit of the poor Christians, who by being such, had lost the benefit, which they used to have for their support, of eating part of the heathen sacrifices.' Nothing of the kind had been attempted by those to whom Paul wrote, and he deemed it necessary to rebuke sharply their stolid indifference. They professed to be one body in Christ, for they all partook of the one loaf and drank of the one cup, which denoted fellowship with him, yet even in the ceremony itself they flaunted before him their divisions, their selfishness, their disregard of the feelings and welfare of their poorer brethren, the very things which were drawing down upon them, day by day, the penalties inseparable from such conformity to the spirit and custom of the world. Let them henceforth show the respect due to each other and to the occasion by at least sitting down together. 'Wherefore, my brethren, when ye come together to eat, wait one for another.' To avoid the possibility of a repetition of the scandal, let them dispense altogether with the formality of a regular meal, satisfying the appetite at home. 'If any man is hungry, let him eat at home; that your coming together be not unto judgement.' Their meetings in congregation would then no longer serve to parade and emphasise their lack of Christian charity. Whatever other alterations might be requisite, Paul himself would arrange about whenever he visited them. 'And the rest will I set in order whensoever I come.'

There is absolutely nothing in the teaching of Paul with respect to the Lord's supper leading to the conclusion that he attributed any special virtue to the bread and wine received therein. Neither does he say anything about, or to the effect of, 'the strengthening and refreshing of our souls by the body and blood of Christ, as our bodies are by the bread and wine.' That conception was introduced by theologians of a later age, later even than the doctrines of transubstantiation and consubstantiation. The apostolic argument is not encumbered with any discussion as to whether the words, 'This is my body, This is my blood,' are to be understood literally or figuratively. He assumes, as a matter of course, that the bread and wine were mere figures and emblems of the body and blood, and that Christ's saying was no more to be interpreted literally, or mystically, than are the apostle's own words, 'We, who are many, are one bread (or, loaf), one body.' The truth on which he lays hold and insists is this: that the taking of the bread and wine is an act of communion, participation, or fellowship, in the body and blood of Christ, denoting that we all are one body, one bread, or as he elsewhere expresses it, 'members of his body.' We have only to exercise common sense in order to comprehend the spiritual sense; but if either the literal sense or the spiritual, metaphorical sense be put foremost, standing where it ought not, then we drift away from common sense into incomprehensible, incredible doctrines of transubstantiation, consubstantiation, or of a spiritual yet real and actual eating and drinking of the veritable body and blood of the Lord Jesus. It was a huge stride, and at the time a bold one, which our forefathers made in breaking from the Church of Rome and repudiating the dogma of transubstantiation. They did what they could, and we owe them a debt of gratitude for the advance they made. But the ground we still occupy is of their choosing, marked out, fenced round with definitions and prohibitions devised by them : not one step have we advanced in three hundred years. Have we not stood long enough, far too long, in the shoes of these dead men ? For they made this sacrament to signify much more than Christ or his apostles ever did. The Catechism of the Church of England utters an uncertain sound, not one voice, but many voices, as though resulting from a compromise allowing the expression of different and conflicting opinions. We find there the simple doctrine that the Lord's supper was ordained as a feast of remembrance, which was what Jesus made it and Paul described it to be ; we find also the high, inferential doctrine, based upon the application to it of the figurative teaching of Jesus in the 6th chapter of John's gospel, that his body and blood 'are verily and indeed taken and received by the faithful in the Lord's supper :' we find also the somewhat lower doctrine, that the benefits of the body and blood of Christ therein are realised only by the soul, the bread and wine serving to nourish only the body ; and we observe a qualification which seems to make everything contingent on the faith of the recipient. There are expressions in the Communion Service which plainly assert the existence of some hidden virtue in the sacramental elements : Jesus Christ is declared 'to be our spiritual food and sustenance in that holy Sacrament ;' it is eulogised as being 'so divine and comfortable a thing to them who receive it worthily, and so dangerous to them that will presume to receive it unworthily ;' there is the implication of a threat, as to the possibility 'lest after the taking of that holy Sacrament, the devil enter into you, as he entered into Judas ;' then the words of Paul, if not misconstrued certainly misapplied, are applied to it, and we are assured that 'the benefit is great, if with a true penitent heart and lively faith we receive that holy Sacrament ; (for then we spiritually eat the flesh of Christ, and drink his blood ; then we dwell in Christ, and Christ in us ; we are one with Christ, and Christ with us ;) so is the danger great, if we receive the same unworthily. For then we are guilty of the Body and Blood of Christ our Saviour, we eat and drink our own damnation, not considering the Lord's Body ; we kindle God's wrath against us ; we provoke him to plague us with divers diseases, and sundry kinds of death ;' the Priest prays, 'that we, receiving these thy creatures of bread and wine, according to thy Son our Saviour Jesus Christ's holy institution, in remembrance of his death and passion, may be partakers of his most blessed Body and Blood ;' then the plural form is departed from, the 'we' and 'our' are dropped, and 'thee' and 'thy' take their place : 'The Body of our Lord Jesus Christ, which was given for thee, preserve thy body and soul unto everlasting life . . . The Blood of our Lord Jesus Christ, which was shed for thee, preserve thy body and soul unto everlasting life :' these words are uttered *in the very act* of giving first the bread and then the wine ; a strong mind, exercising an independent, unbiassed judgment, can understand the words figuratively and regard the consecrated elements as mere signs and symbols, but everything is against the majority of recipients doing so ; their minds have been worked up by all that went before to the highest pitch of devout expectation ; if they have studied some manual of devotion prepared for the occasion, the effect is heightened, the authorised doctrine probably amplified, stretched still further in the same mysterious direction: it is enough to watch the faces, the folded hands on the way to and from the table, the prayer whilst masticating, to recognise the fact that the promises and benefits announced are deemed to be concentrated, individualised, appropriated at the moment and in the act of participation, if not through and by, at least in connection with the eating of the bread and drinking of the wine; one of the subsequent prayers is so framed as to bind together the reception of the elements with the reception of the body and blood of Christ: 'We most heartily thank thee, for that thou dost vouchsafe to feed *us, who have duly received these holy mysteries*, with the spiritual food of the most precious Body and Blood of thy Son our Saviour Jesus Christ.' To all this must be added the fact that there is a special 'Prayer of Consecration,' during which the hand of the priest is laid upon the bread and the wine cup, without which ceremony the food must not be taken, so that the service is sometimes interrupted for the purpose of consecrating more. Whence comes that claim of priestly power and consecration? Assuredly not from the New Testament, not from any authority derived through Christ or his apostles. Dean Alford, to his honour be it recorded, pronounced emphatically and unreservedly his opinion on that point. On the words, 'the cup of blessing which we bless,' his note is as follows: '*i.e.*, consecrate with a prayer of thanksgiving. Observe, the first person plural is the *same throughout:* the blessing of the cup, and the breaking of the bread, the acts of consecration, were *not the acts of the minister, as by any authority peculiar to himself, but only as the representative of the whole Christian congregation*. The figment of a sacerdotal consecration of the elements by transmitted power, is as alien from the apostolic writings as it is from the spirit of the Gospel.' The passover meal was a purely domestic ceremony; the bread was not broken, nor was the prayer of thanksgiving over the wine uttered, by a priest. If we were to revert to the original institution of the Lord's supper, it would not be celebrated in any temple, church, or other place of worship, but in every household apart, the head of the family directing the proceedings in an appointed way. The meeting of the congregation in one place for the purpose was a matter of convenience, arising out of the changed conditions of life, the segregation of Christian Jews from their unbelieving brethren, and the introduction of converted Gentiles to a rite with which they had not been familiar. In all that Paul says on the matter not a hint is dropped of any apostle or delegate of an apostle being needed to superintend the rite or make it valid. Alford points to the fact that 'the first person plural is the *same throughout*,' as indicating that the act from first to last was congregational and not priestly. The original simplicity and freedom in the administration of the rite have long since been set aside by our spiritual guides, and the very idea of celebrating the Lord's supper except before an altar, or of receiving the elements unconsecrated, or from any hands but those of a consecrated Minister, would now be scouted by many—if not most —members of the Church of England as impious and profane. But those who think for themselves, and whose regard for the truth overrides all claims and customs opposed to it, must have the courage of their opinions. In bygone times martyrs braved the penalties attaching to their denial of the dogma of transubstantiation. Is not an equally vigorous protest needed now against those remaining superstitions which are stereotyped in the Book of Common Prayer? Our

Reformers did their best when it was compiled, but they could not rise above the level of their times and modes of thought. Advancement and Reform should ever be the watchwords of religion, as they are of politics. In both there are two questions which constantly force themselves into prominence? Is this true? Is this right? If these questions are not cried aloud in public, they are none the less either whispered secretly or pondered silently. Only outspoken men can become leaders, and the longer a timid silence is maintained the greater will be the overthrow, and the shock of it, when the decayed foundations of men's faith and practice are tested, found wanting, and are ready to crumble at a touch. The habitual abstention of multitudes of regular worshippers from the Lord's supper is a striking fact. Obviously they do not believe in it, do not care for it, cannot be induced to attend it. Even that is less to be lamented than the fact that they are utterly dumb with respect to it. But if they do not give their reasons, it is partly because they have not formulated them: there is a felt aversion from and disbelief in the sacrament, coupled with an uneasy feeling that they are partly right, partly wrong, and do not care to analyse their sentiments, or inform their judgment further on the matter. Moreover, they are out of sympathy with the clergy who administer the rite and who occasionally from the pulpit urge attendance on it, whose opinions they know, and disregard, yet have neither the wish nor the opportunity to discuss the question. No wonder their minds turn from it to more congenial and profitable topics. But let it not be supposed that there only two classes in our churches, communicants and non-communicants, the attendance of the former being praiseworthy and beneficial, and the absence of the latter blamable and hurtful. The punctilious observances of many may be attributed to the prostration of their individual judgment: they are content to accept without enquiry whatever is offered to them in the shape of doctrine and practice by their clerical guides, who themselves are accustomed to take for granted the truth and wisdom of whatever was decreed and arranged by the original framers of the articles and liturgy of the Church of England. The multitudes who neglect the Lord's table are not necessarily chargeable with wanton indifference, and the lives and characters of most of them will bear comparison with persons of more devout aspect and habits. There is a third class of persons, probably few in number, who are seen at communion very rarely, who disapprove of the superstition and mysticism attaching to the administration of what are proclaimed to be 'holy mysteries,' who contemplate with distrust and sorrow the doctrines taught concerning the eucharist, the assumption of priestly powers in relation to it, and the abject reverence attached to the morsels of bread and sips of wine, which is sufficiently indicated by the demeanour, highstrung, unnatural, fulsomely devout, of some of the participants. Upon the few thoughtful, earnest-minded dissentients, who side neither with the multitude of upholders of the sacrament as now administered, nor with the multitude who deliberately or from utter carelessness ignore it, rest the duty and responsibility of expressing their convictions and acting upon them. Unless such persons make their opinions known, the possibility of any reformation in doctrine and practice must be indefinitely postponed. Large bodies of Dissenters in former times separated from the mother church, and their descendants are still among us, for we all inherit our respective creeds and standing. Whether on the whole Dissenters have any advantage now in breadth of thought and freedom from errors, over members of the Church of England, may well be doubted. It is certainly not worth while to attempt a repetition of the policy of severance, either upon this or any other ground. The apostle Paul's advice is in the opposite direction. He laid down the rule that difference of religion should not separate husband and wife, and then extended its application to every position in life: 'Only, as the Lord hath distributed to each man, as God hath called each, so let him walk:' he desired that principle to be universally acted upon: 'And so ordain I in all the churches;' he urged no dropping of Jewish ordinances by Jews, no assumption of them by Gentiles: 'Was any man called being circumcised? let him not become uncircumcised. Hath any been called in uncircumcision? let him not be circumcised;' and his closing maxim embodies the highest wisdom: 'Let each man abide in that calling wherein he was called.' When the habit of segregation ceases, the tendency towards reunion begins. Unfortunately our ecclesiastical laws are so framed as to prevent the natural process of cohesion and healing. No clergyman of the Church of England is allowed to occupy a Dissenter's pulpit or admit him into his own, even for an hour; nor may any doctrine be preached therefrom, under pain of censure and deprivation, contrary in any respect to that contained in the Prayer Book. How is it possible, under such a system, for truth to flourish and error to decay? Reformation should come from within, working from the clergy as a centre, outwards; but it can only commence and continue in the outer ranks, slowly and painfully labouring to pierce to the charmed and somnolent inner circle; the spiritual heart which should be living and throbbing becomes first motionless and then fossilised; no change in doctrine or practice, however necessary or imperiously called for by advancing light, thought and knowledge, can be initiated by the clergy; the only hope of progress and reform is in, with and from the laity. If the more thoughtful and earnest-minded amongst them fall off into open dissent or indifference, woe to the Church at large. What Paul said of the mariners is true of them: 'Except these abide in the ship, ye cannot be saved.' They only can shift the rudder and guide the vessel out of the rocks and quicksands. What seems to be needed, is an organisation of laymen earnestly bent on Church reform, and which will take up, discuss, impress upon the public mind first one abuse and then another, agitating as well as criticising, until each crying evil is exposed to the glare of day and a remedy applied. That had to be done in the case of the corn laws: no statesman was disposed to attempt their repeal until Cobden, Bright and their coadjutors undertook a crusade with the view of enlightening and influencing the public mind on the question. Something will have to be done in that direction, if the Church of England is to be saved from a gradual process of decay. They are not her friends who fail to discern her errors and who reverentially endorse them, and they are not her enemies who detect and expose them. The questions relating to the Lord's supper need to be brought into prominence; meantime let each man exercise his common sense and judgment with respect to them, and act according to the decision arrived at. Ecclesiastical thunders have no terrors for us in these days; whatever may be the opinions of the clergy, we are free to form our own and to act upon our convictions. We must take the Communion Service as it stands; whenever we attend the Lord's table, the aversion entertained towards what we deem faulty and erroneous in the service must increase. In the first place, therefore, we may wisely resolve to communicate only once a year, at Easter by preference, which seems the most fitting time, because then the largest congregation gathers round the table, and the foremost idea in our minds when there should be that we are one bread, one body in our Lord. There is not the least reason for believing that Jesus ever designed the celebration to be otherwise than annual; he made it part and parcel of the yearly passover feast, and the only doubt with respect to his command, 'Do this in remembrance of me,' is as to whether it was intended for any except 'disciples,' in the true, Scriptural sense of that term, or for Gentiles, on whom the observance of the passover was not incumbent. Having taken upon ourselves this ceremony appertaining to it, it would seem that on every ground a yearly banquet in commemoration of the death of Jesus is most suitable, and that no more can be required. Its repetition quarterly, monthly, weekly or daily is based upon the supposition that some peculiar virtue attaches to it, that it is a 'means of grace.' If, in truth, our souls are strengthened and refreshed by or through it, as we have been taught to believe and expect, then the oftener that bread is eaten and that wine drunk, the better for the participants. That is the central doctrine round which the theological strife has ever raged, and not until it is utterly overthrown, and the minds of Christian men and women are freed from its thraldom, will this feast of remembrance assume its due, true and simple aspect and proportions.

The Romish doctrine has at least the merit of being clear and unmistakeable. The following extracts are from the 'Paroissien Romain,' published in France. The second part of the Mass is thus headed: 'At the Offertory commences the oblation and the celebration of the holy sacrifice. This sacrifice consists in offering to God, on the altar, bread and wine to be changed into the body and into the blood of Jesus Christ, and then to be consumed at the communion.' In one of the hymns of the Feast of the Holy Sacrament (Corpus Christi) are the following passages: *

Verbum caro, panem verum
  Verbo carnem efficit;
Fitque sanguis Christi merum
  Et si sensus deficit
Ad firmandum cor sincerum
  Sola fides sufficit. . .
	Word made flesh, the bread of nature
	  By his word to flesh he turns.
	Wine into his blood he changes;
	  What though sense no change discerns
	Only be the heart in earnest,
	  Faith her lesson quickly learns.

Dogma datur christianis
Quod in carnem transit panis,
  Et vinum in sanguinem.
Quod non capis, quod non vides,
Animosa firmat fides,
  Praeter rerum ordinem. . .
	Hear what holy Church maintaineth,
	That the bread its substance changeth
	  Into Flesh, the wine to Blood.
	Doth it pass thy comprehending?
	Faith, the law of sight transcending,
	  Leaps to things not understood.

* The translations in verse are from the Roman Missal published in England.

Caro cibus, sanguis potus ;
 Manet tamen Christus totus
   Sub utraque specie.
 A sumente non concisus,
 Non confractus, non divisus,
   Integer accipitur.
	Flesh from bread, and Blood from wine,
	 Yet is Christ in either sign
	   All entire confessed to be.
	 They too who of him partake,
	 Sever not, nor rend, nor break,
	   But entire their Lord receive.

Sumit unus, sumunt mille :
 Quantum isti, tantum ille :
   Nec sumptus consumitur.
 Sumunt boni, sumunt mali,
 Sorte tamen inaequali,
   Vitae, vel interitus.
 Mors est malis, vita bonis :
 Vide paris sumptionis
   Quam sit dispar exitus.
	Whether one or thousands eat,
	 All receive the selfsame meat,
	   Nor the less for others leave.
	 Both the wicked and the good
	 Eat of this celestial food :
	   But with ends how opposite !
	 His 'tis life, and there 'tis death ;
	 The same, yet issuing to each
	   In a difference infinite.

The Church of England also holds that Jesus Christ was given by God ' not only to die for us, but also to be our spiritual food and sustenance *in that holy Sacrament,*' which is eulogised as ' so divine and comfortable a thing to them who receive it worthily, and so dangerous to them that will presume to receive it unworthily.' That is equivalent to :

    Mors est malis, vita bonis :
    Vide paris sumptionis
    Quam sit dispar exitus.'

Our Communion Service was framed after the model of the Romish Mass, simply selecting parts and omitting parts. The Absolution beginning, ' Almighty God, our heavenly Father,' is slightly altered from the Latin, ' Misereatur vestri omnipotens Deus...' The chant beginning ' Glory be to God on high,' is an exact translation of ' Gloria in excelsis.' The Nicene Creed occurs in both services. The four sentences beginning ' Lift up your hearts,' are a translation of ' Sursum corda.' ' It is very meet, right and our bounden duty ' is from the Latin form, ' Vere dignum et justum est,' shortened and altered. The words in our service, ' The body of our Lord ... the blood of our Lord ...' agree with ' Corpus Domini ... Sanguis Domini,' but the Romish priest prays that they may preserve the ' soul ' omitting ' body,' and says nothing about remembrance. The doctrine of the Romish sacrifice of the Mass is bold and plain ; the teaching of the Church of England with respect to the sacrament is of doubtful, not to say double meaning, for it may be interpreted in different ways ; it simply shuts out the dogma of transubstantiation, yet claims for the bread and wine the same effects as before ; the mystery attaching to them, or to the taking of them, is not removed or diminished, but insisted on and emphasised. The Church of Rome asserts that the administration of this sacrament was committed by Jesus to the priesthood :

Sic sacrificium istud instituit, Cujus officium committi voluit, Solis presbyteris, quibus sic congruit Ut sumant, et dent caeteris.*	So (Jesus) instituted this sacrifice, Whose office he desired to be committed To the priests alone, to whom it appertains To take, and give to others.

* This is from the Hymn ' Sacris Solemniis,' which is not found in the English Roman Missal.

There is no foundation for that statement in the New Testament. The Church of England is silent on the point, leaving her ministers to exercise the right, without caring to justify or assert their claim to it. All that relates to the Lord's supper, the doctrines hanging to it, and the manner and times of its celebration, require to be reinvestigated and readjusted by modern thought and sentiment. That which seemed right to our forefathers and was adopted by them, is not necessarily right to us and suitable for us. We have outgrown their doctrine of the Real Presence, as they outgrew the doctrine of Transubstantiation. Is it not time for us to imitate their spirit and conduct, and to undertake as they did the work of conscientious innovation? Whenever that task is attempted, we shall have to encounter the same difficulties, probably to make similar compromises, which will result in similar shortcomings. Yet it may be better to take one step forward, halting and short though it be, than it is to attempt no progress whatever. Intelligent, earnest enquiry, with outspoken opinions and honest protest, will do much meantime towards the ultimate triumph of truth and reasonableness over error and superstition. Whenever a change in the mode of administration is adopted, one point, at present overlooked, should receive attention. If it should still be deemed desirable that all who communicate should drink, as now, out of one cup, a due regard to courtesy and decency requires that the edge of the flagon should be wiped after each time of touching it with the lips. It is prescribed that 'the Table, at the Communion time' shall have 'a fair white linen cloth upon it'; one should certainly be attached to the vessel which contains the wine. The Romish Church withholds the cup from the celebrants, the following direction being given: 'The priest divides the Host into three. He then mixes a part of the Host with the precious blood, saying: " Hæc commixtio et consecratio Corporis et Sanguinis Domini nostri Jesu Christi fiat accipientibus nobis in vitam æternam. Amen." "May this mixture and consecration of the Body and Blood of our Lord Jesus Christ procure to us the recipients eternal life. Amen."' This plan of combining the bread and wine obviates the difficulty: but the Church of England passes round the cup, not daring, it would seem, to allow any wiping off of the wine, as though it had become by the act of consecration a symbol, or reality, too sacred to be so dealt with. Probably the above suggestion will be shocking to some minds, and seem nothing less than a deliberate profanation. The proposal may serve as a test: if no superstitious notions are attached to the consecrated elements, it can be received with equanimity, and will bear discussion, at least; but by all who cling to the Romish doctrine, or anything approaching thereto, it will be held in abhorrence and scouted as impious. It is not seemly that we should drink this cup of the Lord together in church after a fashion in which we should deem it a loss of self respect, cleanliness and common courtesy to pass it round in our own houses. Until this simple point can be contemplated and discussed freely by all parties, the time will not be ripe for any public conference as to the best means of making the Lord's supper what it was meant to be, and what the passover was which it should replace—a simple feast of thankful remembrance. Whenever the subject is dealt with practically, it should be in its entirety; the cognate question as to the position and claims of the priesthood or clergy, can hardly be separated from it; the foundation of the rite on the passover will have to be brought into prominence, involving a discussion on the point whether only an annual celebration is requisite. The highest advance we can hope to attain ultimately, would be the framing of the ordinance on the same lines as the passover, making its observance incumbent on Good Friday or Easter day on the head of each family at home, and the adult members of every Christian household sharers in it. Our religion has been too much individualised and made a matter of church-going, church-worship and personal sentiment; it lacks the social element, and in that respect is a departure from the divine plan which was devised for the people of Israel. What the deliverance from Egyptian bondage through Moses was to them, the remission of sins through Jesus should be to us—recognised and celebrated periodically by every Christian family. The commemoration of the death of Jesus oftener than once a year, is as much out of place as would be the keeping of Christmas weekly, or the observance of birthdays and other anniversaries at irregular and frequent intervals. We have got into the habit of thinking that there can be no approach to God, sacramentally, except through the medium of the priesthood; the right of administering baptism and the Lord's supper has been laid hold of and monopolised by the clergy. It should be remembered that the apostles, whose successors they claim to be, were never made priests, but only preachers: that Paul, who could boast: 'I reckon that I am not a whit behind the very chiefest apostles,' thanked God that he had baptised very few of the Corinthians; and that he left to them as a congregation the mode of partaking of the Lord's supper, until it might be possible or convenient for him to visit them and then 'set in order' the previously existing arrangements. To frame our Communion Service in all respects after the model of the passover could not be wrong, for it would be simply to make it the counterpart of the first Lord's supper. Whenever—and the sooner the better—we can revert to that, the last remnant of superstition will have been abolished, together with whatever is false or exaggerated in the claims of sacerdotalism. How long will it be before this new Reformation is inaugurated and consummated? That depends upon ourselves: a continuance of our heedless indifference will delay it; any exercise of honest, earnest thought and effort will help it on.

Mark states that after Jesus had given the bread and wine to the disciples he added: 'Verily I say unto you, I will no more drink of the fruit of the vine, until that day when I drink it new in the kingdom of God.' Luke records a similar saying, but places it, evidently with intention, before the giving of the bread and wine. Alford states: 'This is generally supposed to have been the *first* cup in the Passion-meal, with which the whole was introduced.' There can be no doubt on that point, for Luke himself alludes to a *second* cup, which he, as well as Paul, calls 'the cup after supper.' Mark refers to the latter only.

Although the fourth evangelist does not allude to the institution of the Lord's supper, he gives a very full account of what else happened, and of the conversation at the table. He intimates that before the feast of the passover, Jesus fully anticipated his approaching departure, and manifested an intense affection towards his disciples. 'Now before the feast of the passover, Jesus knowing that his hour was come that he should depart out of this world unto the Father, having loved his own which were in the world, he loved them unto the end (or, to the uttermost).' 'When Jesus knew,' in the Authorised Version, is altered to 'Jesus knowing,' by the Revisers, Young and Alford: the allusion is not to any recently imparted knowledge, but to the consciousness exhibited by Jesus of what was about to happen. The expression, 'his hour was come that he must depart out of the world unto the Father,' must either be a saying of Jesus or based upon some declaration made by him. The Authorised Version continues: 'And supper being ended,' which is now rendered, 'And during supper,' in accordance with the two oldest MSS. Apart from that difference in the text, Alford explains that 'the sense is not, as A.V. *supper being ended* . . . but *supper having begun* or *having been served*.' Young renders: 'And supper having come;' Tischendorf: 'And when supper was ready;' the 'Englishman's Greek New Testament': 'And supper taking place.' The Revised Version continues: 'the devil having already put into the heart of Judas Iscariot, Simon's *son*, to betray him.' The word 'already' replaces 'now' of the Authorised Version; Young renders 'already;' Tischendorf and Alford retain 'now.' This confirms Luke's statement: 'And Satan entered into Judas,' and shows that this was the generally accepted idea and explanation of the traitor's conduct. The fourth evangelist continues: '*Jesus*, knowing that the Father had given all things into his hands, and that he came forth from God, and goeth unto God.' Here are three statements respecting Jesus, which obviously can only have been made on his own authority, from something asserted by himself. 'Was come' is altered by the Revisers to 'came,' and 'went' to 'goeth.' Young renders literally: 'that from God he came out, and to God he goeth.' Having uttered these solemn declarations concerning himself, his delegated powers, his origin and destiny, Jesus proceeded, the impression of these things being fresh in the minds of the disciples, to perform an act which stood out in strong constrast to the claims he made and the reverence with which they regarded him. He rose from his seat at the supper-table, divested himself of his 'garments,'—the word indicates something more than the outer robe merely,—took a towel, wrapped it about him, poured water into the bason at hand for ablutions, and set himself to the task of bathing and wiping the feet of his disciples: 'riseth from supper, and layeth aside his garments; and he took a towel and girded himself. Then he poured water into the bason, and began to wash the disciples' feet, and to wipe them with the towel wherewith he was girded.' The word 'then' replaces 'after that' of the Authorised Version, but the alteration is not adopted by Young, Alford or Tischendorf; they agree with the Revisers in placing the definite instead of indefinite article before 'bason.' There appears to have been no servant present to perform the customary menial office, they had walked together to the city, probably some considerable distance, and had already sat down to the table with the dust of the road clinging to their feet. Jesus could disregard such things, or feel punctilious about them, as the varying occasions might seem to him to make one or the other course desirable. Once he had deliberately scandalised one of the Pharisees, who 'marvelled that he had not first washed before breakfast,' and thereby he took the opportunity of rebuking their hypocritical preference of outside cleansings to inward purity of heart and life. At another time he had mildly reproached a Pharisee whose guest he was by saying : 'Thou gavest me no water for my feet.' Now, as moved by a sudden inspiration, he either delays or interrupts the meal, with the object of impressing on them in a very striking manner a most important lesson. With what astonishment must they have contemplated and yielded to his procedure! In that strange garb and posture he approached the apostle Peter : 'So he cometh to Simon Peter.' The Revisers have replaced 'then' by 'so,' with which rendering Alford agrees, observing : 'the *so* taking up the narrative again after the word *began*, as if it were said, " in pursuance of this intention."' Peter, with his usual outspoken impetuosity, raised an objection : 'He saith unto him, Lord (Sir—Young), dost thou wash my feet?' The personal pronoun appears instead of 'Peter' before 'saith,' as in the two oldest MSS. Jesus replied that his action was incomprehensible for the moment only, and would be explained presently. 'Jesus answered and said unto him, What I do thou knowest not now, but thou shalt understand hereafter.' The word 'understand' has been adopted in place of 'know' by the Revisers, Tischendorf and Alford. The word 'hereafter' is so commonly applied to another life or state in the distant future, that Alford's 'afterwards' or Young's 'after this' is preferable. That assurance of Jesus did not remove Peter's respectful scruples. He was determined never to allow such a reversal of their respective positions : it would be an undue exaltation of himself, an unfitting degradation of Jesus. The feeling of self-condemnation and reproach which at the outset of their intercourse had impelled Peter to cry out, 'Depart from me ; for I am a sinful man, O Lord,' now revived. 'Peter saith unto him, Thou shalt never wash my feet.' Young renders : 'Thou mayest not wash my feet—unto the age.' Jesus met this second refusal with one of his graceful and impressive figures of speech, intimating that the lower Peter's estimate of himself the greater the need of his submitting to this requirement of Jesus. 'Jesus answered him, If I wash thee not, thou hast no part with me.' Peter was quick to catch and admit the truth of that : in such a sense the washing could not be too complete. 'Simon Peter saith unto him, Lord (Sir—Young), not my feet only, but also my hands and my head.' In the Authorised Version the word 'my' is italicised. Young renders literally, 'the hands and the head.' Peter's submission to the purpose of Jesus was well repaid by another simile. 'Jesus saith to him, He that is bathed needeth not save to wash his feet, but is clean every whit.' The Revisers have replaced 'washed' by 'bathed.' Young, Alford and Tischendorf render literally : 'he who hath been bathed.' The Revisers note :. 'Some ancient authorities omit *save* and *his feet*'; the oldest MS., the Sinaitic, does so. The entire cleansing of the corporeal and moral nature, such as Peter craved, would indeed render needless any further ablution ; or, retaining the words 'save' and 'his feet,' the bath having been taken, it was enough to wash off the dust of the road from the uncovered, sandalled feet. Jesus recognised the fact that his disciples were clean in head and heart : ' And ye are clean.' Alas! he must make an exception, adding : ' but not all.' The evangelist explains this as referring to the traitor in their midst. ' For he knew him that should betray him ; therefore said he, Ye are not all clean.' Judas might share in that ablution of the feet, but his head and heart were utterly, hopelessly defiled.

Having gone the round of his disciples, Jesus laid aside the towel, resumed his clothing, again took his seat at the table, and proceeded to explain the motive of his action. 'So when he had washed their feet, and taken his garments, and sat down (Gr. reclined) again, he said unto them, Know ye what I have done to you ?' He reminded them of the position he occupied towards them, and of the reverence with which they habitually treated him, he accepting from them as his due the titles of Lord and Teacher. ' Ye call me Master (or, Teacher), and Lord : and ye say well : for so I am.' It was precisely because they admitted his supremacy that he had taken upon himself this servile function. If he had done it for them, they also should do it for each other. ' If I then, the Lord and the Master (or, Teacher), have washed your feet, ye also ought to wash one another's feet.' He had preferred to teach them by example rather than by simple precept. ' For I have given you an example, that ye should do as I have done to you.' What he stooped to perform could not be considered as beneath their dignity. ' A servant (Gr. bondservant) is not greater than his lord : neither one that is sent (Gr. an apostle) greater than he that sent him.' Let us try to understand the import and the bearing of the Lord's example and advice. The apostles were alone with their Teacher. It was on account of his peculiar and close relationship to them that Jesus performed this action. He never did to others what he now did to them, nor did he urge them to imitate his example towards any outside their own circle. He did not bid them wash the feet of all men, or of other men, or of any man not associated with them in their common enterprise. His counsel went no further than : ' Ye also ought to wash one another's feet.' The water, the bason and the towel were in the room, but no servant being present they had at first all taken their seats without washing. Had it been customary for each guest to rinse his own feet, they would as a matter of course have done so, and Jesus would have been quick to set the example. As it was, he might have done that, thus giving them a lesson of independence and self-help instead of self-sacrifice. The omission on this occasion of the customary ablution would have deprived their banquet to some extent of that sense of comfort and air of refinement which add to the charm of social intercourse. Jesus could not contemplate that with indifference, and it occurred to him that if, for the time being, one of the party would voluntarily make himself servant of all, every requirement of punctilious courtesy could be fulfilled. So he resolved to take upon himself the task, and in spite of protests insisted on accomplishing it, thereby teaching them how easily the spirit of charity among themselves, taking this practical form, could supply the deficiencies and minor inconveniences arising from their lack of worldly wealth and position. Instead of attempting to profess a contemptuous disregard of such things as trifles, let them remember how much of the happiness and grace of life are dependent on them. Jesus would not have his professed disciples sink in any point of delicacy and self-respect beneath the world's level, but seized the occasion to remind them, first by his action and now by his words: 'If ye know these things, blessed are ye if ye do them.' The Revisers have replaced the word 'happy' by 'blessed.' Alford also inserted the note: 'Render, as usual, *blessed*.' But Young here and elsewhere, even throughout the sermon on the mount, translates the word, *makarios*, as 'happy,' and it would be wiser to follow his example than to seek uniformity in the other direction. The minds of ordinary English readers are accustomed to attach to the word 'blessed' the idea of blessing imparted specially by God, which is obviously not its meaning in this place. The true point and natural drift of the incident here related, and of the words of Jesus in connection with it, are generally overlooked, it being taken for granted that the only object was to enforce a lesson of humility. But we must ask: Why in relation to the washing of feet? Why should one out of many thus humble himself? Alford quotes the following from Bengel: 'In these times pontiffs and princes obey this injunction to the letter: but it would be a more wonderful thing to see a pontiff, for example, wash the feet of one equal, than of twelve poor beggars.' That travesty of the injunction of Jesus arises out of a misapprehension of the circumstances and a misapplication of his words. Alford observes: 'The custom of literally and ceremonially washing the feet in obedience to this command, is not found before the fourth century.' If it could be traced up to the first century, that should make no difference in our judgment of the matter: theologians, in their reverence for antiquity, seem often to lose sight of the fact that the men of the first century were as liable to error and perversions of the gospel as we are in the nineteenth century. When we trace a custom or a belief up to the earliest date, it must only be to compare it with the original gospel records, and to say that, in our opinion, at that time the sayings and commands of Jesus were rightly understood and acted upon, or the reverse, as the case may be. Even in the apostle Paul's time the Lord's supper was misconceived, perverted, and had grown into a scandal. From the very first, erroneous opinions and practices have existed, and as time went on they became more and more blended with the truth, leaving to later generations the task of disentanglement. The earliest ages and the greatest names are not credentials of infallibility, and implicit, unreasoning confidence in them is sufficient to account for the perpetuation of various dogmas, principles of action, modes of worship, and sacerdotal claims, which still maintain their hold on Christianity, and which must be exposed and cast aside before we can discern and grasp the pure and simple gospel of 'the kingdom of heaven.'

Alford makes the following comment: 'Notice that our Lord commands us to do, not "*that which* I have done to you," but *as—* in like manner as—I have done to you."' The self-dedication of the individual to the benefit of the community,—that was the point and purpose of his action. Only to a Christian brotherhood resembling that of this apostolic band, can his example and exhortation apply. They were animated by a common purpose, they had joined a common cause, they had given up everything to follow Jesus, they had all one purse, and were so indifferent about it that the thievish Judas was suffered to hold it in his keeping: their voluntary poverty must not lead, as indigence so often does, to any abatement of self-respect, decency, decorum, any deterioration from their proper level of social comfort and refinement; that there would be a tendency in that direction was evident to Jesus when they sat down to the meal without the customary ablution; and to preserve them from that evil, to impart to them a spirit which would guard against it, and a rule of conduct which they could adhere to amidst the lowliest surroundings, he gave them an example in his own person of what a little tact and self-sacrifice on the part of anyone could do for all of them. With houses of our own, with money at our command, with paid servants about us who have no occupation in the world beyond attending to our personal and family comforts, we can read the narrative without any sense of needing to make a practical application of it; but assume the existence of a community of disciples, small or large, be it twelve, twelve hundred, or twelve thousand, all banded together to carry out the gospel scheme of Jesus, who for his sake and for the kingdom of heaven's sake, have relinquished all they had on earth, whose daily recurring need and impecuniosity literalise the petition, 'Give us this day our daily bread:' in such a community there must be a constant interchange of voluntary, unpaid services, the time, the skill, the aptitude of particular members, in a variety of ways, being exercised on behalf of the general body, yet no one member being suffered to degenerate into a mere household drudge, or servant of the rest, but each taking part and turn in those necessary offices of loving service of which the washing of the disciples' feet by Jesus stands forth as a pattern and illustration. He did not say, 'Let each man among you wash his own feet,' nor, 'Let one from among you be chosen to wash the feet of the rest,' but, 'Ye also ought to wash one another's feet:' there must be an established reciprocity of self-sacrificing ministration, a ready, cheerful assumption by each alternately of some lower function, his contribution, for the time being, towards the general welfare, that the entire brotherhood may secure, in spite of general poverty, the ease, grace, comfort, refinement, which are desirable for all, and which the world can pay for but they cannot. This advice of Jesus was not for or suited to the world, nor was it designed to be incumbent on the church,—that is, the assembly of believers,—at large: it was a counsel of perfection for the twelve, and can be laid hold of and applied only by a similar body of 'disciples,' living and labouring under the same conditions and with the same aim and object as the first apostles. Commentators seem to have been altogether at a loss what to make of the incident and lesson. Alford says: 'Our Lord's action was symbolical, and is best imitated in His followers by endeavouring, " if a man be overtaken in a fault, to restore such an one in the spirit of meekness." (Gal. vi. 1.' That is far-fetched and incongruous: Jesus hinted nothing about faults and restoration. That Alford was able to appreciate the real drift of the action, yet to discern no particular ground, direction or scope for its application, is evident from the following note: 'The command here given must be understood in the full light of intelligent appreciation of the circumstances, and the meaning of the act. Bengel remarks, that *one* intent of our Lord's

12 John 6
13 John 2

washing the feet of His disciples must necessarily be absent from any such deed on our part : viz. its *symbolic meaning*, pressed by our Lord on St. Peter, "If I wash thee not, thou hast no part with Me." The demand will rather find its fulfilment in all kinds of mutual condescension and help, than in any literal observance.' Bengel says we cannot imitate the symbolic meaning ; Alford thinks we can best imitate the symbolic meaning, not quite the same as Bengel's, in a particular way, yet at the same time it is perceived and admitted that 'all kinds of mutual condescension and help' constitute the sum and substance of the command.

Having concluded his advice to the apostles with the words, 'If ye know these things, blessed are ye if ye do them,' Jesus added that not to all of them did his words apply : 'I speak not of you all.' He had made choice of them deliberately, but there was one to and through whom no blessedness could come, but from whom there would proceed a wanton and crushing blow. 'I know whom I have chosen (or, chose) : but that the scriptures may be fulfilled, He that eateth my bread lifted up his heel against me.' The Revisers have altered 'bread with me' to 'my bread,' noting that 'many ancient authorities read *his bread with me*.' In the Psalm of David the passage stands :

'Yea, mine own familiar friend, in whom I trusted, which did eat of my bread,
Hath lifted up his heel against me.'

How accurate a picture that of the experience of Jesus in connection with Judas ! It was indeed a 'fulfilment' to the letter. Alford observes : 'This is another instance of the direct and unhesitating application of the words of the Psalms by our Lord to Himself.' It by no means follows that such sayings were not, are not still, applicable to others also. There is nothing in the Psalm to indicate any special reference to the Messiah. Its primary import relates to the troubles, trials, disappointments, deliverances of a man undergoing both the common and exceptional experiences of humanity, and conscious of the divine help and approval. Take this verse :

'The LORD will support him upon the couch of languishing :
Thou makest all his bed in his sickness.'
Surely that cannot refer to Jesus. Again :
'I said, O LORD, have mercy upon me :
Heal my soul ; for I have sinned against thee.'

That is equally inapplicable. Jesus selected one passage as illustrating the conduct of his treacherous disciple : many men, before and since, have undergone similar treatment at the hands of false friends, and to every such instance the words of the Psalmist apply : his experience becomes theirs, his lamentation accurately describes their case, his scripture is again 'fulfilled' in their history. Such frequently recurring expressions as 'that it might be fulfilled which was spoken,' 'then was fulfilled that which was spoken,' 'in them is fulfilled the prophecy of Isaiah,' 'they that dwell in Jerusalem, and their rulers, because they knew him not, nor the voices of the prophets which are read every sabbath, fulfilled *them* by condemning *him*,'—must be understood broadly, and not according to the narrow mode of interpretation which has been so long in vogue. These passages were not quoted as proofs of the authenticity or divine inspiration of Scripture, or of the Messiahship of Jesus : such

passages as, 'Out of Egypt did I call my son,' and 'that he should 2 Mat. 15
be called a Nazarene,' should suffice to obviate that notion. What   „ 23
is prophecy but the records of the lives, teachings, hopes, anticipations, yearnings, forecasts, of men who 'spake from God, being moved 1 ii. Pet. 21
by the Holy Spirit'? 'No prophecy ever came by the will of man:'
it is not purely human or merely mundane, but arises out of the
blending of the earthly with the heavenly, the spirit of man with the
holy spirit. The words of these 'holy men of God' are pregnant
with a wisdom, truth and force far above the ordinary level of
uninspired literature; the vicissitudes of their earthly lot, their
struggles against evil, their triumphs, their defeats, their consolations,
their aspirations, have not only been recorded but passed on, perpetuated, in the lives and labours of men of the same stamp as
themselves; and whoever shares most largely in the common experiences of humanity and also, in combination therewith, the
exceptional experiences of the saints of old, must realise most fully
the appositeness and 'fulfilment,' in varying ways, of what they felt
and wrote. 'The same sufferings are being accomplished in your 5 i. Pet. 9
brotherhood who are in the world.' What the evangelists did, Jesus
himself did: picked out certain passages in the Scriptures, wholly
apart from their context, and applied them, sometimes to himself,
sometimes to those with whom he came in contact, accepting and
regarding them as fulfilments, accomplishments, counterparts, or
recurrences of that particular phase of individual experience. He lived
the holy life so well and thoroughly, that almost every point and
incident therein found its correspondence in the prophetic writings.

Jesus foreseeing the impending blow, thought it well to let it be
anticipated by his disciples also. 'From henceforth I tell you before 13 John 19
it come to pass.' The Revisers have replaced 'now' by 'from
henceforth.' Young, Alford and the 'Englishman's Greek New
Testament' render: 'from this time.' The moment had come when
they must be fully prepared for this disastrous episode in his career.
Their foreknowledge of it would, on the happening of the event,
reduce it to its proper proportions and enable them still to maintain
their confidence in him: 'that, when it is come to pass, ye may
believe that I am *he* (or, I am).' The maginal note of the Revisers   19
indicates that it is open to question whether the italicised 'he' is
properly inserted. Alford puts (*the Christ*), between brackets.
Luther has: 'dass ichs bin,' 'that I am it.' The apostles could
not help entertaining the popular views respecting the office of the
Messiah, and to see their Lord and Master cut off from the earth
instead of reigning over Israel, might well stagger their faith in him.
It would look as though his plan had been abortive, his claim falsified,
when one of themselves gave the death-blow to their hopes and expectations by placing him in the hands of his enemies. To anticipate this trial of their faith and counteract as far as possible its
depressing influence, Jesus dwelt on the fact of his own foreknowledge and prognostication of his destiny. Their office was not to
cease, but in fact to commence at his death. Whatever might
happen to him, he would have their minds impressed with a due and
abiding sense of their commission to the world as his ambassadors,
and with the assurance that their revelation of Jesus would be a
revelation of God to mankind. 'Verily, verily, I say unto you, 13 John 20
He that receiveth whomsoever I send receiveth me; and he that

receiveth me receiveth him that sent me.' Not one whit of his pretensions, or of their confidence in him, must be abated, however dark this crisis of his destiny. Alas! that there should be any defection from among them; that one of the chosen twelve should be a traitor to their Master and his cause. The disclosure of the fact was pain and grief to him. 'When Jesus had thus said, he was troubled in the spirit, and testified, and said, Verily, verily, I say unto you, that one of you shall* betray me.' Such an intimation, uttered so solemnly, and at such a time, filled them with astonishment and consternation. Each man scanned his neighbour in doubt and perplexity. 'The disciples looked one on another, doubting of whom he spake.' This mention of the betrayal appears to be identical with that related by Matthew and Mark, already considered, and also with the following in Luke: 'But behold, the hand of him that betrayeth me is with me on the table. For the Son of man indeed goeth, as it hath been determined: but woe unto that man through whom he is betrayed! And they began to question among themselves which of them it was that should do this thing.' The fourth evangelist supplies further interesting details. Jesus evidently did not intend to disclose the name of the traitor to all present. But the anxiety to ascertain it was natural, and two of the disciples sought to elicit the information privately. One of them, to whom Jesus was much attached, was sitting next him at the table. 'There was at the table reclining in Jesus' bosom one of his disciples, whom Jesus loved.' The words 'at the table' have been added by the Revisers, as '(at meat)' were by Young, to make the sense clear. Alford explains: 'Since the captivity, the Jews lay at the table in the Persian manner, on divans or couches, each on his left side, with his face towards the table, his left elbow resting on a pillow and supporting his head. Thus the second guest to the right hand lay with his head near the breast of the first, and so on.' The next verse stands in the Authorised Version as follows: 'Simon Peter therefore beckoned to him, that he should ask who it should be of whom he spake.' The words, 'that he should ask' down to 'spake' are omitted by the Revisers, and the following reading of the oldest MSS. is adopted: 'Simon Peter therefore beckoneth to him, and saith unto him, Tell us who it is of whom he speaketh.' Alford observes that 'the text is in confusion, some ancient authorities reading' as the Authorised Version and others as the Revised Version. He adds: 'Peter characteristically imagines that John, as the beloved disciple, would know: but he, not knowing, asks of the Lord.' The narrative does not mention John by name, but continues: 'He, leaning back, as he was, on Jesus' breast, saith unto him, Lord (Sir—Young), who is it?' The Authorised Version begins, 'he then lying,' and omits 'as he was.' The Sinaitic MS. has simply, 'He therefore lying'; the Vatican MS., 'He lying thus.' Alford says: 'I understand it, that John, who was before lying close to the bosom of Jesus, now leaned his head absolutely *upon* His breast, to ask the question.' Tischendorf renders: 'He then having fallen back thus on Jesus' breast.' Quietly and privately Jesus gave the information, pointing out the man without naming him, and in

---

* A Reviser of the MS. considers the word 'shall' to be 'arbitrary and objectionable,' and asks: 'Why not *will?*' Young and Tischendorf render 'will.'

such a way as to avoid making him conspicuous and exciting the suspicions of the company. 'Jesus therefore answereth, He it is, for whom I shall dip the sop, and give it him. So when he had dipped the sop, he taketh and giveth it to Judas, *the son* of Simon Iscariot.' Tischendorf agrees with the Revisers in putting 'Iscariot' after 'Simon' instead of after 'Judas.' Young renders 'sop' as 'morsel.' Alford notes : 'Observe the word *sop*, in this sentence, stands for the act in which it played a principal part. This *giving the sop* was one of the closest testimonies of friendly affection.' That act of kindly courtesy, at such a moment, and after all that had been said, was a last appeal to the better nature of Judas. His name not having been disclosed, it was even now not too late for him to repent of his design, refuse to make himself the tool of the enemies of Jesus, return to his allegiance, renounce his scheme of betrayal, and cling, penitent and forgiven, to the side of a Master so patient and so loving. As he partook of the sop, what a conflict of feeling must he have undergone ! How must two opposing voices have sounded in his ears ! What a foretaste must he have had of that remorse which later on made life unbearable ! Had he, or was he without, a good angel contending for the victory ? Be that as it may, an evil angel gained it. 'And after the sop, then entered Satan into him.' Young renders : 'And after the morsel, the Adversary entered into that one.' In the previous verse 26 also, 'He it is' is rendered, 'That one it is ': that one of the twelve. As Jesus watched the man 'eating his bread,' and saw no signs of relenting, but the reverse, he was moved to address him. 'Jesus therefore saith unto him, That thou doest, do quickly.' Tischendorf renders, 'more quickly.' It must have been well-nigh intolerable to see the hypocrite sitting there still, lengthening out his deceptive part, and utterly unmoved by the reticence of Jesus in refraining from denouncing him, or by his last act of courtesy in handing him the sop. It was all said and done in such a way as to fix no suspicion upon Judas, so that even now not one of those sitting at the table regarded the words spoken to him as relating to anything unusual ; knowing him to be the purse-bearer, some imagined that Jesus had directed him to purchase whatever they might require during the holidays, or to give their contribution to the poor. 'Now no man at the table knew for what intent he spake this unto him. For some thought, because Judas had the bag (or, box), that Jesus said unto him, Buy what things we have need of for the feast ; or, that he should give something to the poor.' The Revisers have omitted the needlessly inserted words '*of them*' before 'thought.' The traitor was not slow to act upon the hint and expressed desire of Jesus. 'He then having received the sop went out straightway.' Young renders : 'Having received therefore the morsel, that one immediately went out.' The evangelist adds : 'and it was night.' 'Outer darkness' indeed to Judas ! His departure was another step in the development of the tragedy. Jesus was able to contemplate the approaching crisis steadily, without flinching. In his death he would honour God and God would honour him. 'When therefore he was gone out, Jesus saith, Now is (or, was) the Son of man glorified, and God is (or, was) glorified in him.' Young and Tischendorf adopt the past tense, 'was.' The carrying out of the plot against the life of Jesus could have no other result than this. The Authorised Version continues: 'If God be glorified in him,' which is omitted by the Revisers, in accordance with the two oldest MSS. Alford notes that it is 'omitted by many of the most ancient authorities, but probably by mistake in transcribing, from the two similar endings, *in him—in him*.' Tischendorf inserts it: 'If God was glorified in him.' The Revised Version stands: 'And God shall glorify him in himself, and straightway shall he glorify him.' Dishonour from men would soon be exchanged for honour from God.

13 John 32

According to Luke's narrative there arose during the supper a discussion among the apostles on the question of priority. 'And there arose also a contention among them, which of them is accounted to be greatest (Gr. greater).' Jesus expressed his own views upon precedence and rulership generally, very clearly and emphatically. It was a system known and recognised throughout the world, and was appreciated as a national benefit. 'And he said unto them, The kings of the Gentiles have lordship over them; and they that have authority over them are called Benefactors.' But Jesus deliberately chose, and peremptorily enjoined upon his disciples, a system the very reverse of that. 'But ye *shall* not be so: but he that is the greater among you, let him become as the younger: and he that is chief, as he that doth serve.' Tischendorf renders 'he that is chief' as 'he that leads,' and Young 'he who is leading.' There could be true leadership without any assumption of authority, and the intercourse between Jesus and themselves was a proof and type of that. 'For whether is greater, he that sitteth (Gr. reclineth) at meat, or he that serveth? is not he that sitteth (Gr. reclineth) at meat? but I am in the midst of you as he that serveth.' This may be understood as referring to the washing of the disciples' feet by Jesus at this meal. And throughout the trials attendant upon his career they had continued faithful to him: 'But ye are they which have continued with me in my temptations.' And his object from the first had been the establishment of a kingdom which God had appointed, and to which Jesus had appointed them. 'And I appoint unto you a kingdom, even as my Father appointed unto me (Or, and I appoint unto you, even as my Father appointed unto me a kingdom . . .'). Whatever was for him, was for them also; no special table reserved for himself alone, but one table for him and them, and twelve thrones in his kingdom, all of them taking part jointly and severally in the task of governing God's chosen people: 'that ye may eat and drink at my table in my kingdom; and ye shall sit on thrones, judging the twelve tribes of Israel.'

22 Luke 24

25

26

27

28

29

30

This is to the same effect as 20 Mat. 20—28 and 10 Mark 30—35, which have already been dealt with. But this appears to have been spoken later, has additional ideas, and reverts to a previous mention of twelve thrones in connection with the twelve tribes. To understand that allusion we must bear in mind that at the time of making it ten of the tribes had never returned from exile: they had become and have ever since been utterly lost to human view, mingled with the nations which had carried them captive, or others among whom they

19 Mat. 27–30

dispersed themselves. The two tribes, who had been taken into captivity 133 years later by the Babylonians, had come back, but were under Roman rule. The conception of a revived, active nationality composed of the twelve tribes, was not a vision realisable by the apostles in the then existing state of the world; the promise based on that must have seemed as far-off, visionary, intangible, unworldly, as it would if uttered now. Yet Jesus made it, and we must attach to it a meaning and object. He connected it with the triumph and work of the Messiah: 'Verily I say unto you, that ye which 19 Mat. 28 have followed me, in the regeneration when the Son of man shall sit on the throne of his glory, ye also shall sit upon twelve thrones, judging the twelve tribes of Israel.' The hope of Israel was bound up with the manifestation of the Messiah, and had not become either extinct or transformed. The apostle Paul bore witness to it: 'And 26 Acts 6 now I stand *here* to be judged for the hope of the promise made by God unto our fathers; unto which *promise* our twelve tribes, earnestly „ 7 serving *God* night and day, hope to attain. And concerning this hope I am accused by the Jews.' Through Jesus only could it be fulfilled: and the first thing was to enlarge it, making it include „ 23 Gentiles: 'how that the Christ must suffer, *and* how that he first by the resurrection of the dead should proclaim light both to the people and to the Gentiles.' Here is a prophecy of Isaiah: 'Yea, he saith, 49 Isa. 6 It is too light a thing that thou shouldest be my servant to raise up the tribes of Jacob, and to restore the preserved of Israel: I will also give thee for a light to the Gentiles, that thou mayest be my salvation unto the end of the earth.' That was quoted by Paul and Barnabas, who regarded it as a command of God to them to turn to 13 Acts 47 the Gentiles. That is what Paul terms 'the mystery of Christ . . . 3 Eph. 4 that the Gentiles are fellow-heirs, and fellow-members of the body, „ 6 and fellow-partakers of the promise in Christ Jesus through the gospel.' In the eyes of the apostle, 'the Israel of God' were those 6 Gal. 16 who, apart from circumcision, with it or without it, had become 'a „ 15 new creation' in Jesus Christ. The conception of the promise and the claim of participation therein have become not merely enlarged but transformed: as there is a heavenly Jerusalem so there is an Israel of God; the twelve tribes are replaced by a nobler race, true sons of God, Jews inwardly, whose 'circumcision is that of the heart, in the 2 Rom. 29 spirit, not in the letter.' So fully was this recognised, that Paul when alluding to his countrymen distinguished them as 'Israel after the flesh.' 10 i. Cor. 18

Jesus foresaw that his apostles would be exposed to more than human malice in carring out his policy. Something led him to address Peter specially on the point. 'Simon, Simon, behold, Satan 22 Luke 31 asked to have you (or, obtained you by asking), that he might sift you as wheat.' The Revisers, Tischendorf and Alford have omitted from the beginning of this verse the words, 'and the Lord said,' which are not in the Vatican MS. Alford notes: '*you*, all of you: not Simon alone, as sometimes understood, even by preachers;' the distinction between 'you' and 'thee' must be observed, and the figure of sifting wheat cannot apply to one individual. The Authorised Version has, 'Satan hath desired *to have* you.' Alford renders: 'desired' as 'prevailed,' and notes: 'hath obtained you;—his desire is granted.' In the absence of Jesus they would be tempted to lose faith in him, and he had prayed on behalf of Peter: 'but I made supplication for thee, that thy faith fail not.' Much would depend on him, and when his own moment of weakness should have passed, on him must devolve the task of strengthening his fellow-disciples: 'and do thou, when thou hast turned again, stablish thy brethren.' The Authorised Version has, 'when thou art converted.' Young renders, 'when thou has turned,' Tischendorf, 'when once thou hast returned.' Jesus assumed a temporary defection in all of them, and especially on the part of Peter. Such a suspicion was ill suited to the mood of the apostle. He felt himself strong, devoted, self-sacrificing, more likely to be suffering imprisonment and death with Jesus than to be free and self-reproachful, bewailing his own declension, and seeking to recover the faith and purpose of his brethren and himself. 'And he said unto him, Lord (Sir—Young), with thee I am ready to go both to prison and to death.' Jesus knew him better than he knew himself, foresaw—by what mysterious power or intuition we know not—what was about to happen, and startled the boastful apostle by revealing one incident of the approaching crisis. 'And he said, I tell thee, Peter, the cock shall not crow this day, until thou shalt thrice deny that thou knowest me.' Alford notes: 'This is the only place in the Gospels where our Lord addresses Peter by the name *Peter*. And it is remarkable, as occurring in the very place where He forewarns him of his approaching denial of Himself.' That stony, rock-like disposition could be as firm and immovable in denial as in confession: the chief virtue of such a character, misplaced and misapplied, becomes its chief defect.

This warning to Peter, which Luke introduces abruptly, is represented by the fourth evangelist as arising out of a comment of Peter on a statement made by Jesus. After alluding to the honour which God was about to bestow on himself, Jesus proceeded: 'Little children, yet a little while I am with you.' Alford notes that the term 'little children' is '*here only* used by Christ.' But he had previously applied very similar terms to his disciples: 'Whosoever shall give to drink unto one of these little ones a cup of cold water only in the name of a disciple.' 'Whoso shall cause one of these little ones which believe on me to stumble.' Jesus was deeply conscious of the state of defencelessness and helplessness, from the world's point of view, to which he introduced his disciples, telling them at one time, 'Behold, I send you forth as lambs in the midst of wolves,' and at other times speaking of them as 'little ones,' 'little children.' He must soon leave them, and in his absence they would long for his presence: 'Ye shall seek me;' not in the sense of hoping to find him again on earth, for it would be no more possible for them to go to him than for those to whom he had once said: 'Yet a little while am I with you, and I go unto him that sent me. Ye shall seek me, and shall not find me: and where I am, ye cannot come.' The friends as well as the enemies of Jesus must realise their distance from him while in this world: 'And as I said unto the Jews, Whither I go, ye cannot come; so now I say unto you.' Himself away, Jesus was anxious that they should draw close together: 'A new commandment I give unto you, that ye love one another.' They should exhibit towards each other the same spirit and conduct he had ever manifested towards them: 'Even as I have loved you, that ye also love one another (or, Even as I loved you, that ye also may love one another).' That mutual love must constitute the band and evidence of their profession : 'By this shall all men know that ye are my disciples, if ye have love one to another.' We must not overlook the word 'disciples,' or think to broaden the command by making it include 'believers' generally. It is for that peculiar community of 'brethren' or 'followers' of Jesus who for his name's sake renounce all worldly hopes and possessions, that they 'may gain Christ, and be found in him.' It is as though a father were to exhort his children to love one another, that they might be recognised as one united family: the love of neighbours, friends and distant relatives would be something extraneous, and to interpret the father's wish as in any way referring to it, would be to misconstrue and misapply his words. If the clergy, as a body, could be regarded as disciples of Jesus, the precept would apply to them; and whenever a community of true disciples comes into existence, and not before, there will be scope for the exercise and manifestation of this peculiarly Christian virtue. For the love inculcated must be no mere sentiment, but an active principle of mutual help and oversight, after the pattern exhibited by Jesus towards the twelve apostles, and it can only come into play in a community bound together and labouring in a common cause, no one of them having a private purse or a single selfish aim, but all living the heavenly life and laying up for themselves treasure in the heavens. In such a Christian brotherhood comprising various classes and professions, the free, gratuitous interchange of services on the part of its individual members would go far towards neutralising that childlike helplessness inseparable from a profession and practice of the doctrines of non-resistance to evil and voluntary poverty; the brethren would learn 'to wash one another's feet,' each would strive to be 'as he that serveth,' and by their active love towards each other the world would know them to be the disciples of Jesus.

The apostle Peter took upon himself to question Jesus : 'Simon Peter saith unto him, Lord (Sir—Young), whither goest thou?' Jesus replied that Peter could not now accompany him, but should make the same journey later. 'Jesus answered, Whither I go, thou canst not follow me now; but thou shalt follow afterwards.' The word 'me' before 'afterwards' has been omitted, on the authority of the three oldest MSS. The impetuous disciple was not convinced, and proceeded to argue the question. It was evident that Jesus alluded to death, and Peter was ready to die with him, or even instead of him. 'Peter saith unto him, Lord (Sir—Young), why cannot I follow thee even now? I will lay down my life for thee.' Luke has: 'with thee I am ready to go both to prison and to death.' He would face imprisonment and execution rather than separation. Jesus knew that the performance would fall lamentably short of the intention, and that this boastful spirit would within a few hours become a craven and lying one. For the second time he warned him : 'Jesus answereth, Wilt thou lay down thy life for me? Verily, verily, I say unto thee, The cock shall not crow, till thou hast denied me thrice.'

Luke records some remarkable sayings of Jesus, evidently spoken with the design of bringing forcibly before the minds of the apostles the trying and dangerous position in which they were about to be placed. 'And he said unto them, When I sent you forth without purse, and wallet, and shoes, lacked ye anything? And they said, Nothing.' The unhesitating reply, 'Nothing,' indicates the friendly feelings with which they, their Master and their mission, had been in those days regarded. But Jesus forewarned them that they were now on the eve of very opposite experiences. 'And he said unto them, But now, he that hath a purse, let him take it, and likewise a wallet.' They must no longer rely upon general sympathy for the supply of their daily recurring needs. On the contrary, they would be subjected to attack, and must be prepared to stand on the defensive: 'and he that hath none, let him sell his cloke, and buy a sword (or, and he that hath no sword, let him sell his cloke, and buy one).' Young renders: 'and he who hath not, let him sell his garment, and buy a sword.' Alford explains: 'There is a question how this sentence, which is elliptical in the original, should be filled up. Very many authorities make *a sword* understood after *hath not* (as in A. V.): but the simpler construction and better sense is to place *hath not* in contrast with *hath*, He that hath a purse, &c., and he that hath none, let him, &c. Thus the sense will be complete, for he who *has a purse*, can buy a sword *without selling his garment*.' We know well the extremely emphatic and highly figurative language in which Jesus was accustomed to speak, leaving his hearers to discover for themselves the sense in which his words were to be taken, as when he said, 'I have meat to eat that ye know not,' and again, 'Beware of the leaven of the Pharisees and Sadducees,' and again, 'It is easier for a camel to go through a needle's eye, than for a rich man to enter into the kingdom of God.' We must never cling to the letter and overlook the spirit of such sayings, or attempt to press them beyond the point which was in the mind of Jesus at the time of their utterance. The context, the occasion, the circumstances of the moment, must always be taken into account, in order to grasp the idea intended to be conveyed, especially when, as in this instance, the language is intentionally exaggerated with the object of deepening the impression of the truth sought to be conveyed. It would obviously be unwise, irrational, unjustifiable, to assume that the counsel of Jesus about money, food and clothes, and a sword as being more necessary than a cloke, is to be interpreted as a new system of procedure designed to be suddenly introduced and acted upon in opposition to all that he had previously inculcated. He never intended to lay upon his disciples conflicting commands; the thought should not be entertained for a moment that we have here a deliberate repeal of his previous counsels, and a repudiation of those doctrines of non-resistance and self-renunciation which were deliberately proclaimed in the Sermon on the Mount and again and again enforced in the teaching of Jesus. Yet that such an assumption has been made, and such astounding conclusions, either with or without pretence of argument, broached and adopted, is evident from the following note of Alford: 'The saying is both a description to them of their altered situation with reference to the world without, and a declaration that self-defence and self-provision would henceforward be necessary. It forms a *decisive testimony, from the mouth of the Lord Himself, against the views of the*

Quakers and some other sects on these points. But it does not warrant *aggression* by Christians, nor, as some R. Catholics, *spreading the Gospel by the sword.*' The italics here, as elsewhere in quotations from Alford, are his own. The questions raised by this note are too important and far-reaching in their effects to be dismissed without careful consideration. He admits that it is 'a description to them of their altered situation with reference to the world without,' but he adds that it is also 'a declaration that self-defence and self-provision would henceforward be necessary.' The introduction of the word 'henceforward' transforms the saying into a permanent rule of life, which Alford regards as applicable to the apostles and to Christians generally throughout all time. But the word used by Jesus was not 'henceforward' but 'now,' being the Greek *nun*, which occurs in 137 passages. In 122 it is translated, in the Authorised Version, 'now'; in 4 'this time'; in 5 'present' or 'this'; in 6 'henceforth' or 'hereafter,' and all these last 6 are literally 'from now.' The addition of the 'from,' justifies the rendering in those cases, but there is no justification for Alford's 'henceforward.' A review of all the passages makes it obvious that the word 'now' must be understood in precisely the contrary sense to that of 'henceforward': the term is restrictive, denoting the present time or emergency, and excluding the future altogether. A moment of crisis had come, overthrowing for the time being all previous arrangements; and the strong language of Jesus appears to have been designedly chosen with the view of making the apostles realise the imminence of the difficulties and dangers with which they were threatened. Beyond that it ought not to be pressed. But Alford says: 'It forms a decisive testimony from the mouth of the Lord Himself, against the views of the Quakers and some other sects on these points.' The fact that the saying proceeded 'from the mouth of the Lord Himself,' is good ground for believing that it must be so interpreted as not to clash with his previous and solemnly reiterated teachings. Alford seems to regard it as either rescinding or modifying them. Is it reasonable to suppose that the precise instructions given at various times by Jesus to his disciples were so worded as to be of dubious meaning, so strange in their form and tenour as to mislead 'Quakers and some other sects,' and that their true import and limitations are only to be demonstrated by this casual passage recorded by one of the evangelists only? Surely Jesus did not speak with two voices, laying upon his disciples a certain principle of action to be adhered to only so long as he was with them in the world, and then, in almost the last hour of his life, withdrawing what he had all along insisted on, and calling them back from his own heavenly-minded teachings to conformity with the maxims and practice of the world! The inference drawn by Alford and others from this saying of Jesus amounts to that, and nothing less: they in fact regard it as explaining away and utterly abolishing all that went before, and as placing the apostles thenceforth on the same level of action as the rest of mankind. A few 'Quakers and some other sects' have honestly given a full, literal construction to the peculiar and startling precepts of Jesus with respect to oath-taking and non-resistance, but such views of Christian duty are generally regarded as visionary, inapplicable, unworkable, and are therefore by an immense majority utterly ignored. Some portions of the Sermon on the Mount are really a standing, unsolved puzzle to mankind: our common sense assures us that the world at large cannot adopt such maxims, that any attempt to carry them out thoroughly by all would lead to confusion worse confounded ; and this passing allusion of Jesus to the taking of a purse, scrip, sandals and a sword, is laid hold of as a godsend, a heaven-sent demonstration of the erroneous literalism of interpretation given by a few 'sects' in opposition to the teachings of the Church, to those counsels of Jesus which his apostles certainly understood in their plain, unvarnished sense, adopted as their future course of action, and perseveringly adhered to to their lives' end. A right conception of 'discipleship' supplies the clue to the true import and bearing of those commands which were designed by Jesus for the guidance of his own, whom he had chosen out of the world, and which are undoubtedly too high for the grasp, and altogether unsuited to the duties and positions of ordinary men and women. We must place the 'multitude of them that believe' on a lower level of obligation, in order that the smaller body of professed 'disciples' who have first counted the cost and resolved to forsake all else for the gospel's sake, may carry out unreservedly, to the full, both in the spirit and to the letter, the sublime instructions of their Founder. But now a time had come when his name would be held in execration, and his apostles be compelled to lay aside all thought of conforming to his precepts : 'For I say unto you, that this which is written must be fulfilled in me, And he was reckoned with transgressors.' The Revisers have ommitted 'yet' after 'must,' on the authority of the three oldest MSS. The quotation is from Isaiah : 'He poured out his soul unto death, and was numbered with the transgressors.' Jesus himself was about to die as a criminal, and such a crisis would seem to threaten the overthrow of his scheme and method of evangelisation : 'For that which concerneth me hath fulfilment (Gr. end).' The Revisers have followed the two oldest MSS. in substituting 'that' for 'the things.' Alford notes that 'most ancient authorities read *the matter concerning me*,' and states : '*hath an end* does not merely mean *must be fulfilled*, which would be an assertion without any reference here.' The rendering of the Revisers, 'hath fulfilment,' is anything but synonymous with 'hath an end.' Alford says, apparently by way of explanation : 'The prophecy cited closes the section of Isaiah, which eminently predicts the Lord's suffering.' That is neither clear nor satisfactory, and cannot be accepted as the proper sense. The reversal of the plan of action of Jesus, the return of his apostles to the ordinary routine of life, was equivalent to the ending of all that related to himself, the annihilation of his influence in the world. Jesus couples the two things together : the forsaking of his precepts with the ruin of his cause. Had this foreseen, this enforced departure from his system, been other than temporary, the collapse would have been complete and final ; if the apostles had not only 'now' but 'henceforth' and permanently placed their dependence upon money and arms, they would have become merged with the world around them, and their Master's doctrine and salvation would have ended for ever with his life. Such an ending of his power and his gospel comes to pass whenever and wherever this fundamental principle of action is abandoned by his disciples, or when disciples do not exist who both profess and practise it. Avarice and force are the chief controlling factors in the history and government of the world, apart from Christianity; and the spirit of the gospel can only be maintained and propagated by living witnesses and examples of its precepts. Where they fail to appear, the form and name and profession of Christianity may continue to exist, but its power is lost: we have a mock gospel of peace, which allows war, a salvation unrealised, far off, and which is simply a hope for the next world because its attainment is so hopeless in this.

It is scarcely to be wondered at that the apostles failed to understand the allusion of Jesus to 'a sword,' just as they had once before misunderstood when he told them to beware of the 'leaven of the Pharisees.' 'And they said, Lord (Sir—Young), behold here are two swords.' It was no time for entering into explanations; the precious moments were fleeting, and the mind of Jesus was full of other thoughts. He dismissed their comment in two words. 'And he said unto them, It is enough.' Alford says: 'Our Lord breaks off the matter with *It is enough,*—not *they are sufficient*, but *It is well—we are sufficiently provided,—it was not to this that My words referred.* The rebuke is parallel with, though milder than, the one in Mark viii. 17, as the misunderstanding was somewhat similar.' Does not Alford here refute himself? He began by assuming that the mention of a sword was a declaration of the necessity for self-defence, and he ends by admitting that it was not to this the words of Jesus referred.

22 Luke 38
" 38

Jesus exhorted his disciples to shake off all anxiety, and to place their confidence in God and himself. 'Let not your heart be troubled: ye believe (or, believe) in God, believe also in me.' He directed their thoughts to a heavenly home: 'In my Father's house are many mansions (or, abiding-places).' The idea conveyed seems to be identical with that in one of the Psalms of David, which was probably familiar to them all. It begins:

14 John 1
" 2

'The LORD is my light and my salvation, whom shall I fear?
The LORD is the strength of my life; of whom shall I be afraid?
When evil-doers came upon me to eat up my flesh,
Even mine adversaries and my foes, they stumbled and fell.
Though an host should encamp against me,
My heart shall not fear:
Though war should rise against me,
Even then will I be confident.'

27 Ps. 1
" 2
" 3

That answers to the frame of mind: 'Let not your heart be troubled: believe in God, believe also in me.' The Psalm continues:

'One thing have I asked of the LORD, that will I seek after;
That I may dwell in the house of the LORD all the days of my life,
To behold the beauty of the LORD, and to inquire in his temple.'

" 4

That answers to: 'In my Father's house are many abiding-places.' Jesus would have them regard themselves as ministers dwelling in the house of God, under the divine protection, safe in his temple from the malice of their foes, and able to say:

'For in the day of trouble he shall keep me secretly in his pavilion:
In the covert of his tabernacle shall he hide me.'

" 5

Not for an instant would Jesus hold out to them any false hope. 'If it were not so, I would have told you.' Young instead of 'if it were not so' renders: 'but if not;' Tischendorf: 'otherwise.' Yet not to this world only or chiefly did the saying apply. Jesus added: 'for I go to prepare a place for you.' The word 'for' has been inserted on the authority of the three oldest MSS. Alford notes: 'It is *a place*, not the *many mansions* that He is preparing: *the place* as a whole, not *each man's place* in it.' Sharpe renders 'mansions' as 'chambers;' the 'Englishman's Greek New Testament' as 'abodes:' the allusion seems to be to the chambers or abodes of the priests in the temple. With these before their minds' eyes, the apostles would understand the words of Jesus as pointing to a special sphere of duty, assured rest and peace in the performance of their prescribed work of God for men in the world; so that the mention of 'a place' to be prepared for them elsewhere would naturally convey the idea of an appointed work for them, to be inaugurated by Jesus. The apostle Paul used the same word 'place' (*topon*) in that sense: 'now, having no more any place in these regions.' From the first Jesus had appointed the apostles 'that they might be with him, and that he might send them forth to preach.' Their active career on earth was now about to begin; their Master was on the point of leaving them, to enter himself upon another life, and prepare for them another field of action. His declaration to that effect must be taken to imply the necessity and certainty of reunion. 'And if I go and prepare a place for you, I come again, and will receive you unto myself; that where I am, *there* ye may be also.' The Revisers, agreeing with Young and Tischendorf, have omitted 'will' before 'come.' The 'Englishman's Greek New Testament' renders 'am coming:' the purpose of his departure indicated his intention of returning. We must bear in mind that Jesus was addressing his small chosen band of fellow-labourers, and that their common dedication to his cause was the sole ground of their union with him and with each other. To apply the promise here spoken to them collectively to Christians generally, and to each individual Christian in every age and country, is simply to misapply, exaggerate, distort the words of Jesus. The hope, the grace, the salvation proclaimed in his name to all, are wide enough and sure enough for all, without any such perversion of discourses and assurances vouchsafed specially to the eleven apostles. Who am I, who art thou, that either of us should presume to appropriate to himself or herself all that was uttered privately in their ears in this night of their Lord's betrayal? 'The glorious company of the apostles praise thee:' that may be a right deduction from this promise, which relates to them, and in no way belongs to others. Jesus continued: 'And whither I go, ye know the way.' The Revisers have adopted that reading of the two oldest MSS., noting that 'many ancient authorities read, *And* whither I go ye know, and the way ye know.' The mention of a 'way' involves the idea of a journey, a certain line of progress to be followed. Not by any sudden, involuntary, supernatural translation, could the apostles hope to be placed again by their Master's side, but by pursuing their appointed course of action. But whither Jesus was about to go, they knew not, and in the absence of that knowledge it seemed strange to bid them follow him. One of the apostles gave utterance to that thought: 'Thomas saith unto him, Lord (Sir— Young), we know not whither thou goest; how know we the way?' The Revisers have adopted the reading of the Vatican MS. The Authorised Version has: 'how can we know?' and Young: 'how are we able to know?' 'Jesus saith unto him, I am the way, and the truth, and the life.' To reach the goal of Jesus, the place he spoke of, they must be what he was, they must cling to the truth he taught, they must live the life he lived on earth. He added: 'No one cometh unto the Father, but by (or, through) me.' The word 'cometh' continues the idea of walking in a particular direction, after the example of Jesus, that through him we may reach the Father. Yet this approach to the Father is not connected with the previous promise, 'I come again, and will receive you unto myself; that where I am, *there* ye may be also.' That related to the future, this to the present: it is not, 'no one will come,' hereafter, but, 'no one cometh,' now or at any time. The apostle Paul regarded this coming to the Father as possible and realised both by Jews and Gentiles in this life. He wrote: 'Through him (Christ Jesus) we both have our access in one Spirit to the Father.' Jesus goes on to explain that the knowledge and sight of himself were the mode of their intercourse with and vision of the Father. 'If ye had known me, ye would have known my Father also: from henceforth ye know him, and have seen him.' That declaration harmonises with the doctrine enunciated by the Baptist: 'No man hath seen God at any time; the only begotten Son, which is in the bosom of the Father, he hath declared *him*'; and with Paul's conception of God: 'whom no man hath seen, nor can see.' Jesus told the Samaritan woman that 'God is spirit,' and that the Father must be worshipped in spirit and truth; no locality helps or hinders our approach to him, 'neither in this mountain, nor in Jerusalem,' neither in earth nor in heaven. Instead of, 'if ye had known me, ye would have known my Father also,' Tischendorf adopts the reading of the oldest MS., 'if ye have known me, ye will know my Father also'; the relationship is that of cause and effect, as appears from the following words, which are rendered by Young, 'and from this time,'—of seeing and knowing me,—'ye have known him, and have seen him.' Still Philip did not clearly grasp the truth. 'Philip saith unto him, Lord (Sir—Young), shew us the Father, and it sufficeth us.' Young renders: 'it is enough for us': enough in the way of demonstration and conviction was probably what Philip meant. But if they craved for a material manifestation and embodiment of the heavenly Father, what better one could be presented or desired than the personality of Jesus himself? He was the appointed revelation and representation of the Father to mankind. A voice from heaven had attested, 'This is my beloved Son'; it was not for them to desire, nor for him to grant, a reversal of the divine procedure, to point to some visible presentment of Deity, and say, This is my loving Father. All they could see and know of him must be through the person and character of Jesus. 'Jesus saith unto him, Have I been so long time with you, and dost thou not know me, Philip?' The Revisers, agreeing with Young and Alford, have rendered 'hast thou not known me?' by 'dost thou not know me?' Their intercourse with Jesus had been equivalent to intercourse with his Father. 'He that hath seen me hath seen the Father; how sayest thou, Shew us the Father?' The Revisers have omitted 'and' before 'how,' on the authority of the two oldest MSS., and after 'thou' the word 'then,' which Alford explains is 'not in the original.' Long before, Jesus had declared the same truth: 'No one knoweth who the Son is, save the Father; and who the Father is, save the Son, and he to whomsoever the Son willeth to reveal him.' Between Jesus and the Father there was such an entire identity of character and purpose, that to know one was to comprehend the other, and to be ignorant of either was to be ignorant of both. No superficial meaning of the terms 'see' and 'know' can answer to the stress laid upon them by Jesus. No mere passing glance, no gaze however long and fixed can reveal the inner man; no casual acquaintance in the way of ordinary intercourse, no recognition by form and feature, can constitute knowledge of any person, much less of Jesus. Only by his deeds and words was he truly manifested; and they were interpreted according to the state of mind of those who saw and heard them. Some thought that his miracles were devilish, and his doctrine blasphemous. Of the Jews Jesus said: 'Now have they both seen and hated both me and my Father.' Others were of the very opposite opinion, recognising in his teaching and career the signs of divine power and love. Jesus could confidently appeal to the faith of Thomas: 'Believest thou not that I am in the Father, and the Father in me?' Not in any such sense as that of the Athanasian Creed, but in the spirit of his life-work. 'The words that I say unto you I speak not from myself: but the Father abiding in me doeth his works.' The Revisers have altered 'the works' to 'his works,' in accordance with the two oldest MSS. The expression here used by Jesus must not be interpreted as bearing upon the doctrine of the Trinity subsequently formulated by theologians. The apostle John employed very similar words as applicable to Christians generally: 'He that keepeth his commandments abideth in him, and he in him. And hereby we know that he abideth in us, by the Spirit which he gave us.' And again: 'If we love one another, God abideth in us.' Jesus continued: 'Believe me that I am in the Father, and the Father in me: or else believe me for the very works' sake.' Young, agreeing with the 'Englishman's Greek New Testament,' renders literally: 'but if not, because of the works themselves believe me.' Jesus had before used the same argument to the Jews: 'The works that I do in my Father's name, these bear witness of me.' Yet in saying this, Jesus claimed not for himself any divinity or prerogative above others who, receiving him and through him would become Sons of God like himself. He added: 'Verily, verily, I say unto you, He that believeth on me, the works that I do shall he do also.' Young renders: 'He that believeth on me,' as 'he who is believing in me.' They who have such confidence in Jesus as to accept him for Teacher and Leader will work in his spirit, with the same object and the same results. The intrinsic character of the works, as manifestations of the Father in man and for man, is pointed at, rather than their miraculousness in the eyes of men; yet that also is not excluded: whatever Jesus did, and more than he did, is feasible by his followers: 'And greater *works* than these shall he do;

because I go unto the Father.' 'My Father' is altered to 'the
Father,' on the authority of the three oldest MSS. We are told
that the age of miracles is past; which is true historically, and must
continue so, until the age of faith shall come. Jesus not only
performed miracles, but imparted to his disciples the same power.
It lies within the compass of our nature, yet something hinders.
Jesus could always exercise it; the first disciples did so occasionally; there have been aspirants and imitators, but the secret is lost,
and the earliest records of miracles are now rejected by unbelievers
equally with those of later times. Whoever would do a mighty 9 Mark 39
work in Christ's name must first place himself in the same position
as that in which Jesus lived in this world, yielding implicit, entire
obedience to his precepts: this, not in order to perform miracles,
but for his name's sake, leaving the miracles to follow or not,
as the Spirit may dictate and human needs require. Jesus
characterised his miracles as 'good works': 'Many good works have 10 John 32
I shewed you from the Father.' Instead of such miraculous powers
decreasing and gradually dying out, they ought to have increased
both in number and importance after and in consequence of his
ascension. Their paucity, or entire absence, is attributable to the
want of faith, either in the world or in the church or in both; even
Jesus in his own country 'could there do no mighty work, save that 6 Mark 5
he laid his hands upon a few sick folk and healed them. And he   ,, 6
marvelled because of their unbelief.' After his resurrection, the
preaching and working of his gospel were first opposed and then perverted. He seems to have considered its ultimate success, in the
hands of men and apart from himself, as very doubtful, for he once
dropped the observation: 'When the Son of man cometh, shall he 18 Luke 8
find faith on the earth?' We must not limit the gospel of Christ, its
doctrines, its influence, its effects, to that manifestation or imitation
of it which has descended down to this nineteenth century. We see
what it is, not what it might be and should be; we know it as men
have made it, not as Jesus designed it. His scheme of action for the
regeneration of mankind has become distorted, entangled with the
policy and methods of the world; and the problem of our age is how
to revive the ideal conception of Christianity, how to separate its
heavenly doctrines from their earthly incrustations. Its success is
limited, deferred, thwarted, not by any mysterious procrastination in
the divine purposes of mercy to mankind, not by any lack of inherent
power in the gospel, not by any deliberate withdrawal of efficient aid
on the part of our ascended Saviour, but by our own failure,—
intellectual, moral, spiritual,—to grasp, hold fast and transmit to our
descendants the true, pure, simple gospel preached by Jesus and his
apostles. Whatever help, natural or supernatural, is needful for its
proclamation, he undertook to supply: 'And whatsoever ye shall ask 14 John 13
in my name, that will I do, that the Father may be glorified in the
Son.' The gospel was first preached, as asserted by the apostle Peter,
'in the Holy Spirit sent forth from heaven.' That gift was simul- 1 1. Pet. 12
taneously and visibly bestowed on the twelve apostles: 'they were 2 Acts 4
all filled with the Holy Spirit;' and it was not restricted to them,
for we read that on another occasion 'the Holy Ghost fell on all 10 Acts 44
them which heard the word,' that 'on the Gentiles also was poured   ,, 45
out the gift of the Holy Ghost;' and Peter declared that 'the Holy 11 Acts 15

Ghost fell on them, even as on us at the beginning.' Why did those supernatural spiritual manifestations cease? Why did the power of working miracles depart? Why does the promise of Jesus find no fulfilment now: 'He that believeth on me, the works that I do shall he do also?' Why, but because the method of Jesus has been departed from, and therefore such things can no longer be granted, or even truly asked, in his name. 'Whatsoever ye shall ask in my name:' in those last three words lies the secret. 'In my name' is equivalent to 'for my cause,' 'as my representatives,' 'as followers of me,' 'as preachers of my gospel.' Compare his precepts with our practices, and say whether men, clergy and laity alike, have not mistaken his cause, misrepresented his teachings, professed to follow him after a fashion different from that set by himself and his apostles, preached another gospel,—of formulated theological dogmas, another kingdom of heaven, restricted to the next world and unrealisable in this. We have lost sight of his aims, we have departed from his prescribed mode of life, we have mingled the policy of the world with his heavenly-minded maxims: can we wonder that we no longer feel or discern the presence and working of his Spirit? 'These signs shall follow them that believe:' the signs have ceased because the faith has failed. To the promise, 'Whatsoever ye shall ask in my name, that will I do,' is annexed the qualification, 'that the Father may be glorified in the Son.' The things asked and granted must tend to the honour of the fatherly character of God, and accord with the system laid down by Jesus for the guidance of his followers. If his promised aid is not forthcoming, it must be because he is not supplicated aright, with due regard to his conditions. Jesus repeated the promise: 'If ye shall ask me anything in my name, that will I do.' The Revisers have inserted the word 'me,' with the note that it is omitted by many ancient authorities. It is not in either of the three oldest MSS. 'I will do *it*' has been altered to 'that will I do,' in accordance with the Vatican and Alexandrine MSS. Alford notes that in the original the 'I' is emphatic: 'I myself.' The clause 'in my name' is repeated by Jesus, and restricts the application to missionary enterprise: the promise has no connection with the personal wants and wishes of any man, except so far as he may be engaged in the cause and work of Jesus.

The discourse continues: 'If ye love me, ye will keep my commandments.' The words 'ye will' have been added by the Revisers and by Tischendorf, agreeing with the Vatican MS. The saying constitutes a definition by Jesus himself of the meaning to be attached to the word 'love.' Love is not, as we are apt to conceive it, a sentiment, a mental emotion, the feeling engendered by our cogitations on the divine Being; it must never be dissociated from action. The apostle John seized and retained this idea, and handed it down in his epistle as an axiom: 'This is the love of God, that we keep his commandments: and his commandments are not grievous.' The expression 'my commandments' must obviously have reference to those directions which are peculiar to the teaching of Jesus, including those doctrines of non-resistance to evil and of voluntary poverty which he imposed upon his disciples. Our love to him must take that direction, if it exists at all, and thereby becomes an exhibition of his own course of action: 'We love, because he first loved us:' the life of discipleship, which is the only true Christian life, is the effect and imitation of Christ's life: 'Herein is love made perfect with us . . . because as he is, even so are we in this world.' Apart from such discipleship, our professed 'love' of Jesus is mere verbiage and sentimentalism: we confound 'gratitude' with 'love,' and mistake the former for the latter. Love to Jesus, in its perfection, is supreme and entire devotion to his cause; and when that is forsaken or mistaken, either wholly or partially, our boast of loving him degenerates, more or less, in proportion to our neglect of his commands, into a delusion or a sham. The coldness or fervency of our love is determined by the standard of obedience, not by any self-measurement of our changeful moods and emotions. Each man takes up love to Christ to the same degree as he yields homage to Christ's precepts. He taught us to distinguish between loving him much and loving him little, and Paul prayed for the Philippians, 'that your love may abound yet more and more.' A passage in one of his epistles seems to be misunderstood by some: 'If any man love not the Lord, let him be anathema. Maran atha (This is, Our Lord cometh).' Alford explains that *Maran-atha* is an Aramaic expression for *the Lord cometh*, and is probably unconnected with *Anathema*.' Young and Tischendorf agree with the Revisers in separating the words, which are connected in the Authorised Version. The word 'anathema' occurs also in the following passage: 'For I could wish that I myself were anathema from Christ for my brethren's sake.' The term, as is obvious from the context, is equivalent to excommunication, separation or estrangement from Christ; so that the dictum, 'If any man love not the Lord, let him be anathema,' carries the same meaning as, 'If ye love me, ye will keep my commandments:' there can be no love of Christ, no union with him in any other way. Jesus continued: 'And I will pray (Gr. make request of) the Father, and he shall give you another Comforter (or, Advocate, or Helper, Gr. Paraclete), that he may abide with you for ever, *even* the Spirit of truth.' The word 'and' at the beginning of this verse indicates its connection with the preceding one: the promised prayer of Jesus and bestowal of the Spirit are contingent upon the loving obedience of the disciples: if they adhered to his instructions, he would procure for them this gift. The Revisers, following the two oldest MSS., have altered 'abide with you' to 'be with you.' Young renders 'for ever'—'unto the age.' Tischendorf renders Paraclete as 'advocate.' Alford quotes Olshausen's remark that 'the interpretations of this word range themselves in *two classes*, which again by no means exclude one another: those of *Comforter*, and those of *Advocate*. The etymology of the word requires the *latter* as its strict meaning.' Alford adds that '*Comforter* has been both here and in Germany (Luther has the equivalent term) sanctioned by Christian usage as the most adequate rendering. Wicliff, from whom we have our word *Comforter*, often used *comfort* for the Latin *confortari*, which means to strengthen, as e.g. Luke xxii. 43; Acts ix. 19, &c. Thus the idea of *help and strength* is conveyed by it, as well as of consolation.' To this it must be replied that, in modern usage, the words advocacy and comfort are quite distinct, and therefore the term Comforter should be replaced by Advocate. The allusion to 'another advocate' implies that Jesus also was their advocate: 'I will make request of

4 i. John 17

7 Luke 47
1 Phil. 9

16 i. Cor. 22

9 Rom. 2

14 John 16

the Father.' The God-given Spirit would be in them a ceaseless invocation of divine help and favour. Only disciples would be able to receive that Spirit, whom mankind in general could neither contemplate nor comprehend: 'Whom the world cannot receive; for it beholdeth him not, neither knoweth him.' But the disciples would be intimate with him, and he with them: 'Ye know him; for he abideth with you, and shall be in you.' The Revisers have omitted the word 'but' before 'ye,' on the authority of the two oldest MSS. Alford notes that many ancient authorities have 'is' instead of 'shall be.' The Vatican MS. reads 'is.' The three verses are translated by Samuel Sharpe as follows: 'If ye love me, keep my commands. And I will pray the Father, and he will give you another comforter (or, advocate), that he may abide with you till the end of the age; the spirit of truth, which the world cannot receive, because it seeth it not, nor knoweth it; but ye know it, for it dwelleth with you and will be in you.' The passage is made to assume a different complexion by the omission of capital letters from 'spirit, comforter' and 'advocate,' and by the adoption of 'which' and 'it' instead of 'whom' and 'he.' It must be admitted that, apart from theological preconceptions, it is quite consonant with the genius of our language to adopt the neuter form in speaking of the spirit by which the disciples would be animated. It is impossible to attach the idea of personality to the term 'spirit' in every instance where it occurs. This is evident from the following passages, if only we disregard the arbitrary capitalisation of the word. 'The law of the spirit of life in Christ Jesus made me free from the law of sin and of death.' 'But we received not the spirit of the world, but the spirit which is of God.' 'Being absent in body but present in spirit.' 'He that is joined unto the Lord is one spirit.' 'In one spirit were we all baptized into one body . . . and were all made to drink of one spirit.' 'I will pray with the spirit, and I will pray with the understanding also: I will sing with the spirit, and I will sing with the understanding also.' 'Not of the letter, but of the spirit: for the letter killeth, but the spirit giveth life.' 'Having the same spirit of faith.' 'Or if ye receive a different spirit, which ye did not receive, or a different gospel, which ye did not accept.' 'Walked we not by the same spirit? *walked we* not in the same steps?' 'If we live by the spirit, by the spirit let us also walk.' 'He that soweth unto the spirit shall of the spirit reap eternal life.' 'Be not drunken with wine, wherein is riot, but be filled with the spirit.' There is a passage which in the Authorised Version stands thus: 'The Spirit itself maketh intercession for us,' where the Revisers have altered 'itself' to 'himself.' The word 'itself' may perhaps have been no more intended to obviate the idea of a personality than the word 'which' in 'Our Father which art in heaven.' It should be immaterial to us whether the masculine or neuter form is adopted, or the words 'father' and 'spirit' are capitalised or not: those adventitious aids to translation simply indicate the views of the translators. Sharpe's rendering of the passage and its context is as follows: 'In like wise the spirit also helpeth our weaknesses; for we know not what we should pray for as we ought; but the spirit itself intercedeth for us with unspoken groans. And he who searcheth the hearts knoweth what is the mind of the spirit, that by God's will it intercedeth for the saints.' Is not that the office of an 'advocate' as alluded to by Jesus in the words, 'I will make request of the Father, and he shall give you another advocate, that he may be with you for ever, *even* the Spirit of truth?' The spirit within us, by which we are animated, and which is known to God who searches our hearts, is the only true prayer which man can offer: 'They that worship Him must worship Him in spirit and in truth:' and *that, it, he*—call it what you will—that spirit, its longings and unformulated desires, like those of an infant crying for its food, appeal to the heart of the heavenly Father for the supply of the necessities growing out of that new nature developed and developing in his 'saints,' his 'sons,' God having 'sent forth the Spirit of his Son into our hearts, crying, Abba, Father.' The Scriptural revelations with respect to the holy Spirit have no connection with any dogma relating to God and a Trinity of persons in the Godhead; yet the frequent texts in which mention is made of the spirit have been used by translators and expounders as so many pivots on which to hang and turn that doctrine. Men deem it right to introduce the notion of a personality, by writing 'Spirit' with a capital, but the sense of that term must be determined in every instance by the context, and to use capitals in some cases and not in others, as is done in the Authorised and Revised and other Versions, is not the way to ensure a right interpretation or to arrive at the truth. Take this definition of Paul: 'The spirit is life because of righteousness;' and this of John: 'It is the spirit that beareth witness, because the spirit is the truth.' The spirit is—life, righteousness,—and the spirit is—truth: by them 'Christ is in' us. In the Authorised Version the word 'spirit' is capitalised in both passages; but in the Revised Version in the latter only. If capitals were omitted everywhere, readers would naturally and properly be called upon to exercise their own independent judgment, as the Revisers evidently did in this instance. Tischendorf discards capitals in the first passage, but introduces them into the second, although in the very next verse he omits capitals in 'they that bear witness are three, the spirit, and the water, and the blood.' Samuel Sharpe puts no capitals, thereby not dictating the proper sense, but leaving it open for those who will seek and can grasp it. All that the apostles and first Christians knew about the Spirit was learnt by them not doctrinally but experimentally: 'to each one' was 'given the manifestation of the spirit to profit withal.' The spirit imparted to them may be properly described as an energy, an influence, a power, bestowed supernaturally, in connection with some occult laws of attraction, volition, self-development. It would seem that this spirit lies round about us, an impregnative principle of thought, life, action, which they only can receive who so believe in Jesus as to adopt his precepts and devote themselves to his cause: 'whom the world cannot receive; for it beholdeth him not, neither knoweth him: ye know him; for he abideth with you, and shall be in you.'

[4 Gal. 6]
[8 Rom. 10]
[5 i. John 7]
[8 Rom. 10]
[12 i. Cor. 7]

Jesus continued: 'I will not leave you desolate (or, orphans): I come unto you.' The Authorised Version has 'comfortless,' now replaced by 'desolate (or, orphans).' Young, Tischendorf, Luther and Alford render 'orphans,' which the latter explains is the literal translation of the original word—*orphanous*. The Revisers have omitted 'will' before 'come,' as do Young and Luther. Tischendorf

[11 John 18]

and the 'Englishman's Greek New Testament' render 'I am coming.' Alford states that 'I am going' is the literal rendering. In a little time Jesus would be away from the observation of the world, yet he would not that his apostles should regard him as dead, and themselves left without his presence. He and they would still be alive and together, he 'coming' or 'going' to them. 'Yet a little while, and the world beholdeth me no more; but ye behold me: because I live, ye shall live also (or, and ye shall live).' Young renders, 'and ye shall live.' The next words of Jesus obviate the idea of any corporeal presence: 'In that day ye shall know that I am in my Father, and ye in me, and I in you.' That threefold union could only be brought about in one way: 'He that hath my commandments, and keepeth them, he it is that loveth me: and he that loveth me shall be loved of my Father, and I will love him, and will manifest myself unto him.' Instead of 'keepeth them,' Young has, 'is keeping them:' there must be a life devoted to the cause of Jesus; the promise is contingent upon obedient discipleship, which alone can bring men into perfect harmony and union with him and the Father. There is no 'beholding' of Jesus, no true knowledge of him apart from that. But was he not the Messiah, and how could the manifestation of him be restricted to disciples, and not granted to mankind generally? One of the apostles gave utterance to the objection. 'Judas (not Iscariot) saith unto him, Lord (Sir—Young), what is come to pass that thou wilt manifest thyself unto us, and not unto the world?' The Authorised Version has 'how is it' instead of 'what is come to pass.' Alford notes that some ancient authorities read 'and how is it,' and adds, 'we may remark that *and*, preceding an interrogation, expresses astonishment at what has just been said, and, assuming it, connects to it a conclusion which appears to refute or cast doubt on it—*how is it that*, literally, *what has happened*, that ...?' Young renders: 'Why hath it come to pass, that to us thou art about to manifest thyself, and not to the world?' Tischendorf and the 'Englishman's Greek New Testament' also have 'art about to manifest' instead of 'wilt manifest.' Jesus simply repeated his statement, as if not admitting that there was to be any other kind of manifestation: 'Jesus answered and said unto him, If a man love me, he will keep my word: and my Father will love him, and we will come unto him, and make our abode with him.' Young, Tischendorf and the 'Englishman's Greek New Testament' render 'man' as 'any one:' the revelation would be granted without respect of persons, being entirely contingent upon loving obedience, which would ensure the closest conceivable union with Jesus and his Father: 'we will come unto him, and make our abode with him.' On the other hand, those persons who loved not Jesus would not live by his precepts, which were in truth dictated by the Father. 'He that loveth me not keepeth not my words: and the word which ye hear is not mine, but the Father's who sent me.' To them there could be no possibility of such manifestation or communion. The directions, commands, 'words' or 'things,'—the terms appear to be equivalent,—had been already delivered to them by Jesus. 'These things have I spoken unto you, while *yet* abiding with you.' The italicised word 'yet' appears to be superfluous: Young renders literally, 'remaining with you,' Tischendorf, 'while abiding with you.' But the commands already given needed to be impressed upon them, not merely heard but learnt ; and this teaching would be supplied to them by the promised Spirit. 'But the Comforter (or, Advocate, or, Helper, Gr. Paraclete), *even* the Holy Spirit, whom the Father will send in my name, he shall teach you all things, and bring to your remembrance all that I said unto you.' Young renders : 'and remind you of all things I said to you.' The word 'remind' is not quite the same as 'bring to your remembrance,' which seems to be understood as a strengthening of the natural memory. Alford says : 'It is on the fulfilment of this promise to the Apostles, that their sufficiency as Witnesses of all that the Lord did and taught, and consequently *the authenticity of the Gospel narrative*, is grounded.' But the reference is to the doctrines and commands of Jesus, their import and obligation, not the mere words and phrasing of his discourses : just as to 'remind' one of all the injunctions of a departed friend, would not signify a precise verbal recollection of every utterance, but of their scope and binding character. Samuel Sharpe's translation of this verse is as follows : 'But the Comforter, the Holy Spirit, which the Father will send in my name, he will teach you all things, and remind you of all that I have said to you.' Here the word 'which' appears in place of 'whom,' but the words Comforter, Holy and Spirit are capitalised, which was not the case in verse 16. In the absence of any explanation of this difference, it is only fair to assume that it was based upon some principle, in order to ascertain which, the 94 passages containing the word 'holy' in conjunction with 'ghost' or 'spirit' have been examined. The following 11 passages are the only ones in which Sharpe has capitalised those words. 'She was found with child of the Holy Spirit.' 'What is conceived in her is of the Holy Spirit.' 'Whoever speaketh against the Holy Spirit, it will not be forgiven him,' and the corresponding passages in Mark and Luke. 'The Holy Spirit will teach you in that hour what ye ought to say.' 'The Comforter, the Holy Spirit, which the Father will send in my name, he will teach you all things, and remind you of all that I have said to you.' 'Well spake the Holy Spirit through Isaiah the prophet about our fathers.' 'Therefore, as the Holy Spirit saith.' 'The Holy Spirit signifying this.' 'And the Spirit also witnesseth for us.' In these comparatively few exceptions it will be observed that there is a kind of personification of the Holy Spirit, human actions being attributed to or done against him or it. In such cases only has Samuel Sharpe followed the lead of other translators, that evidently being the utmost extent to which he felt justified in adopting capitals as indicative of a divine personality. But it is open to question whether in each of these instances there is any good and sufficient reason for this departure from his ordinary practice. The angel Gabriel described the miracle performed upon the virgin Mary as the result of a spiritual influence or power : 'Holy spirit will come upon thee, and the power of highest will overshadow thee ; and therefore the holy offspring will be called Son of God.' Blasphemy may be committed against that which is not a person, for the apostle James wrote : 'Do not they blaspheme the honourable name by the which ye are called ?' The passage : 'They were not able to resist the wisdom and the spirit by which he spake,' should be sufficient to prove that allusions to the speaking of a spirit are not always necessarily to be understood as the speaking of a person. The Revisers have cast that passage into the mould of orthodoxy by capitalising the word 'spirit,' which is not done by Young, Tischendorf, Alford, Sharpe, or the 'Englishman's Greek New Testament;' obviously that word ought no more to be capitalised than the word 'wisdom,' the two being connected. In a thoroughly impartial translation there should be no such arbitrary introduction of capitals; they simply indicate the sense attributed by the translator to the passage in which they occur, and it is far better that the reader should be left free to seek the meaning for himself. Neither should he allow his mind to be influenced by the use of pronouns in the masculine or neuter form: where others apply 'he' to the spirit, Sharpe adopts the word 'it.' These are simply conventional modes of expression, and should not be taken as settling the real nature of that to which they refer. The Authorised Version reads: 'The Spirit ITSELF maketh intercession for us,' but in the next verse: 'HE maketh intercession for the saints.' The Revisers have altered 'itself' to 'himself;' Sharpe has: 'the spirit itself intercedeth,' and 'it intercedeth for the saints.'

The discourse of Jesus continues as follows: 'Peace I leave with you; my peace I give unto you.' Instead of 'with,' Young has 'to' and Tischendorf 'unto.' The word (*humin*) is the same after 'leave' as after 'give,' and should therefore be rendered in the same way. Peace, his own peace, was his bequest to his disciples: how different a legacy from that which was customary among men! 'Not as the world giveth, give I unto you:' not a peace founded upon self-defence and power for strife, nor one attributable to other men's silent contempt of their work and influence, but peace in the midst of opposition and persecution, for Jesus adds: 'Let not your heart be troubled, neither let it be fearful.' The Revisers have replaced 'afraid' by 'fearful,' which indicates an habitual tone of mind: with a heart untroubled and bold they could be calm and confident at all times. There is here the same ringing appeal to courage and devotion to his cause as in his former exhortation: 'I say unto you my friends, Be not afraid of them which kill the body, and after that have no more that they can do.' Their Master's approaching death by martyrdom involved no more than a temporary parting: 'Ye have heard how I said to you, I go away, and I come unto you.' The Revisers, agreeing with Young, Tischendorf and Alford, have omitted the italicised word 'again' after 'come.' Alford explaining that it is 'not expressed in the original.' Tischendorf renders: 'I am going away and coming unto you.' If the apostles had understood and regarded his own interest solely, they would have congratulated him upon his approaching departure to the Father. 'If ye loved me, ye would have rejoiced, because I go unto the Father.' The words, 'I said,' before 'I go,' are omitted on the authority of the three oldest MSS. As the reason and explanation of the implied advantage, Jesus adds: 'for the Father is greater than I.' Following the Vatican and Alexandrine MSS., the word 'the' now replaces 'my' before 'Father.' Young has 'because' instead of 'for.' In what sense, and with what application, is the word 'greater' to be understood? Jesus had previously used the term in the same connection: 'My Father, which hath given *them* unto me, is greater than all; and no one is able to snatch *them* out of the Father's hand.' The allusion there is to the greatness or power of God exerted on behalf of Jesus and his sheep. Adopting the same idea here, the connection of the saying with what precedes is obvious. The cause of Jesus would be strengthened by his departure from the world; and inasmuch as love to him was the keeping of his commands, that is, devotion to his cause, their love of him would dictate rejoicing over the fact of his ascension to the Father so mighty to guard and help. It was all for their benefit: he went that he might return to them in another way, by the holy spirit sent from the Father in his name: 'I am going away and coming unto you.' He had thus prepared them for his absence, and foretold its beneficial consequences, in order that when the shock of bereavement came, they might still have the same confidence in him as ever. 'And now I have told you before it come to pass, that, when it is come to pass, ye may believe.' The Revisers have altered 'might' to 'may,' agreeing with Alford, Young and Tischendorf. In the Authorised Version the next verse begins: 'Hereafter I will not talk much with you,' now altered to: 'I will no more speak much with you,' corresponding substantially with the same translators. The word 'hereafter' was open to misapplication: the 'Englishman's Greek New Testament' supplies its place by 'no longer.' Jesus explains the reason for this approaching and unusual reticence on his part: he was anticipating another and far different conference: 'for the prince of the world cometh.' Young and the 'Englishman's Greek New Testament' render 'prince' as 'ruler.' 'This world' is altered to 'the world,' on the authority of the three oldest MSS. The plural form of *archōn*, ruler, is used by Paul as denoting that combination of the military and priestly powers which compassed the death of Jesus: 'Which none of the rulers of this world knoweth: for had they known it, they would not have crucified the Lord of glory.' Peter also said: 'And now, brethren, I wot that in ignorance ye did it, as did also your rulers.' Alford notes: '*the prince of this world*, i.e. Satan: not Satan in Judas, but *Satan himself*, with whom the Lord was in conflict during his passion: see Luke iv. 13, and xxii. 53.' That seems somewhat too bold and peremptory. Paul in one place alludes to 'the god of this world (or, age),' but he works by blinding 'the minds of the unbelieving,' and through 'the principalities ... the powers ... the world-rulers of this darkness.' 'The prince of the world cometh: and he hath nothing in me.' The word 'he' has been introduced by the Revisers, and is in Young and the 'Englishman's Greek New Testament.' Probably there is in that saying a depth of meaning which we cannot fathom: yet we are not justified in assuming that it points to a direct conflict with Satan during the passion. We have no information on the point, nothing to indicate clearly any such spiritual struggle with the evil one, and it becomes us not to go beyond what is revealed to us. 'Of a truth in this city against thy holy Servant Jesus, whom thou didst anoint, both Herod and Pontius Pilate, with the Gentiles and the peoples of Israel, were gathered together:' that mustering of the world's forces is by itself a fulfilment of the words: 'the prince of this world cometh:' Satan works through his ministers. Alford explains that the words, 'and he hath nothing in me,' have been variously understood, 'as

Augustine, *findeth no sin in me.*' Alford adds: 'This is the only true interpretation: *has nothing in Me*—no point of appliance whereon to fasten his attack. But Meyer well observes, that this is rather *the fact to be assumed* as the *ground* of what is here said, than the *thing itself* which is said. Tholuck, and many others render it *has no power over me*, or as Euthymius, *finds nothing worthy of death.*' There is no reference in the words or context to any of these things,—temptation, sin, death or condemnation. The expression 'he has nothing in me,' taken by itself, denotes complete estrangement between the two, an utter absence of sympathy or identity of purpose, the prince of the world and Jesus brought face to face as opposing powers, thereby demonstrating the antagonism and irreconcilableness of their policy and principles. Jesus had brought into the world a new doctrine and mode of life; he manifested to mankind the course of action which would commend them to the favour of the heavenly Father, from whom he had received his authority and commission, and in accordance with whose will he spoke and acted. 'But that the world may know that I love the Father, and as the Father gave me commandment, even so I do.' Observe the inference which necessarily attaches to the words: 'that the world may know that I love the Father ... so I do.' Love, in the speech of Jesus, is inseparable from conduct: it is more than a sentiment, a mental emotion of affection,—for what could the world know about that in the heart of Jesus? Love, as defined by him, is in the life and actions, not merely in the brain and feelings.

At this point of the discourse Jesus gave the signal for departure, by saying, 'Arise, let us go hence.' Yet without any other break the narrative proceeds with two chapters of monologue, followed by a lengthy prayer. The Reverend J. J. Halcombe supposes that they left the supper chamber and went to a room elsewhere. He says: 'The near approach of Judas appearing to have been the immediate cause of Christ's leaving the Supper Chamber, the place at which the discourse was spoken was probably some house or room of which it could not be said, "And Judas which betrayed him knew the place."' The following suggestion of Alford appears more probable: 'These words imply a movement from the table to depart. Probably the rest of the discourse, and the prayer, ch. xvii., were delivered when now all were standing ready to depart. There would be some little pause, in which the preparations for departure would be made. But the *place* is clearly the same, see ch. xviii. 1, "when Jesus had spoken these words, He went forth:" besides which, we can hardly suppose, as Grotius and others, discourses of a character like those in ch. xv., xvi. to have been delivered to as many as eleven persons, while *walking by the way*, and in a time of such publicity as that of the Paschal feast.' These were veritable last words of Jesus. We can picture to ourselves the scene: the earnestness of the Speaker, and the strained, reverential attention of the disciples grouped round him in the quiet of the night. We must needs suppose, too, that one of them, probably John, was and had been noting down, as best he could, the words as they fell from the lips of Jesus. These and other discourses are too long to have been compiled from memory. It would be equally natural and proper that arrangements should be made by the disciples for preserving, day by day, some record of the sayings and doings of their Teacher; and there are supposed to be evidences of some such original document in that underlying verbal agreement which is common to the three Synoptic Gospels, and which, being extracted out of those narratives, is held to constitute the 'Common Tradition'* But the fourth gospel stands on a different footing. It was obviously prepared from other and fuller material, records which the other evangelists did not include in their narratives. Matthew, Mark and Luke relate the public and formal teaching and works of Jesus. John wrote with another object: chapter after chapter is filled with discourses of Jesus more or less private, or outside his public ministry and not reported elsewhere. Of the thirty-eight parables, three are recorded in two gospels, six in three gospels, the remainder in one gospel only, and not one in the fourth gospel. So that of the two narratives which have been handed down under apostolic names, that of Matthew embodies a large amount of the public teaching, entirely omitted by John, and that of John contains the inner teachings and deeper revelations of Jesus respecting himself and his work for mankind, one third of the narrative being 'occupied with the sayings and doings of the last twenty-four hours of his life.'† Yet Matthew did not record one half of the discourses delivered to the multitude, by far the most in number and importance of the parables being preserved to us through Luke's gospel only. It can scarcely be doubted that the Synoptics, if they had had at command the information supplied by John, would have incorporated it, or at least some portion of it, in their histories. We owe John's narrative to the fact, not that he remembered what others did not, but that he possessed material prepared by him at the time, which he afterwards collated and gave to the world. That presents itself as a reasonable explanation of the genesis and peculiarities of John's gospel. In 'Helps to the Study of the Bible' it is stated: 'His (John's) Gospel was written at the close of the first century, or beginning of the second, long after the others had become well known throughout Christendom. He had all of them before him: he supplemented what they had omitted, corrected false impressions formed by reading them, and gave the clue to their deeper interpretation. He indirectly refers to and corroborates much that they have recorded, but abstains from traversing the same ground.' That very positive statement appears to be purely imaginary. Alford, in his Introduction, wrote as follows: 'It belongs to the present section of our subject to enquire how far it may be supposed that John had seen or used the three other Gospels. I confess myself wholly unable to receive the supposition *that any of them, in their present form, had ever been seen by him*. On such a supposition, the phenomena presented by his Gospel would be wholly inexplicable .... In no part can it by the most ingenious application of the supplementary theory be shown, that he in any respect produces or aims at the effect of a work designed to fill up and elucidate those which have gone before.'

We come now to the last parable delivered by Jesus. 'I am the

* "The Common Tradition of the Synoptic Gospels."
† "Helps to the Study of the Bible."

true vine, and my Father is the husbandman.' The vine provides mankind with food, shade, refreshment, stimulus; but the application of the simile lies not in that direction. Jesus uses it to illustrate the connection between himself and his disciples. They must live and flourish conjointly: he the root and stem, they the branches growing out of him. Only through them can his life and spirit be developed, transformed into fruit visible, tangible, beneficial to humanity. If any one of them should become fruitless, that branch must fall beneath the stroke of divine Providence. 'Every branch in me that beareth not fruit, he taketh it away': a complete eradication. 'And every *branch* that beareth fruit, he cleanseth it, that it may bear more fruit.' Young renders this: 'And every one bearing fruit, He cleanseth by pruning it, that it may bear more fruit.' Union with Jesus involves divine oversight and interference: no branch in him is suffered to grow in the shape and direction it would have chosen for itself. It lives not for itself, but for the good of others; its tendrils, luxuriant, beautiful, natural though they be, must be pruned, trammelled, made subservient to the one object of fruit-bearing. Fit emblem this of that discipleship of which Jesus spoke the hard saying: 'If any man cometh unto me, and hateth not his own father, and mother, and wife, and children, and brethren, and sisters, yea, and his own life also, he cannot be my disciple.' This grand act of self-renunciation, this pruning, purging, cleansing process, had already been performed on the apostles: 'Already ye are clean because of the word which I have spoken unto you.' That word they had obeyed, and could say, 'Lo, we have left all, and have followed thee.' As they had begun, so they must continue. 'Abide in me, and I in you.' Only by close, continuous, entire obedience to his precepts and example could they accomplish the purpose for which he had chosen them out of the world. 'As the branch cannot bear fruit of itself, except it abide in the vine; so neither can ye, except ye abide in me.' He would have them lay hold of the simile in the way of self-application. 'I am the vine, ye are the branches.' If their union with him was perfect and permanent, their mission would be abundantly successful. 'He that abideth in me, and I in him, the same beareth much fruit.' No personal characteristics could ensure success; only by adhering to him, his plan and principles of action, could they gain power and influence: 'for apart from me ye can do nothing.' The Revisers have altered 'without' to 'apart from.' Young renders: 'because apart from me ye are not able to do anything.' Utter barrenness is the doom of any man who, having become incorporate with Jesus as a disciple, ceases to imbibe his spirit, relinquishes his mode of life, withers away from his influence and control, and so falls off into the world, adopting its maxims, customs, policy. 'If a man abide not in me, he is cast forth as a branch, and is withered.' Young renders: 'If any one may not remain in me, he was cast out as the branch, and was withered.' He thereby deteriorates from his high and heavenly calling, and is made to serve mankind's lower uses: 'and they gather them, and cast them into the fire, and they are burned.' Alford notes: 'He is gathered up with other such (Matt. xiii. 40) by the angels at the great day: is cast into the fire, as the result of that judgment, and finally *burneth*; not, *is burned*, in any sense of being *consumed; and must burn*, as Luther renders it.' But there is no mention of 'angels' or of 'judgment' here: the idea conveyed is simply that of becoming dead fuel for the world's fire, instead of living to bear fruit for the world's need. There are no limits to the success of those who continue in union with Jesus and steadfastly loyal to his instructions. 'If ye abide in me, and my words abide in you, ask whatsoever ye will, and it shall be done unto you.' Young renders: 'If ye remain in me, and my sayings in you remain, whatever ye wish ye shall ask, and it shall be done to you.' The Revisers, following the Vatican and Alexandrine MSS., have altered 'ye shall ask' to 'ask.' The desires of firm and faithful disciples must needs prevail, because their cause is the cause of God, and their success his glory. 'Herein is (or, was) my Father glorified, that ye bear much fruit; and *so* shall ye be my disciples.' The Revisers note: 'Many ancient authorities read, *that ye bear much fruit, and be my disciples*.' Alford reads and renders: 'and so shall ye become my disciples.' Young's rendering seems to meet both readings: 'In this was my Father glorified, that ye may bear much fruit, and ye shall become my disciples.' The Revisers have italicised the inserted word 'so,' which was not done in the Authorised Version. 15 John 7

,, 8

Jesus continues: 'Even as the Father hath loved me, I also have loved you.' The Revisers have introduced the word 'even,' and 'also' instead of 'so.' Young renders: 'According as the Father loved me, I also loved you.' This is in close connection with 'ask whatsoever ye will,' and 'that ye bear much fruit.' Jesus had previously spoken to the Father's love to himself, connecting it in the same way with powers and privileges. 'The Father loveth the Son, and hath given all things into his hand;' and again: 'For the Father loveth the Son, and sheweth him all things that himself doeth: and greater works than these will he shew him, that ye may marvel.' Love is indissolubly bound up with acts and gifts: the love of God to Jesus was manifested by giving all things into his hand, shewing him all things that himself did, and greater works than any actually exhibited to the world. The love of Jesus to his disciples was the same in kind and in effect: 'He that believeth on me, the works that I do shall he do also; and greater *works* than these shall he do; because I go unto the Father.' It rested with themselves whether that love, with all that appertained to it, which Jesus had bestowed on them, should continue. He counselled them: 'abide ye in my love.' That could only be in one way: by obedience to his precepts: 'If ye keep my commandments, ye shall abide in my love.' Their life and their experience would then resemble his own: 'even as I have kept my Father's commandments, and abide in his love.' That tallies with a previous declaration of Jesus, in which he attributes his works and words to his conformity to the Father's good pleasure: 'I do nothing of myself, but as the Father taught me, I speak these things. And he that sent me is with me; he hath not left me alone; for I do always the things that are pleasing to him.' On that depended the continuance of the power of Jesus, which was the testimony of the Father's love. So would it be with the apostles. Jesus had done 'works which none other did'; he had assured to those believing in him the same ,, 9

3 John 35
5 John 20

14 John 12

15 John 9

,, 10

,, 10

8 John 28
,, 29

15 John 24

powers: 'the works that I do shall he do also.' This was contingent on the love of Jesus, which was contingent on their obedience. 'To our Saviour, this world was as plastic as any world need be; and to His true disciples, He promised the like powers, and the like obedience from the world. In short, he inaugurated the miraculous as the order of nature, and the realisation of this we look upon as the outward measure and standard of the human regeneration.'* Jesus himself plainly intimated that if he had not continued obedient to the Father's commandments, he would not have retained the Father's love, and so would have lost his power of working 'the works of God,' amongst which he classed the opening of blind eyes. If we ask, How came it to pass that 'by the hands of the apostles were many signs and wonders wrought among the people'? or by what means the impotent man was made whole? no answer can be given but that of Peter: 'In the name of Jesus Christ of Nazareth.' If then we ask, How is it that this wonder-working power extended so little, faded away so soon, and became again utterly lost to mankind, the answer surely must be, Because the faith of Jesus Christ has departed from among us; because his disciples did not keep his commandments, and so did not abide in his love. If he has 'left us alone,' it is because we do not 'always the things that are pleasing to him.' 'The Christian church had been declining from the days of the apostles, by whom it was first founded in love and simple faith. It had declined through the anger and hatred of the Christians; through their violence and bloody wars; through their love of dominion in a kingdom where all were to be servants; through their love of the world in a state whose early builders had all things in common, and in which the Lord's morrow would take care of itself; through their councils where the human mind erected itself in session upon the truths of God, and made them into coverings for human sins; through the popedom, which sat upon the vacant throne of the Messiah; through the reformation, which kindled fresh hostilities and passions, and brought into clear separation the mind and heart of the church, writing up justification by faith on the hall of the concourse of evil-doers: finally through the wide-spread Atheism which found too valid an excuse in the manifold abominations of the Christians.'* In brief, the race of true disciples of Jesus, living by his precepts and animated by his spirit, has become extinct, unrecognisable upon the earth: therefore the signs of discipleship exist no more.

The commandments which Jesus had laid upon his disciples were not imposed as burdens, but as the means of bringing them into that joyous frame of mind experienced by himself. 'These things have I spoken unto you, that my joy may be in you.' The Revisers and Tischendorf, following the Vatican and Alexandrine MSS., have replaced 'remain in you' by 'be in you.' In proportion to the depth of their devotion and self-abnegation would be the height of their rejoicing: 'and *that* your joy may be fulfilled.' Tischendorf renders the last word 'made full.' Between the disciples themselves, Jesus desired the existence of a love as perfect as that which he had manifested towards them. 'This is my commandment, that ye love one

---

* "Emanuel Swedenborg." By James John Garth Wilkinson.

another, even as I have loved you.' Here, again, love does not signify simply an emotion of the mind and heart, but an act of self-sacrifice: 'Greater love hath no man than this, that a man lay down his life for his friends.' Neither was friendship a mere sentiment, but had the same basis as love,—obedience. 'Ye are my friends, if ye do the things which I command you.' Instead of 'whatsoever' the Revisers have put 'the things which,' agreeing with Tischendorf. If Jesus indeed laid down his life for friends devoted to his precepts, it follows that the object of his death is frustrated by neglect of his commands. He had exalted his disciples from the level of servitude to that of friendship. 'No longer do I call you servants (Gr. bondservants); for the servant (Gr. bondservant) knoweth not what his lord doeth: but I have called you friends; for all things that I heard from my Father I have made known unto you.' The Revisers, agreeing with Tischendorf, have replaced 'henceforth' by 'no longer,' rendered by Alford and Young 'no more.' Jesus recalls to the minds of the apostles the circumstances under which their intimacy began. The union had been initiated by him. With ulterior purposes in view, he had selected them, constituting them his messengers, binding them as closely to himself as the branches to the vine, that they might themselves develop in practical form his life and doctrine, and become the firstfruits of the salvation proffered by him to mankind. 'Ye did not choose me, but I chose you, and appointed you, that ye should go and bear fruit, and *that* your fruit should abide.' The Revisers, agreeing with Young, Tischendorf and Alford have replaced 'ordained' by 'appointed.' Alford observes: '*Ordained*, in A. V., is objectionable, as conveying a wrong idea, that of *appointing to the Ministry*, which is not here present.' The measure of their success in the cause of Jesus would be limited only by their own desires: 'that whatsoever ye shall ask of the Father in my name, he may give it you.' This is the third time Jesus impressed that fact upon them. All that was revealed as within the compass of his own power, was within their reach: 'the works that I do shall he do also; and greater *works* than these shall he do . . . And whatsoever ye shall ask in my name, that will I do . . . Ask whatsoever ye will, and it shall be done unto you.' 'Divine commissions are intended to be common whenever men can receive them.'*

Jesus continued: 'These things I command you, that ye may love one another.' The expression is peculiar. He had already said: 'This is my commandment, that ye love one another.' He now explains that to be the result aimed at by his precepts,—'these things I command you,'—in their entirety. His object was to introduce into the world a new society, in which mutual love should be the predominant principle of action. By his own example he had taught them that they ought to wash one another's feet; 'even as I have loved you,' should be their motto in every point of their intercourse. The apostle John urged this in one of his epistles: 'Hereby know we love, because he laid down his life for us: and we ought to lay down our lives for the brethren.' It is doubtful whether we clearly grasp the sense of this laying down of life for the sake of others. It involves something distinct from the confronting of death, which is

---

* "Emanuel Swedenborg." By J. J. G. Wilkinson.

otherwise expressed: 'Scarcely for a righteous man will one die:' it would not be often that one person could in that sense die for another, secure a brother's life by sacrificing his own: all that Paul ventured to say with respect to so exceptional an occasion was: 'peradventure for the good man some would even dare to die.' A thing so rare was outside the range of ordinary experience and obligation; but the apostle John speaks of a common, recognised duty: 'we ought to lay down our lives for the brethren.' To 'lay down' seems to be equivalent to 'dedicate, devote,' which broadens the meaning and application, making it include the course as well as the ending of life, living rather than dying for others: the will of a tyrant might perchance necessitate the latter, but our own wills could habitually accomplish the former. This interpretation throws light on other passages where the same Greek verb (which is rendered in 19 different ways in the Authorised Version) occurs. 'The good shepherd layeth down his life for the sheep.' This is in opposition to the hireling who 'leaveth the sheep and fleeth.' The shepherd risks his life by meeting the wolf; in that sense, he has actually laid down, devoted his life, although he may slay the wolf instead of the wolf him. It is assumed that every good shepherd 'lays down his life for the sheep,' though his skill and fitness as a shepherd will be best shown by overcoming the wolf, as David slew both the lion and the bear. 'I lay down my life for the sheep:' that is spoken in connection with knowing and leading the sheep, superintending more than one fold, and finally uniting them, and suits better the idea of dedicating the life to the sheep than of losing it. So also what follows: 'Therefore doth the Father love me, because I lay down my life, that I may take it again,' which indicates the temporary relinquishment of a former life. Then comes: 'No one taketh it away from me, but I lay it down of myself.' The Revisers note: 'Some ancient authorities read *took it away*.' The two oldest MSS. have: 'no man hath taken it from me,' which evidently refers to the past, not to the future death of Jesus on the cross: he alludes to the life he had forsaken voluntarily, and he adds concerning it: 'I have power (or, right) to lay it down, and I have power (or, right) to take it again;' this agrees with his subsequent declaration: 'I came out from the Father, and am come into the world: again I leave the world, and go unto the Father.' This makes the closing words intelligible: 'This commandment received I from my Father,' which they are not on the supposition of any reference to the taking away of his life upon the cross: to that the words of Jesus cannot apply, 'no one taketh it away from me,' otherwise Peter was wrong in saying to the Jews: 'ye ... killed the Prince of life.'

The Christian society, based upon mutual love, would stand forth in strong contrast to the rest of mankind. Between the disciples of Jesus, living by his heavenly maxims, and those who walk according to the spirit and practice of the present world, there can be no sympathy, but the reverse. The experience of Jesus would be that of his disciples. 'If the world hateth you, ye know (or, know ye) that it hath hated me before *it hated* you.' The Authorised Version stands, 'If the world hate you,' which seems to imply a doubt: the Revisers, agreeing with Young, Tischendorf and Alford, have replaced the subjunctive by the indicative. The words, 'it hated,' are italicised, being only once repeated in the original, whereas the English has it three times; Tischendorf renders: 'ye know that it has hated me first.' Alford notes: 'The verb rendered in the A. V. *ye know*, is most likely imperative, *know ye*. The *assertion* of their knowledge of the fact would in all likelihood have been otherwise expressed in the original.' Hatred of the system and its followers argues hostility to its Founder; the world's approval is to be secured by conformity to the world: 'If ye were of the world, the world would love its own.' But between his disciples and the world Jesus had drawn broad lines of demarcation: 'but because ye are not of the world, but I chose you out of the world, therefore the world hateth you.' Nonconformity is at once the badge and the reproach of discipleship. 'Woe *unto you*, when all men shall speak well of you!' was not a warning applicable to disciples, to whom such an experience would be impossible, but to self-constituted teachers, 'false prophets,' able to gain the ear and approbation of the world. The apostles knew what treatment their Master had received, and he could not promise, nor could they hope for, any better. 'Remember the word that I said unto you, A servant (Gr. bondservant) is not greater than his lord. If they persecuted me, they will also persecute you; if they kept my word, they will keep yours also.' The Revisers, Young, Tischendorf and Alford omit the word 'have' which is before 'persecuted' and 'kept' in the Authorised Version. Loyalty to Jesus would expose them to the same afflictions. 'But all these things will they do unto you for my name's sake.' This persecuting spirit Jesus attributed to ignorance of God: 'because they know not him that sent me.' The coming and preaching of Jesus were the occasion of this new outburst of sin. 'If I had not come and spoken unto them, they had not had sin.' Alford renders: 'they would not have sin:' Young: 'they were not having sin.' The touch of heavenly truth bared their hearts and revealed their hidden character: 'but now they have no excuse for their sin.' Instead of 'excuse,' which Alford prefers 'for perspicuity,' the Authorised Version has 'cloke.' Young renders: 'but now pretence they have none concerning their sin:' the doctrine of Jesus tore away their flimsy robe of false righteousness, compelled them to side either with or against him, and ranked them as opponents to him and his Father. 'He that hateth me hateth my Father also.' Young renders: 'He who is hating me.' Hatred, like love, is an active principle, not a feeling shut up in the heart: these persecutors knew not the Father, their minds received nothing with respect to him, yet they hated him, as they hated Jesus, in the sense of opposing his will and purposes. Doubtless they could disclaim all personal animosity against Jesus or any of his followers; but acts and facts, not names and words, constitute the true indices and nomenclatures of character. There had been unprecedented displays of divine power, worked through and for humanity, and these also had evoked, not admiration and gratitude, but blasphemy and opposition; the new revelation had drawn forth a fresh current of sin: 'If I had not done among them the works which none other did, they had not had sin: but now have they both seen and hated both me and my Father.' Alford understands the allusion to be to 'the sin of hatred to Him and His.' The decalogue does not contain a complete summary of all the crimes possible to mankind. 'What then is the law? It was added because of transgressions.' The apostle John laid down the doctrine: 'All unrighteousness is sin:' whatever is not strictly 'right' between man and man, that is sin, albeit no prohibition and no punishment can be found written against it in laws divine or human. The apostle James carries us a step further,—to this conclusion: 'To him therefore that knoweth to do good, and doeth it not, to him it is sin.' The gospel has enlarged both our views of sin and our occasions of sinning: 'This is the judgement, that the light has come into the world, and men loved the darkness rather than the light; for their works were evil.' The opposition to Jesus was causeless, not consistent with moral sanity. 'But *this cometh to pass*, that the word may be fulfilled that is written in their law, They hated me without a cause.' Alford notes that there is nothing in the original corresponding to the italicised words, 'this cometh to pass.' Young omits them, without any loss of sense: 'But—that the word may be fulfilled which hath been written in their law—They hated me without a cause.' There are passages in the Psalms to that effect. 'Yea, I have delivered him that without cause was mine adversary.' 'They shall be ashamed that deal treacherously without cause.' 'For without cause have they hid for me their net *in* a pit.' 'Without cause have they digged *a pit* for my soul . . . Neither let them wink with the eye that hate me without a cause.' 'They that hate me without a cause are more than the hairs of mine head.' 'They compassed me about also with words of hatred, and fought against me without a cause.' 'Princes have persecuted me without a cause.'

But all this hatred of Jesus would be shortly overborne by testimony in his favour. 'But when the Comforter (or, Advocate, or, Helper, Gr. Paraclete) is come, whom I will send unto you from the Father, *even* the Spirit of truth, which proceedeth from (or, goeth forth from) the Father, he shall bear witness of me.' Animated by that Spirit of truth, the apostles would undertake the task of making known what manner of person Jesus was, what he said and did, their intercourse with him from the beginning of his ministry enabling them to do so. 'And ye also bear witness (or, And bear ye also witness), because ye have been with me from the beginning.' The Authorised Version has: 'And ye also shall bear witness,' rendered by Alford, 'And ye also are witnesses,' and by Young, 'And ye also do testify.' Instead of 'ye have been with me,' Young and Tischendorf render, literally, 'ye are with me.'

Throughout this discourse, and elsewhere, Jesus refers repeatedly to his 'words,' 'sayings,' 'commandments,' the terms appearing to be synonymous. When alluding to the words or things he spoke, the reference was to more than any particular discourse. For instance: 'If any man hear my sayings, and keep them not, I judge him not . . . He that rejecteth me, and receiveth not my sayings, hath one that judgeth him: the word that I spake, the same shall judge him in the last day. For I spake not from myself; but the Father which sent me, he hath given me a commandment, what I should say, and what I should speak . . . The things therefore which I speak, even as the Father hath said unto me, so I speak.' These declarations constitute a clue to similar observations on the same topic made subsequently. When Jesus said, in the course of his last address to the apostles, 'The words that I say unto you I speak not from myself,' they would not suppose him to be claiming a particular inspiration for what he was saying at the moment, but for the whole drift and body of his teaching. 'If ye love me, ye will keep my commandments . . . If a man love me, he will keep my word . . . The word which ye hear is not mine, but the Father's who sent me . . . These things have I spoken unto you, while *yet* abiding with you.' It is obvious that 'the words that I say unto you,' 'the word which ye hear,' 'these things I have spoken unto you,' are equivalent to 'my commandments.' His teaching and their obedience are kept prominently in view throughout the discourse. 'If ye keep my commandments, ye shall abide in my love . . . These things have I spoken unto you, that my joy may be in you . . . This is my commandment, that ye love one another . . . Ye are my friends if ye do the things which I command you . . . These things I command you, that ye may love one another.' But at one point in the discourse Jesus introduces the same expression, 'these things,' to describe, not his own things or words, but those of his adversaries,—the persecutions they had begun and would continue : 'But all these things will they do unto you for my name's sake,' immediately adding, 'If I had not come and spoken unto them, they had not had sin.' The things of Jesus are placed in opposition to the things of the persecutors, both being described as 'these things.' In continuing the discourse, the context will indicate to whom and what the phrase applies. Jesus proceeds : 'These things have I spoken unto you, that ye should not be made to stumble.' The Revisers have replaced 'offended' by 'made to stumble.' Young renders : 'that ye may not be stumbled.' The meaning is not lest the apostles should be 'offended,' disgusted, disheartened, by their trials coming unexpectedly, but lest any conformity to the world's maxims and customs should interfere with their heavenly walk and calling. That was the reason for giving them his distinctive and peculiar precepts. Alford's explanation is as follows : '*These things*, viz. ch. xv. 18—27, not only the warning of the hatred of the world, but the promise of the testifying Spirit.' The true sense of the expression, 'these things,' does not lie thus upon the surface. Not what readers might take it to be on a cursory perusal, but what Jesus meant and what the apostles understood by it, is the important question. Adherence to the things spoken to them by Jesus, must needs have a most disastrous effect on their worldly position and prospects. 'They shall put you out of the synagogues.' And not only would the preaching of their Master's doctrine be prohibited, but blind opposing bigots whould deem themselves promoters of God's service in putting to death the preachers. 'Yea, the hour cometh, that whosoever killeth you shall think that he offereth service unto God.' The Revisers, agreeing with Tischendorf, have replaced 'the time' by 'the hour.' Young renders 'an hour cometh.' 'Doeth God's service' is altered to 'offereth service unto God :' Alford explains that 'the verb in the original is the technical word for *offering a sacrifice*.' Now recurs the previous expression : 'And these things will they do, because they have not known the Father, nor me ;' so that again, in the same breath, the words 'these things' are used in opposite senses, the distinction between the things of Jesus and the things of his adversaries being sufficiently obvious. The words 'unto you' are omitted after 'do,' on the authority of the Vatican and Alexandrine MSS. And now again, without a break, Jesus reverts to his own things : 'But these things have I spoken unto you, that when their hour is come, ye may remember them, how that I told you.' The Authorised Version begins the verse : 'But these things have I told you.' The Revisers have replaced 'told' by 'spoken unto,' which agrees with Alford, Young, and Tischendorf, and brings back the exact wording of verse 1, as in the original. Instead of 'but,' Alford renders 'nevertheless,' and says : '*Nevertheless* here indicates no contrast, but only breaking off the mournful details, and passing back to the subject of ver. 1. If we are to seek any contrast, it will be between the *non-knowledge* of the world, and the *remembering* of the church. The one know not what they are doing : the other know well what they are suffering.' The word 'their' instead of 'the,' now stands before 'hour,' as in the Vatican and Alexandrine MSS. The precepts of Jesus were spoken to his apostles with the very object of being kept through all persecutions. Tischendorf renders : 'But these things have I spoken to you, that when the hour may come, ye may remember them, that I told you ;' Young : 'But these things have I spoken to you, that when the hour may come, ye may remember them, that I said *them* to you.' Alford notes that the 'I is emphatic : that it was I *myself* who told you.' Young discards the word 'told,' which, if adopted as correct, alters the sense to a mere 'telling' of what would happen, instead of a 'speaking' of commands to be remembered, under the most adverse circumstances, as imposed by Jesus himself. 'The hour,' or 'their hour,' is obviously 'the hour' alluded to in verse 2, when the lives of the apostles would be in peril. Now, in opposition to 'these things have I spoken unto you,' Jesus continues : 'And these things I said not unto you from the beginning, because I was with you.' This, of course, cannot refer to the precepts spoken by Jesus, but to the actions of his enemies against his apostles, which it had not been necessary for him to dwell on throughout his teaching, while he was present to guide and keep them. Alford observes : 'A difficulty has been found in the latter part of the verse, because our Lord had repeatedly announced to them future persecutions, and that at least as plainly as here, Matt. v. 10 ; x. 16, 21—28, and elsewhere.' Let it be observed, in the first place, that the Revisers, agreeing with Young, have altered 'at the beginning' to 'from the beginning.' What is the import of that expression when used elsewhere. 'He which made *them* from the beginning made them male and female :' that points out the undeviating course of nature. 'From the beginning it hath not been so :' not in the proper, regular order of things. 'Which from the beginning were eyewitnesses :' that is, throughout the entire period. 'Jesus knew from the beginning who they were that believed not, and who it was that should betray him :' that is, from first to last. 'Even that which I have also spoken unto you from the beginning :' throughout my teaching. 'He was a murderer from the beginning :' throughout all time. 'Ye have been with me from the beginning :' constantly. Therefore 'these things I said not unto you from the beginning,' may be taken to signify, 'I was not continually impressing these things upon you ;' and the reason, 'because I was with you,' implies that more important and profitable subjects of discourse filled his mind and theirs. But now he was on the point of quitting them. 'But now I go unto him that sent me.' The Authorised Version has the words 'my way' after 'go.' Young renders: 'But now I go away;' Tischendorf, 'But now I am going.' And not one of the apostles was now asking, Whither? 'And none of you asketh me, Whither goest thou?' A question on that point had already been put and answered. Peter had enquired: 'Lord, whither goest thou?' and had been told that it was to a place where they as yet could not follow him. They had recognised the fact that it lay beyond their knowledge: 'Thomas saith unto him, Lord, we know not whither thou goest.' The parting was not accepted by them as inevitable. And the only present result of all his teaching was, that he must leave them exposed to dangers and oppressed with sorrow! 'But because I have spoken these things unto you, sorrow hath filled your heart.' His choice of them, his instructions to them, and their fidelity to him, had led up to this sad climax. But though this was the effect of his teaching, still that teaching was the truth: 'Nevertheless I tell you the truth.' Taken in conjunction with, 'I have spoken these things,' this seems to be the sense, and to accord with the use of the word 'truth'—throughout this gospel. 'Full of grace and truth ... Grace and truth came by Jesus Christ ... He hath borne witness unto the truth ... Ye shall know the truth, and the truth shall make you free ... Ye seek to kill me, a man that hath told you the truth, which I heard from God ... And stood not in the truth, because there is no truth in him ... Because I say the truth, ye believe me not ... If I say truth, why do ye not believe me.' But here, instead of connecting the mention of 'the truth' with the 'things spoken,' translators and commentators have attached it, by punctuation and explanation, to what follows,—'It is expedient for you that I go away,' as though Jesus had said simply, 'Nevertheless, verily I say unto you, It is expedient for you that I go away.' That is to read 'the truth' as 'this truth.' One misapprehension has given rise to another: missing the full and proper import of the words, 'These things have I spoken unto you,' it was not possible to understand the bearing of, 'Nevertheless I tell you the truth.' It seems right to let that stand as a sentence by itself, placing a full stop after it. Having thus vindicated his teaching, Jesus proceeds to justify his departure and explain its advantages. 'It is expedient for you that I go away.' Young renders 'expedient' as 'good;' the 'Englishman's Greek New Testament' as 'profitable.' So long as he continued with them, they must remain without the presence and teaching of the promised Spirit of truth. 'For if I go not away, the Comforter (or, Advocate, or, Helper, Gr. Paraclete) will not come unto you.' His presence was contingent upon the absence of Jesus. Why that should be, is not stated, and to this day we know not. It was necessary that Jesus should first depart, in order that he might send to them this mysterious, unknown, spiritual visitant: 'but if I go, I will send him unto you.' In the Authorised Version the next verse stands as follows: 'And when he is come, he will reprove the world of sin, and of righteousness, and of judgment.' In the Revised Version: 'And he, when he is come, will convict the world in respect of sin, and of righteousness, and of judgement.' Young renders:

'And having come, He will convict the world concerning sin, and concerning righteousness, and concerning judgment.' On the word rendered 'convict' Alford observes: 'It is difficult to give in one word the deep meaning of the original term: convince approaches perhaps near to it, but does not express the double sense, which is manifestly here intended—of a *convincing* unto salvation, and a *convicting* unto condemnation: *reprove* is far too weak, conveying merely the idea of an outward rebuke . . . In the word here used is always implied the refutation, the overcoming of an error, a wrong,—by the truth and the right.' No clear, consistent meaning can be gathered from the rendering in the Authorised Version: we cannot understand how the world can be reproved both of sin and of righteousness, these being contraries. The alteration of the word 'of' to 'in respect of' or 'concerning' is an improvement, but then the word 'convict' cannot properly apply to righteousness. From Alford's explanation it appears that an argument, a struggle, a contention, a triumphant refutation, are here alluded to, the Spirit of truth in opposition to the world and overcoming the world. It is not said that this Spirit would be given to the world, but only that he would be sent to the apostles, through whom his work upon the world would be accomplished, he being their Helper, Comforter. This accords with the previous declaration of Jesus: 'He shall give you another Comforter, that he may be with you for ever, *even* the Spirit of truth: whom the world cannot receive: . . . he abideth with you, and shall be in you.' In their contest with mankind, they would engage, the Spirit helping them, in this threefold strife: 'of sin, because they believe not on me; of righteousness, because I go to the Father, and ye behold me no more; of judgement, because the prince of this world hath been judged.' 'My Father' has been altered to 'the Father,' on the authority of the two oldest MSS., and 'is judged' to 'hath been judged,' which agrees with Alford, Tischendorf, Young, and the 'Englishman's Greek New Testament.' Young, agreeing with the last-named, renders: 'concerning sin, because they believe not in me; concerning righteousness, because to my Father I go away, and no more do ye behold me: and concerning judgment, because the ruler of this world hath been judged.' Each of these clauses needs to be considered.

'Concerning sin, because they believe not in me.' There is no reason for understanding this to mean, 'concerning the sin of unbelief in me.' Jesus is describing a process of convincing and refuting, which, as regards sin, had to be undertaken because the world did not believe in him. If the world had believed in him, obeyed him, followed him, instead of opposing and crucifying him, he would have made an end of sin, for 'he was manifested to take away sins.' Jesus had declared: 'Except ye believe that I am *he*, ye shall die in your sins.' An angel had predicted: 'It is he that shall save his people from their sins.' Having rejected him, their Messiah was still to seek, and their sin remained: 'I go away, and ye shall seek me, and shall die in your sin.' The strife against sin had to be taken up and carried on by his apostles, and in proportion as his Spirit worked in and through them the world would become convinced of sin and reformed.

'Concerning righteousness, because to my Father I go away, and no more do ye behold me.' Jesus had been from the first a preacher of righteousness, saying: 'John came unto you in the way of righteousness.' 'Thus it becometh us to fulfil all righteousness.' [3 Mat. 15] 'Blessed are they that hunger and thirst after righteousness.' 'Seek [5 Mat. 6] ye first his kingdom and his righteousness.' 'Except your righteous- [6 Mat. 33] ness shall exceed *the righteousness* of the scribes and Pharisees, ye [5 Mat. 20] shall in no wise enter into the kingdom of heaven.' The world had, and has, a very inadequate notion of righteousness, and that of orthodox religionists, the scribes and Pharisees, was insufficient in the eyes of Jesus. That was equally so in the time of Isaiah, who said: 'Thou meetest him that rejoiceth and worketh righteousness,' but [64 Isa. 5] described the righteousness of the nation as a thing stained, deteriorated, withered, misplaced : 'All our righteousnesses are as a polluted garment : and we all do fade as a leaf ; and our iniquities, like the [,, 6] wind, take us away.' The apostle Paul recognised and admitted the same insufficiency, perversion and faultiness in the Jews generally and in himself : 'For being ignorant of God's righteousness, and [10 Rom. 3] seeking to establish their own, they did not subject themselves to the righteousness of God ;' and : 'That I may gain Christ, and be [3 Phil. 9] found in him, not having a righteousness of mine own, *even* that which is of the law, but that which is through faith in Christ, the righteousness which is of God by faith.' 'What the law could not [8 Rom. 3] do, in that it was weak through the flesh,' Christ came to accomplish : 'For Christ is the end of the law unto righteousness to every one [10 Rom. 4] that believeth.' By 'righteousness' is to be understood rightness, rectitude, uprightness, integrity, justice, in purpose, word and deed, in all that relates to our own personality and our intercourse with others ; not that theological notion of a 'righteousness' which is outside ourselves and apart from our activities, a thing 'imputed' but not possessed, a hazy fiction preached and praised as though it were a solemn and soul-saving reality. Clear thought and bold speaking are necessary on this important question. Here is the 11th Article of the Church of England : 'We are accounted righteous before God, only for the merit of our Lord and Saviour Jesus Christ by Faith, and not for our own works and deservings. Wherefore, that we are justified by Faith only is a most wholesome doctrine, and very full of comfort, as more largely is expressed in the Homily of Justification.' Two words more would make the doctrine true and profitable, and without some such addition it is false and pernicious : 'We are MADE AND accounted righteous.' God does not 'account,' 'impute,' pretend that to exist which is non-existent, however positively we may have been taught that he does so. Against that hideous misconception it should suffice to set the apostle's words : 'Little children, let no man lead you astray : he that doeth righteous- [34 i. John 7] ness is righteous, even as he is righteous : he that doeth sin is of the devil.' The scriptural definition of righteousness in the New Testament has not been changed from that in the Old Testament : it still consists, as described by Ezekiel, in doing 'that which is lawful [18 Eze. 5] and right (Heb. judgement and righteonness).' Jesus detected and exposed its absence in the hypocritical scribes and Pharisees, and because he went to the Father, and was beheld no more on earth, on his apostles, taught by his Spirit, devolved the tasking of bidding all men 'awake to righteousness, and sin not.' Paul declared : 'The law [15 i. Cor. 34 (A. V.)] of the Spirit of life in Christ Jesus made me free from the law of sin [8 Rom. 2] and death ;' he thus interpreted the gospel summons : 'Awake, thou [5 Eph. 14] that sleepest, and arise from the dead, and Christ shall shine upon thee;' and he asserted that 'the fruit of the light is in all goodness and righteousness and truth.'

'Concerning judgment, because the ruler of this world hath been judged.' Jesus had said: 'Now is the judgement of this world: now shall the prince of this world be cast out.' The Father 'hath given all judgement unto the Son.' The laws and customs prevailing among mankind would thenceforth be subject to the revision, repeal or amendment of Jesus. Paul proclaimed this truth: 'The times of ignorance therefore God overlooked; but now he commandeth men that they should all everywhere repent: inasmuch as he hath appointed a day, in the which he will judge the world in righteousness by the man whom he hath ordained.' The sin of the world has to be displaced by the righteousness of Christ, and the works of the devil in the world subjected to the judgment of Christ: and these things can come to pass only through the influence of the Spirit imparted by Jesus to his disciples.

The teaching of Jesus did not include all that he desired to say, or that it was necessary for them to know. His hours were numbered, and the time, in their present state of mind, did not admit of his speaking as much as he would otherwise have done. 'I have yet many things to say unto you, but ye cannot bear them now.' The unfolding of heavenly truths and doctrines must necessarily be gradual. Jesus here states that his teaching was imperfect, his mission and the desire of his heart only partially accomplished. That must be laid to the charge of his enemies: the guilt was theirs, not only of shortening his life, but thereby of robbing the world of the full fruits of his earthly sojourn. That was but another instance of human perversity thwarting the divine will and purposes. The martyr Stephen took that view: 'Which of the prophets did not your fathers persecute? and they killed them which shewed before of the coming of the Righteous One; of whom ye have now become betrayers and murderers.' Religious bigotry, blind fanaticism, unscrupulous power, dense prejudice and ignorance, are responsible for the indefinite postponement upon earth of Messiah's kingdom of righteousness, peace and joy. 'And now, brethren, I wot that in ignorance ye did it, as did also your rulers,' said the apostle Peter. There is no more reason to suppose that an insuperable divine decree limited the term of the teaching of Jesus to the brief period during which it lasted, than there would be for a similar supposition with respect to any other martyr to the truth. The end was foreseen, foretold, provided for, but neither precipitated nor averted. Two opposing forces were in the world: Jesus on the side of God, truth and love, and his persecutors on the side of the devil, error and hatred. Human wills were left free then, as always, to choose which side they would, or to stand aloof in cold neutrality. The world made its choice, and with such an overwhelming majority in Jerusalem the conflict could not be a prolonged one. The crisis soon came: 'Of a truth in this city against thy Holy Servant Jesus, whom thou didst anoint, both Herod and Pontius Pilate, with the Gentiles and the peoples of Israel, were gathered together, to do whatsoever thy hand and thy counsel foreordained to come to pass.' The divine counsel dictated no interference in the strife; the divine hand moved not to the rescue of Jesus: 'For it became him, for whom are all things, [2 Heb. 10] and through whom are all things, in bringing many sons unto glory, to make the captain of their salvation perfect through sufferings.' What the world has lost through the premature death of Jesus, none can say. He had wide-reaching plans for the good of his country, and for the dissemination of truth and righteousness among other nations. He had already been able to send forth in his name, at one time, first the twelve and afterwards seventy missionaries, and had made a beginning of what might be, by placing them on the same plane of desire and action as that occupied by himself, so that they became endowed with a share of his miraculous powers: 'Heal [10 Mat. 8] the sick, raise the dead, cast out demons: freely ye received, freely give.' The task of regenerating society is a mighty one, and many years were needed to inaugurate, develop, watch over and extend the work which Jesus had taken in hand. In the three short years which men allowed him, he had barely done more than begin to be about his Father's business: his life-work was first impeded and then ruthlessly cut short; no sufficient time was given for the growth and ripening of the seed himself had planted; and so little prepared were his apostles for the duties devolving on them and the career which opened out before them, that a profound, hopeless, aimless despondency took possession of their minds: they had 'hoped that it was he [24 Luke 21] which should redeem Israel,' and seven of them, Peter taking the lead, could at first design for themselves no better occupation than to 'go a fishing.' They were far from being prepared to take up at [21 John 2, 3] once in their own hands the thread of their Master's purposes, and he bade them, 'tarry ye in the city, until ye be clothed with power from [24 Luke 49] on high.' He had not been able to complete the instructions necessary for their guidance, and in their interview before he suffered, prolonged as was his discourse to them, he was constrained to tell them, 'I have yet many things to say unto you, but ye cannot bear them now.' But to supply the place of his own teaching, they would receive that of the Spirit. 'Howbeit when he, the Spirit of [16 John 13] truth, is come, he shall guide you into all the truth.' The Revisers, agreeing with Young, Tischendorf and Alford, have translated literally 'all the truth,' instead of 'all truth:' that is, 'as the truth [4 Eph. 21] is in Jesus.' The Spirit would convey to them no new, independent doctrine: 'for he shall not speak from himself.' Here, and in [16 John 13] Young and Tischendorf, 'from' replaces 'of.' The revelations made would not be originated by the Spirit, but derived: 'but what things soever he shall hear, *these* shall he speak.' Young renders: 'but as [,, 13] many things as he may hear he will speak,' acting simply as the medium of communication: 'and he shall declare unto you the [,, 13] things that are to come.' This is altered from the Authorised Version, 'and he will shew you things to come.' The allusion is not to a mere disclosure or prophecy of future events, but to a declaration or instruction concerning the changes to be wrought by the gospel. Alford renders: 'he shall tell you the things to come;' Young, literally: 'the coming things he will tell you.' The result of the Spirit's ministry would be the glorification of Jesus, by the adoption and manifestation of his principles and powers. 'He shall glorify [,, 14] me: for he shall take of mine, and shall declare it unto you.' Jesus added: 'All things whatsoever the Father hath are mine.' These [,, 15]

M

words, dropped so quietly and naturally, are such as no ordinary man would dare to use, or dream of using. And who but Jesus ever made or could make the bold, positive and startling announcement, that after his departure from the world he would send to his followers a Spirit of truth, to comfort and teach them? It all lay outside the range and compass of human experience. Jesus speaks as one to whom unexplored and unimagined mysteries were open and familiar; of heaven, as having dwelt there; of the Spirit as a willing conjutor; of the Father as a Being with whom he was in closest intimacy, and in whose 'things' he participated: 'therefore said I, that he taketh of mine, and shall declare *it* unto you.' The Revisers and Tischendorf have altered 'shall take' to 'taketh,' on the authority of the two oldest MSS. Alford renders: 'for this cause said I, that he receiveth of mine, and shall tell it unto you.'

16 John 15

16 Jesus continued: 'A little while, and ye behold me no more; and again a little while, and ye shall see me.' The closing words of the Authorised Version: 'because I go to the Father,' are omitted by the Revisers, Tischendorf and Alford, on the authority of the two oldest MSS. The apostles were puzzled by the observation, and debated as to its possible meaning.

" 17 '*Some* of his disciples therefore said one to another, What is this that he saith unto us, A little while, and ye behold me not; and again a little while, and ye shall see me; and, Because I go to the Father?' In this and the preceding verse the Revisers, Young, Tischendorf and Alford have brought out the distinction between the two verbs in the original, by rendering them 'behold' and 'see.' Instead of, 'because I go to the Father,' Tischendorf renders, 'I am going to the Father': he omits 'because,' which the 'Englishman's Greek New Testament' retains. The disciples simply quoted the words used by Jesus in verse 10, 'because I go to the Father,' to which he had there added, 'and ye behold me no more.' The two sayings did not seem to agree: after stating, 'because I go to the Father, and ye behold me no more,' Jesus now speaks, not of a permanent departure, but of one for a little while only. Our knowledge of what actually happened makes his meaning clear, but the disciples could not possibly foresee or imagine that Jesus, shortly after his death, would re-appear to them.

18 'They said therefore, What is this that he saith, A little while? We know not what he saith.' Tischendorf renders: 'What is this that he calls the little while? We know not what he speaks of.' It was not dulness of apprehension on their part, but the contrary, which made the saying enigmatical to them. Jesus perceived that they were longing for an explanation, and he himself fixed upon the point with respect to which they were in doubt.

" 19 'Jesus perceived that they were desirous to ask him, and he said unto them, Do ye inquire among yourselves concerning this, that I said, A little while, and ye behold me not, and again a little while, and ye shall see me?' The word 'now' before 'Jesus' has been omitted, on the authority of the two oldest MSS. The Revisers have replaced 'knew' by 'perceived,' but Alford, Young and Tischendorf retain the word 'knew.' Jesus proceeded to make his meaning clear to the disciples, by telling them what was about to happen: they would be plunged into the utmost grief, whilst the world around them would be rejoicing.

" 20 'Verily, verily, I say unto you, that ye shall weep and lament, but the world shall rejoice.' Then a change would come over them, so thorough and so sudden that it would be like a transformation of sorrow into joy: 'ye shall be sorrowful, but your sorrow shall be turned into joy.' The word 'and' before 'ye' has been omitted, on the authority of the two oldest MSS. Their swift revulsion of feeling would be like that of a mother at the moment of her child's birth. 'A woman'—Alford notes: 'The original has the definite article'—'A woman when she is in travail hath sorrow, because her hour is come: but when she is delivered of the child, she remembereth no more the anguish, for the joy that a man is born into the world.' The illustration was appropriate to the condition of the disciples: 'And ye therefore now have sorrow:' their period of waiting and expectation must in a little while reach its crisis: already they were sorrowful, and soon their grievous trial would culminate,— not disastrously, but happily. There would be indeed 'a man born into the world,' 'the first-born from the dead,' and their eyes would marvel and their souls exult at the sight of him : 'but I will see you again, and your heart shall rejoice.' That would be no mere passing emotion, but a life-long and world-wide joy, the realisation of the prophecy : 'Unto us a child is born, unto us a son is given ; and the government shall be upon his shoulder : and his name shall be called Wonderful counsellor, Mighty God, Father of Eternity, Prince of Peace.' Well might Jesus add : "And your joy no one taketh away from you.' When Jesus would be again revealed to them, all his sayings would have become clear by their fulfilment : 'And in that day ye shall ask me nothing (or, ask me no question).' Young renders : 'Ye will question me nothing.' The Authorised Version continues : 'Verily, verily, I say unto you, Whatsoever ye shall ask the Father in my name, he will give it you.' This is now reversed, on the authority of the two oldest MSS. : 'Verily, verily, I say unto you, If ye shall ask anything of the Father, he will give it you in my name.' Alford so renders the passage, explaining it to be the reading of 'the most weighty ancient authorities.' Tischendorf's rendering agrees, except that he retains 'whatsoever ye shall ask' instead of 'if ye shall ask anything.' The difference is one of reading, not of translation. Here is a repetition of the previous promise : 'that whatsoever ye shall ask of the Father in my name, he may give it you.' In both passages there is the same condition or restriction : 'in my name :' 'whatever,' 'whatsoever,' 'anything,' which may be desired and solicited in the name of Christ, will be given. The assurance has no reference to anything private, to personal wants or wishes : it is not said, 'what each one of you may ask for himself or others,' but what 'ye,' collectively, 'ask in my name.' All idea of individual advantage or salvation must be excluded from the application of this promise : no rounding off of our petitions with the formal ending, 'through,' or 'for the sake of,' or 'in the name of thy Son our Saviour Jesus Christ' can amount to a compliance with its terms, or ensure its fulfilment. Jesus continued : 'Hitherto have ye asked nothing in my name : ask, and ye shall receive, that your joy may be fulfilled.' Alford's note is : 'It was impossible, up to the time of the glorification of Jesus, to pray to the Father in His name.' Rather : It was impossible for the disciples to pray in his name, till they had set about his work ; and it is now, and will ever be impossible for any man or any community to pray in his name, unless they are engaged in his work, and then only in respect of his cause.

Jesus now again refers to his teaching, under the expression 'these things,' and to its symbolical character. 'These things have I spoken unto you in proverbs (or, parables).' Young renders: 'These things in similitudes have I spoken to you.' Alford notes: 'The word used here signifies *literally*, as rendered in A. V., *a proverb*: but it is better for the English reader to render it parable, because proverb has the technical appropriated sense of a short pithy saying of concentrated wisdom, whereas this implies generally something dark and enigmatical—deep truth wrapped up in words, as in a parable.' That style of teaching would be superseded by something more clear and open: 'the hour cometh, when I shall no more speak unto you in proverbs (or, parables), but shall tell you plainly of the Father.' 'Time' is altered to 'hour,' by the Revisers, Young, Tischendorf and Alford. 'I shall shew you plainly' is now, 'shall tell you plainly.' Alford renders: 'I shall tell you plainly concerning the Father'; Tischendorf: 'I shall tell you openly concerning the Father'; Young: 'openly of the Father tell you.' The expression 'of' or 'concerning the Father' appears to point to revelations of the divine Being, his nature and attributes. The promise is, 'I shall tell you,' not 'the Spirit will tell you,' of whom Jesus had said, 'He shall teach you all things, and bring to your remembrance all that I said unto you'; 'He shall bear witness of me'; 'He shall take of mine, and shall declare *it* unto you.' Something beyond that is now indicated: a renewed personal teaching by Jesus 'concerning the Father.' The apostles were content to wait for that: they formulated no doctrine concerning the invisible God and Father; they broached no creed descriptive of a Trinity in Unity, and a Unity in Trinity, in the Godhead: that was done by men who claimed to be their successors, and the result of their ambitious, unauthorised, presumptuous work has been division, confusion, uncertainty, bewilderment throughout Christendom from that day to this. The 'Apostle's Creed' is simple: 'I believe in God the Father Almighty, Maker of heaven and earth: And in Jesus Christ his only Son our Lord, Who was conceived by the Holy Ghost, Born of the Virgin Mary. . . . I believe in the Holy Ghost.' Here are declarations of belief without attempts at definition; no mention is made of a Son born from eternity, but of a Son conceived by the Holy Ghost and born of the Virgin Mary. But the members of the Council of Nice went much further, and devised a Creed asserting that Jesus Christ was: 'Begotten of his Father before all worlds,' that the Holy Ghost is 'the Lord and Giver of life, Who proceedeth from the Father and the Son,' and the Divinity was divided into three persons. God the Father, God the Son, and God the Holy Ghost. Instead of leaving to Jesus the fulfilment of his promise, 'The hour cometh when I shall . . . tell you plainly of the Father,' theologians anticipated his hour and revelation, and took upon themselves to define, construct, decree a declaration concerning the Divine nature, which they imposed upon the minds and consciences of believers generally. The Athanasian creed went further still, putting this doctrine in the forefront of the Christian faith: 'The Catholic faith is this: That we worship one

God in Trinity, and Trinity in Unity ; neither confounding the Persons : nor dividing the Substance.' The receptive mind is first saturated with the idea of three personalities, and taught 'to acknowledge every Person by himself to be God and Lord,' and then is led on 'to the statement : 'we are forbidden by the Catholic Religion to say, There be three Gods, or three Lords' : the verbal denial is set against the actual doctrine, as though the two were thereby confirmed and reconciled ! This theological jugglery calls for our scorn and reprobation, not for our reverential acceptance. Not through such guides can we attain to the knowledge of God. Jesus said : 'No one cometh unto the Father, but through me.' Let every one lay aside these perplexing human dogmas concerning the Trinity, and be content to wait for the hour when Jesus will tell us plainly concerning the Father. With that revelation will come a deep interest in the cause of Jesus. 'In that day, ye shall ask in my name.' Jesus continued : 'and I say not unto you, that I will pray (Gr. make request of) the Father for you.' Alford observes : 'This has been variously understood, Grotius' rendering, "I pass by this, as a lesser thing than that which I am about to mention," comes I believe the nearest to the truth, though it does not express the whole meaning.' The apostles possessed already the love of the Father, as a consequence of their love towards and faith in Jesus : 'for the Father himself loveth you, because ye have loved me, and have believed that I came forth from the Father.' The Authorised Version has : 'that I came out from God.' The Vatican MS. reads : 'from the Father.' Tischendorf retains : 'that I came forth from God.' In what sense had the apostles believed that Jesus 'came forth from the Father' ? We have no reason to suppose that they looked upon their Master as 'begotten of his Father before all worlds, God of God, Light of Light, Very God of very God, Begotten, not made, Being of one substance with the Father.' That positive exactitude of definition was formulated three centuries later, at the Council of Nicæa, and after the promulgation of the Nicene Creed 'schisms and controversies followed upon it for generations.' * Not until two centuries later was it generally accepted, for 'it was ordered to be recited at the Holy Communion in the East early in the 6th century, and about fifty years later in the West,' * a controversy to this day unsettled, existing between the Eastern and Western Churches with respect to the words ' and from the Son— *Filioque*,' after 'who proceedeth from the Father.' Our tame, unprotesting acquiescence, century after century, in this and the Athanasian Creed, is an evidence, not of our love of truth, but rather of our indifference about it, what theologians thought and taught fifteen centuries ago being quietly accepted as holding good for all minds in all ages. Jesus said : 'When he, the Spirit of truth, is come, he shall guide you into all the truth.' Have we lost the guidance of that Spirit ? Or does the guiding Spirit stand still ? Was the teaching of the Spirit closed in the 6th century ? What are formal creeds but barriers against free thought ? Timid theologians have always dreaded and opposed it, fearing its attendant errors and uncertainties, not realising the fact that its

---

* "The Teacher's Prayer Book."

rushing, roaring waves, despite all storms and wrecks, are of divine appointment, a 'sea, great and wide,' whereon must 'go the ships,' freighted with their treasures of intellectual wealth and progress. Those solid-looking Creeds, Articles of Religion, Catechisms, Confessions of Faith, on the building up of which our forefathers lavished so much time and painful effort, have long since been undermined, and are now altogether surrounded by the advancing tide; they stand no longer as barriers at the edge of the shore, but in the midst of seething floods, mementos of bygone times, worse than useless to the present generation, unsafe, unstable,—impediments which first by general indifference and then by common consent must be left to crumble and decay. The attempt to insist upon unanimity of belief on Scriptural doctrines has been a grave, fundamental error of judgment. Differences of opinion and of interpretation must naturally exist: they arise from the varying degrees of enlightenment among mankind, and the true bonds of Christian union are patient toleration, enquiry, teaching, not a dogmatic insistence upon any particular exposition of divinely-revealed truths. No individual can claim the right of imposing his own views and conclusions upon another; and the design of one generation of theologians to mould the faith of succeeding generations is as futile as it is unwise. Men differ, not from any lack of reverence for Scripture, not from any desire to misinterpret and pervert it, but from infirmity of mind on the part of some, from undue self-confidence on the part of others, from defects of judgment, and from rash conclusions. This is especially the case with respect to those deep mysteries which relate to the divine Being, and the nature of the union between the Father, the Son, and the Holy Spirit. Our comprehension of such subjects must depend partly on the power of our intellectual grasp, partly on our moral and spiritual condition, partly on the teaching to which we have been accustomed and the point of view which, consciously or unconsciously, we occupy. Let this be borne in mind in considering the next words of Jesus: 'I came out from the Father, and am come into the world: again, I leave the world, and go unto the Father.' In the verse immediately preceding the Revisers have altered 'out' to 'forth:' in this they have altered 'forth' to 'out.' Young has 'out' in both places; Tischendorf has 'forth' in both places; Alford states that the rendering should be the same in the two verses. The expression: 'I came out from the Father, and am come into the world,' certainly indicates pre-existence. The fourth evangelist brought out that mystery in the nature of Jesus in the words: 'knowing . . . that he came forth from God, and goeth unto God.' That exalts Jesus far above ordinary humanity, but to what extent must remain a further mystery, apart from some fuller revelation. The same evangelist boldly asserted that the pre-existence of Jesus dated back to the beginning of creation: 'The same was in the beginning with God. . . He was in the world, and the world was made through him, and the world knew him not.' Startling, incomprehensible though the statement be, we need no more shrink from or reject it than did the evangelist himself. On the contrary, it becomes us to endeavour to seize its full and proper import, carefully considering the meaning of the terms employed: Word, God, Father. Doubtless these assertions of the evangelist were made on the authority of Jesus himself, whose own recorded words we find confirm some and harmonise with all of them. But the full significance of such utterances lies beyond the reach of unassisted human reason. We must needs conceive here the idea of duality, of two distinct individualities—Jesus and the Father, and their reunion after a period of separation: 'I came out from the Father, and am come into the world: again, I leave the world, and go unto the Father.' Altogether in the same direction is the previous saying: 'If ye loved me, ye would have rejoiced, because I go unto the Father: for the Father is greater than I.' That is as clear as it is positive, the natural, inevitable inference being, that Jesus and the Father are as much two persons as are any two members of one family. Numerous passages point to the same conclusion; but professed theologians are not content to let it sink into their own minds or rest undisturbed in ours. No; they say: Father, Son and Holy Spirit together are only one God, meaning thereby not one Ruler, which is the true scriptural sense of God, but one Being, one living Entity. That is a stupendous statement, which we are dared to contradict at our peril. How much less should any mortal man ever have dared to frame it! It has been formulated in face of such declarations as: 'I go unto the Father. . . My Father is greater I. . . Now I come to thee. . . . Then *cometh* the end, when he shall deliver up the kingdom to the God and Father. . . And when all things have been subjected unto him, then shall the Son also himself be subjected to him that did subject all things unto him, that God may be all in all. . . The Revelation of Jesus Christ, which God gave him.' The obvious contradiction between such passages and the Athanasian view of the Trinity, the incomprehensible mysteriousness attaching to the conception of three Persons constituting one Being, is supposed to be obviated by the further inexplicable dogma that one of those Persons possessed a twofold nature, the Son being both God and man, again setting aside the interpretation of God as Ruler, which would make that assertion credible and comprehensible, and assuming that one Person of the Triune Being is both that, or in that, or one Person in that—Supreme Being,—it is difficult to put in words so abstruse a thought,—and at the same time a human Being! There is a sense in which the doctrine of a Trinity in Unity is conceivable and rational: that the Supreme Being, the Father, has two modes of operation, distinguished as the Son and the Spirit, just as from the Sun of the natural universe issue both Light and Heat, which are one with that Luminary, of its very essence, proceed from it, and may be again absorbed by it; or just as from a cloud and the atmosphere proceed both Rain and Dew, which are part and parcel of the cloud and atmosphere, and which descend, the former visibly, the latter invisibly, to water the earth, and reascend as vapour to the source from which they emanated. There can be no objection, and there would scarcely be a limit, to such speculations and analogies concerning the Supreme Being; but our spiritual guides, having formed their own theory, and imposed it on the Church, as an article of faith, forbid all others, however reasonable, and would bind us eternally to a belief in their own crudities and irrationalities. The strange dogma of three Persons in one Being, and of two Personalities in one of those three Persons stands as an obstacle in the way of free thought and further enlightenment. We are sometimes reminded that man himself is a Trinity: body, soul and spirit, and that therefore we ought not to deem the teaching of Athanasius incredible. There is nothing analogous in the two cases: if any one were to assert that the body is one person, the soul another person, and the spirit another person, and that the three persons together were only one person, we should simply laugh in his face. What earthly use in such a jumble of words and contradictions? And what earthly or heavenly use, we are bold to ask, in the prevalent doctrine respecting the Divine Trinity? Far be it from any one who holds the Scriptures in reverence, to reject or minimise their teaching; on the other hand, it becomes us not '*to go beyond the things which are written.*' Revelations concerning the Father, the Son and the Holy Spirit have been given us in a variety of scattered passages, each having its particular context and bearing, conveying some practical lesson, or furnishing matter for thought. If they were all collated and compared by one individual, he might either be at a loss to reconcile the whole of them, or self-confident enough to evolve out of their mass certain conclusions about the Supreme Being and the relationship between Father, Son and Spirit. Another mind, equally honest and bold, would probably arrive at different conclusions. What is a Council of the Church but a number of minds, some broad, some narrow, each having its own leanings and idiosyncrasies, with no guarantee that those most positive, dictatoral and influential, are not at the same time the most partial, illogical and prejudiced? Debates on so mysterious a subject as the nature and existence of the Supreme Being, inevitably give rise to opposite opinions, and open out a controversy which, as history proves, may go on for generations. Not a few days or hours, not a life-time, or ages even, would suffice to make clear to the human intellect that which is infinitely beyond its grasp.

'Canst thou find out the deep things of God?
Canst thou find out the Almighty unto perfection?
It is high as heaven; what canst thou do?
Deeper than Sheol: what canst thou know?
The measure thereof is longer than the earth,
And broader than the sea.'

To set about the task of compiling such a document as the Athanasian Creed, was by itself a proof that the thoughts of its framers were '*corrupted from the simplicity and the purity that is toward Christ.*' How different from his style of teaching and of acting! It was in truth preaching '*another Jesus,*' whom apostles '*did not preach,*' receiving '*a different spirit,*' which the first converts '*did not receive,*' and '*a different gospel*' which they '*did not accept.*' The true work of professed disciples of Jesus is to carry out his precepts, to adopt all his maxims of life; but those who claimed to be his ambassadors and representatives among mankind, having forsaken that '*high calling of God in Christ Jesus,*' applied themselves to work of a vastly different character, and thought to promote his cause by teaching what he never taught, dealing with mysteries which they could not elucidate, and which he and his apostles never attempted to, and then scrupled not to assert further: '*He therefore that will be saved: must thus think of the Trinity.*'

Their mode of dealing with Scripture was like that of hungry men who, instead of eating the food suitable for the body's nourishment, should proceed to analyse it, discuss and seek to determine its constituent elements, and then declare that whoever did not acquiesce in their decisions could not live upon the food. 'Grace to you and peace from God the Father and the Lord Jesus Christ,' was Paul's customary salutation at the beginning of his epistles, without entering upon any abstruse definitions of the nature and union of the Father and the Son; and his doctrine of the Spirit was practical: 'To each one is given the manifestation of the Spirit to profit withal.' Let us dismiss as articles of faith all human speculations regarding the Trinity, and wait for the promised revelation of Jesus, when he shall tell us plainly of the Father. When he added: 'I came out from the Father, and am come into the world: again I leave the world, and go unto the Father,' his apostles were fully satisfied, and craved no further information: 'His disciples say, Lo, now speakest thou plainly, and speakest no proverb (or, parable).' The Revisers have omitted the words 'unto him' after 'say:' they do not appear in the Vatican MS. Alford observes: 'The stress is on *Now:* as if they said "Why announce that as *future*, which Thou art doing *now?*" The hour was not yet come for the *speaking plainly:* so that we must understand the disciples' remark to be made in weakness, however true the persuasion, and heartfelt their confession.' Alford quotes Augustine: 'They so little understood Him, that they did not even understand that they did not understand. For they were as babes;' and Lampe, as follows: 'They are annoyed that they should be accounted by their Master as unskilful and not comprehending His discourses, and wanting another Teacher, the Spirit whom he promised. And thus they go so far as to contradict Christ and dispute His plain words, and deny that He was speaking enigmatically to them.' Lampe, as Alford intimates, overlooks the fact that the promised open revelation was 'of the Father,' and that the observation of the apostles referred merely to the subsequent remark of Jesus, that he had come from and would return to the Father. That assurance they could at once accept, for already they had proofs of his preternatural knowledge, of that marvellous intuition by which he read the thoughts of all and anticipated their questions. 'Now know we that thou knowest all things, and needest not that any man should ask thee.' The last clause defines and restricts the sense of 'all things' to those in the minds of men. The insight of Jesus was so infinitely beyond anything ordinary and natural, that by itself it sufficed to justify the belief that he had a divine mission: 'by this we believe that thou camest forth from God.' Young renders 'by this' literally as 'in this,' and Tischendorf as 'herein.' In the reply of Jesus there was a touch of sadness, if not of reproach. 'Jesus answered them, Do ye now believe?' Alford observes: 'The opening words of our Lord's answer are much better taken *not as a question*, for this very belief was by our Lord recognized and commended, see ch. xviii. 8, also Matt. xvi. 17, 18 . . . He therefore recognizes their faith—"Ye do now believe;"—but shews them how weak it as yet was.' 'Behold, the hour cometh, yea, is come, that ye shall be scattered, every man to his own, and shall leave me alone.' The word 'now' is omitted before 'come,' on the authority of the three oldest MSS. After the word 'own' Young introduces 'things.' The apostolic band would no longer hold together, each one would have regard for himself and his personal concerns, and none for Jesus and his cause. No sooner, however, did Jesus drop the pathetic word 'alone' than he modified it by adding: 'and *yet* I am not alone, because the Father is with me.' The Revisers have italicised *yet*; Young omits it. Throughout his teaching, and at its close, the consciousness of the Father's approval was the only and sufficient consolation of Jesus. The words, 'The Father is with me,' must not be pressed as though they were spoken with the object of claiming and defining any special relationship between Jesus and the Father. The expression was common among the Jews, being used in the Psalms: 'The LORD of hosts is with us,' and applied by Stephen to Joseph: 'God was with him.' The paramount thought in the mind of Jesus was with respect to the teaching he had imparted to his disciples, to which he now again refers in the same words as before, 'these things.' 'These things have I spoken unto you, that in me ye may have peace.' The Revisers have altered the word 'might' to 'may,' therein agreeing with Young, Tischendorf, Alford, and the 'Englishman's Greek New Testament.' In adhering to the precepts given by Jesus, the disciples would realise the promise uttered of old: 'The LORD will bless his people with peace:' 'peace with God through our Lord Jesus Christ,' and peace among themselves. Their outer life, their intercourse with a world hostile to their faith and practice, would needs be the reverse of peaceful. 'In the world ye have tribulation.' The word 'shall' has been omitted before 'have,' on the authority of the three oldest MSS. Opposition to the world is the very root of the Christian system: without it, there can be no growth and no fruit, the branches themselves withering away. The apostles would have to take up the strife waged by their Master, and at the point at which it would seem to men to have culminated in defeat. Not so in the eyes of Jesus: he had now gained the victory, and bids his disciples exult over it with him: 'but be of good cheer; I have overcome the world.' Young renders: 'but take courage;' the 'Englishman's Greek New Testament': 'but be of good courage.' His own sufferings and death would be their example, nerving them for the struggle, and showing them how to conquer.

In the Authorised Version the next chapter begins: 'These words spake Jesus, which Alford understands to refer to 'the foregoing discourse.' But the Revisers, Young and the 'Englishman's Greek New Testament' render: 'These things,' instead of 'these words,' and it is reasonable to attach to that expression the same meaning as before. The sense of it comes out more clearly in the German version: Luther renders throughout the Greek *tauta*, by 'solches,' which is equivalent to 'such things.' Here the phrase is introductory to the prayer which Jesus uttered at the end of his ministry, and which may be taken to denote the closing up of his teaching. His thoughts were now wholly above the world, and in giving them expression he looked upwards: 'and lifting up his eyes to heaven, he said, Father, the hour is come.' He had reached a solemn and long-foreseen turning point in his career, and now, amidst all the dishonour and shame preparing for him by his

adversaries, he could appeal to his Father to honour him : 'glorify 17 John 1
thy Son, that the Son may glorify thee.' 'That thy Son also,' has
been altered to 'that the Son,' on the authority of the two oldest
MSS. Luther connects the sentences : ' Vater, die Stunde ist hier,
dass du deinen Sohn verklärest, auf dass dich dein Sohn auch
verkläre ' : ' Father, the hour is here, that thou mayest glorify thy
Son, that thy Son also may glorify thee.' Jesus ignores his cross
and sufferings, 'despising shame,' and looking only to 'the joy that 12 Heb. 2
was set before him.' The nature and operation of the glory which
Jesus craved are stated in the next sentence : ' even as thou gavest 17 John 2
him authority over all flesh.' 'Power' has been altered to
'authority,' which agrees with Young and Tischendorf. Alford
explains : '*all flesh* is not only *all mankind*, but *all that has life*, all
that is subject to death, all that is cursed on account of sin ' : in
proof of which he refers to the following passages in Genesis : ' They 7 Gen. 15
went in unto Noah into the ark, two and two of all flesh wherein is
the breath of life. And they that went in, went in male and female ,, 16
of all flesh. . . . And all flesh died that moved upon the earth, both ,, 21
fowl, and cattle, and beast, and every creeping thing that creepeth
upon the earth, and every man.' The authority of which Jesus
speaks has never been exercised by him on earth : the writer to the
Hebrews applies the promise of it to another world, saying :
' For not unto angels did he subject the world (Gr. the inhabited earth) 2 Heb. 5-8
to come,* whereof we speak. But one hath somewhere testified, saying,

 What is man, that thou art mindful of him ?
 Or the son of man, that thou visitest him ?
 Thou madest him a little lower than the angels ;
 Thou crownedst him with glory and honour,
 And didst set him over the works of thy hands :
 Thou didst put all things in subjection under his feet.

. . . But now we see not yet all things subjected to him. But we ,, 9
behold him who hath been made a little lower than the angels, *even
Jesus*, because of the suffering of death crowned with glory and
honour, that by the grace of God he should taste death for every
man.' The Revisers have italicised the word 'man': Young and
Tischendorf render 'every one' ; Luther has simply 'alle,' 'all' ;
the 'Englishman's Greek New Testament' renders 'every one
(*or*, everything).' The 'all things' alluded to by the apostle
must include those in the Psalm from which the quotation is made :

 'All sheep and oxen,   8 Ps. 7, 8
 Yea, and the beasts of the field ;
 The fowl of the air, and the fish of the sea,
 Whatsoever passeth through the paths of the seas.'

The next words of Jesus assert such a lordship : ' that whatsoever 17 John 2
thou hast given him, to them he should give eternal life.' The
Authorised Version has : 'that he should give eternal life to as
many as thou hast given him.' The rendering of the Revisers
corresponds with that of Alford, and agrees with that of Tischendorf ; Young renders : ' that—all that Thou hast given to him—
he may give to them life age-during.' Jesus here holds himself out

---

* Note by the Reviser of the Author's MS. 'And so not here yet. See also
Pss. xcvi. 13, xcviii. 9 ; in both of which, in the LXX., *oikoumenē* occurs as
synonymous with "earth."'

as the source of life to 'everything that hath breath.' It is a huge and startling claim, but we know him who made it, and that 'he received from God the Father honour and glory, when there came such a voice to him from the excellent glory, This is my beloved Son, in whom I am well pleased.' Sharpe's rendering differs from that of other translators, and is as follows : 'that he may give to them everything that thou hast given to him, even life everlasting.' Omitting the inserted word 'even,' Sharpe's version is word for word the same as Young's, except that the latter has 'all' for 'everything' and 'age-during' for 'everlasting'; but the order in which Young places the words, strictly corresponding with the original Greek, gives them a very different meaning from that of Sharpe, whose construction appears to be erroneous, for it makes 'everlasting life' comprise 'everything' given to Jesus. To reach the true signification we must adopt Young's rendering of 'eternal' or 'everlasting,' that is—'age-during.' The apostle John declares concerning Jesus Christ : 'this one is the true God and the life age-during,' that is, the true Ruler and source of the age-during life ; and again : 'the Life was manifested, and we have seen, and testify, and declare to you the Life the age-during, which was with the Father, and was manifested to us.'

<blockquote>
'Thou takest away their breath, they die,
And return to their dust.
Thou sendest forth thy spirit, they are created.'
</blockquote>

In common with all creatures, we are simply receptacles of life, as we are of light : we lie open to their influx, and when they are withdrawn we return to death or darkness ; yet with the hope of a renewed life, as sure and certain as that of a new day. Having regard to the words 'whatsoever (all things—Young) thou hast given him,' we are unable to restrict the promise to mankind, but must take it to include all living creatures, in their varying, 'age-during,' periods of existence. 'We see not yet all things' thus 'subjected' to Jesus : the mystery of universal life emanating from him, as light and heat from the sun, must be unfolded in 'the world to come, whereof we speak.' It is enough that Jesus here asserts the fact, adding the explanation: 'And this is life eternal, that they should know thee the only true God, and him whom thou didst send, even Jesus Christ.' The Revisers have altered 'might' to 'should,' and 'hast sent' to 'didst send,' and they have introduced the word 'him' and the italicised word 'even.' Young renders, literally, 'And this is the age-during life.' This is the only recorded instance in which Jesus speaks of himself by the name Jesus, which indicates both his power to save and his humanity : 'thou shalt conceive in thy womb, and bring forth a son, and shalt call his name Jesus' ; in that human form 'the Life the age-during which was with the Father . . . was manifested,' so that the apostle John regarded him as the only revelation of Deity, saying of Jesus Christ : 'this one is the true God and the life age-during.' Alford observes : 'The knowledge of *God and a creature* could not be eternal life, and the juxtaposition of the two would be inconceivable.' In these thoughts of Jesus, and in the words in which he clothed them, there is a depth of meaning which it is probably beyond our power to fathom, and least of all can we hope to do so by taking them in connection with any humanly-devised doctrine concerning a divine Trinity.

Alford notes: 'The Latin Fathers, Augustine, Ambrose and Hilary, anxious to avoid the inference unwarrantably drawn by some from this verse against the Godhead of Christ, tried to arrange it thus: "that they might know Thee, and Jesus Christ whom Thou didst send (*to be*) the only true God." But this treatment of the original is inadmissible. Others, as Chrysostom and Euthymius, construing rightly, yet regarded Jesus Christ as included in the words "the only true God."' From such high and profitless discussions let us turn away. A day may come when all will be made clear, but it has not dawned upon us yet. Our first effort must be to fix the proper sense of 'life eternal'; our next, to understand what kind of knowledge of God and Jesus is referred to: even over these primary questions much uncertainty hangs. 'Age-during' life is not synonymous with 'endless' life: the promised boon is not immortality, but the continuance of existence throughout a prescribed term or age. Our present earthly life comes not direct from Christ, but through Adam: 'Your life is hid with Christ in God'; the realisation of the promise must be in another state of existence. On the words: 'That they should know thee ... and Jesus Christ,' Alford comments as follows: 'The knowledge spoken of is no mere head or heart knowledge,—the mere information of the mind, or excitation of the feelings,—but that living reality of knowledge and personal realization—that oneness in will with God, and partaking of His nature, which IS itself life eternal: the knowledge, love, enjoyment of Him who is infinite, being themselves infinite.' The three last words are startling, going far beyond the text; the promise is not 'knowledge, love, enjoyment,' but 'age-during life' through knowledge. Alford defines that knowledge as 'personal realization, oneness in will with God, and partaking of His nature.' But it must be remembered that the gift applies to 'all flesh,' 'all things,' 'whatsoever' is given to Christ. God and Jesus are in heaven, and can be 'known' by any and every creature only as they know the sun in the heavens, far off, glorious, ineffable, incomprehensible, yet also within themselves, universally and individually, consciously or unconsciously, by the light and heat which emanate therefrom: even so, the age-during life of all streams forth to all from a similar knowledge and realization of the true God and Jesus Christ. The statement is not a theological dogma, but an actual fact and experience of life.

Looking back upon his earthly career, Jesus was comforted by the thought that he had honoured his Father, and had fulfilled his appointed task. 'I glorified thee on the earth, having accomplished the work which thou hast given me to do.' 'Having' now takes the place of 'I have,' in accordance with the three oldest MSS. Tischendorf renders: 'by completing the work.' Jesus was now free to look forward to his own future in another state of existence. 'And now, O Father, glorify thou me with thine own self with the glory which I had with thee before the world was.' Young translates the passage literally, placing the words in the same order as in the original: 'And now glorify me, Thou Father, with thyself: with the glory which I had before the world was, with Thee.' Had Jesus been merely human, his mind could not have dared to conceive, nor his lips to utter, a desire and an assertion so solemn and stupendous. He was conscious within himself of a state of pre-existence, dating back to remotest ages, 'before the world was,' of an acknowledged rank and equality with the heavenly Father of whom he had so often spoken, and he unhesitatingly claims the restoration of his original position and privileges. It becomes clear to us now, that the sublime statements concerning Jesus which stand at the forefront of this fourth gospel were based upon his own declarations, which were abundantly confirmed, and unhesitatingly accepted by the apostles. This last prayer of Jesus appears to have been uttered in presence of the eleven: it was authenticated by all that went before in his unique and inimitable career, and by the astounding facts of his resurrection and visible ascension which followed.

17 John 6   Jesus continued: 'I manifested thy name unto the men whom thou gavest me out of the world.' That was the accomplished work upon which Jesus looked back with satisfaction. The world needed a better, truer conception of God, which Jesus had imparted by his words and works. It had been necessary to make choice of a few, to whom the mysteries of the kingdom of God might be manifested; that had been done, and those chosen had submitted to the new teaching of Jesus: 'thine they were, and thou gavest them to
,, 6   me: and they have kept thy word.' The expression 'thine they were,' must carry some definite meaning. Alford explains: '*Israelites—Thy people before:* not only outwardly, but Israelites indeed, and thus prepared to receive Christ.' He had discerned in those men, engaged in their rough and humble callings, a devotion to the divine will excelling that of the scribes and Pharisees. From the latter he had encountered scorn and opposition, but by his disciples
7   he was believed in as a Teacher sent from God: 'Now they know that all things whatsoever thou hast given me are from thee.' Jesus was a manifestation of the Father: what he was, God was, to the disciples and to the world. Instead of the strange doctrine taught by many, that the Son was and is occupied in diverting from us the Father's wrath, Jesus declares that his words were God's words, that
8   he was the Father's messenger and representative: 'for the words which thou gavest me I have given unto them; and they received *them*, and knew of a truth that I came forth from thee, and they believed that thou didst send me.' Being thus assured of the faith of his disciples, Jesus could confidently appeal to the Father on their
,, 9   behalf. 'I pray (Gr. make request) for them.' For mankind, apart
,, 9   from them, he entertained no hope and could frame no prayer. 'I pray (Gr. make request) not for the world, but for them whom thou hast given me.' Only through them could the world be influenced and transformed. The prayer aimed not at their personal happiness or prosperity, but at their work and its effects. Young renders: 'I ask in regard to them: not in regard to the world do I ask, but in regard to those whom Thou hast given to me, because thine they are.' After the departure of Jesus, they would be the sole representatives of God's cause in the world, the only pioneers, teachers
,, 10   and exemplars of the kingdom of heaven upon earth. 'For they are thine; and all things that are mine are thine, and thine are mine: and I am glorified in them.' The Revisers have introduced the word 'things,' agreeing with Tischendorf and Alford, the latter explaining that 'the gender is neuter.' The doctrine and method of Jesus were framed according to the Father's will: his instructions were those of 'a teacher come from God,' and by their observance

and propagation he would be honoured. That work must now devolve upon the disciples. 'And I am no more in the world, and these are in the world, and I come to thee.' Before 'I am' the word 'now' has been omitted, not being in the original. The Authorised Version continues : 'Holy Father, keep through thine own name those whom thou hast given me.' On the authority of the three oldest MSS. this is now altered to : 'Holy Father, keep them in thy name which thou hast given me.' Alford notes that this is 'not only the best supported, but the *best* reading.' Here, as elsewhere, we must understand by 'name' power, authority, much more than a mere title : 'Behold, I send an angel before thee, to keep thee by the way, and to bring thee into the place which I have prepared. Take ye heed of him, and hearken unto his voice ; provoke him not : for he will not pardon your transgression ; for my name is in him.' As the word 'holy' denotes separateness, the prominent idea here is separation from the world, and the sentence ends : 'that they may be one, even as we *are*.' There can be no 'keeping,' no preservation of the disciples, except by and through unity. They must have the same oneness of will, purpose, design, as existed between Jesus and the Father. Hitherto Jesus had held them thus together. 'While I was with them, I kept them in thy name which thou hast given me.' The words 'in the world' before 'I kept' are omitted by the Revisers on the authority of the two oldest MSS. ; the construction is also altered, 'those that thou gavest me' being omitted, 'which' taking the place of 'whom' or 'those that.' The divine 'name,'—power, authority, influence,—which was given to Jesus, and in which he kept his disciples, did not include any miraculous deliverance from opposition, for Jesus himself was about to fall as the first martyr in the cause, and he asks for them nothing which was not given to himself. Neither was the prayer offered for them individually, but collectively ; had they ceased to have one bond, aim, intention, the prayer on their behalf would have failed of accomplishment. Jesus had watched over them, and with one exception, inevitable and foretold, the company of apostles remained intact : 'and I guarded them, and not one of them perished, but the son of perdition ; that the scripture might be fulfilled.' The life which now lay before Jesus was a heavenly one ; upon earth his new doctrine had been delivered, by adhering to which his disciples would be able to attain to the same joy as himself. 'But now I come to thee ; and these things I speak in the world, that they may have my joy fulfilled in themselves.' The rejoicing would be internal, 'in themselves,' accompanied by opposition from without. 'I have given them thy word, and the world hated them, because they are not of the world, even as I am not of the world.' It was the deliberate purpose of Jesus that they should continue in the midst of a hostile world, not be removed from it, but kept free from surrounding evils. 'I pray (Gr. make request) not that thou shouldest take them from (Gr. out of) the world, but that thou shouldest keep them from (Gr. out of) the evil *one* (or, evil).' The italicised word 'one' has been introduced by the Revisers. Luther and Young agree with the Authorised Version ; Sharpe renders simply 'from evil' ; Alford notes : 'Not *from the evil*, as A.V., but *from the evil one :* see the usage of our apostle in 1 John ii. 13, 14, v. 18, and compare iii.

12.' In the last named of those four passages, Sharpe renders 'evil:' in the others he agrees with the Authorised Version, Young and Alford: 'evil one.' If either interpretation will stand, the mention of 'the world' certainly points to 'evil' generally, especially having regard to what follows: 'They are not of the world, even as I am not of the world.' The apostles were 'called with a holy calling,' consecrated to the office of making known the truth: 'Sanctify (or, consecrate) them in the truth.' 'Thy' has been altered to 'the,' on the authority of the three oldest MSS., and 'through,' which Alford states was a wrong translation, to 'in.' The 'truth' alluded to is not mere truth of doctrine, a right conception of matters intellectual or spiritual, but truth of aim and life, based on obedience, for Jesus added: 'thy word is truth.' The 'word' of God includes commands, instructions, precepts. The office which had been undertaken by Jesus must now devolve upon his apostles. 'As thou didst send me into the world, even so sent I them into the world.' The entire devotion, the self-dedication of Jesus to his work, was with the view of giving these disciples an example for their imitation. 'And for their sakes I sanctify (or, consecrate) myself, that they themselves also may be sanctified in truth.' Sanctification or consecration signifies the setting apart of their lives and labours to their Master's cause, as appears by the apostle's words: 'For both he that sanctifieth and they that are sanctified are all of one: for which cause he is not ashamed to call them brethren.'

Anticipating the success of the apostolic labours, Jesus formulated his request for all who through their preaching would believe in him. 'Neither for these only do I pray (Gr. make request), but for them also that believe on me through their word.' The word 'shall' has been omitted before 'believe,' in accordance with the three oldest MSS. The same unity which he desired for the apostles he desired for all: 'that they all may be one; even as thou, Father, *art* in me, and I in thee; that they also may be in us.' In the Authorised Version the word 'one' stands before 'in us,' but Alford notes that it is 'omitted by many ancient authorities,' and Tischendorf omits it. The desired union is obviously that of heart and purpose, and it is also clear that the words 'even as thou, Father, in me, and I in thee,' must not be strained beyond that sense: the church, the assembly of believers, must be engaged with, at one with, the Father and the Son, in carrying out the gospel scheme; the work must be not individual, but collective, not unseen, in the soul of each, but visible, seen and known of all men: 'that the world may believe that thou didst send me.' In this unity, the glory of Christ and of his church consists. 'And the glory which thou hast given me I have given unto them; that they may be one, even as we *are* one; I in them, and thou in me, that they may be perfected into one.' The Authorised Version has, 'may be made perfect in one,' but the Revisers, Young, Tischendorf and the 'Englishman's Greek New Testament' agree in rendering 'may be perfected into one.' The design of Jesus is here plainly revealed: he desired the formation and continuance of a compact body of believers, all animated by a common purpose, separated from the world while living in the world, adopting the high and heavenly maxims of Jesus, which are so contrary to the spirit of the world, and relying for protection, guidance, safety, not on resistance to evil, not on the wielding of the sword of self-defence, but on that divine love whereon Jesus cast himself and taught his followers to depend: 'that the world may know that thou didst send me, and lovedst them, even as thou lovedst me.' Opposition from mankind, and martyrdom for the cause, involve no separation from 'the love of God, which is in Christ Jesus our Lord,' but are evidences that 'as he is, even so are we in this world.' 17 John 23 8 Rom. 39 4 i. John 17

The Authorised Version continues: 'Father, I will that they also, whom thou hast given me, be with me where I am,' now altered to: 'Father, that which thou hast given me, I will that, where I am, they also may be with me,' the Revisers noting: 'Many ancient authorities read *those whom*.' Tischendorf renders: 'what thou hast given me.' Alford notes that 'the genuine original text has here, Father, (as to) that which thou hast given me,' and he observes: 'The neuter gender has a peculiar solemnity, uniting the whole Church together as *one gift* of the Father to the Son.' Jesus added: 'that they may behold my glory, which thou hast given me.' He says not, 'which thou wilt give me,' but 'which thou hast given me.' The reference is to some past experience, as appears from the following words: 'for thou lovedst me before the foundation of the world.' The thought of Jesus pierced back to remotest ages; his words here harmonise with those of the evangelist at the opening of this gospel: 'The same was in the beginning with God.' Standing now as a man among men, Jesus alone possessed that supernatural knowledge of God, and was deeply conscious of the dense ignorance of the world. 'O righteous Father, the world knew thee not, but I knew thee.' The literal rendering is: 'Father righteous, and the world thee knew not.' Tischendorf renders this as an exclamation of astonishment: 'Righteous Father! and the world knew thee not!' To dissipate human ignorance and misconceptions of God, was the mission of Jesus; and by revealing himself to his disciples as one sent from God, he had made known to them the Father's name, his loving power and attributes: 'and these knew that thou didst send me; and I made known unto them thy name.' That teaching of Jesus was not yet complete; he added: 'and will make it known.' His disciples were as capable of receiving and rejoicing in the Father's love as he was: 'that the love wherewith thou lovedst me may be in them;' but only through discipleship, through oneness of mind with Jesus, could that come to pass: 'and I in them.' 17 John 24 ,, 24 ,, 24 1 John 2 17 John 25 ,, 25, 26 ,, 26 ,, 26 ,, 26

It was probably after the conclusion of this prayer that Jesus proceeded with his disciples to the neighbouring mount of Olives. 'And when they had sung a hymn, they went out unto the mount of Olives.' Tischendorf renders, 'the hymn.' The verb in the original, *humneō*, is 'to sing a hymn, to sing praise.' Alford says: 'The *hymn* was in all probability the last part of that which the Jews called the Hallel, or great Hallel, which consisted of Psalms cxv.—cxviii.; the former part (Psalms cxiii., cxiv.) having been sung during the meal.' Jesus now told his disciples that before the morning their devotion to him would be sorely tried and found wanting. 'Then saith Jesus unto them, All ye shall be offended (Gr. caused to stumble) in me this night.' The blow directed against himself 26 Mat. 30 ,, 31

N

would recoil upon them : 'for it is written, I will smite the shepherd, and the sheep of the flock shall be scattered abroad.' The reference may be to this passage in Zechariah : 'Awake, O sword, against my shepherd, and against the man that is my fellow, saith the LORD of hosts: smite the shepherd, and the sheep shall be scattered : and I will turn mine hand upon the little ones.' Young's rendering is as follows :

<blockquote>
'Sword, awake against My shepherd,
And against a hero, My fellow,
Affirmeth the LORD of Hosts :
Smite the shepherd,
And scattered is the flock :
And I have put back My hand on the little ones.'
</blockquote>

Sharpe's version is : 'Awake, O sword against my shepherd, and against the man of my friendship, Jehovah of hosts hath said it. Smite the shepherd, and the sheep shall be scattered : and I will turn my hands against the vile ones.' Alford observes : 'This is a very important citation, and has been much misunderstood; *how much* may appear from Grotius' remark : that Zechariah's words are not directly alluded to : nay, that in them rather is the saying used of some *bad* shepherd. But, on the contrary, if we examine Zech. xi., xii., xiii., we must I think come to the conclusion that the shepherd spoken of xi. 7—14, who is *rejected* and *sold*, who is said to have been *pierced* (xii. 10), is also spoken of in ch. xiii. 7. Stier has gone at length into the history of the whole prophecy, and especially that of the word *my fellow*, and shewn that the reference can be to *no other than the Messiah*.' The differences of translation or of reading, as that of 'vile ones' for 'little ones' and of 'friendship' for 'fellow,' the fact that the prophet's words must have had an application to current events (Sharpe understands by 'my shepherd' Jehoiachin), and the varying opinions of Commentators, indicate the difficulty of justifying any particular interpretation. Nor did Jesus quote the words for the purpose of proving his Messiahship, but obviously as a mere incidental illustration of the fact he stated, that the smiting of the shepherd would result in the scattering of the sheep. Mark, according to the Authorised Version, gives the quotation as in Matthew, omitting the words 'of the flock ;' but the Revisers, following the two oldest MSS., also omit in Mark, 'because of me this night.' The scattering of the disciples would not be permanent. Jesus bade them look forward to a time when he would be with them and lead them back to Galilee. 'But after I am raised up, I will go before you into Galilee.' 'Howbeit, after I am raised up, I will go before you into Galilee.' Young renders, literally, 'after my having risen.' Jesus, foreseeing the end from the beginning, speaks in the most natural way of that stupendous miracle the mention of which on a former occasion had led them to question 'among themselves what the rising again from the dead should mean.' But now one of the apostles was more eager to assert and vaunt his own fidelity than to enquire about that future visit to Galilee. 'But Peter answered and said unto unto him, If all shall be offended (Gr. caused to stumble) in thee, I will never be offended (Gr. caused to stumble).' The Revisers have here without any loss of sense or emphasis, omitted two italicised words, 'men' after 'all' and 'yet' after 'thee.' Mark has: 'But Peter said unto him, [14 Mark 29] Although all should be offended (Gr. caused to stumble), yet will not I:' literally, 'yet not I.' He could contemplate the possibility of the defection of others, of all the rest, but not his own, being conscious of the sincerity and earnestness of his determination. But Jesus knew him better than he knew himself, and repeats—it would seem to be for the third time—his sad, prophetic warning. 'Jesus [26 Mat. 34] said unto him, Verily I say unto thee, that this night, before the cock crow, thou shalt deny me thrice.' Young renders, 'before a cock crows:' so soon would the mood of the self-confident apostle change, and his courage evaporate. Mark records the saying more accurately and emphatically. 'And Jesus saith unto him, Verily I [14 Mark 30] say unto thee, that thou to-day, *even* this night, before the cock crow twice, shalt deny me thrice.' Alford notes: 'The *first* cock-crowing is at midnight; but inasmuch as *few hear it*,—when the word is used *generally*, we mean the *second* crowing, early in the morning, before dawn. If this view be taken, the cock-crowing and double cock-crowing amount to the same—only the latter is the *more precise* expression.' The solemn, well-weighed words of Jesus made no impression on the mind of the apostle, who did not hesitate to set them aside, even to contradict them. 'Peter saith unto him, Even if [26 Mat. 35] I must die with thee, *yet* will I not deny thee.' Here again Mark gives an additional touch. 'But he spake exceeding vehemently, If [14 Mark 31] I must die with thee, I will not deny thee.' Alford notes: 'The original implies, *went on* repeating superabundantly.' What Peter said so boastfully and arrogantly, the others expressed as their own determination: they were all ready to die with Jesus rather than repudiate their connection with him. 'Likewise also said all the [26 Mat. 35] disciples.' 'And in like manner also said they all.' [14 Mark 31]

This conversation took place either at or on the road to the mount of Olives. Luke has not recorded it, nor does he mention the previous singing of the hymn, but simply says: 'And he came out, and [22 Luke 39] went, as his custom was, unto the mount of Olives; and the disciples also followed him.' The word 'his' before 'disciples' has been replaced by 'the,' on the authority of the three oldest MSS. The fourth evangelist, after recording the lengthy prayer of Jesus, says: 'When [18 John 1] Jesus had spoken these words, he went forth with his disciples over the brook (or, ravine, Gr. winter torrent) Kidron, where was a garden, into the which he entered, himself and his disciples.' Tischendorf renders: 'over the brook of the cedar.' Alford notes: 'The name given to this brook in the oldest text, *of the cedars*, seems to furnish an instance of the common practice of changing foreign, or unmeaning names, into other words bearing sense in the new language: the Hebrew word Ce- or Ke-dron signifying *of cedars* in Greek.' The word 'himself' has been introduced, from the original, by the Revisers, Young and Tischendorf. The garden appears to have been known as 'Gethsemane,' the name signifying 'an oil press,' for Matthew says: 'Then cometh Jesus with them unto a place (Gr. an [26 Mat. 36] enclosed piece of ground) which was named Gethsemane.' In both passages Tischendorf renders 'place' as 'enclosure.' From Luke's passing remark: 'And when he was at the place . . .' it appears that [22 Luke 40] it was a customary resort, and this is confirmed by the words of John: 'Now Judas also, which betrayed him, knew the place: for Jesus [18 John 2] oft-times resorted thither with his disciples.' On arriving there, Jesus desired them to seat themselves, while he went further into the garden to pray. 'And saith unto his disciples, Sit ye here, while I go yonder and pray.' Here the Revisers, on the authority of the three oldest MSS., have replaced 'the' by 'his,' before 'disciples.' Mark agrees : 'and he saith unto his disciples, Sit ye here, while I pray.' Luke states that he charged them to pray for themselves, that they might be kept from temptation : 'he said unto them, Pray that ye enter not into temptation.' The hour was full of peril to them all. Then he took with him three of the disciples, and being alone with them his composure, so long maintained, utterly broke down, and he was overwhelmed with grief and dejection. 'And he took with him Peter and the two sons of Zebedee, and began to be greatly amazed, and sore troubled.' The Revisers have altered 'very heavy' to 'sore troubled,' which Tischendorf renders as 'dejected,' and the 'Englishman's Greek New Testament' as 'greatly depressed.' Jesus made no attempt to conceal his emotion, but, on the contrary, told his three companions that the sorrow of his soul was so intense as to endanger life, 'reaching even to the *utmost limit of endurance*, so that it seemed that *more* would be *death itself*' (Alford). 'Then saith he unto them, My soul is exceeding sorrowful, even unto death.' The word 'even' has been added by translators to the Greek *heōs*, 'until' or 'up to.' Young renders : 'Exceedingly sorrowful is my soul— unto death.' Mark stands in the Authorised Version : 'And saith unto them, My soul is exceeding sorrowful unto death,' but there also the Revisers have inserted 'even.' In the extremity of his anguish Jesus craved for solitude. He bade the three stay where they were, but to be vigilant : 'abide ye here, and watch.' Matthew adds 'with me :' 'abide ye here, and watch with me.' Mark continues : 'And he went forward a little, and fell on the ground ;' Matthew: 'And he went forward a little, and fell on his face.' Tischendorf gives a different reading in Matthew : 'and he approached a little nearer.' According to Tischendorf, Matthew represents Jesus as going *from* the disciples, and Mark as coming *towards* them. The two accounts are reconcilable on the supposition that Jesus walked up and down, which we know to be natural, if not absolutely necessary, to any man labouring under strong emotion, and that having left the disciples and then turned back, he then fell prostrate. Tischendorf's rendering of Luke confirms this idea. The Authorised Version stands : 'And he was withdrawn from them about a stone's cast :' the Revised Version : 'And he was parted from them about a stone's cast.' Luther renders : 'Und er riss sich von ihnen bey einen Steinwurf,' which agrees with Tischendorf : 'And he tore himself away from them about a stone's throw.' The verb is *apospaō*, which is defined : 'to tear or drag away, sever or part from.' The expression well describes the excitement, nervous, physical and mental, exhibited by Jesus ; the bodily agitation corresponded in intensity with the perturbation of the soul, and as he paced up and down, his fall to the ground as he again approached the disciples may have been due partly to bodily weakness and partly to spiritual anguish. In that position they heard him praying ; Luke describes him as deliberately kneeling : 'and he kneeled down and prayed ;' but as he prayed to the same purport thrice, that may describe his posture subsequently, when he had regained greater calmness. He was now lying on the ground, 'and prayed that, if it were possible, the hour might pass away from him.' His words, or some of them, reached the ears of the disciples, and are recorded by the three evangelists, with such slight differences and general agreement as are natural in independent accounts. Matthew: 'saying, O my Father, if it be possible, let this cup pass away from me: nevertheless, not as I will, but as thou wilt.' Mark: 'And he said, Abba, Father, all things are possible unto thee; remove this cup from me: howbeit not what I will, but what thou wilt.' Luke: 'saying, Father, if thou be willing, remove this cup from me: nevertheless not my will, but thine, be done,' which Young renders literally: 'Father, if thou be willing to remove this cup from me— : but, not my will, but thine be done.' Alford explains that the sentence is broken off at 'me,' and adds: 'The A. V.' (which is adopted by the Revisers)* 'is not a correct reading in grammar.' The evangelists left the sentence unfinished, rugged, but our translators have rounded and smoothed it. The short, broken utterance denotes the struggle in the breast of Jesus: his own desire checked by the will of God, his petition stayed in its course, submissively modified by 'nevertheless' or 'howbeit.' Martyrdom for the truth's sake had been long foreseen; it was the destined portion of Jesus and of his disciples: 'If any man serve me, let him follow me:' that was spoken in connection with the loss of life. But even while exhorting his disciples to follow him, his own soul was full of trouble at the terrible prospect: 'Now is my soul troubled;' human nature could not face the bitter ordeal without a longing to escape: 'and what shall I say? Father, save me from this hour? But for this cause came I unto this hour.' Now, as the last hour approached, the trouble had again laid hold of him, and reached its climax. To leave the world and go to the Father, was joy and gain to him; but to leave it in the way he must,—by a violent death at the hands of those he had failed to convince and convert, his work unhonoured, unfinished, his disciples insufficiently instructed, their shoulders all too weak for the burden laid upon them,—that was an end repugnant to his aim and life-work. Was there no other way, simpler, better, more natural, for inaugurating the salvation of mankind? The mind of Jesus wrestled with the problem. O that his life and labour of love might be prolonged! Was it utterly impossible for him to remain upon earth, teaching and doing his Father's will? 'O my Father, if it be possible, let this cup pass away from me.' 'Abba, Father, all things are possible unto thee; remove this cup from me.' No voice from heaven in reply? No inward consciousness of a favourable answer? Then let the will of God be done; let his purpose, dark and enigmatical though it be, have free course and be glorified: 'Lo, I am come (in the roll of the book it is written of me) to do thy will, O God.' 'Not what I will, but what thou wilt.' The writer to the Hebrews seems to have regarded the matter in this light, representing the prayer of Jesus to have been for deliverance from death: 'Who in the days of his flesh, having offered up prayers and supplications with strong crying and tears unto him that was able to save him from death.' Of death, simply

---

* Note suggested to the Author: 'Yes, but as representing another Greek reading — *parenengke*, not *parenengkein* — therefore without breach of grammar.'

as death, Jesus had, could have, no dread: he knew that after three days he would rise again; nor did its manner and circumstances appal him, 'who for the joy that was set before him endured the cross, despising shame.' But to have his career cut short after only three years of labour, and when he must tell his apostles, 'I have yet many things to say unto you, but ye cannot bear them now,'—from that destiny his soul recoiled and desired passionately, yet in vain, a way of escape. He was not wont to pray in vain: at the grave of Lazarus he had said, 'Father, I thank thee that thou heardest me. And I knew that thou hearest me always;' but now his earnest wish must needs be thwarted; always hitherto 'having been heard for his godly fear,' he now, 'though he was a Son, yet learned obedience by the things which he suffered.' We seem to get here a glimpse of the divine plan and purpose: 'For it became him, for whom are all things, and through whom are all things, in bringing many sons unto glory, to make the captain of their salvation perfect through sufferings:' the free will and free action of mankind must not be interfered with, even for the sake and in the cause of God's own beloved Son; their hostility was foreseen, but not impeded: 'him, being delivered up by the determinate counsel and foreknowledge of God, ye by the hand of lawless men did crucify and slay.' The kingdom of heaven upon earth, the salvation of God to the world, are preached and offered, but there is not, must not be, from first to last, any compulsion of the human will: men believe or disbelieve, accept or reject, honour or crucify the Christ of God; our prejudices and misconceptions, inherited or self-generated, our sins of heart and life, our crimes and virtues, our sordid earthliness and heavenly aspirations, all work together, against us or for us, and there can be no deliverance from evil, no progress towards good, except in proportion to our acceptance of 'the gospel preached unto us by the Holy Spirit sent forth from heaven.' The spiritual, as much as the secular history of mankind, is of their own making. Jesus longed, even prayed, for divine interference, but it could not be granted. There is a deep, insuperable philosophy in the apostolic exhortation, 'work out your own salvation with fear and trembling; for it is God which worketh in you both to will and to work for his good pleasure.' Only by accepting his gospel, and willing and working through his Spirit, can the salvation of society, as tending to which the salvation of an individual is chiefly important, be attained. 'God our Saviour willeth that all men,' not some, not one here and another there, 'should be saved;' and in the prosecution of that grand design there will be no local, temporary, partial overruling and compelling of mankind: they are left free to choose the evil or the good, the false or the true, and Jesus in this world was left, as his followers were and must ever be, exposed to the full brunt and outburst of an ever-shifting popular sentiment and policy. The spirit of the age, the prevailing tone and temper of society, assert and maintain supremacy in all mundane affairs. Jesus sought to counteract the evil rampant in his day and generation, and he fell a victim to bigotry, self-satisfied intolerance, popular prejudice and clamour. If supernatural interference had been vouchsafed then, on his behalf, how would that have benefited the after ages? God stretched forth no hand to the rescue of his Son, who was left, as the prophets which went before him, to be persecuted even to death for righteousness' sake. The same divine policy has run throughout all past ages, is continued now, and will last as long as the world stands. Herein lies the secret of that apparent aloofness of God from the world he has made: it is not that he does not rule, but that he rules us in his own way: 'Not by might, nor by power, but by my spirit, saith the Lord of hosts.'   4 Zech 6

Calmed and comforted through prayer, Jesus returned to the spot where he had left the three disciples. He found them wrapped in slumber. 'And he cometh unto the disciples, and findeth them sleeping.'   26 Mat. 40
'And he cometh, and findeth them sleeping.' Jesus ex-   14 Mark 37
pressed his surprise at this, addressing himself specially to him who had boasted so confidently his readiness to die with his Master: 'and saith unto Peter, Simon, sleepest thou? couldest thou not watch one hour?' Matthew also represents the expostulation to have been addressed to Peter, but to have included the others: 'and saith unto Peter, What, could ye not watch with me one hour?' And he   „ 37
26 Mat. 40
„ 41
repeats his previous injunction: 'Watch and pray, that ye enter not (or, Watch ye, and pray that ye enter not) into temptation: the spirit indeed is willing, but the flesh is weak.' The Revisers have altered 'ready' to 'willing,' rendered by Young 'forward.' The reiterated direction to watch, and seek freedom from temptation, indicates that Jesus apprehended danger to them. Whatever might come upon himself, he was anxious that they should escape. At any moment they might be surprised: if that happened when Jesus was not at hand to direct and control them, they might attempt to meet force by force, thereby laying themselves open to the charge of resisting lawful authority. How would that have told against him and them, as well as against the cause of the gospel! For it would have been an abnegation of his precepts, and a reversal of the principles on which his kingdom must be founded. Having roused them, Jesus again left them, and became absorbed in prayer. Their listening ears caught something of his utterances. Mark says: 'And   14 Mark 38
again he went away, and prayed, saying the same words.' Matthew   „ 39
reports a slight variation: 'And again a second time he went away, and prayed, saying, O my Father, if this cannot pass away, except I drink it, thy will be done.' The Revisers have altered 'may not' to 'cannot,' agreeing with Young and Tischendorf, and they have omitted 'cup' after 'this,' and 'from me' after 'away,' the former on the authority of the three, and the latter on the authority of the two oldest MSS. The recorded words of Jesus indicate entire submission and a growing conviction of its necessity: 'as' would have been stronger than 'if,' before 'this cannot pass away;' we seem to see Jesus in the very act of 'learning obedience.' The Authorised Version continues: 'And he came and found them asleep again,' which is altered in accordance with the two oldest MSS. to: 'And he came again and found them sleeping.' In Mark the Authorised Version stands: 'And when he returned, he found them asleep again,' now altered on the same authorities to: 'And again he came, and found them sleeping.' Exhausted nature could hold out no longer. Matthew explains: 'for their eyes were heavy;' Mark: 'for their eyes were very heavy.' Even when partly wakened they showed no power of coherent thought and speech: 'and they wist not what to answer him.' Matthew, however, was able to tell us: 'And he left them again, and went away, and prayed a third time, saying again   26 Mat. 42
„ 43
14 Mark 40
26 Mat. 43
14 Mark 40
„ 40
26 Mat. 44

the same words.' His coming and going must have roused one or more of them sufficiently to observe thus much. The word 'again,' after 'saying,' has been inserted by the Revisers from the oldest MS. The bare account of a thrice repeated prayer is simple enough, but only consider what it involves: the earnest longing, the inward strife, the agony of suspense, the shrinking from what is every moment more and more realised as inevitable, albeit well-nigh unendurable!

<small>12 ii. Cor. 8</small> Saint Paul knew what it was to pray repeatedly and be denied: 'I besought the Lord thrice, that it might depart from me, and the un-<small>5 Heb. 7</small> granted prayer of Jesus is described as accompanied 'with strong crying and tears.' Luke's account of the circumstances brings the scene vividly before us. He tells of supernatural aid vouchsafed to <small>22 Luke 43</small> Jesus during the struggle. 'And there appeared unto him an angel from heaven strengthening him.' The burden of distress was more than unassisted human nature could bear. After recording the prayer and the supernatural help, Luke relates a fact of terrible significance. The deadly sorrow became yet more poignant, the prayer more urgent, and the body, sympathising in the spiritual <small>,, 44</small> conflict, was bathed in a sweat of no ordinary kind. 'And being in an agony he prayed more earnestly: and his sweat became as it were great drops of blood falling down upon the ground.' The phenomenon, so deliberately described, calls for our reverential consideration. Alford observes: 'The intention of the evangelist seems to be, to convey the idea that the sweat was (not *fell* like, but *was*) *like drops of blood*,—i.e. *coloured with blood*, for so I understand the *as it were*, as just distinguishing the drops *highly coloured with blood* from *pure blood*. Aristotle, speaking of certain morbid states of the blood, says, "when the blood is watery, grievous disease ensues: for it becomes serous and milky, to such an extent that some have been known to *perspire a bloody sweat*." To suppose that it only *fell like drops of blood* (why not drops of anything else? and drops of blood *from what*, and *where?*) is to nullify the force of the sentence. We must not forget, in asking on what testimony this rests, that the marks of such drops would be visible after the termination of the agony. An interesting example of a sweat of blood under circumstances of strong terror, accompanied by loss of speech, is cited in the Medical Gazette for December, 1848. It occurred in the case of certain Norwegian sailors in a tremendous storm.' The account of the ministering angel and the bloody sweat rests only on the testimony of Luke. From the narratives of the other evangelists it must be inferred that only from Peter, James or John could the information have originated. No mention is made of the occurrence in the gospel or epistles of John, nor in the epistles of Peter. But that omission is no argument against its credibility. John's gospel up to this point is restricted chiefly to a record of the discourses of Jesus; there was no reason for introducing into it, any more than into epistles written long after with definite objects, any mention of this passing and personal episode in the history of Jesus. It was a private matter, rather to be whispered and pondered reverently than to be proclaimed publicly. But when Luke resolved to 'draw up a narrative concerning those matters which have been fully established among us,' he would naturally include therein everything which he knew to be authentic, and reject anything which was unreliable. The Revisers note: 'Many ancient authorities omit ver. 43, 44;' and

Alford: 'Verses 43, 44 are omitted in some of our oldest MSS., but contained in others, and in the most ancient versions.' Tischendorf has included them in his Critical Text, though he points out that they are omitted from the three oldest MSS., having been erased in the Sinaitic, which is the oldest. Alford observes: 'With the early and weighty evidence cited in my Gr. Test. in favour of verses 43, 44, it is impossible that they should have been an apocryphal insertion. The passage was perhaps expunged by the orthodox, who imagined they found in it an inconsistency with the divine nature of our Lord.'

Luke continues: 'And when he rose up from his prayer, he came unto the disciples, and found them sleeping for sorrow, and said unto them, Why sleep ye? rise and pray, that ye enter not into temptation.' The definite article now replaces 'his' before 'disciples,' on the authority of the three oldest MSS. The expression 'sleeping for sorrow' indicates that the evangelist saw reason for attributing the drowsiness to that cause; that the accounts handed down, by tradition or otherwise, represented them to have been outworn by the reaction of grief, rather than by mere bodily fatigue. The three were fishermen, and in that capacity were accustomed to lengthy vigils. Peter had once said: 'Master, we toiled all night'; but in this last night with their Master, instead of strong physical exertion, they had undergone intense mental emotion; they were harassed by the apprehension of the dangers unseen, impalpable, not to be guarded against, which surrounded him and them, knowing only that one of their own company had mysteriously departed for the purpose of delivering him to his enemies; they had been distressed by the trouble of his spirit at the supper table, and by his solemn words of parting: no wonder they were outworn by sorrow. As Luke's account ends with the exhortation, 'rise and pray that ye enter not into temptation,' the occasion must have been the first or second return of Jesus, for on his third return he told them that the necessity for watchfulness had passed. 'And he cometh the third time, and saith unto them, Sleep on now and take your rest: it is enough.' Young renders: 'Sleep on henceforth, and rest.' Matthew: 'Then cometh he to the disciples, and saith unto them, Sleep on now, and take your rest.' Here again 'his' before 'disciples' has been replaced by 'the,' on the authority of the three oldest MSS. The Revisers have omitted here and in Mark to italicise, as in the Authorised Version, the word 'your.' Young renders, 'Sleep on henceforth, and rest.' Jesus simply withdraws his command to watch on his behalf and their own: henceforth they could sleep when they would, free from reproach and danger. The crisis anticipated was now come: 'behold, the Son of man is betrayed into the hands of sinners.' 'The hour is come; behold, the Son of man is betrayed into the hands of sinners.' The word 'betrayed' seems to be not well chosen, the prominent idea in connection with it being treachery, which finds no place in Young's rendering 'delivered up,' corresponding with Luther's 'überantwortet.' What Jesus had shrunk from, but was now resigned to endure, was the triumph of evil over good, the power of wickedness, embodied in his enemies, over righteousness in the person of himself. He, the Son of man, the Messiah, the appointed Teacher,

Leader, Hope of mankind, must pass through this adversity; his personal influence in the world for good must cease, and be numbered with the things that are past; his light of life must be extinguished by the foul breath of sin; his followers must continue to suffer the same martyrdom; the wail of the Psalmist must still be prolonged through the ages:

_{94 Ps. 3}   'LORD, how long shall the wicked,
          How long shall the wicked triumph?'
'Lo, the Son of man is delivered up into the hands of the sinful.'

Yes: the redemption of mankind must be worked out in this fashion. The will of the Father admits of no other, shorter, better way: his Son, and all his saints, must drink this cup of affliction; there can be no immunity for any, no divine interposition even on behalf of Jesus himself. And he was now ready to be offered; _{10 Luke 21} 'Yea, Father; for so it was well pleasing in thy sight.' Sub- _{26 Mat. 46} missively, courageously he went forth to meet his destiny. 'Arise, _{14 Mark 42} let us be going: behold, he is at hand that betrayeth me.' 'Arise, let us be going: behold, he that betrayeth me is at hand.' This would seem to have been spoken to the three disciples, and to signify an intention of at once returning to the other eight. But at the very instant in which Jesus made the proposal, Judas Iscariot was seen approaching: and behind him a crowd of persons, armed and _{26 Mat. 47} carrying lights. 'And, while he yet spake, lo, Judas, one of the twelve came, and with him a great multitude with swords and _{14 Mark 43} staves.' 'And straightway, while he yet spake, cometh Judas, one of the twelve, and with him a multitude with swords and staves.' The word 'great' is here omitted before 'multitude,' on the authority of the two oldest MSS. In this verse the similarity of diction points to the adoption by Matthew and Mark of a common document which, being in a condensed form, became slightly varied in the narratives of the two evangelists, Mark adding 'straightway' before 'while,' and omitting 'great' before 'multitude.' Matthew's 'lo, Judas one of the twelve came,' being in Mark 'cometh Judas, one of the twelve.' A similar difference in construction is noticeable in the preceding verse, Matthew having, 'he is at hand that betrayeth me,' and Mark 'he that betrayeth me is at hand.' Luke's _{22 Luke 47} account is less detailed: 'While he yet spake, behold, a multitude, and he that was called Judas, one of the twelve, went before them.' The Revisers, following the three oldest MSS., have omitted 'and' _{26 Mat. 47} before 'while.' Matthew states that the armed band came 'from the _{14 Mark 43} chief priests and elders of the people.' Mark: 'from the chief priests and the scribes and the elders.' The fourth evangelist omits all mention of what had previously happened in the garden, and _{18 John 3} takes up the narrative at this point. 'Judas then, having received the band (or, cohort) *of soldiers*, and officers from the chief priests and the Pharisees, cometh thither with lanterns and torches and weapons.' The Revisers have altered the italicised words 'of men' to 'of soldiers.' Judas had prearranged a signal by which the soldiers, or constables, should be able to identify the person they _{26 Mat. 48} were sent to apprehend. 'Now he that betrayed him gave them a sign, saying, Whomsoever I shall kiss, that is he: take him.' The Revisers have altered 'hold him fast' to 'take him.' Young renders, 'lay hold on him'; Tischendorf, 'lay hold of him'; the 'Englishman's Greek New Testament, 'seize him.' Mark adds something: 'Now he that betrayed him had given them a token, saying, Whomsoever I shall kiss, that is he; take him, and lead him away safely.' Alford notes: 'It does not quite appear whether *safely* is to be subjectively taken, *with confidence*, or objectively, *in safety*.' Probably the former, for no harm was intended against Jesus by any other persons. But when Judas approached with the evident intention of kissing Jesus, he was received with a reproachful glance and words: 'and he drew near unto Jesus to kiss him. But Jesus said unto him, Judas, betrayest thou the Son of man with a kiss?' Still Judas would not, or could not, draw back. 'And straightway he came to Jesus, and said, Hail, Rabbi, and kissed him (Gr. kissed him much).' 'And when he was come, straightway he came to him, and saith, Rabbi: and kissed him (Gr. kissed him much).' Tischendorf renders, 'kissed him tenderly'; the 'Englishman's Greek New Testament,' 'ardently kissed him.' Alford notes: 'The word in the original implies, *kissed him eagerly*, with ostentation, as a studied and pre-arranged sign.' The verb used by Mark in verse 44 is *phileō*; in verse 45 *kataphileō*. Then again Jesus spoke to Judas. The Authorised Version reads: 'And Jesus said unto him, Friend, wherefore art thou come?' The Revised Version: 'And Jesus said unto him, Friend, *do* that for which thou art come.' The relevancy of such an observation is not apparent, Judas having already done that for which he had come. The word 'do' is an insertion of the Revisers. Young renders: 'Comrade, for what art thou present?' There is some difficulty about the proper translation. Alford says: 'It is more than doubtful whether the words can properly be rendered as a *question*. More likely do they mean, "Friend, there needs not this show of attachment: I know thine errand,—do thy purpose." But the command itself is suppressed.' Without adding the word 'do,' or supplying a note of interrogation, the saying stands, 'Friend—that for which thou art come.' It was enough to contrast the two things,—the show of friendship—'Friend!' and the object of the visit—'That for which thou art come.' The brief exclamation was full of reproach,—another form of the expostulation, 'Betrayest thou—with a kiss?' John's narrative appears to come in at this point. We can picture to ourselves the scene. The eleven apostles would naturally be standing close about Jesus. Judas, after giving the kiss, would not venture to join them, but fell back towards those with whom he came. Without delay, Jesus stepped forward, and enquired who was the person sought. 'Jesus, therefore, knowing all the things that were coming upon him, went forth, and saith unto them, Whom seek ye?' Note the expression, 'Knowing all the things that were coming upon him:' the evangelist is not careful to justify the assertion in any way, although he could have told of the prayers and agony of Jesus in anticipation of what was about to happen. The same reticence is observable in other parts of John's narrative: 'He knew all men . . . He himself knew what was in man . . . He himself knew what he would do . . . Jesus knew from the beginning who they were that believed not, and who it was that should betray him.' These statements were not made rashly; no doubt the writer had his reasons, and could have supplied them in every instance. A true witness is not anxious to give proof of everthing he asserts.

<small>18 John 5</small> The officers gave a plain answer to the enquiry of Jesus. 'They answered him, Jesus of Nazareth.' Young and Tischendorf render, literally, 'Jesus the Nazarene.' He forthwith admitted his identity. <small>" 5</small> 'Jesus saith unto them, I am *he*.' Still there seemed to be irresolution, delay. Judas was now standing with the cohort, which, instead <small>" 5, 6</small> of advancing, retired. 'And Judas also, which betrayed him, was standing with them. When therefore he said unto them, I am *he*, they went backward.' There was something very strange in that: <small>" 6</small> something still more so in the additional fact: 'and fell to the ground.' No hint is given as to whether this retirement and prostration were voluntary or involuntary, except that the expression 'went backward' naturally indicates the former. Young renders: 'they went away backward, and fell to the ground. Alford writes very positively on the matter: 'The question on the miraculous nature of this incident is not whether it was a miracle *at all* (for it is evident that it *must* be regarded as one) but whether it were an act *specially intended* by our Lord, or a result of the superhuman dignity of His person, and the majestic calmness of His reply. I believe the latter alternative to be the right one. Commentators cite various instances of the confusion of the enemies of *innocent men* before the calmness and dignity of their victims : how much more was this likely to be the case when He in whom was no sin, and who spake as never man spake, came forth to meet His implacable foes as the self-sacrificing Lamb of God. So that I regard it rather as a miracle *consequent upon* that which Christ said and did, and the state of mind in which His enemies were, than as one, in the strict sense, *wrought* by Him : bearing however always in mind, that to Him nothing was *unexpected*, or a *mere result*, but everything foreknown.' Whether the evangelist regarded the circumstance in that or a totally different light, we cannot know ; he has recorded it simply as any observer might who had no clue to the proper explanation. It is not said that the men were struck down ; on the contrary, the words might without any strain be paraphrased thus : 'they retired, and prostrated themselves.' Alford's view admits as much, only he assumes that they could not help doing what they did, that the cohort were simultaneously overcome by the majestic demeanour and words of Jesus, and all instinctively manifested their amazement and confusion in the same way. That would be altogether so contrary to nature, that the suggestion involves a miracle of the most astounding kind. The event admits of a natural interpretation. The men appear to have been trained soldiers. Alford considers the 'great multitude' to have consisted ' of (1) a detachment of the Roman cohort which was quartered in the tower of Antonia during the feast in case of an uproar, called *the band*, John vv. 3, 12. (2) The servants of the council, the same as the *captains of the temple*, Luke ver. 52. (3) Servants and others deputed from the high priest to assist, see Mat. ver. 51. (4) Possibly, if the words are to be taken exactly (Luke ver. 52), some of the chief priests and elders themselves, forward in zeal and enmity.' The question of Jesus, ' Whom seek ye ?' would naturally be addressed to those by whom the arrest was to be made ; they were men acting under orders, and probably among

them were some who had heard of Jesus and honoured him. If their foremost officer happened to be such an one, a word of command from him to retire would be instantly obeyed, and would sufficiently account for the sudden and unexpected movement; the act of prostration may have been a recognized form of homage to which the troops were disciplined, or may have been in imitation of their leader, a voluntary act on the part of most or all, and expressive of the men's sympathy in the respect manifested by him to the well-known Teacher whom they were bound to apprehend as though he had been a criminal. That task might be highly distasteful to many or most of those compelled to undertake it. What! go and seize the man who had done so many miracles, who had opened the eyes of the blind, raised Lazarus from the dead, and whom the populace had lately hailed with enthusiasm, crying out, 'Hosanna: Blessed *is* he that cometh in the name of the Lord, even the King of Israel.' At least, before a hand was laid upon him, they would mutely testify their intense respect for his person and character: it is possible that their action was not a momentary impulse, but deliberately planned from the first. Another explanation has been suggested. The treachery of Judas is supposed to have been part of an ambitious scheme for making Jesus assume his rightful position as the Jewish Messiah. Pretending to play into the hands of his enemies, Judas did not scruple to place his Master within their grasp, convinced that he would then be forced to free himself, even by supernatural power if necessary. The avarice of Judas is assumed to have been subordinate to his cunning. He wanted to expedite the time when Jesus would become a King indeed, and he one of the twelve greatest men in his kingdom. Having been entrusted with the cohort, which was instructed to carry out his directions, he partly revealed his plan to the men composing it, told them to take Jesus, but be careful to lead him away safely, and first of all to join with himself in tendering an unmistakeable act of homage. Up to the last, he could truly say, 'Hail, Master,' and there was sincerity in his kiss, if only the heart of Jesus would chime in with the ambitious project. Though the kiss was received coldly and reproachfully, the plan must be carried through: surely this attitude of the soldiers and himself must convince Jesus that he had only to speak the word, and they were ready to do his bidding, to turn their arms against those who sent them, and make Jesus the king they were anxious he should be. The scheme of Judas failed, and from that moment he was a disappointed, baffled man. This theory of his conduct is plausible, has been carefully conceived, and might be further elaborated; but it is best dismissed: nothing is easier than to form theories, and the character of even the worst of men ought not to be sported with. The work of the historian is restricted to facts; only the Omniscient can deal with motives. Imagination is out of place in any sober record of events. Historical romances are the least desirable form of fiction. It is legitimate enough to invent purely fictitious characters, to mould, drape and analyse them as we will; but the deeds and words of men who were once alive should never be altered or added to. This applies equally to Scriptural and to secular history.

Whatever the cause of the hesitation manifested by the soldiers, Jesus sought no personal advantage from it. He simply repeated his

18 John 7	enquiry as to their errand. 'Again therefore he asked them, Whom seek ye?' And they said, Jesus of Nazareth,' probably a quotation of the words of the warrant placed in their hands. To that, Jesus urged them to adhere. They were authorised to take him, and no one else : therefore his disciples must be allowed to depart in peace.
,, 8	'Jesus answered, I told you that I am *he* : if therefore ye seek me, let these go their way.' Young renders : 'suffer these to go away ;' Tischendorf : 'leave these to go away.' Probably they were all surrounded by the cohort, Jesus standing somewhat in advance of the apostles, to whom his words were an intimation of his desire that they should at once depart. This anxiety for their safety made a deep impression on the evangelist, who adds : 'that the word might be fulfilled which he spake, Of those whom thou hast given me I lost not one.'
,, 9	
17 John 12	This appears to refer to his recorded saying : 'I guarded them, and not one of them perished.' Alford comments as follows : 'An unquestionable proof, if any were wanted, that the words of chap. xvii. are no mere description of the mind of our Lord at the time, nor free arrangement of His words, but His very words themselves. On the application of the saying, we may remark that the words unquestionably had a much deeper meaning than any belonging to this occasion : but that the remarks so often made in this commentary on the fulfilment of prophecies must be borne in mind ;—that to *fulfil* a prophecy is not to *exhaust* its capability of being again and again fulfilled :—that the words of the Lord have many stages of unfolding ;—and that the temporal deliverance of the apostles now, doubtless was but a part in the great spiritual safe-keeping which the Lord asserted by anticipation in these words.'
26 Mat. 50	The appeal of Jesus was respected : the apostles were not arrested, but Jesus only. 'Then they came and laid hands on Jesus, and took
14 Mark 46	him.' 'And they laid hands on him, and took him.' The word in the original here rendered 'took him,' is rendered by Young in Matthew 'kept hold on him,' and in Mark 'held him fast,' and by Tischendorf in both places 'laid hold of him :' from that moment Jesus was a prisoner.
22 Luke 49	The apostles were in no haste to act upon the hint of Jesus and 'go their way.' But to see him treated as a criminal, and yet stand idly by, was more than they could bear. 'And when they that were about him saw what would follow, they said, Lord (Sir—Young), shall we smite with the sword?' The Revisers, following the two oldest MSS., have omitted 'unto him' after 'said.' One of the apostles, in hot anger, without permission, and reckless of consequences, aimed a blow at the high priest's servant, the sword barely
,, 50	escaping the man's head, and actually severing one of his ears. 'And a certain one of them smote the servant (Gr. bondservant) of the high priest, and struck off his right ear.' Matthew and Mark, as well
26 Mat. 51	as Luke, withhold the name of the striker. 'And behold, one of them that were with Jesus stretched out his hand, and drew his sword, and smote the servant (Gr. bondservant) of the high priest, and struck off
14 Mark 47	his ear.' 'But a certain one of them that stood by drew his sword, and smote the servant (Gr. bondservant) of the high priest, and struck off his ear.' Alford observes that why the name 'was not mentioned, is idle to enquire : one supposition only must be avoided—that there is any *purpose* in the omission. It is absurd to suppose that the

mention of his name in a book current only among Christians, many years after the fact, could lead to his apprehension, which did not take place *at the time*, although he was recognised as the striker in the palace of the High Priest, John, ver. 46.' That is not quite accurate: the fourth evangelist does not say that 'he was recognised as the striker,' but simply that he was identified as being present at the time by a kinsman of the person struck. Moreover, the 'book current only among Christians, many years after the fact,' is composed of records which were extant from the first, and from which—at first —it may have been deemed right to exclude the name, lest the person named should be exposed to obloquy, or worse. At the same time, it is quite possible, even probable, that in the confusion prevailing at the time, which was midnight, it was not known generally who had struck the blow ; if one only of themselves, John for instance, could have identified the striker, he would have chosen to be silent on the point. But when the fourth gospel was written, which Alford considers could not have been earlier than A. D. 70—85, no reason for reticence existed ; accordingly, the fourth evangelist did not scruple to declare the name. 'Simon Peter therefore having a sword drew it, and struck the high priest's servant (Gr. bondservant), and cut off his right ear. Now the servant's (Gr. bondservant's) name was Malchus.' Sternly and peremptorily Jesus bade the apostle sheathe his sword. 'Jesus therefore said unto Peter, Put up the sword into the sheath.' 'Thy' has been altered to 'the,' on the authority of the three oldest MSS. Matthew's account is fuller. 'Then saith Jesus unto him, Put up again thy sword into its place : for all they that take the sword shall perish with the sword.' Young renders : 'for all who have taken the sword, by the sword shall perish' ; Tischendorf : 'for all they that have taken a sword will perish by a sword.' All efforts to defend Jesus or his cause by brute force are out of place and doomed to fail. 'The weapons of our warfare are not of the flesh.' The only aid in which Jesus could trust must come from above, and that was even now available to him. 'Or thinkest thou that I cannot beseech my Father, and he shall even now send me more than twelve legions of angels ?' The Revisers and Tischendorf have supplied the word 'or' ; 'pray to' is altered to 'beseech ;' Tischendorf has 'entreat ;' Young 'call upon.' By 'pray to' some are apt to understand a set form of petition, as though some virtue attached to the prayer itself ; at least, that notion is too common with respect to our own prayers. In the Authorised Version the word 'now' stands after 'cannot,' and 'presently' after 'shall.' The former is omitted in the two oldest MSS., and the Revisers have replaced the latter by 'even now.' Alford says : 'One of these, *now*, or *presently*, should be omitted. The word is read by some authorities in the former clause, and by some in the latter : but by none in both.' In place of 'send me,' Tischendorf renders, 'furnish me with,' and Young has, 'place beside me more than twelve legions of messengers.' Alford explains : 'The complement of the legion was about 6000 men.' That absence of defence, which Peter foolishly attempted to supply by his own puny arm, arose from no lack of divine sympathy, but was consonant with the heavenly Father's will, and deliberately acquiesced in by Jesus. One word of command from God, or of entreaty by Jesus, would have sufficed to set all the hosts of heaven in movement for the

18 John 10

,, 11

26 Mat. 52

9 ii. Cor. 4

26 Mat. 53

succour of the beloved Son. But that word must not be spoken, nor that petition uttered: 'How then should the Scriptures be fulfilled, that thus it must be?' The word 'but' before 'how' is omitted by the Revisers, Young and Tischendorf, not being in the original. 'Thus it must be:' if the prayer of Jesus, 'Remove this cup from me,' could not be granted, how much more was the sword of Peter out of place! The fourth evangelist supplies the closing words: 'the cup which the Father hath given me, shall I not drink it?' Young renders: 'may I not drink it?' without any officious interference on the part of those whom he had undertaken to teach, by precept and example, to suffer and to die. That no evil consequences might remain from the blow so rashly and unwarrantably given, Jesus craved permission to stretch out his hand for healing. 'But Jesus answered and said, Suffer ye thus far.' Alford observes: 'His hands were held, and He says, *Suffer, permit me, thus far*: i.e. to touch the ear of the wounded person.' 'And he touched his ear, and healed him.' Tischendorf renders 'the ear,' in accordance with the two oldest MSS. From the expression 'touched the ear,' Alford infers that 'the (external) ear, though severed, was apparently still hanging on the cheek.'

Although Jesus would not permit the lifting of a hand on his account, he protested indignantly against the manner of his apprehension. 'In that hour said Jesus to the multitudes, Are ye come out as against a robber with swords and staves to seize me?' The Revisers, agreeing with Young and Tischendorf, have omitted 'same' before 'hour.' Mark reports precisely the same words, prefacing them with: 'And Jesus answered and said unto them.' Luke states that he addressed himself to the leaders, who naturally would be standing nearest to him. 'And Jesus said unto the chief priests, and captains (magistrates—Young) of the temple, and elders, which were come against him, Are ye come out, as against a robber, with swords and staves?' In each of the three narratives Young and Tischendorf render 'ye are' instead of 'are ye?' omitting the note of interrogation. The only charge which could be devised against Jesus must be with respect to his teaching, and they had suffered him to go on with that unmolested and in public day after day. 'I sat daily in the temple teaching, and ye took me not.' 'Ye laid no hold on me' has been altered to 'ye took me not,' but Young renders, 'ye laid not hold on me,' Tischendorf, 'ye did not lay hold of me,' the 'Englishman's Greek New Testament, 'ye did not seize me,' and Alford left the Authorised Version unaltered. The words 'with you' are omitted after 'daily,' on the authority of the two oldest MSS. Probably they were inserted to agree with the other evangelists. Mark: 'I was daily with you in the temple teaching, and ye took me not.' Luke: 'When I was daily with you in the temple, ye stretched not forth your hands against me.' To this protest Jesus added an explanation: 'But all this is come to pass, that the scriptures of the prophets might be fulfilled.' The Authorised Version has: 'But all this was done,' leaving it doubtful whether the words were spoken by Jesus or added by the evangelist. Young's rendering admits of no uncertainty: 'but all this hath come to pass, that the writings of the prophets may be fulfilled.' Tischendorf also has 'is' for 'was' and 'may' for 'might.' Mark: 'but this is done that the scriptures might be fulfilled:' Young: 'but that the Writings may be fulfilled:' Tischendorf: 'but it is that the scriptures may be fulfilled.' Luke omits this saying of Jesus, but records another: 'but this is your hour, and the power of darkness.' Tischendorf renders 'power' as 'authority.' The gloom of midnight well beseemed the blackness of their deed. [22 Luke 53]

It was evident that the apostles could do nothing for their Master, and they now acted upon his suggestion that they should 'go their way.' 'Then all the disciples left him, and fled.' The Revisers, Young and Tischendorf have altered 'forsook' to 'left.' It could not properly be called a 'forsaking' of Jesus: nothing would have been gained by following the crowd, and it was time to think of their own safety, especially after the blow given by the impetuous Peter to the priest's servant. The word 'fled' indicates some attempt to lay hands upon them. Young renders: 'then all the disciples, having left him, fled,' as though, their departure having been observed, they were compelled to evade pursuit. Mark relates the occurrence in the same words: 'And they all left him, and fled:' and he tells what happened to one person who did follow by the side of Jesus. 'And a certain young man followed with him, having a linen cloth cast about him, over *his* naked *body*: and they lay hold on him.' The Revisers have altered 'young men' to 'they,' on the authority of the two oldest MSS., which also omit the word 'certain.' The unusual garb must have been assumed hastily: perhaps its wearer had been roused from sleep suddenly, and rather than miss seeing what was about to happen, had followed with all speed, careless about dressing, and with the eagerness of youth had placed himself in this prominent position. Whether he was a disciple of Jesus, or intended thus to show respect to him, or was simply actuated by curiosity, we cannot tell; but whatever his motive, the captors of Jesus would now have no prying or sympathising stranger among them, and laid hold of him. One can imagine their astonishment and derision, when he slipped out of their hands, leaving his only garment behind him: 'but he left the linen cloth, and fled naked.' The words 'from them' are omitted after 'fled,' on the authority of the two oldest MSS. [26 Mat. 56; 14 Mark 50; ,, 51; ,, 52]

Luke's narrative continues: 'And they seized him, and led him *away*, and brought him into the high priest's house.' The Revisers have introduced the italicised word 'away.' Tischendorf renders, literally: 'And when they took him, they led and led him into the high priest's house.' Jesus was 'led' as any other unresisting prisoner might be, and he was subjected to the further indignity of being manacled. 'So the band (or, cohort) and the chief captain (or, military tribune, Gr. chiliarch), and the officers of the Jews, seized Jesus and bound him, and led him to Annas first.' The Revisers, Tischendorf and Alford have replaced 'then' by 'so,' which Young renders as 'therefore.' The word 'away' is omitted after 'him,' in accordance with the two oldest MSS. Only the fourth evangelist mentions Annas, and relates the examination of Jesus by him. The reason for taking the prisoner 'to Annas first' is thus explained: 'for he was father-in-law to Caiaphas, which was high priest that year.' The word 'same' is omitted before 'year.' Young and Tischendorf render 'of that year.' Alford notes: 'The influence of Annas appears to have been very great, and Acts iv. 6, he is called [22 Luke 54; 18 John 12; ,, 13] *the High Priest,* in the year following this. The narrative evidently rests upon some arrangement with regard to the High Priesthood now unknown to us, but accountable enough by foreign influence and the deterioration of the priestly class through bribes and intrigues, to which Josephus and the Talmud sufficiently testify.' Luke states that at the commencement of John the Baptist's preaching, Annas and Caiaphas were high priests, indicating either that there were two high priests, or that there was a joint high-priesthood. The fourth evangelist twice alludes to Caiaphas as 'high priest of that year,' but he now mentions Annas in conjunction with him, and as exercising jurisdiction, apparently in the same palace. He adds: 'Now Caiaphas was he which gave counsel to the Jews that it was expedient that one man should die for the people.' Young renders 'expedient' by 'good;' the 'Englishman's Greek New Testament' by 'profitable.' There was small hope for Jesus in coming before a man who had already expressed that opinion with reference to him. Two of the disciples appear to have returned after fleeing from the cohort, and to have followed the procession. It was a bold thing to do, and we are not surprised to find that one of them was the boastful Peter, the name of the other not being disclosed by the evangelist. 'And Simon Peter followed Jesus, and *so did* another disciple.' The Revisers have italicised the words 'so did.' Alford and Young, following the original reading, render 'the other' instead of 'another.' On the part of that disciple there could be no thought of concealment, for he was known to the high priest, and he was therefore permitted to follow Jesus into the palace. 'Now that disciple was known unto the high priest, and entered in with Jesus into the court of the high priest.' The word 'now,' rendered 'and' by Young and Tischendorf, has been added by the Revisers. 'Palace' is altered to 'court,' rendered by Young 'hall.' Peter was obliged to remain outside until his companion came out, spoke to the doorkeeper, and obtained admission for him: 'but Peter was standing at the door without. So the other disciple, which was known unto the high priest, went out and spoke unto her that kept the door, and brought in Peter.' His friend being known as a disciple of Jesus, and having thus interested himself to introduce a companion who had accompanied him thither, what more natural than to suppose that the connection between the two men and Jesus must be the same? A question on the point was at once put to Peter. 'The maid therefore that kept the door saith unto Peter, Art thou also *one* of this man's disciples?' Here was the opportune moment for Peter to carry out the determination he had but a few hours ago so deliberately formed and emphatically expressed: 'If I must die with thee, I will not deny thee.' He had begun boldly, albeit not wisely, when in the garden he had struck a blow for his Master, and though he had fled with the rest, yet he was soon back again, and is now here in the same building with Jesus. Alas, alas! Can this be the voice of Peter? Does he know what he is saying? 'He saith, I am not.' Imagine the amazement of his fellow-disciple! Well: it is not for him to interfere, to denounce Peter as a liar and a coward, although nothing can justify so shameless a denial. What can have been his motive? Did he fear to be excluded if he spoke the truth? Did some evil spirit suggest the impromptu lie, and move the apostle's lips to its vile utterance? Surely he will, on reflection, retract, or at least whisper a word of regret or explanation to his companion! Surely he is not himself: the strain, physical and mental, has been too much for him; anxiety, want of rest, and cold, have benumbed the mind as well as the body, unnerved him, made him both timid and callous here, as he had been before both bold and reckless in the garden! Well: having abjured his Master, he is his own master now, and must be left to himself! That eventful night was trying enough to all who took part in it. There was no thought of sleep for anyone; the servants and officers were standing about, a fire was made up, the night being chilly, and they grouped themselves round it. 'Now the servants (Gr. bondservants) and the officers were standing *there*, having made a fire of coals (Gr. a fire of charcoal); for it was cold: and they were warming themselves.' Peter made no attempt to avoid observation, but placed himself in the midst of the group: 'and Peter also was with them, standing and warming himself.' The attention of all present must now have been centred upon Jesus, who was being examined by the high priest. 'The high priest therefore asked Jesus of his disciples, and of his teaching.' Jesus practically refused to supply any information, alleging that his teaching had been in public, and that the proper course for obtaining any testimony with respect to it, would be to examine those who had heard his preaching. 'Jesus answered him, I have spoken openly to the world.' Alford notes: '*plainly* (referring to the character of the *things said*): not *openly* (referring to the outward *circumstances under which* they were said), which the word will not bear.' In Jerusalem his discourses had invariably been delivered either in a synagogue or in the temple, places which all Jews were in the habit of frequenting: 'I ever taught in synagogues, and in the temple, where all the Jews come together.' The Revisers have altered 'the synagogue' to 'synagogues,' adding the note, '(Gr. synagogue).' There were many synagogues, and only one temple, which Tischendorf—following another reading—indicates, not by altering the singular to the plural, but by rendering 'a synagogue.' 'Always' has been replaced by 'all,' on the authority of the three oldest MSS. Not the slightest approach to secret teaching had been made by Jesus: 'and in secret spake I nothing.' Why should the ordinary course of judicial investigation be departed from, by questioning the prisoner instead of witnesses? 'Why askest thou me?' His hearers would be the proper persons to supply the required information: 'ask them that have heard *me*, what I spake unto them.' Witnesses were not far to seek: 'behold, these know the things which I said.' The Revisers have replaced 'they' by 'these.' Alford observes: 'Our Lord appeals to persons *there present* in court, pointing at or otherwise designating them. The word "they" in the A. V. makes it appear as if He meant *those which heard Me*. The *officers* mentioned in ch. vii. 46 may have been present.' The reply of Jesus was as unanswerable as it was bold. He was entitled at least to the treatment of an ordinary prisoner, and he stood within his right in making this vigorous and uncompromising protest. The judge made no attempt to silence or reprove him, but an officious underling took upon himself to resent what he deemed an impertinent reply. 'And when he had said this (Young

—these things) one of the officers standing by struck Jesus with his hand (or, with a rod), saying, Answerest thou the high priest so?' The Revisers have omitted 'the palm of' before 'his hand.' Young renders: 'gave Jesus a slap.' Alford explains: 'It is not quite certain whether the word here used implies a blow with the hand, or with a staff.' Even that did not disturb the equanimity of Jesus. With quiet dignity he reproved his assailant. 'Jesus answered him, If I have spoken evil, bear witness of the evil; but if well, why smitest thou me?' In the absence of a tittle of evidence, or even of accusation, how could it be justifiable thus to insult and assault him? The Authorised Version continues: 'Now Annas had sent him bound unto Caiaphas the high priest.' The Revised Version has: 'Annas therefore sent him bound unto Caiaphas the high priest.' The omission of the word 'had' gives a different sense to the statement. Tischendorf's rendering is word for word the same as the Revisers', and Young's agrees: 'Annas then sent him bound to Caiaphas the chief priest.' Alford renders: 'So Annas sent him ...' and against the word 'had' notes: 'not according to the original,' adding: 'I cannot acquiesce in the *pluperfect* rendering of this word *sent*, to bring about which the opening particle, *so*, has apparently been omitted by the copyists. I believe the verse simply to describe what followed on the preceding—*So Annas* (or *Annas therefore*) *sent him bound to Caiaphas the High Priest.* "Then," says Chrysostom, "not being able even thus to make progress in their decision, they send Him bound to Caiaphas." There is no real difficulty in this rendering, if Annas and Caiaphas lived in one palace, or at all events transacted public affairs in one and the same. They would naturally have different apartments, and thus the sending from one to the other would be very possible.' Luther also renders: 'Und Hannas sandte ihn ... And Annas sent him ...' We are almost forced to the conclusion that the word 'had' was introduced in order to conform to the idea that the examination of the prisoner related by the fourth evangelist took place before Caiaphas, not before Annas. That might seem to harmonise this account with the narratives of the other evangelists, who do not mention Annas, and also to explain the remark of the fourth evangelist himself, four verses lower down, 'They lead Jesus therefore from Caiaphas into the palace.' The addition of the word 'had' might seem at the same time to get rid of this further difficulty: the fourth evangelist states twice that Caiaphas 'was high priest that year,' then alludes to Annas under that title,—'The high priest therefore asked Jesus ...' yet shortly after again calls Caiaphas 'the high priest.' But there was as little need as there could be justification, to tamper with the text. Luke alludes to a previous joint high-priesthood, the fourth evangelist, who 'was known unto the high priest,' and must therefore have been fully cognizant of the facts, seems to intimate an alternate yearly assumption of the office, and in the Acts we find the two mentioned thus: 'Annas the high priest, and Caiaphas, and John, and Alexander;' although both sat at the same tribunal, Annas only is called 'the high priest,' and the name of Caiaphas is merged with that of others present. As the Jewish year began with the passover, it is probable that the office was on the very point of transfer from Caiaphas to Annas, which would account for Jesus being taken before both. There may have been a friendly purpose on the part of the 'chief captain and officers,' who seem to have voluntarily prostrated themselves at the feet of Jesus before apprehending him, in leading 'him to Annas first;' there was small hope of justice from Caiaphas, with his counsel that it was good that one man should die for the people, and if Annas had remanded the prisoner until his own term of office commenced, instead of at once sending him to his son-in-law, a fairer trial might have been anticipated.

The examination by Annas seems to have been merely tentative and preliminary, and the three other evangelists confine themselves to what occurred before Caiaphas. 'And they that had taken Jesus led him away to *the house of* Caiaphas the high priest.' The words, 'the house of' are not in the original, and would seem to have been inserted by the Revisers as explanatory of this which follows: 'where the scribes and the elders were gathered together.' Mark says: 'And they led Jesus away to the high priest,' adding that he was accompanied by many others of rank and influence: 'and there come together with him all the chief priests and the elders and the scribes.' Luke, confining himself at present to what happened to Peter in the palace, makes no mention of the high priest: 'And they seized him, and led him *away*, and brought him into the high priest's house.' The italicised word 'away' is an insertion by the Revisers. Tischendorf renders, literally: 'And when they took him they led and led him into the high priest's house.' 26 Mat. 57

,, 57

14 Mark 53

,, 53

22 Luke 54

The narrative is now taken up by the three synoptic gospels at the point where Peter was sitting by the fire. Matthew: 'But Peter followed him afar off, into the court of the high priest, and entered in, and sat with the officers, to see the end.' Mark: 'And Peter had followed him afar off, even within, into the court of the high priest; and he was sitting with the officers, and warming himself in the light *of the fire*.' In both passages the word 'servants' is now rendered 'officers,' which agrees with Young. Tischendorf has 'attendants.' Tischendorf renders simply 'at the light.' The mention of firelight seems designed to indicate that Peter braved recognition rather than courted concealment. Luke states that he actually sat down in the centre of the group. 'And when they had kindled a fire in the midst of the court, and had sat down together, Peter sat in the midst of them.' 26 Mat. 58

14 Mark 54

22 Luke 54, 55

A meeting of the Sanhedrim had been summoned, and met at daybreak. 'And as soon as it was day, the assembly of the elders of the people was gathered together, both chief priests and scribes; and they led him away into their council.' Young, Tischendorf being nearly the same, renders: 'the eldership of the people, chief priests also, and scribes, and they led him up into their sanhedrim.' Their first effort was to obtain evidence sufficient to make Jesus amenable to a charge entailing capital punishment. 'Now the chief priests and the whole council sought false witness against Jesus, that they might put him to death.' The words 'and elders,' after 'priests,' are omitted on the authority of the two oldest MSS. Tischendorf renders 'Sanhedrim' literally, instead of council. The omission here made by the Revisers brings this wording of Matthew into close correspondence with Mark, which is as follows: 'Now the chief priests and the whole council sought witness against Jesus to ,, 66

26 Mat. 59

14 Mark 55

put him to death.' Young and Tischendorf render 'council' as 'Sanhedrim.' Matthew's bold assertion that 'false' testimony was sought requires no confirmation: any evidence to swear away the life of one so innocent as Jesus must of necessity be perjured. But this weapon of attack broke in their hands: 'and they found it not, though many false witnesses came.' The Revisers have omitted the word 'yea' before 'though,' and the concluding words '*yet* found they none,' on the authority of the two oldest MSS. Mark explains that the evidence was too weak or contradictory to warrant a conviction: 'and found it not. For many bare false witness against him, and their witness agreed not together.' Alford notes: 'literally, *their testimonies were not equal.*' Tischendorf and the 'Englishman's Greek New Testament' render 'not alike.' At last two men came forward stating that they once heard Jesus say something about pulling down the temple and building another. 'But afterwards came two, and said, This man said, I am able to destroy the temple (or, sanctuary), and to build it in three days.' The words 'false witnesses' have been omitted after 'two,' on the authority of the two oldest MSS. Instead of 'man' the Authorised Version has 'fellow' in italics. Alford notes: 'Not expressed in the original. Better, *This man.*' Mark relates: 'And there stood up certain, and bare false witness against him, saying, We heard him say, I will destroy this temple (or, sanctuary) that is made with hands, and in three days I will build another made without hands.' This seems to indicate the contradictions and discrepancies between the two. 'I am able to destroy' becomes 'I will destroy,' and the addition, 'made without hands,' placed the saying, be it what it might, outside the range of human action and jurisdiction. No legal accusation or sentence could be formulated in respect of words so vague and visionary, especially as the witnesses differed: 'And not even so did their witness agree together.' The charge attempted to be made involved sacrilege. It appears to have been based on a reminiscence, exaggerated and perverted, of the saying of Jesus: 'Destroy this temple, and in three days I will raise it up:' words enigmatical even to the disciples, who came eventually to understand, after his resurrection, that 'he spake of the temple of his body,' which not he but his enemies would destroy. Jesus had listened in silence to the evidence tendered against him. The high priest therefore rose and addressed him: 'And the high priest stood up, and said unto him . .' 'And the high priest stood up in the midst, and asked Jesus, saying, Answerest thou nothing? what is it which these witness against thee?' In the Authorised Version the words 'is it which' are italicised, but in both gospels the Revisers have omitted to italicise them. Tischendorf renders: 'Answerest thou nothing to what these witness against thee?' which is strictly literal except the inserted word 'to.' Jesus nevertheless maintained his imperturbable silence. 'But Jesus held his peace.' 'But he held his peace, and answered nothing.' Unless something could be extracted from his own mouth, there was absolutely nothing of which to accuse him. Annas had already attempted to draw admissions from him respecting his disciples and his teaching, but without success, Jesus having refused to answer any of his questions. Up to this point he had preserved the same policy of silence before Caiaphas. Luke represents Jesus to have been questioned by the council generally: 'and they led him away into their council, saying, If thou art the Christ, tell us.' Jesus replied that what he might say on that point they would not believe, and if he attempted to argue with them, they would not deign to answer. 'But he said unto them, If I tell you, ye will not believe: and if I ask *you*, ye will not answer.' Following the two oldest MSS. the Revisers have omitted 'also' after 'I,' and 'me, nor let me go' after 'answer.' But now the question was put officially by Caiaphas. 'And the high priest asked him, and saith unto him, Art thou the Christ, the Son of the Blessed?' Alford notes that 'the Blessed' is, 'in Hebrew, the ordinary name for God,' and he quotes Meyer: 'This is the only place in the New Testament where the well-known name constantly used by the Rabbis is thus absolutely given.' Matthew explains that in order to draw an answer from Jesus the most solemn form of adjuration was employed: 'And the high priest said unto him, I adjure thee by the living God, that thou tell us whether thou be the Christ, the Son of God.' The words 'answered and' are omitted before 'said:' they are not in the Vatican MS. and had been erased from the Sinaitic MS. by a later hand. To an appeal of that character, Jesus would not hesitate to respond. His answer was immediate, bold and clear. But from Luke's narrative it may be inferred that the question had a twofold bearing, arising from the statement which had been made by Jesus: 'But from henceforth shall the Son of man be seated at the right hand of the power of God.' The word 'but' has been added in accordance with the three oldest MSS. 'Hereafter' has been altered to 'from henceforth.' This assertion respecting the exaltation of humanity to the power of Deity was an addition to the recognised anticipations of the Messiah, and naturally led to the enquiry whether Jesus claimed to be both the Christ, as generally conceived of, and also this Son of God with power. The assembly fixed on the latter as the crucial question. 'And they all said, Art thou then the Son of God?' The demand of the high priest combined the two questions: Art thou (1) the Christ, (2) the Son of the Blessed? Jesus replied in the affirmative. 'Jesus saith unto him, Thou hast said.' Mark: 'And Jesus said, I am.' Luke: 'And he said unto them, Ye say that I am (or, Ye say *it*, because I am),' rendered by Young and Tischendorf, 'Ye say it, for I am.' But of the two claims, that of a glorified humanity would be pre-eminent: 'nevertheless I say unto you, Henceforth ye shall see the Son of man sitting at the right hand of power, and coming on the clouds of heaven.' Instead of 'nevertheless' the 'Englishman's Greek New Testament' renders 'moreover:' the word, *plēn*, is defined as '(properly contracted from *pleon*, more than), beyond.' The Revisers, agreeing with Tischendorf and the 'Englishman's Greek New Testament,' have altered 'hereafter' to 'henceforth,' denoting a continuous manifestation, not merely a single event at some future time. Mark has: 'and ye shall see the Son of man sitting at the right hand of power, and coming with the clouds of heaven.' Although 'henceforth' is omitted, the word 'sitting' denotes a continuous session. The expression 'sitting on the right hand of power, and coming with the clouds of heaven,' is obviously figurative. The apostle Paul held that 'there is no power but of God.' Jesus here asserts that to himself, as the Messiah, would appertain all power, from its source and in its fulness, and a rulership high above the world as the clouds of heaven are high above the earth. The revelation of these things is not for earth, but will be in heaven, not for this life but in the life to come. ' Ye shall see,' said Jesus to his judges : but they never saw it on this side the grave, and if there were no life beyond in which they could see it, the declaration of Jesus would be visionary, baseless, untrue, ' for if there is no resurrection of the dead, neither hath Christ been raised.' They looked for a Messiah who would visibly *sit* to judge and *come* to save his people ; but his judgment would be divine, not human, and his appearance to salvation would be in a higher world than this. All this was contrary to Jewish hopes and aspirations. We know that Caiaphas nourished expectations of Jewish nationality ; he argued that by the death of Jesus the nation would be saved from perishing, that it would therefore be a national benefit, ' Jesus should die for the nation,' thereby making possible the gathering together into one of all scattered Israelities. The evangelist added that in a different and far loftier sense than the speaker's own, his inspired words would come to pass, but we can judge of the state of mind of Caiaphas by the contemptuous tone of his observation : ' Ye know nothing at all, nor do ye take account that it is expedient for you that one man should die for the people.' He had far-sighted political views, overlooked by others, and nothing must be allowed to stand in the way of putting Jesus to death. The Baptist had pointed to him as the hope of Israel, but the scribes and Pharisees did not take John for a prophet, and the teaching and labours of Jesus had no reference whatever to a redemption of Israel answering to popular expectation. Now from the lips of Jesus himself they had heard words which, if heeded, would give the death blow to long cherished desires of national recovery and aggrandisement. On every ground Jesus stood condemned : he claimed to be the Messiah, without moving a step towards the accomplishment of what were held to be the objects of Messiah's coming ; he declared himself to be the Son of God, which they deemed flat blasphemy ; he would postpone to another life in another world the jurisdiction and regality attaching to the Messiah's kingdom. Out of his own mouth let him be judged. ' Then the high priest rent his garments, saying, He hath spoken blasphemy : what further need have we of witnesses ? ' ' And the high priest rent his clothes, and saith, What further need have we of witnesses ? ' Young renders ' blasphemy ' as ' evil speaking.' It only remained to put the question formally to the council and take their vote upon it. ' Ye have heard the blasphemy : what think ye ? ' ' Behold, now ye have heard the blasphemy : what think ye ? ' In Matthew the Revisers and Tischendorf, following the oldest MS., have altered ' his ' to ' the ' before ' blasphemy.' As was to be anticipated, the decision was adverse to Jesus : ' They answered and said, He is worthy of (Gr. liable to) death.' Mark states that the vote in favour of capital punishment was unanimous : ' And they all condemned him to be worthy of (Gr. liable to) death.' Luke, whose account of the matter is condensed throughout, does not record the putting of the question or the voting on it : ' And they said, What further need have we of witnesses ? for we ourselves have heard from his own mouth.'

As soon as the sentence was pronounced, Jesus was assailed with a torrent of insult and abuse. Those who had been his judges gave vent to their prejudice and hatred in this cruel and unmannerly fashion. 'Then did they spit in his face and buffet him.' Alford notes: 'The word rendered *buffet* denotes *strike with the fist*.' Tischendorf so renders it. Matthew continues: 'and some smote him with the palms of their hands (or, with rods).' Alford explains that the verb *smite* is, '*generally, to strike a flat blow with the back of the hand*, but also . . *to strike with a staff*.' Young renders: 'and others slapped *him*.' In addition to these indignities Jesus was subjected to rude, rough banter: 'saying, Prophesy unto us, thou Christ: who is he that struck thee?' A coarse way, truly, of ridiculing his claim to the Messiahship. Mark informs us that they had first rendered identification impossible by covering the face of Jesus. 'And some began to spit on him, and to cover his face, and to buffet him, and to say unto him, Prophesy.' Young renders 'prophesy' by 'divine.' The Authorised Version continues: 'and the servants did strike him with the palms of their hands.' This is rendered by the Revisers, according to a different reading: 'and the officers received him with blows of their hands (or, strokes of rods),' and by Tischendorf: 'and the attendants with blows took him in charge.' The servants did but imitate their masters; the members of that priestly council themselves set the despicable example of violence and opprobrium, and the soldiers were not slow to follow it. Luke, indeed, only mentions the latter: 'And the men that held *Jesus* (Gr. him) mocked him, and beat him. And they blind-folded him, and asked him, saying, Prophesy: who is he that struck thee?' In the two oldest MSS. the word 'him' stands in place of 'Jesus.' The Revisers have notified the fact, but could not depart from the Authorised Version, as the personal pronoun would refer back to Peter, not to Jesus. This is an indication of some misplacement in this portion of Luke's narrative, which it has been necessary to take out of order here in incorporating it with Matthew and Mark. Following the two oldest MSS. the Revisers have omitted before 'asked,' 'struck him on the face and.' The brutal jesting did not soon cease. It was a carnival of scoffs and ribaldry for the soldiers, Jesus being the victim. 'And many other things spake they against him, reviling him.' The Revisers have changed 'blasphemously' to 'reviling him,' which corresponds with Young's 'speaking evilly.'

In the account of the denial of Jesus by Peter there is a close agreement between the four evangelists. They all tell of his sitting with the servants by the fire in the court. Matthew and Mark drop the matter for a time, and then take it up again at the same point. Luke's account of it is unbroken, resulting in a dislocation of his narrative with respect to the trial. John devotes six intermediate verses to the hearing before Annas. Matthew, having interposed ten verses, says: 'Now Peter was sitting without in the court: and a maid came unto him, saying, Thou also wast with Jesus the Galilæan.' Mark, after a break of twelve verses, continues: 'And as Peter was beneath in the court, there cometh one of the maids of the high priest; and seeing Peter warming himself, she looked upon him, and saith, Thou also wast with the Nazarene, even Jesus.' Luke: 'And a certain maid seeing him as he sat in the light *of the fire*, and looking steadfastly upon him, said, This man also was with him.' The Revisers have altered 'by the fire' to 'in the light,' adding in italics 'of the fire.' Young and Tischendorf render literally 'at the light.' The question has been raised, whether the maid here spoken of was the same as previously mentioned by the fourth evangelist. That can scarcely be, for the following reasons: (1) John alludes to the maid 'that kept the door,' the inference being that the question was put by her and the answer given by Peter immediately upon his entrance; (2) after that, John tells of the fire, and of Peter standing by it; (3) John describes an enquiry, 'Art thou?' the other evangelists a recognition, 'Thou also wast,' 'This man also was'; (4) John now proceeds to relate what happened by the fire: 'Now Simon Peter was standing and warming himself. They said therefore unto him, Art thou also *one* of his disciples?' To reconcile the accounts, it is only necessary to make the very natural assumption, that the positive identification by the maid led to this direct challenge by others present. Matthew describes Peter's reply as being made to several: 'But he denied before them all, saying, I know not what thou sayest.' Young and Tischendorf omit 'them.' Mark: 'But he denied, saying, I neither know, nor understand what thou sayest (or, I neither know, nor understand: thou, what sayest thou?') The Revisers have followed the two oldest MSS. Luke: 'But he denied, saying, Woman, I know him not.' The Revisers have omitted 'him' after 'denied,' on the authority of the two oldest MSS. John: 'He denied, and said, I am not.' Each of the evangelists records the words of Peter differently, but all are to the same effect. Doubtless each expression was uttered and fairly reported, but one listener retained one and another another. Observers describe facts as artists paint from nature: each from his own point of view, according to his own observation; four painted landscapes of the same scene will all differ, but each may be true to nature. Their distinctive touches and mannerisms are evidences, not disproofs, of personal observation. So here: except in the case of John, the reports must have been obtained from various persons who were not disciples, and the slight verbal discrepancies between them corroborate their accounts.

After a time Peter moved from the fire and went out into the vestibule. There again the sharp eyes of another female detected him, and she called the attention of those about to the fact of his presence and his discipleship. 'And when he was gone out into the porch, another *maid* (female—Young) saw him, and saith unto them that were there, This man also was with Jesus the Nazarene.' The Revisers, Alford and Tischendorf have replaced the opprobrious word 'fellow' by 'man'; Young renders 'this one.' Mark's account is as follows: 'And he went out into the porch (Gr. forecourt); and the cock crew.' The Revisers note: 'Many ancient authorities omit *and the cock crew*.' Those words are not in the two oldest MSS.' 'And the maid saw him, and began again to say to them that stood by, This is *one* of them.' 'The maid,' here, does not necessarily mean the maid previously mentioned by Mark, but the maid having charge of the porch, who is described by Matthew as 'another.' 'But he again denied it.' Alas! what craven, lying spirit has taken possession of this devoted, boastful apostle? Has he altogether forgotten, or has he deliberately renounced, his repeated promise of fidelity? Certainly he has altogether ignored his Master's precept, 'Swear not at all.' 'And again he denied with an oath, I know not the man.' Luke, whose account is obviously derived from another observer, says nothing about this second maid, but relates that a man charged Peter with discipleship, and received a denial. 'And after a little while another saw him, and said, Thou also art *one* of them. But Peter said, Man, I am not.' The italicised word 'one' has been needlessly inserted by the Revisers: it is not in the Authorised Version, and is omitted by Young and Tischendorf. 14 Mark 70

26 Mat. 72

22 Luke 58

Too much attention had now been attracted to Peter to allow of his being left long in peace. He was surrounded by watchful eyes, and soon found himself subjected to renewed comments and questions. 'And after a while they that stood by came, and said to Peter, Of a truth thou also art *one* of them; for thy speech bewrayeth thee.' Young renders, literally: 'for even thy speech makes thee manifest.' He had the unmistakable brogue of Galilee. 'And after a little while again they that stood by said to Peter, Of a truth thou art *one* of them; for thou art a Galilæan.' The Revisers and Tischendorf have omitted, 'and thy speech agreeth *thereto*,' those words not being in the two oldest MSS. Alford observes: 'Wetstein gives many examples of various provincial dialects of Hebrew. The Galileans could not pronounce properly the gutturals, and they used *t* for *s*.' Luke defines the 'little while' as about an hour, and he quotes the remark of one of the accusers. 'And after the space of about one hour another confidently affirmed, saying, Of a truth this man also was with him: for he is a Galilæan.' The Revisers have replaced 'fellow' by 'man.' Peter gave him a positive denial. 'But Peter said, Man, I know not what thou sayest.' He affected an entire ignorance and indifference about the matter. It is stated by the fourth evangelist that either this man or another of the questioners declared that he had actually seen Peter in the garden of Gethsemane. 'One of the servants (Gr. bondservants) of the high priest, being a kinsman of him whose ear Peter cut off, saith, Did I not see thee in the garden with him?' No, Peter asserted: the man's eyesight had deceived him. 'Peter therefore denied again.' But when the bystanders persisted in reiterating the charge, he lost all self-control, together with the last vestige of truth and self-respect. 'Then began he to curse and to swear, I know not the man.' 'But he began to curse, and to swear, I know not this man of whom ye speak.' Young gives the word 'curse' in its Greek form, 'anathematize': Peter attempted still to brazen out the matter by reprobating in strong and solemn phraseology all those who thus accused him of consorting with a man to whom he was a perfect stranger! Alas! alas! a greater fall from truth and rectitude there could not be. And at the very instant, joining in with and, as it were, seeking to drown the lying voice of Peter, the shrill cry of a cock was heard. 'And immediately, while he yet spake, the cock crew.' 'And straightway the cock crew.' 'And straightway the second time the cock crew.' Each of the four

26 Mat. 73

14 Mark 70

22 Luke 59

„ 60

18 John 26

„ 27

26 Mat. 74
14 Mark 71

22 Luke 60
26 Mat. 74
18 John 27
14 Mark 72

^{22 Luke 61} evangelists introduces that fact as the climax. Luke adds: 'And the Lord turned, and looked upon Peter.' So the shameless denial of Jesus had actually been made in his own presence! The voice of the bird was enough to bring to the mind of Peter the warning of Jesus, which had been repelled at the time, but the accuracy of which was now so fully and lamentably proved; but how much more must that look of Jesus have done towards melting the stony heart of the renegade apostle! A flood of recollection swept across his ^{26 Mat. 75} mind, and a flood of tears followed thereupon. 'And Peter remembered the word which Jesus had said, Before the cock crow, thou shalt deny me thrice. And he went out, and wept bitterly.' ^{14 Mark 72} Mark: 'And Peter called to mind the word, how that Jesus said unto him, Before the cock crow twice, thou shalt deny me thrice. And when he thought thereon, he wept (or, And he began to weep).' On the words, 'when he thought thereon,' Alford observes: 'No entirely satisfactory meaning has yet been given for the original word thus rendered. Referring to my Greek Testament for the discussion, I may sum it up by stating that the sense in the text, though not elsewhere found, seems to suit both the word and the context better than any other that has been suggested.' Luke states that Peter retired from the place to reflect and weep alone. ^{22 Luke 61} 'And Peter remembered the word of the Lord, how that he said unto him, Before the cock crow this day, thou shalt deny me thrice. And he went out, and wept bitterly.' The words 'this day' have been added, and 'Peter' replaced by 'he' before 'went out,' on the authority of the two oldest MSS.

When the narratives are combined, the result differs from the impression derived from viewing them separately. The account of each of the four evangelists indicates that Peter's denial occurred three times; but when all the facts related are combined, it becomes evident that the apostle was questioned, and replied, more than thrice; indeed, it seems that Peter's mouth was as full of denials as the place was of questioners. Alford observes: 'This narrative furnishes one of the clearest instances of the *entire independency of the four Gospels of one another*. In it, they all differ; and supposing the denial to have taken place *thrice*, and *only thrice*, cannot be literally harmonized . . . I do not see that we are obliged to limit the narrative to *three sentences* from Peter's mouth, each expressing a denial, *and no more*. On *three occasions* during the night *he was recognized*, —on *three occasions he was a denier* of his Lord: such a statement may well embrace *reiterated expressions of recognition*, and *reiterated* and *importunate denials*, on *each* occasion.' That disposes of the matter satisfactorily enough, on the supposition that there were three and only 'three occasions,' but the synoptic gospels supply three, and the fourth evangelist adds another, representing Peter to have repudiated discipleship immediately upon entering the palace. The word 'thrice' cannot be got rid of, for it occurs in each of the three warnings given by Jesus; yet it is open to question whether it is right to interpret it rigidly, as signifying three and no more. Was it not rather a common colloquial expression, well understood to be equivalent to 'frequently' or 'repeatedly'? That appears to be the case, for the ^{12 ii. Cor. 8} apostle Paul apparently adopts it in that sense, saying: 'Concerning this thing I besought the Lord thrice, that it might depart from me.'

The Sanhedrim which had voted the death of Jesus had assembled at daybreak, 'as soon as it was day.' The trial was short, and it was 22 Luke 66 yet early morning when another council was summoned to decide as to the means to be adopted for carrying out the sentence. 'Now 27 Mat. 1 when morning was come, all the chief priests and the elders of the people took counsel against Jesus to put him to death.' Mark intimates that this second council followed quickly upon the first. 'And straightway (immediately—Young) in the morning the chief 15 Mark 1 priests with the elders and scribes, and the whole council (Sanhedrim —Young and Tischendorf) held a consultation.' This construction differs from that of the Authorised Version, which stands as follows: 'the chief priests held a consultation with the elders and scribes and the whole council.' This represents the chief priests as taking the lead in the matter; Young's rendering puts them foremost: 'the chief priests having held a consultation, with the elders and scribes, and the whole Sanhedrim'; Tischendorf's version also attributes the initiative to the priests: 'the chief priests having prepared counsel with the elders and the scribes and the whole Sanhedrim.' The expression 'having prepared counsel' may be taken to signify that the necessary formalities had been arranged previously: from the first the result had been anticipated as a foregone conclusion and the next step contemplated beforehand. This is the more probable from the mention of 'the whole Sanhedrim': it could only be possible to ensure the attendance of the entire body on so short a notice by taking active measures to summon all promptly and peremptorily. Alford notes: 'Lightfoot quotes from Maimonides a precept which declares that of the Sanhedrim of 71 members it is not necessary for business that all be present: but when *all* were specially summoned, attendance was compulsory.' They decided that it was best to treat Jesus as a common criminal, and to hand him over as one worthy of death to the judicial authorities: 'and they bound him, and led him 27 Mat. 2 away, and delivered him up to Pilate the governor.' The Revisers and Tischendorf have omitted 'Pontius' on the authority of the two oldest MSS. Mark: 'and bound Jesus, and carried him away, and 15 Mark 1 delivered him up to Pilate.' This similarity of diction between the two evangelists in a statement which is purely explanatory, appears to indicate that they compiled from the same original document. In recording the sayings of Jesus, such similarities are to expected, but otherwise they are naturally attributable to some common origin. Luke's account is obviously independent: 'And the whole company 23 Luke 1 of them rose up, and brought him before Pilate.' Probably it was considered that the attendance of the whole body would give greater weight and authority to their application to Pilate. Such unanimity in the condemnation of Jesus is a phenomenon to ponder over and marvel at. These men were of the highest class, chosen representatives of the intelligence and policy of the Jews. Was not one protesting voice heard among them all? There may have been adverse votes, overborne by a large majority; and if the council was not declared to be dissolved until after the visit to Pilate, the attendance of every member before him may have been compulsory. The fourth evangelist records the fact very briefly: 'They lead 18 John 28 Jesus therefore from Caiaphas into the palace (Gr. prætorium).' The Authorised Version has 'hall of judgment.'

Although the treacherous Judas had deliberately formed and remorselessly carried out his plan of action, yet when its result became apparent he was filled with misery and self-reproach. Urged by the pangs of an accusing conscience, he sought out the chief priests and elders, and protested that the man he had delivered up, and whom they had sentenced as a criminal to death, was innocent. As far as possible, Judas was anxious to repudiate his own share in the base transaction into which he had been tempted; he took the thirty silver coins in his hand, as though by returning them he could cancel the contract he had made and carried out. 'Then Judas, which betrayed him, when he saw that he was condemned, repented himself, and brought back the thirty pieces of silver to the chief priests and elders, saying, I have sinned in that I betrayed innocent blood.' Tischendorf renders 'repented himself' as 'seized with remorse,' and 'pieces of silver' as 'shekel-pieces.' Following all the ancient MSS. the Revisers have omitted the word 'the' before 'innocent.' From the statement in Mark that money was 'promised' to Judas, and in Luke that they 'covenanted to give him money,' it may be inferred that the thirty shekels were merely a deposit, and that Judas now, instead of claiming the balance, was anxious to refund the earnest-money. Alford however says: 'Observe it was *the thirty pieces of silver* which he brought back—clearly *the price* of the Lord's betrayal, not *earnest-money* merely.' 'Clearly' is too strong a word: if quite clear Alford would not have needed to add the following weak suggestion by way of argument: 'for by this time, nay when he delivered his Prisoner at the house of Annas, he would have in that case received the *rest*.' How could the balance have been paid before Judas applied for it? When he presented himself, it was to repay what he had already received. In the givers of the bribe there does not appear to have been a spark of repentance. With an assumption of cool and callous dignity they refused to concern themselves in any way about Judas and his scruples. 'But they said, What is that to us? see thou *to it*.' The Revisers have omitted to italicise the words 'is that;' Young renders literally: 'What—to us? thou shalt see.' As they refused to take back the money and Judas was determined not to keep it, he threw it down on the floor of the temple, leaving both it and them. 'And he cast down the pieces of silver into the sanctuary, and departed.' He was utterly reckless now, caring as little for his life as he did for the money; both were hateful to him; he was realising the full truth of his Master's words: 'Woe unto that man through whom the Son of man is betrayed.' The burden of existence was unbearable to him: 'and he went away and hanged himself.' Young renders: 'and having gone away, strangled himself.' Alford notes: 'hanged (or strangled).' The word 'strangled' does not denote what we understand by 'hanging:' 'The lion did tear in pieces enough for his whelps, and strangled for his lionesses.' 'My soul chooseth strangling, and death rather than *these* my bones.' The priests were constrained to gather up the silver, and then arose the question what was to be done with it. Legal scruples forbade putting it into the sacred chest, because it was blood-money. 'And the chief priests took the pieces of silver, and said, It is not lawful to put them into the treasury (Gr. *corbanas*, that is, *sacred treasury*), since it is the price of blood.' The question how to dispose of the money was formally discussed, and the resolution come to was to the effect that they should purchase with it a plot of ground known as the potter's field, which could thenceforth be reserved for the burial of strangers. 'And they took counsel, and bought with them the potter's field, to bury strangers in.' Alford notes: 'Not Gentiles, but *stranger Jews* who came up to the feasts.' That was probably the intention: to provide a cemetery for those who died away from home and were without friends who would undertake to bury them. It is added: 'Wherefore that field was called, The field of blood, unto this day.' Alford observes: 'This expression shews that a considerable time had elapsed since the event, before St. Matthew's Gospel was published.' That must be the case, whether the passage was in the original manuscript or was introduced by a compiler subsequently.

_{27 Mat. 7}
_{,, 8}

Let us now turn to the account of this matter as recorded in the Acts of the Apostles. '(Now this man obtained a field with the reward of his iniquity; and falling headlong, he burst asunder in the midst, and all his bowels gushed out. And it became known to all the dwellers at Jerusalem; insomuch that in their language that field was called Akeldama, that is, The field of blood).' The two accounts are not only quite independent, but at first sight and until compared carefully, appear to be contradictory. Alford observes: 'The statement, that he *bought a field*, does not appear to agree with the account in Matt. xxvii. 6—8; nor, consistently with common honesty, can they be reconciled, *unless we know more of the facts than we do* . . . The various attempts to reconcile the two narratives, which may be seen in most of our English commentaries, are among the saddest examples of the shifts to which otherwise high-minded men are driven by an unworthy system. A notable example occurs in a solution lately proposed, that as the *Jews* are said to have crucified our Lord when they were only the occasion of his being crucified, so Judas may be said to have bought the field when he only gave occasion to its being bought by the Chief Priests. I need hardly say to any intelligent and ingenuous reader, that this is entirely precluded here by the words *with the reward of his iniquity*, which plainly bind on the purchase to Judas as his personal act.' The 'unworthy system' alluded to by Alford is that of upholding by any and every means the theory of Scriptural inspiration. Apart from that, and dealing with the accounts as we should deal with any other historical records, we are justified in suggesting such probabilities and reconcilements as naturally arise upon reflection. It is to be inferred from the phraseology of Mark and Luke, that the thirty shekels were simply a deposit paid to Judas on entering into the 'covenant' which involved the 'promise' of a larger sum. It would have been indeed a strange coincidence, although overlooked by commentators, that the thirty shekels should happen to be the precise sum required for the purchase of the field. It is clear that Judas did not pay those thirty shekels for it: it is not said that he bought it for thirty shekels, but that he 'obtained a field with the reward of his iniquity.' The Revisers have altered 'purchased' to 'obtained;' the 'Englishman's Greek New Testament' renders 'got a field.' That must have been before he was seized with remorse, before the condemnation of Jesus, possibly immediately after the covenant was

_{1 Acts 18}
_{,, 19}

made with the priests. The sum he was promised emboldened him to treat for and become the purchaser of the land. If it had been paid for by him, and legally transferred to him, the priests could not have bought it. This points to, indeed necessitates the conclusion, that the contract for purchase was found not to have been completed by Judas, so that the vendor was able at once to accept the offer of the priests, transferring the lot to them instead of to him. On this point Alford observes: 'Whether Judas, as Bengel supposes, began the purchase, and so gave occasion for its being completed by the Chief Priests, we cannot say: such a thing is of course *possible*, but is certainly not contemplated by St. Matthew's account, where the priests settle to buy the field, on deliberation what they should do with the money.' Yet there must have been something to give rise to the suggestion. Matthew does not explain how it originated, but what more probable than that the knowledge of the purchase having been made by Judas, and the fact of his death, or simply of his repudiation of the whole transaction, should have led to the proposal. The two accounts, far from being contradictory, fit into and supplement each other. Again: the idea of an apparent inconsistency between them has arisen in connection with the mode of death. That difficulty begins to disappear as soon as it is recognised that the word rendered 'hanged himself' does not signify death by actual suspension, but 'strangulation' by whatever means brought about. Still, it is evident that Matthew indicates suicide in some form, and without some further consideration it does not appear what is meant by Luke's phrase 'falling headlong.' Alford notes: '*Falling headlong* will hardly bear the meaning assigned to it by those who wish to harmonize the two accounts, viz. that, having hanged himself, he fell by the breaking of the rope.' That certainly would not be falling headlong. Alford continues: 'It would rather point, as the word used is explained, to a sudden fall forward on the face by a stroke from God, or by an accident.' But to assume (and it is only assumption) death by the visitation of God or by accident, is to introduce an absolute discrepancy between the two accounts. Falling headlong or head-foremost, whether by accident or otherwise, on level ground, would be an impossibility. Here again the two narratives dovetail into and corroborate each other. Matthew describes the ground as 'the potter's field.' Alford says: 'The field originally belonged to a potter, and was probably a piece of land which had been exhausted of its clay fit for his purposes, and so was useless. Jerome relates that it was still shown on the South side of Mount Zion, in which neighbourhood there is even now a bed of white clay.' That fact explains everything. The land must have been hollowed out to a considerable depth, just as we see in the case of chalk pits, and from the top of its precipitous side Judas deliberately fell 'headlong,' and so 'strangled himself.' Not only was the neck broken by the fall, but 'he burst asunder in the midst, and all his bowels gushed out.' A tragedy so terrible excited universal comment; doubtless multitudes flocked to the spot where it occurred: so deeply was the public mind impressed by the catastrophe, that the place from that time forth was generally alluded to by a name suited to the event which had brought it so prominently into notice: 'insomuch that in their language that field was called Akeldama, that is, The field of blood.'

The Revisers have placed the whole of this account between brackets, as if to notify that it forms no part of the speech of Peter, but is an interpolation of the evangelist, like the previous one in verse 15: '(and there was a multitude of persons *gathered* together, about a hundred and twenty).' The use of the past tense, 'it became known,' and the expression 'in their language,' clearly indicate that the passage was not uttered by Peter; besides which, his speech was delivered too soon after the event to have allowed the adoption and general recognition of any popular nomenclature. Alford, however, takes a contrary view. Of verse 18 he says: 'This verse *cannot be regarded as inserted by St. Luke*: for, 1, the place of its insertion would be most unnatural for a historical notice: 2, the form of its introduction in the original forbids the supposition; 3, the whole style of the verse is rhetorical, and not narrative, e.g. *this man, the reward of iniquity*;' and of verse 19: 'It is principally from this verse that it has been inferred that the two verses 18, 19, are *inserted by St. Luke*. But it is impossible to separate it from verse 18; and I am disposed to regard both as belonging to Peter's speech, but freely given by St. Luke, inserting *into the speech itself* the explanations, *in their proper tongue*, and *that is to say, the field of blood*, as if the speech had been spoken in Greek originally.' The statement itself, whether made by Peter or Luke, has been supposed to contradict that found in Matthew. Alford says: 'In Matt. xxvii. 8, the name, "the field of blood," is referred to the fact of its having been *bought with the price of blood*: here, to the fact of *Judas* having there *met with a signal and bloody death*. On the whole, I believe the result to which I have above inclined will be found the best to suit the phænomena of the two passages, viz. that, with regard to the *purchase of the field*, the more circumstantial account in Matthew is to be adopted, with regard to the *death of Judas*, the more circumstantial account of Luke.' This seems to mean: Here are two historians apparently at variance on two points; we cannot reconcile them, so let us assume that one is right with respect to one fact, and the other is right with respect to the other fact. That cannot be regard as a satisfactory or logical conclusion, and it would simply impugn the accuracy of both narrators. There is really no contradiction between them. It is difficult to trace the origin of names which have become current by common consent. The appositeness of the title must have commended itself to various minds before the public seized upon it; in this instance, the fact that there were two reasons for fixing it, may have conduced to its speedier and more general adoption. Matthew states one reason; Luke the other; either might have been sufficient by itself to originate the name, and men would attribute it to the one or the other with equal truth. The priests bought the field with what was admittedly blood-money; the field was stained with the blood of the suicide; everything about the spot being thus tinged with the horror of blood, 'the field of blood' became its common designation; if one person started it in connection with the outlay of the price of blood, others would adopt it because of the bloody tragedy enacted there. Does not Alford go too far in saying: 'The clue which joins these has been lost to us'? On the contrary, the apparent discrepancy between the two accounts disappears on a close investigation, and they are seen actually to confirm and supplement each other.

More than that: it is not altogether impossible to harmonise them with a tradition of the death of Judas quoted by Alford, which seems at first sight to be diametrically opposed to both. 'Another kind of death is assigned to Judas by Œcumenius, quoting from Papias: "Papias, the disciple of the apostle John, relates, that Judas, as he walked about, was a great example of God's judgments on impiety in this world: for that he swelled up to a fearful size, and once on attempting to pass through (a gateway) at the same time with a waggon which left ample space, he was crushed with the waggon, so that his bowels gushed out." This tradition may be in accordance with, and may have arisen from an exaggerated amplification, of our text.' The words of Matthew: 'and he went away and hanged himself,' do not compel the conclusion that the suicide took place immediately. Had that been the case, the priests would hardly have bought the field: and they had first to summon a council, which required some necessary formalities, and the discussion and decision could not have taken place until some time after they had waited upon Pilate. Matthew is as terse as possible, dismissing Judas in a sentence, without troubling himself to enter into details of the time, place or manner of the death, except by saying that it was self-inflicted. And Papias does not say that the enormous bulk of Judas arose on a sudden, but that 'as he walked about' men observed it. The accident with the waggon may have occurred, and may have been the culmination of his physical and mental misery, leading him to commit suicide, and accounting for the strange fact of the bursting asunder in the midst and the rupture of the intestines, as recorded by Luke. Dean Alford did not care to enter upon the consideration of all or any of the suppositional probabilities tending to harmonise the various accounts, because he had set himself to oppose the efforts which had been made, and were still making in his days, to uphold the infallibility of the New Testament by asserting and attempting to prove an utter absence of contradiction between the gospel narratives, regardless of common sense and to the prejudice of the truth sought to be upheld. He preferred rather to face, point out, insist upon obvious or apparent discrepancies, avoiding speculations as to the probable solutions of such difficulties, and preferring to say, as in this instance, 'the clue has been lost to us.' The allusion in the Acts to the tragic end of Judas in connection with the name which had been given to the field, was natural and proper, leading up to the Scriptural quotation applied to him:

1 Acts 20

'Let his habitation be made desolate,
And let no man dwell therein.'

The allusion of Matthew to the name in connection with the blood-money, was equally natural and apposite, because he discerned therein

27 Mat. 9, 10 the fulfilment of another prophecy: 'Then was fulfilled that which was spoken by (or, through) Jeremiah the prophet, saying, And they took (or, I took) the thirty pieces of silver, the price of him that was priced, whom *certain* of the children of Israel did price (or, whom they priced on the part of the sons of Israel): and they gave (*some ancient authorities read*, I gave) them for the potter's field, as the Lord appointed me.' Alford explains: 'The citation is not from Jeremiah, and is probably quoted from memory and unprecisely; we have similar instances in two places in the apology of Stephen,

Acts vii. 4, 16—end and in Mark ii. 26. Various means of evading this have been resorted to, which are not worth recounting. Jer. xviii. 1, 2, or perhaps Jer. xxii. 6—12, may have given rise to it : or it may have it arisen from a Jewish idea (see Wordsworth here) that "Zechariah had the spirit of Jeremiah." The quotation here is very different from the Septuagint,—and not much more like the Hebrew.' Alford adds : ' I put it to any faithful Christian to say, whether of the two presents the greater obstacle to his faith, the solution given above, or that given by a commentator of our own day, that the name of one prophet is here substituted for that of another, to teach us not to regard the prophets as the *authors* of their prophecies, but to trace them to divine Inspiration.' The quotation is from Zechariah : ' And I said unto them, If ye think good, give me my hire ; and if not, forbear. So they weighed for my hire thirty *pieces* of silver. And the LORD said unto me, Cast it unto the potter, the goodly price that I was priced at of them. And I took the thirty *pieces* of silver, and cast them unto the potter, in the house of the LORD.' On the words, ' unto the potter,' the Revisers note : '.The Syriac reads, *Into the treasury.*' [11 Zech. 12, 13]

The fourth evangelist states that it was yet early in the morning when the chief priests with the whole council led Jesus to Pilate, and he records the fact that they refrained from entering into the judgment-hall, holding that they would thereby have become ceremonially unclean, and so debarred from eating the passover. ' And it was early ; and they themselves entered not into the palace (Gr. prætorium), that they might not be defiled, but might eat the passover.' Alford here quotes from Friedlieb, as follows : ' The entrance of a Jew into the house of a Gentile made him unclean till the evening. It is surprising, that according to this declaration of the Holy Evangelists, the Jews *had yet to eat the Passover*, whereas Jesus and His disciples had already eaten it in the previous night. And it is no less surprising, that the Jews in the early morning should have been afraid of rendering themselves unclean for the Passover,—since the Passover could not be kept till *evening*, i.e., *on the next day*, and the uncleanness which they dreaded did not, by the law, last till the next day. For this reason, the passage in John labours under no small exegetic difficulties, which we cannot altogether solve, from want of accurate knowledge of the customs of the time. Possibly the law concerning Levitical defilements and purifications had in that age been made more stringent or otherwise modified ; possibly, they called some other meal, besides the actual Passover, by its name. This last we certainly, with our present knowledge of Hebrew antiquities, must assume : for the law respecting uncleanness will not allow us to interpret this passage of the *proper* Passover on the evening of the 14th of Nisan, nor indeed of any *evening meal* at all.' Alford states the difficulties fully and fairly, as follows : ' Over all three narratives extends the great difficulty of explaining *the first day of unleavened bread* (Matt., Mark), or *the day of unleavened bread* (Luke), and of reconciling the impression undeniably conveyed by them, that the Lord and his disciples *ate the usual Passover*, with the narrative of St. John, which not only does not sanction, but I believe absolutely excludes such a supposition. I shall give, in as short a [18 John 28] compass as I can, the various solutions which have been attempted, and the objections to them; fairly confessing that none of them satisfy me, and that at present I have none of my own. I will (1) state the *grounds of the difficulty itself*. The day alluded to in all four histories as that of the supper, which is unquestionably one and identical, is Thursday, the 13th of Nisan. Now the day of the Passover being slain and eaten was the 14th of Nisan (Exod. xii. 6, 18; Lev. xxiii. 5; Numb. ix. 3; xxviii. 16; Ezek. xlv. 21), *between the evenings*, which was interpreted by the generality of the Jews to mean the interval between the first westering of the sun (3 p.m.) and his setting,—but by the Karaites and Samaritans that between sunset and darkness;—in either case, however, *the day* was the same. The feast of unleavened bread began at *the very time of eating the Passover* (Exod. xii. 18), so that the *first day of the feast of unleavened bread was the 15th* (Numb. xxviii. 17). All this agrees with the narrative of St. John, where (xiii. 1) the last supper takes place *before the feast of the Passover*—where the disciples think (ib. ver. 29) that Judas had been directed to buy the things *which they had need of against the feast*—where the Jews (xviii. 28) would not enter into the judgment-hall, lest they should be defiled, *but that they might eat the Passover*—and where it could be said (xix. 31) *for that Sabbath day was an high day*,—being, as it was, a *double Sabbath*,—the coincidence of the first day of unleavened bread, which was sabbatically hallowed (Exod. xii. 16), with an actual sabbath. But as plainly, it *does not agree* with the view of the three other Evangelists, who not only relate the meal on the evening of the 13th of Nisan to have been a Passover, but manifestly regard it as the *ordinary legal time* of eating it: *on the first day of unleavened bread*, WHEN THEY KILLED THE PASSOVER (Mark xiv. 12), *when the Passover* MUST BE KILLED (Luke xxii. 7), and in Matthew by implication, in the use of THE PASSOVER, &c., without any qualifying remark.' This formidable list of difficulties may be thus summarised :—

(1) Jesus and his disciples ate the passover some hours before the Jews.
(2) The dread of defilement is inexplicable, because the passover might not be eaten till evening.
(3) The passover might only be eaten on the 14th of Nisan, whereas Jesus and his disciples ate it on the 13th.
(4) 'Between the evenings' means either from 3 p.m. to sunset, or from sunset to darkness.
(5) The feast of unleavened bread began simultaneously with the passover.
(6) The last supper is stated by John to have taken place 'before the feast of the passover.'
(7) After the supper allusion was made to 'the things which they had need of against the feast.'
(8) The 'first day of unleavened bread,' the 15th, happened to coincide with the weekly sabbath, and therefore the night of Thursday was too soon for the passover to be kept.
(9) Yet the meal is described as a passover held at the ordinary legal time.

Now turn to the law of the passover as laid down in the four passages referred to.

'Ye shall keep it up until the fourteenth day of the same month: and the whole assembly of Israel shall kill it at even (Heb. between the two evenings).' — Ex. 12:6

'In the first *month* on the fourteenth day of the month at even, ye shall eat unleavened bread, until the one and twentieth day of the month at even.' — 18

'In the first month, on the fourteenth day of the month at even (Heb. between the two evenings) is the LORD's passover. And on the fifteenth day of the same month is the feast of unleavened bread unto the LORD.' — Lev. 23:5,6

'In the fourteenth day of this month, at even (Heb. between the two evenings) ye shall keep it in its appointed season.' — Num. 9:3

'And in the first month, on the fourteenth day of the month, is the LORD's passover. And on the fifteenth day of this month shall be a feast.' — Num. 28:16,17

The expression 'between the two evenings,' indicates that the passover day was not reckoned from sunrise to sunrise, but from sunset to sunset. The passover might be kept at any time between the evening of one day and the evening of the next day; the 14th of Nisan began at evening and ended at evening. In 'Helps to the Study of the Bible' it is stated: 'The *Civil* Day was from sunset one evening to sun-set the next. The *Natural* Day was from sun-rise to sun-set.' Colloquially there must have been some merging of the two: the eating of unleavened bread began at even, and the twelve hours of daylight preceding would naturally be called 'the day' or 'the first day of unleavened bread.' Jesus resolved to keep the feast with his disciples at the earliest moment possible; therefore 'when it was evening he cometh with the twelve,' and 'when' (that is, 'as soon as') the hour was come, he sat down, and the apostles with him.' The fact that 'he said unto them, With desire I have desired to eat this passover with you before I suffer,' and his message to the householder, 'My time is at hand,' are, to say the least, quite consistent with the earliest possible partaking of the passover. It might not be killed till evening: most Jews doubtless allowed some hours to elapse before eating it, the law prescribing only that it must be 'between the two evenings.' Jesus, knowing all things that were about to come upon him, chose to anticipate by some hours the general time of observance: the chief priests and others had no reason for doing so, and inasmuch as they must needs eat the passover some time *before* the close of the 14th, they were careful not to enter the judgment hall, as that would have rendered them unclean till the evening. The passover was always killed at sunset: 'Thou shalt sacrifice the passover at even, at the going down of the sun;' — Deut. 16:6
then it had to be roasted, and eaten before the next sunset. Jesus did not eat the passover on the 13th, but very early on the 14th, and the chief priests and others did not eat it after the 14th, but only many hours later on that day. This meets the objections numbered 1, 2 and 3.

— Mark 14:17
— Luke 22:14, 15
— Mat. 26:18

(4) Alford understands 'between the evenings' to signify either some hours before or some hours after sunset. Sharpe inclines to a similar restricted meaning, by translating 'at twilight,' but he evinces uncertainty by giving the alternative rendering, 'or between the evenings.' The French version has, 'entre les deux vêpres,' the

German, 'zurischen Abends.' Young, 'between the evenings.' Alford's opinion appears to be based solely upon the interpretations of 'the generality of the Jews' and of 'the Karaites and Samaritans,' but as the Jews were not unanimous and the two other sects differed from the majority of them, it is obvious that no reliance is to be placed on either. There is great probability that the differences were not of interpretation but of practice, and simply indicate the hours 'between the two evenings' which by common consent had come to be regarded as most convenient. Admitting that the killing of the passover always took place 'at even, at the going down of the sun,' it is certain that the eating of it must have been later. There was first a small margin as to the time of sacrifice, and afterwards a much larger margin as to the time of the meal.

(5) Alford's statement that 'the feast of unleavened bread began at *the very time of eating the passover*,' appears to be an error, the passover being on the 14th, and the feast of unleavened bread on the 15th. The *eating* of the unleavened bread began on the 14th 'at even,' not 'between the evenings,' but the feast of unleavened bread was held on the 15th. Alford seems to have confounded the two.

(6) The fourth evangelist does not state that 'the last supper took place before the feast of the passover,' but that 'before the feast of the passover,' that is, before the last supper, and 'when supper was ready' (Tischendorf), Jesus rose up from it and washed the disciples' feet.

13 John 2

20

(7) The expression, 'Buy what things we have need of for the feast,' would be applicable to the feast of unleavened bread on the 15th.

(8) Reckoning the passover day from sunset to sunset, the keeping of the feast by Jesus was on the 14th, not on the 13th as is supposed.

(9) Not only are the synoptics unanimous as to its being kept at the 'legal time,'—Alford's words, 'the ordinary legal time' are too strong,—but the more closely the matter is investigated the more clearly do the recorded facts appear to confirm their statement.

Unless some flaw can be found in the view here taken, all idea of a contradiction between the first three gospels and the fourth may be dismissed, together with the guesses by the aid of which commentators have sought to reconcile them, and which Alford has enumerated as follows: '(1) That the Passover which our Lord and his disciples ate, was not the ordinary, but an *anticipatory* one. (2) That our Lord and his disciples ate the Passover, but at the time observed by *a certain portion of the Jews*, while He Himself was sacrificed at the time *generally* observed. (3) That *our Lord* ate the Passover at the strictly legal, *the Jews* at an inaccurate and illegal time. (4) Our Lord ate only a *commemorative* Passover, such as the Jews now celebrate, and not a sacrificial Passover (Grotius). (5) Our Lord *did not eat the Passover at all*. (6) The Council did not eat their Passover at the proper time, but on another day, and broke the law, because of their eagerness about this execution . . . they chose even to neglect the Passover, that they might fulfil their murderous desire. (Chrysostom, and so Eusebius).' Alford set himself to refute these suppositions seriatim, and added a 'few hints,' without 'pointing to any particular solution.' Was there anything to solve? Let that be the primary question.

As the religious scruples of the Jews forbade their entering into the Prætorium, the Roman governor went outside to them for the purpose of ascertaining what was the crime of which they accused Jesus. 'Pilate therefore went out unto them, and saith, What accusation bring ye against this man?' Following the two oldest MSS., the Revisers have altered 'said' to 'saith.' There must have been no small difficulty in answering such a question. Their charge of blasphemy would have seemed an idle one to Pilate. In what way had Jesus transgressed the Roman laws? The members of the council sought to evade the difficulty by an informal reply. Could Pilate possibly imagine that they all with one consent would have brought this prisoner for punishment, if he had not been a criminal? 'They answered and said unto him, If this man were not an evil doer, we should not have delivered him up unto thee.' Assuming that to be the case, Pilate naturally suggested that their proper course was to judge and sentence the criminal at their own tribunal. 'Pilate therefore said unto them, Take him yourselves, and judge him according to your law.' They replied, in effect, that their difficulty was not with respect to his condemnation, but his execution. 'The Jews said unto him, It is not lawful for us to put any man to death.' Everything was leading up to the end which Jesus had foreseen and foretold : 'that the word of Jesus might be fulfilled, which he spake, signifying by what manner of death he should die.' The necessary legal charge was soon formulated. Luke was able to state the three heads of it : (1) alienating the Jewish nation ; (2) arguing against the payment of tribute ; (3) claiming the throne of Cæsar. 'And they began to accuse him, saying, We found this man perverting our nation, and forbidding to give tribute to Cæsar, and saying that he himself is Christ a king (or, an anointed king).' The word 'our' replaces 'the' before 'nation,' on the authority of the two oldest MSS. The framing of this indictment was equally artful and unscrupulous, well worthy of those who had 'sought false witness against Jesus to put him to death, and found it not.'

Abruptly and briefly Matthew introduces the following verse. 'Now Jesus stood before the governor : and the governor asked him, saying, Art thou the king of the Jews? And Jesus said unto him, Thou sayest.' Following the two oldest MSS, Tischendorf omits the words 'unto him.' Mark is equally brief. 'And Pilate asked him, Art thou the king of the Jews? And he answering saith unto him, Thou sayest.' Following the two oldest MSS, the Revisers have altered 'said' to 'saith.' The same brevity is observable in Luke. 'And Pilate asked him, saying, Art thou the king of the Jews? And he answered him and said, Thou sayest.' Obviously these three accounts are from the same original record. Turning to the fourth gospel, we are able to understand why they are so terse and similar. This examination of Jesus took place inside the palace, while the Jews waited outside. It was therefore in comparative privacy, and the bare record of question and answer was probably obtained from some soldier or other person who happened to be present. But John has already told us that one of the disciples, apparently meaning himself, 'was known unto the high priest' and had free access 'into the court of the high priest.' It would seem that he was able also to obtain admission into the Prætorium, for the account he gives is very graphic, and is characterised by that fulness and self-evident accuracy which prevails throughout his narrative. The more closely the fourth gospel is considered, the more is the conviction pressed upon us, that it was composed from notes made by the author at the time, and with the skill and reliableness appertaining to a swift and accomplished writer. That is the only natural and satisfactory way of accounting for the preservation of lengthy discourses of Jesus, of which his last address to the disciples and his prayer for them, occupying the 14th, 15th, 16th and 17th chapters, are a conspicuous example. The interview between Pilate and Jesus is described in detail, as follows: 'Pilate therefore entered again into the palace (Gr. Prætorium), and called Jesus, and said unto him, Art thou the king of the Jews?' The question must have arisen out of the accusation: 'saying, that he himself is Christ a king.' Before replying, Jesus enquired whether that idea had originated in Pilate's own mind, or had been suggested to him by others. 'Jesus answered, Sayest thou this of thyself, or did others tell it thee concerning me?' The accusation may have been made in writing, or if verbally, not in the hearing of the prisoner. Pilate intimated that, inasmuch as he was not a Jew, it was not to be supposed that he felt any personal interest in the question. 'Pilate answered, Am I a Jew?' The charge had been broached by the Jewish people and priesthood. 'Thine own nation and the chief priests delivered thee unto me.' The question, however, was not about what he had claimed, but as to what he might have done: 'what hast thou done?' Towards claiming or establishing any earthly kingship, absolutely nothing: 'Jesus answered, My kingdom is not of this world.' Had it been, there would have been the usual appeal to arms, the adherents of Jesus would have rallied round him, and his capture by the Jews would not have been effected without bloodshed: 'if my kingdom were of this world, then would my servants (or, officers) fight, that I should not be delivered to the Jews.' Young renders: 'my officers would have struggled.' A kingdom which did not rely for its establishment on physical force, must be altogether apart from worldly aims and ambitions: 'but now is my kingdom not from hence.' Alford notes: 'The word *now* has been absurdly pressed by the Romanist interpreters to mean that at some time His Kingdom would be *from hence*, i.e. of this world: as if its essential character could ever be changed. But *now* implies, "as the case now stands;" it conveys an ocular demonstration, from the fact that no servants of His had contended or were contending in his behalf; see similar usages of *now*, ch. viii. 40; ix. 41; xv. 22, 24; Rom. vii. 16, 17.' A reference to these passages corroborates the view of Alford. But the mention of 'my kingdom' pointed to Jesus as its King, and Pilate put to him a question on that point. 'Pilate therefore said unto him, Art thou a king then?' The reply of Jesus was unhesitating, unequivocal: 'Jesus answered, Thou sayest that I am a king (or, Thou sayest it, because I am a king.' Young renders: 'Thou sayest it; king I am'; Tischendorf: 'Thou sayest it, for I am a king.' Alford explains: '*Thou sayest*. A formula frequent in the Rabbinical writings: and conveying assent to the previous enquiry.' Jesus continued : ' To this end have I been born, and to this end am I come into the world, that I should bear witness unto the truth.' The words ' have I been born,' must naturally and properly be taken to refer to his birth in this world, and if the expression ' am come into the world ' does not refer to his mission and manifestation to mankind, which seems its probable sense, it must be connected with the word ' born.' Alford, however, contends against any such view. He says : Our Lord implies that He was *born* a King, and that He was born with a definite purpose. The words are a pregnant proof of an Incarnation of the Son of God. This truth is further expressed by what follows,—" I have been born, but not therein commenced my being—I am (or, have) come into the world." Thus certainly are the words to be understood, and not of his public appearance, nor as synonymous with His *having been born*. It is this saying which began the *fear* in Pilate, which the charge of the Jews, ch. xix. 7, increased.' The positive tone here assumed must not interfere with the reader's free judgment. Of course this saying of Jesus harmonises with the truth of his pre-existence, which he had plainly asserted to his disciples : ' I came out from the Father, and am come into the world '; but the point of the question and answer turned not upon the fact but upon the object of Christ's birth and coming : ' to this end have I been born, and to this end am I come into the world, that I should bear witness unto the truth.' If by ' truth ' we are to understand ' the truth ' of his incarnation, then Alford is right ; but that is not the sense, for it is added : ' Every one that is of the truth heareth my voice,' whereas the doctrine of the incarnation was known to none, and had only lately been revealed to and apprehended by the eleven apostles. Pilate caught no such drift in the words, but simply expressed his inability or disinclination to determine what might or might not be the truth on which Jesus laid so much stress : ' Pilate saith unto him, What is truth ?' Having gained sufficient insight into the character, motives and aims of his prisoner, whom he probably deemed a harmless religious enthusiast, he closed the examination and went back to the Jews who were waiting outside. ' And when he had said this, he went out again unto the Jews.' Then the accusers stated publicly what they laid to his charge. We are simply told that ' many things ' were brought against him, and that to none of them did Jesus make the slightest reply. ' And when he was accused by the chief priests and elders, he answered nothing.' Mark now stands : ' And the chief priests accused him of many things,' to which the Authorised Version adds : ' but he answered nothing.' Young puts these four words in italics ; Luther, the Revisers and Tischendorf omit them, although the latter gives no indication of their absence from either of the three oldest MSS. They are not in the Greek Text of Stephens of 1550, nor in the Textus Receptus of 1624. Alford retains the words, without comment. Jesus stood there as mute and impassive as though he had been deaf and dumb. Pilate sought to elicit a reply, by asking him if he did not hear what was passing. ' Then saith Pilate unto him, Hearest thou not how many things they witness against thee ?' Was he really determined not to attempt any vindication ? ' And Pilate again asked him, saying, Answerest thou nothing ? behold how many things they accuse thee of.' Still the same grave, imperturbable silence. 'And he gave him no answer, not even to one word.' In Mark the Authorised Version has: 'But Jesus yet answered nothing,' which now stands: 'But Jesus no more answered anything,' agreeing with Young. Alford renders: 'made him no further answer.' He had already justified himself before Pilate by declaring the high and holy objects of his life and actions: let his accusers say what they will; it was for them to support their charges, and for Pilate to determine whether they had proved them. Jesus had previous experience of the uselessness of any defence of himself before his persecutors, and the event shows that none was necessary in order to convince Pilate of his innocence. But Pilate could not understand and was astonished at the persistent silence of a person whose life hung upon the issue, and who, obviously so able to defend himself, would not utter a word even in response to the invitation of his judge: 'insomuch that Pilate marvelled.' 'Insomuch that the governor marvelled greatly.' 'Never man spake like this man': never man kept silence like this man.

The fourth evangelist having stated that Pilate 'went out again unto the Jews,' adds in the same sentence: 'and saith unto them, I find no crime in him.' After hearing all the accusations, and in spite of the absence of any attempt at defence, Pilate retained his opinion, and pronounced judgment to the effect that nothing had been proved against the prisoner. 'And Pilate said unto the chief priests and the multitudes, I find no fault in this man.' The Jews were not content to accept that decision, and thereupon reiterated their charges, declaring that Jesus had excited the populace in every part of the country. 'But they were the more urgent, saying, He stirreth up the people, teaching throughout all Judæa, and beginning from Galilee even unto this place.' The Revisers have altered 'fierce' to 'urgent,' agreeing with Young; Tischendorf renders 'violent'; Alford explains that the 'words may mean, *they strengthened, redoubled the charge*—or perhaps, *they became urgent*.' At the mention of Galilee, it occurred to Pilate to enquire whether Jesus came from that province. 'But when Pilate heard it, he asked whether the man were a Galilæan.' After 'heard' the Revisers have omitted 'of Galilee,' on the authority of the two oldest MSS.: the word 'it' is an insertion. Having ascertained that Jesus was properly amenable to the jurisdiction of Herod, who happened then to be at Jerusalem, Pilate decided to hand over the prisoner to him. 'And when he knew that he was of Herod's jurisdiction, he sent him unto Herod, who himself also was at Jerusalem in these days.' Alford notes: 'Grotius observes that this was the regular practice among the Romans, to *remit* a criminal to the ruler or judge of the district in which his crime was alleged to have been committed.' Herod was delighted at this unexpected arrival, for he had heard much about Jesus, and had long been curious to see him. 'Now when Herod saw Jesus, he was exceeding glad: for he was of a long time desirous to see him, because he had heard concerning him.' The words 'many things' are omitted after 'heard,' on the authority of the two oldest MSS. Herod expected to see now some display of the reported miraculous powers of Jesus: 'and he hoped to see some miracle (Gr. sign) done by him.' To the unbelieving, especially at such a time, no sign could be vouchsafed. Herod proceeded to examine the prisoner upon many points; probably some questions were dictated by curiosity, and others suggested by the accusation. 'And he questioned him in many words.' Again Jesus kept silence: 'but he answered him nothing.' There stood his enemies, launching out their complaints: 'And the chief priests and the scribes stood, vehemently accusing him.' And he 'as a sheep that before her shearers is dumb: yea, he opened not his mouth.' Was this the man who, according to the indictment, had claimed kingship over the Jews? Herod thought meanly of him, openly expressed his contempt, encouraged his guards to join in deriding his claims. 'And Herod with his soldiers set him at nought, and mocked him.' Their jesting assumed a practical form: with cruel, bitter sarcasm, they decked him out in some imitation of royal robes, and in that garb sent him back to Pilate: 'and arraying him in gorgeous apparel sent him back to Pilate.' The Revisers, agreeing with Young, have altered 'robe' to 'apparel.' Tischendorf renders, 'bright clothing.' Alford explains that 'a gorgeous robe' is 'variously interpreted: either *purple*, as befitting a king, or *white*, as the word rendered *bright* is understood by some.'

The sending of Jesus to Herod was appreciated by the latter as an act of courtesy, and served to mollify a spirit of hostility which had previously existed between himself and Pilate. 'And Herod and Pilate became friends with each other that very day: for before they were at enmity between themselves.' The Revisers have reversed the names, putting Herod before Pilate, on the authority of the two oldest MSS. Those two world-rulers shook hands, as it were, over the outraged body of Jesus. But although Pilate cared nothing about the indignity to which Jesus had been illegally subjected, he nevertheless preserved a judicially impartial mind. After the return of the prisoner he again summoned his accusers before him, and pronounced what should have been a final decision in opposition to their wishes. 'And Pilate called together the chief priests and the rulers and the people, and said unto them, Ye brought unto me this man, as one that perverteth the people: and behold, I, having examined him before you, found no fault in this man touching those things whereof ye accuse him.' And Herod's opinion would seem to have been the same; for although both Jesus and his accusers had appeared before him, no sentence of death had been pronounced, the prisoner having been sent back, with marks of indignity and contempt, certainly, but with nothing to indicate that he deserved capital punishment: 'no, nor yet Herod: for he sent him back unto us; and behold, nothing worthy of death hath been done by him.' The words, 'I sent you to him,' have been altered to 'he sent him back unto us,' the two oldest MSS. having 'he sent him to us.' That correction has led to another, 'done unto him' being now 'done by him,' which agrees with Young, Tischendorf and Alford. Having regard to all the circumstances, Pilate had determined to release the accused, but first inflicting upon him the punishment of scourging. 'I will therefore chastise him, and release him.' The Revisers have omitted the next verse: '(For of necessity he must release one unto them at the feast),' adding this note: 'Many ancient authorities here insert ver. 17 *Now he must needs release unto them at the feast one* prisoner. Others add the same words after ver. 19.' The oldest MS., the Sinaitic, has the verse; the two next in point of age, the Vatican and Alexandrine, are without it. The fact, however, is alluded to by the other evangelists, and from them it appears that Pilate suggested that the release of Jesus need not be regarded as an acquittal, but as a simple compliance with a periodical custom. 'But ye have a custom that I should release unto you one at the passover: will ye therefore that I release unto you the King of the Jews?' That is the account of John, whose narrative at this point is very condensed: what took place in comparative privacy he relates with some detail, but gives in briefest words what happened before the multitude. For the former purpose he must have been inside the palace; probably he was not an eye witness of what went on outside; it seems unlikely that he would have liberty to go in and out with Pilate. The proposal of release was made to the assembled populace, not merely to the chief priests and leading citizens. Matthew and Mark are in close accordance. Matthew: 'Now at the (or, a) feast the governor was wont to release unto the multitude one prisoner, whom they would.' Alford explains that 'at the feast' is 'literally *feast by feast*, i.e. at every feast.' Mark: 'Now at the (or, a) feast he used to release unto them one prisoner, whom they asked of him.' Matthew gives the name of the most prominent one. 'And they had then a notable prisoner, called Barabbas.' Mark mentions his crime: 'And there was one called Barabbas, *lying* bound with them that had made insurrection, men who in the insurrection had committed murder.' Mark adds the further fact that the multitude began to clamour for their customary boon. 'And the multitude went up and began to ask him *to do* as he was wont to do unto them.' Following the two oldest MSS., the Revisers have omitted after 'multitude' the words 'crying aloud,' and have inserted in their place 'went up and.' On the same authority, 'had ever done' is altered to 'was wont to do.' Pilate seized the opportune moment to suggest that they should make choice of Jesus. 'And Pilate answered them, saying, Will ye that I release unto you the King of the Jews?' Matthew states that Pilate brought the name of Barabbas into competition. 'When therefore they were gathered together, Pilate said unto them, Whom will ye that I release unto you? Barabbas, or Jesus which is called Christ?' The use of the two titles, 'Christ' and 'King of the Jews,' was a covert appeal to Jewish national vanity. If there was any ground for the charge made against Jesus that he had 'stirred up the people,' they would surely now adopt Pilate's hint, and vote for his release. The judge may have been in some doubt whether Jesus had or had not pandered to popular prejudices and passions; it may well be that some of the mud thrown by his unprincipled accusers may have seemed to stick, in the judgment of Pilate, and to have justified the infliction of the scourge; but apart from the guilt or innocence of the prisoner, of one thing Pilate was confident: that envy on the part of the clergy was the real cause of the apprehension and accusation of Jesus. Both evangelists agree on that point. 'For he knew that for envy they had delivered him up.' 'For he perceived that for envy the chief priests had delivered him up.'

At this momentous crisis in the fate of Jesus, a strange thing happened. As Pilate sate upon the judgment-seat a message was delivered to him from his wife, begging him to hold himself entirely aloof from 'that righteous man,' the only, but as she deemed it, the sufficient ground for the entreaty being a dream about him which had greatly troubled her. 'And while he was sitting on the judgment-seat, his wife sent unto him, saying, Have thou nothing to do with that righteous man: for I have suffered many things this day in a dream because of him.' Young renders literally: 'Nothing —to thee and to that righteous one.' The message came at the most opportune moment; it must have increased the perplexity of Pilate, and may account for some of his hesitancy and vacillation. If he had been moved by it to withdraw from the case, to release Jesus at once and without the scourging, at least the show of a sham legality would have been removed from the execution: Pilate would have appeared to us under a better aspect, and the 'betrayers and murderers' of Jesus would have stood forth in the eyes of all men in their true colours. Alford notes: 'In the apocryphal gospel of Nicodemus, c. 2, we read that Pilate called the Jews and said to them, "Ye know how that my wife is a worshipper of God, and is rather of your religion than mine. They say unto him, Yea, we know it." . . . The Jews are made to reply, "Did we not tell thee that he is a magician? behold, he hath sent a dream-token to thy wife."' Whether that account be true or imaginary, something must have taken place to make the message to Pilate public. His reliance upon the acquiescence of the populace in his proposal was doomed to disappointment. The clergy and their influential allies, the elders, exerted all their influence in persuading the people to make choice of Barabbas, and to vote for the death of Jesus. 'Now the chief priests and the elders persuaded the multitudes that they should ask for Barabbas, and destroy Jesus.' It was necessary to play upon their passions and prejudices, for Mark says: 'But the chief priests stirred up the multitude, that he should rather release Barabbas unto them.' After an interval, the momentous question was put. 'But the governor answered and said unto them, Whether of the twain will ye that I release unto you?' Young and Tischendorf replace the archaic form 'Whether of the twain,' by 'Which of the two.' The decision of the multitude was adverse to Jesus. 'And they said, Barabbas.' This failure of the temporising policy of Pilate placed him in a dilemma: he had appealed to the people, and they had gone contrary to his wish and expectation. What strange infatuation induced him to trust them again? His course was clear: Barabbas had escaped; it rested with Pilate to carry out the sentence he had pronounced, to scourge Jesus and then release him. But instead of acting upon his own judgment and responsibility, he once more sought the opinion of the populace. 'Pilate saith unto them, What then shall I do unto Jesus which is called Christ?' That in asking this he laid stress upon the claim of Jesus to the Messiahship is evident from the somewhat different wording of Mark. 'And Pilate again answered, and said unto them, What then shall I do unto him whom ye call the King of the Jews?' Having themselves given that title to Jesus, they could hardly wish him to be punished on account of it; the voice of the multitude would surely be contrary to the envy of the priesthood. Again the hope of Pilate was disappointed.

'And they cried out again, Crucify him.' Matthew describes them as unanimous. 'They all say, Let him be crucified.' The words 'unto him' are omitted after 'say,' on the authority of the three oldest MSS. Luke is to the same effect. 'But they cried out all together, saying, Away with this man, and release unto us Barabbas.' The Revisers have put 'all together' instead of 'all at once,' which is retained by Tischendorf. Young renders: 'the whole multitude': the 'Englishman's Greek New Testament': 'in a mass.' Luke explains: 'one who for a certain insurrection made in the city, and for murder, was cast into prison,' and then tells how, and how vainly, Pilate sought to reason with the fickle multitude. 'And Pilate spake unto them again, desiring to release Jesus; but they shouted, saying, Crucify, crucify him.' Instead of 'spake,' Young renders 'called out'; the 'Englishman's Greek New Testament,' 'called to': as though it needed no small effort for Pilate to make himself heard at all. Thrice he addressed them, and managed to make his question heard plainly and to reiterate his former decision. 'And he said unto them the third time, Why, what evil hath this man done? I have found no cause of death in him. I will therefore chastise him and release him.' Matthew and Mark also report the question. 'And he said, Why, what evil hath he done?' 'The governor' has been altered to 'he,' on the authority of the two oldest MSS. 'And Pilate said unto them, Why, what evil hath he done?' No expostulation availed to stem this sudden torrent of popular frenzy. 'But they cried out exceedingly, saying, Let him be crucified.' 'But they cried out exceedingly, Crucify him.' 'But they were instant with loud voices, asking that he might be crucified.' The account of the fourth evangelist is very succinct. 'They cried out therefore again, saying, Not this man, but Barabbas. Now Barabbas was a robber.' The word 'all' has been omitted after 'they,' on the authority of the two oldest MSS. On the word 'again' Alford notes: 'They have not *before* "cried out" in this narrative: so that some circumstances must be presupposed which are not here related.' Obviously John's narrative is much condensed. It became apparent to Pilate that his words produced no effect, and that to resist further the will of the people would endanger the public peace. In the midst of the prevailing uproar, he had recourse to a symbolical action: taking some water, he washed his hands before them all. This strange proceeding naturally attracted general attention, and was probably the means of silencing the noisy crowd, enabling Pilate to explain to them the significance to be attached to what he was doing. 'So when Pilate saw that he prevailed nothing, but rather that a tumult was arising, he took water, and washed his hands before the multitude, saying, I am innocent of the blood of this righteous man: see ye *to it*.' The Revisers note: 'Some ancient authorities read *of this blood:* see *ye* &c.' Alford observes: 'The *washing of the hands*, to betoken innocence from blood-guiltiness, is prescribed Deut. xxi. 6—9, and Pilate uses it here as intelligible to the Jews.' Nothing better could have been devised to impress them with a due sense of the reponsibility entailed upon them by the vote they had given. They realised it at once, yet swerved not from their course. As Pilate would not accept the onus of the deed, let it rest upon themselves. Where the chief priests led, the people held them-

selves justified to follow. 'And all the people answered and said, His 27 Mat. 25
blood be on us, and on our children.' Upon that understanding the
crucifixion of Jesus was assented to. Pilate inflicted, and was
content to be accountable for the scourging of Jesus, but shook off
from himself in this fashion the guilt of innocent blood. 'Then ,, 26
released he unto them Barabbas: but Jesus he scourged and delivered
to be crucified.' Mark attributes the conduct of Pilate to his anxiety
to comply with the popular will. 'And Pilate, willing to content 15 Mark 15
the multitude, released unto them Barabbas, and delivered Jesus,
when he had scourged him, to be crucified.' Luke says briefly:
'And their voices prevailed.' The words 'and of the chief priests' 23 Luke 23
are omitted, on the authority of the two oldest MSS. Luke adds:
'And Pilate gave sentence that what they asked for should be done.' ,, 24
The Authorised Version has, 'that it should be as they required';
Young renders: 'And Pilate gave judgment for their request being
done'; Tischendorf: 'And Pilate gave sentence that it should be
as they asked.' The judgment did not order the crucifixion of
Jesus, but simply that whatever his accusers desired should be done
to him, thus throwing upon them the entire responsibility. This
view is confirmed by what follows: 'And he released him that for ,, 25
insurrection and murder had been cast into prison, whom they asked
for; but Jesus he delivered up to their will.' The words 'to their
will' denote that they were to act as they would in the matter.
After 'released' the words 'unto them' are omitted, on the authority
of the three oldest MSS.

Sentence being given, Jesus was left in the hands of the soldiers.
Some of these had probably been present when Pilate questioned
him, 'Art thou the King of the Jews?' and had heard the reply of
Jesus, 'Thou sayest.' His solemn words, 'My kingdom is not of
this world,' would be interpreted by coarse minds as contradictory
rather than explanatory. The claims and the person of Jesus were
now treated with contempt and derision. The soldiers were bent on
making sport of their prisoner. They took him into the common
hall, and there, the whole of them having surrounded him, they
dressed him up again in a mock imperial robe, amused themselves by
plaiting an imitation crown made of some thorny shrub, put it round
his head, forced a reed into his right hand, as though he held a
sceptre, made a pretence of offering him royal homage, smote the
sham crown deep into his brow with the sham sceptre, and actually
spit upon him. 'Then the soldiers of the governor took Jesus into 27 Mat. 27-30
the palace (Gr. Prætorium), and gathered unto him the whole band
(or, cohort). And they stripped him, and put on him a scarlet robe.
And they plaited a crown of thorns and put it upon his head, and a
reed in his right hand; and they kneeled down before him, and
mocked him, saying, Hail, King of the Jews! And they spat upon
him, and took the reed and smote him on the head.' On the word
'stripped' the Revisers note: 'Some ancient authorities read
clothed.' That is the reading of the Vatican MS., and the later reading of the Sinaitic MS. Young renders 'a scarlet robe' as 'a
crimson cloak.' The Revisers have altered 'bowed the knee' to
'kneeled down;' very likely both postures were adopted. Mark's
catalogue of the indignities is similar: 'And the soldiers led him 15 Mark 16-19
away within the court, which is the Prætorium (or, palace), and they

call together the whole band (or, cohort). And they clothe him with purple, and plaiting a crown of thorns, they put it on him: and they began to salute him, Hail, King of the Jews! And they smote his head with a reed, and did spit upon him, and bowing their knees worshipped him.' Alford notes: '*Purple*, in Greek, is vaguely used, to signify different shades of red, and is especially convertible with *scarlet*, as St. Matthew.' Luke does not record this scene. The fourth evangelist describes it as follows: 'Then Pilate therefore took Jesus, and scourged him. And the soldiers plaited a crown of thorns, and put it on his head, and arrayed him in a purple garment; and they came unto him, and said, Hail, King of the Jews! and they struck him with their hands (or, with rods) (Young—were giving him slaps).' The words 'and they came unto him' have been added by the Revisers, on the authority of the two oldest MSS. Tischendorf renders: 'and they kept coming to him.' Alford inserts: 'and they approached him,' with the note: 'This has been probably erased by the copyists, as not being understood. It was their mock-reverential approach, as to a crowned king: coming probably with obeisances and pretended homage.'

¹⁹ John 1-3

Pilate, in accordance with his decision to let the Jews do what they would to Jesus, next brought him out to them. While thus delivering up the prisoner 'to their will,' Pilate stated plainly that he himself held Jesus to be innocent of any crime. 'And Pilate went out again, and saith unto them, Behold, I bring him out to you, that ye may know that I find no crime in him.' Just as he was, decked out with the mock purple and thorn crown, Jesus was placed in sight of his accusers. Pilate bade them look at him: the sight was one which, if it did not move their pity, must prove at least that no ambitious usurpation was to be dreaded on the part of one who stood alone, unfriended, and who, after having been flagellated, had undergone such contumely. 'Jesus therefore came out, wearing the crown of thorns and the purple garment. And *Pilate* saith unto them, Behold the man!' But at sight of him his enemies again clamoured for his execution. 'When therefore the chief priests and the officers saw him, they cried out, saying, Crucify *him*, crucify *him*.' It was nothing to them that the judge pronounced him innocent; they cared not about justice, being swayed by bigotry and rancour, and they wanted to make Pilate the tool of their vengeance. That he positively refused to become. 'Pilate saith unto them, Take him yourselves, and crucify him: for I find no crime in him.' Seeing that their charge of treason against Cæsar and disturbance of the public mind, had broken down, they contended that although the Roman law did not recognise his guilt, according to the Jewish law he stood condemned to death for having arrogated to himself the title 'Son of God.' 'The Jews answered him, We have a law, and by that law he ought to die, because he made himself the Son of God.' That complete shifting of the ground of accusation served to perplex Pilate, and made him more anxious than before. He re-entered the Prætorium, and began again to question the prisoner. 'When Pilate therefore heard this saying, he was the more afraid; and he entered into the palace (Gr. Prætorium) again and saith unto Jesus, Whence art thou?' Again the same absolute silence at which the governor had previously 'marvelled greatly.'

'But Jesus gave him no answer.' The question touched a point [19 John 9] which lay altogether outside the range of judicial cognizance. Then Pilate began to expostulate. Why persist in this reticence? Before a crowd of howling accusers, or in face of absurd and unprovable charges, it might be natural and dignified, but now why should he refuse to speak? Could he be ignorant of or indifferent to the fact that his questioner had in his hands the power of life or death? 'Pilate therefore saith unto him, Speakest thou not unto me? Knowest thou not that I have power (or, authority) to release thee, [,, 10] and have power (or, authority) to crucify thee?' The Revisers, following the three oldest MSS., have reversed the position of the words 'release' and 'crucify.' To that remark Jesus at once responded, not by giving any explanation about himself or his origin, but reminding Pilate that he, as judge, possessed only a delegated authority, coming from a higher source. 'Jesus answered him, Thou [,, 11] wouldst have no power (or, authority) against me, except it were given thee from above.' The word 'him' has been inserted, being in the two oldest MSS. The italicised words 'at all' after 'power' have been omitted. Although not in the original, and therefore better away, they served to indicate that the expression 'thou couldest have no power' did not refer to any supernatural restraint put upon its exercise, nor to any divine permission for what was about to be done, but to the official status of Pilate and the responsibility attaching to his judicial functions. The Sinaitic and Vatican MSS. read, 'thou hast no power.' He could have no authority except against evil-doers. That being the case the delivering up of Jesus to the civil power was a monstrous act of injustice and impiety: 'therefore he that delivered me unto thee hath greater sin.' [,, 11] Alford notes: 'Beyond question Caiaphas—to whom the initiative on the Jewish side belonged; by whose authority all was done.' The omission by the Revisers of 'the' before 'greater sin' helps to make it clear that no comparison is intended between the guilt of Pilate and that of Caiaphas, but a strong condemnation of the evil policy and passions which had prevailed to drag Jesus before this criminal tribunal. The impression produced by the words and demeanour of Jesus was so great that, in the words of the Authorised Version, 'from thenceforth Pilate sought to release him.' This is altered by the Revisers to: 'Upon this Pilate sought to release him.' Alford notes: [,, 12] 'Upon this: or from this time: but the words in the original hardly bear so much as the latter meaning.' There was not a tinge discoverable either of mad, reckless enthusiasm or of guilt in this remarkable prisoner. What steps Pilate now took on his behalf, we are not told. The position was a difficult one, the accused having been already judicially consigned to the Jews, with full authority to them to crucify him. They now perceived in Pilate an increased leaning in favour of Jesus, and they sought to counteract it by reminding the governor that the release of one charged with claiming kingship would be construed by them as an act of hostility to the emperor: 'but the Jews cried out, saying, If thou release this man, [,, 12] thou art not Caesar's friend: every one that maketh himself a king speaketh against (or, opposeth) Caesar.' The multitude took up and shouted out that argument: Young renders 'cried out' as 'were crying out,' and Tischendorf as 'kept crying.' Alford observes:

Q

'This was a terrible saying, especially under Tiberius, with whom, as Tacitus assures us, the undefined charge of disaffection to the person of the emperor was used to fill up all other accusations.' That home-thrust was artfully planned and well dealt, and it sufficed to shake the mind and change the purpose of Pilate. 'When Pilate therefore heard these words, he brought Jesus out.' 'That saying' has been altered to 'these words,' on the authority of the three oldest MSS. That the Jews might have no pretence that Pilate shirked his duty, he proceeded to close the matter with all formality, sitting on the seat of judgment: 'and sat down on the judgment-seat at a place called The Pavement, but in Hebrew, Gabbatha.' Alford explains: 'The judgment seat, or *bema*, was in front of the *prætorium*, on an elevated platform called Gabbatha, which was paved with a tessellated pavement. Such a pavement, Suetonius informs us, Julius Cæsar carried about on his expeditions.' Samuel Sharpe translates Gabbatha: 'Behind the palace.' The evangelist interpolates the remark: 'Now it was the Preparation of the passover.' Alford notes: 'This *preparation day* is *the vigil of the Passover*, i.e. the day preceding the evening when the passover was killed. And so it must be understood here.' That conclusion is open to question, because (1) the word *day* is an insertion by Alford, and (2) the word *preparation*, by itself, denotes simply the actual getting ready of the meal, as appears from the passage rendered in the Authorised Version: 'Where wilt thou that we prepare (make ready—Revised Version) for thee to eat the passover?' where Young and Tischendorf retain the word 'prepare.' The meaning of the evangelist appears to be, that at the time when Pilate took his seat on Gabbatha, the preparation of the passover meal was going on among the Jews, so that it was necessary to bring the matter to an issue without further delay. The additional words: 'it was about the sixth hour,' have occasioned much uncertainty and discussion. They will need to be considered later on.

When Pilate had previously presented Jesus to the people it was with the words, 'Behold, the man!' Now we read: 'And he saith unto the Jews, Behold, your King!' Alford observes: 'The words *Behold your King* seem to have been spoken in irony to the Jews,— in the same spirit in which afterwards the title was written over the cross: partly perhaps also, as in that case, in consequence of the saying in ver. 12,—to sever himself altogether from the suspicion there cast on him.' Knowing what we do of Pilate's frame of mind, his increased fear on learning that Jesus had claimed to be 'the Son of God,' his perplexed question, 'Whence art thou?' and remembering that he was seeking to release him, we can scarcely suppose that any sarcasm against Jesus was intended. He was no criminal: Pilate had already declared that. The only substantial ground of accusation was the claim to be a king; Jesus had accepted that title: 'Thou sayest, because I am a King;' the Jews had been obliged to fall back upon that charge; coupled with it was the mention of divinity, on which question Jesus had refused to answer. Pilate could not but feel that he was dealing with one who professed to be the long expected Messiah of the Jews, and who, on that account, out of envy, had been laid hold of by the priesthood; in that character he now introduces him to the people, throwing upon them the responsibility of acknowledging him as such or of rejecting him. Perhaps even at this last moment such an appeal might turn the tide of popular feeling in his favour, and quell the opposition which had been manifested against his proposed release. Any hope of that was doomed to disappointment; the suggestion was met by a clamour for the execution of the prisoner. 'They therefore cried out, Away with *him*, away with *him*, crucify him.' But it was not incumbent upon Pilate to become the executioner of one whose only fault was that of holding himself out as their Messiah. 'Pilate saith unto them, Shall I crucify your King?' It was not for him to resent and quench in blood the pretension to a royalty so shadowy, unearthly, unsubstantial. Then the chief priests repudiated any concern about the question of a Jewish Messiah, and professed their entire loyalty to the Roman emperor. 'The chief priests answered, We have no king but Cæsar.' Thereupon Pilate ceased his efforts: if these representatives of the religion and hopes of their nation chose deliberately and persistently to repudiate the aims and claims of this man, be they what they might, and were bent on ending them by taking away his life, let them do with him what they would. It was their concern rather than his, and it must be, as he had already decreed, their act and deed, not his. 'Then therefore he delivered him unto them to be crucified.'

19 John 15

„ 15

„ 15

„ 16

Jesus was now indeed delivered over into the hands of his enemies. The scourging and mocking had not been inflicted until it was known that his execution was permitted. Then came the final interview with the Jews, resulting merely in delay; they now proceeded to carry out the crucifixion. 'And when they had mocked him, they took off from him the robe (cloak—Young), and put on him his garments, and led him away to crucify him.' Mark evidently drew from the same narrative: 'And when they had mocked him, they took off from him the purple, and put on him his garments. And they led him out to crucify him.' The fourth evangelist mentions the fact that the cross was laid upon the shoulders of Jesus himself. 'They took Jesus therefore. And he went out, bearing the cross for himself.' According to another reading the word 'therefore' now takes the place of 'and led him away.' The words 'for himself' have been added, on the authority of the two oldest MSS. Tischendorf renders: 'So they took Jesus with them; and he bearing his own cross went forth.' Probably the strength of Jesus was seen to be unequal to the task, for the other evangelists state that on the road a passing countryman was laid hold of, and compelled to carry the hideous burden. 'And as they came out, they found a man of Cyrene, Simon by name: him they compelled (Gr. impressed) to go *with them*, that he might bear his cross.' The words 'to go *with them*' have been added by the Revisers: they are not in the original, nor in the versions of Young and Tischendorf. From Mark's account it may be inferred that two sons of this countryman became afterwards known in the church. 'And they compel (Gr. impress) one passing by, Simon of Cyrene, coming from the country, the father of Alexander and Rufus, to go *with them*, that he might bear his cross.' Here again the Revisers have inserted the same words. Luke also reports the circumstance. 'And when they led him away, they laid hold upon one Simon of Cyrene, coming from the country, and laid on him the cross, to bear it after Jesus.' The word 'after'

27 Mat. 31

15 Mark 20

19 John 17

27 Mat. 32

15 Mark 21

23 Luke 26

is of doubtful meaning: it must not be understood to signify after the cross had been first borne by Jesus, but 'behind Jesus:' Sharpe so renders it. That a stranger was impressed to undertake the task, may have been owing to the fact that the details of the crucifixion devolved upon the chief priests : 'Take him yourselves, and crucify him,' Pilate had said : his soldiers were not bound, possibly refused, to perform a distasteful work at their bidding.

A crowd followed the procession, including a number of women who gave free expression to their feelings of sympathy and sorrow. 'And there followed him a great multitude of the people, and of women who bewailed and lamented him.' Following the Vatican and Alexandrine MSS. the Revisers have omitted the word 'also' before 'bewailed.' Jesus halted, turned and addressed them, with as much calm and solemn dignity as had ever marked his public teachings. 'But Jesus turning unto them said, Daughters of Jerusalem, weep not for me, but weep for yourselves, and for your children.' He had striven, and had failed, to avert from the city its impending doom. Upon that generation would fall such evils as would make life itself unendurable. 'For behold, the days are coming, in which they shall say, Blessed are the barren, and the wombs that never bare, and the breasts that never gave suck.' No figure of speech used in prophecy could be too strong to portray the agony of terror which would overtake the people. 'Then shall they begin to say to the mountains, Fall on us; and to the hills, Cover us.' The simile is the same as in 10 Hosea 8. Alford says : ' It was partially and primarily accomplished, when multitudes of the Jews towards the end of the siege sought to escape death by hiding themselves in the subterranean passages and sewers under the city, as related by Josephus : who adds that more than two thousand were found dead in these hiding-places, besides those who were detected there and killed.' Jesus added ; 'For if they do these things in the green tree, what shall be done in the dry?' Sharpe renders 'green tree' as 'green wood,' which agrees with Luther : 'Denn so man das thut am grünen Holz, was will am dürren werden?' 'For if one does that to the green wood, what will be to the dry (or, withered)?' The word 'they' is used generally : if the state of society permits this wanton disregard of the life of the innocent and harmless, to what monstrous cruelty will it not lead hereafter, when rebellion actually exists, and the power which now unjustly crushes out my life will, in self-defence and for mastery, be let loose upon you and your children?

No distinction was made between Jesus and the vilest criminals. First, his name had been coupled with that of a robber, and now in the same procession walked two malefactors, that the three might be executed together. 'And there were also two others, malefactors, led with him to be put to death.' The procession halted at the well-known spot : 'And they bring him unto the place Golgotha, which is, being interpreted, The place of a skull.' There they invited him to drink a beverage compounded of wine and myrrh. 'And they offered him wine mingled with myrrh.' The words 'to drink' after 'him' are omitted on the authority of the two oldest MSS. Alford explains : 'It was customary to give a stupefying drink to criminals on their way to execution.' Matthew's account stands in the Authorised Version as follows: 'And when they were come unto a place called Golgotha, that is to say, a place of a skull, they gave him vinegar to drink mingled with gall.' Alford notes: 'We may observe here (and if the remark be applied with caution and reverence, it is a most useful one) how St. Matt. often adopts in his narrative *the very words of prophecy*, where one or more of the other Evangelists gives the matter of fact detail; see above on ch. xxvi. 15, and compare with this verse, Ps. lxix. 21.' This appears to mean that Matthew intentionally made his statements of what happened, conform to prophecies rather than to actual facts. He is the only one of the evangelists who mentions thirty pieces of silver as paid to Judas. Here is Alford's note on that point: 'St. Matthew is the only Evangelist who mentions the sum. De Wette and others have supposed that the accurate mention of the *thirty pieces of silver* has arisen from the prophecy of Zechariah (xi. 12), which St. Matthew clearly has in view. The others have simply *money*.' If this is an insinuation that Matthew said the sum paid was so much, simply because Zechariah's prophecy alluded to that sum, the 'remark' deserves to be characterised as the very reverse of 'a most useful one.' Again, the Psalm referred to is as follows:

'They gave me also gall for my meat;
And in my thirst they gave me vinegar to drink.'

Can Alford really have meant that Matthew spoke of 'wine' as 'vinegar,' and of 'myrrh' as 'gall,' in order that his narrative might correspond with the Psalmist's words? He says: 'Although *wine* and *vinegar* might mean the same thing, *myrrh* and *gall* cannot.' The Revisers have altered 'vinegar' to 'wine,' not because they mean the same thing, but on the authority of the two oldest MSS. The passage now stands as follows: 'And when they were come unto a place called Golgotha, that is to say, The place of a skull, they gave him wine to drink mingled with gall.' It looks as if copyists finding 'gall' in Matthew had changed 'wine' to vinegar,' rather than that Matthew named both ingredients wrongly to make them correspond with a passage to which he did not allude. The latter assumption is gratuitous and dishonouring; for the former, the oldest copies furnish some ground. There is nothing surprising in the fact that the component parts of the drink should be matter of report only, for no such narcotic was brewed for ordinary use, and it is quite possible that both myrrh and gall may have been used in its composition. The nauseous compound was refused by Jesus. Mark says simply: 'but he received it not.' Matthew states that he tasted before rejecting it: 'and when he had tasted it, he would not drink.' The Revisers have inserted 'it' in place of the italicised 'thereof': neither word is necessary; Young and Tischendorf make no such insertion. This circumstance is not mentioned by Luke or John. The latter merely says that Jesus went out 'unto the place called The place of a skull, which is called in Hebrew Golgotha; where they crucified him.' The former: 'And when they came unto the place, which is called The skull, there they crucified him.' In the Authorised Version the place appears as 'Calvary;' the Revisers note: 'According to the Latin, Calvary, which has the same meaning,' as *kranion*. As the power of inflicting capital punishment was in the hands of the Romans, the place of execution would naturally be named by them in their language, and in writings intended for Jews it was equally natural to give the Hebrew signification. Luke and John mention simultaneously with the crucifixion of Jesus that of the two malefactors. Luke: 'and the malefactors, one on the right hand and the other on the left.' John: 'and with him two others, on either side one, and Jesus in the midst.' But from the narratives of Matthew and Mark it appears that some time elapsed before that happened. In Luke we read: 'And Jesus said, Father, forgive them, for they know not what they do.' The Revisers note that 'some ancient authorities omit' this verse. It does not appear in the Vatican MS. and was erased by a later hand in the Sinaitic MS. Tischendorf retains it. One would not willingly part with it, and it is difficult to conceive how it could have been introduced without warrant.

To the sufferings of Jesus his executioners were callous. They were too much accustomed to scenes of cruelty and bloodshed to exhibit the least spark of feeling. When he had been nailed to the cross they proceeded to appropriate to themselves his garments. Luke says: 'And parting his garments among them, they cast lots.' Mark: 'And they crucify him, and part his garments among them, casting lots upon them, what each should take.' Alford explains: 'The garments of the executed were by law the perquisite of the soldiers on duty.' Matthew: 'And when they had crucified him, they parted his garments among them, casting lots.' The Authorised Version continues: 'that it might be fulfilled which was spoken by the prophet, They parted my garments among them, and upon my vesture did they cast lots.' This is not in either of the three oldest MSS., and is omitted by the Revisers. Alford notes: 'The words omitted in the text are not found in *any of the ancient manuscripts*, are clearly interpolated from John. ver. 24, with just the phrase *that which was spoken by the prophets* assimilated to St. Matthew's usual form of citation.' The fourth evangelist supplies details which are evidently direct from an eye-witness. He describes the division into four parts, one to each soldier, and makes it clear why the lot was cast. 'The soldiers therefore, when they had crucified Jesus, took his garments, and made four parts, to every soldier a part; and also the coat (or, tunic): now the coat (or, tunic) was without seam, woven from the top throughout. They said therefore one to another, Let us not rend it, but cast lots for it, whose it shall be.' The evangelist points out that therein was a fulfilment of a passage in the 18th verse of Psalm 22: 'that the scripture might be fulfilled, which saith,

They parted my garments among them,
And upon my vesture did they cast lots.'

Tischendorf omits the words 'which saith,' they not being in the two oldest MSS. It is added: 'These things therefore the soldiers did.'

Mark makes a statement with respect to the time of the crucifixion. 'And it was the third hour, and they crucified him.' On this Alford comments as follows: 'This date is in agreement with the subsequent account, ver. 33, and its parallel in Matthew and Luke, but, as now standing unexplained, *inconsistent with John* xix. 14, where it is said to have been about the *sixth hour* at the time of the exhibition of our Lord by Pilate. I own I see no satisfactory way of reconciling these accounts, unless there has been some very early erratum in our copies, or unless it can be shewn *from other grounds than the difficulty before us*, that John's *reckoning of time* differs from that employed in the other Evangelists. The difficulty is of a kind in no way affecting the authenticity of the narrative, nor the truthfulness of each Evangelist ; but requires some solution to the furnishing of which *we are not competent*. It is preposterous to imagine that two *such accounts as these* of the proceedings of *so eventful a day* should differ by *three whole hours* in their apportionment of its occurrences. So that it may fairly be *presumed*, that some *different method of calculation* has given rise to the present discrepancy. Meanwhile the chronology of *our text*,—as being carried on through the day, and as allowing time both for the trial, and the events of the crucifixion,—is that which will I believe be generally concurred in. All the other solutions (so called) of the difficulty are not worth relating.' On the passage in John alluded to, Alford notes : 'There is an insuperable difficulty as the text now stands. For St. Mark relates that the *crucifixion* took place at the *third hour*: and that it certainly was so, the whole arrangement of the day testifies. For on the one hand, the judgment could hardly have taken the whole day till noon : and on the other, there will not thus be time left for the rest of the events of the day, before the sabbath began. We must certainly suppose, as did Eusebius, Theophylact, and Severus, that there has been some very early erratum in our copies ; whether the interchange of 3 and 6, which when expressed in Greek numeral letters, are not unlike one another, or some other, cannot now be determined. We certainly may bring the two accounts nearer together by recollecting that, as the crucifixion itself certainly did not take place *exactly* at the third hour, and as here it is ABOUT *the sixth hour*, some intermediate time may be described by both Evangelists. But this is not satisfactory. The solution given by Dr. Wordsworth, after Townson and others, that St. John's reckoning of the hours is different, and like our own, so that the sixth hour would be 6 A.M., besides being unsupported by any authority, would leave here the difficulty that there must thus elapse three hours between the hearing before Pilate and the Crucifixion.' Let us see whether Alford's hopelessness of finding any solution of the apparent discrepancy, as well as the somewhat rash guesses put forward by others, may not be owing to some misconception as to what John really intended by his allusion to the sixth hour. Here are his words, according to the Revised Version : 'Now it was the Prepara- [19 John 14] tion of the passover : it was about the sixth hour.' The Authorised Version stands : 'And it was the preparation of the passover, and about the sixth hour.' The word 'and' before 'about' is omitted by the Revisers, not being in the three oldest MSS., but in lieu thereof they have inserted, not in italics, 'it was.' Young's version, omitting the 'and,' is : 'And it was the preparation of the passover, . . . as it were the sixth hour.' Sharpe puts in brackets the words which he thought it necessary to insert : 'And it was (to be at night) the Preparation for the Passover, and (it was) about the sixth hour.' So the correct translation of the oldest MSS. would seem to be : 'And (or, Now) it was the preparation for (or, of) the passover about the sixth hour.' This is confirmed by the literal translation in the 'Englishman's Greek New Testament,' which is as follows: 'And it was preparation of the passover (the) hour was about the sixth.' The sixth hour refers either to the passover or to the preparation of the passover. That disposes of the idea of Alford and others, that by 'the preparation' the preparation *day* was meant. Luther, in order to give it the same sense as Alford, rendered the words as 'Rüsttag in den Ostern,' 'Preparation day in Easter :' but it has been already shown (page 226) that the word 'preparation' in connection with 'the passover,' did not convey that meaning. The 'passover' signified not the *day*, but the *meal*, and 'the preparation of the passover' *the preparation of the meal*, as is clear from the question : 'Where wilt thou that we prepare for thee to eat the passover?' Thus viewed, the passage in John is simple enough : 'Now it was the preparation for the passover (meal), about the sixth hour.' It is not necessary to introduce any additional words, but if any are inserted they should not be 'it was,' but 'which was,' before 'about the sixth hour.' The sixth hour was 12 at noon. John explains that when the last stage of the trial was reached, and Pilate, after long delay, sat on the judgment seat, the preparations were in progress for the banquet which the Jews generally would keep about mid-day. They were anxious to make an end of the matter and get home. This statement of the fourth evangelist in no wise clashes with the other gospel narratives. From this passage in John's account we simply deduce the fact that while Jesus was hanging on the cross the Jews were feasting.

²⁶ Mat. 17

Matthew continues : 'And they sat and watched him there.' The word 'they' refers to the soldiers mentioned in the preceding verse, and this watching of Jesus was simply the performance of their duty : Tischendorf renders 'watched' by 'were keeping,' and the 'Englishman's Greek New Testament' by 'kept guard over.' Above the cross they fixed a placard, specifying the nature of the accusation which had been made against the sufferer. 'And they set up over his head his accusation written, This is Jesus the King of the Jews.' Mark : 'And the superscription of his accusation was written over, The King of the Jews.' Luke : 'And there was also a superscription over him, This is the King of the Jews.' On the authority of the two oldest MSS., the Revisers have omitted the word 'written' before 'over ;' they have also omitted : 'in letters of Greek, and Latin, and Hebrew,' which are not in the Vatican MS. and were erased in the Sinaitic MS. The fourth evangelist enters more into details. He states that the notice had been written by Pilate : 'And Pilate wrote a title also, and put it on the cross. And there was written, Jesus of Nazareth, the King of the Jews.' The word 'also' introduced by the Revisers is in the original, and appears likewise in Young and Tischendorf : Alford renders it 'moreover.' As the title was above the head of Jesus, yet *on* the cross, it is supposed to have been 'on the projecting upright beam of the cross' (Alford). With respect to the superscription Alford observes : 'It is not known whether the affixing of this title was customary. In Dio Cassius and others, we read of such a title being hung round the neck of a criminal on his way to execution. On the difference in the four

Gospels as to the *words of the inscription itself*, it is hardly worth while to comment, except to remark, that the advocates for the verbal and literal exactness of each gospel may here find an *undoubted* example of the absurdity of their view, which may serve to guide them in less plain and obvious cases. *A title was written containing certain words; not four titles, all different,* but *one,* differing probably from all of these four, but certainly from three of them. Let us bear this in mind, when the narratives of words spoken, or events, differ in a similar manner.' The nature and extent of scriptural inspiration are involved in so much uncertainty, that it becomes no man upon earth, unless himself divinely inspired, to lay down any fixed rules of faith or judgment on the question. We may venture to assert that whatever is not true and right cannot be inspired of God; and who will be bold enough to say that anything which is true and right is *not* inspired of Him?

We read of none of the apostles, with the exception of the fourth evangelist, being present at the crucifixion. The reported words, however few, of a public notification, must naturally differ when quoted from memory by such persons as happen to have read the document, and especially where it is written in three different languages. Probably John's wording is strictly accurate : ' Jesus of Nazareth, the King of the Jews.' The title attracted much attention. 'This title therefore read many of the Jews.' The nearness of the place of crucifixion is stated as the explanation of this : 'for the place where Jesus was crucified was nigh to the city (or, for the place of the city where Jesus was crucified was nigh at hand).' The morbid curiosity which now attracts such crowds to a public execution, is partly owing to the fact that the crisis is instantaneous : the sightseers have only the trouble of going and returning in order to see the whole tragedy from beginning to end. But the long, lingering death upon the cross offered no such opportunity. The proximity of the place induced many, however, to visit the scene ; these persons would gaze at it for a time, observe all that was going on, and then return home or pursue their interrupted journey. Pilate was evidently anxious that all who did see Jesus on the cross should be in no doubt about the charge under which he had been condemned to this ignominious death, for not only was it placed conspicuously over him, but in characters decipherable by Jews, Greeks and Romans : 'and it was written in Hebrew, *and* in Latin, *and* in Greek.' The order of the two last-named languages has been reversed by the Revisers, on the authority of the two oldest MSS. Alford explains : 'The Latin was the official language, the Greek that usually spoken, the Hebrew (*i.e.* Aramaic) that of the common people.' The priests who had accused Jesus, and upon whom rather than upon Pilate rested the responsibility of the crucifixion, were far from pleased with the wording of the displayed title, and they suggested that an alteration should be made in it. It read like the announcement of a fact, and they begged that just two or three words might be added to make it clear that nothing more was meant than that the dying man had laid claim to such a title. 'The chief priests of the Jews therefore said to Pilate, Write not, The King of the Jews ; but, that he said, I am King of the Jews.' Alford observes : 'The same spirit of mockery of the Jews shewed itself in the title, as before, ver. 14. They had prevailed on Pilate by urging this point, that Jesus had set Himself up as a king; and Pilate is willing to remind them of it by these taunts. Hence their complaint, and his answer.' Without going so far as to accuse Pilate of deliberately taunting the Jews, he must have had some object in view in thus flaunting the title in the sight of all men. He had conceived for Jesus a feeling of respect and even awe, which the chief priests, scribes and elders had never felt. He had not scrupled to hint to them the conclusion which would be drawn from the crucifixion of one who had claimed to be their king, who was deemed the king of the Jews by many of them, and against whom Pilate himself could find no other ground of accusation. But in vain had he appealed to them. 'Behold your King,' and 'shall I crucify your King?' The expectation of a Messiah had been a long-standing cause of disaffection and insurrection among the Jews. Gamaliel quoted the instances of Theudas, who had given 'himself out to be somebody,' and of 'Judas of Galilee in the days of the enrolment,' against whom it had been necessary to take strong measures, annihilating them and their followers. It may have seemed desirable to Pilate to make an end once for all of such hopes and pretensions, and here and now was the opportunity for doing so. They had taken Jesus and crucified him: all men should know why and wherefore: thenceforth, when any talked of the anticipated restoration of Israel, the answer would be forthcoming: Yes, the promised Messiah appeared, and many hoped that it was he who should redeem Israel, but they took him, and slew him—he suffered death under Pontius Pilate. That title on the cross was the highest and only homage Pilate could pay to the character of the man of whom he had been constrained tremblingly to ask, 'Whence art thou?' and at the same time it subserved the imperial policy, emphasised the declaration of the Jews, 'We have no king but Cæsar,' and read like an announcement of the fact that the cherished hope of a revived Israelitish nationality must needs die with Jesus on the cross. Whatever the motives of Pilate in drawing up and affixing the title, the chief priests and their coadjutors may have felt a personal interest about it. Not much was needed to turn the fickle populace, and it might well happen that the accusers and executioners of Jesus might find themselves charged with having crucified the true Messiah: any holding of him out in that character was to be dreaded. If that was their apprehension, they did but forecast what actually happened, when Peter stood up with the eleven and said: 'Let all the house of Israel therefore know assuredly, that God hath made him both Lord and Christ, this Jesus whom ye crucified.' But Pilate had already yielded too much to their passions and prejudices, and he refused emphatically and somewhat curtly to comply with their request: 'Pilate answered, What I have written I have written.'

At this point of the narrative Matthew introduces the statement: 'Then are there crucified with him two robbers, one on the right hand, and one on the left.' The Revisers have altered 'were' to 'are,' agreeing with Young and Tischendorf,—an important difference, for the present tense, 'then are,' indicates that this did not take place, as might have been inferred from John and Luke, simultaneously with the crucifixion of Jesus. Mark states: 'And with him they crucify two robbers; one on his right hand, and one on his left.' The word 'with' denotes in the same place, in his company, but not necessarily quite at the same time. The next verse in the Authorised Version is omitted in the three oldest MSS. The Revisers note in the margin: 'Many ancient authorities insert ver. 28 *And the scripture was fulfilled, which saith, And he was numbered with transgressors.* See Luke xxii. 37.' 15 Mark 28

As is the case in our own days at similar spectacles, a motley crowd was attracted to the execution. 'And the people stood beholding.' The place appears to have abutted on the high road, for the demeanour and remarks of the passers by are described. That any observations made by them publicly and ostentatiously should be unfriendly, might well be expected, for all who honoured Jesus would either keep away from so sad a sight, or if present would contemplate it with silent horror and compassion. His enemies had spread abroad reports of the charges brought against him in the sanhedrim, and the perverted sense of words he was there charged with having once uttered was now caught up and turned into a gibe. Matthew says: 'And they that passed by railed on him, wagging their heads, and saying, Thou that destroyest the temple (or, sanctuary), and buildest it in three days, save thyself: if thou art the Son of God, come down from the cross.' Mark: 'And they that passed by railed on him, wagging their heads, and saying, Ha! thou that destroyest the temple (or, sanctuary), and buildest it in three days, save thyself, and come down from the cross.' Tischendorf renders 'railed' literally 'blasphemed,' and Young 'speaking evil.' Ignorance and prejudice were only too ready to scoff at that which deserved the highest reverence. All these mockers knew of Jesus and his doctrine was, that he had made certain claims which they, without examination, characterised as visionary, fanatical, absurd; it was enough for them that his teaching had been rejected and opposed by chief priests and scribes, men whose lives were devoted to the study of theology, who had branded Jesus as a deceiver, and had thought it their duty to condemn him to death. Alas! for the errors of humanity, the falsehood which darkens truth, and the evil passions born of prejudice and pride. The voice of the multitude served but as echo and chorus to that of their recognised spiritual guides. These latter were the leaders, if not originators, of that detestable and cruel ribaldry which assailed the ears of Jesus as he hung upon the cross. 'In like manner also the chief priests mocking *him* among themselves with the scribes said, He saved others; himself he cannot save (or, can he not save himself?). Let the Christ, the King of Israel, now come down from the cross, that we may see and believe.' This wording of Mark coincides so closely with that of Matthew, that both seem to be based upon the same original manuscript, yet not without variations and additions. 'In like manner also the chief priests mocking *him*, with the scribes and elders, said, He saved others: himself he cannot save (or, can he not save himself?). He is the King of Israel; let him now come down from the cross, and we will believe on him. He trusted on God; let him deliver him now, if he desireth him: for he said, I am the Son of God.' The words 'if he be' have been altered to 'he is,' in accordance with the two oldest MSS. These men must have treasured up in their minds various sayings dropped by Jesus in the course of his teaching; they had long lain rankling there, and now when he cannot vindicate or attempt to explain them, they are deemed to have been falsified and proved incredible. Jesus and God himself were challenged to demonstrate the authenticity of the claims and doctrines promulgated: let Jesus step down from his cross, or let God send down deliverance from heaven; that, and nothing else than that, would convince these gainsayers. God's ways were not their ways. They could not grasp his scheme for the salvation of the world. The Divine silence and impassiveness proclaimed, more loudly than any words could do, the solemn, sober truth, that men must work out their own salvation, God working in them both to will and to suffer. There can be no salvation except on these terms, no Messiah for those who do not believe and obey him.

<small>23 Luke 35</small>　　Luke's account is brief. 'And the rulers also scoffed at him; saying, He saved others: let him save himself, if this is the Christ of God, his chosen.' After 'also' the words 'with them,' referring to 'the people,' are omitted, on the authority of the two oldest MSS. The soldiers were only too ready to join their insults with the rest.

<small>,, 36, 37</small> 'And the soldiers also mocked him, coming to him, offering him vinegar, and saying, If thou art the King of the Jews, save thyself.' Alford notes: 'It was about the time of the mid-day meal of the soldiers,—and they in mockery offered Him their *posca* or sour wine, to drink with them.' All treated the claim of Jesus to kingship as a farce, a subject rich in material for jesting. Even the two malefactors who were crucified with him took part in ridiculing him.

<small>27 Mat. 44</small>　Matthew says: 'And the robbers also that were crucified with him cast upon him the same reproach.' The Authorised Version has 'cast the same in his teeth.' Young renders, 'reproached him;' Tischendorf, 'reproached him in the same fashion;' Alford, 'in like manner did the thieves also revile him.' Mark: 'And they that were crucified with him reproached him.' The Revisers and Tischendorf have altered 'reviled' to 'reproached:' Young renders, 'were reproaching;' the word is the same as in Matthew. Luke's account

<small>15 Mark 32</small>

<small>28 Luke 39-42</small> is not only much fuller, but very different. It is as follows: 'And one of the malefactors which were hanged railed on him, saying, Art not thou the Christ? save thyself and us. But the other answered, and rebuking him said, Dost thou not even fear God, seeing thou art in the same condemnation? And we indeed justly; for we receive the due reward of our deeds: but this man hath done nothing amiss. And he said, Jesus, remember me when thou comest in thy kingdom.' On the authority of the two oldest MSS. the Revisers have altered, 'If thou be Christ' to 'Art thou not the Christ?' and 'unto Jesus, Lord' to 'Jesus.' It is noted that 'Some ancient authorities read *into thy kingdom*.' Young renders 'in thy reign.' Alford explains: 'The A. V. following the Latin Vulgate (so also Luther), renders this *into thy kingdom*, which is a sad mistake, as it destroys the force of the expression.' Alford's further comments are as follows: 'Neither St. Matthew nor St. Mark is in possession of the more particular account given by St. Luke . . . St. Matthew and St. Mark have merely a general and less precise report of the same incident.' English readers generally, however, cannot fail to perceive an apparent discrepancy, if not an absolute contradiction, between the narratives. Matthew says that both robbers reproached

Jesus, and Mark confirms that statement, whereas Luke is understood to represent 'one of the malefactors' only as doing that, the other taking a precisely opposite course; that appears also to be Alford's view, judging from his remark: 'the evil-minded thief, perhaps out of bravado before the crowd, puts in his scoff also.' Some expounders have attempted to reconcile the narratives by assuming Luke to refer to a somewhat later period, as though both thieves did at first revile Jesus, and one of them afterwards altered his mind, or his heart somehow suddenly became changed, so that from being a mocker he was transformed into a respecter and defender of Jesus; and lessons are thence deduced about the omnipotence of divine grace, and the possibility of repentance at the eleventh hour, one of the vilest being thus 'saved,' that none might despair, and only one, that none might presume. This mode of evading the difficulty by hazarding a guess, is reprehensible, and the exhortations thence derived are injudicious and out of place. A more careful consideration of the text and of the circumstances needs to be made. If the two evangelists really contradict the third, let the fact be admitted: but no such admission should be made except upon clearest evidence. The probability lies in the other direction. It is not likely that Matthew and Mark used the plural, by mistake, for the singular; it is equally improbable that the account handed down by an independent observer can have been in direct conflict to that on which they relied. Much hangs upon niceties of translation. If the word 'but,' in Luke's narrative, be altered to 'and,' the matter becomes susceptible of a totally different explanation, and the three accounts may be found to harmonize. The introduction of the conjunction disjunctive places the conduct of the one thief in opposition to that of the other, whereas Matthew and Mark put them in the same category. The first question to be decided is as to the sense of the word rendered 'but.' The Greek word is *dè*, which is generally rendered by 'and,' sometimes by 'but.' A translator exercises his judgment as to which is most suitable, and, as a matter of course, subsequent translators follow in his wake, unless there should appear reason to the contrary. In this 23rd chapter of Luke the Greek *dè* occurs 35 times: once (verse 17) it is rendered 'now;' 8 times (verses 5, 6, 9, 18, 21, 23, 40, 41) it is rendered 'but;' in the remaining 26 instances it is rendered 'and.' We are fully justified, therefore, in discarding the word 'but,' and putting in its place the word 'and.' Their import differs in English, whereas no difference can be attributed to the original when one and the same word is employed. 'And the other answered,' by no means necessarily denotes opposition, but simply a continuation of the subject, and, according to the words of Matthew, of the same policy and method of reproach, for he uses the expression 'cast upon him the same reproach,' that is sarcastic, derisive addresses similar to those of the chief priests, or, as rendered by Tischendorf, 'reproached him in the same fashion.' That supplies an answer to the second question for consideration: How can the robber be supposed to be speaking ironically, in face of the statement that he was 'rebuking' the other? He was simply imitating the example which others around him had been setting, and his 'rebuke' was no more meant to be taken seriously and literally than were the expressions, 'He saved others. . .

Let the Christ, the King of Israel, now come down from the cross.' It was a veritable pandemonium of ribaldry: the sorry jests at the expense of the august sufferer flew thick and fast, and these two criminals, exhibiting obduracy and bravado to the last, joined their voices to the common chorus. The mention of saving others, and of coming down from the cross, excited a feeling of contempt in the mind of one robber: the idea of any man claiming such a power was as tantalising to him as it was absurd to others. By all means let any such superhuman ability be exercised now: 'Art not thou the Christ? save thyself and us.' His companion, not to be outdone, took up the idea, improved upon it, amplified the jesting taunt, exhibited his talent for mimicry and sarcasm. He adopted a tone of sham reproof, of feigned humility, addressing his companion in crime as a paragon of virtue and religion, of whom better things were expected: 'Dost not even thou fear God?' Let him remember that he and Jesus were on the same level, fellow-sufferers: 'seeing thou art in the same condemnation:' but with this difference,—and here the irony becomes more intense,—that they were punished justly, and that this man crucified between them, was innocent in all respects: 'And we indeed justly: for we receive the due reward of our deeds: but this man hath done nothing amiss.' Imagine the jeers with which such a statement was likely to be greeted by those passers by who had stayed to wag their heads at Jesus, saying, 'Ha! thou that destroyest the temple, and buildest it in three days, save thyself.' This scoffing thief carried the grim joke still further: to him, as to others present, all pretensions on the part of Jesus to Messiahship over Israel and a throne, must have seemed incredible, utterly annihilated. 'We hoped that it was he which should redeem Israel,' was the despairing remark of two disciples three days later. If they could not understand the matter, much less could this criminal now undergoing the last penalty of the law. It must surely have been with a scornful disbelief that he now addressed Jesus, pretending to regard him as a monarch about to reign, and soliciting his royal influence on his behalf when he came into possession of his kingdom and authority: 'And he said, Jesus, remember me when thou comest in thy kingdom.' This mock petition was the very acme of unbelief and sarcasm. We are bold to say that on the testimony of two evangelists: they did not report his words, but Luke did, and we take them to have been uttered in that spirit of reproach attributed to them by Matthew and Mark. There is no more reason for assuming them to have been dictated by faith and reverence than the words of the priests and scribes, 'Let the Christ, the King of Israel, now come down from the cross,' for Matthew distinctly says, according to Tischendorf, that the robbers 'reproached him in the same fashion,' or, according to the 'Englishman's Greek New Testament' '(with) the same thing.'

From the position occupied by the incident in the three narratives, and from the wording, it appears that the two malefactors were actually hanging, each upon his cross, when they thus joined in mocking Jesus. That is very remarkable. It might well be imagined that the agony of crucifixion would have diverted their thoughts from aught else, and have rendered them incapable, physically if not mentally, of anything of that kind. But it was a lingering mode of death; the act of speaking was not likely to cause any increase of pain; and robbers—men accustomed to risk and take life—would even pride themselves on facing death with a show of indifference. Probably, too, they had partaken of that stupefying drink which Alford says it was customary to give before execution, and which Jesus had refused to take. It may have had the twofold effect of deadening pain and of exciting the mind: to the wine contained in it may be attributable the unloosing of the tongue and the outburst of invective.

Up to this point Jesus had heard, seen, felt everything, in silence. But now, when the slowly-dying thief's railing voice had ceased, his own was heard in reply. Calm, solemn, unimpassioned, prefaced by his accustomed 'verily,' his words were addressed to the man who had last spoken. 'And he said unto him, Verily I say unto thee, To-day shalt thou be with me in Paradise.' The word 'Jesus' has been altered to 'he,' on the authority of the two oldest MSS. The answer implies that the kingdom of Jesus was in the world beyond the grave, where they two would be that day together. There he would see Jesus in his true character, and be remembered according to his own. Alford notes that the word paradise ' is used of the *garden of Eden* by the LXX. Gen. ii. 8, &c.' That sense corresponds with the passage: 'To him will I give to eat of the tree of life, which is in the Paradise of God.' The only other place where the word occurs is where used by Paul: 'And I know such a man (whether in the body, or apart from the body, I know not; God knoweth), how that he was caught up into Paradise.' Jesus spoke with a perfect knowledge of the destiny and location of departed spirits. May it not be that to all, upon their first entrance into the life to come, there is granted admission to a state or place of quiet and refreshment, such as every new-born infant has on its mother's bosom, and that subsequently each finds 'his own place' in the new world? The proper thought for every man on such a subject is that of Paul: 'I know not; God knoweth.' But these words of Jesus point that way, and they are in harmony with the 'supernatural experiences' of Emanuel Swedenborg, one of whose revelations is as follows: '450. The celestial angels who attend upon a resuscitated person do not leave him, because they love every one; but if he is of such a quality that he cannot remain with celestial angels, he wishes to leave them; and angels from the Lord's spiritual kingdom then approach, and give him the use of light; for as yet he only thought, but saw nothing . . . . They now tell him that he is a spirit. After they have given light to the new-comer, the spiritual angels render him all the kind offices which he can possibly desire, and instruct him concerning the things of another life, so far as he is able to comprehend them: but if he is not disposed to receive instruction he wishes to leave them. These angels also do not leave him, but he separates himself from them; for angels love every one, and desire nothing more than to perform kind offices to all, to instruct them, and to take them to heaven, for this is their highest delight. When the spirit thus separates himself from the attendant angels, he is received by good spirits, who also render him all kind offices whilst he continues with them; but if his life in the world has been such that he could not endure the society of the good, he wishes to leave them also, and these changes continue, until at length he associates himself with spirits who are in perfect agreement with his life in the world. With them he finds his life, and, wonderful to say, he then leads a similar life to that which he had led in the world. 451. This first state of man's life after death does not continue longer than a few days; but in what manner he is afterwards led from one state to another, and at last either into heaven or hell, will be shown in what follows from the ample experience which has been granted me.' *

19 John 25 — Amidst the hostile crowd about the cross there stood a few of those who loved Jesus. 'But there were standing by the cross of Jesus his mother, and his mother's sister, Mary the *wife* of Cleopas, and Mary Magdalene.' The word 'but' represents the Greek *dè*, which is here rendered in the Authorised Version as 'now,' and by Young and the 'Englishman's Greek New Testament' as 'and.' The mother of Jesus, now so highly honoured, must have suffered throughout her life a silent, unknown martyrdom. Highest joy and deepest sorrow were her lot. She must have felt oppressed by the weight of a secret, that of her first-born's birth, which she could not tell, and she must have watched with painful interest that mysterious career which she could neither understand, direct nor influence. How must she have been tried and grieved by the open hostility of her other sons towards Jesus! And this frightful, incomprehensible catastrophe, following upon the persecution, the accusation, the trial, the condemnation, must have overwhelmed her with the sorest agony a woman's heart can know. She was now realising to the full the truth of old Simeon's

2 Luke 35 — prophecy: 'A sword shall pierce through thine own soul.' At whatever cost to her own feelings, she must needs take one last look at her son before his eyes should close in death, and while they could yet exchange glances of love and sympathy. So there she stood, with her two or three female friends, with the favourite disciple who had leaned upon his Master's breast during the last supper, who had followed him to the high priest's palace, who appears to have been the only one of the twelve who stood by to the last, and to whom we owe the precious legacy of the fourth gospel. For a time the little group may have remained unrecognised, but when Jesus turned his gaze upon them, and saw his mother and that disciple standing side by side, he addressed first to her and then to him one pregnant, loving, trustful sentence, intimating that thenceforth they two should dwell

19 John 26 — together, he regarding her as a mother and she him as a son. 'When Jesus therefore saw his mother, and the disciple standing by, whom he
„ 27 — loved, he saith unto his mother, Woman, behold thy son! Then saith he to the disciple, Behold thy mother!' That dying wish was acted
„ 27 — on, that sacred charge thenceforth sedulously kept. 'And from that hour the disciple took her unto his own *home*.' The last word, not expressed in the original, is inserted by Young as 'friends.' The experiences of Mary are unique in human history. 'Blessed art thou among women!'

At the sixth hour, when Jesus had been three hours upon the
27 Mat. 45 — cross, a strange phenomenon occurred. 'Now from the sixth hour there was darkness over all the land (or, earth) until the ninth hour.'
15 Mark 33 — Mark: 'And when the sixth hour was come, there was darkness over

---

* "The Future Life. Heaven and Hell."

the whole land (or, earth) until the ninth hour.' Luke : ' And it [23 Luke 44]
was now about the sixth hour, and a darkness came over the whole
land (or, earth) until the ninth hour, the sun's light failing (Gr. the
sun failing).' The wording of the Authorised Version : ' and the
sun was darkened,' has been altered in accordance with the two
oldest MSS. The evangelists confined themselves to a simple statement of the fact : it becomes us not to speculate and dogmatize about
its cause and significance, albeit a higher wisdom than our own might
discern the import of this portent, as the eastern Magi were able to
read the mystic meaning of the star which heralded Messiah's birth.

When the supernatural darkness had passed or was about to pass,
Jesus shouted out four words of solemn import. ' And about the [27 Mat. 46]
ninth hour Jesus cried with a loud voice, saying, Eli, Eli, lama
sabacthani ? that is, My God, my God, why hast thou forsaken me
(or, why didst thou forsake me) ? ' Alford explains : ' The words
are Chaldee, and not Hebrew. Our Lord spoke them in the ordinary
dialect, not in that of the sacred text itself.' They are the opening
words of the 22nd Psalm. Their loud utterance at that critical
moment would seem to have been designed to call attention to that
Psalm, which stands forth as an inspired and marvellously accurate
picture of our Lord's experiences, down to the piercing of his hands
and feet, the dividing and raffling for his clothes, and which ends by
portraying the consequences to mankind at large of his final deliverance and exaltation. On the word ' cried ' Alford observes : ' Better
cried out, or even *cried mightily*, or *shouted forth*: it is the same word
as in Mark xv. 8 ; Luke ix. 38 : in which two places only it occurs.'
Mark's record is as follows : ' And at the ninth hour Jesus cried with [15 Mark 34]
a loud voice, Eloi, Eloi, lama sabacthani ? which is, being interpreted, My God, my God, why hast thou forsaken me ? (or, why
didst thou forsake me ?).' After ' voice ' the word ' saying ' has been
omitted, in accordance with the two oldest MSS. Alford notes :
' Elöi, the Syro-chaldaic form, answering to *Eli* in Matthew. Meyer
argues that the words in Matthew must have been those actually
spoken by our Lord, owing to the taunt, that He *called for Elias*.
The last word is pronounced *Sabacthani*, not *Sabachtani*.' There is
much variation in the oldest MSS. in the words : the Sinaitic has
lema, the Alexandrine *lima*; the original reading of the Sinaitic was
sabactani; the Alexandrine has *sabacathani*; the Vatican *zabaphthani*.
In Matthew the Sinaitic and Vatican have *Eloi, Eloi* and *lema*, and
the Alexandrine *lima*.

The Psalm to which Jesus, with his dying breath, so emphatically
called attention, is an epitome of his life, his sufferings, his tragic
end, his deliverance, not *before* but *at* death, and his final triumph
and rejoicing subsequent thereto. Its opening ejaculation is a
declaration of despairing innocence, on behalf of which God put
forth no helping hand, in despite of strong crying and prayer for
succour. The ways of divine providence were in this case reversed.
In old times God had delivered his people, but he left Jesus exposed
to the reproach and contempt of men :

   'Our fathers trusted in thee : [22 Psa. 4]
    They trusted, and thou didst deliver them :
    They cried unto thee, and were delivered :   „ 5
    They trusted in thee, and were not ashamed.
   But I am a worm, and no man ;   „ 6

A reproach of men, and despised of the people.

22 Ps. 7
All they that see me laugh me to scorn :
They shoot out the lip, they shake the head, *saying*,

„ 8
Commit *thyself* unto the LORD ; let him deliver him :
Let him deliver him, seeing he delighteth in him.'

All this came upon him in spite of a life-long devotion to and confidence in God :

„ 9
'Thou didst make me trust *when I was* upon my mother's breasts.'

At last came the crisis of his fate, which he must meet in lonely helplessness :

„ 11
'Be not far from me ; for trouble is near ;
For there is none to help.'

There came round about him the 'strong bulls of Bashan,' and he is powerless before them :

„ 15
'My strength is dried up like a potsherd.'

'Dogs' and 'evil doers' compass him while he lies in 'the dust of death' ; his hands and feet are pierced ; he becomes a gazing-stock ; his raiment is apportioned—he will never need it more—yet even then his faith stands firm :

„ 19
'But be not thou far off, O LORD :
O my succour, haste thee to help me.

„ 21
Save me from the lion's mouth.'

Then, not till then, comes the answer to the prayer for salvation :
' Yea, from the horns of the wild oxen thou hast answered me.'

The rest of the psalm is hopeful and exultant : Jesus and his brethren—disciples—praise God, Messiah's work is accomplished :

„ 28
'For the kingdom is the LORD'S ;
And he is ruler over the nations.'

Little thought had they who heard that great cry, of all that was in the mind of Christ in uttering it. Catching only at the first two words, some of the bystanders conceived it to be a call for Elijah.

27 Mat. 47
'And some of them that stood there, when they heard it, said, This

15 Mark 35
man calleth Elijah.' Mark : 'And some of them that stood by, when they heard it, said, Behold, he calleth Elijah.'

The fourth evangelist, after relating the care shown by Jesus for

19 John 28
his mother, continues : 'After this Jesus, knowing that all things are now finished, that the scripture might be accomplished, saith, I thirst.' The same evangelist has alluded previously to the perfect

13 John 1
knowledge of Jesus : 'Jesus knowing that his hour was come that he should depart out of this world unto the Father ;' and again :

18 John 4
'Jesus therefore, knowing all the things that were coming upon him, went forth.' The object of mentioning this must be to impress us with the conviction that Jesus was fully aware that no exception would be made in his favour, no deliverance granted to him from above, no interference with the free action of his enemies ; he had chosen his course of life, a new one in the history of the world, holding himself out to his disciples as their leader in a crusade on behalf of truth and love, based upon the principle of relinquishing all worldly property, hopes, ambitions, coupled with absolute and entire non-resistance to evil. He foresaw that he must suffer in consequence, to the extremity of physical and mental torture, and now he knew also that the utmost had been undergone, that human malice could do no more against him, that he lay, as it were, 'in the lion's mouth,' and between 'the horns of the wild oxen,' that all

things were now finished that the scripture might be accomplished. Simultaneously with that welcome thought, there came upon him the sense of an overpowering thirst; the cessation of the mental strain gave room for the realisation of the physical discomfort. Beyond that, there seems no ground for imagining any connection between the words 'I thirst' and the statement by which it is preceded.

The evangelist continues: 'There was set there a vessel full of vinegar: so they put a sponge full of the vinegar upon hyssop, and brought it to his mouth.' Alford explains: 'The *vinegar* was the sour wine, or vinegar and water, the common drink of the Roman soldiers.' So the act was one of kindness: what they had they gave, and in the only possible way, for drink to one in that posture and extremity could only be administered by suction. This consideration may tend to remove still further from our minds the idea of Alford that Jesus, in saying 'I thirst,' was 'only speaking because He so willed it, and because it was an ordained part of the course which He had taken upon Him.' As to this, Alford quotes from Lampe as follows: 'He would not have sought this alleviation of His sufferings, had He not known that this also pertained to the distinguishing signs of the Messiah as given in the Prophets.' Now the only reference to the Old Testament in the margin is to a passage in the Psalms: 19 John 29

'They gave me also gall for my meat; 69 Ps. 21
And in my thirst they gave me vinegar to drink.'

That is obviously a figure of speech, the allusion being not to one isolated occasion but to the regular supply of food: there is no justification for applying it to the offering of wine mixed with gall, which was previously mentioned by Matthew; still less can it be held to refer to the incident now mentioned in John's gospel: that stands out as the one act of compassion shown towards Jesus, whereas the Psalmist insinuates deliberate malice. 27 Mat. 34

The other evangelists do not allude to the saying of Jesus. 'I thirst.' They relate, however, the giving of the draught. Mark says: 'And one ran, and filling a sponge full of vinegar, put it on a reed, and gave him to drink.' Matthew: 'And straightway one of them ran, and took a sponge, and filled it with vinegar, and put it on a reed, and gave him to drink.' There is nothing in those two narratives to account for the giving of the vinegar: John's gospel explains the reason, which Matthew and Mark seem to have been ignorant of. As they were not present, there is no cause for surprise at the imperfection of their description. The close similarity of the wording indicates that both evangelists drew their information from the same source; yet there is a slight discrepancy between them. Mark proceeds: 'saying, Let be; let us see whether Elijah cometh to take him down.' Tischendorf, on what authority does not appear, omits the words 'let be;'* their application is not plain, for only the man himself was doing anything to Jesus. Matthew, however, puts the matter in a clearer light, telling us that it was not the man, but his companions, who said 'let be.' 'And the rest said, Let be; let us see whether Elijah cometh to save him.' Yet here again Tischendorf omits the words 'let be.'* 15 Mark 36 27 Mat. 48 15 Mark 36 27 Mat. 49

---

* Mark: 'Saying, Let us see whether Elijah is coming. . .' Matthew: 'But the rest said, Let us see whether Elijah is coming. . .'

Merging John's narrative with the others, circumstances otherwise inexplicable become clear. There was no apparent reason why drink should be given to Jesus on his crying out 'Eloi, Eloi :' the words 'I thirst' supply one. Why was there such haste : 'Straightway one of them ran'? Probably because the obtaining of the vinegar and hyssop required some time, and the man was anxious to comply with the sufferer's wish yet to be back speedily in order to see what might happen. Here, as often elsewhere, the omission or insertion of a detail makes a great difference in our comprehension of the narrative.

To Matthew's account the Revisers have appended the following note : 'Many ancient authorities add, *And another took a spear and pierced his side, and there came out water and blood*. See John xix. 34.' Those words are found in the two oldest MSS., but they are not retained by Tischendorf.

<small>19 John 30</small> The fourth gospel continues : 'When Jesus therefore had received the vinegar, he said, It is finished.' That exclamation explains and justifies the previous statement about his 'knowing that all things are now finished.' The three Synoptics agree that there was a loud outcry by Jesus which they do not put into words, and which to most <small>27 Mat. 50</small> may have sounded only like an inarticulate cry. 'And Jesus cried <small>15 Mark 37</small> again with a loud voice.' 'And Jesus uttered a loud voice.' 'And <small>23 Luke 46</small> when Jesus had cried with a loud voice (or, And Jesus crying with a <small>„ 46</small> loud voice).' Only Luke records his last words : 'he said, Father, into thy hands I commend my spirit.' On 'commend' Alford notes : <small>„ 46</small> 'Better, *deliver up*.' Young renders 'commit.' 'And having said this, he gave up the ghost ;' this is rendered by Young : 'and these things having said, he breathed out the spirit ;' Tischendorf : 'and <small>15 Mark 37</small> having said this, he expired.' Mark : 'and gave up the ghost,' rendered by Tischendorf 'expired,' and by Alford, 'breathed his last.' <small>27 Mat. 50</small> Matthew : 'and yielded up his spirit,' rendered by Young, 'let away <small>19 John 30</small> the spirit.' John gives the touch of an eye-witness : 'And he bowed his head, and gave up his spirit.' Alford notes that in Mark 'the words are not as in Matthew,' and he observes : 'None of the Evangelists say, He *died :* although that expression is ever after used of His death stated as one great fact : but it is *yielded up his spirit*, Matthew ; *breathed his last*, Mark, Luke ; *delivered up his spirit*, John.' On the words, 'Father, into thy hands I deliver up my spirit,' Alford says : 'These words have in them an important and deep meaning. They accompany that, which in our Lord's case was strictly speaking the *act* of death. It was *His own act* . . . a determinate delivering up of His spirit to the Father . . . See John x. 18—*no man taketh it from Me*, but *I lay it down of Myself.*' This can only mean that, notwithstanding the crucifixion and the draining away of the life-blood, Jesus must have continued to live on for an indefinite period, in fact for ever, if he had not himself voluntarily separated his spirit from his body. That strange notion is supported by the <small>10 John 17.</small> quotation, which has already been considered : 'I lay down my life, <small>18</small> that I may take it again. No one taketh it away from me, but I lay it down of myself.' Tischendorf's version does much towards removing the idea of Alford, by adopting the word 'expired' in Mark and Luke. That being the simple meaning of those two evangelists, the sense of the other two must be held to harmonise with it. Apart

from theological dogmas there would have been no attempt at stretching the expressions in the direction indicated by Alford. The word 'commend' or 'commit,' *paratithēmi*, on which he lays so much stress, is the same as that used in the passage: 'Let them also that suffer according to the will of God COMMIT their souls in well-doing unto a faithful Creator.' The dying cry of Stephen: 'Lord Jesus, receive my spirit,' is analogous to that of Jesus: 'Father, into thy hands I commit my spirit.' In the passage: 'I lay it down of myself,' the original word, *tithēmi*, is the same as in the passage: 'We ought to LAY DOWN our lives for the brethren.' To suppose that Jesus did not, and could not, die upon the cross like other men, or without a voluntary determination on his part, by 'his own act,' is to repudiate the reality of his human nature. [i. Pet. 19] [7 Acts 59] [3 i. John 16]

Simultaneously with the dying cry and passing away of Jesus, a strange prodigy or portent is recorded. The three synoptics agree in describing it. Matthew: 'And behold, the veil of the temple (or, sanctuary) was rent in twain from the top to the bottom.' Mark: 'And the veil of the temple (or, sanctuary) was rent in twain from the top to the bottom.' Luke: 'And the veil of the temple (or, sanctuary) was rent in the midst.' It is evident from the similarity of the wording that the statement was taken from the same original document; and that the fact was generally accepted and believed is clear from its introduction into the three narratives. The evangelists report it without comment; they make no attempt to explain its cause or significance. That such a circumstance must have been supernatural, admits of no doubt; and after all the other marvels which have been so gravely, simply, unhesitatingly related, there can be no valid reason for rejecting this. Spiritual beings were not merely interested beholders, but active agents in connection with this unexampled tragedy and its wide-reaching consequences. Spiritual insight, wide and deep, is needed to grasp the hidden meaning of what then took place. Is it not a fact that the Jewish ritual, the temple, the veil, the holy of holies, were arranged by Moses in accordance with divine command? Unless the history of Israel be regarded as a monstrous and inexplicable myth,—and against any such rash assumption the continued existence of the people and their unique literature testify to this day—it is an indubitable truth that their mode of worship was prescribed by the supreme Ruler of the universe; it was representative and symbolical; the writer of the epistle to the Hebrews describes the things appertaining thereto as being 'copies of the things in the heavens,' and Stephen reminded the Jews that they had 'received the law as it was ordained by angels.' Doubtless the rending of the veil by an unseen agency conveyed to higher minds than ours a sacred and solemn meaning; it becomes us not to guess or dogmatise, but we cannot err in connecting with the recorded fact the apostolic exhortation: 'Having therefore, brethren, boldness to enter into the holy place by the blood of Jesus, by the way which he dedicated for us, a new and living way, through the veil, that is to say, his flesh, and *having* a great priest over the house of God, let us draw near with a true heart in fulness of faith.' [27 Mat. 51] [15 Mark 38] [23 Luke 45] [9 Heb. 23] [7 Acts 53] [10 Heb. 19]

In addition to the mysterious rending of the veil, Matthew groups together various other phenomena which occurred at that eventful crisis: 'and the earth did quake, and the rocks were rent; and the tombs were opened; and many bodies of the saints that had fallen asleep were raised: and coming forth out of the tombs after his resurrection they entered into the holy city and appeared unto many.' Here are six distinct statements: (1) an earthquake; (2) the rending of rocks; (3) the opening of tombs; (4) the resurrection of dead bodies; (5) the entrance of men dead and buried into the city: (6) their appearance to many persons. All these marvels hang together and may be deemed contingent upon the first: without an earthquake there would have been no dislocation of the rocks, no opportunity of egress from the tombs, and consequently no revisiting of the living by the dead. Alford accepted the account in its entirety, without qualm or question. He wrote: 'It would not be right altogether to reject the testimonies of travellers to the fact of extraordinary rents and fissures in the rocks near the spot. Of course those who know no other proof of the historical truth of the event, will not be likely to take this as one; but to us, who are firmly convinced of it, every such trace, provided it be soberly and honestly ascertained, is full of interest. The whole transaction was *supernatural* and symbolic: no other interpretation of it will satisfy even ordinary common sense. Was the earthquake a *mere coincidence?* This not even those assert, who deny all symbolism in the matter. Was it a mere *sign of divine wrath* at what was done—a mere *prodigy*, like those at the death of Cæsar? Surely no Christian believer can think this. Then *what was it?* What but the *opening of the tombs*—the symbolic declaration that *the Death* which had happened had broken the bands of death for ever? These following clauses, which have no mythical or apocryphal character, require only this explanation to be fully understood. The graves were opened *at the moment of the death* of the Lord; but inasmuch as He is the first fruits from the dead—*the* Resurrection and the Life—the bodies of the saints in them *did not arise till He rose*, and having appeared to many after his resurrection,—possibly during the forty days,—went up with Him into His glory.' Agreeing with Alford as to the symbolic character of whatever actually happened, it is nevertheless necessary and proper to exercise an independent judgment with respect to the details of the account. What is meant by the word 'saints'? It cannot refer to Christian believers, for we know of no disciples of Jesus previously deceased. The term was of frequent occurrence in the Old, as afterwards in the New Testament. In Job, in the Psalms and in the Prophets, it denotes those in favour with God, devoted to his service. 'The LORD loveth judgement, and forsaketh not his saints; they are preserved for ever.' 'The saints of the Most High shall receive the kingdom, and possess the kingdom for ever, even for ever and ever.' The expression 'holy city' is also borrowed from the prophets. Matthew had introduced it previously: 'Then the devil taketh him into the holy city; and he set him on the pinnacle of the temple.'. In Daniel we read: "Seventy weeks are decreed upon thy people and upon thy holy city.' The adoption of these prophetic forms of speech may be taken to indicate that the fulfilment of prophecy was in the mind of the evangelist when describing the phenomena. But except the earthquake, the torn rocks and the opened tombs, nothing appears to have come under his own personal observation. He writes simply what had been related to him or was currently reported, and he does not say that the *bodies* out of the tombs were those which appeared: Alford inserted 'they,' as applying to the 'saints,' not to the 'bodies,' before 'came out,' noting: 'the gender is masculine, whereas *bodies* is neuter.' It is not asserted, or hinted, that any one saw dead bodies come out of the tombs, but merely that departed saints, after an interval of three days, appeared to many. Neither may the idea be entertained that there was any recognition or identification of the dead by the living, for there is nothing in the text to that effect. They manifested themselves as Moses and Elijah did on the mount, in bodily form, yet not as resuscitations of their dead and gone bodies, but in their spiritual and heavenly bodies. Only gross, crude, unphilosophical, unscriptural notions of what is involved in the doctrine of a bodily resurrection, can have led to the assumption that the dead saints who appeared in material, visible shape, had come out of the yawning tombs. Either Matthew's words, 'came out of the tombs,' simply describe the popular rumour, or if that was his own conception, we must needs attribute it to error of judgment on his part. A cloud of misconception in regard to the resurrection of the dead has long hovered over Christendom; that glorious hope became so perverted, distorted, far-off, unnatural, incredible, that the only wonder is we have not lost it altogether. There could have been no connection, except in the way of symbolism, between the visions of saints and the rending of rock-hewn tombs; but how easily and almost imperceptibly the imagination may blend fictions with facts, appears from the closing words of Alford, gravely uttered as though they had been susceptible of proof, or the fact might be taken for granted: 'the bodies of the saints . . . having appeared to many after his resurrection—possibly during the forty days,—went up with Him into His glory.' That is a mere guess, on a par with that which attributed the appearance of the saints to their having come out of the tombs.

Matthew describes the effect produced on the minds of the soldiers by the convulsion of nature experienced on the death of Jesus. 'Now the centurion, and they that were with him watching Jesus, when they saw the earthquake, and the things that were done, feared exceedingly, saying, Truly this was the Son of God (or, a son of God).' The physical commotion had been preceded by three hours of preternatural darkness, and was coincident with the mighty outcry of Jesus just before he bowed his head and died. The lamentable cry, 'My God, my God, why hast thou forsaken me?' was a solemn proclamation to the world of the sufferer's innocence and sincerity of purpose: the soldiers appear not to have understood that, but the words, 'Father, into thy hands I commend my spirit,' were equally expressive of guiltlessness, and evinced a triumphant confidence in God. He whose departure took place under such unparalleled conditions and manifestations, could have been no ordinary man: 'Truly this was a son of God.' Mark's account does not include the earthquake, and he attributes the exclamation to the centurion only, and as having arisen solely out of the manner in which Jesus died. 'And when the centurion, which stood by over against him, saw that he so gave up the ghost, he said, Truly this man was the Son of God (or, a son of God).' The Revisers, following the two oldest MSS., have omitted after 'so' the words 'cried out, and,' noting that many ancient authorities contain them. Being close to the cross, the centurion had the best opportunity of watching the demeanour and hearing the words of Jesus; the gazing crowd was probably kept at some distance; the fact that John was able to bring the women to stand 'by the cross' may have been owing to his having been known to the high priest, which secured him also the opportunity of access to the palace: the words addressed by Jesus to his mother and the beloved disciple were probably not spoken loudly enough to reach the ears of those standing far beyond them: but the centurion and his attendant soldiers saw and heard everything, from first to last, and the mind and heart of Jesus were so plainly disclosed to them by his every look and utterance, that, when all was over, they could not and would not forbear from testifying to their entire conviction of his integrity and superiority: whatever he might have declared himself to be, that man must needs have been: 'Truly this was a son of God.' There is no contradiction between Matthew and Mark: the opinion expressed by the commanding officer might very naturally be adduced by one reporter, and the fact that the other soldiers agreed with it, by another. It was founded primarily on the demeanour and words of Jesus, but was of course strengthened in no small degree by the signs which accompanied his death. The expression of Matthew, 'and the things that were done,' suggesting other reasons than the earthquake, includes the sayings of Jesus as well as the darkness: everything combined to produce the impression; the last utterance was enough by itself, but what preceded and followed must also be taken into account.

The Revisers have placed in the margin the indefinite article 'a,' as an alternative reading to the definite article 'the,' before the word 'son,' which they leave uncapitalised in the margin. The introduction to 'The Englishman's Greek New Testament' contains the following statement, which should always be kept in mind: 'The Greek will not help in the difficulty' (as to capitalisation) 'because in the earliest copies every letter was a capital.' Properly no question arises between 'a' and 'the,' for neither word is in the original. Young's renderings, strictly literal, are, 'Truly this was Son of God,' 'Truly this man was Son of God,' agreeing with Tischendorf's, 'Truly this was God's son,' 'Truly this man was God's son.' It is obvious that no doctrinal significance is to be attached to the term 'son of God.' Alford says: 'It cannot be doubtful, I think, that he used these words *in the Jewish sense*—and with some idea of that which they implied. When Meyer says that he must have used them in a heathen sense, meaning a *hero or demigod*, we must first be shown that *Son of God* was *ever so used*.' It is necessary also to enquire carefully what was its proper 'Jewish sense;' and in connection with that point the account of Luke deserves consideration.

23 Luke 47 It is as follows: 'And when the centurion saw what was done, he glorified God, saying, Certainly this was a righteous man.' Young and Tischendorf render: 'Really this man was righteous:' the 'Englishman's Greek New Testament': 'Indeed this man was just.' Here is Alford's view of the passage: 'Something in the manner and words

convinced him that this man was the Son of God; which expression he used doubtless with reference to what he had before heard, but especially to the words just uttered—"*Father*, into Thy hands I commend my spirit." St. Luke has not expressed the words exactly the same: but the A. V. has wrongly and ungrammatically rendered what he relates the Centurion to have said, and made *a righteous man* (St. Luke) stand in the place of *the Son of God* (St. Mark); whereas the words only give the *general sense* of the persuasion of the centurion. *Truly this man was innocent:* and if innocent (nay more, *just, truthful*), *He was the Son of God, for He had asserted it.* This scarcely harmonises with an observation made by Alford elsewhere: 'I believe St. Luke's to be a different report.' If so, why attempt to mix up the two reports? The word 'righteous' or 'just,' *dikaios*, is not—'truthful,' and is never so rendered. It may perhaps be fairly open to question whether Luke, having the term 'Son of God' before him, did not render it by what he conceived was its equivalent, recognised Jewish sense: a righteous or just man was a son of God, and to own that Jesus was such an one, was to 'glorify God.' If the centurion expressed his personal conviction, the words in which it was couched must have borne a definite meaning, either that given by Luke or the one suggested by Meyer. The plural form used in the Old Testament widens the significance and application of the term: 'The sons of God came to present themselves before the LORD.' 'All the sons of God shouted for joy.' '*Ye are* the sons of the living God.' We may dismiss the exaggerated sense which the scribes and Pharisees attached to the expression, and against which Jesus himself protested. It suited their purpose to accuse him of making himself equal to God by calling him Father, and afterwards to assert: 'According to our law he ought to die, because himself Son of God he made.' The argument of Jesus in opposition to their accusation was very striking: 'If them he called gods, to whom the word of God came .... do ye say, Thou blasphemest, because I said, Son of God I am?' That is the literal rendering. God's servants have been called gods: surely I, as one of them, may be called Son of God: that is the drift of the argument. Be it observed, too, that the word 'blasphemest' is pure Greek, *blasphēmeis*, untranslated, which Young renders into English, 'speakest evil.' To get at the true sense, here and elsewhere, we must discard the definite article before 'son of God,' when it does not occur in the original, we must not be misled by capital letters, we must restrict blasphemy to what it actually signifies, and we must follow the argument and leading of Jesus in opposition to the strained interpretations and dogmatic teachings of an antiquated, inherited system of theology.

Luke informs us that the impression produced on the minds of the spectators of the closing scene was great and manifest. They, like the soldiers, were unable to resist the conviction that the sufferer was innocent, and it would seem that they returned homewards bitterly reproaching themselves for their own share in the transaction. 'And all the multitudes that came together to this sight, when they beheld the things that were done, returned smiting their breasts.' Outside, and at a distance from the crowd, there had been standing other gazers of a very different character, who had been drawn to the spot not by a callous curiosity, but by sympathy and friendship. 'And all his acquaintance, and the women that followed with him from Galilee, stood afar off, seeing these things.' Matthew identifies some of the women. 'And many women were beholding from afar, which had followed Jesus from Galilee, ministering unto him: among whom was Mary Magdalene, and Mary the mother of James and Joses, and the mother of the sons of Zebedee.' Mark's account is evidently based on the same written document, the similarity of the wording being too close to be accidental; but he adds that these women had first followed Jesus in Galilee before coming up with him to Jerusalem. 'And there were also women beholding from afar: among whom were both Mary Magdalene, and Mary the mother of James the less (Gr. little) and of Joses, and Salome; who, when he was in Galilee, followed him, and ministered unto him; and many other women which came up with him unto Jerusalem.' The word 'also,' between 'who' and 'when,' has been omitted, on the authority of the two oldest MSS. As it was customary for families to come from a distance to Jerusalem in order to keep the passover there, it would be quite natural for those who knew Jesus to travel with him thither. The allusion to the women having 'followed him when he was in Galilee,' coupled with the fact that they ministered to his necessities, although not denoting actual discipleship, probably signifies the nearest approach to it which their sex and opportunities permitted.

Alford explains: 'The *Roman custom* was for the bodies to remain on the crosses until devoured by birds of prey. On the other hand Josephus says that the Jews were so careful about burying that they took down even those who had been crucified, and buried them before sunset.' They were particularly anxious on this point now, because it was the Passover festival and the next day would be a sabbath of exceptional solemnity. They therefore requested Pilate to have the bodies removed without delay. 'The Jews therefore, because it was the Preparation, that the bodies should not remain on the cross upon the sabbath (for the day of that sabbath was a high *day*), asked of Pilate that their legs might be broken, and *that* they might be taken away.' Instead of 'it was the Preparation,' Tischendorf renders literally, 'it was preparation.' Alford says that the sabbath was '*a double sabbath:* the coincidence of the first day of unleavened bread with an ordinary sabbath.' He notes also: 'The *breaking of the legs* was sometimes appended to the punishment of crucifixion, but does not appear to have been inflicted for the purpose of causing death, which indeed it would not do. Friedlieb supposes that the term involved in it the *coup de grace*, which was given to all executed criminals.' That would account for the matter of fact way in which the proposal was made and is mentioned. Soldiers were sent to execute it: they broke the legs of the two malefactors, but Jesus being unmistakably dead, they did not trouble to do so in his case. 'The soldiers therefore came, and brake the legs of the first, and of the other which was crucified with him: but when they came to Jesus, and saw that he was dead already, they brake not his legs.' Instead of that, one of the soldiers thrust a spear into his side, and through the wound there instantly issued a stream of—not blood merely, but of blood and water: 'howbeit one of the soldiers pierced his side, and straightway there came out blood and water.'

The evangelist draws special attention to that remarkable phenomenon, asserting that the fact rests upon the direct testimony of an eye-witness, whose veracity was unimpeachable, and who was careful to express his own thorough knowledge with respect to the matter, in order that no doubt might exist in the minds of the readers of the narrative. 'And he that hath seen hath borne witness, and his witness is true: and he knoweth that he saith true, that ye also may believe.' The word 'also' has been introduced from the Sinaitic and Vatican MSS. The expression, 'he that hath seen hath borne witness,' may be equivalent, in modern phraseology, to, 'the observer of the fact has testified thereto by a solemn affirmation.' Alford notes: 'The third person (*he that saw it*) gives solemnity. It is, besides, in accordance with St. John's way of speaking of himself throughout the Gospel.' Alford further observes: 'This emphatic affirmation of the fact seems to regard rather the whole incident, than the mere outflowing of the blood and water. It was the object of St. John to shew that the Lord's Body was a *real body*, and *underwent real death*. And both these were shewn by what took place: not so much by the phænomenon of the water and blood, as by the infliction of such a wound,—after which, even had not death taken place before, there could not by any possibility be life remaining.' To this it must be replied, that the issuing of blood alone from the wound, though amply sufficient to prove death, would have required no such strong asseveration to make it credible, and we must take the marvel in its entirety: if blood alone had come forth, that would have been evidence of 'a real body,' that is, a purely human body, but the outflow of blood *and* water points to the opposite conclusion. As to that, Alford observes: 'The spear perhaps pierced the pericardium or envelope of the heart, in which case a liquid answering the description of *water* may have flowed with the blood. But the quantity would be so small as scarcely to have been observed. It is hardly possible that the separation of the blood into placenta and serum should so soon have taken place, or that, if it had, it should have been by an observer described as *blood and water*. It is more probable that the fact, which is here so strongly testified, was a consequence of the extreme exhaustion of the Body of the Redeemer. The medical opinions upon the point are very various, and by no means satisfactory.' It would seem that the ideas of Alford on the subject were in a chaotic state, for having thus minimised the occurrence to the utmost, as though it were merely the result of extreme bodily exhaustion, he immediately adds: 'Meyer's view after all seems to be the safe and true one—that the circumstance is related as a miraculous sign, having deep significance as to the work of the Redeemer, and shewing him to be more than mortal.' Admit the 'miraculous sign' to be a miraculous fact, proving Jesus to 'be more than mortal,' and the explanation meets the requirements of the narrative, which nothing less than that will do. Alford himself admits as much, saying: 'nor can I see how i. John v. 6 can be understood without reference to this fact.' That is the passage round which a storm of controversy raged for centuries. The Authorised Version stands as follows: 'This is he that came by water and blood, *even* Jesus Christ; not by water only, but by water and blood. And it is the Spirit that beareth witness, because the

<small>1 John 7</small> Spirit is truth. For there are three that bear record in heaven, the Father, the Word, and the Holy Ghost: and these three are one.
<small>,, 8</small> And there are three that bear witness in earth, the spirit and the water, and the blood: and these three agree in one.' The intermediate verse, 7, is not in the three oldest MSS. The Revisers have rejected it, and have included with the 7th the latter portion of verse 6. That alteration frees us from the incubus of a theological dogma, open to misconception because infinitely high above our reasoning powers, and reduces the statement to a matter of fact certified by the writer as within his cognizance. This passage in John's epistle and the solemn declaration in his gospel are in perfect harmony, illustrating and confirming each other. He is speaking of Jesus as the Son of God: 'This is he that came by water and blood, *even* Jesus Christ: not in the water only, but in the water and in the blood.' Tischendorf agrees with the Revised Version, merely omitting the inserted word *even*. Young renders: 'This one is he who came through water and blood—Jesus the Christ, not in the water only, but in the water and the blood.' What could be plainer or more definite? The nature assumed by the Christ, when he 'came' into the world, was a compound of water and blood. The apostle is dealing with a reality, the incarnation of Jesus: his words are no mere figure of speech, however much men may have come to regard them as such, as they have
<small>2 John 3, 6</small> the words to Nicodemus: 'Except a man be born of water and the Spirit, he cannot enter into the kingdom of God. That which is born of the flesh is flesh, and that which is born of the Spirit is spirit.' These are actualities, not metaphors: flesh and blood must have as their vitalised counterparts water and spirit. Do
<small>15 i. Cor. 50</small> we ask why? Because 'flesh and blood cannot inherit the kingdom of God; neither doth corruption inherit incorruption.' That saying of Paul is at one with the statement of Jesus to Nicodemus, that a second birth of water and spirit must precede entrance into the kingdom of God. But with Jesus himself the process was
<small>2 Heb. 14</small> reversed: 'Since . . . the children are sharers in flesh and blood, he also himself in like manner partook of the same.' That is not a figure of speech, but describes an actual, living embodiment: there was in Jesus a double nature, the heavenly—water and spirit, the earthly—flesh and blood; his manifestation to mankind was of a threefold character: 'for there are three who bear witness, the Spirit, and the water, and the blood: and the three agree in one.' Young renders the last clause literally: 'and the three are into the one.' The word 'agree' is merely a guess by translators at the sense. The 'Englishman's Greek New Testament' suggests instead the word 'point.' There is no reason, however, for alteration of or addition to the text, the literal rendering of which is given in the last-named work thus: 'and the three to the one are,' that is, the three are centered in Jesus. No wonder the evangelist insisted so strongly on the phenomenon disclosed to his own eyesight, attesting the physical fact that in the body of Jesus there was water as well as blood, coursing together through the frame, so that on the rupture of the veins they both flowed forth, yet so separated the one from the other that each was distinctly visible, the blood undiluted, the water uncoloured. That is the startling account of a sight of unexampled strangeness, certifying that the union of the divine with the human in Jesus is no

mere myth or dogma, but a real, sober truth, a physical as well as spiritual actuality, the double nature being embodied in him as a living entity. Although born of the Woman he was conceived of the Spirit, having no earthly father, and there was blended with the blood which distended his veins a more ethereal fluid, a divine ichor, to the outflowing of which in the shape of water the astounded apostle bore solemn testimony. This evangelist relates nothing about the miraculous birth of Jesus, but he was able to assert, on the testimony of his own eyesight, that the essential basis of life in Jesus was different from that of other men. How accurately and wonderfully do the gospel narratives fit into and corroborate each other!

The evangelist connects with this incident two scriptural passages indicating that Jesus was no ordinary man, and that what befel him had been prearranged and predicted. 'For these things came to pass, that the scripture might be fulfilled, [19 John 36, 37]

A bone of him shall not be broken (or, crushed).

And again another scripture saith,

They shall look on him whom they pierced.'

The first quotation possibly refers to the command with respect to the paschal lamb: 'neither shall ye break a bone thereof,' but more probably to this passage in a psalm of David: [12 Ex. 46]

'Many are the afflictions of the righteous: [34 Ps. 19]

But the LORD delivereth him out of them all.

He keepeth all his bones:

Not one of them is broken.'

The second quotation corresponds with the passage: 'They shall look unto me whom they have pierced,' where the Revisers note that 'according to some MSS.' *me* is *him*. [12 Zech. 10]

The object of the Jews who made request to Pilate to have the bodies removed, was simply to avoid the scandal of letting them hang throughout the sabbath: as to what became of the corpse of Jesus they were utterly indifferent, probably supposing that the three bodies would be taken away together. But there was one person of repute among them who determined, if possible, to bestow upon Jesus an honourable burial. The time pressed, for it was evening, so it was necessary to act promptly and decisively. Nothing could be done without the authority of Pilate, and he was appealed to openly and unhesitatingly. 'And when the even was now come, because it was the Preparation, that is, the day before the Sabbath, there came Joseph of Arimathæa, a councillor of honourable estate, who also himself was looking for the kingdom of God; and he boldly went in unto Pilate, and asked for the body of Jesus.' The word *paraskeue*, rendered 'Preparation,' is the same which occurs in 19 John 14 and 31. It is generally assumed to signify 'Paschal Friday,' as to which Alford notes: '(the preparation—*Parasceve*, "the name by which Friday is now generally known in Asia and Greece." Words.).' This reliance upon a quotation from Wordsworth shows that the meaning of the term is a matter of opinion, and the idea thus handed down seems to have been held too rigidly, and to have led to some misconception. Let it be observed that in one place John uses the expression 'preparation of the passover,' and in another place 'preparation' simply, and that the second passage applies to a time some hours later than the first, and when the passover had already been eaten. Mark, [15 Mark 42, 43] apparently in order to avoid the possibility of mistake, lest the 'preparation' should be supposed to be that of 'the passover,' adds the explanation, 'that is, before sabbath,' rendered by Young, 'that is, the fore-sabbath:' the words 'the day,' are an insertion by the translators, although not italicised. It seems clear enough, that the word 'preparation' was applicable both to the passover and the sabbath, just as we use the word 'vigil' in connection with different festivals: the preparation of the sabbath was, of course, on every Friday, the preparation of the passover denoting, in the same way, the making ready of all things for that festival.

Each of the four evangelists says something in praise of the character of the man who took upon himself the pious duty of burying Jesus. Mark mentions his high position, alludes to his moral courage, and says that he 'was looking for the kingdom of God.' Luke uses those same words, and adds that he was noted for goodness and rectitude, and either had failed to attend the Sanhedrim, or had voted there against the death of Jesus. 'And behold, a man named Joseph, who was a councillor, a good man and a righteous (he had not consented to their counsel and deed), *a man* of Arimathæa, a city of the Jews, who was looking for the kingdom of God: this man went to Pilate, and asked for the body of Jesus.' The words 'also himself' are omitted after 'who,' on the authority of the two oldest MSS. Matthew informs us that Joseph was actually a disciple of Jesus. 'And when even was come, there came a rich man from Arimathæa, named Joseph, who also himself was Jesus' disciple: this man went to Pilate, and asked for the body of Jesus.' John qualifies the statement about discipleship, saying that it had been secret on account of the peril involved in any open confession of belief in Jesus, the penalty for which we know was excommunication. 'And after these things Joseph of Arimathæa, being a disciple of Jesus, but secretly for fear of the Jews, asked of Pilate that he might take away the body of Jesus.'

The mental attitude attributed to Joseph—that of 'looking for the kingdom of God,' is still, alas! the highest aspiration which the most hopeful and enthusiastic Christian is able to form. Century after century has dragged out its weary length of strife, oppression, degradation, crime, and still the cry of suffering humanity, unsanctified, unregenerated, unredeemed, rises up to heaven, as if in mockery of the announcement, long since outworn and overborne, 'The kingdom of heaven is at hand.' The high and pure ideal of Christ's gospel has never yet been realised on earth: there has been no experience of a 'common salvation.' Be the causes what they may, let the responsibility of them rest on whom it may, the sad, solemn, awful fact is undeniable: the social condition of the mass of mankind is not such as our Lord would have it. Is it because his scheme of salvation has failed through some inherent weakness or defect? Or is it because we have failed to apprehend it, and so have not abided by it? Scribes, Pharisees and chief priests blundered frightfully in their treatment of the gospel, its Founder, and his apostles. What about the ecclesiastical system and polity of our own and bygone generations? Are we quite sure there is no grave, gross, hideous misconception generally prevalent, both among our spiritual guides and their flocks, with respect to the fundamental aims and method of

Christianity? What of the papacy, with all its past abominations and persecutions? of sacerdotalism, with its dogmatic teachings and assumption of spiritual powers and privileges? of Calvinism, and every other 'ism,' putting in the place of the simple teaching of Jesus their peculiar tenets, creeds, modes of worship, and so-called means of grace and salvation? what of the solemn conclave assembled in 1889 at Lambeth, where the Archbishop of Canterbury sat in judgment on the Bishop of Lincoln, and learned lawyers discussed and argued about the details connected with the administration of the Eucharist, the prayer of consecration, the mixing of water with the wine, the posture and gestures of the celebrant, and so forth? How alien are all these things from the gospel of Jesus and the true spirit of Christianity! Until they are supplanted by something better, higher, more heavenly, aye! more rational, we can only still go on 'looking for the kingdom of God,' but never finding it.

Death by crucifixion was so lingering that Pilate had considerable doubt whether it had taken place when the application was made to him for the body. To be certain on the point, he summoned the centurion and enquired of him, not simply if Jesus was dead, but whether he had been long dead. 'And Pilate marvelled if he were already dead: and calling unto him the centurion, he asked him whether he had been any while dead.' The Revisers note: 'Many ancient authorities read *were already dead*.' As Jesus expired about the ninth hour, the centurion was able to report that some hours had elapsed, on hearing which Pilate complied with Joseph's request. 'And when he learned it of the centurion, he granted the corpse to Joseph.' Probably his application was made shortly after that of the Jews; they cared only to secure the removal of the body anyhow and anywhere, whereas Joseph offered to take upon himself its disposal. The other evangelists do not record the hesitation of Pilate: Matthew says briefly: 'This man went to Pilate, and asked for the body of Jesus. Then Pilate commanded it to be given up.' Following the two oldest MSS., the Revisers have omitted 'the body,' the word 'it,' which they put instead, being an insertion. John says merely: 'and Pilate gave *him* leave.'

15 Mark 44

,, 45

27 Mat. 58

19 John 38

Armed with this authority Joseph proceeded to remove the body from the cross. 'And he took it down, and wrapped it in a linen cloth.' Matthew: 'And Joseph took the body, and wrapped it in a clean linen cloth.' Mark: 'And he bought a linen cloth, and taking him down, wound him in the linen cloth.' Young and Tischendorf render 'linen cloth' as 'fine linen.' The fourth evangelist states that Joseph was aided in his pious task by another person, Nicodemus, who brought a quantity of spices for the corpse. 'He came therefore, and took away his body. And there came also Nicodemus, he who at the first came to him by night, bringing a mixture of myrrh and aloes, about a hundred pound *weight*.' Following the Vatican and Alexandrine MSS., the Revisers and Tischendorf have replaced 'Jesus' by 'him.' The Revisers note that instead of 'mixture' 'some ancient authorities read *roll*.' 'So they took the body of Jesus, and bound it in linen cloths with the spices, as the custom of the Jews is to bury.' The Alexandrine MS. reads, 'the body of God,' which was probably a mistake of some transcriber. On the words, 'as the custom of the Jews is to bury,' Alford notes: 'Little is

23 Luke 53

27 Mat. 59

15 Mark 46

19 John 38, 39

,, 40

known with any certainty of the Jews' ordinary manner of burying.' The body was placed in a rock-hewn tomb. 'And laid him in a tomb which had been hewn out in a rock.' Matthew states that the sepulchre belonged to Joseph, having been lately excavated by him: 'and laid it in his own new tomb, which he had hewn out in the rock.' John adds that it was in a garden, near the place of crucifixion, and he seems to hint that but for the approach of the sabbath some other place might have been chosen, or more publicity given to the funeral. 'Now in the place where he was crucified there was a garden; and in the garden a new tomb wherein was never man yet laid. There then because of the Jews' Preparation (for the tomb was nigh at hand) they laid Jesus.' Luke intimates that the sabbath was on the point of beginning. 'And laid him in a tomb that was hewn in stone, where never man had yet lain. And it was the day of the Preparation, and the sabbath drew on (Gr. began to dawn).' To prevent intrusion, a stone was placed against the door of the cave. 'And he rolled a stone against the door of the tomb.' Although this is spoken of as the act of Joseph, of course that does not mean that he employed no assistants: Matthew alludes to the largeness of the stone. 'And he rolled a great stone to the door of the tomb, and departed.'

No mention is made of any of the apostles being present at this last scene, but the women from Galilee, who had not shrunk from the sight of the cross, now assembled to show the last tribute of respect to Jesus. 'And the women which had come with him out of Galilee, followed after, and beheld the tomb, and how the body was laid.' The word 'also,' after 'women,' has been omitted on the authority of the three oldest MSS. Here and in verse 49 Tischendorf omits the definite article before 'women.' These faithful followers had an object in inspecting the tomb and the position of the body. They intended to revisit the spot, and busied themselves after leaving it in preparing aromatics for the corpse. 'And they returned, and prepared spices and ointments.' Luke mentions no names, but Mark and Matthew again specially designate the two Marys. 'And Mary Magdalene and Mary the *mother* of Joses beheld where he was laid.' They seem to have lingered about the sepulchre, for Matthew says: 'And Mary Magdalene was there, and the other Mary, sitting over against the sepulchre.'

Matthew relates that the day after the burial the accusers of Jesus presented themselves to Pilate with a request that he would take means for the safe-keeping of the body. They explained that they had called to mind a saying of Jesus to the effect that after three days he would rise. 'Now on the morrow, which is *the day* after the Preparation, the chief priests and the Pharisees were gathered together unto Pilate, saying, Sir, we remember that that deceiver said, while he was yet alive, After three days I rise again.' The Revisers have omitted 'will' before 'rise,' but they retain the word 'again.' Young renders, 'I rise;' Tischendorf, 'I am raised.' The application of the term 'deceiver' to Jesus is noteworthy. We should not be justified in assuming that his accusers regarded him in any other light: what they said, they thought about him, and doubtless considered themselves to be opponents of error, upholders of religious truth, defenders of the public interest; they probably classed Jesus and his disciples as fanatics, whose career it was imperative on them to stop at any cost, by any means within their power. The chief priests and Pharisees were simply bigots blinded by prejudice and passion, men incapable of perceiving the necessity for any change in the system of theological belief and practice to which they had been so long wedded, too self-opinionated to be taught, believing themselves to be the only authorised teachers, so sure of their own orthodoxy as to be incapable of receiving new ideas, and prone to impute bad motives to those by whom they were disseminated. That evil spirit is still rampant in our midst, that class still exists, fighting, embittering, maligning, and sometimes prevailing. We see this now in politics; in former days it was felt in religion: whether in Church or State it is a thing to be deplored, watched against, denounced, but it can only be extirpated by the infusion of a better spirit and the persuasive force of a better example. The chief offenders now are the writers in the public press, whose lucubrations are day by day greedily and unquestioningly devoured by thousands. Feeding constantly on such intellectual garbage, what wonder that the minds of the readers lose the healthy tone essential to the formation of any sound, impartial judgment? The writers of these partisan articles seem to become incapable of looking on more than one side of the questions which they oppose or defend; like hired advocates, they make the best of their own cause and paint that of their opponents in the blackest colours, and unfortunately the public, who in this case constitute the jury, are not bound as in other trials of truth to hear counsel on both sides, but are accustomed to listen to the arguments of one side only, and to give their votes accordingly. The highest intellectual attainments, in both writers and readers, cannot withstand the evil consequences inherent in such a system of political warfare. 'From such turn away.' No true light or wise leading can be gained from these self-constituted and arrogant Mentors. They and their kind transform patriots into criminals, sagacious statesmen into selfish imbeciles, martyrs into heretics, apostles into brawlers, and Jesus Christ himself into a 'deceiver.' 3 II. Tim. 5

That the statement of Jesus that he would 'after three days rise again,' should have reached the ears of his enemies, is not to be wondered at, for we are told that 'he spoke the saying openly.' They now suggested that the tomb should be watched, not permanently, but up to the third day. 'Command therefore that the sepulchre be made sure until the third day.' The reason given was characteristic of these scandal-mongers: they assumed that the disciples of Jesus were base and unscrupulous enough to form and carry out a plot for the removal of the corpse, and would then spread abroad the report that their crucified Teacher had risen as he foretold: 'lest haply his disciples come and steal him away, and say unto the people, He is risen from the dead.' The words 'by night' have been omitted after 'come,' on the authority of the three oldest MSS. What a gratuitous and foul slander was contained in the insinuation! Yet those who conceived it were actuated, forsooth, by the best of motives: they had crucified 'that deceiver,' and must now be careful to guard the people against even worse deception: 'and the last error will be worse than the first.' Pilate granted their request: he bade them take whatever steps they deemed necessary to secure their object. 'Pilate said unto them, Ye have a guard (or, Take a guard): go your 8 Mark 32
27 Mat. 64
,, 64
,, 64
,, 65

s

way, make it *as* sure as ye can (Gr. make it sure, as ye know).' They themselves accompanied the soldiers to the place, and took the precaution of affixing a seal to the stone, so that no one should enter the tomb without the fact being detected. 'So they went, and made the sepulchre sure, sealing the stone:' the Authorised Version adds: 'and setting a watch,' which is altered by the Revisers to: 'the guard being with them.' Alford renders: 'besides (posting) the guard;' Young: 'together with the guard;' Tischendorf, literally: 'sealing the stone with the guard;' probably the officer of the guard attached his seal, together with the seals of some of the chief priests and Pharisees.

27 Mat. 66

Matthew continues his narrative as follows: 'Now late on the sabbath day, as it began to dawn toward the first *day* of the week, came Mary Magdalene and the other Mary to see the sepulchre.' The end of the sabbath was at sunset, and it would seem that the expression 'began to dawn toward,' must be understood accordingly. It occurred previously in Luke: 'And it was the day of the Preparation, and the sabbath began to dawn.' The same word is used in both places, the reference being to the evening. The 'Englishman's Greek New Testament' renders: 'it was getting dusk toward.' Young translates the passage: 'And on the eve of the sabbaths, at the dawn, towards the first of the sabbaths.' That differs considerably from other translations, but it corresponds substantially with Luther's: 'Am Abend aber des Sabbaths, welcher anbricht am Morgen des ersten Feyertages der Sabbathen.' 'But on the evening of the sabbath, which dawns to the morning of the first feast-day of the sabbaths.' Turning to the original, the word 'day' is not found there, although in the Authorised Version it occurs once and in the Revised Version twice. Moreover the Greek word *sabbatōn* is first rendered 'sabbath' and then 'week.'

28 Mat. 1

23 Luke 54

Matthew describes the visit to the tomb to have been just before the close of the ordinary sabbath: the three other evangelists state that it took place immediately afterwards. This involves no contradiction, for the women may have started before the sabbath had ended, arriving at the tomb after the day had closed, and have lingered some hours about the spot waiting for daylight. Mark says: 'And when the sabbath was past, Mary Magdalene, and Mary the *mother* of James, and Salome, bought spices, that they might come and anoint him.' Matthew and Mark first mention three women as witnessing the crucifixion; then both evangelists allude to two only as present at the burial; then Matthew tells how the same two went to see the sepulchre before the sabbath ended, and Mark informs us that the three women were there somewhat later. Salome may have arrived after the others, the object of the three being to anoint the corpse together. 'Had bought sweet spices' is now altered to 'bought spices,' which agrees with Young. Alford notes: 'To suppose *two parties* of women (Greswell) or to take *bought* as *pluperfect* (as the A. V.) is equally arbitrary and unwarranted.' The buying of the spices could not take place till after the sabbath, and probably the impatience of the two Marys to be at the tomb would not brook any delay. Luke alludes to the fact that the anointing was deliberately and punctiliously postponed until the termination of the sabbath. 'And on the sabbath they rested according to the commandment.' Even then it was necessary to wait for daylight.

16 Mark 1

23 Luke 56

Luke is thus continued: 'But on the first day of the week, at early [24 Luke 1] dawn, they came unto the tomb, bringing the spices which they had prepared.' The dawn here spoken of is that of the natural day, not the dawn toward the day after the sabbath. Alford renders: 'at deep (i.e. dusk) dawn'; the 'Englishman's Greek New Testament': 'at early dawn.' After 'prepared' the words 'and certain *others* with them,' have been omitted on the authority of the two oldest MSS. Instead of: 'but on the first day of the week' Young renders: 'but on the first of the sabbaths;' Luther: 'aber an der Sabbather einem :' 'but on one of the sabbaths.' Luke uses the same word in the two verses, *sabbaton* (singular), *sabbatōn* (plural), but our translators, except Young, render the former 'sabbath,' and the latter 'day of the week.' Mark's narrative is continued as follows: 'And very early on the first day of the week, they come to [16 Mark 2] the tomb when the sun was risen.' 'At the rising of the sun' is altered to 'when the sun was risen,' which Tischendorf states is the reading of 'all MSS.' Of course the women could not attempt to enter the tomb until daybreak. Young renders: 'And early in the morning of the first of the sabbaths;' Luther: 'an einem Sabbather sehr frühe :' 'on one of the sabbaths very early.' Here again the same Greek word, singular and plural, in the two consecutive verses, has been rendered first as 'sabbath' and then as 'day of the week.' John's narrative stands as follows: 'Now on the first *day* of the [20 John 1] week cometh Mary Magdalene early, while it was yet dark, unto the tomb.' Young renders : 'and on the first of the sabbaths'; Luther: 'an der Sabbather einem': 'on one of the sabbaths.' By English translators generally a rendering has been adopted in each of the four gospels which ignores the plural form of the Greek word, introduces the word 'day' which is not in the original, and translates 'sabbath' as 'sabbath' in one sentence and 'sabbaths' as 'day of the week' in the next. It is well worth while to ascertain, if possible, how this apparent mistranslation came about, and why it has been so persistently adhered to. Besides these four passages the word 'week' [20 Acts 7] occurs only thrice in the English New Testament, and in each case [16 i. Cor. 2] it represents the Greek *sabbaton* or *sabbatōn*. In two of those passages Young and Luther render it properly as 'sabbaths,' but in the third they both translate it 'week.' 'I fast twice in the [18 Luke 12] week' stands in Greek : 'Nēsteuō dis tou sabbaton.' The reason for translating 'sabbath' in that place as 'week' may have been twofold : (1) the idea of a 'fast' as being synonymous with a 'fast-day'; (2) a reputed custom of the Jews, for Alford notes : 'This was a *voluntary fast*, on the Mondays and Thursdays.' Neither of those reasons justifies the transformation of 'sabbath' into 'week.' 'I fast twice in the sabbath' would mean, 'I abstain from two meals on the sabbath.' Johnson's dictionary defines Sabbath as 'an Hebrew word signifying *rest*.' As the word was not Greek, it can scarcely have had in that language a recognised meaning apart from its original signification. How could the one day of rest be synonymous with a period of seven days? So many sabbaths might indeed represent so many weeks, just as so many 'pipes' in some countries represent in common talk so many miles: but there would be no more reason for translating 'sabbath' as 'week' than 'pipe' as 'mile.' The Greek word *sabbaton* or *sabbata* occurs sixty-four times in the New Testament. Why should it be rendered literally fifty-seven times, and seven times changed into 'week'? It may have arisen from the fact that either the translators themselves did not understand what was meant by 'one' or 'first of the sabbaths,' or that they feared ordinary readers would be at a loss to comprehend what day was meant, so to avoid all uncertainty they put aside the expression, and felt justified in rendering it freely by the words 'first day of the week,' which the day actually was. Liddell and Scott's Greek Lexicon defines *Sabbaton* as 'the Hebrew *Sabbath*, i.e. *Rest*,' adding as a secondary meaning: '(2) *a week*'; but it must be remembered that the Authorised Version has been in existence for some centuries, and the compilers of a lexicon could not omit giving the translation which had been so long upheld. Luther's rendering dates back as far, and deserves equal respect, and now that it has been deliberately confirmed by a modern scholar like Dr. Robert Young, we need have no hesitation in setting aside the strange and obvious misconstruction which has been so long the only translation presented to English readers, and which commentators generally have been content to pass without an attempt at criticism or explanation. There is another passage in which a difficulty occurs in connection with the word 'sabbath.' The reading of the Authorised Version is: 'the second sabbath after the first,' rendered by Luther: 'einen Aftersabbath,' 'an aftersabbath,' and by Young literally: 'the second-first sabbath.' The Revisers, following the two oldest MSS., put 'a sabbath' in the text, and in the margin 'second-first.' On that expression Alford notes: 'The word thus rendered presents much difficulty. None of the interpretations have any certainty, as the word is found nowhere else, and can only be judged of by analogy'; and he did not scruple to add that it was 'omitted by some ancient authorities, perhaps on account of its difficulty.' Our original translators seem to have cut the knot of the difficulty about 'first of the sabbaths' in a somewhat similar fashion, not by omitting the passage, but by mistranslating it, yet in such a way that the new signification given to it represented an actual fact, 'the first of the sabbaths' having happened to fall on 'the first day of the week.' The passover held on the fourteenth of the first month, was followed by the feast of unleavened bread, lasting a week from the fifteenth, and there were two sabbaths in connection with that feast: 'In the first day shall be an holy convocation: ye shall do no servile work ... And on the seventh day ye shall have an holy convocation; ye shall do no servile work.' The 'first of the sabbaths' obviously refers to that of the fifteenth. There are two other passages in which that particular sabbath appears to have been referred to, but in both cases the allusion is lost sight of owing to a similar mistranslation. 'And upon the first day of the week, when we were gathered together to break bread.' The Revisers have not even italicised the word 'day,' which was done in the Authorised Version. Young renders: 'And on the first of the sabbaths'; the original is: '*En de tēi miai tōn sabbatōn*,' which Luther renders 'Auf einen Sabbath aber,' 'But upon a sabbath.' When the ordinary sabbath is alluded to, a different expression is used: 'And on the sabbath day,' so rendered also by Young, the original being: *Tēi te hemerai tōn sabbatōn*, which Luther translates

[margin notes: 6 Luke 1; 28 Num. 18; ,, 25; 20 Acts 7; 16 Acts 13] literally, 'Des Tages der Sabbather,' 'On the day of the sabbaths,' that is, 'Every sabbath day. An inspection of the context respecting the breaking of bread on the first of the sabbaths, shows that it was passover time, and if the passage bears at all upon the celebration of the Lord's supper, it points only to its observance at that annual festival. Alford's 'New Testament for English Readers' gives no hint of the word 'sabbaths' being in the original; on the contrary, he says: 'We have here an intimation of the continuance of the practice, which seems to have begun immediately after the resurrection (see John xx. 26), of assembling on the first day of the week for religious purposes.' The 'first day of the week' is arbitrarily introduced into the text, and then it is argued that the passage proves the observance of that day! Alford continues: 'Perhaps the greatest proof of all, that this day was thus observed, may be found in the early (see i. Cor. xvi. 2) and at length general prevalence, in *the Gentile world* of the *Jewish seven-day period* as a *division of time*,—which was entirely foreign to Gentile habits.' But the passage here referred to is another instance of mistranslation. It stands in the Authorised Version thus: 'Upon the first *day* of the week,' the word 'day' being italicised to indicate that it is not in the original. The only alteration made by the Revisers is the omission of the italics. Young renders: 'On every first of the Sabbaths'; Luther: 'Auf einen jeglichen Sabbather,' 'Upon every one of the Sabbaths.' The original is: '*Kata mian sabbatōn.*' Why is the word 'sabbaths' eliminated in the translation? And by what strange process of linguistic alchemy has it come to pass that the Hebrew word which signifies 'rest' and denotes the *seventh* day of the week, being introduced unaltered into Greek, comes to represent in that language the *first* day of the week? According to Young's rendering the reference would seem to be to the first extra sabbath following the passover, and the injunction to 'lay by in store' at that period would be an argument in favour of Easter offerings, the practice of which must have originated in some such exhortation. The words 'as he may prosper' are more applicable to a yearly than to a weekly reckoning up of profits. If, however, Luther's rendering be adopted, the passage simply points to the observance by Christians of the Jewish weekly sabbath: it has nothing to do with the following day. The discovery and rectification of a mistranslation is all the more important, because of the erroneous arguments arising out of it.

Still more important are the questions which arise in connection with the introduction into the Gentile world of a weekly sabbath, and its transference from the seventh to the first day of the week. That the Jewish preachers of the gospel should have taught their Gentile converts to observe the weekly sabbath, is what might have been expected; but that the Gentiles should have taken upon themselves to change the day is not a little remarkable. Even if it could be proved, as Alford assumes, that the resurrection-day was immediately observed weekly, the adoption of that festival on the first day of the week in lieu of the appointed sabbath of the seventh day, shows a freedom of judgment and a boldness of practice which could scarcely have been anticipated either in Jews or Gentiles. The sanctity of the sabbath, and the call to its observance, could only rest upon the divine command, and the modification of the Jewish custom simultaneously with its acceptance, must have arisen from some deep conviction of expediency and propriety. No obligation was laid upon Gentile Christians to receive circumcision or to live as do the Jews. The apostle Paul argued strenuously against any teaching in that direction. But the ordinance of the sabbath was embedded in the ten commandments, and formed part of the moral law equally with the prohibition of murder, adultery, theft and covetousness. To regard the sabbath only or chiefly as a form and time of divine worship, is to misconceive its scope and purpose. On the highest authority we are assured that 'the sabbath was made for man.' If we would observe it rightly, the command must be received and urged in its simplicity, apart from those extraneous ideas of religious ceremonialism which, however naturally and properly they have come to be associated with the day, have no inseparable and necessary connection with it. We cannot enhance the dignity of the divine command, neither do we promote its due and true observance, by adding aught thereto. The day was designed to be simply that which its name imports, a Sabbath, that is—a Rest. To that end it has been set apart, or made 'holy.' Abstention from ordinary labour is the sum total of this divine command. And as we may not add, neither may we diminish aught therefrom. The obligation is not merely personal, but social : ' Six days shalt thou labour, and do all thy work : but the seventh day is a sabbath unto the LORD thy God : *in it* thou shalt not do any work, thou, nor thy son, nor thy daughter, thy manservant, nor thy maidservant, nor thy cattle, nor the stranger that is within thy gates.' The one and only thing insisted upon is abstention from work : ' Six days shall work be done, but on the seventh day there shall be to you an holy day, a sabbath of solemn rest to the LORD : whosoever doeth any work therein shall be put to death.' All, without exception, must rest from labour on the sabbath : ' that thy manservant and thy maidservant may rest as well as thou.' The essence of the command is—Rest ; in that respect, and in no other,—if in any other respect it could be infringed,—was its infraction punishable ; and so important was cessation from labour deemed that in one case death was actually inflicted : ' they found a man gathering sticks upon the sabbath day . . . . And the LORD said unto Moses, The man shall surely be put to death.' There may be differences of opinion as to what is meant by the expressions : ' a sabbath unto the LORD thy God,' and ' a sabbath of solemn rest to the LORD,' but there can be no question that all labour was forbidden, and that all persons were to be exempt therefrom. But the developments of civilisation and the complicated relationships of our social life, make it practically impossible that all should rest upon the same day. Recognising that fact, we can appreciate the wisdom of the early Christians in freeing themselves from a slavish adherence to the observance of the seventh day. They did well to change the sabbath to a day of their own choosing, for it was not written, 'Remember the seventh day,' but 'Remember the sabbath day, to keep it holy.' That all may enjoy their sabbath, it is imperative that some should keep it on one day and some on another. Through greed, oppression, thoughtlessness, many of those whose lot it is to labour for others are

2 Mark 27

20 Ex. 10

35 Ex. 2

5 Deu. 14

15 Num. 32

deprived of God's boon of a sabbath day ; and so long as one day in the week only is regarded as the appointed day, there will be an apparent excuse for those who consider its universal observance to be an impossibility. It is high time that our spiritual teachers and guides should set free their own minds from inherited conventional ideas with respect to the sabbath : by attempting to make too much of it in the direction of religious observances, they make far too little of it in its most essential point of simple rest from labour. Only by adopting broader and truer views, can they hope to touch the national conscience, and help to bring about such an observance of the sabbath as will benefit humanity to the full extent and redound to the glory of God. And it equally behoves laymen, as heads of households, to ponder this matter. It is our boast and our comfort that, with certain exceptions (about which and the possibility of obviating them we have as yet scarcely begun to think), the pulse of labour each sabbath day stands still : the bulk of employers and employees, clerks, workmen, shopmen, enjoy the sabbath as a matter of undoubted right. But there is one exception, one class of persons who seem to be overlooked, who neither have, nor claim, nor expect to obtain their sabbath day : domestic servants. They live with us, side by side, and they minister constantly to our needs and enjoyments, yet it is only too true to say, that no man cares for their souls, at all events not for their bodies by arranging to give them one day's rest each week. Neglect of this latter and lesser duty involves indifference to the former and greater one. We flatter ourselves upon our personal and family observance of the sabbath, and—more or less—upon our regular attendance at church or chapel, wholly oblivious of the sad fact that our menservants and our maidservants do *not* rest as well as ourselves. Are we not responsible for this, and verily guilty concerning our brother ? Or have we received a special dispensation exempting us from our obligation to that portion of the divine command ? How can we say that we observe it, while that plain direction is set at naught ? We have drifted into this state of callousness. Household duties are light, and we want more rather than less waiting upon on Sundays, and our servants are docile and content, and things have gone on like this for generations : yes ; and will for generations longer, unless we wake up to our neglect of duty and set ourselves to perform it. So long as we have omitted it blindly, through heedlessness, we may find excuse ; but as soon as it comes home to us, there is only one honest, straightforward and safe course to take. If our sabbath-keeping is not to be hypocritical, we must determine to keep the command in its entirety, making no exceptions, but including in its scope every manservant, every maidservant, and every beast of burden. That can only be done in one way ; only by observing the spirit of the command can we obey it in the letter. To each one his sabbath day : that must be the rule, and the carrying of it out a matter of arrangement. The first step in that direction will make it clear that some additional household expenditure will be entailed,— not much, certainly not beyond our means, which must needs be in proportion to the number of our servants, but sufficient to remind us that hitherto we have been profiting at their expense, and that probably a wretched, undue parsimony may originally have led to the evil we are called upon to remedy. These remarks upon this serious subject are made in all humility; and for the guidance of others who may be disposed to do their parts towards righting this wrong the following rules, which were drawn up for the occasion and put in practice, are here submitted. Would that some such rules could be placed in a conspicuous position in every household, to be seen and known of all men as the divinely-appointed *Magna Charta* of servitude. There is a temptation to add to them some words of counsel as to the way in which servants should employ their newly-granted leisure; but it is well to remember that we only give them what God decreed they, as well as ourselves, should have, and that He did not see fit to attach to his bestowal of a sabbath day any directions as to the mode of its observance.

'*Household Rules for the Sabbath.*'

'Every servant in this house is entitled to—and is expected to take—one day's REST each week.

'Sunday will be observed by each in turn as a day of rest, so that when there are three Servants each will have every third Sunday free, the other days of rest being on week days.

'Each Servant will, on her Rest-day, be exempted from labour of every kind, and her fellow Servants will on that day supply her place with respect to household duties as far as may be necessary.

'The Rest-day may be spent entirely at discretion, in or out of the house, wholly or partially, as may be preferred, and with liberty to return at meal times.'

How much better to grant that simple boon at once and voluntarily, than to withhold it until those entitled to it by the law of God rise up and demand it! Together with a pleasant sense of liberty it will bring to our servants opportunities of health, of recreation, of mental improvement, of friendships, which have too long been wanting to the class. Let us begin by reforming our homes in this respect, and the movement will extend to railway officials, omnibus drivers and conductors, coachmen, waiters, and a multitude of persons who have been so long robbed of their Sabbath-day birthright as to have become unconscious of their claim to it.

Erroneous ideas with respect to the Sabbath have led to wrong efforts in the direction of its enforced observance. Here is an extract from a daily newspaper of 23 November, 1891:—

'The Lord's Day Society and the Sunday League.

'Proceedings Threatened.

'Notices have been served upon the National Sunday League by the Lord's Day Observance Society, warning them that if they continue to give Sunday evening lectures and concerts they will proceed against them in the Law Courts. These notices have been served at the Bermondsey Town-hall, Shoreditch Town-hall, The Horn's Assembly Rooms, Kennington, and the Myddleton Hall, Islington, where the lectures and concerts are being given. The National Sunday League have intimated their intention of fighting the question if necessary.'

That spirit of persecution has sprung out of the false notion that the Sabbath is to be kept holy, that is sacred, not to Rest, but to what is supposed to be 'divine worship,' church and chapel-going, prayers, devotional singing, and sermons; to all which our Lord's rule applies: 'These ought ye to have done, and not to leave the other undone.' On this subject these words of John Ruskin are as wise as they are strong: 'By the perverseness of the evil Spirit in us, we get to think that praying and psalm-singing are "service." . . . Begging is not serving: God likes mere beggars as little as you do—He likes honest servants,—not beggars. . . Neither is singing songs about God, serving God. It is enjoying ourselves, if it's anything, most probably it is nothing; but if it's anything it's serving ourselves, not God. And yet we are impudent enough to call our beggings and chauntings "Divine service": we say, "Divine service will be *performed* (that's our word—the form of it gone through) at so-and-so o'clock." Alas; unless we perform Divine service in every willing act of life, we never perform it at all. The one Divine work—the one ordered sacrifice—is to do justice; and it is the last we are ever inclined to do. Anything rather than that.' *

The term 'Sabbatarian' has become one of reproach; but we really need Sabbatarians in the true sense of the word: men who will advocate and help forward organised efforts for the extension of the boon of a weekly day of Rest for all. The Lord's Day Observance Society seems to be occupied rather in attempts to prevent what they unwarrantably and unwisely assume to be profanations of the Sabbath, than to enforce its universal obligation and observance; and the National Sunday League is engaged in fighting against such interference; instead of which, a crusade needs to be undertaken for securing to every man, woman, child, and beast of burden, God's gift of one day's Rest in seven. Only in one way can the Sabbath be profaned: that is by Work in place of Rest; and that, no matter what the object of the work or the person who performs it. Jesus did not scruple to assert 'that on the sabbath day the priests in the temple profane the sabbath.' Our clergy do the same; both 'are guiltless': but if these ministers about holy things do not themselves *rest* upon some other day than Sunday, they lose their sabbath, which God designed should be observed and enjoyed by all. In any movement having that object ministers of Christ should take the lead, claiming the privilege for themselves, and urging on behalf of all men the duty of giving and taking *one day's Rest in seven*. 12 Mat. 5

When the three women were on their way to the sepulchre, the question naturally arose among them as to whose services they could employ for the removal of the stone which had been placed against the entrance. 'And they were saying among themselves, Who shall roll us away the stone from the door of the tomb?' It is not surprising that they knew nothing about the arrangements which had been made for watching the place and sealing the stone. But on looking towards the spot, they perceived that there was now nothing to impede their entrance: 'and looking up, they see that the stone is rolled back: for it was exceeding great.' Alford notes: '*For it was very great* is stated as a reason why *they could see that it was rolled away on looking* 16 Mark 3

,, 4

---

* "The Crown of Wild Olive. 39 Work."

up, possibly at some distance. This explanation is according to St. Mark's manner of describing minute circumstantial incidents; but to refer this clause back as the *reason why* they questioned who should remove the stone, is not only harsh, but inconsistent with the usage of this gospel.' Luke states: 'And they found the stone rolled away from the tomb;' John mentions Mary Magdalene only, probably because he records her account of the matter: 'and seeth the stone taken away from the tomb.' Matthews tells much more. 'And behold, there was a great earthquake.' Alford notes: 'This must not be taken as pluperfect, *there had been &c*., which would be altogether inconsistent with the text.' Accepting that statement, it does not necessarily follow, as Alford says: 'The words here must mean that the women were *witnesses of the earthquake* and *that which happened*.' If Matthew had meant that, surely he could have said so as plainly as Alford does. The whole tenor of the narrative is against his supposition. Tischendorf renders: 'a great earthquake took place.' That the evangelist introduces merely the statement of an event, without reference to those who witnessed it, seems clear from the opening words, 'And behold,' as it was said of Saul, 'Behold, he prayeth.' Matthew's description is very solemn and impressive: 'And behold, there was a great earthquake; for an angel of the Lord descended from heaven, and came and rolled away the stone, and sat upon it. His appearance was as lightning, and his raiment white as snow: and for fear of him the watchers did quake, and became as dead men.' The words 'from the door,' after 'stone,' are omitted on the authority of the two oldest MSS. The astounding, supernatural occurrence could not have been told in simpler or more appropriate words. By 'great earthquake' is not to be understood such a convulsion of nature as overturns houses and whole cities, but a localised trembling of the ground in connection with the opening of the tomb. Alford says: 'It was not *properly* an earthquake, but was the sudden opening of the tomb by the descending angel, as the *for* shews. The rolling away was not done naturally, but by a shock.' The account must have been supplied by an eye-witness of the event. An unearthly Being was seen to descend from above, at whose presence, if not by whose hands, the stone was displaced; on it, the angel seated himself, a human form indeed, but of more majestic aspect than any mortal man, his face as radiant as a lightning-flash, and the vesture which draped his body glittering in pure, snow-like whiteness. The sight of him struck the keepers with terror and amazement, and the first effect of the vision was to deprive them of all power of motion. On recovering themselves they must have gone away, for when the women came there were no earthly guards about the tomb. From the absence of the stone it might well be inferred, not only that the grave had been opened, but that the corpse must have been removed. Mary therefore hastened, her eagerness impelling her to run, to tell the fact to two of the disciples. 'She runneth therefore, and cometh to Simon Peter, and to the other disciple whom Jesus loved.' The fourth evangelist always refers to himself by this title: that, at least, is the natural inference from the persistent withholding of the name. He was with Peter in the palace, with the women by the cross, and had received the mother of Jesus into his own home. That Peter should still be with him, and that Mary Magdalene should now seek out the two, is very natural and consistent with other parts of the narrative. The exact words in which Mary announced the distressing news have been preserved : 'and saith unto them, They have taken away the Lord out of the tomb, and we know not where they have laid him.' Although this evangelist only mentions this one woman, whose account he relied upon and handed down, her words 'we know not' show that others had been with her : much may have happened which is not recorded, and it is quite possible that one or more of the women may have looked into the sepulchre before Mary started off to announce the fact of the removal of the body : the words 'we know not where they have laid him' seem to imply that some search had been made in the vain hope of tracing, by footsteps or otherwise, the direction which might have been taken by the supposed riflers of the tomb. Peter and his fellow disciple decided to investigate the matter by personal inspection. 'Peter therefore went forth, and the other disciple, and they went toward the tomb.' As every moment might be of consequence in their attempt to discover what had become of the body, they both ran at their utmost speed, Peter being outdistanced by his companion. 'And they ran both together : and the other disciple outran Peter, and came first to the tomb.' The Authorised Version proceeds : 'And he stooping down, *and looking in*, saw the linen clothes lying,' the words 'and looking in' being italicised to intimate that they are an insertion. The Revisers have omitted the italics : 'and stooping down and looking in, he seeth the linen cloths lying.' Luther renders : 'Gucket hinein, und siehet die Leinen gelegt,' 'Looks in, and sees the linen cloths laid.' Of course Peter must have been 'looking in,' or he would not have seen : but that is no good reason for introducing the words into the text, neither should the word 'stooping' be omitted, as by Luther. Young renders : 'And having stooped down, seeth the linen clothes lying.' The observer did not enter into the tomb : 'yet entered he not in.' But Peter, when he arrived, did enter the tomb, and there found nothing except the grave clothes, the handkerchief which had been used to bind round the head being carefully folded up and placed apart. 'Simon Peter therefore also cometh, following him, and entered into the tomb ; and he beholdeth the linen cloths lying, and the napkin, that was upon his head, not lying with the linen cloths, but rolled up in a place by itself.' The Revisers have in this verse altered 'seeth' to 'beholdeth' ; Alford explains : '*seeth* represents the original word used of the cursory glance of John, who did not go in,—*beholdeth*, that which describes the exhaustive gaze of Peter, who did.' If there had been simply a removal of the corpse, why should it have been stripped, and why such an obvious absence of haste, and such evidences of care about the clothes? The inspection of Peter made the matter still more mysterious. His companion proceeded to investigate for himself : he entered the tomb, found everything as Peter had reported, and nothing more. Then and there, amidst the gloom of the sepulchre, a new light darted into his mind : Jesus was risen, literally risen out of his grave as he had foretold ! 'Then entered in therefore the other disciple also, which came first to the tomb, and he saw, and believed.' Up to that moment he had not realised 'what the rising again from the dead should mean': the question had been discussed, but not settled, and such a solution as this had never until now dawned upon their minds. 'For as yet they knew not the scripture, that he must rise again from the dead.' Young renders: 'For up to this time they knew not the writing, that it behoveth him from the dead to rise again.' Their present conviction rendered any further search for the body altogether needless, albeit they could as yet have had no expectation of seeing Jesus again alive upon earth. 'So the disciples went away again unto their own home.' Young renders: 'to their own friends.' Mary they left still standing by the tomb, having doubtless told her that nothing therein supplied any clue to the mystery. The narrative proceeds: 'But Mary was standing without at the tomb weeping: so, as she wept, she stooped and looked into the tomb.' Here again the Revisers have failed to italicise the words 'and looked,' which have nothing corresponding with them in the original. Young, Tischendorf and the 'Englishman's Greek New Testament' render: 'she stooped down into the tomb'; the same words in the original are used here as in verses 3 and 4, *eis to mnēmion*, which are rendered by the Revisers 'toward the tomb' and 'to the tomb.' It is clear that in those verses *eis* does not signify 'into,' but merely an approach 'to'; but in verse 6 the same word is translated 'into,' which is there and in this verse 11 its obvious meaning, the expression being the same in both places, *eis to mnēmion, kai theōrei*, 'into the tomb, and beholds,' the last word, according to Alford, signifying not a mere looking but an 'exhaustive gaze,' such as could be obtained only in the tomb itself. What must have been Mary's amazement to perceive that it was not now tenantless! Two angelic Beings, draped in white, were sitting there at some distance apart: 'and she beholdeth two angels in white sitting, one at the head and one at the feet, where the body of Jesus had lain.' Probably the corpse had been placed on a bier of some kind, at either end of which these heavenly 'messengers' were now seated. There was nothing terrible in their aspect; on the contrary, with kindly sympathy they asked Mary why she wept. 'And they say unto her, Woman, why weepest thou?' It was all so quiet, so natural even, in spite of its marvellousness, that she was able to reply without a tremor. 'She saith unto them, Because they have taken away my Lord, and I know not where they have laid him.' At that instant something impelled her to turn round, and lo! some one was standing behind her. Some one! it was Jesus himself, though as yet she recognised him not. 'When she had thus said, she turned herself back, and beholdeth Jesus standing, and knew not that it was Jesus.' The word 'and' has been omitted before 'when,' on the authority of the three oldest MSS. Alford notes as follows: '*She turned herself back*—having her attention attracted by consciousness of some one being present near her—not perhaps by the *approach* of Jesus. Or it might be with intent to go forth and weep again, or further to seek her Lord. Chrysostom's reason is very beautiful, but perhaps hardly probable, from the fact that Mary on turning round did not recognize our Lord: "It seems to me that while she was saying these words, the sudden appearance of Christ behind her struck the angels, who saw their Lord, with amazement: and that they immediately showed both by their posture and by their look, that they saw the Lord: and this caused Mary to turn round and look behind her." We need not surely enquire too minutely, *why* she did not know Him. The fact may be psychologically accounted for—she did not *expect Him to be there*, and was wholly preoccupied with other thoughts : or, as Dräseke says, "Her tears wove a veil, which concealed Him who stood before her. The seeking after the Dead prevents us from seeing the Living.'" Jesus spoke to her, asking why she wept and whom she sought. 'Jesus saith unto her, Woman, why weepest thou ? whom seekest thou ?' Even then she did not recognise him, but assumed that her questioner must be the person who had the care of the garden, and who, therefore, would probably know about the removal of the body. In her grief she may have imagined that he objected to its presence in the garden, and had himself placed it elsewhere. If so, let him tell her whither he had taken the corpse, and she, without troubling him, would have it reinterred somewhere else. 'She, supposing him to be the gardener, saith unto him, Sir, if thou hast borne him hence, tell me where thou hast laid him, and I will take him away.' One word Jesus spoke—her name, and at that word she knew him on the instant, and herself by one word—Teacher—expressed her consciousness of his identity. 'Jesus saith unto her, Mary. She turneth herself, and saith unto him in Hebrew, Rabboni ; which is to say, Master (or, Teacher).' The words 'in Hebrew' have been added on the authority of the two oldest MSS. The expression 'she turneth herself' may denote some natural gesture indicating her intention to greet him by a friendly touch, as by a handclasp : but whatever the movement, Jesus checked it. 'Jesus saith to her, Touch me not (or, Take not hold on me).' As in explanation of the prohibition, he added : 'for I am not yet ascended to the Father.' Until then, no mortal hand might touch him : so much we may infer from the saying, but it is full of mystery to us, as the mention of a rising again from the dead had been to the disciples. That proved to be an actual physical fact, a visible return and manifestation of Jesus after death to the living. For the realisation of that marvellous event a fixed period, three days, was necessary : 'after three days I rise again.' The women were early at the tomb, not indeed before Jesus was risen, but before he was ready to exhibit himself to his disciples. On showing himself first to Mary, he alluded to another physical fact, his ascension to the Father, which must be accomplished before her hands might touch him. Why that should be, we know not, any more than we can explain the interval of three days required for the resurrection. The word 'ascension' is not in common use with us, being chiefly restricted to the recorded visible uprising of Jesus from the earth, but the Greek word used by Jesus, *anabaino*, was applied in a variety of ways : it occurs in a multitude of passages, as for example : 'Behold, we *go up* to Jerusalem'; 'fruit *that sprang up* and increased'; 'when his brethren *were gone up*, then *went* he also *up* unto the feast'; 'they went forth and *entered* into a ship'; 'they *went up* into an upper room.' It is clear, therefore, that the word 'ascend' now used by Jesus was an ordinary form of speech, the phrase being equivalent to : 'I have not yet gone to the Father.' Alford notes : 'In the words *I ascend* is included His temporary stay which He was now making with them—*I am ascending*—i.e. I am on my way.' Mary was bidden to tell the disciples that Jesus was about

20 John 15

„ 15

„ 16

„ 17

„ 17

27 Mat. 63

20 Mat. 18
4 Mark 8
7 John 10
21 John 3
1 Acts 13

to undertake that mysterious journey: 'but go unto my brethren, and say to them, I ascend unto my Father and your Father, and my God and your God.' What words could be chosen to express more plainly the fact of an absolutely identical relationship: that Jesus and his brethren were children of the same Father, subjects of the same King? Yet this plain and simple sense will not suit theologians. Alford observes: 'This distinction, *my* . . and *your* . . . when *Our seems* so likely to have been said, has been observed by all Commentators of any depth, as indicating an *essential difference in the relations*. Cyril of Jerusalem says, "*My* Father, by nature: *your* Father by adoption." Similarly Augustine; adding, "Nor did He say *Our God*": wherefore here also is a difference in the relation.' Is not this a strange way of arguing: What is *mine* and *yours* cannot be *ours?* Rather: It is so entirely *ours*, in common, that I call it *mine* and *yours*. In the mouth of Jesus the words 'God' and 'Father' were not mere titles of nomenclature, but were used to express an actual relationship arising out of life and character. That outcry upon the cross, 'My God, my God, why hast thou forsaken me?' derived its force and application from the consciousness of devotion to the divine will and laws, 'God' being synonymous with 'Ruler' or 'King.' Jesus would not allow the unbelieving, persecuting Jews to claim God as their Father: 'If God were your Father, ye would love me: for I came forth and am come from God'; nor would he admit that his Father was in any sense their God, except in their own vain imagination: 'of whom ye say that he is your God; and ye have not known him.' Their spiritual parentage was the very opposite, their actions being regulated by him who is the adversary of God: 'Ye are of *your* father the devil, and the lusts of your father it is your will to do.' The fourth evangelist proclaimed the same truth: 'But as many as received him, to them gave he the right to become children of God, *even* to them that believe on his name: which were born, not of blood, nor of the will of the flesh, nor of the will of man, but of God.' The claim to divine parentage comes through Jesus, God's children becoming such by a spiritual birth which is outside the natural and ordinary worldly life. To the 'brethren,' that is, to the 'disciples' of Jesus, to those who 'receive him,' who having been 'baptized into Christ did put on Christ,' the promise applies and is restricted. The aim of theologians and ecclesiastical rulers has been to augment the number of the 'children of God,' not by insisting upon 'discipleship' to Jesus in its proper sense of absolute obedience to all his precepts and imitation of his mode of life, but by including in the circle those who take the far lower ground of a practical conformity to the world, its maxims, aims and ambitions, coupled with a theoretical, professed, but not actual devotion to the cause and cross of Jesus. The external rite of baptism was originally a badge of discipleship: 'the Pharisees had heard that Jesus was making and baptizing more disciples than John.' And Jesus saw fit to say: 'Whosoever doth not bear his own cross, and come after me, cannot be my disciple': the cost had to be counted and the choice made, before baptism could be claimed. But in process of time that salutary rule was dispensed with, and now we rather assume and are taught the contrary, as though baptism made us Christians, that is, disciples, instead of disciples needing to be made before they can be baptised. When the apostles went forth to proclaim salvation through Christ, what could the subject-matter of their preaching be except the precepts of Jesus, not diluted as now with worldly wisdom and made conformable to social customs, but in their integrity, free from gloss or exception of any kind? When baptism was offered and accepted, what did it, could it mean but the entrance upon a new mode of life based upon the new faith in Jesus as its originator and director? The kingdom of heaven among men could be established only by the apostles conforming themselves to the example of their Master, and by inducing others to follow them even as they followed Christ. Baptism was therefore the sign and seal of non-conformity to the world, and Christians were a body of believers and practisers of Christ's maxims, by the observance and promulgation of which society was to be regenerated. Therefore it is not to be wondered at that the apostolic epistles should be pitched in a high tone respecting the privileges and position of those to whom they were addressed. The General Epistle of James asserts an absolute equality among the 'brethren.' 'Let the brother of low degree glory in his high estate : 1 James 9, 10 and the rich, in that he is made low.' 'My brethren, hold not the 2 James 1 faith of our Lord Jesus Christ, *the Lord* of glory, with respect of persons.' Community with the apostles in faith, life and status is the key-note of John's epistles : 'that which we have seen and heard 1 i. John 3 declare we unto you also, that ye also may have fellowship with us : yea, and our fellowship is with the Father, and with his Son Jesus Christ.' 'Behold what manner of love the Father hath bestowed 3 i. John 1 upon us, that we should be called children of God : and *such* we are. For this cause the world knoweth us not, because it knew him not.' In those days, they only were sons of God who maintained the same aloofness and separation from the world as did the apostles ; but now we claim the title well nigh universally, the result being that we have the name without the reality. It is only to Christ's 'brethren,' in the true and full sense of that term, that his words apply : 'my Father and your Father, and my God and your God.'

That Mary Magdalene was the first person who saw Jesus after his resurrection, is plainly stated in Mark's gospel. 'Now when he was 16 Mark 9 risen early on the first day of the week, he appeared first to Mary Magdalene, from whom he had cast out seven devils (Gr. demons).' Here again we have the expression 'the first day of the week,' a strange mistranslation pertinaciously adhered to. The original is *prōtēi sabbatou*, which is rendered by Young 'first of the sabbaths,' and by Luther, 'am ersten Tage der Sabbather,' 'on the first day of the sabbaths.' The word *prōtos*, 'first,' is not the word rendered first in the analogous six passages which have been referred to, where the Greek term is *mia*, which is defined in the Greek Lexicon as 'one.' Luther renders it 'one' in five instances, and why he makes an exception by rendering it 'first' in 28 Matt. 1 is not apparent. The word *mia* occurs 71 times in the New Testament, and only 7 times is it translated 'first' instead of 'one,' six of the passages being those in which 'sabbaths' is so curiously rendered as 'day of the week.' That obviously free and incorrect translation seems to have led to a transmutation of 'one' into 'first:' if the word 'one' had been retained, the expression 'one day of the week' would have become meaningless, and 'one of the sabbaths' (which is the accurate rendering) is not comprehensible without consideration, for which reason it would seem that Dr. Young followed the lead of the Authorised Version by rendering 'one' as 'first.' The seventh exception is the passage: 'after the first and second admonition,' where Luther keeps to the word 'one:' 'wenn er einmal und abermal ermahnet ist,' 'when he has been once and again admonished.' The 'Englishman's Greek New Testament' renders literally: 'one and a second admonition.' Even in that work, in which the interlinear translation is professedly literal, under the word *mia* in those six passages *only*, is printed 'first,' whereas *mia* is simply the feminine form of εἷς, 'one.' Assuming the word 'day' to be understood, the proper rendering would be 'one *day* of the sabbaths,' equivalent to 'one of the sabbath days.'

3 Tit. 10

To this portion of Mark's gospel the Revisers have appended the following note: 'The two oldest Greek manuscripts, and some other authorities, omit from ver. 9 to the end. Some other authorities have a different ending to the Gospel.' Tischendorf prints it as 'an appendix from the received text and Lachmann.' Lachmann's object was 'to recover the text as it was in the *fourth* century.* Of this closing portion of Mark, Alford says: 'It is quoted as early as Irenæus, in the 2nd century: but Jerome in the 3rd says that *nearly all the Greek MSS. in his time did not contain it.* The legitimate inference is, that it was placed as a completion of the Gospel soon after the apostolic period,—the Gospel itself having been, for some reason unknown to us, left incomplete.' Alford sums up the evidence as follows: 'Internal evidence is, I think, very weighty *against St. Mark's being the author.* No less than *twenty-one words and expressions occur in it* (and some of them several times), which are *never elsewhere used* by St. Mark,—whose adherence to his own peculiar phrases is remarkable. The inference therefore seems to me to be, that *it is an authentic fragment, placed as a completion of the Gospel in very early times:* by whom written, must of course remain wholly uncertain; but coming to us with very weighty sanction, and having strong claims on our reception and reverence.'

This addition to Mark's gospel supplies an important and absolute confirmation of the statement in the fourth gospel to the effect that the first manifestation of the risen Lord was to Mary Magdalene. The accounts of Matthew and Luke are to be interpreted accordingly. They describe what the women saw and heard together, which by no means excludes the possibility, or diminishes the probability, of their being separated and investigating apart from each other during the long period of their lingering in the neighbourhood of the tomb. From John's account it may reasonably be inferred that Mary Magdalene went by herself to tell the disciples about not finding the body, and it is naturally to be supposed that during her absence the other women would be investigating for themselves. Let us for the moment assume that to have been the case: then the following particulars relate to their experiences apart from those of Mary Magdalene. Mark says: 'And entering into the tomb, they saw a young man sitting on the right side, arrayed in a white robe; and

16 Mark 5

---

* "Englishman's Greek New Testament." Introduction.

they were amazed.' Matthew seems to take it for granted that this was the angel who had descended from heaven and rolled away the stone, but whose appearance in the eyes of the women was not terrible, but the reverse. 'And the angel answered and said unto the women, Fear not ye: for I know that ye seek Jesus, which hath been crucified. He is not here: for he is risen, even as he said. Come, see the place where the Lord lay (many ancient authorities read *where he lay*).' That is the reading of the two oldest MSS. This corresponds very closely with Mark, whose account must have been based upon the same information. 'And he saith unto them, Be not amazed: ye seek Jesus, the Nazarene, which hath been crucified: he is risen; he is not here: behold, the place where they laid him!' The narratives of the two evangelists continue as follows. Mark: 'But go, tell his disciples and Peter, He goeth before you into Galilee: there shall ye see him, as he said unto you.' Matthew: 'And go quickly, and tell his disciples, He is risen from the dead; and lo, he goeth before you into Galilee: there shall ye see him: lo, I have told you.' The mention of Peter in Mark, and the additional words in Matthew, indicate that the two accounts were independent. Luke's account differs entirely, and evidently relates to some other angelic manifestation, probably to other persons, although about the same time and at the same place. Luke does not refer to three women only, but generally to 'the women which had come . . . out of Galilee,' 'among whom' were the three specially mentioned. That these last should have been followed later on to the tomb by others who, being there and venturing into it, should also see a similar vision, is not to be wondered at, but is highly probable, especially when we bear in mind the fact that the Vatican and other ancient MSS. include in verse 1 of this 24th chapter of Luke the words, now omitted by the Revisers, 'and certain *others* with them.' Luke says; 'And they entered in, and found not the body of the Lord Jesus. (Some ancient authorities omit *of the Lord Jesus*.) And it came to pass, while they were perplexed thereabout, behold, two men stood by them in dazzling apparel. And as they were affrighted, and bowed down their faces to the earth, they said unto them, Why seek ye the living (Gr. him that liveth) among the dead? He is not here, but is risen (some ancient authorities omit *He is not here, but is risen*): remember how he spake unto you when he was yet in Galilee, saying that the Son of man must be delivered up into the hands of sinful men, and be crucified, and the third day rise again. And they remembered his words, and returned from the tomb (some ancient authorities omit *from the tomb*).' This is obviously a different interview altogether from that with the other women, who were charged with a special message to the disciples, and lost not a moment in conveying it to them: 'And they departed quickly from the tomb with fear and great joy, and ran to bring his disciples word.' Mark describes the excitement and perturbation of mind resulting from the vision. 'And they went out, and fled from the tomb; for trembling and astonishment had come upon them: and they said nothing to anyone; for they were afraid.' The word 'quickly' is omitted after 'went out,' on the authority of the three oldest MSS. Of course the expression 'they said nothing to any one; for they were afraid,' means simply that overpowering emotion forbade for the time being any attempt to describe what they had seen, not that they maintained silence permanently or long: that would have been to disobey the command laid upon them. As they were on their way to fulfil it, Jesus himself met them and greeted them. 'And behold, Jesus met them, saying, All hail.' The words, 'as they went to tell his disciples' are omitted, on the authority of the two oldest MSS. The word rendered 'all hail,' *chairete*, denotes joy, being the same as in the passage: *Chairete kai agalliasthe*, 'Rejoice and exult.' This friendly greeting emboldened them to approach him, albeit with lowliest demonstrations of loving respect. 'And they came and took hold of his feet, and worshipped him.' Tischendorf renders 'came' as 'came up;' Young, literally, 'having come,' and 'worshipped him' as 'bowed to him.' Why might not Mary Magdalene touch him, while these women were permitted to grasp his feet? We cannot say; but the touching and even kissing of the feet carried with it a very different significance from a similar greeting on the face or the giving of the hand as a sign of fellowship. The women were still disposed to tremble at his presence, and Jesus sought to calm their fears. 'Then saith Jesus unto them, Fear not.' Let them take from his own lips the angel's message: 'go tell my brethren that they depart into Galilee, and there shall they see me.' That invitation was not confined to the apostles: the term 'brethren' included all 'disciples.'

As Mary Magdalene had been the first to announce the disappearance of the dead body of Jesus, so she was the first to bring tidings of his resurrection. 'Mary Magdalene cometh and telleth the disciples, I have seen the Lord; and how that he had said these things unto her.' Tischendorf in place of 'cometh and telleth' renders 'comes bringing word.' With the Revisers he adopts another reading, altering 'that she had seen' to 'I have seen.' This message and the effect it produced are recorded in Mark's appendix. 'She went and told them that had been with him, as they mourned and wept.' The words of Jesus were coming to pass: 'Ye shall be sorrowful, but your sorrow shall be turned into joy.' But as yet the disciples were sceptical: they had but the word of a woman, excited, overwrought, perhaps imaginative or hysterical, and against it the sure evidence of death and burial. Admitting, even, that he had been raised from the dead, how should he become manifested to the living. In vain did Mary assert the facts and her own sure conviction. 'And they, when they heard that he was alive, and had been seen of her, disbelieved.' Luke bears testimony to the same effect: 'and told all these things to the eleven, and to all the rest.' They told of all that had been communicated to them in the tomb by the two angels, and of their present recollection of the prophecy which had been uttered by Jesus. Luke adds: 'Now they were Mary Magdalene, and Joanna, and Mary the *mother* of James: and the other women with them told these things unto the apostles.' The word 'which' has been omitted before 'told,' on the authority of the three oldest MSS., and this has necessitated a somewhat different construction of the sentence, a colon instead of a comma being introduced after 'James.' This slight alteration brings Luke into clearer agreement with Matthew and Mark. There were three separate accounts: that of Mary Magdalene, that of Joanna and the other Mary, and that of 'the other women.' The disciples were told that two angels in white were seen by Mary Magdalene, sitting opposite each other in the tomb, that Jesus had shown himself to her in or close to the tomb, had been recognised by her, and had sent a loving message to his disciples; they heard also that one angel, a young man arrayed in a white robe, had been seen sitting on the right side, who had invited the two women to inspect the resting place of the body of the now risen Jesus, and had bidden them tell the disciples to go to Galilee, where they would see him, and that Jesus had met the women on their way; the other women also came, asserting that they had seen in the tomb two men in dazzling apparel, standing, not sitting, who had explained that they should not seek among the dead for him who was alive, reminding them that Jesus himself had foretold his betrayal, crucifixion and resurrection. The independent accounts, however different, harmonised to a certain extent; yet they found no credence with the apostles; there was room for uncertainty, exaggeration, trickery; the only certain fact was that the body had disappeared; it might have been removed by enemies, who might have deliberately concocted these deceptive appearances, playing upon the minds of the timid women, hoping through them to delude the followers of Jesus and then turn round, confess the plot, and thereby bring ridicule upon his memory and his teaching. That all the women spoke in good faith could not be doubted; but they told a tale such as had never been heard before since the beginning of the world, and the disciples, exercising cautious judgment and strong common sense, arrived at the conclusion that it was incredible. 'And these words appeared in their sight as idle talk: and they disbelieved them.' The word 'their' has been replaced by 'these,' on the authority of the two oldest MSS. The Revisers have altered 'idle tales' to 'idle talk,' which agrees with Young, but Tischendorf renders 'an idle tale,' which corresponds to Luther's 'Mährlein,' and seems preferable: the definition of the Greek word *leros* is 'idle talk; frivolousness, nonsense;' the apostles cannot have supposed that the women's chatter was the only basis of their various statements, but decided that what they reported as having seen and heard was too frivolous and nonsensical to be really true: some prank had been played, some idle tale believed in, which must be treated with the contempt it merited. 24 Luke 11

The next verse is as follows: 'But Peter arose, and ran unto the tomb; and stooping and looking in, he seeth the linen cloths by themselves; and he departed to his home, wondering (or, departed, wondering with himself) at that which was come to pass.' The Revisers note: 'Some ancient authorities omit ver. 12.' Lachmann and Tregelles mark it as doubtful. Tischendorf omits it. But it is in the three oldest MSS. and must therefore not be disregarded. Here it seems out of place: it appears to be the same incident which is recorded by the fourth evangelist, when Peter and John ran together to the tomb, and if so, we must needs suppose that Luke had the recorded fact without its circumstantial details, and inserted it where it seemed best in his narrative, so, in fact, misplacing it. The reading of the Authorised Version: 'then arose Peter,' would naturally lead to that inference; but this faulty rendering is now ,, 12 altered by the Revisers to: 'But Peter arose,' which agrees with Alford, Young rendering, 'and Peter having arisen.' Dismissing the idea conveyed by the word 'then,' that Peter rose up after the apostles had rejected the statement made by the women, no particular time is referred to by Luke, and there is nothing against the conclusion that the visit to the tomb to which he alludes had taken place previously. Alford observes: *'The similarity in diction to John xx. 5, 10 (stooping down he beheld the linen clothes laid by themselves, and went away home, being common to the two passages) indicates a common origin, and, if I mistake not, one distinct from the rest of the narrative in this chapter.'* Luke's expression, 'ran unto the tomb,' also corresponds with John's account, so that everything points to the existence of some original record of that incident in the hands of Luke. Taking the verse as it now stands, it simply amounts to a notification of the fact that all the apostles knew about the matter was the assurance given them by Peter to the effect that the body was not in the tomb, but only the cerements, and that its disappearance was to him marvellous and inexplicable.

Matthew informs us that just about the time when the women were hastening to communicate their marvellous news to the apostles, some of the soldiers who had been set to watch the tomb entered the city, went to the chief priests, and told them all that had happened.[28 Mat. 11] 'Now while they were going, behold, some of the guard came into the city, and told unto the chief priests all the things that were come to pass.' It was a strange tale they brought: the quaking of the ground, the descent of the angel, his rolling away of the stone and sitting upon it, his luminous form and pure white raiment, and the mortal terror which overcame them at the sight. Whatever the chief priests may have thought about all this, it was at least clear to them that their object in guarding the sepulchre had been defeated. Something, be it what it might, had happened to induce these men to forsake their post of duty. These priests had been, and probably were still, firmly persuaded that Jesus was a 'deceiver': they were not disposed to stultify themselves now by admitting the contrary, even had it been possible for them to uproot in a moment the convictions and prejudices which had long been growing up in their minds and directing their policy. It might even be open to question whether the guards, knowing the anxiety of the chief priests about the safekeeping of the tomb and their reasons for it, had not plotted together to make money out of the affair by trumping up an imaginary tale, breaking the seal, removing the stone, and quitting the spot: if so, they were now masters of the situation, for they could spread abroad this story, and so bring about the result which had been dreaded, making 'the last error worse than the first.' The matter required careful handling, and the chief priests laid it before the elders, and discussed with them the course to be adopted. The larger the number assembled, the greater the scepticism: for if one or two might be disposed to place reliance on the account given by the soldiers, the strong 'common sense' of the majority would naturally enough refuse to believe in a miracle upon the testimony of a band of hirelings who confessed themselves cowards and were probably traitors. Such would be the arguments likely to be used in debating the question; moreover, it would not be difficult to make the soldiers understand how completely they were at the mercy of their employers, who could at any moment charge them before Pilate with neglect of duty, or worse, —conspiracy. It was to the interest of all parties to hush up the matter, and a liberal offer of money would suffice to close the mouths of the soldiers. They would readily understand that by spreading abroad their tale they had nothing to gain, but on the contrary stood in peril of being denounced and punished, for the military governor would not be likely to accept their extraordinary explanation as an excuse for breach of discipline and duty. Would it not be far better for them to take a considerable sum in cash, and in return for it confess, if questioned, that they had fallen asleep at their post, and on awaking found that the disciples had come and stolen the corpse? By so doing they would secure the friendship instead of the enmity of these city magnates, who, if any enquiry should be instituted by the governor, pledged themselves to find a way of satisfying him and holding the soldiers harmless. 'And when they were assembled with the elders, and had taken counsel, they gave large money unto the soldiers, saying, Say ye, His disciples came by night, and stole him away while we slept. And if this come to the governor's ears (or, come to a hearing before the governor), we will persuade him, and rid you of care.' The tempting bribe was accepted, the bargain struck and carried out: 'So they took the money, and did as they were taught.' The passing of the money sufficiently indicates the nefariousness of the transaction on both sides, yet it should be borne in mind that the council probably believed that they were simply paying the soldiers to speak the truth: if the apostles deemed the account of the women incredible, how much more readily would the chief priests persuade themselves that the tale of the soldiers was fictitious. The former were speedily convinced by many infallible proofs, and gave witness to the resurrection of Jesus; the latter remained unconvinced, and disseminated the false report of the concealment of his dead body: 'and this saying was spread abroad among the Jews, *and continueth* until this day.' Alford notes: 'Justin Martyr says that the Jews sent men far and wide to disseminate this report.'

28 Mat. 12–14

,, 15

,, 15

Mark, in briefest words, reports another appearance of Jesus. 'And after these things he was manifested in another form to two of them, as they walked, on their way into the country.' The facts here condensed into a sentence are amplified by Luke into a detailed and interesting narrative. Although subsequent—'after these things'— the incident occurred on the same day. 'And behold, two of them were going that very day to a village named Emmaus, which was threescore furlongs from Jerusalem.' In this walk of 6 or 7 miles they, being disciples of Jesus—'two of them'—had naturally much to talk and speculate about. 'And they communed with each other of all these things which had happened.' While they were thus conversing Jesus himself overtook them and walked beside them. 'And it came to pass, while they communed and questioned together, that Jesus himself drew near, and went with them.' They did not recognise him, however: 'But their eyes were holden that they should not know him.' The word 'holden,' *ekratounto*, is from the verb *krateō*, which is found 46 times in the New Testament and is variously rendered, as *rule*, *lay hold of*, *seize*, &c. The writer's meaning is clear:

16 Mark 12

24 Luke 13

,, 14

,, 15

,, 16

some power or influence was exercised over their eyes to prevent recognition; and this was doubtless the explanation of the men, for no one but themselves could be able to express an opinion on the point. The seeming stranger entered into conversation with them.

24 Luke 17 — 'And he said unto them, What communications are these that ye have one with another (Gr. what words are these that ye exchange one with another), as ye walk?' The Authorised Version adds, before the note of interrogation, 'and are sad?' On the authority of the

„ 17 three oldest MSS. this is now altered to: 'And they stood still, looking sad.' In the Vatican MS. that was the original reading, altered by a later hand. Tischendorf reads: 'And they stood with a sad countenance.' The sudden question caused them to halt, and for the moment they hesitated, either unable or unwilling to disclose the sacred subject of their doubts and sorrows. When one of them answered, it was with an expression of surprise that the questioner should not have gathered from what he must have overheard enough

„ 18 to indicate the matter of their talk. 'And one of them named Cleopas, answering said unto him, Dost thou alone sojourn in Jerusalem and not know the things (or, Dost thou sojourn alone in Jerusalem, and knowest thou not the things) which are come to pass there in these days?' The Authorised Version stands: 'Art thou only a stranger in Jerusalem..'; Young renders: 'Art thou alone such a stranger..'; Tischendorf: 'Art thou the only sojourner in Jerusalem that knowest not...' Be that as it might, the inquirer

„ 19 begged them to be explicit: 'And he said unto them, What things?' Something in his tone and manner invited their confidence, and they gave it freely. They told him of Jesus of Nazareth, recognised as a prophet, of his preaching and miracles, his persecutions, trial, cruci-

„ 19, 20 fixion. 'And they said unto him, The things concerning Jesus of Nazareth, which was (became—Young) a prophet mighty in deed and word before God and all the people: and how the chief priests and our rulers delivered him up to be condemned to death, and crucified him.' They admitted too, their hope, now seen to be falla-

„ 21 cious, that he would have proved the Saviour of their nation. 'But we hoped that it was he which should redeem Israel.' Then they alluded to the fact that this was the third day since his death, a day to which his words, mysterious, inexplicable, had sometimes pointed

„ 21 as the turning-point in his career. 'Yea, and beside all this, it is now the third day since these things came to pass.' And something strange had indeed been disclosed at the dawning of that day: his corpse was missing, and certain women who were among the adherents of his cause reported that they had seen angels, who had told them

„ 22, 23 that Jesus was living. 'Moreover certain women of our company amazed us, having been early at the tomb; and when they found not his body, they came, saying, that they had also seen a vision of angels, which said that he was alive.' Young renders: 'an apparition of messengers, who say he is living.' The word *angelos* occurs 84 times in the New Testament. In the following 7 instances only it is ren-

11 Mat. 10
1 Mark 2
7 Luke 24
9 Luke 52
12 ii. Cor. 7
2 James 25

dered 'messenger' in the Authorised Version. 'I send my messenger.' 'When the messengers of John were departed.' 'And sent messengers before his face.' 'The messenger of Satan.' 'She had received the messengers.' The distinction made by our translators is not apparent in the Greek, and is best avoided.

The expression, 'certain women of our company,' throws light upon the results realised during the life of Jesus from his preaching. There were the twelve disciples, styled apostles; seventy others sent forth at one time to preach and heal; Luke speaks of the eleven and 'all the rest;' Mark of 'many women which came up with him unto Jerusalem,' some of whom are now alluded to by 'two of them,' that is, of 'the rest' of the disciples, as 'of our company.' As whole families migrated to Jerusalem at passover time, it would be natural for the band of disciples to go thither with their Teacher. There may have been also some secret disciples, like Joseph of Arimathæa. Paul states that 'above five hundred brethren at once' saw Jesus after his resurrection. When 'Peter stood up in the midst of the brethren,' it is added: '(and there was a multitude of names together, about a hundred and twenty),' probably meaning open, professed disciples, who at first were not afraid to cast in their lot with the apostles, although we read later that the apostles were 'all with one accord in Solomon's porch. But of the rest durst no man join himself to them.' 15 Mark 41
15 i. Cor. 6
1 Acts 15
5 Acts 12, 13

Although the two disciples mentioned the report of the women, they expressed no faith in it, merely saying that they had been 'amazed' by it, and adding that some of their number had confirmed the women's statement about the tomb, but had not seen Jesus, either dead or alive. 'And certain of them that were with us went to the tomb, and found it even so as the women had said: but him they saw not.' This may refer either to the visit of Peter and John to the sepulchre, or to some search undertaken subsequently by others. As no mention is here made of any manifestation of Jesus to Mary Magdalene or her companions, it is to be inferred that these two disciples had not heard of it: probably that part of the news had not been communicated when they left the apostolic company: some of the women saw the angels but not Jesus, and the whole of the information did not arrive at once. 24 Luke 24

The first comment of the stranger on this recital was one of surprise and reproach. 'And he said unto them, O foolish men, and slow of heart to believe in (or, after) all that the prophets have spoken! Behoved it not the Christ to suffer these things, and to enter into his glory?' Those were the opening words of a long discourse in which he took up the prophetical books one after the other from the very first, pointing out in each of them the various references to 'the sufferings of Christ and the glories that should follow them.' These words of Peter show that to his subsequently-enlightened mind such testimonies abounded in the prophets. Alford notes: 'De Wette remarks, It were much to be wished that we knew what prophecies of the death and triumph of Christ are here meant. There are but few that point to the subject.' That opinion must be owing to our imperfect comprehension, for we are told: 'And beginning from Moses and from all the prophets, he interpreted to them in all the scriptures the things concerning himself.' Our first step towards the study of that subject must be to gain a right notion of what is meant by 'prophets' and 'prophecy.' There is still a lingering idea that the essence of prophecy is the foretelling of future events, which in truth is but its incidental and occasional ,, 25, 26
1 i. Pet. 11
24 Luke 27 adjunct. Moses and David are called prophets, yet how small a portion of their teaching had reference to forecast and prediction. The Greek words to *prophesy, prophet, prophecy*, have been incorporated into our language. Here are their definitions : *prophēteuō*, 1, to be an interpreter of the gods. 2, to expound publicly, preach ; *prophētēs*, 1, one who speaks for another, an interpreter of the will of a god, *generally* an interpreter, proclaimer. 2, an interpreter of scripture, inspired teacher, preacher. 3, a foreteller, prophet : *prophēteia*. 1, the gift of interpreting the will of the gods. 2, the gift of expounding of scripture, public instruction, preaching. De Wette takes too narrow a view in thinking only of 'the death and triumph of Christ:' the 'things concerning him' embraced the whole of his career, not merely its close ; neither is 'triumph' synonymous with 'glory,' which we are too apt to restrict to regal splendour. The word *doxa* is generally translated 'glory,' but the following passages are sufficient to indicate its proper sense. 'Then shalt thou have glory in the presence of all that sit at meat with thee :' the Authorised Version has 'worship.' 'Which receive glory one of another, and the glory that *cometh* from the only God ye seek not :' the Authorised Version has 'honour.' 'If I glorify myself my glory is nothing :' the A. V. has 'honour.' There are some passages in which the word 'honour' occurs in conjunction with 'glory,' as 'unto praise and glory and honour,' where the word rendered honour is *timē*. An examination of the passages in which *timē* occurs, indicates that it is really equivalent to 'worth' or 'worthiness,' being sometimes rendered by 'price,' 'sum,' 'preciousness,' as well as by 'honour.' The Lexicon defines the word : 1, the price, cost, worth of a thing. 2, the honour in which one is held, worship, esteem, respect. External marks of glory and honour there must needs be, but they are merely the appendages and outward signs of intrinsic excellence of character, certifying the approval of God or man. The expression, 'to enter into his glory,' denotes the introduction of Christ into a state of existence carrying with it the evidences of divine approbation. In the frequently recurring expression, 'that it might be fulfilled,' the Greek verb is *plēroō*, which is defined : 1, to fill, make full. 2, to satiate, satisfy. 3, to complete. The word is used in the following passages : 'which, when it was filled, they drew up on the beach.' 'Fill ye up then the measure of your fathers.' 'His decease which he was about to accomplish at Jerusalem.' 'Sorrow hath filled your hearts.' 'That your joy may be fulfilled.' These and similar uses of the word are sufficient to show that when applied to the scriptures it does not necessarily mean the coming to pass of a foretold event, but rather the realisation of an experience, a condition, a state of things, a circumstance recorded in the scriptures. In that way, for instance, must be understood the words of Peter : 'Brethren, it was needful that the scripture should be fulfilled, which the Holy Ghost spake before by the mouth of David concerning Judas.' There must have been in Peter's mind some passage of the Psalms which alluded to treachery like that of Judas, probably : 'Yea, mine own familiar friend, in whom I trusted, which did eat of my bread, hath lifted up his heel against me.' He quotes another passage, probably from 69 Psalm 25 : 'For it is written in the book of Psalms,

'Let his habitation be made desolate,
Let no man dwell therein.'

And then another: 'His overseership let another take,' which corresponds with: 'Let his days be few: *and* let another take his office.' As there had been a realisation of the one scripture, Peter urged that they should set themselves to realise the other, by choosing some one else in place of Judas to fulfil his office.

In the same way Peter asserted that there had been a realisation or fulfilment of another prophecy: 'This is that which hath been spoken by the prophet Joel.' And here we are carried a step farther, the prophet himself intimating that his words were a forecast of the divine purpose: 'And it shall be in the last days, saith God.' Peter elsewhere asserts: 'No prophecy ever came by the will of man: but men spake from God, being moved by the Holy Spirit.' Quoting from another Psalm: 'Thou wilt not leave my soul in Hades, neither wilt thou give thy Holy One to see corruption,' he concludes that David 'foreseeing spake of the resurrection of the Christ, that neither was he left in Hades, nor did his flesh see corruption.' That cannot mean that in no sense did the words apply to David or express his personal hope, but that in their fullest sense and highest aspiration they appertained to Jesus, finding in him alone their perfect literal fulfilment. The Revisers, on the authority of the two oldest MSS., have altered 'his soul' to 'he,' so that the apostle's quotation of the passage can no longer be adduced in favour of the idea that the future life is a life of the soul only apart from a spiritual body. The original passage stands:

'For thou wilt not leave my soul to Sheol;
Neither wilt thou suffer thine holy (or, godly, or, beloved) one to see corruption (or, the pit).'

There is nothing in the bare words of David to lead to the conclusion that he was thinking of more than his own deliverance from ordinary death so long as God stood by to help him against his enemies: 'Because he is at my right hand I shall not be moved.' David was a man of war, always relying upon his God for strength and safety:

'The God that girdeth me with strength,
And maketh my way perfect.
He maketh my feet like hinds' *feet*:
And setteth me up upon my high places.
He teacheth my hands to war;
So that mine arms do bend a bow of brass.
Thou hast also given me the shield of thy salvation;
And thy right hand hath holden me up.'

The literal sense applied to David, the spiritual sense to Christ, in whose career of spiritual warfare all these things became susceptible of a higher and celestial meaning. The epistle to the Hebrews is a splendid dissertation on prophecy, showing how things in the law and prophets and patriarchal history pointed to Christ and waited to find in his day their ultimate fulfilment. Scriptural interpretation, if not a lost science, is one which has become ignored and obscured, and only in proportion as we have the mind of Christ and are able to assimilate his teaching can we hope to comprehend that science.

The walk to Emmaus was all too short for the interesting discourse which occupied the minds of the travellers during the journey. When they approached the village, the stranger showed no intention of halting, his purpose being evidently to go forward. 'And they drew nigh unto the village whither they were going: and he made as though he would go further.' Young renders: 'he made an appearance of proceeding further;' the 'Englishman's Greek New Testament': 'he appeared to be going farther.'* Alford notes: 'It is not implied that He *said* anything to indicate that He would go further—but simply, that he was passing on.' The verb *prospoieomai*, here rendered 'made as though,' occurs no where else in the New Testament. Bishop Jeremy Taylor alluded to the passage as follows: 'Our blessed Saviour pretended that He would pass forth beyond Emmaus: but if He intended not to do it, yet He did no injury to the two disciples.' The definition of the word is 'to take to oneself, pretend to, lay claim to. *Latin* affectare ; *generally*, to pretend, feign, affect.' If the latter meaning is inseparable from the word, we must needs think that the narrator chose too strong a term: for how could the original or any subsequent recorder of the fact possibly know what was in the mind of Jesus, and take upon himself to say that any dissimulation, even the very least conceivable, was practised? Doubtless villages lay wide apart, and it might well excite astonishment to see this traveller apparently bent on going forward at so late an hour. But time and distance were now of no account to Jesus; it may well be that he had designed only to make himself the companion of their journey in order to instruct them: that object accomplished, he would, but for their persuasion, have passed onward without any disclosure of his personality. They, deeming him an ordinary traveller, thought of the lonely route, the darkness and fatigue, and took upon themselves to persuade him to stay with them. 'And they constrained him, saying, Abide with us: for it is toward evening, and the day is now far spent.' Jesus acquiesced in their proposal: 'And he went in to abide with them.' The Revisers have altered 'tarry with them' to 'abide with them.' It is the same word, *menō*, as in 'abide with us,' which occurs 112 times in the New Testament, and in every instance denotes continuance, permanency for the time being. 'They came therefore and saw where he abode: and they abode with him that day.' 'Your sin remaineth.' 'Stuck, and remained unmoveable.' The two disciples fully expected that the stranger intended to spend some hours in their company. And there was every appearance of his doing so, for he sat down with them as if to share in their repast. They watched him as he took the loaf into his hands, blessed, brake it and handed it to them. 'And it came to pass, when he had sat down with them to meat, he took the bread (or, loaf), and blessed it, and brake, and gave to them.' The Revisers have omitted to italicise the word 'it,' which is not in the original and is omitted by Young and Tischendorf. There was no benediction or consecration of the loaf. The word *eulogeō*, rendered 'bless,' occurs 43 times in the New Testament. An inspection of the passages leads to the conclusion that the sense is best indicated by our form of the Greek, to *eulogize*. That meaning

---

* 'He made for journeying further': "New Testament Critically Emphasised."

lies upon the surface in such passages as the following. 'Blessed art [Luke 42] thou among women, and blessed the fruit of thy womb.' 'And he [" 64] spake, blessing God.' 'Blessed the King that cometh in the name of [Luke 38] the Lord.' 'The cup of blessing which we bless.' 'Therewith bless [i. Cor. 16] we the Lord.' 'Else if thou bless with the spirit, how shall he that [James 9] filleth the place of the unlearned say the Amen at thy giving of [i. Cor. 16] thanks, seeing he knoweth not what thou sayest?' This last quotation seems decisive on the point. In the following passages the word *eulogeō* appears, on reflection, to carry the same import. 'Looking [Mat. 19] up to heaven, he blessed.' The upward gaze showed that the Giver of the bread, not the bread itself, was eulogized. 'He took them in [Mark 16] his arms, and blessed them, laying his hands upon them.' 'The less [Heb. 7] is blessed of the better.' 'Isaac blessed Jacob and Esau, even concerning things to come.' [Heb. 20] A correct notion of the word used tends to modify the prevalent idea that the act of 'blessing' was a kind of magic ceremony, not only involving foresight and commendation, but actually imparting all that was foreseen and eulogized. 'In thy [Acts 25, 26] seed shall all the families of the earth be blessed (*eneulogēthēsontai*) ... God .. sent him to bless you (*eulogounta*), in turning away every one of you from your iniquities:' that must be the means whereby to obtain the promised eulogy. 'Blessed (*eulogētos*) the God and [Eph. 3] Father of our Lord Jesus Christ, who hath blessed (*eulogēsas*) us with every spiritual blessing (*eulogia*) in the heavenlies with Christ:' the divine eulogy is contingent upon a heavenly and Christlike character and life. 'Bless them that persecute you; bless, and curse [Rom. 14] not.' If the command to bless (*eulogeite*) persecutors is obligatory upon all Christians, what better can be understood by it than to *eulogize*? An invocation would come under the definition of praying for them, not blessing them; to confer a benefit upon them is generally out of the question; but to speak good and nothing but good about them is possible, for all men have salient points of character, some open to praise and some to condemnation: to pass by the latter in silence and to dwell upon the former, is the duty here made incumbent upon Christians, a very easy one, however much neglected. The absence of scandal and evil insinuation in matters social, political and religious would be a purification of the moral atmosphere, rendering it healthy and invigorating instead of mephitic and depressing. This modified and simple view of what is meant by blessing others must alter our conception of what is meant by cursing them: the latter requires for its realisation no priestly form of anathema, no witch-like incantation, no launching of opprobrious epithets: the Latin form—malediction—speaking evil, sufficiently indicates the true sense, and that is equivalent to the Greek *blasphēmia*, which has become incorporated into our language, and the meaning of which is sufficiently obvious from the following passage: 'Every sin and blasphemy shall be forgiven unto men, but [Mat. 31] the blasphemy against the Spirit shall not be forgiven. And whosoever shall speak a word against the Son of man, it shall be forgiven [" 32] him; but whosoever shall speak against the Holy Spirit, it shall not be forgiven him.' Young renders the first verse as follows: 'All sin and evil speaking shall be forgiven to men; but the evil speaking of the Spirit shall not be forgiven to men."' Blasphemy, malediction, cursing, are synonymous with evil speaking, and blessing is the opposite to these, that is—eulogy. If theologians, instead of disputing and dogmatising about the meaning of texts relating to the Divine nature and personality, dividing themselves into Trinitarians and Anti-trinitarians, would set themselves to the study and elucidation of the words and scope of the practical and unique precepts of Christianity, they would labour far more usefully than at present: a mine of wealth lies at our feet, and only proper tools and willing hands are needed to bring to light many a buried truth which would flash in the eyes of men like a jewel in God's sunlight.

When Jesus took into his hands the loaf, blessed, brake and gave it to the two disciples, something in his manner, attitude and look seemed like a sudden revelation of his personality: 'And their eyes were opened, and they knew him.' The expression 'their eyes were opened' stands in opposition to 'their eyes were holden.' The word here rendered 'were opened,' *diēnoichthēsan*, is the same as in the passage 'his ears were opened.' It occurs 8 times in the New Testament, and denotes something which had been previously closed physically, or had remained undisclosed mentally. But their recognition of Jesus was as fleeting as it was sudden and unexpected: no sooner did they know him than they ceased to see him; he was gone in an instant, as though he had been a phantom: 'and he vanished out of their sight.' Young renders: 'and he became unseen by them.' Alford notes: '*He vanished out of their sight* does not imply His Body to have remained, though *invisible to them*; but plainly indicates in the original, besides the supernatural disappearance, a real objective *removal from them*.' But the narrative can only be an account of what they saw and what they ceased to see; if it 'plainly indicates' that Jesus went from them when he became invisible to them, it states something which they could not know anything about. The translation in the 'Englishman's Greek New Testament' is: 'and he disappeared from them.' More than that they could neither say nor mean to say. It was a mystery to them, and so much the more because on entering he had given them to understand, either verbally or by implication, that he intended to stay with them: 'he went in to abide with them.' We must needs believe that there were good and sufficient reasons why everything should have happened as it did. The object of Jesus in visiting them is apparent from his conversation: he wished to make them understand how the whole tone and tenor of the scriptures harmonised with the life he had led and the sufferings he had undergone. That could only be attempted by quiet converse and prolonged explanation; any revelation of himself as risen from the dead, would have overwhelmed them with astonishment; their minds, filled with wonder and fear, as was the case with the women, would have been unfitted for the calm exercise of their reflective and reasoning powers. How it came to pass that they were withheld from recognition, must remain a mystery to us, as it was to them. Strange things are recorded, even in our own days, of the influence of the mind of one person upon the percipient faculties of others, and we can place no limit to the effects which might result from the mere volition of Jesus. So long as he wished to remain unknown, he was not identified; when he chose to remove the veil from their eyes, they saw him clearly. Some sufficient cause, we know not what, forbade his remaining visibly in their company when they had realised the fact of his presence. The recorded appearances and disappearances of celestial Beings have always been sudden and inexplicable; we cannot tell to what extent their manifestation is contingent upon the mental and spiritual condition of those who are permitted to behold them. Our outward bodily eyes are but windows through which our internal spiritual eyes look. Was not that the idea of Solomon when he spoke of 'those that look out of the windows'? If the inward vision fails, even natural things may become more or less invisible; if the inward vision is strengthened, it may perceive spiritual things which mortal men are not generally privileged to behold. Saint Paul's doctrine about the natural and the spiritual body needs to be carefully pondered. According to the Authorised Version he says: 'There is a natural body, and there is a spiritual body.' That must not be understood to mean: 'there *is* a natural body, and there *will be* a spiritual body': the word *estin*, 'is,' indicates the simultaneous existence of both. The Revised Version, following the three oldest MSS., reads: 'If there is a natural body, there is also a spiritual': they exist conjointly; the former cannot be without the latter. The Authorised Verson renders: 'Howbeit that *was* not first which is spiritual, but that which is natural; and afterward that which is spiritual.' The old translators were careful to italicise 'was,' indicating thereby that it was an insertion. The Revisers have replaced 'was' by 'is,' not italicised, and instead of 'and afterward' they put the word 'then.' The word translated 'first' is *prōton*, which is distinguished in the 'Englishman's Greek Concordance' from *prōtos*. *Prōtos* is defined in the Lexicon as 'first, foremost, front, of Number or Place; of Time, first, earliest, Lat. primus.' *Prōton* is defined: 'first, in the first place, Lat. primum: first of all, above all.' Therefore: 'that is not first which is spiritual, but that which is natural,' signifies that the spiritual body is not manifested first, or in the first place, or first of all, or above all, but the natural body takes precedence. The word 'first' does not mean in this passage first in time, but that foremost, above all, stands the natural or, properly speaking, psychical—Greek *psuchikon*—body. The Greek word *epeita*, rendered by the Revisers 'then' instead of 'afterward,' is thus defined: 'Marks the Sequence of one thing *upon* another: thereupon, thereafter, then, Lat. deinde.' Therefore: 'then that which is spiritual,' *epeita to pneumatikon*, refers to no new creation, but signifies that the spiritual (pneumatic) body stands behind the natural (psychical) body, the former coming forth when the latter perishes. The apostle, in order to convey his idea about the psychical and spiritual bodies of man, refers to the account of his creation. 'So also it is written, The first man Adam became a living soul.' The Revisers have properly altered 'was made' to 'became,' the Greek *egeneto* being from the verb *gignomai*, which is defined: to become, to happen: to be born: to be. It may be observed in passing that this Greek verb is rendered in the translation of the New Testament by no less than 47 different English words: a fact which shows the necessity of careful investigation when dealing with important doctrines. The passage referred to by Paul appears to be this: 'And the LORD God formed man of the dust of the ground, and breathed into his nostrils the breath of life; and man

12 Eccl. 3

15 1 Cor. 44

„ 46

„ 45

2 Gen. 7

became a living soul.' That was the primary form of his development. The term 'first man Adam' would seem to have been chosen by the apostle as denoting the nature of the human race in its origin and entrance upon this earthly life. The word rendered 'first' in 'the first man Adam,' is not *prōton* but *prōtos*, and stands in opposition to 'last,' numerically—not as pre-eminently. In the original there is a word—*eis*—in, or into, or unto, which has been omitted by translators. The passage reads literally: 'Became the first man Adam into a soul (*psuchēn*) living; the last Adam into a spirit (*pneuma*) quickening.' Out of the many hundreds of passages in which *eis* occurs, only in 47 instances is it omitted in our translation, and then on account of a different construction, not because the word had no value: indeed, in some cases, as in this passage of Paul, the sense would come out as well or better had it been introduced; for example: 'I will send (unto) them prophets'; the Revisers have supplied 'unto.' 'It grew and became (into) a tree.' 'Might be spoken to them (in) the next sabbath.' 'They returned (unto) home again.' 'Let their table be made (into) a snare, and (into) a trap, and (into) a stumbling-block, and (into) a recompense.' The quotation of the apostle ends with the word 'living': 'Became the first man Adam into a *psuchēn* living'; he adds the second development: 'the last Adam into a *pneuma* life-giving' (Young). Then comes the statement, already considered, about the living *psuchēn* standing foremost and the life-giving *pneuma* succeeding to it, after which the Revised Version proceeds: 'The first man is of the earth, earthy: the second man is of heaven.' The Revisers have considerably modified the sense by altering: 'the second man *is* the Lord from heaven,' into 'the second man is of heaven.' The latter is the reading of the two oldest MSS., and is adopted by Lachmann, Tischendorf, Tregelles and Alford. Assuming it to be the genuine original reading, the words 'the Lord' must have been inserted by some commentator who supposed that addition brought out the proper sense of the passage. This is the more probable, because Alford notes that 'the last Adam' was an 'expression well known among the Jews as indicating the Messiah. A Rabbinical work says, *The last Adam is the Messiah:* and other instances are given.' Our only concern is to know what Paul meant by it in this passage, and that must be ascertained by the context: his opinions often differed from those of other Jews. 'Of the earth' is *ek gēs*; 'of heaven' is *ex ouranou*: *ek* and *ex* are identical, the latter form being used before a vowel. Its radical sense is defined as 'from out of, away from,' and it is used of (1) place, (2) time, (3) origin, (4) motive, the Lexicon including under the third head 'the materials of a thing, as *pōma ek xulou*, a cup *of* wood.' That is obviously its import in this passage, and how necessary it is to fix the meaning by the context is evident from the fact that the word *ek* is rendered in the New Testament by 40 different English words. The word rendered 'earthy' is *choïkos*, which is defined as 'of rubbish, of earth *or* clay.' It occurs only in these three verses of the New Testament. Let us take their literal rendering: 'But not foremost the pneumatic, but the psychic, then the pneumatic. The first man of earth, earthy; the second man of heaven: such as the (one) earthy, such also those earthy; and such as the (one) heavenly, such also those heavenly. And according as we bore the image of the (one) earthy, we shall also bear the image of the (one) heavenly.' By omitting the inserted words 'is' and 'are,' the passage assumes the form of a simple definition and corollary: the apostle is arguing, not making a new revelation: he starts with the assertion that man possesses a psychic body and a pneumatic body, the former being of earthy material, that of the first man, the latter being of heavenly material, that of the second, ultimate man. Take the literal rendering of verse 45: 'So also it has been written, Became the first man Adam into a soul (*psuchēn*) living; the last Adam into a spirit (*pneuma*) life-giving.' The word rendered 'last' is *eschatos*, which is defined as 'the furthest, uttermost, extreme,' and as signifying either, (1) the uppermost, highest (Latin *summus*), (2) the lowest (Latin *imus*), (3) the innermost (Latin *intimus*).' Therefore 'the last Adam' is in fact 'the highest Adam,' or 'the innermost Adam.' The two first-manifested Adams are the typical forerunners of the human race: 'For since by man death, by man also the resurrection of the dead. For as in Adam all die, so also in the Christ shall all be made alive.' That important word 'all' must neither be overlooked nor explained away: the resurrection is as universal as the death. Alford explains the passage thus: '*In community with*, as partakers of a common nature with *Adam* and *Christ*: who are respectively the sources, *to the whole of that nature* (all men), of death and *life*, i.e. (here) *physical death*, and *rescue from physical death*.' He adds: 'The ancients, and the best of the moderns, keep to the *universal* reference.' That this is the meaning of the apostle is clear from the argument he had previously adduced: 'For if the dead are not raised, neither hath Christ been raised.' His resurrection equally with his death, was in accordance with the universal law and common experience of mankind. This is strongly insisted upon: 'But if there is no resurrection of the dead, neither hath Christ been raised.' 'The dead' is plural: German, *Todten*, French, *des morts*, Latin, *mortuorum*. This reasoning of the apostle stands in direct opposition to the prevalent idea that but for the resurrection of Christ there would have been no resurrection for others: Saint Paul's assumption is the very reverse of that, and the discrepancy between his view of the matter and that generally entertained points to some grave misconception of his doctrine both here and elsewhere. One error naturally leads to another, and one truth clearly grasped will be a guide to other truths. The exultant cry: 'Thanks be to God, which giveth us the victory through our Lord Jesus Christ,' does not refer to a victory over death, but over sin, which is the sting of death, and the law, which is the power of sin. The resurrection of Christ was not the conquest over death: 'For he must reign, till he hath put all his enemies under his feet. The last enemy that shall be abolished is death.' Our resurrection from death is a natural, not a miraculous process: it is the birth of our second or innermost Adam into the unseen world, corresponding to the birth of our first or outer Adam into the visible world.' 'Flesh and blood cannot inherit the kingdom of God; neither doth corruption inherit incorruption.' The flesh-clothed form in which we walk this world is all unsuited to the next stage of existence; the gradual process of decay in this 'earthy' body exceeds its power of reparation, and the time of its dissolution cannot be far prolonged. The change of nature, place and state which comes to

1 Cor. 21
,, 22
,, 16
,, 13
,, 57
,, 25
,, 26
,, 50

us through death, is a step in advance, the uprising into a higher sphere of spiritual activity. Of the innumerable hosts of the departed, Jesus alone returned to manifest himself repeatedly during a period of forty days to the chosen witnesses of his resurrection. The mystery attaching to his sudden appearances and disappearances arose out of the changed conditions of his being; all that relates to the other life must be strange and inexplicable to us who have had no experience of the attributes and powers bestowed upon the inhabitants of the heavenly world. The recorded visions of angels resemble, in many points, the interviews which Jesus had with his disciples after his rising again: they, like him, appeared in human form, at unexpected times and places, came and went no man could say how or whence, held short converse with mankind, and were seen no more. We have no reason to suppose that these celestial messengers were other than what they seemed: the human form is indicative of the human race, and instead of regarding them as a different order of Beings, it would be reasonable to assume that they were men like ourselves, but who had passed through the grave and gate of death to a joyful resurrection. We cannot wonder that they should never have been manifested except for some definite and important purpose; terror sometimes fell upon those who saw them; knowing the weakness of our nature, how wildly the heart may pulsate at any shock of surprise at what is unexpected and unaccustomed, these angelic visitants must exercise caution in their method of approach. That may have been the reason why Jesus only partially revealed himself to the two disciples on the road to Emmaus and, as soon as they recognised him, vanished out of their sight. When that happened, they began to talk over the matter, and recalled the unusual feeling of interest they had experienced in listening to the discourse on the road. 'And they said one to another, Was not our heart burning within us, while he spake to us in the way, while he opened to us the scriptures?' The word 'and' has been omitted before 'while he opened,' on the authority of the two oldest MSS. They resolved to return immediately to Jerusalem to acquaint their fellow disciples with all the circumstances. 'And they rose up that very hour, and returned to Jerusalem.' There they found the apostles and others engaged in conversation on the subject of another manifestation of Jesus which had been granted to Simon: 'and found the eleven gathered together, and them that were with them, saying, The Lord is risen indeed, and hath appeared to Simon.' The two from Emmaus then related their own strange experiences. 'And they rehearsed the things *that happened* in the way, and how he was known of them in the breaking of the bread.' Mark says that their tale met with no credence. 'And they went away and told it unto the rest: neither believed they them.' That is not what we should have expected, because in the mood in which the disciples now were, they would naturally be disposed to welcome any confirmation of the fact they now admitted, 'The Lord is risen indeed.' But it would seem that although they attached great importance to the account of Simon, they placed small reliance on that from Emmaus. The inference is, that they were more careful to weigh evidence than to collect it. Only clearest proof would satisfy them; anything at all vague or visionary they rejected; the accounts of the women had seemed too incoherent and excited, and the momentary glimpse of recognition at Emmaus was not to be relied upon. The disbelief could not proceed from any doubt of the good faith of the narrators, who were well known and of their company, but it was possible they had been either intentionally deluded or were unconsciously self-deceived. Only overwhelming evidence of the bodily, tangible presence and personality of Jesus could convince them of the fact that he was really risen from among the dead. And that evidence was now forthcoming. While they were still talking—reasoning about the question, lo! Jesus himself was seen to be standing among them. 'And as they spake these things, he himself stood in the midst of them, and saith unto them, Peace be unto you.' 'Jesus' has been altered to 'he,' on the authority of the two oldest MSS. The Revisers note: 'Some ancient authorities omit *and saith unto them, Peace be unto you*.' Tischendorf does so, although he notes no such omission in the three oldest MSS. Those present gazed upon Jesus with the utmost consternation, deeming that he could be no living man who revealed himself to them in this sudden and inexplicable manner. 'But they were terrified and affrighted, and supposed that they beheld a spirit.' They were as slow to trust the testimony of their own senses as they had been to believe that of others, assuming that any such appearance of Jesus in bodily form could only be spectral or spiritual, not corporeal. The word rendered 'spirit' is *pneuma*: the disciples thought this must be the spiritual or pneumatic body, which we have seen was believed by Paul, probably therefore by the Jews generally, to underlie and outlast the natural or psychic body. It was only the sceptic Sadducees who said that there was 'no resurrection, nor angel (*angelos*) nor spirit (*pneuma*).' When the apostles in the storm saw Jesus walking on the sea, and cried out, they used a different word—*phantasma*, phantom: 'It is an apparition,' an appearance merely, not the man himself. But now their idea seems to have been altogether different: they doubted not the identity of Jesus, but the fact of this being his earthly body resuscitated; they supposed it to be his spiritual, pneumatic body. That assumption, however natural, was erroneous, and Jesus proceeded to convince them that the same body which was crucified and laid in the tomb was now before them, no longer dead, inanimate, but revived, quickened by the 'life-giving pneuma.' Why should they doubt the fact, or be alarmed at his reappearance? 'And he said unto them, Why are ye troubled? and wherefore do reasonings arise in your heart? See my hands and my feet, that it is I myself: handle me, and see; for a spirit (*pneuma*) hath not flesh and bones, as ye behold me having.' The next verse stands: 'And when he had said this, he shewed them his hands and his feet.' The Revisers note that some ancient authorities omit this. Tischendorf does so, although it is in the three oldest MSS., and Tregelles marks it as doubtful. On the previous verse Alford notes: 'Observe *flesh and bones*—but not *blood*. This the Resurrection Body probably *had not* —as being the *animal life* . . . His Flesh and Blood were *sundered* by Death. Death was the shedding of His precious Blood, which (most probably) *He did not afterwards resume*.' As a matter of fact, the body was drained upon the cross by the final spear-thrust, and the streaming forth of the blood was followed by an outflow of water. The pneumatic life is an aërial existence, the word *pneuma* signifying

24 Luke 36

,, 37

23 Acts 8

14 Mat. 26

24 Luke 38, 39

,, 40

3 John 5 *wind, air, breath* or *spirit*. 'Water and spirit' (*hudōr kai pneuma*) are
15 i. Cor. 50 the elements of the new birth, as 'flesh and blood' (*sarx kai haima*)
are the constituents of the earthy body. The *pneuma* of Jesus took up and reanimated his earthly form, but the natural, corporeal life which is contingent upon the presence and circulation of the blood was wholly laid aside: the material frame was there, no longer vivified and energised by blood, but by water and spirit, and therefore no longer subject to the limitations attaching to a merely natural body. Jesus, like other heavenly beings, became visible and invisible at will, and the spirit brought him and carried him away, whence, how, whither, we cannot tell, not knowing the laws of volition, motion, contraction, expansion, dissolution, materialisation, which exist in the life to come.

The disciples were overwhelmed with astonishment at this marvellous manifestation of their crucified, dead and buried Master. The joyous fact seemed too good to be true. Still further to con-
24 Luke 41 vince them, Jesus asked for food, and ate it in their presence. 'And
while they still disbelieved for joy, and wondered, he said unto them, Have ye here anything to eat? And they gave him a piece of a broiled fish. And he took it, and did eat before them.' The Revisers note that, after *fish*, 'Many ancient authorities add *and a honeycomb*.' Those words are omitted on the authority of the three oldest MSS.

Luke states that the journey to Emmaus was made on the day of
" 13 the resurrection: 'that very day,' and that the two travellers
" 33 returned on the same evening: 'they rose up that very hour, and
returned to Jerusalem,' where they found the apostles and others gathered together. The manifestation of Jesus to the disciples related by the fourth evangelist is evidently identical with that of Luke, for John states that it took place at the same time, and that Jesus introduced himself in the same way and with the same
20 John 19 greeting. 'When therefore it was evening, on that day, the first *day*
of the week, and when the doors were shut where the disciples were, for fear of the Jews, Jesus came and stood in the midst, and saith unto them, Peace *be* unto you.' Here we have again the same translation, 'the first *day* of the week.' Young renders: 'the first of the sabbaths;' Luther: 'Am Abend aber desselbigen Sabbaths,' 'But on the evening of the same sabbath:' the original reading, according to Lachmann, Tischendorf, Tregelles, Alford and Wordsworth, is *tēi miai sabbatōn*.* The word 'assembled' has been omitted after 'were,' on the authority of the three oldest MSS. John's account is condensed: he does not allude to the terror of the disciples, nor record the words with which Jesus allayed it, but passes
" 20 on at once to the ocular demonstration he vouchsafed. 'And when
he had said this, he shewed unto them his hands and his side.' The expression, 'and when he had said this' must not be taken to imply that the act followed immediately upon the words, no others being spoken: it seems merely to denote a sequence, equivalent to 'and
18 John 38 afterwards:' the same form is used elsewhere: 'And when he had
" 1 said this he went out again unto the Jews,' and similarly, 'When
Jesus had spoken these words, he went forth.' Although John

* For further information on this subject see Note A in the Appendix.

alludes to the 'side' and Luke does not, there is no discrepancy, and the wording of the respective accounts is very natural: 'See my hands and my feet,' they being open to view: the further invitation, 'handle me,' would lead to an examination of the spear-wound; 'he shewed unto them his hands and his side,' which, unlike the feet, could be closely inspected without stooping. The demonstration resulted in a joyful recognition: 'The disciples therefore were glad, 20 John 20 when they saw the Lord,'—the state of mind described by Luke. Jesus, anxious that his first words should not be deemed a mere courteous form of greeting, repeated them. 'Jesus therefore said to ,, 21 them again, Peace *be* unto you.' That had been his parting legacy to them: 'Peace I leave with you; my peace I give unto you.' The 14 John 27 promotion of peace being the sum and substance of the mission of Jesus and his apostles, he immediately adds: 'as the Father hath 20 John 21 sent me, even so send I you.' Their undertaking was both new and solemn, and could only be performed through the same holy Spirit by which Jesus himself was animated. By deed and word he now impresses upon them their duty, privilege and responsibility. 'And ,, 22, 23 when he had said this, he breathed on them, and saith unto them, Receive ye the Holy Ghost (or, Spirit): whose soever sins ye forgive, they are forgiven unto them; whose soever sins ye retain, they are retained.' The Revisers have omitted to italicise 'them' after 'breathed on,' and they have altered 'remit,' 'remitted' into 'forgive,' 'forgiven.' The interlinear literal translation in the 'Englishman's Greek New Testament' is as follows: 'And this having said he breathed into, and says to them, Receive Spirit Holy: of whomsoever ye may remit the sins, they are remitted to them; of whomsoever ye may retain, they have been retained.' The word *enephusēsen*, which is from *emphusaō*, to breathe in, into *or* upon, occurs only here, and no similar action is recorded elsewhere. The significance of the act can therefore only be judged of by the context. Jesus emitted his breath, and bade the disciples receive it as *pneuma hagion*, the word *pneuma* signifying both *breath* and *spirit*. Alford calls attention to the fact that *labete*, rendered *receive*, is the same word rendered *take* in Matt. xxvi. 26 and the parallels: 'Jesus *took* bread .. *Take*, eat.' It would seem therefore to denote a voluntary appropriation by the recipient; and this is confirmed by the definitions in the Lexicon of the verb *lambanō*, from which *labete* comes: 1, To take, take hold of, grasp, seize; 2, (of things) to take away, carry off; 3, to take in, receive hospitably, entertain; 4, to gain, win, procure, acquire. That holy spirit of peace which Jesus possessed and eulogised, which he bequeathed as his sole legacy to his disciples, he would have them accept direct from him and carry with them into the world. We are told of the breathing, but not of the attitude which accompanied it, nor that it was on each of them separately. Jesus, standing in the midst, sent forth his breath towards them and 'saith unto them,' collectively, 'Take, *or* take hold of, *or* take away holy spirit. Luther renders: 'Nehmet hin den heiligen Geist,' 'Take away the Holy Spirit.' From him alone they received it, and on their possession and cultivation of it would depend their influence upon the world. Jesus had previously told them that the Holy Spirit in them would 'convict the world in 16 John 8 respect of sin, and of righteousness, and of judgement.' The word *elenxei*, rendered 'convict,' is from *elenchō*: 1 to disgrace, put to shame, dishonour; 2 to convince, refute, accuse, reprove. The Authorised Version has 'reprove the world of sin.' In the 17 instances in which the word *elenchō* occurs in the New Testament it signifies *reprove*. The lives of the disciples of Jesus, animated and guided by his holy Spirit, would be a standing reproof of the conduct of the world. He now solemnly reminds them of the fact that the world can be thus changed through them, and will not be changed except through them. The Revisers have rather marred than improved the sense by altering 'remit' to 'forgive.'

The important doctrine attached to this text calls for a careful investigation as to the proper meaning of the words both in the original Greek and in the English translation. There are three Greek words rendered 'forgive': *apoluō, aphiēmi* and *charizomai*.

The word *apoluō* is thus defined: 1, to loose from, to set free or release from; 2, to release for oneself, redeem; 3, *passive* to be released, let free from. *Apoluō* is rendered in the New Testament by the following 11 words: depart, dismiss, divorce, forgive, let depart, let go, loose, put away, release, send away, set at liberty. It is rendered forgive in one passage only: 'Forgive, and ye shall be forgiven,' *apoluete kai apoluthēsesthe*: but here Young, Tischendorf and the Revisers have altered forgive, forgiven to release, released.

6 Luke 37

The word *aphiēmi* is thus defined: 1, to send forth, discharge; 2, to send away, let go; 3, to give up: 4, to let, suffer, permit. *Aphiēmi* is rendered in the New Testament by the following 16 words: cry, forgive, forsake, lay aside, leave, let, let alone, let be, let go, let have, omit, put away, remit, send away, suffer, yield up. It is rendered 'forgive' in the following passages: 'Forgive us our debts, as we forgive our debtors. For if ye forgive men their trespasses, your heavenly Father *will* also forgive you. If ye forgive not men . . will your Father forgive your trespasses.* Thy sins be forgiven thee.* Power on earth to forgive sins. Blasphemy shall be forgiven. *Shall* not be forgiven. And I forgive him? I forgave thee all that debt. Forgive not everyone his brother. Who can forgive sins but God?* All sins shall be forgiven. Their sins should be forgiven. Forgive, if ye have aught against. May forgive your trespasses. If ye do not forgive. To forgive sins. Little is forgiven. Thy sins are forgiven. That forgiveth sins. Forgive us our sins, for we also forgive. It shall be forgiven. Forgive him. Thou shalt forgive him. Father, forgive them. Sins ye remit (forgive, R. V.), they are remitted (forgiven, R. V.). May be forgiven thee. Whose iniquities are forgiven. They shall be forgiven him. To forgive us our sins. Your sins are forgiven.'

6 Mat. 12
" 14
" 15
9 Mat. 2
" 5
12 Mat. 31
18 Mat. 21,
27
32, 35
2 Mark 5
" 9
3 Mark 28
4 Mark 12
11 Mark 25
" 26
5 Luke 23, 24
7 Luke 47,
48, 49
11 Luke 4
12 Luke 10
17 Luke 3, 4
23 Luke 34
20 John 23
8 Acts 22
4 Rom. 7
5 James 15
1 i. John 9
2 i. John 12
14 Mark 6
9 Luke 60
10 Luke 42
13 Luke 8
17 Luke 34
18 Luke 28
16 John 12
16 John 28
7 i. Cor. 4
6 Heb. 1
15 Mark 37

Now let us take a few passages in which the word *aphiēmi* is otherwise translated. 'Jesus said, *Let* her *alone. Leave* the dead to bury their own dead. Not to *leave* the other undone. *Let* it *alone* this year also. The other *shall be left. We have left* all. *Leaveth* the sheep. I *leave* the world. Let not the husband *put away* his wife. *Leaving* the principles. *Cried* with a loud voice!: *apheis phōnēn megalēn, having sent forth* a loud voice.' These and the rest of the 16 words by which translators have rendered *aphiēmi* all carry the sense

* And the parallel passages: 2 Mark 5, 10; 5 Luke 20, 21, 23.

of *let go, let be, let alone:* forsake, lay aside, omit, send away, suffer, yield up, come under one or other of those three synonyms, as do also the terms forgive or remit. The forgiveness or remission of sins is a letting go or letting alone of sins: forgiveness from God to man, or from man to man signifies the letting go of sins without retaliation, so that where there is punishment, either by God or man, there cannot be forgiveness; forgiveness as regards the sinner himself, signifies the letting go of sins absolutely, so that where sin continues there cannot be forgiveness. The substantive derived from the verb *aphiēmi* is *aphesis*, which is rendered either as deliverance, forgiveness, liberty or remission. However the verb or substantive may be translated they represent an actuality, the letting go of something, and in the case of sin either the putting away of the punishment or the putting away of the sin itself.

A mere change of mind, feeling or disposition towards a sinner or a debtor is not forgiveness, but benignity, and is represented by the word *charizomai*, which is thus defined : 1, to show favour *or* kindness ; 2, to offer willingly, offer as a free gift ; 3, *passive*, to be pleasing, agreeable, to be granted as a favour. *Charizomai* is rendered in the New Testament by the words deliver, forgive, frankly forgive, give, give freely, grant. We need only consider the passages in which it appears as *forgive.* 'He *frankly forgave* them both. 7 Luke 42. He to whom he *forgave* most.' Here the allusion is to the free gift of the amount owed : *freely gave* and *gave* would more accurately express the sense. 'Ye ought rather *to forgive* him': it is clear from 2 ii. Cor. 7 the context that *to show favour* is the proper sense, the word being connected with 'encourage' or 'comfort,' and opposed to 'rebuke' or 'punishment.' 'To whom ye *forgive* anything . . For if I *forgive* ., 10 anything, to whom I *forgave* it . .': the apostle simply ratifies and adopts any favour shown. '*Forgive* me this wrong': equivalent to 12 ii. Cor. 13 'look kindly on my wrong.' '*Forgiving* one another, even as God 4 Eph. 32 for Christ's sake *hath forgiven* you.' The preceding words manifest the sense to be rather *show favour :* 'Be ye kind one to another, tender hearted, *showing favour* to each other, even as God for Christ's sake hath *shown favour* to you.' '*Having forgiven* you all tres- 2 Col. 13 passes': Luther adheres to the Greek sense : 'Und hat uns geschenket alle Sünden.' 'And *forgiving* one another, even as Christ *forgave* 3 Col. 13 you, so also do ye.' This is part of an exhortation to mercies, kindness, longsuffering, and applies to the case of 'a quarrel against any.'

The word *charizomai* expresses the sentiment of forgiveness, that is—compassion ; the word *aphiēmi* represents the reality of forgiveness, that is—the letting go of sin. It is the latter word which occurs in the passage, 'Whose soever sins ye *remit*, they are *remitted* unto them.' The true sense of this is apparent from what follows : 'whose soever ye *retain*, they are *retained*.' 'Retain' or cling to, is placed in opposition to 'remit' or let go. The verb *krateō* is rendered in the New Testament as follows : hold, hold by, hold fast, keep, lay hand on, lay hold on, obtain, retain, take, take by. In what sense could the disciples of Jesus retain, hold, keep the sins of others ? Out of the 46 passages in which the word *krateō* occurs, this is the only one in which it is rendered by 'retain.' It invariably denotes an actual taking, holding, or keeping in possession, as appears by the following examples: 'And *took* her *by* the hand.' '*Will* he not *lay hold on* it.' 'And he *laid hands on* him.' 'They that *had laid hold* on Jesus.' 'And *laid hold upon* John.' '*Holding* the tradition of the elders.' 'They *kept* that saying with themselves.' 'But their eyes *were holden*.' 'Supposing that they *had obtained*.' '*Let* us *hold fast* (our) profession.' 'Them *that hold* the doctrine of Balaam.' The import of the word is clear. Surely to *hold the doctrine* of others and to *hold the sins* of others, must be interpreted in the same manner: they both signify a personal retention of the things alluded to. 'Whose soever sins ye let go, they are let go unto them; whose soever ye hold, they are held': you, my disciples, having my holy Spirit, can only abolish the sins of the world in this way: those which you drop, the world will drop; those which you keep, the world will keep. That stands out as the plain, natural, straightforward sense of this saying of Jesus. There is no allusion here, or anywhere else, to the 'absolution' of sin by word of mouth or priestly authority: that doctrine was invented long afterwards, and led to the practice of auricular confession. That has been laid aside by Protestants, although the Church of England still holds, more or less, in a half-hearted, shamefaced, perfunctory way, to the theory of sacerdotal powers and privileges, based partly on this passage, on which Dean Alford commented as follows: 'The words, closely considered, amount to this: that with the gift and real participation of the Holy Spirit, comes the conviction, and therefore the *knowledge* of *sin*, of *righteousness*, and *judgment*; and this knowledge becomes more perfect, the more men are filled with the Holy Ghost. Since this is so, they who are pre-eminently filled with His presence are pre-eminently gifted with the discernment of sin and repentance in others, and hence by the Lord's appointment authorized to pronounce pardon of sin and the contrary. The apostles had this in an especial manner, and by the full indwelling of the Spirit were enabled to discern the hearts of men, and to give sentence on that discernment: see Acts v. 1—11; viii. 21; xiii. 9.' The word 'repentance,' which Alford found it necessary to introduce into his argument—'discernment of sin and repentance'—is not in the passage under consideration; and surely to 'let go' sin must mean more than to 'discern sin and pronounce pardon of sin,' and to 'hold sin,' more than 'the contrary.' Alford continues: 'And this gift belongs to the Church in all ages, and especially to those who by legitimate appointment are set to minister in the Church of Christ.' Is it not evident that Alford, instead of arguing from the text alone, is seeking to justify the existing doctrine and practice, with respect to which, however, he boldly adds: 'not by *successive delegation* from the Apostles,—*of which fiction I find in the New Testament no trace*,—but by their mission from Christ, the Bestower of the Spirit for their office, when *orderly and legitimately conferred upon them by the various Churches*. Not however to them exclusively,— though for decency and order it is expedient that the outward and formal declaration should be so: but in proportion as *any disciple* shall have been filled with the Holy Spirit of wisdom, is the inner discernment, the *judgment*, his.' All that chopping of logic and trimming of doctrine would not have been needed, if the solemn words of Jesus had been rightly understood. They contain no hint of any class of men being set apart to pronounce and withhold absolution, but they point out the vast responsibility resting upon disciples, and the influence which their conduct must have upon the world. 'The kingdom of heaven is like unto leaven, which a woman took, and hid in three measures of meal, till it was all leavened.' There can only be a gradual process of ameliorative change in the condition of society, and the disciples of Jesus are, or should be, its pioneers. The salvation of Jesus was never meant to be individual, one here and another there, but social: 'who willeth that all men should be saved.' Our habit is to look upon salvation as a personal concern, and to overlook the grand design of Christ—the establishment of a heavenly kingdom upon earth. The expression 'whose soever sins' alludes to class sins, as distinguished from individual sins; indeed, the use of the plural form throughout is significant. Jesus did not say: If one of you remits the sins of any one, they shall be remitted unto him; if one of you retains them, they are retained. His words have unfortunately been misread in that sense, which has led to the setting up of the confessional. But he spoke to his disciples as a holy community, living in the midst of mankind, and reminded them that the morality of the world would be determined by and fluctuate according to their standard, and would in nothing rise above it: 'whose soever sins ye let go, they are let go unto them; whose soever ye hold fast, they are held fast.' The charge was not restricted to the apostles, for at the interview there were others 'with them,' and all the apostles were not included in it, Thomas being absent: 'But Thomas, one of the twelve, called Didymus (that is, Twin), was not with them when Jesus came.' He must have left the room immediately after the arrival of the two from Emmaus, who had 'found the eleven gathered together.'

On his return, the astounding news of the visit of Jesus was communicated to him. 'The other disciples therefore said unto him, We have seen the Lord.' To one who had not actually seen and handled his risen body, strange questions would naturally arise respecting it. Was it in all points what it had been originally? Were the veins again filled with the blood which had formerly circulated therein, but which had been drained away on the cross? All they could reply was, that the flesh and the bones were there, and the indentations of the nails and the spear; but how it had been possible for him to come unperceived through the closed doors, they could not explain. The manner of his going we are not told: it may have resembled his sudden and inexplicable disappearance at Emmaus. In spite of the number who testified to the facts, their unanimity, and their admitted trustworthiness, Thomas remained sceptical. They had become convinced by sight and touch, and nothing less than the same ocular and tangible evidence would suffice for him. 'But he said unto them, Except I shall see in his hands the print of the nails, and put my finger into the print of the nails, and put my hand into his side, I will not believe.' It must have been explained to him that such a test was possible: that the wounds were somehow healed, yet still open and deep-seated, neither cicatrised scars nor raw punctures, and that they could be probed by the touch.

For a week or more the apostle remained in this frame of mind. Then came another manifestation, which transformed him from a sceptic into an adoring believer. 'And after eight days again his disciples were within, and Thomas with them.' On this occasion also the doors were closed, and, as before, they formed no obstacle to the approach of Jesus, who appeared suddenly, standing among them, and repeating his former greeting. 'Jesus cometh, the doors being shut, and stood in the midst, and said, Peace *be* unto you.' He showed himself acquainted with all that had passed between Thomas and the rest, and without waiting for any application from him, at once invited him to satisfy himself in the way he had desired. 'Then saith he to Thomas, Reach hither thy finger, and see my hands; and reach *hither* thy hand, and put it into my side: and be not faithless but believing.' The Revisers have retained, but have italicised, the second 'hither,' and they have altered 'thrust' to 'put,' the word in the original being the same as before used by Thomas. Here indeed was evidence as irrefragable as it was welcome. No particle of doubt remained in the mind of Thomas, from whose lips there fell instinctively a cry of joyful, reverential recognition. 'Thomas answered and said unto him, My Lord and my God.' The word 'and' has been omitted before 'Thomas,' on the authority of the two oldest MSS. Alford refutes 'the Socinian view that these words, *My Lord and my God,* are *merely* an *exclamation*.' But they have really no connection with the doctrine of the Trinity. Neither of the words 'Lord' or 'God' is restricted to the Supreme Divinity. 'Lord' is equivalent to 'Ruler, and 'God' is equivalent to 'King.' This simple fact has been lost sight of, owing to the deplorable determination of our translators to exclude the word 'Jehovah,' and to supply its place by 'Lord' or 'the Lord.'

'Give ear to my words, O Jehovah,
Hearken unto the voice of my crying, my King and my God.'
' My soul longeth, yea, even fainteth for the courts of Jehovah;
My heart and my flesh cry out unto the living God.'

It is not necessary to multiply examples: these two are sufficient to show the proper sense of the word 'God.' The outcry of Thomas was no mere confession of faith in a dogma, but a declaration of homage and loyalty.

The fact of the bodily resurrection of Jesus being now demonstrated to the satisfaction of Thomas, Jesus reminded him that only good could result to those who believed in it and him without ocular evidence. 'Jesus saith unto him, Because thou hast seen me, thou hast believed: blessed are they that have not seen, and *yet* have believed.' The Revisers, on the authority of the three oldest MSS., have omitted 'Thomas' after 'me.' The introduction of the word 'yet,' which is not in the original, reads as though faith in spite of difficulties in the way of its exercise, is here commended. That is not the case. Young renders: 'Happy those who have not seen, and have believed.' The acceptance of truth as truth, of fact as fact, is necessarily beneficial to him who believes and acts accordingly, albeit he may have had no opportunity of personally investigating the evidence upon which it rests. We believe that the earth is a revolving ball, and that the sun is stationary, and are happy in so believing: for though we may never have mastered or studied the science of astronomy, by its aid and the calculations based upon it our mariners traverse the deep and circle the globe. A comparatively small number of astronomers are our 'chosen witnesses' for the truth of the science, and on their testimony we rely implicitly, much to our advantage. It is even so with respect to the supernatural facts on which our faith in Jesus has been founded. The sceptics and semi-sceptics who start their examination of Christianity on the assumption that none of the recorded miracles of the New Testament can possibly be accepted as true, are of the same class with those who refused to believe in the rotation of the earth and laughed at the notion of antipodes. These facts seemed to them contrary to common sense and to experience; which is precisely the ground of argument taken up by those who impugn the gospel narratives. The spiritual world has its mysteries as well as the natural world, and if those of the latter can be safely accepted on human testimony, surely those of the former can be vouched by similar evidence. The disbelief of a truth may be as hurtful as the belief of an error.

The fourth evangelist records only the words which Jesus spoke to Thomas. Doubtless more took place at this interview, to which Mark's gospel seems to refer. We there read: 'And afterward he was manifested unto the eleven themselves as they sat at meat.' 'The eleven' are said to have been present, whereas on the former occasion one apostle was absent and others were with them; now they were reclining at the table and partaking of a meal, so that this cannot have been the occasion when Jesus enquired, 'Have ye here anything to eat?' Jesus not only alluded to the advantage of a ready faith, but also reproved its absence in the apostles generally: 'and he upbraided them with their unbelief and hardness of heart, because they believed not them which had seen him after he was risen.' Alford and Young omit the words 'them with' after 'upbraided:' the reproach was directed against their state of mind and heart. Jesus did not regard with equanimity that scepticism from which not one of the apostles had been free. He had already described them as 'foolish men and slow of heart to believe.' Imagine, if one can, a designer of one of the marvellous inventions of our day,—the telegraph, the telephone, the phonograph,—to encounter the same incredulity, so that results the most momentous should be disbelieved, albeit vouched for by persons of known credit, simply on the ground that their accounts were unprecedented and too astounding for credence. Would not the master-mind which had brought the wonder to pass, be moved to a similar impatience of human ignorance and incredulity? Our forefathers would have laughed to scorn any one who should have foretold to them those scientific discoveries which we have come to regard as everyday matters of course. The eastern potentate could not believe the European traveller who told him that elsewhere, every winter, water became solid and strong enough to bear the crossing of an army. We are in the same state of crass ignorance with respect to the things of the world to come and its to us invisible inhabitants, with their unearthly attributes, and we evince, not judgment, but want of judgment, not wisdom but folly, not reasonable caution but blind prejudice, if we dismiss as fictitious, impossible, unworthy of credit, those solemnly attested facts called miraculous which have come down to us stamped with the unreserved belief of those who lived when the recorded events took place. Human testimony does not become suddenly and utterly unreliable, whenever it deals with things outside the range of common experience. Whoever begins the investigation of the gospel histories by ignoring it altogether—when he chooses—and accepting it, wholly or partially—when he chooses—makes the greatest demand upon our credulity when he asks us to follow his leading.

20 John 30 The fourth evangelist continues : ' Many other signs therefore did Jesus in the presence of the disciples, which are not written in this book.' Before ' disciples ' ' his ' has been replaced by ' the,' according to the Vatican and Alexandrine MS. Alford's note is as follows : ' *Yea, and,*—or *Moreover :* meaning. "This book must not be supposed to be a complete account." *Signs :* not, as many interpret the word, "proofs of his resurrection," but, as ch. xii. 37 and elsewhere in this Gospel, *miracles*, in the most general sense—these after the Resurrection included : for St. John is here reviewing his whole narrative, *this book.*'

As the incredibility and impossibility of 'miracles' is generally taken for granted by Rationalists, it is worth while to gain a clear notion of what is the proper meaning of the term. The word invariably used by the fourth evangelist is *sēmeion*, which properly signifies ' sign ' or ' token,' including a ' flag ' or ' ensign ' and ' the device upon a shield or seal.' Our first translators rendered the word sometimes by ' sign ' and sometimes by ' miracle,' but the Revisers throughout the New Testament have either altered ' miracle ' to ' sign ' in the text, or noted the proper sense in the margin. The word *dunamis*, which signifies ' strength, might, power, ability,' is also rendered as ' miracle ' in the Authorised Version in the following passages : 9 Mark 39, 2 Acts 22, 8 Acts 13, 19 Acts 11, 12 i. Cor. 10, 28, 29, 3 Gal. 5, 2 Heb. 4 ; but the Revisers have in every instance made a similar rectification, either rendering the word ' power ' or noting that as its proper meaning. So the word ' miracle ' is now banished, as it should be, from the New Testament, and any dispute upon the possibility of one must henceforth be as to whether a ' sign ' can have been given and a ' power ' exercised. There is a vast difference between regarding the mighty works of Jesus and his apostles as effects without a cause, breaches of the great natural laws which rule the universe, and regarding them as the result of new powers vouchsafed to men, as signs and firstfruits of a new spirit capable of influencing both mind and matter. ' Miracle ' is synonymous with ' marvel ' or ' wonder,' which is represented by the Greek word *teras*. We find the three words together 2 Acts 22 in the passage : ' By powers (*dunamesin*) and wonders (*terasin*) and signs (*sēmeiois*), which God did by him in the midst of you.' God granted to Jesus—what Jesus sought to bestow upon his disciples generally and did bestow upon such as could receive the gift— marvellous powers which would be signs of his influence. The fourth evangelist recorded only seven of the signs performed by Jesus : the transmutation of water into wine, the healing of a nobleman's son, of an impotent man at Bethesda, and of a blind man, the feeding of the multitude, the walking on the sea, and the raising of Lazarus. These few were selected out of a multitude, as being 20 John 31 sufficient for the object the writer had in view : ' but these are written, that ye may believe that Jesus is the Christ, the Son of God ; and that believing ye may have life in his name.' The expression, ' the Christ, the Son of God,' is an indication that the terms are synonymous. The word *Christos*, the Anointed One, from the Greek *chriō*, to anoint, is a translation of the Hebrew *Messiah*: 'We have found the Messiah (which is, being interpreted, Christ).' 1 John 41 The three titles, Messiah, Christ, Son of God, are synonymous and interchangeable, and therefore the latter cannot properly be held to denote Divinity in the sense of the Trinitarian creed.

What is the meaning of the sentence: 'and that believing ye may have life in his name'? It cannot signify, except in a metaphorical sense, a resurrection from death to life: for the persons spoken of are living, otherwise they would not be 'believing.' The act of faith changes the aim, the current, the scope and character of the life.* The words of Paul are clearly to that effect: 'that *life* which 2 Gal. 20 I now live in the flesh I live in faith, *the faith* which is in the Son of God.' That was no mere figure of speech, but the vivid description of a reality; and this experience of the apostle appertains equally to all believers. To live 'in the name' of Christ, is to live by his will and precepts, under his guidance and protection. 'He that 6 John 47 believeth hath eternal life': it is not 'shall have,' but 'hath'; the life of faith is holy, sinless, freed from whatever tends to prematurely shorten it. The word which is here rendered 'everlasting' in the Authorised Version, 'eternal' by the Revisers, and 'age-during' by Young, is *aiōnios* from *aiōn*, which is thus defined: 1, a space or period of time, a lifetime, life. 2, *of longer periods*, an age, generation, period. 3, an infinitely long space of time, eternity; this last meaning is quite subsidiary, and should not be put foremost, especially as it is succeeded by the following definition: II. one's age or time of life. The word *aiōn* is from *aiō*: to breathe; to breathe out, expire: it cannot be separated from the idea of a terminable existence. In the Revised Version the word *aiōnios* is always rendered 'eternal,' but by Young 'age-during,' which is far preferable. In the Authorised Version the word *aiōn* is rendered in various ways: ages, course, eternal, ever, evermore, never, world, world began, beginning of the world, while the world standeth, world without end. The Revisers have done much towards introducing order into that chaos, by frequently inserting the proper translation of the Greek in the margin; Young has performed a still greater service by his literal renderings, the absence of which has been the cause of much error and perplexity.

The deliberate reticence of the fourth evangelist is remarkable and significant. Out of the multitude of the mighty works of Jesus seven only were chosen, but they are overwhelmingly convincing as signs of superhuman powers. At his will the water turned to wine; he healed, first by a word, spoken at a distance, then a man who had been paralysed nearly forty years, then a man blind from birth; the substance of bread and of fish, on merely passing through his hands, gained bulk enormously, his touch and volition doing instantaneously the work of increase which we look for only through the gradual process of growth—by air, moisture, sunlight and natural development; he walked on the sea as though it had been solid earth; he called a departed spirit back to its body, and the body out of the tomb. These things are told that we may believe in Jesus as the Messiah,

---

* It has been asked: 'Does *zōē* ever in John mean behaviour?' Not by itself: but 'life *in his name*' is taken to mean—life in his cause, under his rule and guidance.

and so believing may live according to his will and precepts. Yet the bulk of John's gospel, although made up chiefly of the sayings of Jesus, does not record his practical directions: the sermon on the mount, his instructions to disciples, and all the parables, touching on human duties and illustrating the nature of the kingdom of God—these things are omitted, and in place of them we find solemn declarations of the pre-existence of Jesus and of his incomparably supreme and incomprehensible nature, arguments with the Jews and others, and discourses with his disciples, all displaying the highest degree of self-assertiveness and claiming for himself power and influence alike in earth and heaven, and stretching out into eternity. 'These are written, that ye may believe that Jesus is the Christ, the Son of God; and that believing ye may have life in his name.' And yet the evangelist does not describe what sort of life Jesus would have his disciples lead, nor what the nature of the change expected in the lives of believers generally. Yet in this absolute indifference and carelessness about any provision for written directions, the apostle did but resemble his Master. There is not a hint anywhere of the slightest anxiety on the part of Jesus to perpetuate his doctrine by written documents; the fragments of his teaching which have come down to us are replete with wisdom, truth, grace, spirituality, and we learn from them clearly what commandments he laid upon his disciples. But to his words, as sayings merely, he attached no importance: they might be preserved, as they have been, and yet the spirit of them might be lost, as alas!

_{6 John 63} it has been. 'The words (sayings—Young—*rhema* not *logos*) that I have spoken unto you are spirit, and are life:' only as their spirit became embodied in the lives of men, could they be of any benefit. Jesus looked to perpetuate his doctrine, not through books and catechisms and dissertations, but through the lives of his disciples.

_{3 ii. Cor. 3} They must be epistles of Christ, 'written not with ink, but with the Spirit of the living God; not in tables of stone, but in tables *that are* hearts of flesh.' The maxims and duties which Jesus imposed upon his disciples were never intended by him for universal adoption, much less to be professed by all alike, and then not carried out by any. That is the position into which Christendom has drifted. The professed ministers of Christ are no more his 'disciples,' in the true and full sense of the term, than are the rest of men who have been baptised as Christians. There exists no body of men pledged to a literal obedience to all the precepts of Jesus, and who, by carrying them out in their integrity, can be recognised as his disciples, a community within the community, in the world yet not of the world, Christ's city set on a hill which cannot be hid, his salt of which every man may take a little, his leaven ever working throughout the mass until the whole be leavened. Failing to realise that high ideal, it has come to be taken for granted that the peculiar directions given by Jesus to his disciples are actually impracticable: all men say so by their lives, though few indeed venture to put their belief into words, as did the late Dr. Magee, Bishop of Peterborough (made Archbishop of York in 1891)—to his honour be it recorded. Speaking at the Diocesan Conference at Leicester, his words are reported as follows: 'Christianity, however, made no claim to rearrange the economic relations of men in the State and in society, and he hoped he would be understood when he said plainly that it

was his firm belief that any Christian State carrying out in all its relations the Sermon on the Mount could not exist for a week. It was perfectly clear that a State could not continue to exist upon what were commonly called Christian principles, and it was a mistake to attempt to turn Christ's kingdom into one of this world. To introduce the principles of Christianity into the laws of the State would lead to absolute intolerance. The law of Christianity was self-sacrifice, impelled by love; the principle of the State was justice, impelled by force.'* Bold words, and wise. It is a step in advance when Christ's precepts are looked upon at all from a practical point of view. By all means let the truth be recognised, that they are impracticable in statecraft, and unsuited to any form of human government. That may lead to the further consideration, that they are equally unsuited for adoption by individuals generally, and were never meant to be acted upon except by willing disciples, who must first count the cost, resolve to give up all things for Christ's sake, and ever thereafter be able to say, 'as he is, so are we in this world,'— 4 I. John 17 divorced from wealth, laying up treasure in heaven only, pledged to patient sufferance and absolute non-resistance, let come what come may. That was the broad line of demarcation drawn by Jesus between 'his own which were in the world' and other men. True, 13 John 1 a State, on such principles of action, 'could not exist for a week,' could not exist at all; true, a solitary individual in some places might not exist a day,—Jesus was not suffered longer than three years,—but nevertheless the apostles and their co-disciples did continue to exist, and if discipleship were now to become what it was then, the flock of Christ, however little, would live, and grow, and spread, until the world, taught and animated by example and not merely by barren precepts regarded as impracticable, would gradually assimilate the gospel to itself and itself to the gospel, and move fast onward to that foretold day when it will be proclaimed: 'The kingdom of the 11 Rev. 15 world, is become *the kingdom* of our Lord, and of his Christ: and he shall reign unto the ages of the ages.'

The various accounts of the appearances of Jesus after his resurrection are condensed, fragmentary, disjointed, and all that can be done is to collate and compare them carefully. With respect to the manifestation which took place on the evening of the resurrection day, Luke supplies additional particulars, telling us what Jesus said, and in what way the interview was terminated. 'And he said unto them, 24 Luke 44 These are my words which I spake unto you, while I was yet with you, how that all things must needs be fulfilled, which are written in the law of Moses, and the prophets, and the psalms, concerning me.' 'The' has been altered to 'my' before 'words,' on the authority of the Vatican and Alexandrine MSS. Jesus proceeded so to explain the scriptures as to make their import clear to them. 'Then opened ,, 45 he their mind, that they might understand the scriptures.' The Old Testament, from Moses to Malachi, was seen, when interpreted by him, to be full of references, forecasts, anticipations, prophecies of the Messiah, his death, his resurrection, and the salvation which through him would be proclaimed to the ends of the earth: 'and he ,, 46, 47

* *Pall Mall Gazette*, 26 October, 1889.

said unto them, Thus it is written, that the Christ should suffer, and rise again from the dead the third day; and that repentance and remission of sins should be preached in his name unto all the nations, beginning from Jerusalem.' After 'written' the words 'and thus it behoved' are omitted, on the authority of the two oldest MSS. The Revisers note that between 'repentance . . remission' some ancient authorities read *unto* instead of 'and.' Tischendorf renders. 'repentance for remission.' as being the reading of the two oldest MSS., but *eis*, which there takes the place of *kai*, is properly *unto* or *to*. Whether the word be 'and' or 'to,' it binds repentance and remission together, so that the latter cannot exist apart from the former. The Greek of 'repentance' is *metanoia*, which Dr. Young renders in every instance except one by 'reformation.' The Lexicon definition is 'after-thought; change of mind on reflection, repentance.' The word *aphesis*, remission, as has been already shown, signifies 'a letting go, setting free.' The word *hamartia*, 'sin,' is defined as 'a failure, error, sin.' As Gentiles,—'all the nations,'—are here alluded to, it is evident that 'sins' here must not be understood in a theological sense, as transgressions of the laws given by God to Israel, but as failures or errors in conduct. 'Repentance to remission of sins' is equivalent to 'change of mind to the letting go of errors and faults,' change of heart and purpose leading on to amendment of life. There is no ground for attributing the word 'repentance' to man and the word 'remission' to God, as though Jesus had said, The nations will repent and God will forgive them. Repentance leads to an actual, not merely forensic remission of sins. 'Repentance' is a new heart, and 'remission' is a new life. That is the salvation of Jesus, and it was not meant to be simply individual and personal, but national, preached 'unto all the nations, beginning from Jerusalem.' The gospel which the disciples were to proclaim, was 'the gospel of the kingdom:' their task was the establishment of a new community in the midst of the world, which only disciples of Jesus, animated by his spirit and obedient to his peculiar precepts, could hope to found, for it must be based on his principles of abnegation of the world and its wealth, absolute non-resistance to evil, and patient sufferance in the effort to overcome evil with good. Round such men a church, an assembly of believers would gather: 'Ye are witnesses of these things.' The word 'and' before 'ye' having been omitted, on the authority of the two oldest MSS., the Revisers note that the punctuation is open to question: the passage may be read, 'beginning from Jerusalem, ye are witnesses.' 'Of these things' includes the repentance and remission of sins, as well as the death and resurrection of Christ. For that great work,—the conversion and regeneration of humanity, special gifts were needed, promised, and would be bestowed. 'And behold, I send forth the promise of my Father upon you.' Until they felt themselves endowed with supernatural powers, let them not commence their mission: 'but tarry ye in the city, until ye be clothed with power from on high.' After 'city' the words 'of Jerusalem' are omitted, on the authority of the two oldest MSS. Alford argues that 'after the command given in this verse 49, the disciples would not have gone away into Galilee:' but the word *kathizō*, which is here rendered 'tarry,' is in 45 instances out of the 47 in which it occurs translated by 'sit' or 'sit down.' The other exception is in the passage: 'And he dwelt (continued—A. V.) *there* is Acts 11 a year and six months,' from which no one would infer that the person spoken of could not have been absent elsewhere for a few days during that period. Luke's narrative at this point is obviously consecutive, and he continues as follows: 'And he led them out until 24 Luke 50 *they were* over against Bethany:' the disciples not only talked but walked with Jesus after his resurrection; yet not for long, for on approaching Bethany he made a solemn gesture of farewell and benediction: 'and he lifted up his hands, and blessed them.' In ,, 50 that attitude, and with his friendly voice yet sounding in their ears, he separated himself from them, the mode of his departure being as sudden and inexplicable as his entrance had been. 'And it came to ,, 51 pass, while he blessed them, he parted from them.' There, in some of the oldest authorities, the sentence ends, so that the added words, 'and was carried up into heaven,' are open to question. In the Sinaitic, which is the oldest MS., they were inserted by a later hand. If they formed part of the original narrative, they may have been omitted lest this ascension into heaven should be confounded with that elsewhere recorded; if they were subsequently introduced, it may have been by a transcriber who supposed that this account of Luke combines what happened on the first day of the resurrection with what took place subsequently. That was Alford's view. He says: 'The following discourse apparently contains a summary of many things said during the last forty days before the ascension; they cannot have been said *on this evening:*' but the only basis on which he rests that idea is the command 'tarry ye in the city,' which does not warrant the inference of Alford. The narrative proceeds: 'And they worshipped him, and returned to Jerusalem with great ,, 52 joy.' Alford considers this as 'a solemn act of worship, now paid to him as exalted to God's right hand.' That is on the assumption, apparently erroneous, that this was the final ascension of Jesus. Young renders: 'And they, having bowed before him . . .' With bent heads and knees they responded to his parting salutation. The Revisers note: 'Some ancient authorities omit *worshipped him, and.*' Tischendorf does so, although he records no such omission in either of the three oldest MSS. The souls of the disciples overflowed with joy, and, observing the injunction to reside in Jerusalem, they spent most of their time in the temple: 'and were continually in the ,, 53 temple, blessing God.' The words 'praising and' have been omitted, on the authority of the two oldest MSS., and the word 'Amen' on that of the Sinaitic MS.

Here Luke's gospel ends. In it he carried forward the history no further than the events of the first day of the resurrection. But Jesus had said to the women: 'Go tell my brethren that they depart 28 Mat. 10 into Galilee, and there shall they see me.' Until they were brought to believe what the women told them, they may not even have thought of going, but when Jesus had appeared to them they could not suppose that his command about establishing themselves in Jerusalem was meant to override his previous injunction, and to forbid that temporary absence which it necessitated. On the contrary, Matthew states that they went to Galilee, Jesus having previously fixed the place where he would meet them there. 'But ,, 16 the eleven disciples went into Galilee, unto the mountain where Jesus had appointed them.'

The fourth evangelist supplies, in careful and loving detail, an account of one manifestation which Jesus made of himself in Galilee, not to all the disciples but to seven of them who happened to be together. 'After these things Jesus manifested himself again to the disciples at the sea of Tiberias.' The way in which he revealed himself was so peculiar and striking as to call for an exact description: 'and he manifested *himself* on this wise.' The apostles, or most of them, had travelled to Galilee as commanded, there expecting the promised vision of Jesus. They had not yet entered upon the work of their appointed ministry, and being in the neighbourhood of their home and former occupations, they naturally sought to fill up that gap in their time which followed upon the absence of their Master and the cessation of their attendance upon him. Peter, as usual in everything, took the lead in proposing to return for the time being to their old employment. 'There were together Simon Peter and Thomas called Didymus (that is, Twin), and Nathanael of Cana in Galilee, and the *sons* of Zebedee, and two other of his disciples. Simon Peter saith unto them, I go a fishing.' The six others volunteered to accompany him. 'They say unto him, We also come with thee.' So they entered the ship and set about their task. 'They went forth, and entered into the boat.' The word 'immediately' is omitted, on the authority of the two oldest MSS. On eleven chosen men the propagation of the gospel and the salvation of mankind now depended. As yet they were not endowed with power from on high for the accomplishment of their office, and here are seven of them engaged in their old occupation! Surely their crucified and risen Lord and Master must be watching them, waiting to pour out upon them at the fitting moment the foretold holy Spirit, and careful meantime to keep them from falling back into their original state of earthly-mindedness and unspirituality. The night was spent in fruitless toil: 'and that night they took nothing.' And at daybreak Jesus himself was standing on the lonely shore, seen by them, but not recognised. 'But when day was now breaking, Jesus stood on the beach: howbeit the disciples knew not that it was Jesus.' He called to them, enquiring whether they were supplied with food. 'Jesus therefore saith unto them, Children, have ye aught to eat?' The Greek diminutive is used—'little children,' the term which Jesus had bestowed upon his disciples as indicative of that state of innocent helplessness and dependence to which he had called them. On receiving their reply in the negative, he told them that if they changed the position of the net, they would find fish. 'They answered him, No. And he said unto them, Cast the net on the right side of the boat, and ye shall find.' His object seems to have been to make them realise their own impotence, and to demonstrate his power to help them. They threw out the net according to his suggestion, and found it so heavily laden that they could not pull it up. 'They cast therefore, and now they were not able to draw it for the multitude of fishes.' That miraculous draught recalled a previous similar manifestation of the power of Jesus, and was enough by itself to identify him. 'That disciple therefore whom Jesus loved saith unto Peter, It is the Lord.' Peter, impetuous as ever, must needs get at once to land: instantly he bound his outer garment about his body and threw himself into the sea, to swim or wade ashore. 'So when Simon Peter heard that it was the Lord, he girt his coat about him (for he was naked), and cast himself into the sea.' The Authorised Version has 'fisher's coat': the word in the original is *ependutēs*, which is defined as 'a tunic worn over another,' from *ependunō*, 'to put on over.' The distance was about a hundred yards, and the other disciples attached the overladen net to a small boat and towed it ashore. 'But the other disciples came in the little boat (for they were not far from the land, but about two hundred cubits off) dragging the net *full* of fishes.' On landing, they perceived that a meal had been prepared for them: a fire was burning, a fish was frying on it, and there was a loaf. 'So when they got out upon the land, they see a fire of coals (Gr. charcoal) there, and fish (or, a fish) laid thereon, and bread (or, a loaf).' It was all weird, mysterious. Jesus addressed them, bidding them bring some of the fish they had just caught. 'Jesus saith unto them, Bring of the fish which ye have now taken.' Peter went to the boat and hauled in the net, the fish were taken out, and being large were counted. 'Simon Peter therefore went up (or, aboard), and drew the net to land, full of great fishes, a hundred and fifty and three.' How the meshes could have borne the strain, was another marvel in the midst of marvels: 'and for all there were so many, the net was not rent.' From first to last Jesus was demonstrating to them his possession and exercise on their behalf, of supernatural, inexplicable powers. He now invited the disciples to partake of the meal which had been provided for them. 'Jesus saith unto them, Come *and* break your fast.' With what strange feelings must they have sat down to that welcome morning meal! Not one of them ventured to question the personality of their host, all being fully convinced that he was none other than Jesus himself. 'And none of the disciples durst enquire of him, Who art thou? knowing that it was the Lord.' Chrysostom thus realised the scene: 'They no longer had their former confidence... but in silence and much fear and reverence they sat down, looking on Him... seeing His form changed and very wonderful, they were much amazed, and wanted to ask him respecting it, but their fear, and their knowledge that it was no other than He himself, hindered them.' Jesus now approached, broke the bread and handed it to them, and apportioned the fish between them. 'Jesus cometh, and taketh the bread (or, loaf) and giveth them, and the fish likewise.' The evangelist here observes in passing: 'This is now the third time that Jesus was manifested to the disciples, after that he was risen from the dead.' 'His' has been altered to 'the' before disciples, on the authority of the three oldest MSS. This statement is important, serving as a reliable clue in our attempts to piece together the few historical records relating to the forty days which followed the resurrection of Jesus. He appeared to his disciples on the evening of that day, again after eight days, and next in Galilee to these seven.

When the meal was over, Jesus put a question to Peter. 'So when they had broken their fast, Jesus saith to Simon Peter, Simon *son* of John (Gr. Joanes), lovest thou me more than these?' Alford explains: 'More than these thy fellow-disciples,' and notes: 'The word *these* has been strangely enough understood (Whitby, and others) of the *fish*, or the employment and furniture of a fisherman.' That idea involves the assumption that Jesus in speaking pointed to the fish, or to the fish, boats and appendages: an inference we are scarcely justified in drawing. The supposition arose out of the fact that Jesus ordered some of the fish to be brought, although fish was already on the fire, and nothing is said of more being required or used; but it is possible, and would be very natural, that the command was understood to mean that a further supply, sufficient for the seven who sat down, should be placed upon the fire. The enquiry, Do you love me more than these fishes? meaning, Do you love me more than you love these fishes? would have been strained and strange, nor—supposing it to have been intended,—would it have been necessary to bring some of the fish to the spot: the mere pointing of the hand to the outcome of the bulging net, and the question, Do you love more than those? would have sufficed. Dismissing that interpretation as far-fetched and untenable, our knowledge of the circumstances sufficiently elucidates the question. Peter had always placed himself in the forefront of the apostles, crying up his own steadfastness and devotion as superior to theirs. [26 Mat. 31] When Jesus said: 'All ye shall be offended in me this night,' [„ 33] Peter proudly claimed exemption: 'If all shall be offended in thee, I will never be offended.' The boast had been falsified, the boaster having thrice denied his Master. Yet now he is again making himself as prominent as ever: he must needs jump into the sea in order to be first on shore, and when some of the fresh-caught fish are called for, it is Peter who hastens to draw the net to land. Jesus watched his actions and read his mind, and by this sudden, unexpected, disconcerting question, compelled him to contrast his promises with his performances, and to ask himself whether, comparing himself with his fellow disciples, his love in any respect exceeded theirs. Peter would not, could not face that issue. He would fain drop all comparison of himself with others, and simply [21 John 15] appeal to Jesus as to the sincerity of his own affection. 'He saith unto him, Yea, Lord, thou knowest that I love thee.' That, 'yea, Lord,' must have meant acquiescence in the view of his conduct which Jesus thus impressed upon him: Whether more or less than these, I say not, know not; but thou knowest my heart and the depth of its love to thee. The Revisers note: '*Love* in these places represents two different Greek words.' Young renders: 'Thou knowest that I dearly love thee.' Alford explains: 'We may note that two Greek words, both signifying *to love*, are used in this conversation. The one (*agapain*) is applied to the ordinary love which men have to one another, or to the reverential love which is borne towards God and man by the child of God; the other (*philein*) to the closer love of a man for his own friend or his dearest relatives. The *former* word is used in ch. xi. 5, where it is said "Jesus *loved* Martha and her sister, and Lazarus:" the *latter* by the Jews in in ch. xi. 37, when judging by the tears of Jesus for Lazarus, they exclaimed, "See how he *loved* him" . . . Peter in his two answers uses a less exalted word, and one implying a consciousness of his own weakness, but a persuasion and deep feeling of personal love.' On [„ 15] the reply of Peter, Jesus based a charge. 'He saith unto him, Feed my lambs.' The word used (*arnion*) is the diminutive of *arnos*, and is defined as 'a young lamb, lambkin.' The metaphor chosen carried with it a call to prompt action, lest the innocent and helpless 'little ones' of Christ should suffer, stray, perish, for lack of oversight and care. Peter should take the lead in looking after them, and not be saying, 'I go a fishing:' he must turn shepherd instead of fisherman. Jesus deemed it necessary to repeat and insist. 'He saith to him again a second time, Simon, son of John (Gr. Joanes), lovest thou me?' The same question was met with the same answer. 'He saith unto him, Yea, Lord; thou knowest that I love thee.' Again the direction, slightly varied in terms: 'He saith unto him, Tend my sheep.' The word rendered 'tend' is *poimainō*, from *poimēn*, a shepherd, and the translation in the 'Englishman's Greek New Testament' is, 'shepherd my sheep:' this was a permanent call to that pastoral office. Here, and in the next verse, Tischendorf renders 'little sheep;' Alford explains: 'The word *sheep* is the diminutive, expressive of affection.' Christ's flock are all and always 'little ones' in his eyes, and their true shepherds carry but the crook to guide them, wielding no weapon of offence or defence, yet ready always to give their lives for the sheep. To impress the charge the more deeply on the apostle's mind, Jesus once more repeats his question. 'He saith unto him the third time, Simon, son of John (Gr. Joanes), lovest thou me?' Here Jesus uses instead of *agapas* the word *phileis*, which had been adopted by Peter. The word *phileō* signifies not only 'to love,' but 'to show signs of love, especially to kiss.' It is thus rendered in the passage: 'Whomsoever I shall kiss, that is he.' In the 24 instances in which it occurs, it either denotes a preference, or is coupled with an action, as in the passage: 'They love to stand and pray in the synagogues and in the corners of the streets.' Peter, oblivious of his former threefold denial, was vexed by the reiteration of the question thrice. 'Peter was grieved because he said unto him the third time, Lovest thou me?' His reply was unhesitating: 'And he said unto him, Lord, thou knowest all things; thou knowest (or, perceivest) that I love thee.' Omniscience or supernatural knowledge is not intended by the words, 'Thou knowest all things:' the verb is *eideō*, which is defined: to see, to be seen, to know. Here are a few examples out of a multitude: 'When Herod *saw* Jesus he was exceeding glad: for he was of a long time desirous *to see* him ... and he hoped to *see* some miracle done by him.' '*Seeing* the multitudes, he went up into the mountain.' 'Thou *knowest* the commandments.' 'Master, we *know* that thou art true.' Peter simply referred to the fact that Jesus was well acquainted with his life and conduct, his long-continued adherence as well as his declension and repentance on the night of the betrayal, and knowing all these things must needs be persuaded of his affection: the verb now is not *eideō* but *ginōskō*, which is thus defined: to perceive, gain knowledge of, mark, to examine, to form an opinion. The love which Peter possessed and Jesus recognised must take this practical form. 'Jesus saith unto him, Feed my sheep.' In no other way could it be demonstrated, for no other purpose had it been evoked. Peter must take up this task of shepherding, with its attendant toil and risk. Jesus would have him do so under the consciousness that he would be called upon as a good shepherd to give his life for the sheep. Now, in the vigour of maturity, he was full of energy, making light of obstacles standing in the way of his purpose. 'Verily, verily, I say unto thee, When thou wast young, thou girdest thyself and walkedst whither thou wouldest.' By Tischendorf, Young and the 'Englishman's Greek New Testament' the word 'young' is rendered 'younger.' The time would come when impetuous strength must give place to passive suffering; just now he had girded himself, swimming through the waves and clambering over the shore to come to Jesus: in old age he would have to rejoin his Lord in a far different way; he would stretch forth his hands to be bound by another, and then be carried to a place not of his own choosing: 'but when thou shalt be old, thou shalt stretch forth thy hands, and another shall gird thee, and carry thee whither thou wouldest not.' The evangelist regarded this as a prophecy of the kind of martyrdom which the apostle would finally undergo. 'Now this he spake, signifying by what manner of death he should glorify God.' Alford notes: 'Thou shalt stretch forth thy hands—but not as just now in swimming; in a more painful manner, on the transverse beam of the cross; and another—the executioner—shall gird thee,—with the cords binding to the cross. Such is the traditional account of the death of Peter.' Having uttered this solemn warning, Jesus called upon the apostle to nerve himself for his Master's work and cross. 'And when he had spoken this, he saith unto him, Follow me.'

The conversation took place while Jesus was walking with Peter, for we are told that at its close Peter turned round and saw that one of his fellow disciples was following, probably foremost among the rest. 'Peter turning about, seeth the disciple whom Jesus loved following, which also leaned back on his breast at the supper, and said, Lord, who is he that betrayeth thee?' The word 'then' (*de*) before 'Peter,' has been omitted on the authority of the Vatican and Alexandrine MSS. The Sinaitic MS. omits the word 'following.' There had always been a connection between Peter and John, who had been partners in fishing when Jesus called them to discipleship. Latterly the intimacy had been very close, as appears from the fact that they went together to the high priest's palace, and ran together to the tomb. It was natural that Peter should, on learning his own future destiny, feel a desire to know whether his chosen companion was appointed to undergo a similar trial. 'Peter therefore seeing him saith to Jesus, Lord, and what shall this man do?' The word 'do' is needlessly introduced, and makes the enquiry signify, What shall be this man's course of action? The Revisers note that the Greek is simply, 'and this man, what?' Young renders: 'but what of this one?' Alford notes: 'literally, This man, what? *i.e.* how shall this man fare?' Jesus checked this spirit of curiosity. The ultimate destiny of another man could have no practical lesson for Peter. If the career of the beloved disciple should be lengthened out till Jesus came to take him hence, what concern was that of Peter's? 'Jesus saith unto him, If I will that he tarry till I come, what *is that* to thee?' Happen what might to others, upon Peter was laid the duty of taking up his cross and suffering as his Lord had done: 'follow thou me.' How unwise the question, was shown by the misconstruction of the answer. 'This saying therefore went forth among the brethren, that that disciple should not die; yet Jesus said not unto him, that he should not die; but, If I will that he tarry till I come, what is that to thee?' Instead of 'should not die,' Young renders 'doth not die,' and Tischendorf, 'is not to die.' The present tense indicates that this was written while the person spoken of was still living. He attempts no explanation of the saying of Jesus, but merely repudiates the popular construction which had been attached thereto. And now at the close of his narrative, the author reveals his personality, which he had all along seen fit to keep in the background. The evangelist himself was the individual referred to, the disciple whom Jesus loved, who had leaned back on his breast at the last supper, had stood beside the cross of Jesus, and to whom the care of his mother had been committed. 'This is the disciple which beareth witness of these things, and wrote these things.' No one could have had better opportunities of making a faithful record. His narrative was compiled under a solemn sense of responsibility: 'which beareth witness of these things.' The change of tense from the present to the past deserves consideration: 'which beareth witness' is followed, not by 'and writes,' but by 'and wrote:' the written records had been made previously, probably at the time the events happened and the discourses were delivered. Had that not been the case, we should not expect to find, or be able to rely upon, the long and exact accounts of the discourses of Jesus with which this fourth gospel abounds. Alford notes: 'The words *these things* certainly refer to the whole Gospel, not merely to the Appendix (chapter xxi.), and are quite in St. John's style: see xii. 41; xx. 31.' The verse ends with the words: 'and we know that his witness is true.' Some have taken this to indicate that,—this gospel having presumably been compiled by other persons from information supplied by John,—they now attest their own conviction of the truthfulness of the accounts he had supplied to them. But there is nothing in this form of expression to justify such a supposition; on the contrary, the phrase is one which is peculiar to this apostle, whose habit it was to identify himself in this way with those to whom he wrote. In his epistles we find the very same words: 'We know that, if he shall be manifested, we shall be like him.' 'We know that we have passed out of death into life.' 'We know that we have the petitions which we have asked of him.' 'We know that whosoever is begotten of God sinneth not.' 'We know that we are of God.' 'We know that the Son of God is come.' 'We also bear witness; and thou knowest that our witness is true.' Although Alford considers the last chapter of John's gospel to be an appendix, 'added by him, some years probably after the completion of the Gospel,' he asserts: 'In every part of it, his hand is plain and unmistakeable: in every part of it, his character and spirit is manifested in a way which none but the most biassed can fail to recognize ... It certainly contains several words and constructions not met with elsewhere in John: but, on the other hand, the whole cast of it is his;—the coupling particles are his:—the train of thought, and manner of narration. The last two verses, from their contents, we might expect to have more of the epistolary form; and accordingly we find them singularly in style resembling the Epistles of John.'

The evangelist would have his narrative viewed as a record designedly restricted to a few examples of the doings of Jesus: an account of them all, one after another, would have been, in his opinion, beyond the world's capacity of reception. 'And there are also many other things which Jesus did, the which if they should be written every one, I suppose that even the world itself would not contain the books that should be written.' Alford terms that 'a popular hyperbole.' But is it clear that the intention of the apostle was to dismiss the idea in that fashion, as though it were a task too huge for human hands to undertake? In the first place, the closing words, 'that should be written,' do not correctly represent the original word, which is simply 'written.' What the apostle says is this: that if the books 'should be written,' the world would not contain the books when written. That gives a different turn to the sentence. Here is Dr. Young's rendering, which aims at literality: 'which, if they may be written one by one, not even the world itself I think to have place for the books written.' The verb rendered 'contain,' or 'have place,' is *chōreō*, which occurs 9 times in the New Testament. In two instances it denotes merely capacity in relation to space: 'so that there was no longer room.' 'Containing two or three firkins.' The same word is used in the passage: 'passeth (is received —Young) into the belly.' In the 6 remaining passages it denotes *a voluntary act of reception*. 'All men cannot receive this saying.' 'He that is able to receive it, let him receive it.' 'My word hath no place in you.' 'Make room for us.' 'That all should come (go forward— Young) to repentance.' The apostle is speaking of 'the world itself,' not hyperbolically of its libraries and bookshelves; and he expresses the opinion that the world itself, as distinguished from the body of believers who were not of the world, would not *receive*, *have place*, or *make room* for such marvellous, unprecedented facts. The amplest consecutive records would not suffice to gain credence with the world. This last verse was found inserted by a later hand in the oldest MS. The closing word, 'Amen,' has been omitted, as in the Vatican and Alexandrine MSS.

The manifestation of Jesus in Galilee described by John, was on another occasion than that alluded to by Matthew, the former being on the sea shore and the latter on a mountain. Matthew says: 'But the eleven disciples went into Galilee, unto the mountain where Jesus had appointed them. And when they saw him, they worshipped *him*.' The second 'him' is omitted in the two oldest MSS., but the Revisers have only italicised it. It is added: 'but some doubted'; Young renders: 'they bowed to him, even those who doubted.' It does not follow from Matthew's saying that 'the eleven disciples went into Galilee,' that they only were present on the occasion. They had gone with the definite expectation of seeing Jesus on a certain mountain designated by him: secrecy was neither necessary nor natural; on the contrary, as the preaching of Jesus had been chiefly in Galilee, believers in him, whether professed disciples or not, most likely abounded in that neighbourhood; to them the words of Jesus and the hope of the apostles would be, as a matter of course, communicated, and probably a considerable number of persons were waiting and watching with the apostles. Alford notes: 'Verse 17 seems to present an instance of this fragmentary narrative. The impression given by it is that the majority *of the eleven* worshipped Him, but some doubted (not, *whether they should worship Him;* which is absurd, and, not implied in the word). This however would hardly be possible, *after the two appearances at Jerusalem* in John xx. We are therefore obliged to conclude that *others were present.* Whether these others were the 500 *brethren at once* of whom St. Paul speaks 1 Cor. xv. 6, or some other disciples, does not appear. Olshausen and Stier suppose, from the previous announcement of this meeting, and the repetition of that announcement by the angel, and by our Lord, that it probably included *all the disciples* of Jesus ; at least, all who would from the nature of the case be brought together.' As the eleven had at first obstinately refused to believe those who brought them the first tidings of the resurrection, it is quite as likely that their own statements failed to produce entire conviction in the minds of all who heard them. Matthew's words may signify, especially as rendered by Young, that when Jesus appeared his presence and his identity were so overwhelmingly convincing that all, including those who had been sceptical, immediately recognised and honoured him with a reverential greeting ; or, if a doubt still lingered in the minds of any, it must have been dissipated when Jesus approached them and they heard once more his well known voice. 'And Jesus came to them and spake unto them.' Young renders : 'And having come, Jesus spake to them.' His words were very solemn and authoritative : 'Saying, All authority hath been given unto me in heaven and on earth.' In connection with this we may do well to revert to the words of Jesus to Mary : 'Touch me not (or, Take not hold on me).' The verb in the original is *haptomai*, and although in the 35 instances in which it occurs it is rendered *touch* in the Authorised Version, the primary definition is ' to fasten oneself to, *hence* to cling to, hang on by, grasp ': so that the proper sense seems to be: 'Cling not to me, for I am not yet ascended to the Father: but go , .' There must at the moment be no detention : let her be as eager to run with the news to the disciples, as he was to ascend to the Father. The physical and the spiritual were bound together, so that under the new conditions of existence time and space had still to be taken into account. 'Tarry ye in the city, until ye be clothed with power from on high.' 'Ye shall be baptized with the Holy Ghost not many days hence.' There was a necessity, in the nature of things, for the delay: forty days had to pass before it could be said of Jesus : 'Being therefore at the right hand of God exalted, and having received of the Father the promise of the Holy Ghost, he hath poured forth this, which ye see and hear.' Step by step Jesus must needs proceed : there must be a three days' sojourn in the tomb, and then immediately an ascension to the Father ; next Jesus showed himself at intervals ; after some further lapse of time, he again appeared, announcing the fact that he was now invested with universal supremacy.

But this possession of unbounded power throughout the universe, altered in no respect his predetermined policy and plan of action for the amelioration of the world. The work which he had begun must be continued by his disciples on precisely the same lines. 'Go ye therefore, and make disciples of all the nations.' The word ' therefore ' is not in the Sinaitic or Alexandrine MSS.; it is omitted by

[28 Mat. 18]
[,, 18]
[20 John 17]
[24 Luke 49]
[1 Acts 5]
[2 Acts 33]
[28 Mat. 19]

Griesbach, Tischendorf and Alford, and is marked as doubtful by Lachmann and Tregelles. The Authorised Version stands: 'teach all nations,' altered by the Revisers to 'make disciples of all the nations.' Young renders: 'having gone, then, disciple all the nations.' The literal rendering in the 'Englishman's Greek New Testament' is: 'Going therefore disciple all the nations.' Tischendorf has: 'Go ye and disciple all the nations.' Alford agrees with the Revisers. Obviously the proper rendering is neither 'teach' nor 'make disciples of,' but simply 'disciple.' The Greek noun *mathētēs*, disciple, is converted into the verb *mathēteuō*, to disciple. The substantive occurs 261 times in the New Testament, and in every instance is rendered 'disciple.' The feminine form, *mathētria*, appears once, in the passage: 'a certain disciple named Tabitha.' The verb occurs only here and in the following three passages.

9 Acts 36

	Authorised Version.	Revised Version.	Young.	Englishman's Greek New Testament.
13 Mat. 52	Every scribe *which is* instructed unto the kingdom of heaven.	Every scribe who hath been made a disciple to the kingdom of heaven.	Every scribe having been instructed as to the reign of the heavens.	Every scribe discipled into the kingdom of the heavens.
27 Mat. 57	Who also himself was Jesus' disciple.	Who also himself was Jesus' disciple.	Who also himself was a disciple of Jesus.	Who also himself was discipled to Jesus.
14 Acts 21	And had taught many.	And had made many disciples.	And having made many disciples.	And having discipled many.

From the consistency of the renderings in the fourth column it is clear that the correct translation of the passage under consideration is: 'Going, disciple all the nations.' What does that mean? Clearly the wording of the Authorised Version, 'teach all nations,' is altogether inadequate to the sense: to teach is not to disciple; Jesus taught multitudes, very few of whom ever became disciples. Discipleship requires a voluntary submission to the teacher, and implicit obedience to the teaching. It is equally clear that the wording of the Revised Version, 'make disciples of all the nations,' as far exceeds the true sense as 'teach all nations' falls short of it. 'Make disciples of all the nations' can only be understood to signify that either every individual in the world or the bulk of the inhabitants of the world was to be transformed into a disciple of Jesus. That would be directly opposed to his own aim and method of proceeding: he never sought to gain disciples in that wholesale fashion, but on the contrary insisted upon every one counting the cost beforehand,

14 Luke 33

and in plain unmistakable words he declared: 'Whosoever he be of you that renounceth not all that he hath, he cannot be my disciple.' The disciples were commissioned, not to overthrow and reverse the policy of Jesus, but to continue and extend it: 'Going, disciple all the nations:' the very act of going would be, by itself, a realisation of the scheme, were no immediate result to follow; for to disciple a nation is to plant disciples, be they many or few, in the midst of it. Jesus did not impose upon his apostles the huge, impossible task of converting all mankind; the small success of his own efforts demonstrated the hopelessness of that; they could only

10 Mat. 23

go from place to place, obeying his injunction: 'when they persecute you in this city, flee into the next.' Is it to be supposed that Jesus issued a command which could not be executed? The duty assigned to his followers did not exceed their power of performance. The word 'nations' indicated a restriction rather than an enlargement of their functions. They were to go everywhere preaching the gospel: first from nation to nation, in order to disciple the nations; afterwards it would be from town to town, in order to disciple the entire community. The first pioneers could but touch the outskirts of the work, 'the nations,' leaving it to their successors to carry it on in cities and villages.

The effect of thus discipling the nations is described by Jesus in the solemn words: 'baptizing them into the name of the Father and of the Son and of the Holy Ghost.' Alford noted: 'It is unfortunate again here that our English Bibles do not give us the force of this word (*eis*). *In* should have been *into*.' The Revisers have made the necessary alteration. The expression 'into the name,' or 'to the name,' is equivalent to 'into the power, or authority, or influence.' 'Far above all rule, and authority, and power, and dominion, and every NAME that is NAMED.' 'Wherefore also God highly exalted him, and gave unto him the NAME which is above every NAME; that in the NAME of Jesus every knee should bow.' 'Baptizing them into the name of the Father and of the Son and of the Holy Ghost' means, Baptizing them into the rule, authority, power, dominion—of the Father and of the Son and of the Holy Ghost. Putting that deep and true sense of the words into the background, they have come to be regarded superficially, chiefly as the prescribed formula to be used in the administration of the rite of water-baptism. Alford energetically upheld that view. He considered the words to constitute an instruction to the disciples, and commented on them as follows: 'As regards the command itself, no unprejudiced reader can doubt, that it regards the *outward rite* of BAPTISM, so well known in this gospel as having been practised by John, and received by the Lord Himself. And thus it was immediately, and has been ever since, understood by the Church. As regards all attempts to explain away this sense, we may say—even setting aside the testimony furnished by the Acts of the Apostles,—that it is in the highest degree improbable that our Lord should have given, at a time when he was summing up the duties of his Church in such weighty words, a command couched in figurative or ambiguous language—one which He must have known would be interpreted by his disciples, now long accustomed to the rite and its name, otherwise than He intended it.' If this saying of Jesus had been understood as a command, how comes it to pass that when baptism was administered in apostolic times we find no indication of the use of such a form of words, but some evidence to the contrary? Philip the deacon had been appointed under the auspices of the apostles, and he 'baptized both men and women,' of whom we are told that 'they had been baptized *into the name of the Lord Jesus:*' no mention of the Father and Holy Spirit. Paul reckoned himself 'not a whit behind the very chiefest apostles,' yet he declared: 'Christ sent me not to baptize, but to preach the gospel.' How can that be reconciled with Alford's idea that the administration of baptism was the very essence of apostleship, and that Jesus had prescribed the form of words to be used by them in administering the rite? Even when the Holy Spirit is specially alluded to in connection with baptism, we are simply told: 'they were baptized *into the name of the Lord Jesus.*' Paul elsewhere alludes to 'all we who were baptized *into Christ Jesus;*' and again he wrote: 'as many of you as were baptized *into Christ.*' To the mind of Paul, baptizing 'into the name' meant something very different from a form of words; he asks: 'Were ye baptized *into the name* of Paul?' meaning, evidently, into the leadership of Paul. He wrote: 'I thank God that I baptized none of you, save Crispus and Gaius; lest any man should say that ye were baptized *into my name.*' Of course there could have been no question about the words which had been used in baptism, but whether baptism involved subjection to Paul instead of to Christ. The words 'baptize' and 'baptism' are untranslated Greek. The verb *baptizō* from *baptō*, to dip, dip under, to dye, colour, steep,' is thus defined: 'to dip repeatedly, dip under, to bathe; 2 to baptize.' The passage: 'that he had not first washed before dinner,' is rendered literally by Young: 'that he did not first baptize himself before the dinner.' The word 'baptize' carried a twofold meaning, that in relation to the ceremony initiated by John the Baptist being the secondary one. If in every one of the 72 instances in which the word 'baptize' occurs, and the 22 instances in which 'baptism' occurs, we substitute mentally the verb 'bathe' and the noun 'bathing,' we shall bring our minds into the same position as that occupied by those who lived in the times of Christ and the apostles. By adopting this plan, we shall get that double sense of the expression which was always present to their minds. The Baptist himself taught the people to expect from Jesus a very different kind of baptism than that of immersion in water, saying: 'I indeed bathe you in water unto repentance: but he that cometh after me is mightier than I . . . he shall bathe you in the Holy Ghost and fire.' Jesus certainly set the sign of his approval on water-baptism, not only by receiving it himself, but by adopting it as the badge of admission for his disciples: 'After these things came Jesus and his disciples into the land of Judæa; and there he tarried with them, and bathed.' Yet the same evangelist tells us that Jesus did not administer baptism himself, but simply allowed his disciples to do so: '(although Jesus himself bathed not, but his disciples).' He never commanded water-baptism, which John contrasted with that higher spiritual baptism to be anticipated from Jesus: 'He that sent me to bathe in water, he said unto me . . . the same is he that batheth in the Holy Spirit.' Immersion in water was to be regarded merely as typical of saturation with the Holy Spirit: John was led to give the former: Jesus was commissioned to bestow the latter. The symbol must not be taken for the thing signified, nor the reality—the Holy Spirit—tied to the figure—water. Every recorded allusion of Jesus to baptism in connection with himself and his work, is altogether independent of and apart from water-baptism. 'Are ye able to drink the cup that I drink? or to be bathed with the bathing that I am bathed with? . . . The cup that I drink ye shall drink; and with the bathing that I am bathed withal shall ye be bathed.' 'I have a bathing to be bathed with; and how am I straitened till it be accomplished!' 'John indeed bathed with water; but ye shall be bathed in the Holy Ghost.' All these passages are obviously, undeniably figurative in regard to the word bathe. Now consider the passage: 'bathing them into the name of the Father and of the Son and of the Holy Ghost.' Is not that equally so? On two occasions only Jesus mentioned water-baptism, speaking of it as the baptism of John. The expression, 'bathing them into the name,' is undoubtedly figurative; to assert that it means, 'bathing them with water into the name,' is to make an unauthorised addition to the words of Jesus. The 'Teacher's Prayer Book,' in quoting the passage, actually inserts the words 'with water,' between brackets: a clear admission that otherwise it does not carry that sense. True, the apostles continued the practice of water-baptism, but that they did not, could not have regarded it as the medium for imparting the holy Spirit, is evident from the fact that the gift of the holy Spirit followed, not upon baptism, but upon the laying on of the apostle's hands. We read that Peter and John, 'when they were come down, prayed for them, that they might receive the Holy Ghost: for as yet he was fallen upon none of them: only they had been bathed into the name of the Lord Jesus. Then laid they their hands on them, and they received the Holy Ghost.' Again: 'They were bathed into the name of the Lord Jesus. And when Paul had laid his hands upon them, the Holy Ghost came on them.' But what the apostles did not claim for baptism, has been and is still claimed for it by others. After administering the rite, the Priest (of the Church of England) thanks God, 'that it hath pleased thee to regenerate this Infant with thy Holy Spirit.' It is so easy a thing for parents to bring their children to the font for baptism, that there is no temptation to omit the custom; to decline, on any ground, to have a child baptized, would be to assume a position which is in itself undesirable, and a responsibility which is uncalled for. The ceremony can do the child no harm, and the responsibility attaching to the rite rests properly on the clergyman who administers it. The practice, with all that appertains to it, is not likely to be called in question by laymen generally, until the time comes when deep and earnest thought shall take the place of indifference, half-heartedness, easy, unenquiring acquiescence in what is taught and preached by the clergy. Habitual church-goers are not disposed to undertake a crusade against infant baptism. But in another quarter there is a sign of the times which deserves to be read and considered. There is a large portion of the community who have long lived among us as sheep not having a shepherd, frequenting neither churches nor chapels, and whose ears and hearts the clergy have never gained. Over large multitudes of them the leaders of the 'Salvation Army' have secured an influence as complete as it is peculiar. The system of doctrinal theology enunciated by the 'General,' is accepted by his followers with as little doubt and difficulty as that of the Church of England is by its professed adherents. If there be in the 'Army' any inclination whatever towards the existing priesthood, with its claims and sacraments, it certainly is not in the direction of infant baptism. Here is an account of the 'DEDICATION OF THE GENERAL'S GRANDCHILD. La Maréchale, and, after la Maréchale, la Maréchale's baby girl Victoire, granddaughter of General Booth, who yet in its long clothes, was solemnly dedicated to the service of God and of the Salvation Army, formed the central figures at the crowded gathering at Exeter Hall last evening. This

[8 Acts 15, 16]
[19 Acts 5, 6]

was in celebration of the ninth anniversary of the commencement of the campaign in France and Switzerland under the direction of la Maréchale and her husband, Commissioner Clibburn. The General presided, and the hall was fairly decorated with tricolour banners and hangings, and upon the platform were the "band of the household Troops" and the Junior Staff Band, in their bright uniforms, whilst further colour was supplied by the native costumes worn by several Asiatics. After singing and prayer, and an address by the General, la Maréchale rose and sang a solo in French, her husband's bass voice coming in with the chorus "En Avant" repeated several times, and a cornet taking up the air at first pianissimo, and swelling gradually louder as the hymn proceeded. Then la Maréchale sang the hymn in English, and the audience quickly took up the chorus, "Go on, Go on," repeating it again with ever increasing fervour. At length it ceased, and la Maréchale, in straightforward, earnest words, gave an account of the work of the Army in Paris, speaking at considerable length, but holding her audience fast until she finished with a verse or two of the hymn and the chorus "Go on." Commissioner Clibburn, Captain (Mademoiselle) Roussell, and several others spoke, a Swiss captain and a French captain addressing the audience in French, which was translated sentence by sentence, by an English captain, who was, if possible, more energetic and gesticulatory than the officers supplying the speeches in the original. This done, the General said very audibly to some one on the platform, "Now," and there was a stir of expectation, which was intensified as la Maréchale appeared carrying the little one in her arms. Then standing one on each side of the General, the red and blue staff banner being held over their heads by a scarlet jerseyed officer, the child was dedicated. The General reminded his audience of the three great points of the Salvation Army theology. The first was separation from all evil, the second an entire surrender to God to do His will, and the third a consecration of themselves and all they had to promote the glory of God, with the object of removing the sins and miseries of mankind. In this case the child was dedicated to the service of God and of Jesus Christ. During the ceremony the General took the child in his arms as a token of its surrender by its parents to God . . . Returning it to la Maréchale, he said, "Mother, I give it back to your arms, in the name of the Lord Jesus Christ, and I join your hands here in mine" (suiting the action to the word) "that you may fulfil the promises that you have made." Then he asked the audience to join with him in prayer with "fixed bayonets," and all hands having been raised in response a mighty "Amen" followed, the Maréchale broke into a hymn, in which everybody joined, the General pronounced the blessing, and the ceremony ended.' *

That remarkable scene indicates a determination to set aside clerical and 'Church' dogmas, and to replace the ordinance of infant baptism by a totally different ceremony. It can scarcely be denied that General Booth has grasped at the substance of which baptism also is a shadow. He has adopted the idea of dedication to God and Christ, casting ruthlessly aside the superstitious notion that only in and through the sacrament of baptism an infant is 'made a

* *Daily Graphic*, 19 March, 1890.

member of Christ, the child of God, and an inheritor of the kingdom of heaven.' Any truth there may be in that doctrine, is equally true of the dedicatory service inaugurated by Mr. Booth: infant baptism was instituted by the 'Church,' infant dedication has been devised by the 'Army:' the Church is nothing more and the Army is nothing less, than an 'assembly' of believers. The 'Church,' in that true sense of the word, which has the most of love, truth and wisdom, and the least of error and false pretensions, will best represent and carry out the purpose of its Founder—Jesus Christ. 'If any man hath not the Spirit of Christ, he is none of his;' if any Church has not the Spirit of Christ, it is none of his. To say the least, it is doubtful whether Jesus ever insisted upon water-baptism, and it is certain that he did not ordain infant baptism. But the things which he did command, he was most anxious should be kept in memory and practice: 'teaching them to observe all things whatsoever I commanded you.' Tischendorf renders 'observe' as 'keep;' the original word is *tēreō*, which is thus defined: 'to give heed to, watch narrowly, to take care of, keep, guard.' What were the things he would have his disciples so careful about? What was the peculiar and distinctive teaching of Jesus? The answer of the Church of England to this question would seem to be: 'Only two sacraments, as generally necessary to salvation, that is to say, Baptism, and the Supper of the Lord.' Of Baptism it can only be said that it rests upon the foundation of universal practice, rather than upon any direct command of Jesus: he does not say, 'whatsoever I now command,' but, 'whatsoever I commanded you,' and no previous command of baptism exists in the gospel narratives. In the last supper the words 'take this,' 'take, eat,' 'take ye,' 'drink ye all of it,' applied to the paschal feast, and the instruction 'this do in remembrance of me,' 'this do ye, as oft as ye drink *it*,' to its yearly celebration. The expression, 'all things whatsoever I commanded you,' obviously includes a variety of precepts imposed upon the disciples in their character of disciples: and those things lie plainly open to our discovery and comprehension. 'Swear not at all . . . Resist not him that is evil (or, evil) . . . Love your enemies, and pray for them that persecute you . . . Lay not up for yourselves treasures upon the earth . . but lay up for yourselves treasures in heaven . . . Judge not . . . Be not anxious for *your* life, what ye shall eat; nor yet for your body, what ye shall put on . . . Seek ye his kingdom . . . Sell that ye have, and give alms; make for yourselves purses which wax not old, a treasure in the heavens that faileth not . . . Whosoever he be of you that renounceth not all that he hath, he cannot be my disciple . . . Ye also ought to wash one another's feet . . . A new commandment I give unto you, that ye love one another . . . By this shall all men know that ye are my disciples, if ye have love one to another.' These, and others of the same character, are the distinctive precepts of Jesus, and by the observance or neglect of them must his disciples be judged. His commands were supplemental to those contained in the law and in the prophets. 'If thou wouldest enter into life, keep (*tēreō*—the same verb) the commandments,' said Jesus. 'Which?' asked the man, and on being referred to the decalogue answered, 'All these have I observed.' That foundation of morality and justice had been laid ages ago. Had Jesus nothing more to teach and enjoin? 'What lack I yet?' Yes: here, if he would receive it, was one of the commands of Jesus: 'If thou wouldest be perfect, go, sell all that thou hast, and give to the poor, and thou shalt have treasure in heaven: and come, follow me.' That is still the touchstone of discipleship, and no sacraments, no doctrines, no preaching of a gospel apart from it, can serve the cause of Jesus or help towards the establishment of his kingdom. Strange! that the very precepts which constitute the groundwork, the glory, the hope and power of Christianity, should be precisely those which have fallen into desuetude. They have come to be regarded as visionary, impracticable, as unsuited to professed disciples of Jesus as they are to that outside 'world' which he sought, through them, to teach and save. These commands of his, so peculiar, so unearthly, so unwelcome, so hard to receive and to obey, are those which he was so urgent on his disciples to 'observe.' The word in the original denotes careful and vigilant holding: it is rendered variously in that sense, as in the passages: 'charging the jailor *to keep* them safely;' 'May your spirit and soul and body *be preserved* entire;' '*reserved* in heaven for you.' The apostles by precept and example did indeed teach, keep, preserve Christ's sayings, but that high standard of life has not been maintained by those who have claimed to be their duly appointed successors, and so we cherish a pseudo gospel, acknowledge Christ as king, proclaim his kingdom, but fail to realise it. Not to such a condition of society does his promise apply: 'and lo, I am with you alway (Gr. all the days), even unto the end of the world (or, the consummation of the age).' The word, 'Amen,' has been omitted, as in the three oldest MSS.

The closing words of Jesus recorded in Mark's gospel seem to be an independent account of what was said to the disciples in Galilee as related by Matthew. 'And he said unto them, Go ye into all the world, and preach the gospel to the whole creation.' The word 'proclaim' is preferable to 'preach,' the latter word being too much bound up with the idea of delivering sermons. 'Every creature' has been altered by the Revisers to 'the whole creation.' Young renders literally: 'Having gone into all the world, proclaim the good news to the whole creation.' Alford explains: 'This word *creation*, or *creature*, appears never in the New Testament to be used of *mankind alone* . . . The expression is the same as in Rom. viii. 22: "the whole creation groaneth and travaileth in pain together (or, with *us*) until now."' The original word *ktisis*, is thus defined: 'a founding, settling, foundation; 2, a making, creating: the creation *of the universe*. II. the world or universe itself. 2, a created thing, creature.' Therefore the passage must not be understood as: 'proclaim to the whole creation—the good news,' but, as it stands: 'proclaim—the good news to the whole creation.' Christ's message is a 'gospel to the whole creation,' for it aims at nothing less, and can compass nothing more, than the refounding, resettling of the constitution of the world, leading up to the foretold 'times of restoration of all things' through the regeneration of humanity.

Jesus continued: 'He that believeth and is baptized shall be saved.' Young renders: 'He who hath believed, and hath been baptized, shall be saved'; Tischendorf: 'He that believed and was baptized shall be saved.' Baptism is here joined to faith, which is its antecedent; the submission to baptism is the sign and seal of that faith which must precede the ceremony of initiation into the company of disciples. 'He that believeth and is bathed shall be saved': bathed with water if you will, but none the less, rather so much the more evidently, as shown by the voluntary adoption of that figure or symbol, 'bathed into the name of the Father and of the Son and of the Holy Ghost.' Being bathed with water was merely significant of being bathed into that 'name,' or 'into the name of the Lord Jesus,' or 'into Christ Jesus,' or 'into his death,' or 'into Christ': the expression might be varied, but the thing signified was the same: 'For in one Spirit we were all bathed into one body,' as the Israelites 'were all bathed into Moses in the cloud and in the sea.' These passages are sufficiently clear as to the views of Paul respecting water-baptism, and that the apostle Peter regarded it as merely typical, appears from his comparison of it to the salvation of Noah and his family 'through water.' Here is Young's literal rendering: 'The long-suffering of God did wait, in the days of Noah—an ark being a preparing—in which few, that is, eight souls, were saved through water; to which also an antitype doth now save us—baptism.' The apostle is careful to add, that not the act of bathing (baptism) availed, but the state of mind it indicated: '(not a putting away of the filth of the flesh, but the question of a good conscience in regard to God)': not the ceremony itself, but the requirement annexed thereto: the word 'question' is rendered in the Authorised Version 'answer,' by the Revisers 'interrogation' or 'inquiry,' by Tischendorf 'inquiry,' by Luther 'Bund,' 'covenant.' The term 'save' is used both by Jesus and Peter in connection with baptism and the faith it symbolises. The verb in Greek is *sōzō*. Although rendered by the translators in 7 ways: 'heal, preserve, save, save self, do well, be whole, make whole,' the English words 'save' or 'preserve' cover the definitions given in the Greek-English Lexicon. To 'be saved or preserved' means simply either to be kept from an evil threatened, or delivered from an evil actually incurred: one who is 'saved' is merely retained in or restored to his natural condition. It must therefore be a mistake to suppose that the 'salvation' of an individual or of mankind denotes more than a restoration to that state of being which accords with the constitution of our nature and the original design of our Creator. An inspection of the 106 passages in which the verb 'save,' *sōzō*, occurs, and of the 49 passages in which the noun 'salvation' *sōtēria*, *sōtērion*, occurs, will be found to justify this conclusion. Faith in Jesus, in his 'good news,' in 'the reign of God,' in his method of bringing it to pass, coupled with a 'bathing into his name' as significant of discipleship to him, will put a man into his right position towards God and men, now in this world, and hereafter in the life to come. Is not that the true and full sense of the assurance given by Jesus: 'He that believeth and is baptized shall be saved'? There can be no 'salvation' apart from discipleship, which is the sole, divinely-appointed remedy for all the evils which afflict humanity. Whoever disbelieves that grand, heaven-revealed truth, whoever lacks faith in the efficacy of the 'gospel of the kingdom' and the discipleship which must introduce and perpetuate it, is chargeable with folly, if not with guilt: 'but he that disbelieveth shall be condemned.' The Authorised Version has: 'but he that believeth not shall be damned.' Young and Tischendorf render 'condemned.' Alford did not change the word, but noted: '*shall be damned*, i.e. in the most solemn sense.' As a theological sense has come to be attached to the word, it is all the more important to ascertain its proper import. The original verb is *katakrinō*. There is another verb *krinō*, from which come the substantives *krima* and *krisis*. *Krinō* is thus defined: 'to separate, divide, put apart, to decide a contest or dispute, to judge of, estimate, to question, examine, bring to trial, to pass sentence upon, condemn.' The word is rendered in the Authorised Version in 15 ways, but the word 'judge' will correctly convey its meaning in the 99 passages in which it occurs. The word *krima* is rendered in 7 ways, but the word 'judgment' applies to each of the 28 passages. The word *krisis* is rendered by accusation, condemnation, damnation and judgment, which might properly be restricted to 'judgment' in the 48 passages. *Krinō*, *krima* and *krisis* all relate to the act of investigating and adjudicating upon a matter, in a way more- or less judicial. The verb *katakrinō* is simply defined: 'to give judgment against: to condemn, sentence,' and appears to relate to the mere delivery of a judgment, apart both from the trial and the execution of the sentence. This sense is confirmed by a consideration of the 19 passages in which the word occurs. The Authorised Version renders it in only two ways, 'condemn' and 'be damned,' and the Revisers by the former word only. Its scope is evident from the following instances: 'The queen of the south shall rise up in the judgement with the men of this generation, and shall condemn them': 'condemn' obviously does not mean to examine, pronounce and execute a judicial sentence, but denotes only a comparison and contrast. 'They all condemned him to be liable to death': that was the expression of their opinion, not a decree of execution, for they admitted: 'It is not lawful for us to put any man to death.' 'Through which he condemned the world,' that is: the faith of Noah stood out in strong contrast to the unbelief of the world. 'Turning the cities of Gomorrah into ashes condemned them with an overthrow:' which is explained to mean, 'made them an example.' The nouns *katakrima*, 'condemnation, sentence,' and *katakrisis*, 'condemnation,' carry a similarly restricted sense of *krima* and *krisis*, the 5 passages in which they occur relating to a condemnatory decision apart from any trial or sentence. The object of choosing the word *katakrinō* instead of *krinō* is, therefore, perfectly obvious. Jesus was not referring to any doom of judgment or punishment, but simply asserting, in fact foretelling, the folly and mistake of those who have no confidence in his appointed method for the salvation of the world: 'he that disbelieveth shall be condemned,' as his own generation would stand condemned by the queen of the south and the men of Nineveh. The charge of 'disbelief,' in the sense in which Jesus used the term, does not properly apply to those who reject the doctrines of theology now current and the system of Christianity universally prevalent. Before any man can be justly reproached with a rejection of the salvation of Jesus and of the gospel of the kingdom which he commanded his disciples to proclaim, it must be shown that the salvation, the gospel and the kingdom now offered and existent among us accord with his teaching and with the subsequent embodiment of his idea by his apostles. A careful, honest, rigid, impartial investigation of the gospels, has led up to the lamentable conclusion that the scheme of salvation promulgated and inaugurated by Jesus has been departed from, misunderstood, distorted. In its present shape, it is little better than a parody of his method, that which is vital to it being absent and replaced by dogmas and practices which have no essential connection with it. We, the professed followers of Jesus, have ceased to insist upon what he taught, and are engaged in teaching much which he taught not ; we have failed to do the things he commanded, which were to constitute the peculiarity and ensure the permanence of his doctrine, and we rely instead upon creeds, observances, modes and forms of worship which he commanded not. The precepts delivered in the sermon on the Mount, and elsewhere, for the guidance of disciples, are practically repudiated by us : they have become a dead letter, as though they had never been laws of Christ at all, or as if they were laws repealed. To this departure from the first principles of Christianity, must be attributed its non-success ; its social power is gone, and in place of it we fondly imagine and seek a salvation which is individual ; the 'body of Christ,' the nucleus of devoted disciples round which adherents from the world without should gradually gather, has no tangible, visible existence ; we are baptised Christians, as a matter of course, from infancy, or we may have been baptised as adults, and the results of that baptism are supposed to be a secret locked up in our own breasts, for such a profession of discipleship involves no renunciation, beyond a verbal one : there is nothing about us, except church or chapel-going and worship, to mark us out as followers of Jesus, nothing to entitle us to an application to ourselves of his chosen simile, 'a city set on a hill,' and which 'cannot ⁵ Mat. 14 be hid.' For want of faith in Jesus we need to reproach, not the sceptic or agnostic, but rather ourselves ; 'he that disbelieveth shall be condemned :' we have long since ceased to believe in the efficacy of the plan and precepts of action enunciated by our Lord, and must stand condemned before him and the world, both for our departure therefrom and the evil consequences thereby entailed. We have to choose between admitting the self-application of this condemnation, or confessing that we are not and never have been 'disciples' of Jesus, in the only true and real sense of that designation. Which of these alternatives shall we adopt ? For the system of religious belief which has come down to us by inheritance, no man living, be he clergyman or layman, can be held responsible ; but each man's responsibility begins from the moment when the truth is first apprehended by him. A mere intellectual assent to this new aspect of Christianity will be the first and natural result of changed ideas on the subject, and for most of us that will suffice. If we believe that 'discipleship' to Jesus was made and left by him optional and not compulsory, then our altered and enlarged opinion with respect to the duties incumbent upon 'discipleship' will not trouble us, if only we are content to take the lower place of simple 'believers' in Christ, instead of calling ourselves his 'disciples' or 'followers.' But if, yielding to the same conviction, we wish to become truly his 'disciples,' we must shrink from nothing he has commanded, but must accept his call with all its consequences. The raising and determining of such a question must necessarily be accompanied by great searchings of heart. How will our ecclesiastical systems, and the rulers in our spiritual hierocracy, bear such a strain as that? It will be found that the taking up of a true 'discipleship' involves the putting away of all that is extrinsic from it. A return to 'the simplicity and the purity that is toward Christ' will be no easy matter. The priestly system exists throughout the whole of Christendom, and we are all alike entangled by it. The clergy are no more chargeable than the laity with its existence and continuance; we were all born into it, as we were into our respective political systems and nationalities, and all that we can do, rulers and the ruled alike, is to make the best of our conditions of existence, and seek to modify them acording to our convictions and requirements. Our ecclesiastical polity is no institution of Christ; it is the natural outgrowth of the best intentions, founded indeed upon his teaching, but largely intermixed with human errors and additions. The things which Jesus commanded his disciples were few, but of the utmost importance. The 'Church' has made them fewer still, has, in fact, dropped the whole of them, and taken up as his two things only, Baptism and the Lord's Supper, which were not so plainly and positively enjoined. When true discipleship ceased, sacerdotalism took its place. The plan of Jesus for the salvation of mankind was despised and rejected, as being too simple for the world's requirements. Only by a return to it can our faith in him as our Saviour and Redeemer be shown. Whether we can discern its advantages and foresee its results, or not, his disciples are equally bound, in loyalty to him, to adopt and adhere to it. But we need be at no loss to forecast its effects and appreciate its wisdom. Imagine the beneficial influence which would have been exerted on society by the existence in its midst of a body of men living in strict accordance with the rules laid down by Jesus; not all of them preachers and teachers like our clergy, but employed in the various businesses and avocations of life, excepting such as were contrary to their profession. Soldiers they could never be, and must at all hazards refuse to become, having been commanded not to resist evil, and never to return blow for blow. Neither could they undertake any judicial or legal functions, acting on the precept, 'Judge not, that ye be not judged.' Of course such men would lie open to insult and injury, being as helpless against violence as are children and women; but who would think of harming those who were innocent and without offence, recognised followers of their Master, 'who, when he was reviled, reviled not again; when he suffered, threatened not?' Some simple symbol might be needed to distinguish them from others: a cross worn upon the breast would then carry a significance which it cannot have now, and it would be deemed as infamous to attack its wearer as it would be to trample on a child or strike a woman. A literal compliance with the precept: 'If any man would go to law with thee, and take away thy coat, let him have thy cloke also,' might seem to leave disciples exposed to fraud and chicanery; but a judicious choice of the persons with whom they dealt would obviate that risk, and legal contention is certainly not a blessing to be desired, nor its avoidance, at any cost, an evil to deplore. True disciples of Christ would, indeed, have little beyond the 'coat' and the 'cloke' to tempt the cupidity of covetous and unprincipled men. Daily labour for the supply of daily needs would be the normal condition of their existence. The apostolic injunction, 'If any will not work, neither let him eat,'[3 ii. Thes. 10] would obviously be incumbent on all who had relinquished both the right and the wish to hold property. Consider how the conjoined laws of work and poverty would act. The disciples would be paid for their labour like other men, and yet no individual among them would amass a store for himself; heartily and literally each one of them must be able to pray, 'Give us this day our daily bread.' To earn upon the one hand, and to spend upon the other, would be twin duties of life, in opposition to the principle of hoarding up for the future, with a view to living at some time, either from necessity or choice, without labour. To the worldly minded, the precept: 'Be not therefore anxious for the morrow: for the morrow will be anxious for itself,'[6 Mat. 34] sounds shockingly indiscreet, only they are withheld by a sentiment of reverence from criticising it. Yet Jesus shrunk not from enunciating it, and his followers must not shrink from acting upon it. Nor would their risk in doing so be greater, or as great, as that which is always run by those who act upon the contrary principle: 'They that desire to be rich fall into a temptation and a snare and many foolish and hurtful lusts, such as drown men in destruction and perdition. For the love of money is a root of all evils.'[6 i. Tim. 9, 10] From that, the disciples of Jesus would be exempt; the obligation to get rid of their money as soon as earned, would be deemed by them as sacred as the duty of earning it. The first, the natural and proper effect of that would be—the prevalence of a more elevated condition of existence. No thought of spending money in vice, excess, selfish indulgence of any kind, would harbour in the mind of a disciple; the only question with him would be, as to how his money could be most judiciously expended. There would be no stinting of suitable food and raiment; the comforts of the household would be the primary care, and the best education would be sought for the children. To provide a permanent home would no more be a holding of property than to provide the body with clothing, and a certain sum might well be set apart towards the purchase of a house; that object attained, the rent saved would be an addition to the income. Insurance against accidents, and as a provision for the family at the bread-winner's death, would be deemed a legitimate expenditure. On the means of mental culture, recreation, and all that appertains to social refinement and rejoicing, there would be an ungrudging outlay, not restricted to the few, but freely participated in by all. For the barrier of class distinctions between the disciples would crumble away and disappear, he who now stands highest in position and respect being not one whit degraded, and the brother of low degree becoming gradually exalted to the same level. Such a state of existence would work, in one generation, a marvellous change in the tone and conditions of society, and if perpetuated, the transformation would be like that from earth to heaven. When a man having great possessions becomes a disciple, his first thought will be how best to deal with his property conformably to the will of Christ. Imagine him to be a millowner, with extensive premises and machinery, and employing some hundreds of workers. To sell everything and give to the poor, would be the height of folly in these days; Jesus only advised that in the case of one wealthy person, and if the young man had parted with his estate, the responsibility of distributing the proceeds, not all at once but judiciously, would still have rested upon his shoulders. A wealthy manufacturer would naturally consider foremost the interests of his workpeople. To shut up the mill and make huge donations, would certainly be no real benefit to them, but would be an encouragement to improvidence, and another step towards the pauperisation of the masses. No: it would be best for him still to hold everything as a steward for his Master, simply resolving thenceforth to retain as his own no unspent profits. His style of living need not be altered; there would be no obligation to reduce his personal and family expenditure, everything lawful and expedient in that direction being not only allowable but praiseworthy. Suppose his yearly surplus income to amount to £10,000. He will decide how much of that ought to be disposed of in the shape of increased wages; how much in providing better dwellings and surroundings and means of physical recreation and mental improvement for all in his employment. He would probably open in his ledger a 'Workmen's Capital Account,' crediting it with a percentage of the annual profits, and letting it be known that, under certain necessary restrictions and conditions, in the framing of which they themselves should be consulted, it would belong to them jointly, and represent their share in the concern and its future profits. When all this had been done, there would probably be little left to dispose of, and little call, legitimately, for help elsewhere: for as this system extended, the need for our so-called 'Charities' would disappear. Dispensaries for the sick, asylums for those past work, orphanages for children, and such like, are the outgrowth chiefly of the inadequate remuneration of labour and the strain and greed of competition in business. With the removal of these causes their effects would gradually cease; nor would there be much room for home missionary societies, with their armies of paid agents in the shape of Scripture readers. True discipleship must needs laugh to scorn the idea that money and printing, even the printed Scriptures, can avail much for the propagation of the gospel.

Assume the new disciple to be a landed proprietor with a large rent-roll. What shall he do? His existing position is anomalous, and would be deemed a strange one, if we had not become accustomed to it. For he claims as his individual property the very soil itself, not only so much of it as he cultivates or builds on, but gardens and farms on which other men's capital and labour are employed, and houses, after the lapse of a term of years, on the erection of which not one penny of his own or his ancestors' money was ever expended. That is a law, not of right but of might, and its spirit is in direct contravention to the Mosaic law of Jubilee, which provided that every fiftieth year land sold should revert to its original owner, and mortgages should be cancelled, whereas under our system of leaseholds, houses built by one man revert, in less than a century, to the descendants of another man. It is no proper answer to this charge of spoliation, to assert that a bargain has been made: the landowners practically dictate its terms by refusing to part with the freehold.

The title of the fee-simple—real estate, that is, estate of the realm or royal estate, elucidates the origin of the custom. The king as supreme ruler granted land to his favourites, with or without conditions of service, which have gradually fallen into desuetude; the system is to blame, not the aristocracy who inherit under it. Like air, water and light, land—apart from human labour—is God's gift; the clearing or reclaiming of it, like the planting, or sowing, or building, appertains to individuals, who are entitled to reap the fruits of their toil. The enfranchisement of leaseholds is a matter which should be undertaken by the legislature. A law needs to be passed making any contract invalid which provides for the handing over of property at a future date without an assessment of its value. Under the existing system, the new disciple of Jesus might wake to a realisation of the fact that he was in possession of a huge income bringing with it no labour or responsibility. Beyond the servants of his establishment, only his tenants have any direct claim upon him, and if they are fairly prosperous there would be no call for largess to them. Of course, if they were poor, as multitudes of them are in Ireland, his first duty would be to reduce their rents to the level of their means, in some cases even remitting them altogether for a period. But to find an outlet for all his wealth, he would have to scan the horizon for opportunities of using it, that is, of consuming its annual increment. That would be no easy problem, no light task. He could no longer be an idle man, responding as he must to his Lord's question and call: 'Who then is the faithful and wise servant, whom his Lord hath set over his household, to give them their food in due season? Blessed is that servant, whom his lord when he cometh shall find so doing.' Schemes would have to be devised for the welfare of the community: sanitary improvements, gymnasiums, parks, technical institutions, art exhibitions, dwellings replete with comforts and conveniences,—all undertaken and maintained so as to pay only a low rate of interest. All that would not exhaust the store; and the outlay on such things would not be occasional and spasmodic, but must continue year after year, the duty and object of the benefactor being to guard against any accumulation of riches kept under his own control. What an incalculable amount of good and happiness would result from such a course of action on the part of only one of the world's many millionaires! And if several of them joined the ranks of the disciples, what a transformation would a few years accomplish in the aspect of the world and the state of society! Jesus decreed that the renunciation of wealth should be inseparable from discipleship, and he knew well what he was about in insisting upon it. It was the only means of equalising mankind, and of elevating the masses to that level of virtue and culture which is the proper condition of humanity. God has joined together body, soul and spirit, and together they must rise or fall: there is no salvation of the one apart from the other. Here is what Sir James Crichton Browne, M.D., LL.D., said in a lecture on 'Brain pressure': 'There were thousands of children in this highly favoured land who were insufficiently fed. Could a wholesome diet be secured to every English child until it was twelve years of age one-third of the disease, pauperism, and crime with which the

24 Mat. 45

country is burdened would disappear in the next generation.' *
Through the material Jesus would have his disciples work upward to
the spiritual. It is a monstrous blunder, a deplorable blindness, to
assume that the divine Providence arranges or acquiesces in that
system of competition, of self-seeking, of cutting down wages, of
individual hoarding up, which prevails universally. That is man's
plan of life, and the plan devised by the Christ of God is its very
opposite. It is not in accordance with the divine Will that any one,
except through his own default, should lack the common necessaries
of existence. It is only man's unequal mode of distribution which
reduces multitudes to a state of semi-starvation. There is enough
for all, and to spare, if only we would divide heaven's bounties
fairly. In our selfishness and greed we really forget our absolute
dependence upon God, who gives us from heaven rains and fruitful
seasons, filling our hearts with food and gladness. To counteract
that ingrained habit of forgetfulness, Jesus sought and seeks a band
of disciples, whom he calls upon to practise self-abnegation to the
utmost, never to hold property for their own benefit, and never to
resist wrong by force, that so the world may learn from and through
them to trust in God and live in peace. True discipleship is a
voluntary Socialism, based, not upon claiming and taking, but upon
relinquishing and imparting. Ministers of religion, of various ranks
and orders, claiming, some more some less, to be ambassadors of
Christ and descendants of the apostles, abound throughout the world;
Christendom is full of baptised believers: but disciples—such as
Jesus sought, made and led—where are they? Judging ourselves
by his word and standard, we must needs confess their absence.
That conclusion, a very solemn one, must be faced and dealt with.
Is it true or false? The more carefully, earnestly, methodically,
this question is investigated by the light of the New Testament, the
more important and absorbing does it become. The truth flashes
out upon us here, there, everywhere. The gospels disclose it, the
epistles confirm it, the history of the earliest Church and the lives of
the apostles enforce and illustrate it.

The last words of Jesus, which have yet to be considered, refer to
the external evidences of a true faith in him. 'And these signs shall
follow them that believe.' Young connects the word 'these' with
'believe,' instead of with 'signs': 'And signs shall accompany those
believing these things.' The signs enumerated all lie outside the
range of ordinary experience. Alford admits: 'This promise is
generally made, without limitation to the first ages of the Church.'
That is obvious enough from the words recorded, which are literally:
'signs shall follow THOSE believing,' not 'YOU believing.' Why, then,
have the signs ceased? Alford anticipates the question by saying:
'*Should occasion arise for its fulfilment*, there can be no doubt that it
will be made good in our own or any other time.' Is not that a
solemn trifling with the words of Jesus? He introduced no such
qualification or restriction, but asserted clearly and positively that
the signs would attach themselves to believers. Alford assumes a

---

* *Pall Mall Gazette*, 19 March, 1890.

reason for the absence of the signs: 'But we must remember that *signs* are not needed where Christianity is *professed*.' On the contrary, they cannot exist where Christianity is not professed. Alford continues: 'nor by missionaries who are backed by the influence of powerful Christian nations.' By 'powerful' we can only understand 'warlike,' and it is an utter perversion and degradation of Christ's gospel and teaching to suppose that his 'missionaries' can be backed by the influence of nations which rely on brute force. Alford adds: 'There are credible testimonies of miraculous powers having been exercised in the Church considerably after the Apostles' times.' Then, why not in our own times? Some better answer to the question should be sought than that propounded by Alford. The signs are thus described: 'in my name shall they cast out devils (Gr. demons): they shall speak with new tongues; they shall take up serpents, and if they drink any deadly thing, it shall in no wise hurt them; they shall lay hands on the sick, and they shall recover.' If only that awkward question could be disposed of by saying that all this is figurative language! But that is impossible: there is plain evidence to the contrary. The power of exorcism was exhibited. It is now so absolutely unknown as to be beyond our comprehension, and sceptics regard the accounts of its exercise simply as evidence of the credulity which is assumed to have flourished in past ages. But we cannot so dismiss the plain, unvarnished statements of the evangelists, nor that wonderfully graphic account of the casting out of the spirit of Python by Paul, and its results. The gift of speaking with new tongues is still more incomprehensible by us. The Revisers note: 'Some authorities omit *new*.' Tischendorf retains it. That a heaven-sent, spiritual influence did impart to believers a new and strange power of utterance, is abundantly testified, although its precise nature baffles our investigation. The Holy Spirit was imparted in a perceptible manner, and this celestial language was a sign of the presence of that Spirit. 'On the Gentiles also was poured out the gift of the Holy Ghost. For they heard them speak with tongues, and magnify God.' 'And when Paul had laid his hands upon them, the Holy Ghost came on them; and they spake with tongues, and prophesied.' Paul describes the gift as varying in character: 'kinds of tongues.' In enumerating the various manifestations of the Spirit granted to believers, he separates the interpretation of tongues from the speaking with tongues: 'to another *divers* kinds of tongues; and to another the interpretation of tongues.' The power of interpretation, however desirable, was not generally possessed by the speaker: 'greater is he that prophesieth than he that speaketh with tongues, except he interpret, that the church may receive edifying.' To the listeners, all that was uttered might be, and generally was, incomprehensible: 'For he that speaketh in a tongue speaketh not unto men, but unto God; for no man heareth; but in the spirit he speaketh mysteries.' The apostle desired to see the two gifts combined in one person: 'Wherefore let him that speaketh in a tongue pray that he may interpret.' The mysterious utterances seem to have been chiefly devotional: 'For if I pray in a tongue, my spirit prayeth, but my understanding is unfruitful': that is, my own comprehension of what I mean does not extend to others. 'If I pray' agrees with 'speaketh not unto men, but unto God.' Sometimes this took the form of praise: 'Else if thou

16 Mark 17, 18

5 Acts 16
8 Acts 7

16 Acts 18, 19

2 Acts 4

10 Acts 45, 46
19 Acts 6

12 i. Cor. 10, 28

„ 10

14 i. Cor. 5

„ 2

„ 13

„ 14

„ 16

bless with the spirit, how shall he that filleth the place of the unlearned say the Amen at thy giving of thanks, seeing he knoweth not what thou sayest?' It was a natural and profitable exercise to the speaker himself: 'He that speaketh in a tongue buildeth up himself.' So many possessed and exhibited this gift that the apostle laid down a rule restricting the number of such speakers: 'If any man speaketh in a tongue, *let it be* by two, or at the most three, and *that* in turn; and let one interpret.' Failing an interpreter, it would be best to refrain from disturbing others, and to speak with hushed voice: 'but if there be no interpreter, let him keep silence in the church: and let him speak to himself and to God.' However mysterious all this appears to us, such plain directions indicate the existence of a mode of speech prevalent among believers, as distinguishable as a foreign language would be to us, and as incomprehensible and unedifying in the absence of an interpreter. An endowment so miraculous, instantaneously bestowed, and thenceforward spontaneously and exultingly exercised, demonstrated in the most convincing way the impartation of a power, influence or spirit emanating from without, the holy Spirit which Jesus had promised to send, and did send in a form both visible and audible, so that Peter could say: 'He hath poured forth this, which ye see and hear.' The exaltation of spirit and freedom of utterance were so great and prominent that they might be mistaken for symptoms of drunkenness or madness: 'They are filled with new wine,' said some; and Paul apprehended a similar unjust criticism: 'If therefore the whole church be assembled together, and all speak with tongues, and there come in men unlearned or unbelieving, will they not say that ye are mad?' The unbelievers here alluded to are assumed not to understand, being of the same nationality as the speakers, but unbelievers—foreigners—who did understand the language used* would see no cause for mockery, but the reverse: 'tongues are for a sign, not to them that believe, but to the unbelieving.' However marvellous the fact may be, it is impossible to evade the conclusion that the holy Spirit entered into believers, just as evil spirits are represented to have inhabited demoniacs, and that the Spirit influenced and taught both mind and tongue, so that new thoughts were conceived and uttered sometimes in one language, sometimes in another. It was just as though the mind of an Englishman should enter the body of a Russian, and thereupon the Russian should begin, without any previous instruction, to think and speak in English. That is the marvel and the mystery which the Author of the Acts of the Apostles calls upon us to believe, and which the Apostle Paul writing to the Corinthians alludes to as a well known and indubitable fact. We read that on the day of Pentecost 'there were dwelling at Jerusalem Jews, devout men, from every nation under heaven.' The word rendered 'dwelling' is *katoikountes* from *katoikeō*, 'to dwell in, inhabit.' There is nothing in the definition, nor in any one of the 47 instances in which the verb occurs, to restrict its meaning to a temporary sojourn or lodging in a place; on the contrary, it denotes a fixed residence, and the

---

* This assumption—that the gift of tongues was the speaking in foreign languages—is the basis of the following observations, and if it can be disproved or set aside, the argument falls to the ground. The whole subject is obscure, and our best efforts to explain it can only be regarded as tentative.

allusion here is to a colony of foreign Jews settled in Jerusalem. These persons were perfectly familiar with the language of the Jews, so much so that they could detect the Galilæan brogue of the apostles: 'Behold, are not all these which speak Galilæans?' they said, just as it had once been said to Peter: 'Of a truth thou art *one* of them; for thou art a Galilæan . . . for thy speech bewrayeth thee.' Every one of these foreign Jews, like those of our own day, had the advantage of being perfectly familiar with at least two languages, the Hebrew derived from their parents, and the speech of the country in which they had been born. When the apostles 'began to speak with other tongues, as the Spirit gave them utterance,' these men were able to understand what they said, and were astounded to hear the twelve Galilæans discoursing in no less than fifteen languages: 'the multitude came together, and were confounded, because that every man heard them speak in his own language. And they were all amazed and marvelled, saying, Behold, are not all these which speak Galilæans? And how hear we, every man in our own language, wherein we were born?' Alford notes: 'The words *in our own tongue* (literally *dialect*) *wherein we were born* are very decisive as to the nature of the miracle. The hearers could not have thus spoken had they been *spiritually uplifted* into the comprehension of some *ecstatic language* spoken by the disciples. *They* were not spiritually acted on at all, but *spoke the matter of fact:* they were surprised at each recognizing, so far from his country, and in the mouths of Galilæans, his own native tongue.' There were twelve speakers in many languages, but only one subject of discourse: 'we do hear them speaking in our tongues the mighty works of God.' To put the matter in plain, homely words: the Spirit which entered into the apostles, informing their minds and directing their tongues, was a most accomplished linguist. Each apostle was possessed and influenced by a Personality distinct from and infinitely superior to himself, in fulfilment of the promise of Jesus: 'I will make request of the Father, and he shall give you another Helper, that he may be with you for ever, *even* the Spirit of truth: whom the world cannot receive; for it beholdeth him not, neither knoweth him: ye know him; for he abideth with you, and shall be in you.' Not twelve Spirits, but 'one and the same Spirit, dividing to each one severally even as he will.' Boldly, honestly, and reverently let us look this recorded marvel and mystery in the face. 'Suddenly there came from heaven a sound as of the rushing of a mighty wind.' Young renders: 'a sound as of a bearing violent breath;' the 'Englishman's Greek New Testament': 'a sound as of a violent breath rushing.' Alford observes: 'To treat this as a natural phenomenon, —even supposing that phenomenon *miraculously produced,* as the earthquake at the crucifixion,—is contrary to the text, which does not describe it as *a sound of a rushing mighty wind,* but *a sound* as *of a rushing mighty wind.'* Precisely so: as in everything else that appertains to spirit and life, there was a blending of the spiritual with the material, the possible existence of spirit apart from matter being purely imaginary. Alford continues: 'It was the *chosen vehicle* by which the Holy Spirit was *manifested to their sense of hearing, as by the tongues of fire to their sense of seeing.'* We must not assume that the 'vehicle' was arbitrarily 'chosen,' but rather that it was both natural and necessary. Something invisible was there, and the sound was the result of its swift entrance, as much as is the noise from the flapping of a bird's wing or the thunder which accompanies the lightning. The peculiar rushing or breathing was heard throughout the building: 'and it filled all the house where they were sitting.' The sound was followed by something visible: a lambent flame like a cloven tongue was seen, which came and perched on each of the apostles. 'And there appeared unto them tongues parting asunder, like as of fire; and it sat upon each one of them.' That this was merely symbolical is more than we should venture to assert; a Real Presence was among them, a Living Entity was about to enter into them; the breath and the fire appertained to the Spirit, as much as flesh and blood appertained to themselves. And that a spiritual Being had actually taken up his abode in each of them, was demonstrated by the fact that they at once began to speak in languages they had never learnt. Jesus had commanded them to go and disciple all the nations, bidding them tarry in the city till they were clothed with power from on high. The first requisite towards the work of evangelisation was a knowledge of the languages of the nations they were commanded to visit and teach. That was now supernaturally granted them. And not to them alone, but subsequently to others, Gentiles as well as Jews. The meaning and import of this miraculous gift were plainly indicated by the mere fact of its possession. It could have but one meaning: it pointed to the duty of propagating the gospel in foreign parts. But it was long before the divine leading in that direction began to be followed. The disciples clung to Jerusalem, and not until persecution arose did they go elsewhere, and then no great distance. 'And there arose on that day a great persecution against the church which was in Jerusalem; and they were all scattered abroad throughout the regions of Judæa and Samaria,'—that is, in places where the gift of tongues was not required, and even then the apostles did not depart, for it is added: 'except the apostles.' They must have found full employment among their own countrymen, and were doing good work in and about the metropolis of Judæa. The first extension of the gospel was to Samaria. Although it was in the land of Israel, it was no slight success to have overcome the prejudices existing between the Samaritans and the Jews, who had hitherto had no dealings together. We read: 'Now when the apostles which were at Jerusalem heard that Samaria had received the word of God, they sent unto them Peter and John.' That was a step in advance, but by no means the stride to which the gift of tongues pointed. When Paul was converted and began his ministry, there had been no extension of the gospel outside the land of Israel. We are merely told: 'So the church throughout all Judæa and Galilee and Samaria had peace, being builded up, and, walking in the fear of the Lord and in the comfort of the Holy Ghost, was multiplied.' A vision was needed to induce Peter even to pay a visit to a Gentile, and the apostle opened it by words of explanation and apology: 'Ye yourselves know how unlawful it is for a man that is a Jew to join himself or come unto one of another nation; and *yet* unto me hath God shewed that I should not call any man common or unclean: wherefore also I came without gainsaying, when I was sent for.' Think of that! One of the apostles, who had been charged to go into all the world and proclaim the gospel, waited till he was sent for, and then went doubtfully, hesitatingly, with apologetic words of self-justification in his mouth. That was the first stroke, however halting and feeble, directed against what the apostle Paul termed 'the middle wall of partition' between Jew and Gentile. On that first visit the gift of tongues, which had been so useless being unemployed, was bestowed upon Gentiles: 'for they heard them speak with tongues, and magnify God.' The Jews were scandalised by what Peter had done. 'And when Peter was come up to Jerusalem, they that were of the circumcision contended with him, saying, Thou wentest in to men uncircumcised, and didst eat with them.' Peter justified himself by pointing out that he had found himself unable to 'withstand God.' That silenced his accusers, who were compelled to admit: 'Then to the Gentiles also hath God granted repentance unto life.' The narrator continues as follows: 'They therefore that were scattered abroad upon the tribulation that arose about Stephen travelled as far as Phœnicia, and Cyprus, and Antioch, speaking the word to none save only to Jews.' The word 'therefore,' following upon the account respecting Peter, seems to be introduced in connection with this event and in order to explain why the preaching of others was 'only to Jews.' It is added: 'But there were some of them, men of Cyprus and Cyrene, who, when they were come to Antioch, spake unto the Greeks also, preaching the Lord Jesus.' These 'men of Cyprus and Cyrene' were, obviously, converted Jews who had been compelled to leave Jerusalem, and it is doubtful whether 'the Greeks' does not signify 'Grecian Jews,' which is the reading of 'many ancient authorities.' Paul's missionary labours were commenced among the Jews, for we always find him, at first, in synagogues addressing them. But this was not to continue; we are told: 'The Holy Ghost said, Separate me Barnabas and Saul for the work whereunto I have called them.' Paul's preaching was so attractive that in Antioch of Pisidia on a certain sabbath 'almost the whole city was gathered together to hear the word of God.' That irruption of Gentiles was resented: 'But when the Jews saw the multitudes, they were filled with jealousy.' That led to the momentous decision of Paul to preach thenceforth to Gentiles rather than to Jews. 'And Paul and Barnabas spake out boldly, and said, It was necessary that the word of God should first be spoken to you. Seeing ye thrust it from you, and judge yourselves unworthy of eternal life, lo, we turn to the Gentiles.' For that work, the gift of tongues was necessary, and Paul possessed it in the highest degree, for he says: 'I thank God, I speak with tongues more than you all.' He valued the gift, and desired its extension: 'Now I would have you all speak with tongues,' yet only for the purpose of teaching: 'but rather that ye should prophesy: and greater is he that prophesieth than he that speaketh with tongues, except he interpret, that the church may receive edifying.' This supernatural linguistic gift was so perfect, that its possessors became to all intents and purposes for the time being, foreigners in speech and thought; so much so, that the speaker often did not possess the power of interpretation, but lost his own language utterly. The ability to understand and interpret, but not to speak, the strange language, was granted to others. What a call was this to preach the gospel to the Gentiles! The gift was useless, puzzling, confusing, when not directed to that object. He who spoke the language of foreigners ought to be labouring among them. But in too many instances in vain was the gift bestowed, and in vain did the Spirit call to the work. What an extraordinary and anomalous state of affairs does the apostle picture to us! 'What is it then, brethren? When ye come together, each one hath a psalm, hath a teaching, hath a revelation, hath a tongue, hath an interpretation.' The last two gifts were worse than useless, unless exercised in conjunction, and only under strict regulations could they be profitably allowed in a native congregation. The possessor of a tongue should be addressing foreigners; the interpreter of a tongue should be translating the thoughts uttered by foreigners. There was no place for such men among their fellow-countrymen: whoever possessed the gift of tongues, and stayed at home, was an incumbrance in respect of the very thing which should have most helped the spreading of the gospel. That this was generally admitted, is shown by the plea put forward by the apostle against the proposed suppression of any exercise of the gift: 'Forbid not to speak with tongues'; he preferred to restrain rather than to prohibit it. But that such a question should ever have been mooted, is sufficient proof by itself of some departure from or neglect of the divine purpose in bestowing so startling and miraculous a power. To what extent, if at all, the apostles — Paul excepted — exercised it, we know not. Did this spiritual weapon rust in their hands for want of use? Were they restrained from undertaking such a crusade as that of Paul and Barnabas by any fear of its effect upon the believers of their own nation? Or did they, later in life, go and labour among the Gentiles, albeit we have in the 'Acts of the Apostles' no account of their having done so? 'To each one is given the manifestation of the Spirit to profit withal.' The apostles were not without their prepossessions and prejudices, and they certainly had to contend against mountains of misconception and opposition on the part of others. That the gift of tongues was so little prized, understood, and put to good use in apostolic times, is an indication of weakness and insufficiency somewhere. That the kingdom of God is not yet, after nineteen centuries, prevalent throughout the world, is not owing to any defect in the plan or power of Christ, but to the fact that we have failed to carry out his plan and exercise his powers.

Jesus also promised to his disciples an entire immunity from the effects of poisonous substances, whether animal or vegetable: 'they shall take up serpents, and if they drink any deadly thing, it shall in no wise hurt them.' The Spirit dwelling in them would so invigorate their physical constitution that it would be able to resist the action of anything deleterious. One remarkable instance of this is recorded: 'When Paul had gathered a bundle of sticks, and laid them on the fire, a viper came out by reason of the heat, and fastened on his hand. And when the barbarians saw the beast hanging from his hand, they said one to another, No doubt this man is a murderer, whom, though he hath escaped from the sea, yet Justice hath not suffered to live. Howbeit he shook off the beast into the fire, and took no harm. But they expected that he would have swollen, or fallen down dead suddenly: but when they were long in expectation, and beheld nothing amiss come to him, they changed their minds, and said that he was a god.' With respect to the harmlessness of deadly potions, Alford says: 'We have no instance of this given in the Acts: but later, there are several stories which, if to be relied on, furnish examples of its fulfilment. Eusebius says that "a wonderful thing was related of Justus, who was surnamed Barsabas—that he drank deadly poison and felt no evil, trhough the grace of the Lord."' The apostle Paul wrote: 'Be filled with the Spirit,' which was no mere figure of speech, for it meant an invigoration and exaltation of mind and body, so marked, that he contrasted it to being 'drunken with wine.' Jesus would place his disciples on the same physical and spiritual level as himself; that indwelling, health-sustaining and health-giving power which had appertained to him would be granted to them also, enabling them not only to resist the natural effect of poison in themselves, but also to inherit his power of healing by a touch: 'they shall lay hands on the sick, and they shall recover.' [5 Eph. 18] [16 Mark 18]

Mark's gospel ends as follows: 'So then the Lord Jesus, after he had spoken unto them, was received up into heaven, and sat down at the right hand of God. And they went forth, and preached everywhere, the Lord working with them, and confirming the word by the signs that followed. Amen.' That is ancient history. Men still go forth, and—more than ever—preach everywhere, and they say that the Lord works with them, and confirms his word. But if we ask for the signs of that confirmation, they cannot point to anything at all resembling the signs which Jesus said should follow them that believe. Is that the natural outcome and development of the gospel? Or does it denote a retrogression from the gospel? Or is it because we have another gospel? [„ 19, 20]

APPENDIX.

NOTE A. (See Part III., pp. 259—261, 271, 290 and 95.)

The adoption by the Author of Dr. Young's and Luther's rendering, 'the first of the sabbaths,' instead of 'the first day of the week,' did not meet the approval of the able and scholarly critic by whom the proof-sheets were revised, and whose suggestions and emendations on various points have proved of great advantage, as may be partly seen from the occasional footnotes. On page 259 of Part III. he remarked as follows:—

'It is humbly submitted that Lev. xxiii. 15, Mark xvi. 9, and Luke xviii. 12 are proof positive of the second meaning of *sabbaton* as "week." Mark xvi. 9, with its genitive singular, is *invulnerable*. Probably all the confusion has arisen through the LXX., which in Ex. xx. 8; xxxv. 2; Nu. xv. 32, 33; Deut. v. 12, 15, has *sabbatōn*, notwithstanding that the Hebrew is singular in all these cases. The LXX. may have (gratuitously) indulged themselves in a "plural of excellence or intensity" = "day of restings"—for every one, all round. It is respectfully but earnestly submitted that Young and Luther are hopelessly wrong.'

A protest so earnest and vigorous, coming from one exceptionally qualified to criticise and judge, deserves and must receive the most careful consideration. The Author's reply was to the following effect.

In Matthew xxviii. 1 the word 'sabbaths' (third declension neuter plural) occurs twice. The Englishman's Greek New Testament renders: 'Now late on Sabbath.' Put that quite literally, 'Now late on Sabbaths,' and it seems, in conjunction with what follows, to signify that when the sabbaths had well advanced, one being almost ended and another—known as 'one of the sabbaths' or the 'first sabbath'—about to begin, the women went to the tomb. I fail to see any justification for rendering the first neuter plural by the singular 'Sabbath' and the second neuter plural by the singular 'first day of the week.' The word 'sabbath,' by itself, denoted the weekly sabbath; to distinguish other sabbaths from it, a prefix was needed, and it seems clear that 'one of the sabbaths,' or the 'first sabbath,' denoted the first sabbath at the beginning of the feast of unleavened bread; and it also seems probable that the term 'second-first sabbath' (Luke vi. 1) which has so puzzled commentators, may have denoted the second sabbath at the end of the same feast. It is admitted that translators did not understand the title 'second-first sabbath,' so in the Authorised Version they changed it to 'second sabbath after the first'; as little did they understand 'one of the sabbaths' and 'first sabbath,' and they took upon themselves to alter both, here in Matthew rendering 'sabbaths' as 'sabbath day,' and 'one of the sabbaths' as 'first *day* of the week,' disregarding the plural and changing 'one' to 'first.' Even if it be admitted that 'sabbath' means 'week,' the proper translation of the second clause would be 'one of the weeks.' The entire verse taken literally is very clear: 'Now late on the sabbaths, as it was getting dusk towards the one of the sabbaths, came Mary the Magdalene and the other Mary to see the sepulchre.'

These ideas are confirmed by a consideration of Mark xvi. There, in verse 1, the word 'sabbath' (second declension singular) denotes the weekly sabbath: 'And when the sabbath was past.' Then, in verse 2, the first sabbath at the beginning of the feast of unleavened bread is alluded to as 'one of the sabbaths' (third declension neuter plural): *tēs mias sabbatōn* (read by Lachmann and Tregelles *miāi tōn sabbatōn*, and by Tischendorf *tēi miāi tōn sabbatōn*), literally, as rendered by Luther, 'one of the sabbaths.' Afterwards, in verse 9, where begins the supplement to Mark, 'bearing traces of *another hand* from that which has shaped the diction and construction of the rest of the Gospel' (Alford), a different form of expression is used: 'Now when he was risen early *prōtēi sabbatou*' (second declension genitive singular), literally, 'first of the sabbath.' There was a 'double-sabbath,' two sabbaths together: the two, being continuous, might—I venture to think—be sometimes spoken of as one sabbath, just as we may speak of any two consecutive holidays in the year either as two holidays or as one holiday. If I grasp the fact rightly, this second sabbath was generally called either 'one of the sabbaths' or 'first sabbath.' The word 'first' sufficiently indicates that it was the first sabbath of the feast of unleavened bread.

At the request of the Author, the critic of the MS. has been good enough to amplify his arguments. He writes:

'The critical question which you raise is two-fold. I. Does *sabbaton*, in the singular, ever mean "week"? II. What ought to be done with these remarkable plurals, *sabbatōn*?

'I. The three passages cited in my note were not adduced in the belief that each passage was by itself conclusive. The *first*—that from Lev. xxiii. 15—was given merely to show how early counting *weeks* by "sabbaths" came in. "Seven sabbaths" became practically equivalent, in certain contexts, to "seven weeks." That was the seed-bed out of which grew the secondary meaning of sabbath as "week." It is pleasant to see that at the foot of p. 259 of your work, Part III., you are alive to the facility with which this signification might come in. That it actually did arise, the remaining two texts satisfactorily evince. I take the third (Luke xviii. 12) second, as being just a shade less convincing than the one left till the last. Sure I am that to most competent and unbiased minds even this, about fasting twice per sabbaton, must appear so strong as to leave scarcely anything to be desired. My first thought on coming to your citation of it was an amused one: "Oh dear! why *I* generally fast three times on every sabbath." Your ingenuity however did not fail to suggest the (to your mind) possible meaning of fasting to the extent of two meals on every sabbath. But now, appealing to your less imaginative self, Can you seriously think that any man would *boast* of having omitted two meals? If he fasted at all, is it likely he would do less than that? My remembrance of accounts of fasting is to the effect that little or no food was usually taken until sunset. But that a man should do this *twice a week*, is good enough for a self-righteous boast—which is all the text needs. I have tried the effect of your exposition on one or two minds, with the result of fully assuring myself that your exegesis is very far-fetched.

'Coming now to Mark xvi. 9, I hold this passage to be absolutely conclusive, for the simple reason that the term "first OF the (or, a) sabbath" splits up the sabbath into portions smaller than its whole self. If "sabbath DAY" is here essential, the word "first" (standing before it and throwing it into the genitive case) must mean the first hour or minute of that day: just as "the first of the month" cannot mean "the first month of the month," but must denote the first day or hour or minute of the month—certainly "day," usage being our guide. Unless, then, the intention in this passage was to say, "On the first hour or minute of the sabbath" Jesus arose (which you do not assert, and which would be untrue if you did) the only grammatical way out of the difficulty is to take *sabbaton* in the extended sense of "sabbath-bounded period of time," namely "week." "On the first of the WEEK" Jesus arose, &c., &c. To say "first of the sabbaths" in the face of that *sabbaton* (singular number) is downright bad grammar, whoever is guilty of it (Young or Luther makes no difference, in so plain a case).'

Admitting that this closing remark is not too strong, as against Young and Luther, it must also be admitted that whereas they, in this passage, transformed a singular into a plural, other translators, in several passages, have transformed the plural into the singular. Of course they all were honest, and gave what seemed to them the right sense, but it might have been better if none of them had ventured beyond the letter of the original, even though they left the true sense uncertain. It was seen that the expression 'first of the sabbath' splits up the sabbath, and it was assumed that the only possible explanation of that was by taking 'sabbath' to mean 'week,' whereas it may have been the 'double-sabbath' which was so split up.

'II. I now come to the irregular plural *sabbatōn*; and say at once that if by usage *sabbaton* (singular) can sometimes denote "week" so can *sabbatōn* (plural); for to say "a sabbath-bounded period of days" is practically the same thing as to say "a period of days bounded by two sabbaths, namely one just before it and one concluding it, and so on indefinitely." Now here is a test for you: Give me a consistent and not ungrammatical rendering of Mat. xxviii. 1. In my "New Testament Critically Emphasised" I have, I think, a consistent and grammatical rendering, which has been before the world twenty years; for it is exactly so long since the 1st edition appeared. Here it is: "And late in [the] week, when it was on the point of dawning into [the] first of the week." If the correctness of that rendering has ever been challenged, the circumstance has not come to my knowledge. Before I say what seems necessary concerning Dr. Young's rendering "On the eve of the sabbaths," &c., it is proper that I should guard myself from being for a moment supposed to unduly depreciate the ability or labour on the Holy Scriptures of that scholar. It is true that I have seen, all along, that you were relying just a little too implicitly upon him. Still, it would be folly to deny him great merit, and on the whole I can easily believe that his translation of the Bible has done immense service, though not unmixed with harm. The gentleman who revised for him his New Testament told me, years ago, that he considered Dr. (then Mr.) Young "rather as a clever linguist than as a philosophic philologian." Be that as it may, I am certain of two things—on the one hand that Young is not always as "literal" as you take him to be: this I have several times had the honour of pointing out to you in detail, during the progress of your work; and on the other hand, that his version is *too* "idiomatic," in the sense of having in it so much of foreign idiom as to make it need to be further translated by the reader in a manner and to a degree quite beyond the capacity of average Englishmen. Having said this much—not without some care not to defame a most able and worthy scholar now departed—it may be that you are measurably prepared for the inevitable remarks derogatory to Dr. Young's rendering of Mat. xxviii. 1, and parallels, in which you have unfortunately placed such unbounded confidence. As to the place just above cited, what I have to say is this: Dr. Young has unwittingly practised on his own and his readers' understanding. He has actually made "late" mean "early." "The eve of the sabbaths" means *before* the sabbaths—very early indeed! "Christmas eve" is not Christmas at all. And so Dr. Young has transferred the resurrection to Friday, or the beginning of Saturday. When you can make "late on Christmas day" mean "Christmas eve," then you may plant the Resurrection so late on the sabbath as to be just as the sabbath was beginning!'

This argument appears to have arisen out of a verbal misconception. The word 'eve' has three significations, according to Nuttall: 'The latter part or close of the day; the evening before a holiday; the time immediately preceding some important event.' Why discard, against Young, the primary definition? The sabbaths began and ended at evening, and the junction of the two evenings, the ending of one sabbath and the beginning of another sabbath, is well described as 'on the eve (*i.e.* evening) of the sabbaths.' Luther had used the same expression: 'Am Abend,' 'On the evening,' but he added, 'of the sabbath,' instead of rendering the plural. His object seems to have been to give what he understood to be the meaning of the passage by a free translation, for he continued: 'which dawns to the day of the first holiday of the sabbaths.' Young's rendering might have been made plainer, and Luther's more accurate, but obviously they both took pains to give the true sense of the passage.

'Struck afresh by these plurals (*sabbatōn*) the other day, it occurred to me to see whether they could be tracked back to the Septuagint ("LXX."): when I found, to my amazement, that the LXX. had actually employed plurals (in the cases cited in the appended Table, besides no doubt others) for the Hebrew singular *shabbāth*, "sabbath." How they came to do this I know not. Very possibly they intended to do no more than to say (by a to them familiar though in this case gratuitous "plural of excellence or intensity") "Day of Restings," where their venerable original merely said, "Day of Rest." Whether we can get at the reason of this their procedure or not makes no difference. Having traced this plural to its probable source, I feel free to say that practically for New Testament students it is a bastard plural; and we are not called upon to agglomerate imaginary special festal sabbaths merely at its bidding. I say this guardedly, as not being disposed to shut my eyes to any valid proofs of a concurrence and succession of sabbaths, ordinary and extraordinary; although, indeed, it might be well to enquire whether the first festal day of unleavened bread was correctly speaking a sabbath at all; seeing that not "all work," as on the seventh-day sabbath, but only "servile work" was prohibited to be done thereupon. It was probably, to the Hebrews, simply a "holiday" religiously observed. In fine: Since we know that *sabbatōn* is sometimes equivalent to "restings" = "rest" = *sabbaton* = "week," we are not going to violate grammatical law, and then foist in imaginary sabbaths to help us out of the pit into which we have fallen. . .

'TABLE *giving examples of the way in which the Septuagint has rendered* BY PLURALS (*sabbata, sabbatōn*) *the Hebrew singular* SHABBÂTH, "*Sabbath.*"

	HEB.	LXX.
Ex. XVI. 23.	Shabbâth, sing.	sabbata, pl.; but followed by hagia, sing.
25.	,,	,, ,, semeron, sing.
26.	,,	,, but preceded by hemeran, sing.
29.	,,	,, but followed by hemeran, sing.
XX. 8.	,,	tōn sabbatōn, pl.; preceded by hemeran, sing.
10.	,,	sabbata, pl.; preceded by hemeran, sing.
11.	,,	hebdomēn (seventh), sing.
XXXI. 13.	Shabbethothai, pl.	sabbata, pl.
14.	Shabbath, sing.	sabbata, pl.
15.	,,	,,
—	,,	hebdome, sing.
16.	,,	sabbata, pl.
XXXV. 2.	,,	,,
3.	,,	sabbatōn, pl.
Lev. XVI. 31.	,,	sabbata, pl.
XIX. 3.	Shabbethothai, pl.	sabbata, pl.
XXIII. 3.	Shabbath, sing.	,,
—	,,	,,
11.	,,	tēs prōtēs.
15.	,,	tōn sabbatōn; followed by day in sing.
—	Shabbathoth, pl.	hepta hebdomadas.
16.	Shabbath, sing.	tēs eschatēs hebdomados.
32.	,,	sabbata sabbatōn.
—	,,	sabbatieite ta sabbata humōn.
38.	Shabbethoth, pl.	tōn sabbatōn.
XXV. 8.	,,	hepta anapauseis etōn.
—	,,	hepta hebdomades etōn.

'REMARKS ON THE ABOVE.

'In the above list of passages several things are observable:

'1. That the LXX. has the *habit* of putting the plural *sabbata, sabbatōn* where the Hebrew is singular. Did they intend to depart in sense from their original? I do not believe it. There is always ready for us to fall back upon the facility of the Hebrew mind in using a plural for the mere sake of intensity, and to put us on our guard lest we unjustly charge them with being untrue to their sacred exemplar.

'2. There is contextual proof positive that the intensification of the idea of *resting* is all they aimed at: they actually, in several instances, construe their plural *sabbata* with adjectives in the singular. Their *sabbata* is an "IT" over and over again.

'3. To carry the argument to a climax,—they render the "seven sabbaths" of the Hebrew as "seven sevens"; proving that they could freely regard a "sabbath" as = "seven days" = a "week."

'4. It may be added that they render seven sabbaths of years as "seven restings of years" and "seven sevens of years." See last text in Table.

'5. In several instances they use their genitive plural *sabbatōn* to render the Hebrew shabbathōn, *which is no plural at all* (im and oth being the two Hebrew plural endings, masculine and feminine), but merely a word with a special intensifying ending, and so *shabbath shabbathōn* in the Hebrew is "a sabbath of sacred rest," the essential idea of rest being not pluralised but emphasised.

'6. I thought I had reached the climax some little ago, but that remains to come: Lev. xxiii. 32: "From evening to evening shall ye sabbatize your sabbath," says the Hebrew; "From evening to evening shall ye sabbatize your *sabbata*," says the Septuagint. There the adverse critic may be safely left, shut up, to pass his *sabbata*, between those two evenings.

'Let me now add that, on turning anew to my Englishman's Hebrew Concordance, in order to refresh my memory before writing this note, I was rather taken aback to find pencilling showing that years ago the usage of the LXX. was fully gone into. To this precaution perhaps may be attributed my having escaped the trap into which others have fallen. The Septuagint cannot safely be ignored in translating the New Testament. I do not myself attach so much importance to it as some do; but a very high value, for certain purposes, remains to it: it often helps in translating the Hebrew, and it bears witness to the text which it must have employed; but, perhaps above all its other uses, it serves as a linguistic connecting link between Old Testament and New,—preparing a vocabulary for the latter and colouring its terminology. Before we too heavily censure its authors for real or supposed shortcomings, let us at least call to mind the training which they brought to their task, and the gigantic difficulties and prejudice they had to confront.'

The author fully appreciates and gratefully acknowledges the care, patience, and weight of learning which are conspicuous in the above arguments. He deems it right to let them speak for themselves, simply appending thereto the following additional quotation from this very able criticism.

'The following extracts will show you that it is no mere private opinion of my own that sabbath sometimes means "week":

'Fuerst, Heb. Lex., under the word *shabbath*: "2 *a week*, i.e., the seven days ending with the sabbath. Lev. xxiii. 15; xxv. 8; so too *shabbath* in the Talmud, *sabbatōn* in the New Testament (Mat. xxviii. 1; Mark xvi. 2; Luke xviii. 12)."

'Davies, Heb. Lex. (under same word): "2 *a week*, Lev. xxiii. 15 (cf. Mark xvi. 9, Luke xviii. 12.)"'

It is very satisfactory to have placed before us the opinions of the ablest Hebrew and Greek scholars, and the grounds on which they based their judgment. We can thus see the idea in process of formation. It involves no derogation from the reputation of these learned men, to bear in mind that an error made by one or more of them at starting has an inevitable tendency to perpetuate itself. The pupils imbibe the opinions of their teachers, and themselves in turn become teachers, and the teachers develop into commentators, translators, lexicographers. Fuerst and Davies considered 'week' to be a proper definition of 'sabbath,' and quoted passages which seemed to them to justify the rendering and in which the word had been so translated. Luther first and Young afterwards, exercising an independent judgment, did not come to the same conclusion. Without presuming to impugn the ability of any one of these intellectual giants, a short and easy way out of the difficulties and uncertainties surrounding the subject may be suggested. There is really no question at all of right or wrong translation; the contention has simply arisen out of the fact that the Hebrew word *shabbath* has either, generally, not been translated at all into Greek or English, or has been—as must be admitted—sometimes translated wrongly, or as some would prefer to call it, 'freely.' In proof of this fact we have only to remember Dr. Johnson's definition of 'sabbath' as 'an Hebrew word signifying Rest,' and to note in Nuttall's Dictionary, after the meanings, the derivation '(Heb. *shabbath*, rest).' Now let us boldly put this real translation of the word in all the passages which have been here alluded to. Lev. xxiii. 15: 'From the morrow after the Rest . . . seven Rests shall there be complete.' Mark xvi. 9: 'Early on the first of the Rest.' Luke xviii. 12: 'I fast twice in the Rest.' Ex. xx. 8: 'Remember the Rest day.' Ex. xxxv. 2: 'A Rest of solemn rest.' Nu. xv. 32: 'Upon the Rest day.' Deu. v. 12, 15: 'Observe the Rest day. . . Keep the Rest day.' Mat. xxviii. 1: 'Now late on the Rests. . . Toward the first of the Rests.' Luke vi. 1: 'On the second-first Rest.' Mark xvi. 1, 2: 'When the Rest was past. . . On one of the Rests.' Lev. xxv. 8: 'Seven Rests of years.' Lev. xxiii. 32: 'A Rest of solemn rest. . . Shall ye keep your Rest.' Lev. xxv. 8: 'Seven Rests of years unto thee, seven times seven years.'

This alteration places us in the same position and under the same necessity of understanding and judging as that which every Hebrew reader occupies. He cannot escape the responsibility of suiting the meaning to the context; neither now can we, although hitherto that duty and privilege have been restricted to translators, who decided for us, and whose lead and opinions, in the absence of strict accuracy of rendering, we could not choose but follow. In the exercise of their discretion they gave us nearly always the original Hebrew word, sometimes the synonym 'week,' when it seemed to them requisite or appropriate, never, or scarcely ever, the foremost meaning—'rest.' We should understand the word 'rest' to signify primarily *repose*, and secondarily *an interval of time*, as when we speak of yearly and half-yearly Rests in the making up of accounts; and the context would fix the sense. All this discussion has been, in truth, not about a right or wrong translation, but about an exercise of judgment: Luther, sometimes, and Young, generally, evidently thought that the plural form in the New Testament referred to more than one sabbath, and they therefore, in many cases, saw no need or justification for departing from the plural; other translators thought otherwise; the author of 'The King and the Kingdom' has ventured to approve the stand made by Luther and Young, and has attempted to show good reasons for it. His friendly critic has detected and hit hard at one weak spot, saying with reference to the suggestion, on page 259, that fasting twice on the sabbath might mean abstaining from two meals on the sabbath: 'But now, appealing to your less imaginative self, can you seriously think that any man would *boast* of having omitted two meals?' Except for the purpose of protesting against the rendering of 'rest' and 'rests' as 'week,' there is no need to imagine it: take it which way you will; you are free to judge, but scarcely free to say it must be translated 'week' because you think it means a week. The aims and methods of translators must widen with the times. New versions are called for by the growing intelligence of those who are prepared to study them; and such readers desire and have the right to expect that as far as possible they may be placed in a position for exercising their own free judgment. When there is a plural in the original, why should it not be rendered as a plural, and vice versâ?

On page 261, Part III., it is observed: 'Still more important are the questions which arise in connection with the introduction into the Gentile world of a weekly sabbath, and its transference from the seventh to the first day of the week.' The author's esteemed critic asked: 'Any real proof of such transference?' and he writes thereon as follows:

'There is not a fragment of evidence in the New Testament in support of the assumption of a change of day by the substitution of the 1st for the 7th. Some observance of the 1st, as a joyful supplement to the 7th, there probably was; but substitution, none... Not until the days of Constantine the Great did the general observance of the 1st day become a public ordinance and custom. But within the range of the New Testament, I am quite confident that no substitution can be found, and the assumption may safely and definitively be dismissed.'

By all means. Good service is done by denying that the Sabbath day was changed as by divine command or apostolic inspiration, although observed by the Gentiles and changed by them, or by converted Jews, it undoubtedly was, otherwise it could not have been handed down to us and by us kept on the 1st day, the Jews still keeping it on the 7th.

INDEX TO QUOTATIONS FROM THE GOSPELS.

The large Roman figures denote the Chapters. The first column shows the Verse, the second column the Series or Part, and the third column the Page.

MATTHEW.

I.			III.			V.			VI.			VII.			IX.			X.		
1	i.	46	1	i.	30	4	i.	115	4	i.	131	17	i.	148	1	i.	99	11	i.	214
2		46	2		31	5		116	5		132	18		148	2		99	12		214
3		46	3		31	6		116	6		132	19		148	3		100	13		214
4		46	4		31	7		116	7		132	20		148	4			14		214
5		46	5		32	8		117	8		132	21		149	5			15		216
6		46	6			9		117	9		134	22		149	6			16		216
7		47	7		32	10		119	10		134	23		149	7			17		216
8		47	8		33	11		119	11		134	24		149	8		103	18		216
9		47	9		33	12		119	12		134	25		149	9		103	19		216
10		47	10		33	13		121	13		134	26		150	10			20		216
11		47	11		34	14		122	14		135	27		150	11		104	21		218
12		47	12		114	15		122	15			28		150	12		104	22		218
13		47	13		37	16		122	16		136	29		150	13		104	23		218
14		47	14		38	17		122	17		136				14		104	24		218
15		47	15		38	18		122	18		136				15			25		219
16		47	16		38	19		122	19		137	VIII.			16		105	26		219
17		48	17		39	20		123	20		137				17		106	27		219
18		14				21		123	21		137	1	i.	96	18		201	28		219
19		14				22		123	22		137	2		96	19		201	29		220
20		14	IV.			23		125	23		138	3			20		201	30		
21		14	1	i.	49	24		125	24		138	4			21		202	31		220
22		14	2		49	25		125	25		138	5		151	22		203	32		220
23		14	3		49	26		125	26		139	6		151	23		204	33		221
24		15	4		50	27		126	27		139	7		151	24			34		221
25		15	5		50	28		126	28		139	8		151	25		205	35		222
			6		50	29		126	29		139	9			26		206	36		
			7		50	30		126	30		139	10			27		207	37		222
II.			8		51	31		126	31		140	11		153	28		207	38		222
1	i.	21	9		51	32		127	32		140	12		153	29		207	39		222
2		21	10		52	33		127	33		140	13		153	30		207	40		223
3		22	11		53	34		128	34		142	14		65	31		207	41		223
4		22	12		58	35		128				15		199	32		208	42		224
5		22	13		58	36		128				16		65	33		208			
6		22	14		59	37		128	VII.			17		66	34		208			
7		23	15		59	38		128				18		192	35		212	XI.		
8		23	16		59	39		128	1	i.	143	19	ii.	82	36		212			
9		23	17		84	40		128	2		143	20		82	37		212	1	i.	227
10		23	18			41		129	3		145	21		82	38		212	2		157
11		23	19		69	42		129	4		145	22		82				3		
12		24	20		69	43		129	5		145	23	i.	192	X.			4		
13		24	21		69	44		130	6		145	24		192				5		
14		24	22		69	45		130	7		146	25		192	1	i.	213	6		
15		24	23		113	46		130	8		146	26		193	2			7		158
16		24	24		113	47		130	9		146	27		194	3			8		
17		25	25		113	48		131	10		146	28		197	4			9		
18		25							11		146	29		197	5		213	10		
19		25	V.			VI.			12		146	30		197	6		213	11		160
20		25							13		147	31		197	7		213	12		160
21		25	1	i.	115	1	i.	131	14		147	32		198	8		214	13		160
22		25	2		115	2		131	15		147	33		198	9			14		160
23		25	3		115	3		131	16		148	34		198	10		214	15		160

*

ii INDEX TO QUOTATIONS FROM THE GOSPELS.

XI.		XIII.		XIV.		XVI.		XVIII.		XX.		XXI.	
16		1	i. 166	10	i. 226	1	i. 299	9	i. 313	7	ii. 221	40	ii. 286
17		2	166	11	226	2	299	10	315	8	221	41	286
18		3	166	12	227	3	299	11	315	9	221	42	288
19	i. 161	4	167	13	227	4	299	12	316	10	221	43	288
20	ii. 87	5	167	14	229	5	300	13	316	11	221	44	288
21	87	6	167	15	230	6	300	14	316	12	221	45	289
22	87	7	168	16		7	300	15	316	13	221	46	289
23	87	8	168	17	230	8	300	16	317	14	221		
24	87	9	168	18		9	300	17	317	15	221		
25	93	10	169	19	231	10	300	18	327	16	222	**XXII.**	
26	93	11	169	20	232	11	302	19	327	17	224		
27	93	12	169	21	231	12	302	20	327	18	224	1	ii. 292
28	94	13	170	22	235	13	255	21	327	19	224	2	292
29	94	14	170	23	236	14	256	22	328	20	226	3	292
30	94	15	170	24	236	15	256	23	328	21	226	4	292
		16	171	25	237	16	256	24	328	22	227	5	292
		17	171	26	237	17	256	25	328	23	227	6	292
		18	171	27	237	18	257	26	329	24	228	7	293
XII.		19	173	28	238	19	258	27	329	25	228	8	295
		20	175	29	238	20	258	28	329	26	228	9	295
		21	175	30	238	21	259	29	329	27	228	10	295
1	i. 107	22	175	31	238	22	259	30	329	28	229	11	298
2	107	23	175	32	239	23	259	31	329	29	238	12	298
3		24	177	33	239	24	260	32	329	30	238	13	298
4		25	177	34	240	25	260	33	329	31	238	14	299
5	108	26	177	35	241	26	261	34	329	32	238	15	305
6	108	27	177	36	241	27	261	35	330	33	238	16	308
7	109	28	177			28	261			34	238	17	308
8		29	177									18	308
9		30	177									19	308
10		31	178			**XV.**		**XVII.**		**XIX.**		20	308
11	110	32	178									21	308
12	110	33	179							1	ii. 3	**XXI.**		22	311
13	110	34	180	1	i. 280	1	i. 262	2	3			23	311
14		35	180	2	280	2	262	3		1	ii. 250	24	311
15	111	36	180	3	281	3	262	4	181	2	250	25	312
16	111	37	181	4	285	4	263	5	181	3	251	26	312
17	111	38	181	5	285	5	263	6	182	4	251	27	312
18	111	39	181	6	285	6	264	7	183	5	251	28	312
19	111	40	183	7		7	264	8	183	6	252	29	312
20	111	41	184	8	285	8	264	9	184	7	254	30	312
21	111	42	184	9		9	267	10	185	8	254	31	315
22	ii. 40	43	185	10	286	10	268	11	185	9	256	32	315
23	40	44	185	11	286	11	268	12	185	10	260	33	318
24	40	45	186	12	287	12	268	13	206	11	260	34	318
25	41	46	186	13	287	13	268	14	206	12	274	35	318
26	41	47	187	14	287	14	270	15	207	13	274	36	319
27	41	48	188	15	287	15	270	16	210	14	274	37	319
28	42	49	188	16	288	16	271	17	210	15	278	38	
29	42	50	188	17	288	17	271	18	212	16	278	39	320
30	43	51	190	18	289	18	274	19		17		40	320
31	43	52	190	19	289	19	274	20	213	18	260	41	323
32	45	53	191	20	289	20	274	21	213	19	260	42	323
33	45	54	209	21	289	21	275	22	213	20	261	43	324
34	46	55	209	22	289	22	278	23	213	21	262	44	324
35	46	56	209	23	289	23	278	24	214	22	263	45	324
36	46	57		24	290	24	304	25	216	23	280	46	327
37	46	58	211	25	290	25	304	26	217	24	281		
38	46			26		26	305	27	217	25	281		
39	47			27	291	27	306	28	217	26	281		
40	47			28	291			29	219	27	282		
41	47	**XIV.**		29	291			30	220	28	283	**XXIII.**	
42	48			30	293	**XVIII.**				29	283		
43	48	1	i. 227	31	293					30	283	1	ii. 335
44	49	2	227	32	295	1	i. 308	**XX.**		31	283	2	335
45	49	3	226	33	296	2	308			32	284	3	335
46	i. 191	4	226	34	296	3	308	1	ii. 220	33	284	4	335
47	191	5	226	35	296	4	309	2	220	34	285	5	335
48	191	6	226	36	296	5	309	3	221	35	285	6	335
49	191	7	226	37	297	6	311	4	221	36	285	7	
50	191	8	226	38	298	7	312	5	221	37	286	8	336
		9	226	39	298	8	313	6	221	38	286	9	336
										39	286	10	336

INDEX TO QUOTATIONS FROM THE GOSPELS. iii

XXIII.	XXIV.	XXV.	XXV.	XXVI.	XXVII.	XXVII.
11	12 iii. 8	1 iii. 40	45 iii. 60	40 iii. 183	5 iii. 206	49 iii. 243
12	13 8	2 40	46 61	41 183	6 206	50 244
13 ii. 338	14 11	3 40		42 183	7 207	51 245
14	15 14	4 40	XXVI.	43 183	8 207	52 246
15 339	16 15	5 40		44 183	9 210	53 246
16 339	17 15	6 40	1 iii. 65	45 185	10 210	54 247
17 340	18 15	7 40	2 65	46 186	11 215	55 250
18 340	19 15	8 40	3 65	47 186	12 217	56 250
19 340	20 16	9 40	4 65	48 186	13 217	57 254
20 340	21 16	10 41	5 65	49 187	14 218	58 254
21 340	22 25	11 41	6 ii. 246	50 187	15 220	59 255
22 340	23 26	12 41	7 246	51 190	16 220	60 256
23 340	24 26	13 41	8 247	52 191	17 220	61 256
24 340	25 26	14 41	9 247	53 191	18 220	62 256
25 340	26 26	15 42	10 247	54 192	19 221	63 256
26 341	27 27	16 42	11 247	55 192	20 221	64 257
27 341	28 27	17 42	12 247	56 192	21 221	65 257
28 341	29 27	18 42	13 217	57 197	22 221	66 258
29 341	30 28	19 43	14 iii. 66	58 197	23 222	
30 341	31 29	20 43	15 66	59 197	24 222	
31 341	32 30	21 44	16 66	60 198	25 223	XXVIII.
32 341	33 30	22 44	17 81	61 198	26 223	
33 341	34 30	23 44	18 82	62 198	27 223	1 iii. 258
34 342	35 34	24 44	19	63 198	28 223	2 266
35 342	36 34	25 44	20 84	64 199	29 223	3 266
36 343	37 35	26 44	21 87	65 200	30 223	4 266
37 258	38 35	27 44	22 87	66 200	31 227	5 273
38 258	39 35	28 44	23 87	67 201	32 227	6 273
39 258	40 36	29 44	24 206	68 201	33 229	7 273
	41 36	30 45	25 88	69 201	34 229	8 273
	42 37	31 46	26 88	70 202	35 230	9 274
XXIV.	43 39	32 48	27 90	71 202	36 232	10 274
	44 39	33 48	28 90	72 203	37 232	11 276
1 iii. 1	45 39	34 48	29 92	73 203	38 234	12 277
2 1	46 39	35 48	30 177	74 203	39 235	13 277
3 2	47 39	36 48	31 177	75 204	40 235	14 277
4 3	48 39	37 49	32 178		41 235	15 277
5 3	49 39	38 49	33 178		42 236	16 303
6 5	50 39	39 49	34 179	XXVII.	43 235	17 310
7 5	51 39	40 49	35 179		44 236	18 311
8	6	41 55	36 179	1 iii. 205	45 240	19 311
9	6	42 55	37	2 205	46 241	20 317
10	7	43 55	38 180	3 206	47 242	
11	7	44 60	39 180	4 206	48 243	

MARK.

I.	I.	I.	II.	III.	III.	IV.
1 i. 48	21 i. 62	41 i. 97	13 i. 103	2	22 ii. 40	4 i. 167
2 31	22 62	42 97	14 112	3	23 41	5 168
3 23		43 97	15 103	4 i. 110	24 41	6 168
4 30	24	44 97	16 104	5 110	25	7 168
5 32	25	45 97	17	6 111	26 41	8 168
6 31	26 63		18 104	7 113	27 42	9 168
7 34	27 63		19 104	8 113	28 43	10 169
8	28 65	II.	20 105	9 113	29 43	11 169
9 38	29 65	1 i. 99	21	10	30 43	12 170
10 39	30 65	2 99	22	11	31 i. 191	13 171
11 39	31	3 99	23 107	12	32	14 173
12 49	32 65	4 99	24 107	13	33	15 174
13 49	33 65	5	25 108	14 112	34 191	16 175
14 58	34 65	6 100	26 108	15 112	35	17 176
15 60	35 66	7 100	27 109	16		18
16 112	36 66	8 100	28 109	17 112	IV.	19
17 112	37 66	9 101		18		20
18 112	38 66	10 101	III.	19	1 i. 166	21 189
19 112	39 66	11 101		20 ii. 40	2 167	22 189
20	40 96	12 103	1	21 40	3 167	23 190

iv INDEX TO QUOTATIONS FROM THE GOSPELS.

IV.		VI.		VII.		IX.		X.		XII.		XIII.	
24	i. 190	5	i. 211	17	i. 288	7	i. 263	25	ii. 214	5	ii. 285	29	
25	190	6	212	18	288	8	264	26	216	6	286	30	iii. 30
26		7	213	19	288	9	267	27	217	7	286	31	34
27		8	214	20	288	10	267	28	217	8	286	32	34
28	180	9	214	21	289	11	268	29	219	9	286	33	37
29	180	10	215	22	289	12	268	30	219	10	288	34	37
30	178	11	215	23	289	13	268	31	220	11	288	35	37
31	178	12	225	24	289	14	270	32	223	12	289	36	37
32	178	13	225	25	290	15	270	33	224	13	305	37	38
33	184	14	227	26	290	16	270	34	224	14	308		
34	184	15	227	27	290	17	270	35	227	15	308		
35	191	16	227	28	291	18	271	36	227	16	308	XIV.	
36	191	17	226	29	291	19	271	37	227	17	308		
37	192	18	226	30	291	20	272	38	227	18	311	1	iii. 65
38	192	19	226	31	291	21	272	39	227	19	311	2	65
39	193	20	226	32	293	22	272	40	227	20	312	3	ii. 246
40	195	21	226	33	293	23	272	41	228	21	312	4	247
41	194	22	226	34	294	24	272	42	228	22	312	5	247
		23	226	35	294	25	273	43	228	23	312	6	247
		24	226	36	294	26	274	44	229	24	312	7	247
V.		25	226	37	294	27	274	45	229	25	313	8	247
		26	226			28	274	46	237	26	315	9	
1	i. 195	27	226			29	275	47	237	27	315	10	iii. 66
2	196	28	226	VIII.		30	278	48	237	28	318	11	66
3	196	29	226			31	278	49	237	29	319	12	81
4	196	30	227	1	i. 295	32	278	50	237	30	319	13	81
5	196	31	228	2	295	33	304	51	237	31	320	14	82
6	196	32	228	3	295	34	308	52	237	32	320	15	84
7	196	33	228	4	296	35	308			33	320	16	84
8	196	34	230	5	296	36	308			34	320	17	84
9	197	35	230	6	296	37	309	XI.		35	328	18	87
10	197	36	230	7	296	38	310			36	328	19	87
11	197	37	230	8	296	39	311	1	ii. 251	37	328	20	87
12	197	38	230	9	298	40	311	2	251	38	335	21	87
13	198	39	231	10	298	41	311	3		39	335	22	89
14	198	40	231	11	298	42	311	4	252	40	335	23	91
15	198	41	232	12	299	43	313	5	252	41	344	24	91
16	198	42		13	300	44		6	252	42	344	25	92
17	199	43	232	14	300	45		7	252	43	345	26	
18	199	44	231	15	300	46	313	8	254	44	345	27	
19	199	45	235	16	300	47		9	256			28	178
20	199	46	236	17	301	48	313	10	256			29	179
21	201	47	237	18	301	49	314	11	260			30	179
22	201	48	237	19	301	50	314	12	260	XIII.		31	179
23	201	49	237	20	301			13	260			32	180
24	201	50	237	21	302			14	260	1	iii. 1	33	180
25	201	51	239	22	302	X.		15	274	2	1	34	180
26	201	52	239	23	303			16	274	3	2	35	180
27	201	53	240	24	303	1	ii. 3	17	274	4	3	36	181
28	202	54	240	25	303	2	181	18	279	5	3	37	183
29	202	55	240	26	303	3	182	19	279	6	4	38	183
30	202	56	240	27	255	4	183	20	261	7	5	39	183
31	202			28	256	5	183	21	261	8	5	40	183
32	202			29	256	6	182	22	262	9	7	41	185
33	202			30	258	7	182	23	262	10	11	42	186
34	203	VII.		31	259	8	182	24	263	11	12	43	186
35	204			32	259	9	182	25	264	12	8	44	187
36	204	1	i. 279	33	259	10	186	26	273	13	8	45	187
37	204	2	279	34	260	11	186	27	280	14	14	46	190
38	204	3	280	35	260	12	186	28	280	15	15	47	190
39	204	4	280	36		13	206	29	281	16	15	48	192
40	204	5	280	37		14	206	30	281	17	16	49	192
41	205	6	280	38	261	15	206	31	281	18	16	50	193
42	205	7	280			16	207	32	281	19	16	51	193
43	205	8	280			17	210	33	282	20	25	52	193
		9	281	IX.		18	210			21	26	53	197
		10	281			19	212			22		54	197
VI.		11	281	1	i. 261	20	213	XII.		23	26	55	197
		12		2	262	21	213			24	28	56	198
1	i. 208	13		3	262	22		1	ii. 284	25	28	57	198
2	208	14	286	4	262	23	213	2	284	26	28	58	198
3	209	15	286	5	263	23		3	285	27	28	59	198
4	211	16		6	263	24	214	4	285	28	30		

INDEX TO QUOTATIONS FROM THE GOSPELS.

XIV.	XIV.	XV.	XV.	XV.	XV.	XVI.
60 iii. 198	72 iii. 203	10 iii. 220	22 iii. 228	34 iii. 241	46 iii. 255	9 iii. 271
61 198		11 221	23 228	35 242	47 256	10 274
62 199	XV.	12 221	24 230	36 243		11 274
63 200	1 iii. 205	13 222	25 230	37 244	XVI.	12 277
64 200	2 215	14 222	26 232	38 245	1 iii. 258	13 288
65 201	3 217	15 223	27 234	39 247	2 259	14 297
66 201	4 217	16 223	28 235	40 250	3 265	15 318
67 201	5 218	17 223	29 235	41 250	4 265	16 318
68 202	6 220	18 223	30 235	42 253	5 272	17 326
69 202	7 220	19 223	31 235	43 253	6 273	18 327
70 203	8 220	20 227	32 235	44 255	7 273	19 333
71 203	9 220	21 227	33 240	45 255	8 273	20 333

LUKE.

I.	I.	II.	III.	IV.	V.	VI.
1 i. 3	53 i. 10	21 i. 18	17 i. 36	27 i. 61	31	40 i. 145
2 3	54 10	22 18	18 36	28 62	32	41 145
3 3	55 10	23 18	19 58	29 62	33 i. 104	42 145
4 4	56 11	24 19	20 58	30 62	34	43
5 4	57 11	25 19	21 37	31 62	35	44 148
6 4	58 11	26 19	22 39	32 62	36 105	45 148
7 4	59 11	27 19	23 46	33 63	37	46 149
8 4	60 11	28 19	24 46	34 63	38	47 149
9 4	61 11	29 19	25 46	35 63	39 106	48 149
10 4	62 11	30 19	26 46	36 63		49 149
11 4	63 11	31 19	27 46	37		
12 4	64 11	32 19	28 46	38 65	VI.	
13 4	65 11	33 19	29 46	39 65		VII.
14 4	66 12	34 20	30 46	40 65	1 i. 107	1 i. 151
15 5	67 12	35 20	31 46	41 66	2 107	2 151
16 5	68 13	36 20	32 46	42 66	3	3 151
17 5	69 13	37 20	33 46	43 66	4	4 151
18 5	70 13	38 21	34 46	44 66	5	5 151
19 5	71 13	39 21	35 46		6 109	6 151
20 6	72 13	40 28	36 46		7 109	7 152
21 6	73 13	41 28	37 46	V.	8 109	8 152
22 6	74 13	42 28	38 46		9 110	9 153
23 6	75 13	43 28		1 i. 67	10	10 153
24 6	76 13	44 28		2 67	11 111	11 154
25 6	77 13	45 28	IV.	3 67	12 111	12 154
26 6	78 13	46 28		4 67	13 111	13 154
27 6	79 13	47 28	1 i. 49	5 68	14 112	14 154
28 6	80 14	48 28	2 49	6 68	15 112	15 154
29 7		49 29	3 49	7 68	16 112	16 154
30 7		50 29	4 49	8 68	17 113	17 154
31 7		51 29	5 51	9 68	18 114	18 157
32 7	II.	52 30	6 51	10 68	19 114	19 157
33 7	1 i. 15		7 51	11 68	20 118	20 157
34 7	2 15		8 52	12 96	21 118	21 158
35 7	3 15	III.	9 50	13 97	22 119	22 158
36 7	4 15		10 50	14	23	23 158
37 7	5 15	1 i. 30	11 50	15 98	24 118	24 158
38 7	6 15	2 30	12 50	16 99	25 118	25 159
39 9	7 15	3 30	13 53	17 99	26 120	26 159
40 9	8 16	4 31	14 58	18 99	27 130	27 159
41 9	9 16	5 31	15 60	19 99	28 130	28 159
42 9	10 16	6 31	16 60	20	29	29 159
43 9	11 16	7 32	17 60	21 100	30 129	30 161
44 9	12 16	8 33	18 60	22	31 130	31 161
45 9	13 16	9	19 60	23	32 130	32 161
46 10	14 16	10 33	20 61	24	33 131	33 161
47 10	15 16	11 33	21 61	25 103	34 131	34 161
48 10	16 16	12 33	22 61	26 103	35 130	35 161
49 10	17 17	13 33	23 61	27 103	36 131	36 162
50 10	18 17	14 33	24 61	28 103	37 143	37 162
51 10	19 17	15 34	25 61	29 103	38 144	38 162
52 10	20 18	16 34	26 61	30 101	39 144	

INDEX TO QUOTATIONS FROM THE GOSPELS.

VII.	VIII.	IX.	X.	XI.	XII.	XIII.	XIV.	XV.	XVI.	XVII.	XVIII.
39 i. 162	1 i. 165	1 i. 213	7 ii. 85	33 ii. 51	47 ii. 71	1 ii. 75	1 ii. 147	1 ii. 157	12 ii. 177	1 ii. 194	1 ii. 201
40 162	2 166	2 213	8 85	34 51	48 72	2 76	2 147	2 157	13 178	2 194	2 201
41 162	3 166	3 214	9 86	35 52	49 i. 221	3 76	3 147	3 158	14 180	3 194	3 201
42 162	4 166	4 215	10 86	36 52	50 221	4 76	4 148	4 158	15 180	4 194	4 201
43 163	5 167	5 215	11 86	37 52	51 222	5 76	5 148	5 158	16 180	5 195	5 201
44 163	6 168	6 225	12 86	38 53	52 222	6 77	6 148	6 158	17 180	6 195	6 201
45 163	7 168	7 227	13 86	39 53	53 222	7 77	7 148	7 158	18 180	7 196	
46 163	8 168	8 227	14 86	40 53	54 ii. 74	8 77	8 148	8 158	19 186	8 196	
47 163	9 169	9 227	15 86	41 53	55 74	9 77	9 149	9 159	20 186	9 197	
48 165	10 169	10 227	16	42 54	56 74	10 78	10 149	10 159	21 186	10 197	
49 165	11 172	11 230	17 89	43 54	57 74	11 78	11 150	11 162	22 186	11 198	
50 165	12	12 230	18 89	44 55	58 74	12 78	12 151	12 162	23 187	12 198	
	13	13 230	19 90	45 55	59 75	13 79	13 151	13 163	24 188	13 198	
	14 175	14 231	20 91	46 55		14 79	14 151	14 163	25 188	14 198	
	15 176	15 231	21 91	47 56		15 79	15 153	15 163	26 188	15 198	
	16 176	16 232	22 91	48 57	XIII.	16 80		16 163	27 189	16 198	
	17 189	17 232	23 93	49 57		17 80		17 163	28 189	17 198	
	18 190	18 256	24 93	50 57		18 i. 179		18 164	29 189	18 198	
	19 191	19 256	25 97	51 57		19 179		19 164	30 189	19 198	
	20 191	20 256	26 97	52 58		20 179		20 164	31 189	20 199	
	21 191	21 258	27 97	53 59		21 179		21 164		21 199	
	22 191	22 259	28 97	54 59		22 ii. 142		22 165		22 199	
	23 192	23 260	29 98			23 142		23 165		23 199	
	24 192	24	30 98			24 142		24 165		24 199	
	25 194	25 261	31 98	XII.		25 142		25 165		25 200	
	26 196	26	32 98	1 ii. 59		26 144		26 165		26 200	
	27 196	27 261	33 98	2 i. 219		27 144		27 166		27 200	
	28 196	28 262	34 98	3 219		28 144		28 166		28 200	
	29 196	29 262	35 99	4 219		29 145		29 166		29 200	
	30 197	30 262	36 99	5 219		30 145		30 166		30 200	
	31 197	31 262	37 99	6 220		31 146		31 166		31 200	
	32 197	32 263	38 100	7 220		32 146		32 166		32 200	
	33 198	33 263	39 100	8 221		33 146				33 200	
	34 198	34 263	40 100	9 221		34 258				34 201	
	35 198	35 263	41 101	10 ii. 60		35 258				35 201	
	36 198	36 264	42 101	11 60				XVI.		36 201	
	37 199	37 270		12 60				1 ii. 167		37 201	
	38 199	38 270		13 60		XIV.		2 172			
	39 199	39 271	XI.	14 60		1 ii. 147		3 173			
	40 201	40 271	1 ii. 136	15 60		2 147		4 173			
	41 201	41 271	2 136	16 61		3 147		5 173			
	42 201	42 271	3 137	17 61				6 173			
	43 201	43 278	4 137	18 61				7 173			
	44 202	44 278	5 138	19 61				8 174			
	45 202	45 278	6 138	20 61				9 175			
	46 202	46 307	7 138	21 61				10 176			
	47 202	47 308	8 138	22 62				11 177			
	48	48 309	9 139	23							
	49 204	49 310	10 139	24 i. 139							
	50 204	50 311	11 139	25 139							
	51	51 ii. 80	12 139	26 139							
	52	52 81	13 139	27							
	53 204	53 81	14 40	28							
	54 205	54 81	15 40	29 140							
	55 205	55 81	16 40	30							
	56 205	56 81	17 41	31							
		57 81	18 41	32 ii. 62							
		58 81	19	33 62							
		59 82	20 42	34 62							
		60 82	21 42	35 62							
		61 82	22 42	36 62							
		62 83	23	37 62							
			24	38 64							
		X.	25 49	39 64							
		1 ii. 84	26 49	40 64							
		2 84	27 49	41 64							
		3 84	28 50	42 65							
		4 85	29 47	43 70							
		5 85	30 47	44 70							
		6 85	31 48	45 70							
			32 48	46 70							

INDEX TO QUOTATIONS FROM THE GOSPELS.

XVIII.	XIX.	XX.	XXI.	XXII.	XXIII.	XXIV.
7 ii. 202	13 ii. 242	14 ii. 286	16 iii. 8	27 iii. 126	4 iii. 218	1 iii. 259
8 202	14 242	15 286	17 8	28 126	5 218	2 266
9 203	15 243	16 286	18 8	29 126	6 218	3 273
10 204	16 243	17 287	19 8	30 126	7 218	4 273
11 204	17 243	18 287	20 14	31 127	8 218	5 273
12 204	18 243	19 289	21 15	32 128	9 219	6 273
13 204	19 243	20 305	22 16	33 128	10 219	7 273
14 204	20 243	21 308	23 16	34 128	11 219	8 273
15 206	21 243	22 308	24 16	35 130	12 219	9 273
16 206	22 244	23 308	25 28	36 130	13 219	10 274
17 206	23 244	24 308	26 28	37 132	14 219	11 275
18 211	24 244	25 308	27 28	38 133	15 219	12 275
19 211	25 244	26 311	28 30	39 179	16 219	13 277
20 212	26 244	27 311	29 30	40 179	17	14 277
21 213	27 245	28 311	30 30	41 180	18 222	15 277
22 213	28 250	29 312	31 30	42 180	19 222	16 277
23 213	29 251	30 312	32	43 184	20 222	17 278
24 213	30 251	31 312	33 34	44 184	21 222	18 278
25 214	31 251	32 312	34 36	45 185	22 222	19 278
26 216	32 252	33 312	35 36	46 185	23 222	20 278
27 217	33 252	34 313	36 37	47 186	24 223	21 278
28 217	34 252	35 313	37 65	48 187	25 223	22 278
29 219	35 252	36 313	38 65	49 190	26 227	23 278
30	36 254	37 315		50 190	27 228	24 279
31 224	37 256	38 315		51 192	28 228	25 279
32 224	38 256	39 318	XXII.	52 192	29 228	26 279
33 224	39 257	40 318		53 192	30 228	27 279
34 224	40 257	41 328	1 iii. 65	54 193	31 228	28 282
35 230	41 257	42 328	2 66	55 197	32 228	29 282
36 235	42 257	43 328	3 66	56 202	33 229	30 282
37 235	43 257	44 328	4 66	57 202	34 230	31 284
38 235	44 257	45 334	5 66	58 203	35 235	32 288
39 235	45 274	46 334	6 66	59 203	36 236	33 288
40 236	46 274	47 334	7 81	60 203	37 236	34 288
41 236	47 279		8 81	61 204	38 232	35 288
42 236	48 279		9 81	62	39 236	36 289
43 236		XXI.	10 81	63 201	40 236	37 289
			11 82	64 201	41 236	38 289
	XX.	1 ii. 344	12 84	65 201	42 236	39 289
XIX.		2 344	13 84	66 197	43 239	40 289
	1 ii. 280	3 345	14 84	67 199	44 241	41 290
1 ii. 240	2 280	4 345	15 84	68 199	45 245	42
2 240	3 281	5 iii. 1	16 84	69 199	46 244	43
3 240	4 281	6 2	17 85	70 199	47 248	44 301
4 240	5 281	7 2	18 85	71 200	48 249	45 301
5 240	6 281	8 3	19 89		49 249	46 301
6 241	7 282	9 5	20 91		50 254	47 301
7 241	8 282	10 5	21 124		51 254	48 302
8 241	9 284	11 5	22 124	XXIII.	52 254	49 302
9 241	10 285	12 7	23 124		53 255	50 303
10 241	11 285	13 7	24 126	1 iii. 205	54 256	51 303
11 242	12 285	14 12	25 126	2 215	55 256	52 303
12 242	13 286	15 12	26 126	3 215	56 256	53 303

JOHN.

I.	I.	I.	I.	I.	II.	II.
1 i. 1	13 i. 41	25 i. 31	37 i. 43	49 i. 45	5 i. 55	17 ii. 276
2 2	14 41	26 34	38 43	50 46	6 56	18 276
3 2	15 42	27 34	39 43	51 46	7 56	19 276
4 2	16 42	28 37	40 44		8 56	20 276
5 2	17 42	29 37	41 44		9 56	21 276
6 13	18 43	30 37	42 44		10 56	22 276
7 13	19 34	31 37	43 44	II.	11 57	23 279
8 13	20 34	32 39	44 44		12 58	24 279
9 13	21 34	33 39	45 44	1 i. 55	13 ii. 274	25 280
10 40	22 34	34 39	46 45	2 55	14 274	
11 40	23 34	35 43	47 45	3 55	15 274	
12 40	24 34	36 43	48 45	4 55	16 274	

viii INDEX TO QUOTATIONS FROM THE GOSPELS.

III.		IV.		V.		VI.		VIII.		IX.		X.	
1 ii.	11	32 i.	77	45 i.	95	65 i.	254	4 ii.	19	12 ii.	105	38 ii.	124
2	11	33	77	46	95	66	254	5	19	13	105	39	124
3	12	34	77	47	96	67	255	6	19	14	105	40	124
4	12	35	77			68	255	7	21	15	106	41	125
5	12	36	77			69	255	8	21	16	106	42	125
6	12	37	77			70	255	9	21	17	106		
7	13	38	77	VI.		71		10	21	18	106	XI.	
8	13	39	78	1 i.	228			11	21	19	106		
9	13	40	78	2	229			12	22	20	111	1 ii.	125
10	13	41	78	3	229	VII.		13	22	21	111	2	125
11	13	42	78	4	229			14	22	22	111	3	125
12	14	43	78	5	229	1 ii.	1	15	22	23	111	4	125
13	14	44	78	6	229	2	1	16	22	24	111	5	125
14	15	45	79	7	229	3	1	17	23	25	111	6	125
15		46	81	8	231	4	1	18	23	26	111	7	125
16	15	47	82	9	231	5	2	19	23	27	112	8	125
17	16	48	82	10	231	6	2	20	23	28	112	9	125
18	17	49	82	11	232	7	2	21	23	29	112	10	125
19	17	50	82	12	232	8	3	22	24	30	112	11	126
20	17	51	82	13	232	9	3	23	24	31	112	12	126
21	17	52	83	14	236	10	3	24	24	32	112	13	126
22 i.	67	53	83	15	236	11	3	25	24	33	112	14	126
23	67	54	83	16	236	12	3	26	25	34	112	15	126
24	67			17	236	13	4	27	25	35	113	16	126
25	69			18	236	14	4	28	25	36	113	17	126
26	70	V.		19	237	15	4	29	26	37	113	18	126
27	70			20	237	16	4	30	26	38	113	19	126
28	70			21	238	17	4	31	26	39	113	20	127
29	70	1 i.	84	22	241	18	4	32	26	40	114	21	127
30	70	2	84	23	242	19	4	33	26	41	114	22	127
31	70	3	84	24	242	20	5	34	26			23	127
32	71	4	85	25	243	21	5	35	26			24	127
33	71	5	84	26	243	22	5	36	27			25	127
34	71	6	84	27	243	23	5	37	27	X.		26	127
35	71	7	84	28	243	24	5	38	27			27	129
36	72	8	86	29	243	25	5	39	27	1 ii.	114	28	129
		9	86	30	244	26	6	40	27	2	114	29	129
		10	86	31	244	27	6	41	27	3	114	30	129
		11	86	32	244	28	6	42	27	4	114	31	129
IV.		12	86	33	244	29	6	43	28	5	114	32	130
		13	86	34	245	30	6	44	28	6	114	33	130
1 i.	72	14	87	35	245	31	6	45	28	7	115	34	130
2	72	15	87	36	245	32	7	46	30	8	115	35	130
3	72	16	87	37	245	33	7	47	30	9	115	36	130
4	73	17	87	38	245	34	7	48	30	10	116	37	130
5	73	18	87	39	88	35	7	49	30	11	116	38	130
6	73	19	88	40	247	36	7	50	30	12	116	39	130
7	73	20	88	41	248	37	7	51	31	13	116	40	130
8	73	21	88	42	248	38	7	52	33	14	116	41	131
9	73	22	88	43	248	39	8	53	33	15	117	42	131
10	73	23	88	44	249	40	8	54	33	16	117	43	131
11	74	24	89	45	249	41	9	55	34	17	118	44	131
12	74	25	89	46	249	42	9	56	35	18	118	45	133
13	74	26	90	47	250	43	9	57	36	19	120	46	133
14	74	27	90	48	250	44	9	58	36	20	120	47	134
15	74	28	90	49	250	45	9	59	36	21	120	48	134
16	74	29	92	50	250	46	9			22	121	49	134
17	74	30	94	51	250	47	9			23	121	50	134
18	74	31	94	52	250	48	9			24	121	51	134
19	74	32	94	53	250	49	10	IX.		25	121	52	135
20	75	33	94	54	251	50	10			26	122	53	135
21	75	34	94	55	251	51	10	1 ii.	102	27	122	54	136
22	75	35	94	56	251	52	10	2	102	28	122	55	245
23	75	36	94	57	251	53	19	3	103	29	123	56	246
24	75	37	94	58	251			4	103	30	123	57	246
25	76	38	94	59	253			5	103	31	123		
26	76	39	95	60	254			6	104	32	123		
27	76	40	95	61	254	VIII.		7	104	33	123		
28	76	41	95	62	254			8	105	34	123	XII.	
29	76	42	95	63	254	1 ii.	19	9	105	35	124		
30	77	43	95	64	254	2	19	10	105	36	124	1 ii.	246
31	77	44	95			3	19	11	105	37	124	2	246

INDEX TO QUOTATIONS FROM THE GOSPELS.

XII.	XIII.	XIV.	XVI.	XVII.	XIX.	XX.
3 ii. 246	3 iii. 117	15 iii. 138	3 iii. 155	19 iii. 176	1 iii. 224	8 iii. 267
4 247	4 117	16 139	4 156	20 176	2 224	9 268
5 247	5 117	17 140	5 157	21 176	3 224	10 268
6 247	6 118	18 141	6 157	22 176	4 224	11 268
7 247	7 118	19 142	7 157	23 177	5 224	12 268
8 247	8 118	20 142	8 157	24 177	6 224	13 268
9 250	9 118	21 142	9 158	25 177	7 224	14 268
10 250	10 118	22 142	10 158	26 177	8 224	15 269
11 250	11 119	23 142	11 158		9 224	16 269
12 254	12 119	24 142	12 160		10 225	17 269
13 255	13 119	25 142	13 161		11 225	18 274
14 255	14 119	26 143	14 161	XVIII.	12 225	19 290
15 255	15 119	27 144	15 161		13 226	20 290
16 255	16 119	28 144	16 162	1 iii. 179	14 226	21 291
17 255	17 120	29 145	17 162	2 179	15 227	22 291
18 255	18 122	30 145	18 162	3 186	16 227	23 291
19 257	19 123	31 146	19 162	4 187	17 227	24 295
20 iii. 67	20 124		20 162	5 187	18 229	25 295
21 67	21 124		21 163	6 188	19 232	26 295
22 67	22 124		22 163	7 190	20 233	27 296
23 67	23 124	XV.	23 163	8 190	21 233	28 296
24 67	24 124	1 iii. 148	24 163	9 190	22 234	29 296
25 68	25 124	2 148	25 164	10 191	23 230	30 298
26 68	26 125	3 148	26 165	11 191	24 230	31 298
27 69	27 125	4 148	27 165	12 193	25 240	
28 70	28 125	5 148	28 166	13 194	26 240	
29 70	29 125	6 148	29 169	14 194	27 240	
30 71	30 125	7 149	30 169	15 194	28 242	XXI.
31 72	31 125	8 149	31 169	16 194	29 243	
32 73	32 126	9 149	32 169	17 194	30 244	1 iii. 304
33 73	33 128	10 149	33 170	18 195	31 250	2 304
34 73	34 128	11 150		19 195	32 250	3 304
35 74	35 129	12 150		20 195	33 250	4 304
36 75	36 129	13 151		21 195	34 250	5 304
37 75	37 129	14 151	XVII.	22 195	35 251	6 304
38 75	38 129	15 151		23 196	36 253	7 304
39 75		16 151	1 iii. 170	24 196	37 253	8 305
40 75		17 151	2 171	25 202	38 254	9 305
41 76		18 152	3 172	26 203	39 255	10 305
42 76	XIV.	19 153	4 173	27 203	40 255	11 305
43 77	1 iii. 133	20 153	5 173	28 205	41 256	12 305
44 77	2 133	21 153	6 173	29 215	42 256	13 305
45 77	3 134	22 153	7 173	30 215		14 305
46 77	4 134	23 153	8 174	31 215		15 305
47 77	5 135	24 153	9 174	32 215		16 307
48 78	6 135	25 154	10 174	33 216	XX.	17 307
49 78	7 135	26 154	11 175	34 216		18 307
50 78	8 135	27 154	12 175	35 216	1 iii. 259	19 308
	9 135		13 175	36 216	2 266	20 308
	10 136		14 175	37 216	3 267	21 308
	11 136	XVI.	15 175	38 217	4 267	22 308
XIII.	12 136		16 176	39 220	5 267	23 308
1 iii. 117	13 137	1 iii. 155	17 176	40 222	6 267	24 309
2 117	14 138	2 155	18 176		7 267	25 310

INDEX TO VARIOUS SUBJECTS.

Age-during, I. 89, 251, 313; II. 15, 31, 122, 128, 212, 273; III. 172
Almsgiving, II. 344—354
Angels, I. 8, 183, 264, 315; II. 313; III. 50—55
Apostles, I. 112, 216
Arnold, Matthew, II. 110, 119, 135
Articles of Religion, II. 58
Athanasian Creed, I. 155, 221; III. 167
Baptism, I. 32, 273, 322; II. 18, 207; III. 313—315
Blasphemy, II. 43; III. 249
Church, I. 187, 257, 316—327; II. 230
Coming, III. 32, 33, 36, 47
Common Tradition, I. 106, 114, 167, 172, 241, 277, 301; II. 282, 289
Confirmation, II. 208
Demons, I. 63, 182, 200, 273; II. 49, 90
Disciples, I. 121, 129, 260; II. 62, 83, 117, 156, 167—172, 176, 179, 215, 231, 271, 296, 307; II. 311, 336—338; III. 6, 7, 49, 56—64, 68, 121, 150, 300, 312, 317, 321—326
Emulation, II. 205
Faith, I. 203, 207, 211, 274; II. 195
Fasting, I. 105
Forgiveness, I. 100—102, 134, 135, 163, 328—330; II. 44, 264; III. 292—294
Gehenna, I. 220, 313; II. 339
Glory, III. 280
God, I. 75, 155, 156; II. 316
Hell. *See* Gehenna.
Holy, I. 8, 40; II. 91
Holy Spirit, II. 8, 12, 91, 140, 328, 330; III. 13, 141, 143, 291
In my name, I. 310, 327; III. 4, 163, 313
Inspiration, I., 3, 12, 53, 56, 78, 232, 237, 281, 308; II. 240, 321, 330—334

Jehovah, II. 324—327
Jews, II. 3, 106—111, 250, 278
Last day, I. 247, 251; II. 127
Lord's Prayer, III. 78
Lord's Supper, I. 225, 252; III. 84—116
Miracles, I. 56—58, 193—195, 233, 239, 274, 297, 306; II. 236, 261; III. 298, 326
Mother of Jesus, I. 17, 209; II. 1, 50
Only-begotten, I. 42; II. 17
Parables, II. 160—162; III. 42
Political Economy, II. 65—72
Politics, III. 257
Prayer, I. 133; II. 55, 137—139, 263 III. 17—25
Preaching, II. 37, 56, 101, 348—352
Prophecies, I. 26, 66
Repentance, III. 302
Resurrection, I. 91; II. 127, 133, 151, 191, 277, 312—318; III. 8—10, 247
Revisers, I. 35
Righteousness, II. 300—305; III. 159
Sabbath, III. 261—265
Salvation, I. 174; II. 145, 223; III. 11, 58, 182, 254, 295, 319—326
Salvation Army, II. 256; III. 315
Scripture-reading, II. 34
Son of God, I. 40, 246, 255; II. 339; III. 249
Son of man, I. 101, 109, 120, 161, 218, 255; II. 64
Spirit, III. 140
Spiritual body, III. 285
Temptation, I. 49
Tongues, III. 327—332
Trinity, III. 167
Vengeance, II. 202
War, II. 272, 298, 305
Word, I. 1, 42
World, III. 3
Yoke, II. 94—96

INDEX TO MIRACLES.

		PAGE			PAGE
Healing of	demoniac	I. 63	Healing of ten lepers		II. 198
,,	Simon's mother-in-law	65	,, two blind men		230
,,	nobleman's son	82	,, Malchus' ear		III. 192
,,	infirm man	84	Casting out of dumb and deaf spirit		I. 273
,,	leper	96	,, ,, demons into swine		198
,,	palsied man	99	Raising of widow's son		154
,,	withered hand	109	,, Lazarus		II. 125
,,	centurion's servant	151	Turning water into wine		I. 55
,,	demoniac	196	Draught of fishes		68
,,	Jairus' daughter	201	,, ,,		III. 304
,,	a woman	201	Multiplication of loaves and fishes		I. 229
,,	two blind men	206	,, ,, ,,		295
,,	a Gentile woman's daughter	289	The fish and the stater		306
,,	deaf, stuttering man	293	Stilling of the storm		193
,,	blind man	303	Walking on the sea		237
,,	deformed woman	II. 78	Cursing of the fig-tree		II. 260
,,	man born blind	102			
,,	man with dropsy	147			

INDEX TO PARABLES.

	PAGE		PAGE
Marriage and fasting	I. 104	The wounded traveller	II. 98
Old and new cloth	105	Door, shepherd, sheep, thieves, and robbers	114
Wine and bottles	106	Shepherd and hireling	116
Old and new wine	106	The friends and the traveller	138
City on a hill	122	The narrow door	143
Blind guides of the blind	144	Seekers of chief seats	148
Good and bad trees	148	The great supper	153
,, ,, treasure	148	The builder of a tower	155
Wise and foolish builders	149	The king going to war	156
Two debtors	162	Savourless salt	I. 121
The sower and the seed	167		II. 157
Good and bad seed	177	The lost sheep	II. 158
Mustard seed	178	,, ,, coin	158
Leaven	179	The father and his sons	162
Growing seed	180	The rich man and his steward	172
Hidden treasure	185	,, ,, Lazarus	186
Merchant seeking pearls	186	The servant and his master	197
Drag-net	187	The unjust judge	201
Lamp under a bushel	122, 189	The Pharisee and the publican	205
Householder and his treasures	190	The camel and the needle's eye	214
Shepherdless sheep	212	The householder and the labourers	220
Harvest and labourers	212	The cup and the baptism	227
Children and dogs	290	The nobleman and his kingdom	242
Leaven of Pharisees and Herod	300	The withered fig-tree	260
Lost sheep	316	The two sons	283
Two debtors	328	The vineyard and the husbandmen	284
Divided kingdom, city or house	II. 41	The royal marriage	292
The lighted lamp	51	Gnat and camel	340
The rich fool	61	The budding trees	III. 30
Servants watching	62	The watchman	37
Unwatchful householder	64	The ten virgins	40
The faithful steward	65	The talents	42
The unfaithful servant	70	The sheep and the goats	48
Cloud and wind	74	Vine, husbandman and branches	148
The slaughtered Galilæans	75	The green tree and the dry	228
The tower in Siloam	76		
The barren fig tree	77		
The dead	82		
The ploughman	83		
Harvest labourers	84		

www.ingramcontent.com/pod-product-compliance
Lightning Source LLC
Chambersburg PA
CBHW021942240426
43668CB00037B/481